BARBAROSSA

DECISIVE CAMPAIGNS

GAME MANUAL

CONTENTS

LIST OF TABLES

1. INTRODUCTION

1.1. SYSTEM REQUIREMENTS ▶

1.1.1. MINIMUM SYSTEM REQUIREMENTS

OS: Windows XP, Windows Vista, Windows 7, Windows 8, Windows 10
CPU: 1.5 GHz Processor or equivalent (running the game in higher resolutions requires more processing power)
RAM: 2 GB
Video/Graphic: 8 MB Video memory
Sound: Any soundcard
Hard Disk space: 750 MB free
DirectX version: Not required
Minimum screen resolution: 1024x768

1.1.2. RECOMMENDED SYSTEM REQUIREMENTS

OS: Windows XP, Windows Vista, Windows 7, Windows 10
CPU: 2 GHz Processor or equivalent
RAM: 2 GB
Video/Graphic: 8 MB Video memory
Sound: Any sound card
Hard Disk space: 1 GB free
DirectX version: Not required

1.2. INSTALLATION ▶

Please ensure that your system meets the minimum requirements listed above. To install the game, either double click on the installation file you downloaded or insert the *Decisive Campaigns: Barbarossa* CD into your drive.

If you have disabled the auto run function on your CD-ROM or if you are installing from a digital download, double click on the installation archive file, then double click on the file that is shown inside the archive. Follow all on-screen prompts to complete the installation.

1.3. UNINSTALLING THE GAME ▶

Please use the Add/Remove Programs option from the Windows Control Panel or the Uninstall shortcut in the games Windows START menu folder to uninstall the game. Uninstalling through any other method will not properly uninstall the game.

1.4. PRODUCT UPDATES ▶

In order to maintain our product excellence, Slitherine Games releases updates containing new features, enhancements, and corrections to any known issues. All our updates are available free on our website and can also be downloaded quickly and easily by the Update link in your Game Menu or by using the Update Game shortcut in your Windows START menu folder for the game.

We also periodically make beta (preview) updates and other content available to registered owners. Keeping up with these special updates is made easy and is free by signing up for a Slitherine Games Member account. When you are signing up, you can then register your Slitherine Games products in order to receive access to these game-related materials. Doing so is a simple two-step process:

Sign up for a Slitherine Games Member account - this is a one time procedure. Once you have signed up you are in the system and will not need to do so again. Go to www.slitherine.com and click the 'Log in' hyperlink at the top right. Select 'Sign up here' and follow the on-screen instructions. When you're finished a confirmation email will be sent to the email account you've supplied.

Once signed up you should register your game purchase using the 'Register Serial number' option under the 'Resources' link at the top of the page.

We strongly recommend registering your game as it will give you a backup location for your serial number should you lose it in the future. Once you've registered your game, when you log in to the 'My Games' section (also found under 'Resources') you can view your list of registered titles.

Patches and updates are found under 'Downloads' (under 'Resources').

Thank you and enjoy your game!

1.5. GAME FORUMS ▶

Our forums are one of the best things about Slitherine (and Matrix) games. Every game has its own forum with our designers, developers and the gamers playing the game. If you are experiencing a problem, have a question or just an idea on how to improve the game, feel free to post a message. Follow the forum link at the top of the main page.

1.6. VR DESIGNS ▶

The VR Designs website contains an archive of articles on the development of the game as well as ongoing posts on this game and future ones.

www.vrdesigns.nl

1.7. THE DIFFERENCES BETWEEN DC2 AND DC3 ▶

Decisive Campaigns 3 is a major evolution in the series and there are many changes throughout. The design focus has pivoted to one of Operational Command and a number of existing mechanics have been redone, replaced or removed for reasons explained within.

The underlying movement and combat model remains, albeit with a number of improvements. While it's probably not helpful to list all the differences as they are numerous, a couple of obvious changes that players of the previous games would notice are as follows.

- There are no Strategic Transfers.
- You can't voluntarily disband units.
- There are no Air or Artillery units on the map, nor can you order a barrage or bombing mission.
- You can't voluntarily reassign units from one HQ to another.

1.8. A WORD FROM THE DESIGNER ▶

Thanks for purchasing the game. It has a lot of new ideas and features that are unique to the war game genre. It's been under development for over two years and builds on a tried and tested Decisive Campaigns engine that's proved to be a reliable and stable platform over several previous games in the series.

This has been a dual effort between Victor Reijkersz and myself, Cameron Harris. Victor has built and extended the DC game engine to accommodate the design and done an excellent job of making the AI the best in the series and, quite likely, an industry benchmark. He's also done sterling duty as Producer and kept some of my wilder ideas from permeating themselves into the game. The design and its implementation is, for better or worse, mine.

As there are many new concepts in the game, I've provided extensive designer notes (at the back) which explain the thinking and reasoning that has resulted in things being the way they are. I also wrote this manual. I've done so with a philosophy of it being visual, plenty of explanation, lots of examples and written in an easily understood manner. Numerous cross references and detail for those who need it. Summaries where ever possible.

It's been a challenge. Hope I got it right. Happy gaming,

Cameron Harris

1.9. SCREENSHOTS ▶

Final art assets were being finalised during the writing of the manual. The number of screen shots and time constraints both colluded to prevent them being redone to reflect the final state of the game.

Most of the differences are cosmetic. The only game-mechanic difference is in how roads and rails are depicted.

You'll notice some screen shots where a road network is visible and the only rail is single tracked.

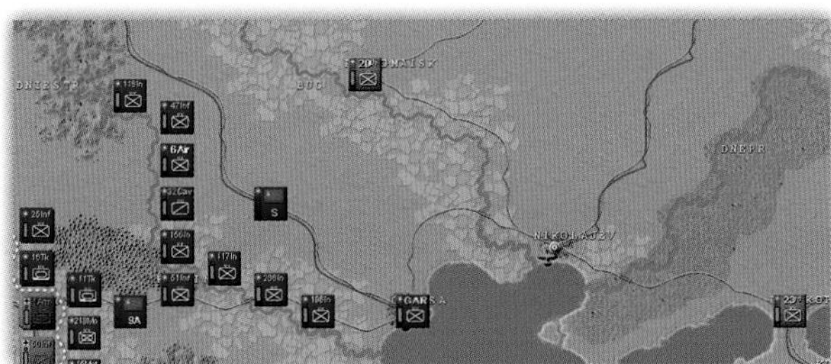

This is the previous style that has been superseded

As roads were assumed to represent single tracked rail lines the decision was made to remove them and depict rail instead. The only roads now shown on the map are all weather ones (sealed) that retain their functionality during the mud season (they don't turn into mush like all the other 'roads').

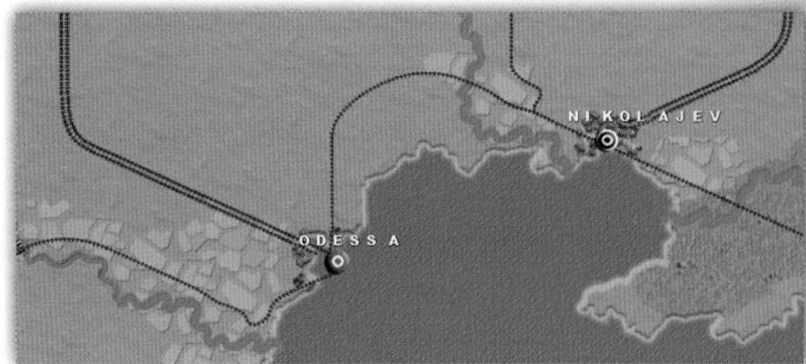

Final game state. The rail lines of previously are now shown properly double tracked and the roads as single tracked rail

Game play has not changed and the rail lines have the road movement rates built into them. So rather than show roads and assume rail, as previously, it's now all rail with the roads being assumed to be where ever the rail is present.

2. GETTING STARTED

2.1. WHICH SIDE TO PLAY?

There are two options but they differ markedly. You are strongly encouraged to play both, but for an initial play through, the following considerations will assist in determining which will be a better fit.

DESIGNER NOTE

A key design goal was to provide the Player with strongly differentiated play experiences for either side. There are major game mechanic and play style shifts involved in going from one to the other.

2.1.1. POINT OF VIEW

As the Germans you are assumed to be Feldmarschall Franz Halder, the Operational Commander of the entire Ostfront. You are required to work within a command hierarchy and have both subordinates and superiors. Your ability to do as you wish requires, at times, adept political manoeuvring. Hitler presents a particular problem and you will have to develop a strategy to counter his interference and micromanagement tendencies.

Playing the Soviets has you representing Joseph Stalin, their Supreme Commander. You have total freedom, answer to no-one, and deal only with subordinates. The biggest obstacle you face is yourself as you are burdened with a high level of paranoia. If you are unable to keep a lid on the pressure cooker that is your mental state you may find yourself walking the corridors of the Kremlin, ranting, raving, and ordering commanders shot indiscriminately.

"I trust nobody, not even myself."

Joseph Stalin

2.1.2. DIFFICULTY

While perfect balance is probably unobtainable, testing has found both sides, in the hands of a competent player, have reasonable chances of victory. Both sides are equally challenging but the type of challenge varies.

The German Player has to deal with the myriad facets of Operational Command. There is a lot going on - more information to digest, more cogs in the wheel, more decisions to make. Operational Command is tough and requires a higher level of attention and input from the Player.

There are options available to lower the bar, but in general, the German side is the one requiring the most thought.

The Soviet Player has a completely different focus. As absolute Commander he has a wide range of levers to pull. Conversely he has a limited resources with which to do so. There are many game mechanics that don't concern him. He makes fewer decisions but they matter more. He has plenty of people to handle the lower level nitty gritty that the German Player must deal with. His focus is firmly on the big picture.

2.1.3. STYLE

The onus of attack is firmly upon the German Player. The arc of the game is of initially overwhelming blitzkrieg thrusts that sweep far and wide. Gradually this changes in tone to a deadly, hard fought battle to the death. The Germans, historically, gambled everything on a fast win. There was no plan B.

In contrast to the historical record, the game allows the German Player to have a fall back position where he can, given good play, survive the winter and hold the Soviets to a Draw, or perhaps eke out a minor victory if he can manage to retain his hard fought gains.

The Soviet Player is the boxer on the ropes, having to absorb a flurry of heavy blows and stay on his feet. If he can last until the bad weather hits there is scope for a winter counter attack. Most of the game he will be on the defensive, trading space for time and looking for opportunities to pounce on any overextended German forces.

2.1.4. HOW TO GET THE MOST OUT OF THE GAME

The game is designed to simulate Operational Command in a realistic manner as is possible, within the realms of a fun experience. The Player is the equivalent of a juggler attempting to juggle more balls than he is capable of. Inevitably he will drop some.

Taking a min max approach will only lead to frustration as an optimal outcome isn't a matter of a correct sequence of decisions done just so. It's more a case of being able to retain focus on what is important amongst the noise and chaos. Figuring out what the vital parts are is the tricky bit as a lot of it is situational and will vary from game to game.

By far the best way to play the game is to accept the fact that you'll make a lot of mistakes, settle back and enjoy the experience. As in life, it's the mistake from which you learn the most.

2.1.5. LEARNING THE GAME

The game is designed to be picked up and played without consulting a manual. It provides a lot of feedback and information and you should be able get a grip on the big picture without too many troubles.

Don't feel overwhelmed by all the reports and decisions. You can ignore just about everything and the wheels won't fall off. Not immediately.

Learning by doing is a good a way as any to get on top of it. When you are ready, dip into the manual to read up on the finer details.

As a starting point the German Player would benefit greatly from browsing the section on Logistics, perhaps before their Panzer Divisions run out of fuel. The Soviet Player would likewise find the section on Activation useful in solving the puzzle of why his armies aren't willing to do anything?

2.2. SCENARIOS ▶

There are none. Instead there is a deep, involved, operational command experience that is heavily geared for replayability.

This isn't the typical approach taken by war games. Most of them offer a range of scenarios covering different aspects of the conflict they are simulating. The philosophy with DC3 has been to provide an epic experience that has a lot of depth and can be replayed many times over rather than smear the development across a range of smaller, shallower, cookie cutter scenarios.

The campaign is not one that takes weeks to play. It's quite manageable. Minimising the unit count and having the map split into three separate theatres serves to make it easily digestible. There is a lot of detail, both in information and game mechanics, but it's presented in a layered form allowing the player to explore different facets when they are ready.

2.3. PBEM++ SCREEN ▶

This screen allows you to play with other players using the Slitherine PBEM++ server. If it is the first time you have gone to the PBEM++ screen and have not yet provided the game with a user name and password, it should prompt you to do so.

STAFF ADVICE

The use of the PBEM++ system is optional. You can still play a regular PBEM game between friends (make sure to select the 'Password' option at game start).

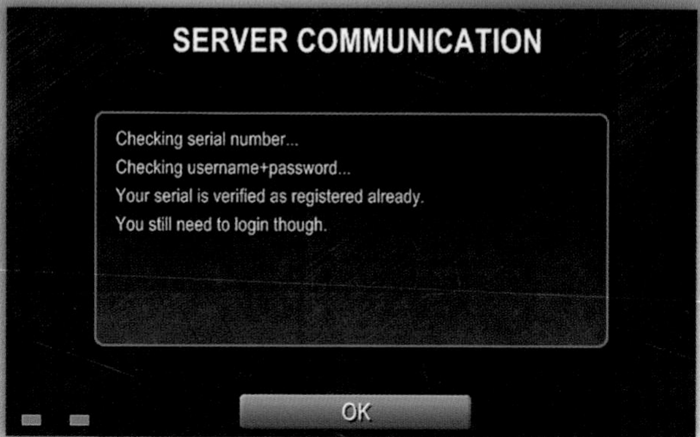

2.3.1. REGISTER

If your serial code is not registered you'll be presented with the registration window. You will have to supply a valid user name, password and email address. The serial code is automatically read from your auto-generated serial file upon installation of the game. If you already have a PBEM++ user/pass than press the button 'already registered' and use the 'login' button in the PBEM++ main menu to connect.

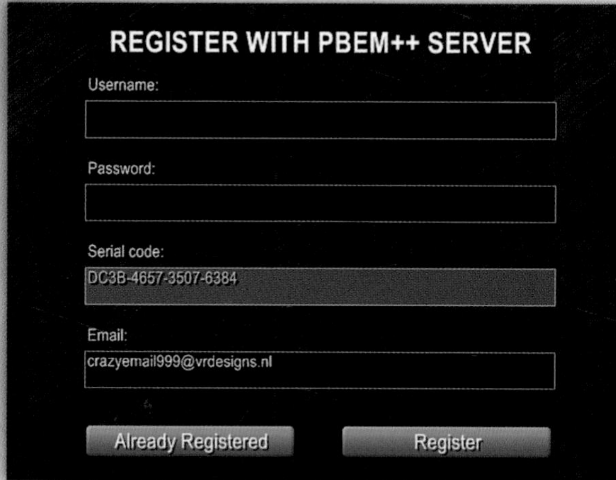

2.3.2. LOGIN

After having registered you should be able to login with your user name and password. The serial code is taken care of automatically but if it isn't, you can manually do it using the login button.

2.3.3. REFRESH

These will be automated after you instigate challenges, but this button makes it possible to do so manually.

The main PBEM screen, buttons on the right

2.3.4. CHALLENGE

When you click the challenge button you can choose to load the game. This is followed by the game set-up screen where you can select the appropriate settings. Don't forget to set each Player to either 'Challenger' and 'Opponent'.

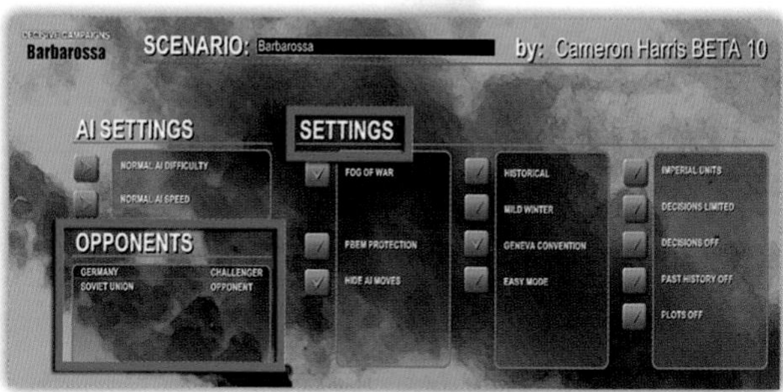

Opponents and Settings

2.3.5. OTHER CHALLENGES

In this tab, all the challenges made by other players are presented. For each challenge you can see if you have the same game version as those of the challenger.

2.3.6. OTHER CHALLENGES - ACCEPT CHALLENGE

If you click "Accept Challenge", the game will be moved to the list of running games. The first player can then make his move.

2.3.7. OTHER CHALLENGES - PREVIEW SCENARIO

Before accepting a challenge you can preview the challengers scenario. If you do this you will load the local file on our computer with the same name as the file the challenger used to make the challenge. You'll be able to inspect the settings used for the game set up and see the mini-map.

2.3.8. YOUR CHALLENGES - CANCEL CHALLENGE

Cancelling a challenge will remove it from the list

2.3.9. RUNNING GAMES - PLAY TURN

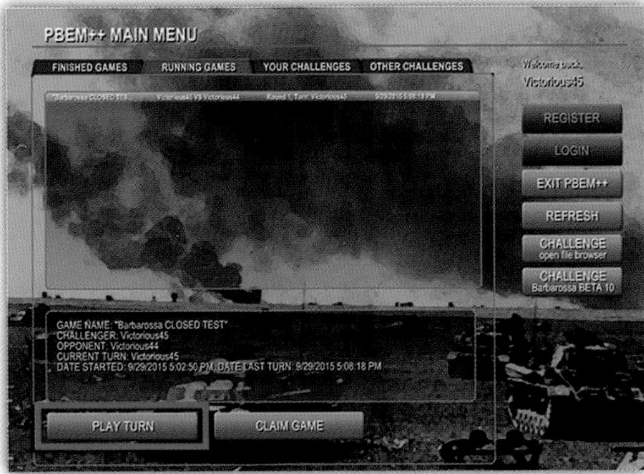

Press 'Play Turn' to start the game

The first turn looks like this. All the settings are locked

If it is your turn for a running game you can press play turn and the turn will be downloaded (found in the 'savedgames/downloadedfile.dc3'). It'll automatically open and start up.

2.3.10. RUNNING GAMES - CLAIM GAME

If the other player has not made a move for the past 30 days you can claim the game and be declared victorious.

2.3.11. END TURN - UPLOAD TURN

After having completed a turn (you've press the 'end turn' button within the game) the game will be ready to be uploaded to the server, ready for your opponent to make their move. In the event of a problem you can reload the game (via 'Load Saved Game' from the Start Screen) and restart the upload process (press 'end turn').

Press to Upload

2.3.12. EXIT PBEM++

Returns you to the main window.

2.3.13. PBEM PROTECTION

If this game option is selected you cannot save the game during your turn. This will serve to minimise any opportunity for your opponent to cheat (repetitive save/reload until they achieve an optimal outcome) but it does remove the luxury of saving in the middle of a long turn.

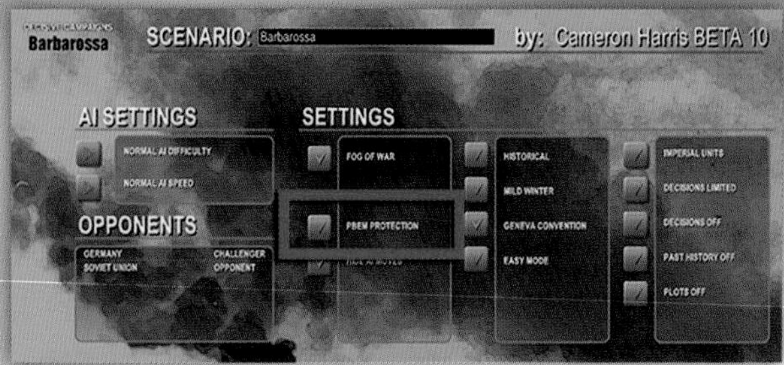

2.3.14. CHALLENGE PASSWORD

When you specify a challenge you can optionally set a password. The challenge can only be accepted by a player who knows this password. This is ideal if you only want a specific player to accept.

2.4. THE BASICS ▶

2.4.1. ACTIONS AND DECISIONS

Depending on what side you play you'll have a range of Action Cards to play that represent the issuing of various orders. There are also, in the case of the Germans, an ongoing series of Decisions that allow you to influence a wide range of operational command matters.

Your ability to make decisions and issue orders via Action cards is constrained by your staff resources, time and goodwill. This is represented by Political Points (PP). Exercising decision options and playing cards both require the expenditure of PP.

2.4.2. GOAL

Your goal when playing the Germans is to take one, or more, of the three objective cities - Leningrad in the northern theatre (AGN), Moscow in the central theatre (AGC) and Rostov in the southern theatre (AGS).

During the special Pre-Start turn you are given the option to choose a strategy via the 'Summonsed to Berlin' decision.

The Soviets have (via a Decision in the Pre-Start turn) the ability to choose one of the same objectives which 'must be held at all costs' and will influence the Victory conditions.

For further information see 4.6 Winning the game.

2.4.3. BOARD AND PLAYING PIECES

The board which the playing pieces (unit counters) are moving on and fighting over, is the map. The objectives mentioned are cities on the map. As the Germans your aim is to try and conquer them by executing actions (moving and engaging in combat) with the units under your control.

The units are either Divisions or Headquarter (HQ) units. There is a hierarchy of command with Divisions being attached to headquarters which, in turn, are attached to higher level HQ's.

2.5. THE SPECIAL PRE-START TURN ▶

This is a special Pre-Start Turn that allows both sides to choose a strategy and make decisions prior to the campaign proper beginning. All units are frozen and the only purpose is to provide the opportunity to do the above. Operation Barbarossa will commence on the following turn.

2.6. GERMAN QUICK START ▶

2.6.1. PRE-START TURN

All your units are frozen. Nothing of a military nature can be done.

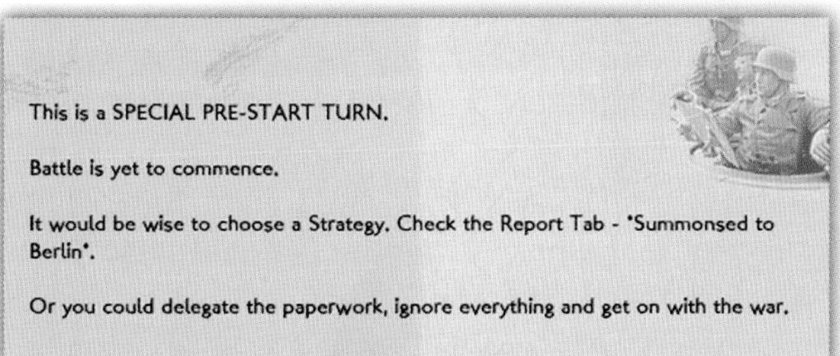

This is a SPECIAL PRE-START TURN.
Battle is yet to commence.
It would be wise to choose a Strategy. Check the Report Tab - 'Summonsed to Berlin'.
Or you could delegate the paperwork, ignore everything and get on with the war.

You could, if you like, ignore this turn but it'd be worth deciding upon a strategy (it'll be decided for you otherwise - 'Support Hitler').

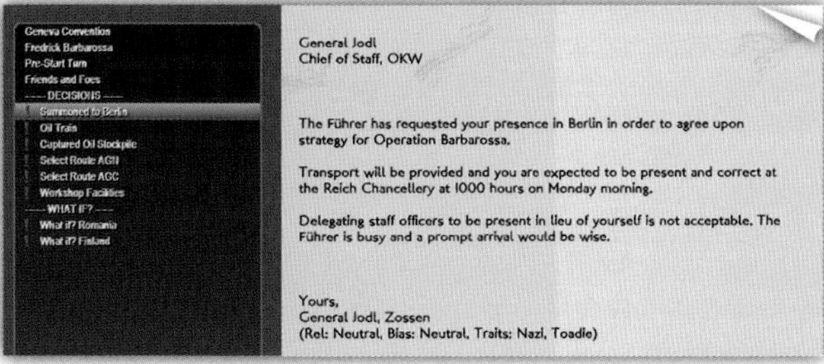

Geneva Convention
Fredrick Barbarossa
Pre-Start Turn
Friends and Foes
--- Military Advisor F.M Keitel, OKW
--- Reichsmarschall Hermann Göring, Aviation Ministry
has a Strong Bias (-2) against you due to you accusing him of losing half the Lufwaffe's Transports in the debacle of Operation Mercury
DECISIONS
Summonsed to Berlin
Oil Train
Captured Oil Stockpile
Select Route AGN
Select Route AGC
Workshop Facilities
WHAT IF?
What if? Romania
What if? Finland
General Jodl
Chief of Staff, OKW
The Führer has requested your presence in Berlin in order to agree upon strategy for Operation Barbarossa.
Transport will be provided and you are expected to be present and correct at the Reich Chancellery at 1000 hours on Monday morning.
Delegating staff officers to be present in lieu of yourself is not acceptable. The Führer is busy and a prompt arrival would be wise.
Yours,
General Jodl, Zossen
(Rel: Neutral, Bias: Neutral, Traits: Nazi, Toadie)

You've been summoned...

There are three possible strategies and these determine your victory conditions as well as providing a baseline for the Führer's opinion of you. Take a moment to read through the information in the report bundle before deciding as this is an important decision.

There are a range of other decisions that you can take but these are optional. If you're playing the game for the first time you can ignore them. If you want to play around here make sure you've chosen a strategy first as this will give you a big boost in Political points (the currency of command) and enable you to exercise your choice of decision options.

In the Report tab is also a list of existing relationships (up the top). These are randomly determined and provide you with a ready made past history with key characters in the game. Who are

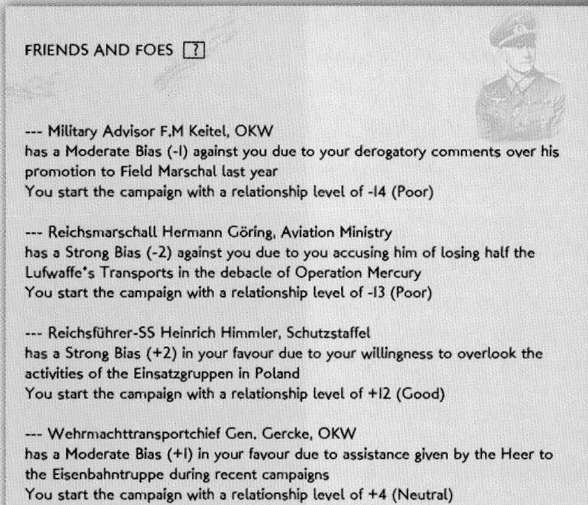

Keitel and Göring are a worry but you've got an ally in Reichsführer-SS Himmler. It appears that you've also got a dubious past as a result of the Polish campaign. Do the ends really justify the means?

you friends with? Is there anyone that you'll need to keep an eye on?

Once you're done, press the end turn button to move onto the campaign proper.

End turn

2.6.2. FIRST TURN

2.6.2.1. First Turn Messages

At the start of every turn there can be a few messages that pop-up.

22 . June . 1941

The morning reports indicate that all Armies (except Eleventh) have started the offensive according to plan. Tactical surprise of the enemy has apparently been achieved along the entire line. All bridges across the Bug river, as on the entire river frontier, were undefended and are in our hands intact.

F.M Franz Halder's Diary ?

There are a lot of quotes for each turn to ensure you'll get different ones with each play through

Often there will be an historical quote from F.M Franz Halder, the commander that the German player is assumed to represent. This is purely chrome but it's interesting as the quotes are extracts from his war diary and correspond to the date in question. Worth a read.

Next will be an official directive from Hitler. This always happens at the start of the campaign and occurs roughly once a month thereafter. These are the campaign priorities as the Führer sees them.

Hitler Directive No.21

The Führer, after listening to all advice, has issued a Directive and expects all Commanders to adhere to his preferred strategy. No further discussion will be entered into. [?]

--- Strategic Intent (in order of priority)

Priority 1: Leningrad (North)
Priority 2: Rostov (South)
Priority 3: Destroy Army HQ's
Priority 4: Moscow (Centre)

Priority 1 is what the Führer is focused on. Any decisions you take to support this will see you gaining a benefit (fewer Political Points required to exercise the option). Going against the wishes of the Führer, priorities 3 & 4, will result in decision options costing more.

AIDE DE CAMP 22 . June . 1941

--- Focus
•AGN: You need to decide who has Command Focus (Card) [?]
•AGC: You need to decide who has Command Focus (Card)
•AGS: You need to decide who has Command Focus (Card)

--- Theatre Artillery
•Your Siege Artillery is sitting idle in Warsaw (Card) [?]
•AGN: You need to assign Theatre Artillery Support (Cards) [?]
•AGC: You need to assign Theatre Artillery Support (Cards)
•AGS: You need to assign Theatre Artillery Support (Cards)

--- Luftwaffe
•The Luftwaffe is currently fully occupied obtaining air superiority [?]

--- Other
•You appear to be delegating a lot of decisions. [?] Delegation doesn't win wars.
•1 Div Failed to deploy, 4 Div's Pending deployment [?]
•4 Decisions outstanding requiring your attention [?]

Command Focus and Theatre based Artillery need sorting out for all three theatres

Finally there is the regular Aide de Camp report. This is a summary of all critical information, put together by your Chief of Staff. It acts as a gentle prod in the ribs for things that need doing.

2.6.2.2. Assignments

As prompted by your Aide de Camp report, you need to assign your theatre based artillery assets. These can be ordered to support an Army (not a Panzergruppe as they won't be able to keep up) or concentrate them behind an individual Division.

Go for the Army. You'll need to play an Action card to do so. Click on the 'Card' tab to get a list and choose the Artillery category. There are two cards for each theatre - Direct Fire or Counter Battery support. Opt for Direct Fire as we are, at this point, definitely on the offensive.

You'll need Political Points to play Action cards (this one will cost 3 PP). These represent your command resources of time, goodwill and staff.

Another task that needs doing is deciding who to assign Command Focus to. Note that this decision, like most in the game, once done, is fire and forget. It'll continue in place automatically until you change your mind.

Command Focus represents you ordering one of your theatre commanders to provide specialist combat battalions and staff resources to an Army, or Panzergruppe, within the theatre. Doing so will generate a set of Officer cards which can be used

The unit selection window. All valid selections have a grey outline. We'll assign the artillery to the 18th Army HQ

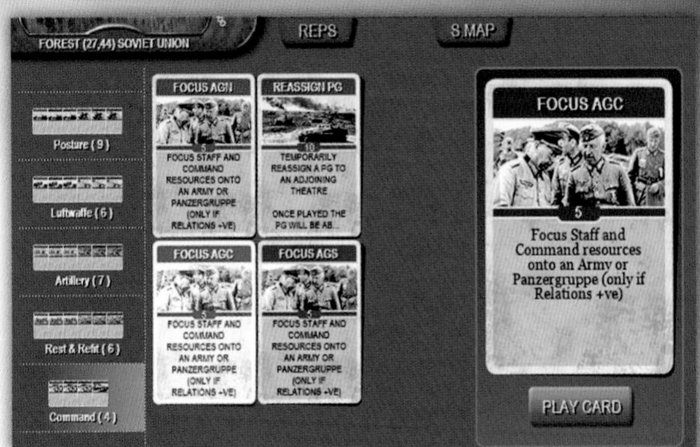

Command Focus can be expensive (5 PP) but it's well worth the cost)

to provide tactical bonuses to the formation in question.

Ideally you want to maximise the effect of your hard hitting Panzergruppes but your theatre commanders will only agree to do so if you have positive (>0) relations with them. You can check the relationship tab down at the bottom of the screen to see if this is the case.

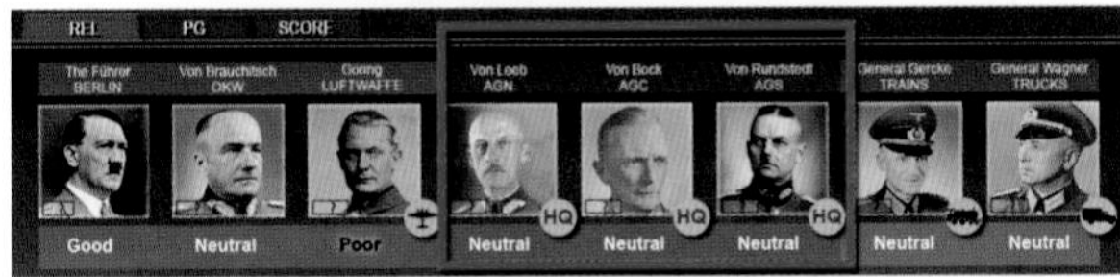

You can hover your mouse over the yellow '?' in the portraits to get more information

As you have marginally positive relationships with all three commanders it would be wise to assign command focus to Panzergruppes in every theatre (don't forget that AGC has two Panzergruppes - you can only choose one).

The other assignment that can make is who to provide Luftwaffe support to? Once again you'll want to maximise your Panzergruppes and have each theatre's Luftflotte give dedicated tactical air ground support where needed. However you can't do that quite yet as the Luftwaffe is still busy beating up the VVS (Soviet Airforce).

There is a decision (always occurs on the first turn), 'D+2 Air Offensive', that lets you decide whether to immediately swing the Luftwaffe over to ground support or have them disrupt Soviet Command and Control (makes it harder for their Armies to activate and retreat).

2.6.2.3. Decisions and Reports

The decisions that appear each turn vary with each play through but there is usually at least one demanding your attention. Sometimes there are a lot more but that's part and parcel of the unpredictability of operational command.

They can be found under the 'Report Tab'. You aren't required to read each and every one. Any that you ignore will be considered to be delegated to your Chief of Staff (who will take a 'cover his rear end' approach to decision making). You can check your Daily Staff Log to see the outcome of any decisions that you delegated the previous turn.

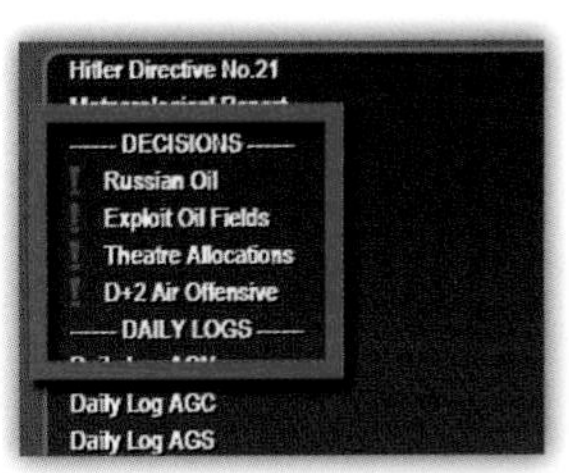

Scan the titles and zoom in for more details if you think the matter warrants your attention. Every time you choose an option, in order to resolve a decision, you are expending Political points (PP). You've got a finite amount of these and it's wise to keep some in reserve. Delegation is part of the game and you aren't expected to personally resolve every decision that comes before you.

Within the Report tab are a hefty list of reports on all manner of things. You're the commander and your staff have compiled these on your behalf. The idea is that you can dip into these if and when required. You'd like to see the maintenance status of the 2nd Panzergruppe? It's there, on your desk.

The only ones that are required reading each turn (unless you really want to wing it) are your three Daily Theatre Logs.

Every important event of note that has happened within a theatre will be listed here.

Daily Summary AG CENTRE 22 . June . 1941

--- Command
•F.M von Bock, AGC, is willing to consider new ideas (Rel +ve) [?]
•F.M von Bock currently has not determined a Command Focus [?]

--- Logistics [?]
•Changes to Truck Maintenance (Decision) +5%, now 25%
•Truck maintenance : Static [?] [?]

--- Organisation and Planning
•4000 bbls of fuel expended to support PG Blitzkrieg Posture [?]
•The Führer is willing to consider alternative PG dispositions [?]

--- Theatre Artillery
•Expected resupply this turn +100 [?]
•Current Ammunition stockpile level 100 [?]
•Siege Artillery at Warsaw [?]

--- Civil Affairs
•Overall Partisan level and risk of activity +0% [?]

--- Luftwaffe
•Main Airfield at Warsaw, Quality 113 (Fine, +3 upgrade) [?]
•Luftwaffe Fuel Level 100 [?]
•Net Effort (Action cards) 100 [?]

--- OOB [?]
•110st Inf Div (9th Army HQ) failed to deploy (50% chance, roll 82) [?]

Tool tips abound. Mouse over for more info

2.6.2.4. Map Operations

You've resolved a curly decision or two, read a few reports, ordered your theatre artillery and command focus assigned to various formations and now you are standing before the great big map of Russia on the wall. The one with all the Army and Divisional tags pinned upon it.

To prevent you from embarrassing yourself in front of your staff on your first real day on the job here is the 'need to know' two minute guide for commanders.

The map is split into three theatres (Armeegruppe North, Centre and South). Units need to stay within their theatre boundaries (dashed red lines) otherwise you'll incur violation penalties.

Click on a unit and press 'M' to move. A handy overlay will let you know where it can move and shows red to highlight a violation situation. Click on any grey shaded hex and the unit will move accordingly.

Movement and combat both expend Action Points (AP). Normally a unit starts with 100 AP per turn (this can vary due to a lot of factors). Once it runs out of AP it can no longer move or fight.

Combat is easy. Click on an enemy unit and press 'A' (to A-ttack). Select the units you want involved (click on them to toggle them in or out) and order the attack.

STAFF ADVICE

Use your infantry to knock a hole in the Soviet defences before ordering your Panzer Divisions through the gap with the aim of encircling as large a pocket as possible. The Germans get special bonuses the first few turns - make the most of them.

At any time you can ask a unit to Report Status! It'll give a full breakdown of all factors affecting it. Very handy. Not much will be there at the start but once the invasion gets underway this will change. Any questions about what's going on, have the unit (or HQ), Report Status!

Report Status! Button

What are all those funny icons on the map? They represent the three logistical 'pipelines' that keep your Panzergruppes supplied in fuel, one for each theatre. Tanks don't move without fuel.

It's a little confusing at the start as everybody is bunched up at the Polish border but it'll soon straighten out. There's a fuel gauge on the top bar that lets you know how much fuel is at the point of use (at your Panzergruppe HQ/s) in each theatre (click on any hex and it'll show an accurate readout for whatever theatre the hex is in).

The gauge is in 'barrels' and will dynamically update every time you move a Fast Division

The logistical pipelines each consist of a Main Depot on the Polish border where your fuel allocations arrive. From here rail links (train icons - none at the start) transport it to your Forward Supply Base (FSB). This will need to be leapfrogged forward as you advance.

From the FSB truck columns (truck icons) transport the fuel to your Panzergruppe HQ/s. Provided you've got enough trains and truck columns whatever fuel arrives at your Main Depots will come out the other end of your 'pipelines', ready for use at your HQ's (it's the amount shown in the fuel gauge up the top).

The logistical icons are colour coded to represent various states. Green is good, yellow is O.K, red is bad (there's a problem somewhere that needs resolving) and grey is 'nothing happening at present'.

There is a nasty big Soviet garrison at Brest-Litowsk (AGC). Surround it and order your Siege artillery to invest the location. A frontal assault will be costly.

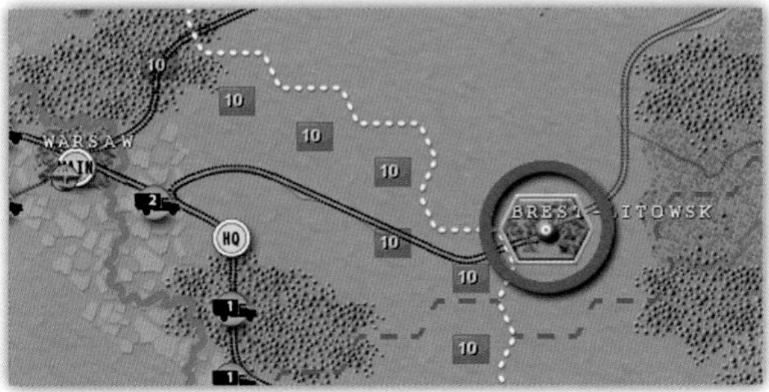

Press '0' to remove the units, '2' to return them

Your siege artillery commences in Warsaw and is rail borne so it's a short hop down to Brest-Litowsk. You'll get status updates from your Daily AGC Log as to what's going on.

That's about it. Keep your Panzergruppe HQ's located on the transport grid (you want to avoid your truck columns going cross country as they'll wear out) and avoid having your Panzergruppe HQ's more than 10 hexes away from your Forward Supply Bases (that's the limit of their effective range).

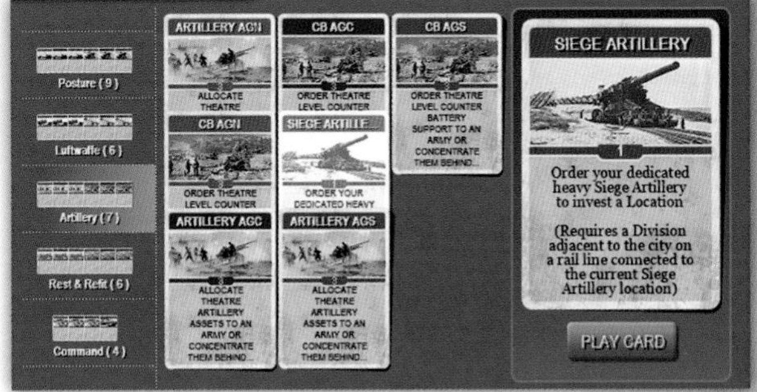

Siege artillery is non-replaceable. Handle with care

Armies, and Panzergruppes, operate as integrated formations. Think of them as your basic units of manoeuvre. If a subordinate Division (other than HQ's, there are only Divisions on the map) moves beyond 5 hexes of its HQ then it will be considered to be outside of 'Command Range' and suffer a range of adverse outcomes. Keep all Divisions of an Army within 5 hexes of the HQ and you'll be fine.

Head east. What could go wrong?

2.7. SOVIET QUICK START ▶

2.7.1. PRE-START TURN

All your units are frozen. Nothing of a military nature can be done.

This is the only time the Soviet Player gets to make decisions. All of them are optional but it is strongly recommended to read 'Stalin Decides'.

This is a SPECIAL PRE-START TURN.

Battle is yet to commence.

It would be wise to choose an Objective. Check the Report Tab - 'Stalin Decides'.

Or you could delegate the paperwork, ignore everything and get on with the war.

This allows you to choose a front (there are three - Northern, Central, Southern) that must be defended at all costs.

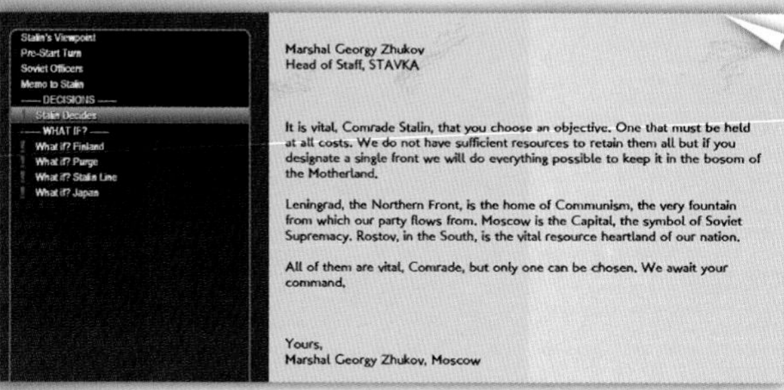

Pick a front that is the one you consider the least likely that your opponent will take. Or perhaps the one you feel you can best defend. If you can manage to retain it (the objective - either Leningrad, Moscow or Rostov) you can positively influence the outcome of the game in your favour.

Once this is done you can click on the 'end turn' button to move onto the campaign proper.

2.7.2. DECISIONS AND REPORTS

There aren't any Decisions. The Soviet command experience is very different to that of the German.

Command is exercised through the use of Action cards. It's more direct and a strong measure of ruthlessness is required to save Russia. Be prepared to remove anybody who stands in the way. Firing squads are on standby.

There are reports and they follow a similar structure to the German ones although there are a number of different ones. A feature of Soviet command is the communication links, between the front line units and STAVKA, often failing. You won't have access to all the information you'd like, when it's needed.

27th Army HQ - 30km's North of Dunaburg

We have been unable to contact the Army, Comrade Stalin, due to an unexplained breakdown in communications.

We are doing what we can to restore telephone and radio links. We regret to inform you that the information you have requested is currently not available.

(chance of occuring 30%, roll 6) [?]

2.7.3. FIRST TURN

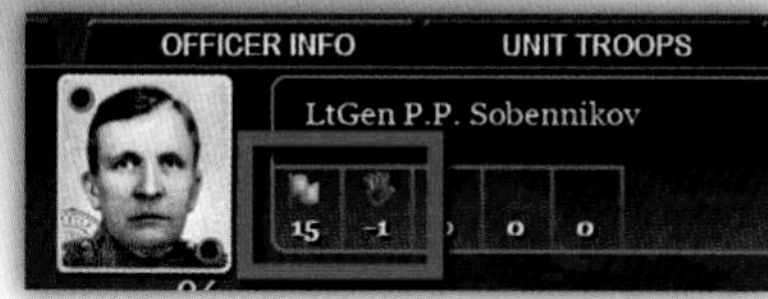

Activation on the left (blue flag), Threat rating on the right (red hand)

Soviet command revolves around two concepts that are unique to their side - Activation and Threat. Each commander (Army and Front) has a rating for both.

Activation is about Armies being able to receive and carry out orders. Because of Stalin's purges, prior to the war, the Soviet Army is full of inexperienced, incompetent officers. Getting things done, at a level of basic military competence, is a challenge.

This is expressed by having each Army HQ make an activation check every turn. Success will grant them and their subordinate Divisions a full 100 Action Point (AP) allowance. Partial success, or worse, failure to activate will see them with progressively less AP. The fewer the AP, the less that can be achieved.

To add to your problems the Luftwaffe may be disrupting command and control right across the entire front and you may find very few armies, if any, achieve activation.

A lot also depends on the quality of your three Front commanders (Fronts are equivalent to German Theatres). You can get a summary of their stats in the Command tab (bottom centre).

Front Commanders are the equivalent of a German Theatre Commander

All Soviet commanders are of a type, eg. TOADIE. Most of them are variations of uselessness but occasionally you find yourself with a TSARIST or a NEW SCHOOL which are the only ones who know what they are doing. A commander's activation rating is a measure of their competence (negative bad, positive good).

To improve your chances of activation you should immediately order Marshal Zhukov, one of your roving troubleshooters, to travel to one of your Front HQ's. His presence will provide a front-wide bonus to all Armies within the Front.

Troubleshooters move around the map going from HQ to HQ

Another worthwhile step is to order a front to be a priority over all others. This will provide another front-wide activation bonus.

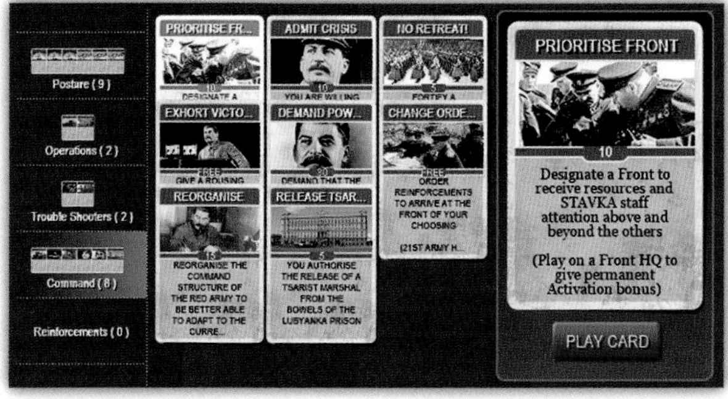

For a more lasting resolution to your activation problems consider 'Reorganising' your command

structure (a necessary evil considering it was in a state of total chaos at the start of the invasion). You can do this a number of times and each instance provides a permanent global activation bonus to all Armies.

A commander's Threat rating is how he is perceived by Stalin (who you represent in the game). Commanders with a negative threat rating are not a concern although they are typically incompetent. Commanders with a positive threat rating are exactly that, a threat. The cumulative threat ratings of all commanders can raise the level of Stalin's paranoia.

Was Stalin actually paranoid? Yes, acutely so. Once his paranoia level rises above zero, a percentage roll is made each turn. If it's less than, or equal to, his level of paranoia, he'll suffer an 'episode'.

There are a range of consequences, most of them bad. To be avoided.

Commissar Khrushchev is your other troubleshooter whose job it is to keep recalcitrant commanders in line. He is authorised to take extreme measures. Send him to a Front HQ and, once there, have him play his 'Intimidate' Officer card to prevent threat levels rising.

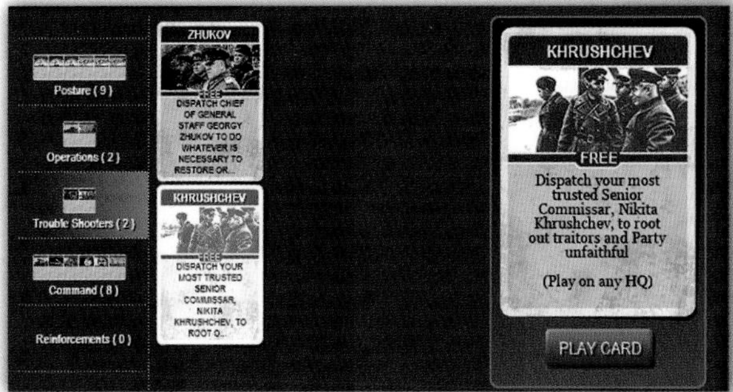

Both troubleshooters can be ordered to travel to any HQ on the map. Once there they receive a set of Officer cards (that vary depending on the level of the HQ) which enable them to take a wide range of actions. Marshal Zhukov is your 'Sort it out, kick backsides and get things moving' guy, Commissar Khrushchev the 'dark Eminence'.

There are several 'Operations' cards that can be played each turn at no cost.

'Fortifications' allow you to construct defences. There is a mini-game involved here as you can build one set per turn while ever the weather remains good. Some forethought as to the bigger picture pays dividends here rather than reacting to whatever tactical crisis is currently looming.

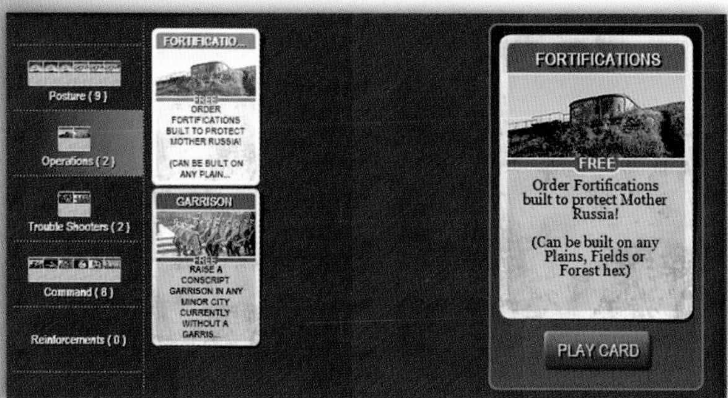

Similarly 'Garrisons' allow you to raise relatively weak garrisons in a selected minor city (grey dot). Coordinating your placement of garrisons with your fortifications can provide the basis of longer term defensive strategy.

Finally the 'No Retreat' card allows you to fortify a major city (red dot) with a powerful, entrenched, garrison which can stymie an unchecked German advance. Raising these in cities that lie on crucial supply routes can force the Germans to make a costly assault or wait for the arrival of siege artillery. Both outcomes work to your advantage.

The Soviet forces suffer heavy penalties for the opening turns of the game. Avoid combat and attempt to pull your forces back and salvage as many regular armies as possible. Consider layering your forces in depth to slow the German Panzer Divisions down. Stack only when you have the benefit of urban, forest, swamp or low mountain terrain (there are specific defensive bonuses for Soviet units in forest and swamp).

Play the 'Admit Crisis' card to reduce the cost of changing the posture of an Army over to a Defensive one. An Army set to this posture is many times more (60%) effective than one on the default 'Offensive' posture.

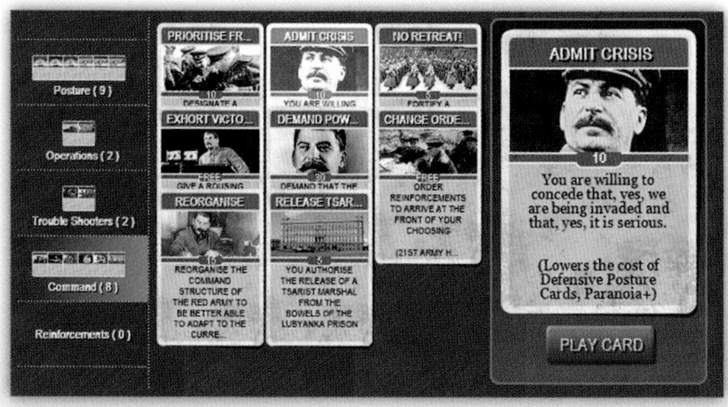

3. THE INTERFACE

3.1. GAME SET-UP SCREEN ▶

This screen allows you to customise the game to your liking.

A range of settings can be tweaked here

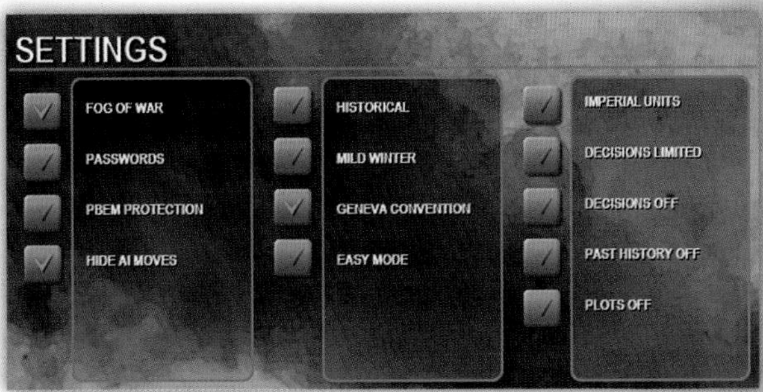

Default settings

3.1.1. AI AND PLAYERS

The AI (artificial intelligence) has two settings. A straight difficulty level which provides escalating bonuses to the AI (mouse over for a tool tip showing details of exactly what these are) and a 'think time' setting. The more time you give the AI to consider its moves, the further it can search its internal decision tree and the more challenging an opponent it will be.

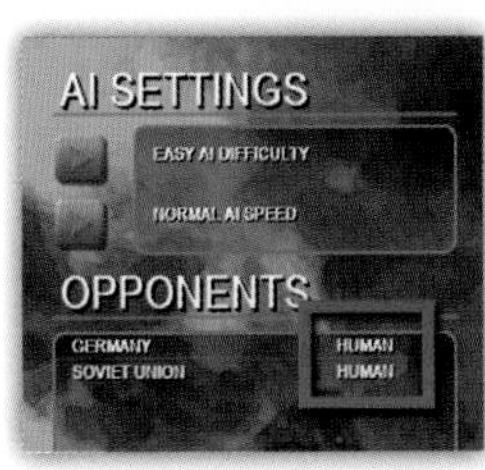

Click on 'Human' to change to 'AI'

Opponents allow you to choose either 'Human' (that's probably you) or 'AI' for a side. Human vs. Human allows you to play yourself.

3.1.2. OPTION SETTINGS

A number of these will change the difficulty level (see 4.5 Difficulty) of the game depending on whether they are toggled ON or OFF.

3.1.2.1. General Settings

Fog of War

With this option selected (default) you have limited information on the enemy. This provides a more realistic game experience as no commander had God-like knowledge of the battlefield.

Difficulty Yourself -15, Opponent +15

Passwords

You'll need to provide a password before starting you turn. Useful in PBEM games. Don't forget the password as it can't be retrieved!

PBEM Protection

Used in Play by Email games it only allows you to save your game once your turn is completed. Doing otherwise informs your opponent that you *may* have been cheating.

Hide AI Moves

When playing the AI, once your turn is completed you will be shown a 'game loop' (please wait) screen that speeds up the AI's turn resolution on older computers with single core processes.

If you have a multi-core processor feel free to leave this option OFF as you'll be able to watch the AI moving. You'll be shown only what is appropriate to the Fog of War setting chosen.

3.1.2.2. Game Settings

Historical

The game restricts itself to dispositions and strategies of an historical nature. This doesn't guarantee an historical outcome but does provide foundations for one. Without this option selected (recommended to be OFF) the game will provide enhanced replayability within the bounds of what's reasonable.

Mild Winter

There is a detailed climatic model that allows for the full range of weather. With 'Mild Winter' selected a decent woolen jumper is all you'll need (the winter will still vary but the extreme cold conditions of '41 won't apply).

Difficulty German -10, Soviet +10

Geneva Convention

The Eastern Front was a bare knuckled fight without an umpire. To avoid causing offence, the game defaults to a CLEAN War where all participants adhere to the Geneva Convention. Deselecting this option (turning it OFF) provides a more realistic DIRTY War where you will find yourself having to deal with an additional moral dimension to the game.

Note that this has been specifically included to highlight the difficulties of Operational Command, not to promote a particular viewpoint, one way or another. Controversial topics have been excluded but if you have strong views in this area it is highly recommended that you ask everybody concerned to act as gentlemen (leave the Geneva Convention option ON).

For a more detailed discussion on this option see 9.3.8 Dark Side.

Difficulty German -10, Soviet +10

(if the 'Decisions Limited' option is also selected then it is -5 and +5 respectively)

Easy Mode

If playing the Germans you are provided with extra trains and truck columns to ensure that Fuel has a higher chance of arriving where it is needed. All logistical related decisions are still in play and there are no differences in their operation. In addition both sides (if played) gain an extra allowance of Political Points (PP's) each turn for a less stressful experience. This is a good choice when you are learning the game.

Difficulty German -15 Soviet +15

Imperial Measurements

Switching this on will have all measurements displayed in Imperial format (for those that don't speak metric).

Decisions LIMITED

This option presents the player with military focused decisions only. There are a lot of decisions that are part and parcel of Operational Command but which aren't directly relevant to the situation on the map.

All Plot decisions will be disabled as well as most Geneva Convention decisions. Select this option for a more focused game with a decreased difficulty.

Difficulty German -10, Soviet +10

Decisions OFF

The entire Decision system is switched off (with the exception of the Pre-Start turn decisions) which also shuts down a lot of other game systems. What's left are the weather, action cards, mechanical reliability and simplified logistical, artillery and Luftwaffe systems.

Overall this option will provide the Germans with a much more streamlined game that captures the essence of the campaign without being overwhelmed.

Difficulty German -20, Soviet +20

Past History

Switching this OFF will ensure that you start the game on an even keel with all key characters (relationship level '0') as if you have just met. You will have neither friends or foe. If ON, Difficulty varies depending on Relationship levels (changes every play through). Switching OFF has no effect.

Plots OFF

Plots are a series of Decisions that are branching story arcs that provide a lot of colour and immersion to the game. They are not historical but they are events that may well have occurred.

They are fun decisions that are there to compliment the serious military focus of the game and provide a more nuanced Command experience. We recognise that they are not to everyone's taste so feel free to switch them off.

If you have selected 'Decisions LIMITED' these are automatically switched off.

Difficult German -5, Soviet +5

3.2. GAME LOOP SCREEN ▶

After you have started the game, or ended a turn, you'll see the game loop screen. This displays while the game is processing the multitude of AI and between turn calculations.

Eventually the game loop screen will complete and the game will require your participation, or if it isn't your turn (in a play by email game) to save and quit, or if in a PBEM++ game, to save and upload. If it is your first turn and you've chosen to use passwords, you must first enter in a password to log into the game. Make sure you pick a password you can remember, because if you lose it, there's no way to reset it or find out what it is.

When you have logged in, you will be updated on what has happened in the previous round. This is the screen where you will see your messages. Pressing any key will continue.

3.3. THE MAIN SCREEN ▶

This is the screen you'll spend most of your time in. Here you can see your units and the field of battle, as well as a number of other interface elements The top bar contains information displays (fuel gauge, hex status, date and round) and a number of drop down tabs.

The terrain window shows the currently selected hex and allows you to mouse over and obtain a detailed tool tip of all movement and combat factors that apply.

The map is where the magic happens!

The Button Bar contains a range of clickable buttons that serve different purposes.

The Information display is multi-purpose and can show unit information or a range of special tabs.

Read on for detailed information of all the above.

3.4. THE MAP ▶

3.4.1. BORDERS

3.4.1.1. Theatres

Red dashed lines mark the theatre borders. There are three theatres (Soviets refer to them as 'fronts') and units are expected to remain in their assigned theatre.

Theatre borders are fixed and don't change.

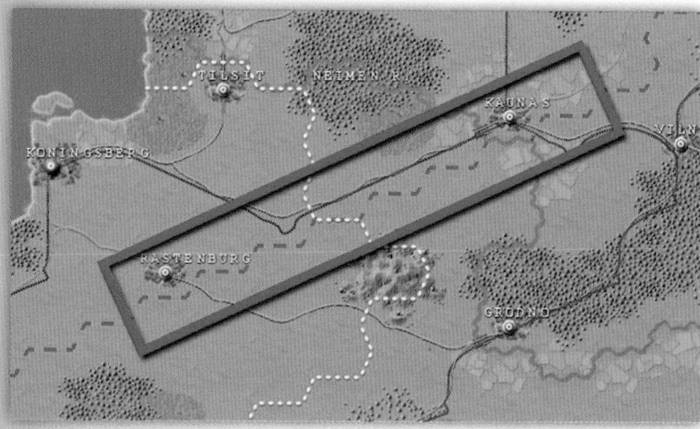

For further information see 4.3 Theaters.

3.4.1.2. Regime Borders

The yellow dashed lines represent the regime border between German (and allied) controlled territory and Soviet controlled. The regime border changes as the tide of battle ebbs and flows.

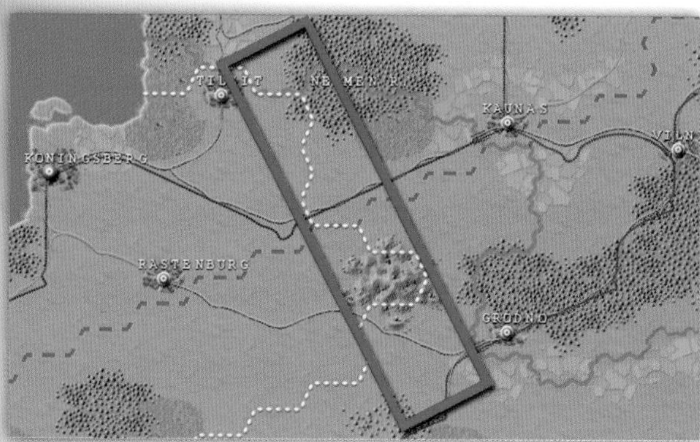

3.4.2. TRANSPORT GRID

The map features a comprehensive transport grid consisting of double and single gauge rail track.

There are two different rail gauges shown. Black is German gauge and dark red is Soviet.

Soviet gauge double track rail running due north out of Bialystok

ASK YOUR STAFF

Why do I have to worry about different rail gauges? The two gauges were incompatible. The German locomotives couldn't be converted to run on Soviet gauge rail and captured Soviet loco's and rolling stock had to be used (which were in short supply and involved a lot of inefficiencies). The Germans were forced to convert vast stretches of Soviet rail over to German gauge, without which they would have been unable to support an advance deep into Western Russia.

Wherever there is a rail line (of whatever type) there is assumed to be a road. There are two types of road in the game. Normal and sealed.

Only sealed, all weather, roads are shown on the map. They are found only in the Baltic States (AGN) and on the main Warsaw - Minsk - Moscow highway. All other roads are 'normal' (unsealed).

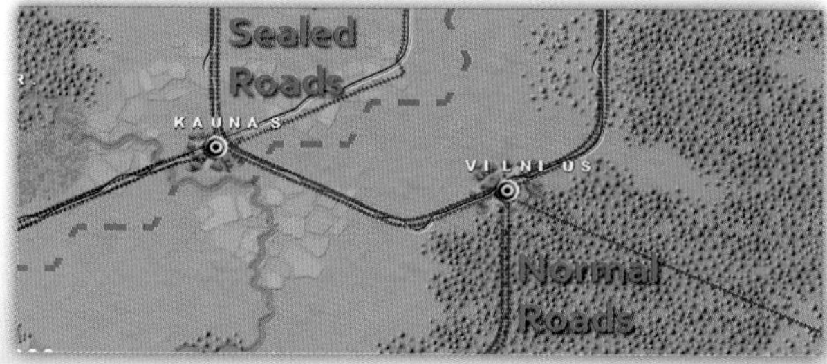

Any road that you can see on the map is automatically a sealed road. If there are no roads visible then it's a normal road

The terrain mouse over tool tips will also let you know if a sealed road is present.

ASK YOUR STAFF

Aren't all roads 'all weather'? Not in Russia in '41 they weren't. Most roads were unsealed and, when it rained, they turned to mush. Trucks bogged to their axles and wheeled movement became impossible (they could struggle forward but as a hex is 30 km's across, in game terms they can't). Only sealed roads held up in the wet conditions and allowed 'all weather' travel.

Rail is used for logistical purposes only (it plays a major role, especially for the Germans) and road for the movement of units.

3.4.3. CITIES

There are two types, Major, or Strategic, Cities (red dots) and Minor (grey dots). The loss of Strategic cities causes Stalin's level of paranoia to rise and provide greater bonus Political Points to the Germans than capturing a minor city does.

The Soviets can place major Garrisons in strategic cities and minor garrisons in minor cities. Theatre airfields can be found in both but Forward Supply bases can be located only in strategic cities (which are on double tracked rail lines).

3.4.4. MAP SYMBOLS

3.4.4.1. Transparent Boxes

These are small transparent boxes that are shown on the map to highlight the additional cost, in Action Points, to move INTO the hex. They don't apply if the unit starts its turn IN the hex, only if they move *into* another hex with a transparent box.

Extra costs can come about from the enemy exerting a Zone of Control over the hex, a previous battle (this turn) in the hex, enemy territory and other causes.

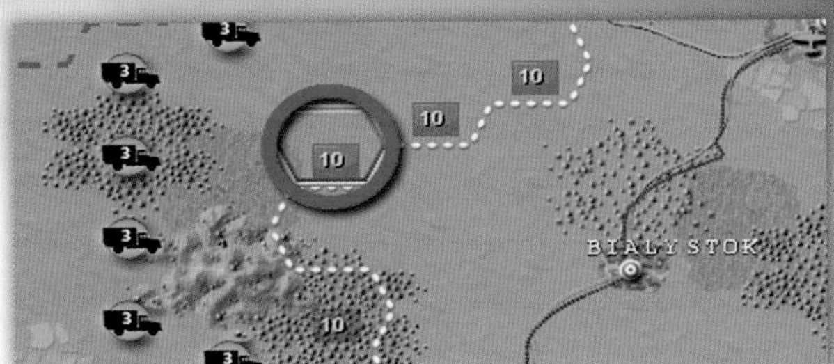

Extra AP costs, above and beyond, normal terrain or road costs

Whatever the reason it can be found in the mouse over tool tip on the terrain window (top centre).

PLAINS (20,38) GERMANY

LANDSCAPE: PLAINS

TROOPTYPE	ATT-MOD	DEF-MOD	A-ENTR	MX-ENTR	CROSS-RIV
INFANTRY	100%	100%	100	100	-
GUNS	100%	100%	100	100	-
MOTORIZED	100%	100%	0	0	-
LIGHT TANKS	100%	100%	0	0	-
MEDIUM TANKS	100%	100%	0	0	-
HEAVY TANKS	100%	100%	0	0	-

MOVETYPE	AP COST	ROAD	RIVER
FOOT	25	-	-
MOTORIZED	15	-	-
CAVALRY	20	-	-
RAIL	NA	-	-
TRACKED	15	-	-
SUPPLY MOVE	10	-	-
IMMOBILE	NA	-	-
RAIL_CAP	NA	-	-

COVER: 0

ZOC PENALTY IN AP = 10

The reasons for the movement boxes are always found down the bottom of the terrain window tool tip

3.4.4.2. Black Circles

These are 'Battlestack points'.

There is a limit to how many forces you can use to attack a single hex before over stacking penalties apply. Successive battles in the same hex, during the same turn, carry over any previous stacking points.

For further information see 5.2.9 Stacking.

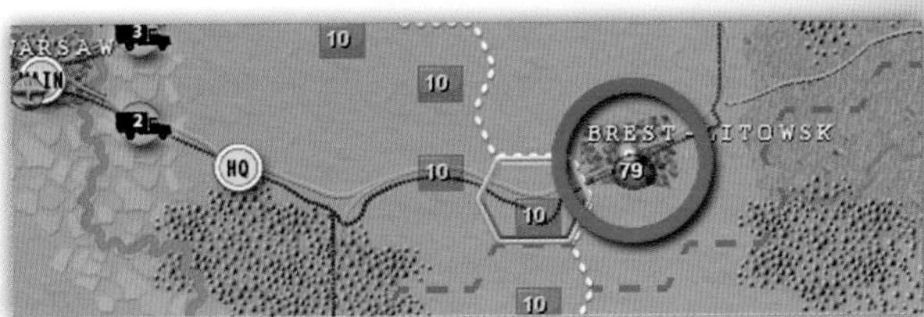

Any future attack on the Brest-Litowsk hex, during the current turn, will have to carry over the 79 stacking points from the previous attack and may result in overstacking penalties

3.4.4.3. Logistical Icons

These display the logistical pipeline that provides the German Panzergruppes with fuel. There are bases, transport links (truck columns and trains) and Baltic Sea convoys.

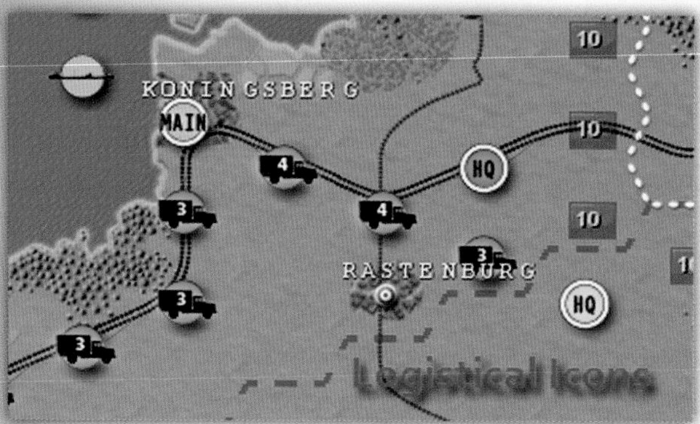

For further information refer to 6.1.6.5 Logistical icons.

3.4.4.4. Airfields

Each theatre has a main airfield (German regime only as airfields aren't shown for the Soviets). They are shown with a blue background and can be overlaid on logistical icons that may be present.

Potential airfield sites are shown on any Soviet city (once they've been captured they are no longer displayed on the map in order to reduce clutter).

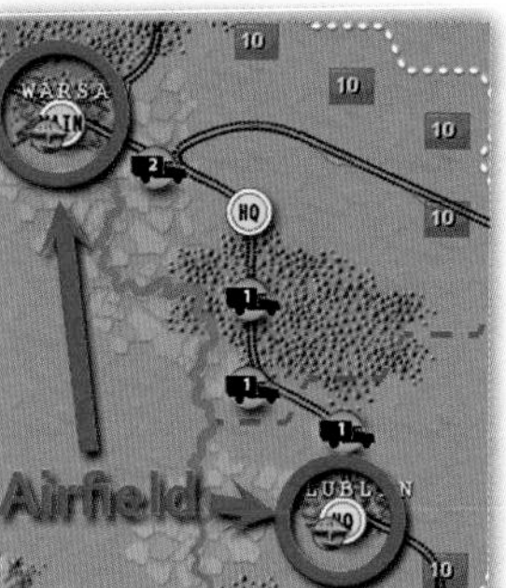

Main airfields at Warsaw, AGC and Lublin, AGS, at the start of the campaign

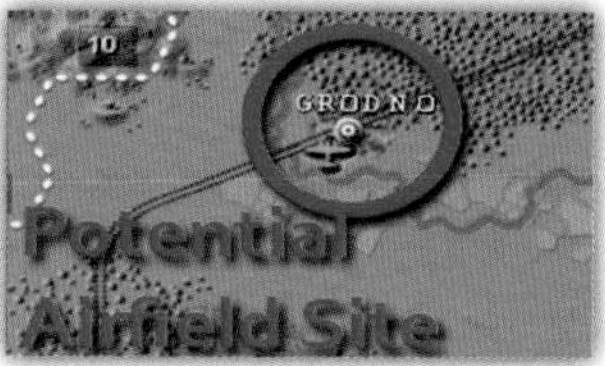

A main theatre airfield could be relocated here

3.5. TOP BAR ▶

This contains a series of 'tabs', the terrain window, hex information, the date and the fuel gauge. It's identical for both sides.

3.5.1. TERRAIN WINDOW

Terrain information is shown here. The type of terrain (Urban in the pic below), the hex coordinates (42,31 below - the x/y coordinate system works with 0,0 being at the top left of the map) and which regime owns the hex (Soviet Union).

The green bar shows the level of destruction of the city (has no game play effect). Fortifications also have a 'health bar' (structural points) and if it drops below zero they are considered destroyed

Hovering your mouse directly over the terrain window produces a detailed pop-up with a range of useful information.

SMOLENSK (42,31) SOVIET UNION

ROADS PRESENT: RAIL SOVIET(SE), HIGHWAY RUSSIAN (ALL WEATHER)(NE,SW)
RIVERS PRESENT: MEDIUM RIVER(SE,S)
BRIDGES PRESENT: SE
LOCATION PRESENT: MINOR CITY
LANDSCAPE: LIGHT URBAN

TROOPTYPE	ATT-MOD	DEF-MOD	A-ENTR	MX-ENTR	CROSS-RIV
INFANTRY	100%	100%	150	150	-30%
GUNS	40%	70%	150	150	-45%
MOTORIZED	50%	75%	0	0	-45%
LIGHT TANKS	50%	75%	0	0	-45%
MEDIUM TANKS	50%	75%	0	0	-50%
HEAVY TANKS	50%	75%	0	0	-55%

MOVETYPE	AP COST	ROAD	RIVER
FOOT	25	25/20	+20
MOTORIZED	15	10/10	+30
CAVALRY	20	20/20	+20
RAIL	NA	3/3	NA
TRACKED	15	10/10	+30
SUPPLY MOVE	1	2/1	+75
IMMOBILE	NA	NA/NA	+0
RAIL_CAP	NA	3/3	+0

COVER: 30
STRUCTURAL POINTS: 2000 OF 2000, AUTO RECOVER POINTS: 250

Terrain window tool tip - there's a lot to look at

TERRAIN WINDOW TOOL TIP	
Item	Explanation
Roads Present	Type of Road and Rail and hex sides that it crosses.
Rivers Present	Type (size) of River and hex sides that it crosses
Location Present	Major city (red dot), Minor city (grey dot) or Fortification
Landscape	Type of terrain
ATT-MOD	Modification of attack values for different troop types. Applies to the attacker
DEF-MOD	Modification of defence values for different troop types. Applies to the defender
A-ENTR	Number of points a unit Automatically Entrenches when first entering the hex' (digging in – see Unit Display 'Entrenchment')
MX-ENTR	Maximum number of Entrenchment points available in the hex for that troop type
CROSS-RIV	Combat penalty if attacking across the river Applies to the attacker
AP Cost	Movement cost to move into the hex in Action Points (AP) Can be over ridden by a road cost if the unit is moving ALONG the road. If the unit has insufficient AP available it can't enter the hex
ROAD	Movement costs in AP (over rides terrain cost). Because there are two type in the hex – Rail and All Weather Road there are two different numbers (in order of the 'roads present' listing so the rail would on the left hand side of the slash and the all weather road on the right) Note: 'Rail' and 'Rail_Cap' Movetypes can be ignored (internal use only)
RIVER	Additional movement cost (in AP) to cross the river
Cover	Provides a Defensive bonus in combat
Structural Points	Only applicable to Fortifications. Destroyed if < 0
ZOC Penalty	AP penalty to enter hex due to enemy Zone of Control (corresponds to the white squares on the map)
Enemy Terrain Penalty	AP penalty to enter hex due to it being enemy owned (corresponds to the white squares on the map)

Note the ROAD movement costs in the pic above. There are two roads present and the costs are separated by a slash ('/').

In the following example there are four different types of road in the hex (rail is considered a road type).

```
KAUNAS (25,32) SOVIET UNION
ROADS PRESENT: RAIL GERMAN(SW), RAIL SOVIET(SE), ROAD SEALED (ALL WEATHER)(NE), HIGHWAY RUSSIAN (ALL WEATHER)(N)
```

The order of the roads shown here is important as it corresponds to their movement costs below

```
MOVETYPE       AP COST   ROAD
FOOT           25        25/25/20/20
MOTORIZED      15        10/10/10/10
CAVALRY        20        20/20/20/20
RAIL           NA        1/3/6/3
TRACKED        15        10/10/10/10
SUPPLY MOVE    1         1/2/1/1
IMMOBILE       NA        NA/NA/NA/NA
RAIL_CAP       NA        1/3/6/3
```

Each movetype has a road cost, in Action Points (AP), for each of the four roads

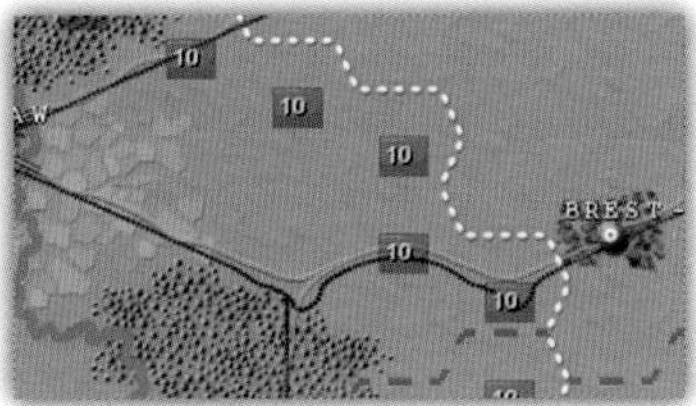

Because there are four road types there will be four separate road movement costs.

The last two entries in the Terrain tool tip table above show possible entries for dynamic conditions that can increase the cost (in AP) to move into the hex (above and beyond the normal cost). These correspond to the white boxes on the map.

If we highlighted one of the hexes the tool tip would show the following.

```
ZOC PENALTY IN AP = 10
```

The 10 AP additional cost is shown on the map in the white squares. Various things can influence these costs and a breakdown can always be found at the bottom of the terrain tool tip

In mud conditions the terrain window will show a 'Mud' prompt to further highlight this.

MUD. Start pushing those trucks

3.5.2. TOP TABS

The top bar has seven different tabs that, when clicked, drop down and provide a wealth of information. There are an additional three 'special' information tabs but they are found at the bottom of the screen and are discussed elsewhere (see 3.6.2 Bottom tabs).

Each tab can be viewed by either clicking on it or by use of an appropriate hot key.

TAB HOT KEYS	
Tab	Hot Key
Preferences	F1
Briefing	F2
Statistics	F3
Order of Battle (OOB)	F4
Reports	F5
Action Cards	F6
Strategic Map	F7

To close a tab you can either press ESC (escape), the appropriate hot key or click on the tab again (it's moved down).

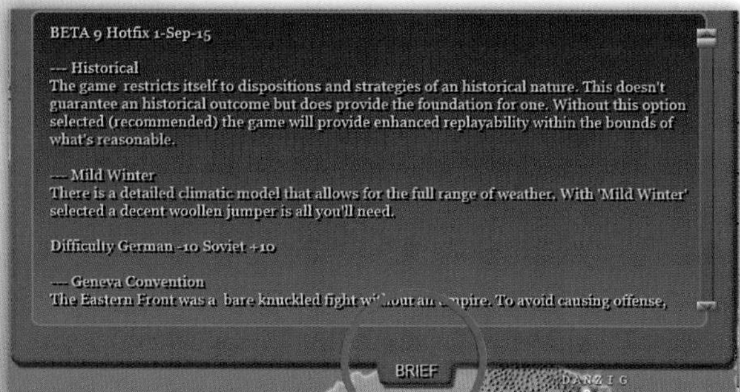

Click here to close

3.5.2.1. Preferences Tab

This gives direct in-game access to the various preference settings

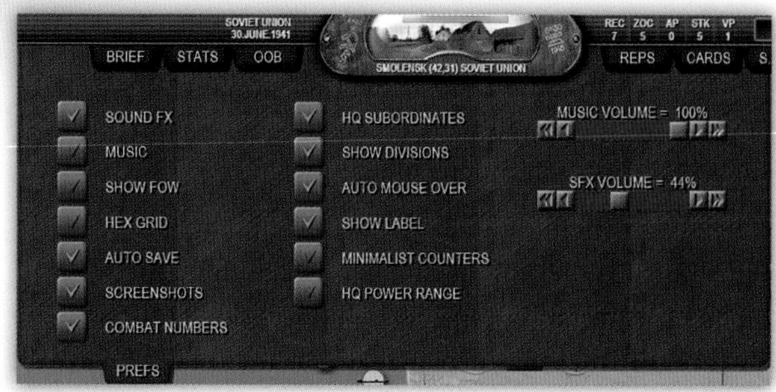

SoundFX toggles combat and movement sound effects. Don't expect Hollywood.

Music is self explanatory with volume sliders for both on the right.

'Show FOW' places a shroud on the map if Fog of War has been selected (highly recommended) as a start game option.

The shroud indicates areas of the map where you have no knowledge of enemy activity

'Hex Grid' toggles the grid on or off.

'AutoSave' creates an 'autosave.dc3' file, every turn, in the /savedgames directory.

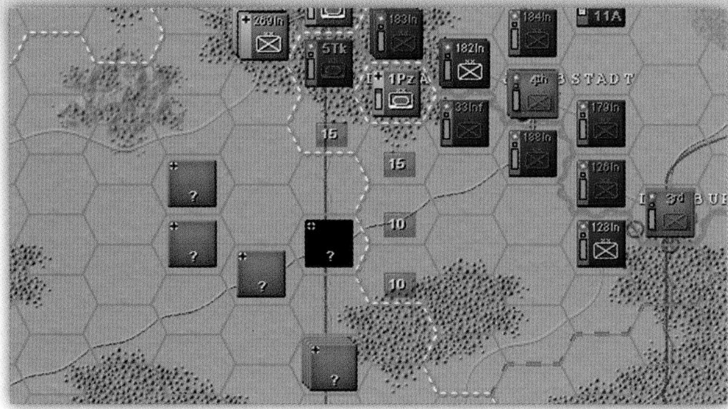

'Screenshots' toggles automatic screenshots on or off. When checked two screenshots are taken: one at the beginning of your turn and one at the end of your turn. Screenshots are stored in the /screenshots directory.

'Combat Numbers' swaps the combat display over to show numbers rather than symbols.

Numbers

Symbols

'HQ Subordinates' allows you to click on an HQ and have all subordinate HQ's, or Divisions highlighted.

AGN highlighting it's three subordinate Army and Panzergruppe HQ's

3rd Panzergruppe highlighting it's subordinate Divisions

'Show Divisions' highlights all subordinate Divisions.

'Auto Mouse Over' toggles tool tips on or off. When off you have to right click on a tool tip to view it. It's highly recommended to leave this option toggled on as tool tips play a vital role in the game displaying, in many cases, dynamic information that changes from turn to turn.

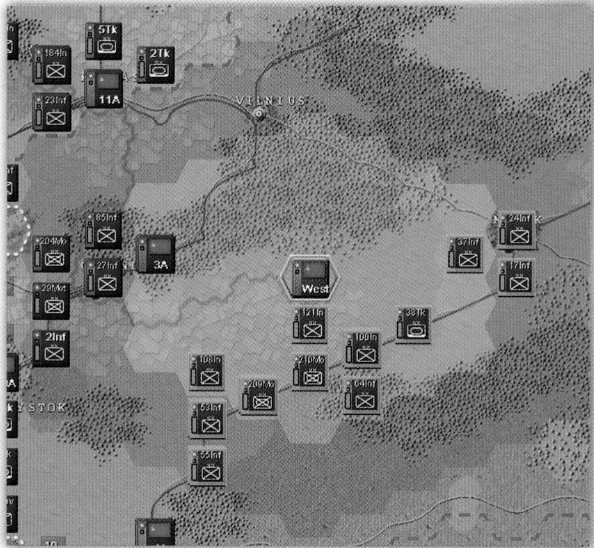

The varying colour bands highlight different ranges from the HQ where different levels of HQ combat bonuses apply (closer to the HQ the better) but the overall colouring shows the 5 hex radius of the command range that extends from each HQ

'Show Label' allows you to toggle place names (cities, rivers etc.) off. As these are important it's also recommended to leave this option on.

'Minimalist Counters' provide a simpler, alternative, unit counter presentation.

'HQ Power Range' allows you to view an HQ's Command Range whenever you click on an HQ.

3.5.2.2. Briefing Tab

This provides access to a range of information. Select a category by clicking on one of the tags along the top of the tab.

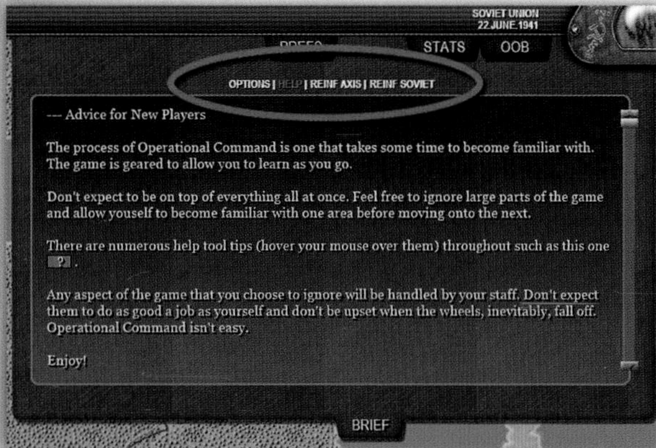

Click on a category where shown. Red text highlights the selected category

3.5.2.3. Statistics Tab

There are two main categories on the left hand side. 'Troops Statistics' allow you to view details on a wide range of troop types.

A range of options can be toggled on or off to filter the data

'Regime Statistics' allow you to see Replacements and a range of custom statistics.

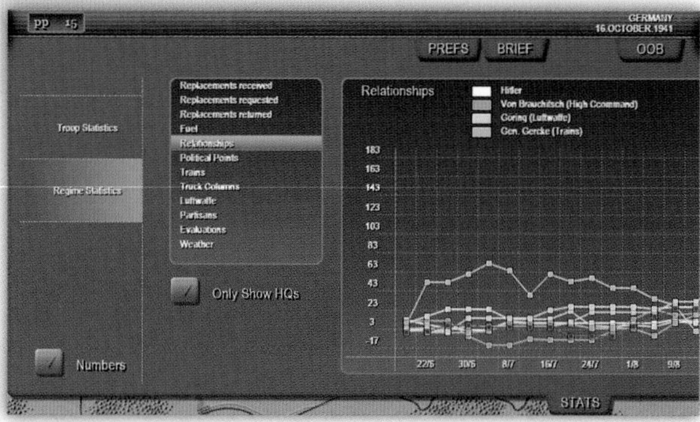

The 'Numbers' toggle (bottom left) layers numerical data points over the line graphs

3.5.2.4. Order of Battle (OOB)

This provides an 'expandable' OOB for the regime. Click on an HQ to display the next level down and double click on any unit to centre the map on it.

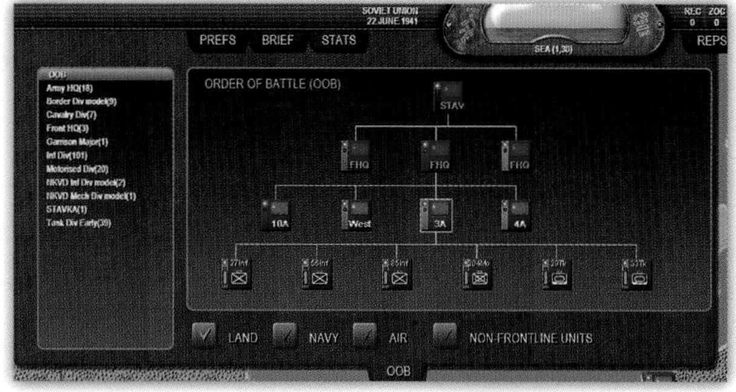

3.5.2.5. Report Tab

Each regime has a complete set of new reports appear in the tab each turn to reflect information compiled by their staff. Scroll through reports by the UP or DOWN mouse arrows or by using the MOUSE WHEEL.

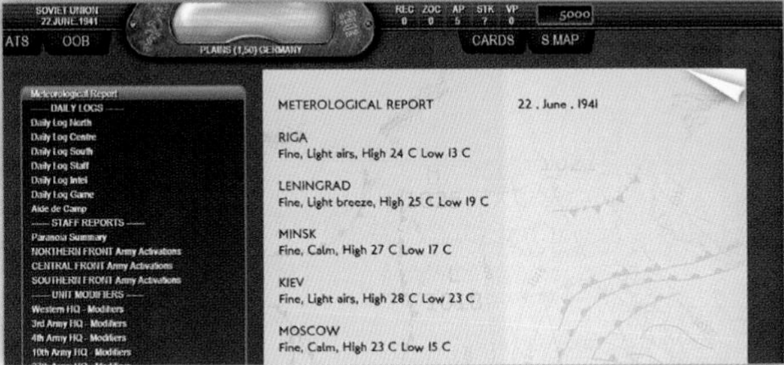
ATS
OOB
CARDS
S MAP
METEROLOGICAL REPORT
22 . June . 1941
RIGA
Fine, Light airs, High 24 C Low 13 C
LENINGRAD
Fine, Light breeze, High 25 C Low 19 C
MINSK
Fine, Calm, High 27 C Low 17 C
KIEV
Fine, Light airs, High 28 C Low 23 C
MOSCOW
Fine, Calm, High 23 C Low 15 C

It's not necessary to read every report every turn. There is a lot there and it's designed to be dipped into as you see fit. Imagine a big pile of reports on your desk. You're running a war and there isn't time to deal with it all. You'll read the ones that you deem to be important. Perhaps you'll make good use of the wastepaper bin and wing it. The game can accommodate a range of management styles

Timing

All the reports found in the tab are compiled by your staff based on information that's arrived at your headquarters at the *beginning of the turn*. Because of this any changes that you make *during* the turn won't show up until the following turn.

Asking a unit to Report Status! (a button on the bottom bar) is a different matter. Here you are establishing a communications link directly with the unit and the information you receive will be up to date, as at that moment.

An example of how this works we'll assign theatre artillery assets to Gen. Von Stülpnagel's 17th Army in AGS.

As this is something that's happened during the turn the 'Unit Modifiers' report for the 17th Army

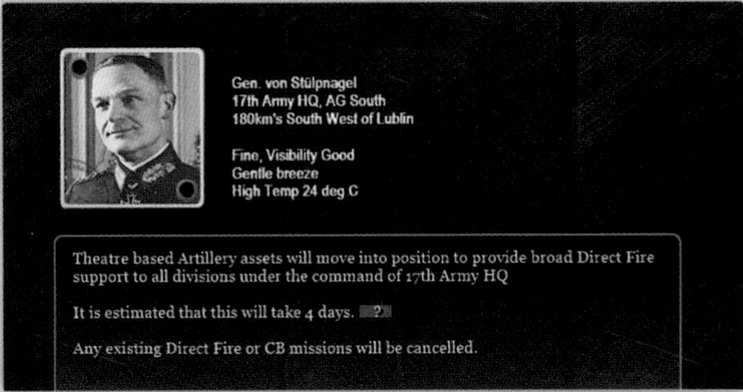
Gen. von Stülpnagel
17th Army HQ, AG South
180km's South West of Lublin
Fine, Visibility Good
Gentle breeze
High Temp 24 deg C
Theatre based Artillery assets will move into position to provide broad Direct Fire support to all divisions under the command of 17th Army HQ
It is estimated that this will take 4 days.
Any existing Direct Fire or CB missions will be cancelled.

Von Stülpnagel is the only German commander in the game that smiled (sort of) when his portrait was taken

won't show it as it is current for the situation at the start of the turn. Same with the Daily Theatre Log and the Aide de Camp report.

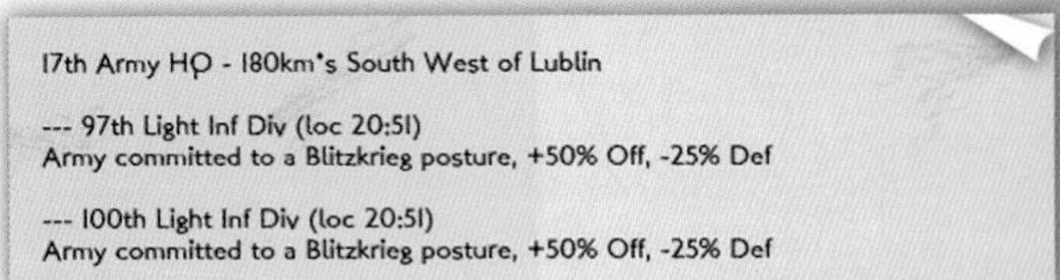
17th Army HQ - 180km's South West of Lublin
--- 97th Light Inf Div (loc 20:51)
Army committed to a Blitzkrieg posture, +50% Off, -25% Def
--- 100th Light Inf Div (loc 20:51)
Army committed to a Blitzkrieg posture, +50% Off, -25% Def

Your headquarters staff do what they can but there is always going to be a lag between the occurrence of an event and when they become aware of it

If one of the 17th Armies Divisions is contacted directly by radio (asked to Report Status!) it will inform you that theatre artillery has been assigned but that it won't be arriving till next turn. You can contact it immediately after assigning the artillery and it will keep you fully up to date with the current situation.

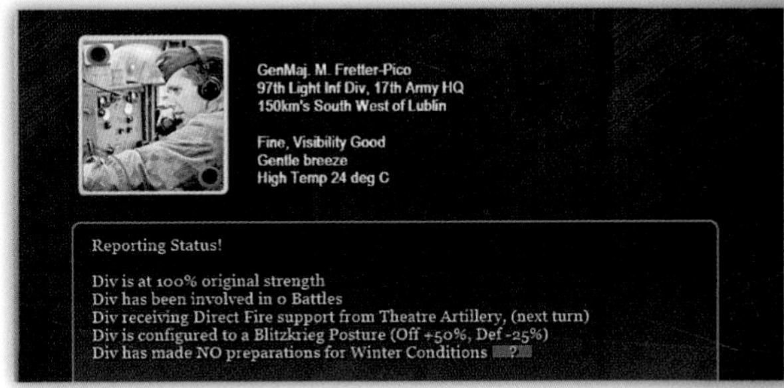
GenMaj. M. Fretter-Pico
97th Light Inf Div, 17th Army HQ
150km's South West of Lublin
Fine, Visibility Good
Gentle breeze
High Temp 24 deg C
Reporting Status!
Div is at 100% original strength
Div has been involved in 0 Battles
Div receiving Direct Fire support from Theatre Artillery, (next turn)
Div is configured to a Blitzkrieg Posture (Off +50%, Def -25%)
Div has made NO preparations for Winter Conditions

GenMaj. Fretter-Pico's 97th Light Infantry haven't packed a jumper. Neither have the rest of the Wehrmacht

3.5.2.6. Cards Tab

Both regimes have a range of Action Cards available in their Card tab split between five different categories.

REPS
S MAP
Posture (9)
Operations (2)
Trouble Shooters (2)
Command (8)
Reinforcements (0)
ADMIT CRISIS
NO RETREAT!
REORGANISE
RELEASE TSAR...
CHANGE ORDE...
DEMAND POWER
Demand that the Poltiburo cede you ever more supreme executive powers!
(+5 PP per turn, increased Paranoia)
PLAY CARD

3.5.2.7. Strategic Map Tab

This provides a big picture overview. Clicking on the tab map will centre the main map on the chosen location. The 'Towns' tab (top right) provides an alphabetic drop down list of all cities in the game.

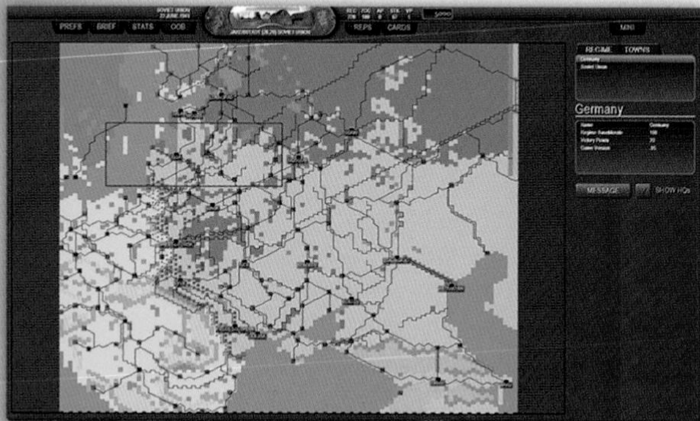

The 'Show HQs' checkbox on the right provides an operational perspective

3.5.3. FUEL

The Fuel 'gauge' shows the amount of fuel, in barrels, for the theatre, or front, in question.

Click on any hex and the fuel gauge will display how much fuel is present. For the Germans this is the fuel present at the point of use - the Panzergruppe HQ's. For the Soviets this represents the general pool of fuel available for all Fast Divisions within a Front.

The gauge is dynamic. Move a Fast Division (one with vehicles that uses fuel) and you can immediately see the fuel gauge decreasing. Same with a Fast Division engaged in combat (heavy fuel use). When it reaches zero there is no more fuel left for that turn.

As mentioned, the fuel gauge always reflects the amount available in the currently selected hex's theatre, or front. A tool tip is available to highlight what theatre, or front, that is. For further information see 6.1.6 Logistics.

3.5.4. DATE AND ROUND

The current date is shown here. Each turn is four days.

The first active turn of the campaign is round 2 (22nd June 1941). Round 1 is the special Pre-Start Turn

Round 1 is a special turn for both sides where no units can be moved but decisions can be made

Hovering your mouse over the date will show the round number.

No date is shown for the special Pre-Start Turn.

3.5.5. HEX INFORMATION

This provides a summary of important hex based information from the point of view of the active regime.

HEX INFORMATION	
Item	Explanation (always from point of view of Regime)
REC	Reconnaissance points see Counter shuffling/reconnaissance
ZOC	Zone of Control points see Counter shuffling/zone of control
AP	Action Points – additional cost to move into hex
STK	Stack points see Counter shuffling/stacking
VP	Victory points see Key concepts/winning the game

3.6. BOTTOM GUI ▶

This provides comprehensive unit details, the button bar and the bottom tabs. It's the same for both regimes.

The button bar, along the top, provides access to a wide range of functions.

There are three bottom tabs (each side has a different set of three).

The unit display is the main source of information on the currently selected unit.

3.6.1. BUTTON BAR

All quick access buttons appear on the bottom button bar. Certain buttons appear only when needed.

3.6.1.1. Minimise GUI

This toggles the bottom GUI display to either the default 'full view' or the 'minimal view' (button bar only visible).

Click the button to swap between the bottom GUI display modes

3.6.1.2. Move

This will allow you to move the selected unit. See 5.1.1 How to Move. Shortcut key 'M'.

3.6.1.3. Group Move

This will allow you to move all units in the selected hex together. -Movement is made at the rate of the slowest unit in the group. +Maximum movement ranged is limited to the unit with the lowest AP.

See 5.1.1 How to move. Shortcut key 'G'.

3.6.1.4. Report Status!

The report status quick action button is found on the bottom tool bar (bottom left) but only when you have a unit (Division or Army level HQ) selected.

It enables you to contact the unit directly by radio (perhaps using intermediate communication links where larger distances are involved) and obtain an up-to-date status report.

The German Player can freely contact as many units as he wishes at any point. The Soviet Player, on the other hand, is burdened by a lack lustre Command and Communications infrastructure and can struggle, at times, to establish a viable communications link from STAVKA to the unit in question.

For more information see 6.2.10 Communication.

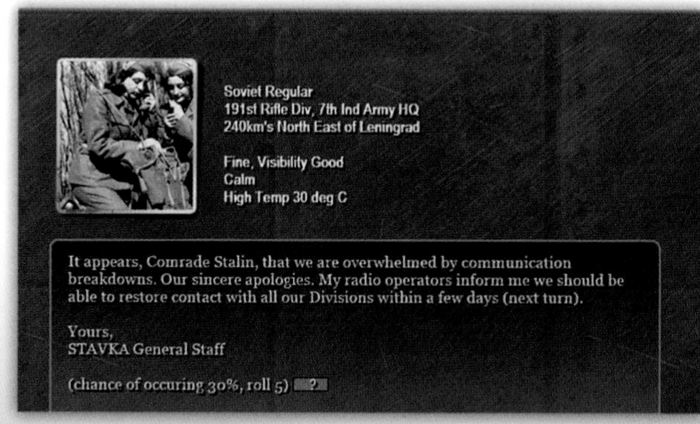

The 191st Rifle Division on the northern Finnish front is unable to be contacted. At least the weather is good

STAFF ADVICE

Make full use of your ability to raise a unit on the radio. A good commander stays in touch with his units.

3.6.1.5. Helpers

These provide special 'helper' actions to a Player in need. Both sides have a different set of Helpers (the Soviets only have one).

Helper buttons are unique in that they are 'double click'. To prevent accidental use they require a two stage process to use.

For more information see 4.5.1 Helpers.

3.6.1.6. Attack

This button only appears once an enemy unit has been selected. It allows the Player to initiate an attack.
Shortcut key 'A'
For more more information see 5.3.1 How to Attack.

3.6.1.7. Unit Display Toggle

This allows you to toggle through three different unit display modes - Nato counters, silhouettes and no counters.

Shortcut keys '2' (Nato counters), '1' (silhouettes), '0' (no counters)

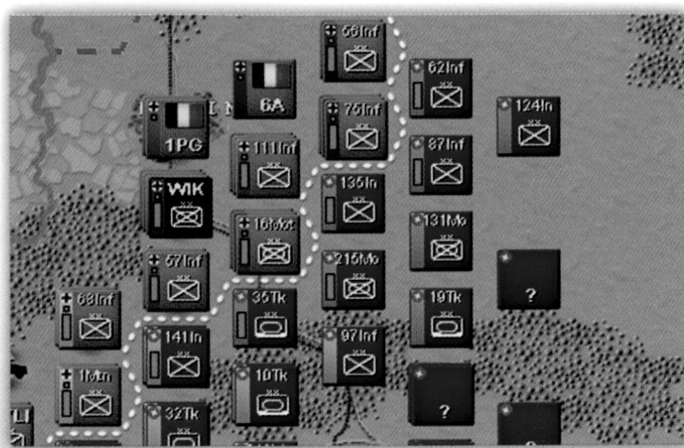

Default Nato counter display ('2')

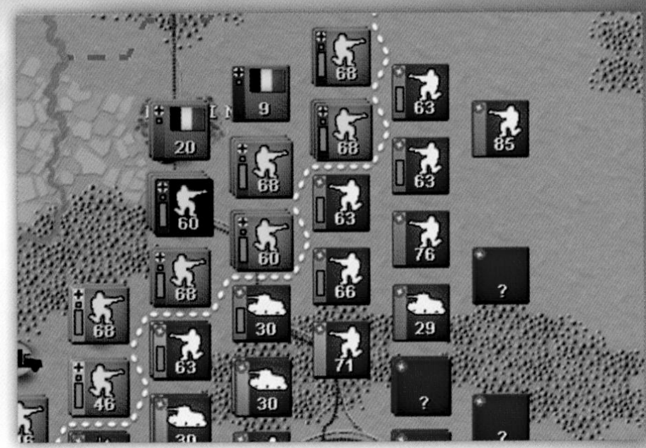

Silhouette counters display ('1')

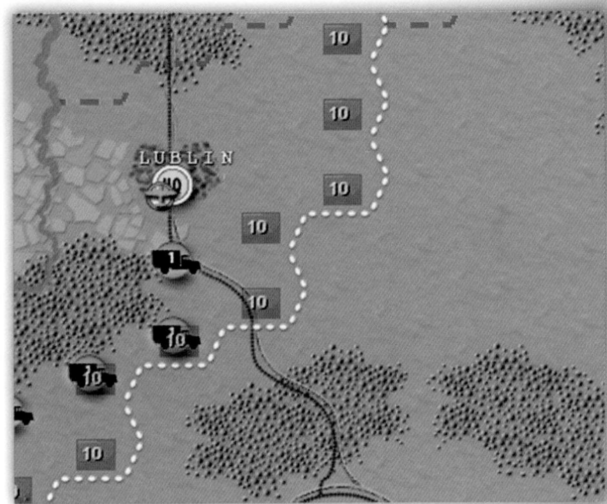

No counters display ('0')

3.6.1.8. Hex Information

This allows you toggle the extra hex information (White boxes and logistical icons) off. It's recommended they are left on for game play reasons but sometimes it's handy to switch them off to see an unadulterated map. Shortcut key '4'

3.6.1.9. Zoom In & Out

There are three levels of zoom.
Shortcut keys '+' & '-' or MOUSEWHEEL

Zoomed out mode allows for a big picture overview of the situation.

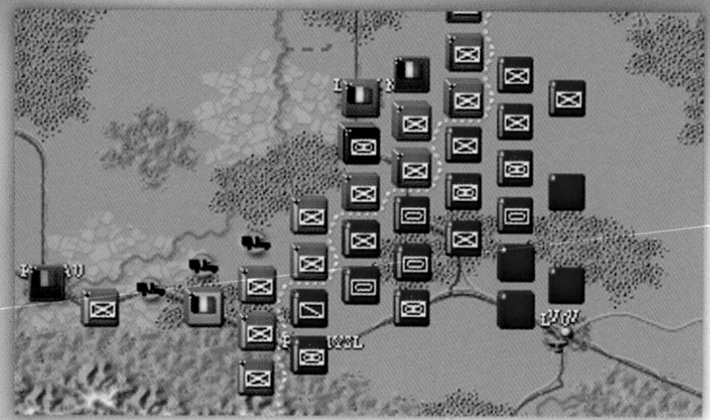

Zoomed in mode provides an additional button that allows you to toggle between two views.

Spread out toggle

Shortcut key '3'

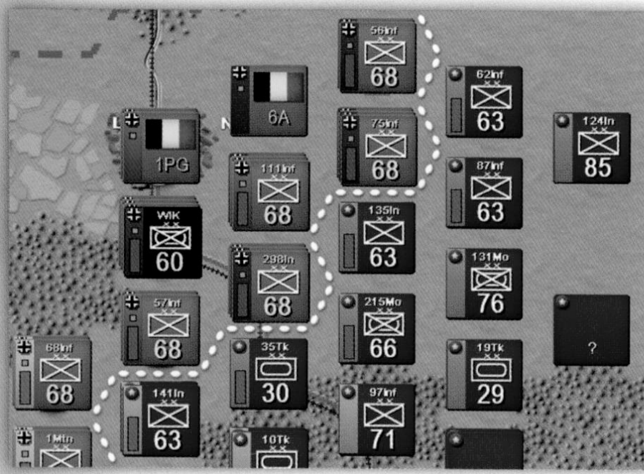

Normal zoomed in mode.

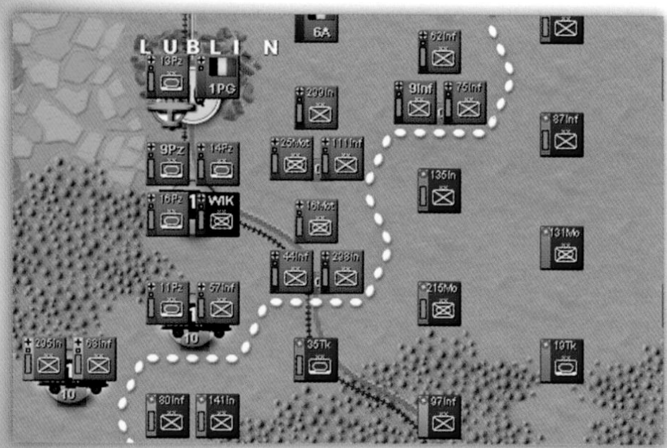

Spread out zoomed in mode.

3.6.1.10. Supply

Places a supply layer overlay on the map. Note that this refers to General Supply, not Fuel for Fast Divisions.

Activate the button to show the overlay. Click on a unit to highlight the supply path. Different colours in the overlay indicate different levels of supply. While light green is best (full supply) while ever the unit is within a hex covered by the shaded overlay, it is receiving some supply.

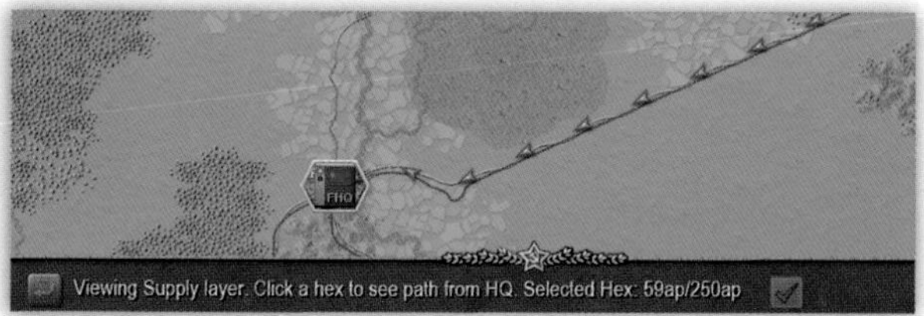

The red arrows show the path that supply travels to the unit

If it is outside of any coloured overlay it isn't receiving any supply and its situation will soon be, if not already, critical.

To exit the supply layer press ESC or press the 'revert' button (bottom left).

For more information see 4.14 Supply.

3.6.1.11. History

This brings up the History screen where the Player can view their opponent's moves during the previous turn. The level of information provided depends on the 'Fog of War' and the 'Hide AI Moves' options (game start) have been chosen.

Once activated the history screen acts as a you tube clip time line with the main map displaying the 'movie' of past moves and battles. 'Play' to view all in sequence or use the arrows to step forward or backwards. You can also grab the slider and drag it along the time line. 'Next Battles' allows you to skip from battle to battle, ignoring all the interim moves.

The history screen controls

Shortcut Key 'P' to start/stop play (P as in 'Pause/Play')

Exit the history screen by pressing ESC or clicking on the 'Revert' button (left).

3.6.1.12. Surrender

Not all campaigns go to plan. Wave the white flag and start again, wiser for the experience.

3.6.1.13. Save

This brings up a file dialogue and allows you to save the game to a named file.

Reloading a previously saved game is done through the main start screen option.

3.6.1.14. End Turn

Press this to end your turn. A confirmation dialogue will appear (press SPACEBAR to say 'Yes')

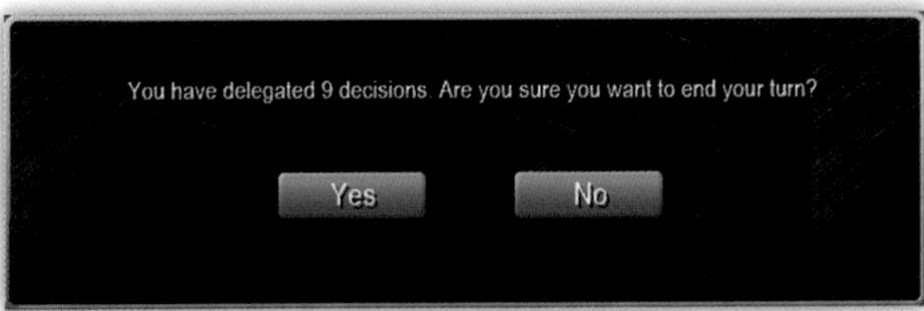

3.6.2. BOTTOM TABS

These provide a range of information that can be accessed at any time (even while you have the report tab open). They enable you to view important facts, at a glance, without having to rummage through the Report tab. Dynamic tool tips provide a further, in depth, layer of information, when needed.

The main difference between the Tabs and the Reports is that the Reports are compiled, by your staff, at the beginning of the turn whereas the information found in the tabs is more recent and takes into account a lot of the actions that you have taken during the turn.

3.6.2.1. German

Relationship Tab

The German Player has a number of characters that he interacts with. The game tracks the level of his relationship in both numeric (eg. '-11') and descriptive (eg. 'Poor') form.

The handful of characters who have the most impact on his ability to prosecute the campaign are shown in this tab. Dynamic tool tips provides a list of all current in-game effects as a result of your current relationship level with each character.

The tab shows the Führer (National leader), F.M Von Brauchitsch (your immediate boss), Reichsmarschall Göring (runs the Luftwaffe), your three theatre commanders (AGN, AGC & AGS) and your two Logistical Generals, Gercke (in charge of trains) and Wagner (in charge of truck columns)

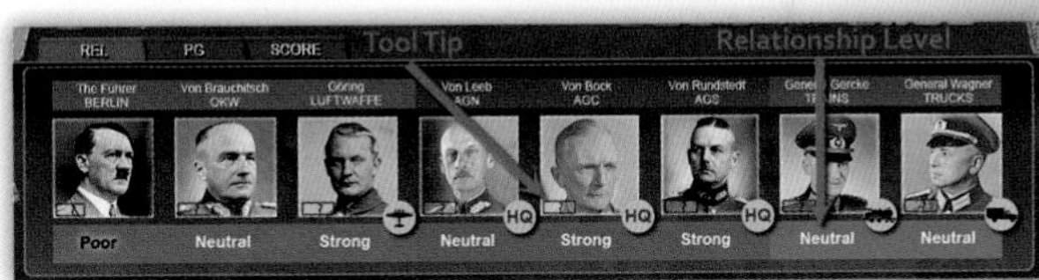

Relationship levels are colour coded. White's good, Black is bad. Notice the 'Poor' relationship with the Führer'

The current relationship level, in descriptive form, can be seen at the bottom. Small icons highlight what each character does.

For further information see 4.8.1 German Characters.

Panzergruppe Tab

This provides summary information on all four Panzergruppes in the German Order of Battle.

There are dynamic tool tips available for each Panzergruppe and they are found in the yellow

boxes within the commander portraits. The numbers on either side show the percentage of 'runners' (vehicles still working) for tanks (Panzers), to the left, and transports (half tracks and trucks) on the right. At the start of the campaign the 'runners' are 100 for both (100%, all working) but battle casualties and break downs reduce this. Replacements and refits serve to increase the number of runners available.

Each Panzergruppe has four 'dials' underneath their commander portraits which provide a quick summary of all critical data.

FUEL		
Icon	Quotas on hand	Effect
UP arrow	Two, or more, Quotas (>=2)	Plenty of fuel. All OK.
SIDE arrow	Between One (>=1) and Two Quotas (<2)	Adequate fuel. All OK.
DOWN arrow	Less than One Quota (<1)	Fuel Rationing needed.
CROSS	No Fuel on hand	Out of Fuel!

For further information see 6.1.6.2 Quotas.

AIRFIELD RANGE		
Icon	Range to Theatre Airfield	Distance Penalty
UP arrow	Close range (<=5 hexes)	<= 10
SIDE arrow	Medium range (>5 and <=10 hexes)	>10 and <=20
DOWN arrow	Long range (>10 hexes)	>20
CROSS	Out of range (>15 hexes away)	Out of range

For further information see 6.1.3 Luftwaffe.

AMMUNITION		
Icon	Ammunition Level	Effect
UP arrow	>= 100	Sufficient Ammunition. All OK
SIDE arrow	Less than 100 and >= 90	Warning. Levels getting low.
DOWN arrow	Less than 90	Ammo Shortages Possible
CROSS	Cut-Off from FSB	No Fuel, No Ammo.

For further information see 6.1.6.13 Ammunition.

COMMAND FOCUS		
Icon	Focus?	Relationship with Theatre Commander
UP arrow	Panzergruppe currently HAS FOCUS	Positive
SIDE arrow	Not applicable	Not applicable
DOWN arrow	Panzergruppe COULD have focus but currently doesn't.	Positive
CROSS	Panzergruppe CAN'T have focus	Negative

For further information see 6.1.1 Command Focus.
For further information see 6.1.2 Panzergruppes.

Score Tab

This provides a summary of where you stand in the game. It shows your objective, the difficulty level that you are playing at and your scores. Two tank 'arrows' move back and forth as the tide of the victory ebbs and flows to provide a visual representation of your, and your opponents, scores.

Your opponent's objective is hidden initially but may be revealed later in the campaign

For further information see 4.6 Winning the Game.

3.6.2.2. Soviet

Command Tab

The Command tab provides an 'all-on-one' information source for the Soviet Player. On the far left is Stalin. His Paranoia level is shown and his tool tip provides a breakdown of all factors influencing it that turn (see 6.2.3 Paranoia).

Next to Stalin are the three front Marshals who command the Front HQ's. Their tool tips give a readout of all armies within their front and their level of activation this turn (full, partial or none). See 6.2.2 Activation.

Below them are their two key qualities (all Soviet front and army commanders have the same qualities) - Initiative and Threat ratings. Initiative provides a global bonus (if positive) or penalty (if negative) to their subordinate armies activation chances.

Threat ratings contribute directly to Stalin's paranoia level (see 6.2.3 Paranoia).

Marshals can, unlike German theatre commanders (their rank equivalents), be changed (the Soviet Player can order them shot, for example) during the game. Any changes will be reflected immediately in the Command tab with a new portrait and set of qualities.

Over on the right are Stalin's two trusted 'Troubleshooters' who answer only to him and move around the map, from HQ to HQ (at the Player's direction), dealing with whatever crisis is on hand.

They have special sets of 'Officer cards' that provide them with a wide range of abilities whenever they are at any HQ (front or army) other than STAVKA (the Soviet equivalent of the German High Command HQ in Berlin).

The current location (or 'in transit' status) is shown below and their tool tips provide further details on their location and activity (see 6.2.4 Troubleshooters).

Score Tab

This provides a summary of where you stand in the game. It shows your objective, the difficulty level that

The Soviet Score tab is the same as the German one in that both have access to the overall scores and difficulty ratings and neither can see the other's objective

you are playing at and your scores. Two tank 'arrows' move back and forth as the tide of the victory ebbs and flows to provide a visual representation of your, and your opponents, scores.

For further information see 4.6 Winning the Game.

Reinforcement Tab

The Soviets receive a lot of reinforcement armies (the invasion triggered a massive internal mobilisation). The tab allows the Soviet Player to view the immediate schedule of reinforcement armies by front. Keep in mind that the timing is for the arrival of the Army HQ. Subordinate Divisions will arrive at least one turn later (probability based unlike the HQ's which are fixed according to the schedule).

The Soviet Player also has the option of reassigning an Army from one front to another by using the 'Change Orders' Action card (see 6.2.5.4 Command).

T+1 indicates next turn, T+2 the turn after, etc. The triple dots at the bottom of the lists (Central and Southern fronts) indicate that there is more to come (off the page but they will gradually move upwards as time progresses)

For further information see 6.2.9 Reinforcements.

3.6.3. UNIT DISPLAY

The unit display is the main source of information on the currently selected unit.

3.6.3.1. Unit Statistics

Underneath the unit name (17th Panzer Division, below) and its HQ (2nd Panzergruppe) are seven statistics that are common to all units.

Action Points

Are used for movement and combat. The normal allowance is 100 AP per turn but this can vary depending on a wide range of circumstances.

Supply Consumption

The rate at which the unit is consuming supplies. Normally 100. Supply is needed to maintain combat effectiveness and to recover Readiness.

For more information see 4.14 Supply and 5.2.1 Readiness.

Integrity

This shows how much of the units original Order of Battle are still present and it influences the chance of a unit breaking in combat.

It has no direct combat effect other than triggering the chance to break below the threshold shown in the tool tip. Low morale can aggravate the situation and combine to increase the chance of breaking.

The tool tip will show the level at which the unit is prone to breaking at. This varies. Normal Wehrmacht units can break at below 50% whereas for SS units it can be 30%. Romanian units, for example, can break at 60% or below.

Readiness

Is the unit sitting, slouched on a chair, or is it on its feet, ready for action? Readiness determines the amount of Action Points a unit receives and influences a unit's combat strength. Readiness decreases as a result of movement and combat. You gain readiness from being in supply.

For more information see 5.2.1 Readiness.

Experience

Units start the campaign with differing levels of experience. The German forces are hardened, combat veterans of recent campaigns in Western Europe and have higher experience levels than the Soviets Regular forces. The Soviet Conscript Armies that are raised en-mass to fend of the invaders have very low levels of experience.

Experience acts as a combat modifiers.

For further information see 5.2.6 Experience.

Morale

Morale is a measure of how well the unit will fight. Morale influences how many casualties a unit will take before breaking (it works in conjunction with Integrity).

Morale recovers automatically, each turn, once the unit is out of combat. The closer a unit is to its HQ the faster the recovery rate.

For further information see 5.2.3 Morale.

Entrenchment

Is a measure of how well the unit is dug in and its level of defensive preparations. Entrenchment levels provide a defensive combat bonus.

For further information see 5.2.7 Entrenchment.

3.6.3.2. Unit Troops

Each unit is made up of a combination of infantry, cavalry, vehicles, guns and staff. The number of each component is tracked and they are shown in the component display.

The numbers in the bottom right of the pictures indicate how many are on hand (there are 5000 infantry in the pic above, for example). The foreground and background of the pictures change to reflect the terrain the unit is currently in.

If the unit is experiencing any combat bonuses or penalties they are shown as coloured boxes. Often there are a number of factors affecting these and the boxes provide the cumulative total. To view a breakdown of combat bonuses and penalties ask the unit to Report Status! (button, bottom centre left).

The RED BOX on the left shows the OFFENSIVE combat bonus/penalty.

The BLUE BOX on the right shows the DEFENSIVE combat bonus/penalty.

You can click on an individual troop type picture to obtain a pop-up with more information.

3.6.3.3. Movement Type

The movement type that the unit is using (Tracked, Motorised, Foot) is shown with a white silhouette icon to the left of the unit name. A mouse over tool tip gives more information.

STAFF ADVICE

If you have a Fast Divisions (has vehicles) that doesn't appear to be moving as fast as it should check the movement type of the unit. If it is showing as 'Foot' it's likely that there aren't enough transports (trucks or half tracks) remaining to carry the unit's complement of soldiers. As the unit moves at the pace of the slowest troop type everybody will be throttling back to walking pace. Hopefully replacements will be arriving shortly.

3.6.3.4. Status Icons

To the right of the unit name can be found the Status Icon zone. Here you can find small icons that represent various states such as posture types, the presence of theatre artillery support or TAC, out of command range warnings etc.

The red/blue arrow to the right of 'Status' is actually an icon indicating that the unit is configured to a Blitzkrieg posture

Mouse over tool tips provide information on each icon.

There aren't that many Status Icons and they provide a handy, quick visual guide, of key factors affecting the unit.

3.6.3.5. Units in Hex

If there are any other units present in the hex they will be shown here. You can click on the unit directly (either on the map or in the unit display as shown below) and they will become the currently selected unit.

3.6.3.6. Unit Settings

These allow you to adjust various parameters that affect the unit.

Click on a setting to toggle through the available options

All three settings are an average of the Division setting and those of its HQ's. For example, if the Division's RETR setting is set at 100% and both its

HQ's (Army and Theatre) are configured to 50% the setting will be averaged to 75%. Being able to configure HQ settings allows you to make broad brush changes quickly (eg. 'All this Army' or 'All this Front').

UNIT SETTINGS	
Setting	Explanation
RETR	Retreat Percentage (what level of loss before the unit retreats) see Combat/Retreat Setting
SUPL	Supply Level (do you want it to receive less than full supply?) see Key Concepts/Supply
RPL	Replacement Priority see Key Concepts/replacements

3.6.3.7. Unit Details

A lot of specific, technical, details on a unit are found here. There are two tabs available, the default 'Basic Details' and the 'Replacements Received'.

Basic Details

Supply Stats

Full details of supply received and supply on hand are found here.

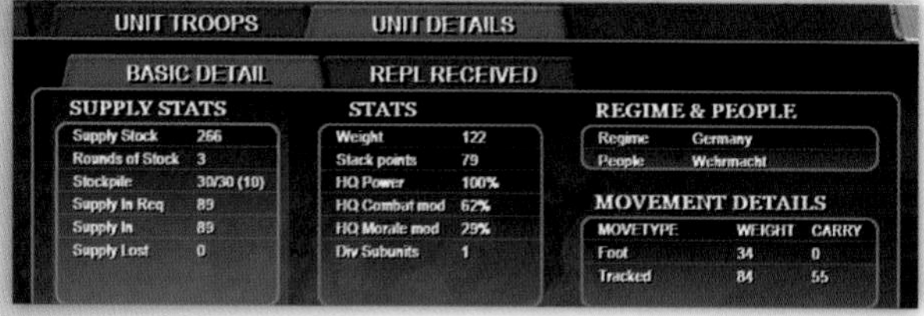

For further information see 4.14.2 Unit Supply Stats.

Stats

Each troop type has a 'Weight'. As you aren't shipping units across the Atlantic their cumulative total is there for completion only.

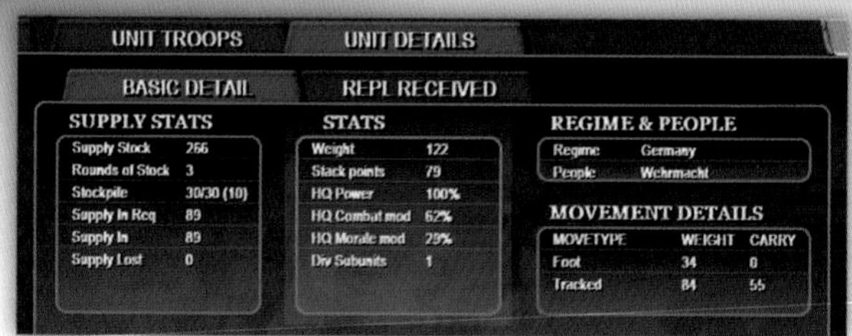

'Stack Points' are more useful and indicate how much the unit will contribute to the hex stacking used in combat calculations (there are penalties for overstacking units in a hex to prevent you from piling up ten units and attacking all at once).

For more information see 5.2.9 Stacking.

The following three items all refer to the units HQ. The first, 'HQ Power' indicates how far the unit is from its HQ. The further away it is the benefits the HQ will provide. If HQ Power is 0% then the unit is considered to be outside of command range (see 4.13 Command Range).

'HQ Combat mod' provides a combat bonus (HQ staff are coordinating and assisting) to the unit.

'HQ Morale mod' provides a morale bonus to the unit.

Both of these bonuses decrease the further the unit is from its HQ.

STAFF ADVICE

It isn't practical to bunch the subordinate Divisions of an Army, or Panzergruppe, around their HQ in order to gain the maximum bonus. Provided the Divisions are within Command Range (5 hexes) they should be O.K but consider pulling a unit under stress back in order to be closer to its HQ.

'Div Subunits' refers to the number of subformations, eg. Regiments, attached to the Division. In Decisive Campaigns 3 all units are Divisions so this value will always be '1' and can be disregarded.

Movement Details

A Division often has a mixture of troop types as shown below for the 17th Panzer Divison. Transports (trucks and half tracks) have a 'Carry' capacity (they can transport passengers). Provided their carry capacity is greater, or equal, than the weight of any 'Foot' troop types, then the entire Division will move at the 'Tracked' movement rate (or 'Motorised' if it had trucks instead of half tracks).

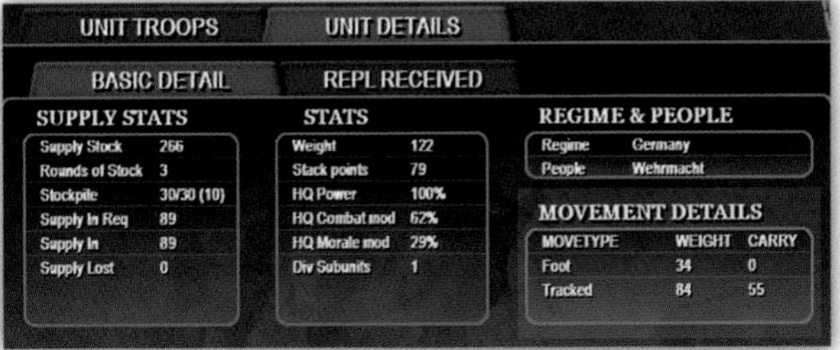

In the example above the half tracks can carry 55 points of weight. The infantry within the Division have a weight of only 34 so there is plenty of spare transport capacity. If, as a result of combat, the number of half tracks dropped to below that of the foot sloggers weight then their would be insufficient transport capacity and a portion of the infantry would have to walk.

This isn't good as the Division will move at the pace of its slowest component, in this case the walking soldiers ('foot'). The Movement type icon (the silhouette to the left of the unit name) will change from 'Tracked' to 'Foot' and the Division will move at the pace of normal infantry.

Replacements Received

Only the Germans receive troop type replacements. The Soviets receive replacement armies instead. The tab shows details of what's requested and what's arrived.

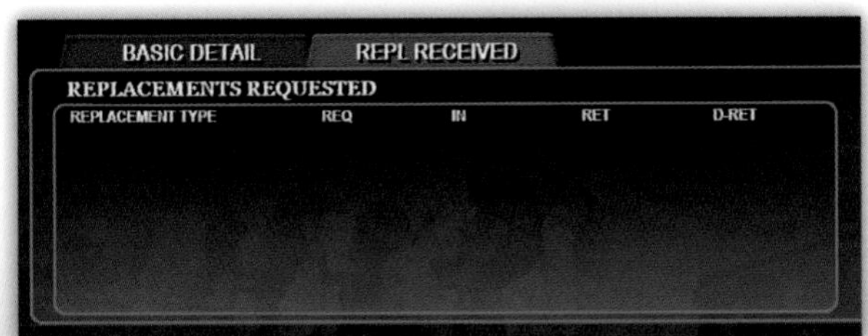

For further information see 6.1.17 Replacements.

3.6.3.8. HQ Units

These are identical to normal Divisions with the addition of a default 'Officer Info' tab. This shows a portrait of the commander (all HQ's have a commander) and a set of officer qualities to the right. Mouse over tool tips let you know which is which.

Officer cards (see 3.9.2 Officer cards) may be present in Army, Panzergruppe, HQ's.

The German officer qualities are Offence, Defence, Manoeuvre, Inspire and Entrench (left to right) and are utilised only when Officer cards are present and being used.

For further information (Germans) see 6.1.5.8 Officer Qualities.

The Soviet officer qualities are Initiative and Threat and are used for determining Activation and raising Stalins Paranoia level respectively (see 6.2 Soviet Command).

For further information (Soviets) see 6.2.1 Commanders.

STAFF ADVICE

Both sides have HQ's with commanders that each have officer qualities but the mechanics of how their commanders work are different.

Immediately below each commander portrait is a large percentage number which is the total combat bonus for all subordinate Divisions (modified by the distance the Division is away

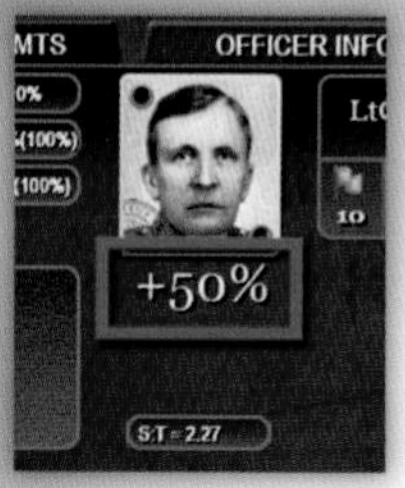

from the HQ). You can see this bonus showing in an individual Division's Basic Details tab under 'Stats' (HQ Combat mod). A mouse over tool tip on the percentage number provides a breakdown.

IN DETAIL

If an HQ Commander has a 50% combat bonus, as in the pic above, then a subordinate Division that is sufficiently close to the HQ, such that its HQ Power rating is 100% (Basic Details tab), will show an 'HQ Combat mod' of the same value, 50%. If the Division is a long distance away, say 5 hexes, it may have an HQ Power rating of only 20% in which case its 'HQ Combat mod' will be 10% (50% x 0.20)

Down the bottom, under the commander's portrait, is the 'Staff to Troops' ratio. Provided this is above 1.0 the HQ has sufficient staff to effectively command all its subordinate Divisions. This will be the case unless the HQ has suffered casualties to its complement of staff in which case all its Divisions will incur combat penalties until enough replacement staff arrive to raise the ratio back above 1.

It's possible to click on a commander portrait for an information pop-up.

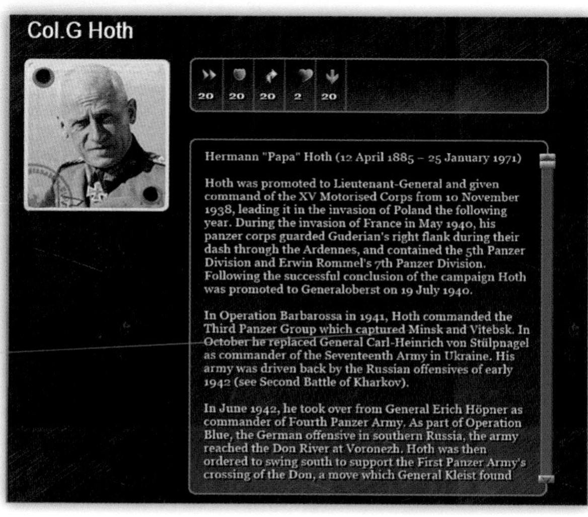

Col.G Hoth
20 20 20 2 20
Hermann "Papa" Hoth (12 April 1885 – 25 January 1971)
Hoth was promoted to Lieutenant-General and given command of the XV Motorised Corps from 10 November 1938, leading it in the invasion of Poland the following year. During the invasion of France in May 1940, his panzer corps guarded Guderian's right flank during their dash through the Ardennes, and contained the 5th Panzer Division and Erwin Rommel's 7th Panzer Division. Following the successful conclusion of the campaign Hoth was promoted to Generaloberst on 19 July 1940.
In Operation Barbarossa in 1941, Hoth commanded the Third Panzer Group which captured Minsk and Vitebsk. In October he replaced General Carl-Heinrich von Stülpnagel as commander of the Seventeenth Army in Ukraine. His army was driven back by the Russian offensives of early 1942 (see Second Battle of Kharkov).
In June 1942, he took over from General Erich Höpner as commander of Fourth Panzer Army. As part of Operation Blue, the German offensive in southern Russia, the army reached the Don River at Voronezh. Hoth was then ordered to swing south to support the First Panzer Army's crossing of the Don, a move which General Kleist found

3.7. UNITS ▶

There are two types of units - Headquarters of varying levels and Divisions. Headquarters are easily identifiable as they have a large national flag on their counter. Divisions have a collection of symbols and numbers.

3.7.1. HEADQUARTERS

The German Command structure has four levels of headquarters. High Command in Berlin, OKH at Posen (where the German Player is assumed to reside), an HQ for each of the three theatres (AGN, AGC, AGS) and a lot of Army, or Panzergruppe (army equivalents), HQ's that do the hard work.

The Soviet structure has only three levels - STAVKA (where the Soviet Player is assumed to reside), an HQ for each of the three fronts (Northern, Central, Southern) and many Army HQ's (there are no Panzergruppes in the Red Army).

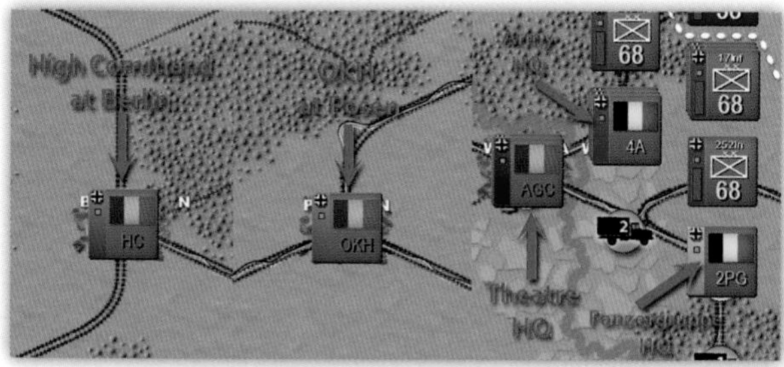

Why are the higher level HQ's greyed out? Because they are fixed in position (immobile)

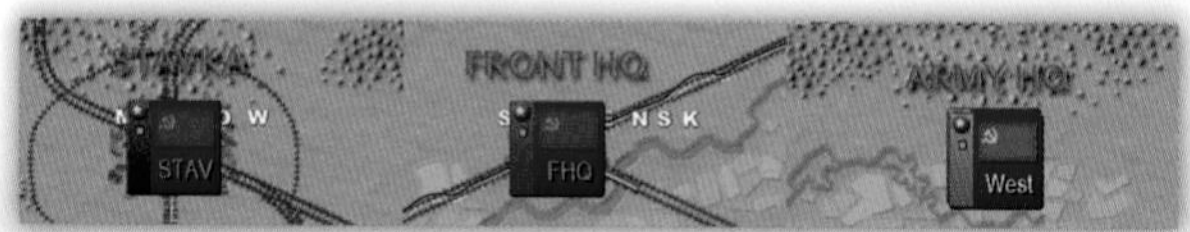

'STAV' represents STAVKA and 'FHQ' is a Front HQ (there are three)

For further information see 4.7 Command Structure.

3.7.2. UNIT TYPES

Divisions are one of four basic types - Armoured, Motorised, Cavalry or Infantry. Each has a unique NATO (Western military) symbol. There can be a wide range of differences and naming conventions within types. A German Armoured Division is called a Panzer Division, for example, whereas a Soviet one could be a Tank or Shock Division.

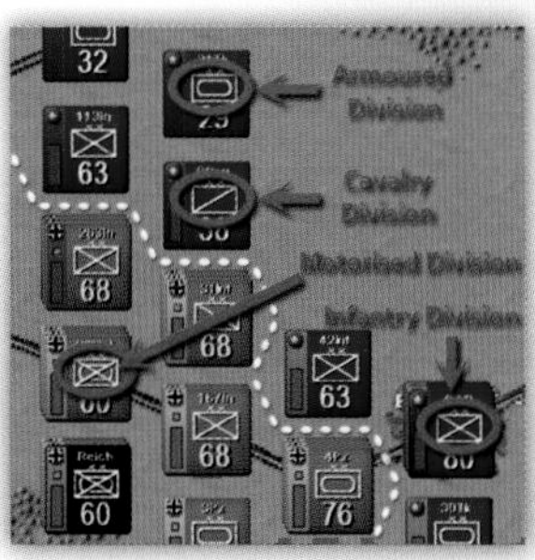

A Division's type provides a quick reference for its purpose. Infantry are going to be full of marching soldiers. Cavalry will be mounted and have more mobility. Motorised are going to have trucks to transport the soldiers. Armoured are going to have tanks.

STAFF ADVICE

There are big differences between regimes. A German motorised Division will have enough trucks to transport all its soldiers and will move at the motorised (wheeled) movement rate. A Soviet equivalent will likely to be chronically short of trucks and won't have enough to transport everybody resulting in the Division moving at the rate of the slowest, marching, soldier. Likewise a German Panzer Division will, at the start of the campaign, be a powerful, fast moving force of destruction unlike a Soviet Tank Division full of old tanks and poorly trained crews.

The type of a Division has no game play effect beyond the fact that motorised and armoured Divisions have vehicles and are considered 'Fast' Divisions and require fuel. All the rest, those without vehicles, are considered 'Slow' Divisions.

3.7.3. COUNTERS

Regardless of the regime, all Divisional counters display the same information.

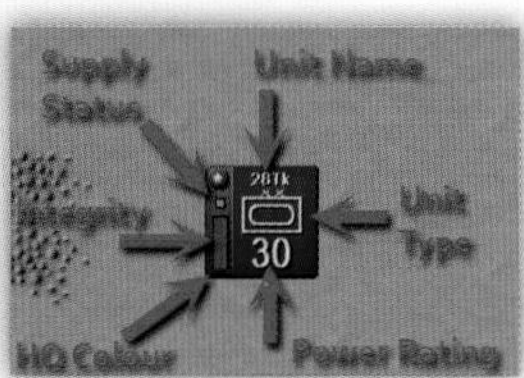

28th Tank Division, 8th Army

The unit name is a shortened version of that found in the unit display. Power Rating is an abstract combat value that allows you to compare units on a roughly equivalent basis. It incorporates soft factors such as readiness, experience and morale.

The vertical Integrity bar is a direct representation of how much of the troops in the unit's OOB are remaining (see 5.2.2 Integrity). Think of it as the unit's 'Health Bar'.

Each Division is attached to an HQ which has a distinctive colour. All subordinate Divisions of an HQ show the same colour in their side bar on the left of the counter ('HQ Colour'). This allows you to visually identify which HQ a Division belongs to.

The small coloured box at the top left ('Supply Status') tells you what percentage of supply arrived at the unit compared to what it requested. Green means everything is OK; yellow indicates some problems but nothing serious. Blue signals major problems (supply shortfall) and red flags a critical situation (little, or no, supply arrived this turn).

3.8. GENERAL INTERFACE ADVICE ▶

There are a handful of keyboard shortcuts (see 8.2 Hotkeys) that make playing the game a lot easier.

'0', '1', '2' toggle the unit display. 'M' & 'G' allow you to move units individually, or as a group. 'A' allows you to instigate an attack against a selected enemy unit.

There are two general purpose keyboard shortcuts that work universally. ESC allows you to exit screens and SPACEBAR acts as a 'Yes' when asked to acknowledge a pop-up screen. SPACEBAR performs a number of other contextual message related functions and it's worth using it generously. If in doubt, press SPACEBAR.

3.8.1. TOOL TIPS

Throughout the game there are many tool tips. Just about all interface elements will produce a tool tip if you hover the mouse over them.

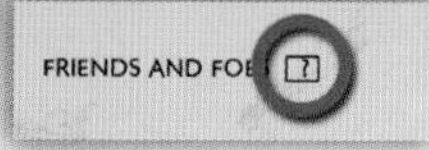
FRIENDS AND

Yellow boxes with '?' are also tool tips

3.9. CARDS ▶

3.9.1. ACTION CARDS

These are found in the 'Cards' tab (top centre right). All work the same. Choose a card and, depending on the purpose of the card, the effect will immediately occur or a pop-up selector window will open allowing you to choose a unit or a hex for the effect. In both cases you'll receive a confirmation message of what has happened.

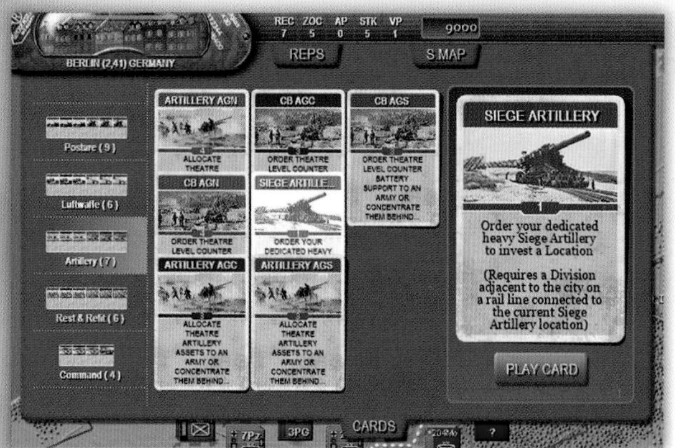
REC ZOC AP STK VP
7 5 0 5 1
9000
BERLIN (2,41) GERMANY
REPS
S.MAP
Posture (9)
Luftwaffe (6)
Artillery (7)
Rest & Refit (6)
Command (4)
ARTILLERY AGN
CB AGC
CB AGS
CB AGN
SIEGE ARTILLE...
ARTILLERY AGC
ARTILLERY AGS
SIEGE ARTILLERY
Order your dedicated heavy Siege Artillery to invest a Location
(Requires a Division adjacent to the city on a rail line connected to the current Siege Artillery location)
PLAY CARD
CARDS

The Cards tab has a number of categories on the left, each with it's own set of cards. The number in the brackets indicate how many cards are in each category. Cards are dynamic and can appear, or be removed, depending on the game situation

A card does not activate until the 'Play Card' button is pressed. You can click on as many cards as you wish. Each time the relevant card will appear on the right (larger size) but unless you hit the button underneath there will be no effect.

DEMAND POWER
30
Demand that the Poltiburo cede you ever more supreme executive powers!
(+5 PP per turn, increased Paranoia)

There aren't enough PP's available for Stalin to Demand more Power

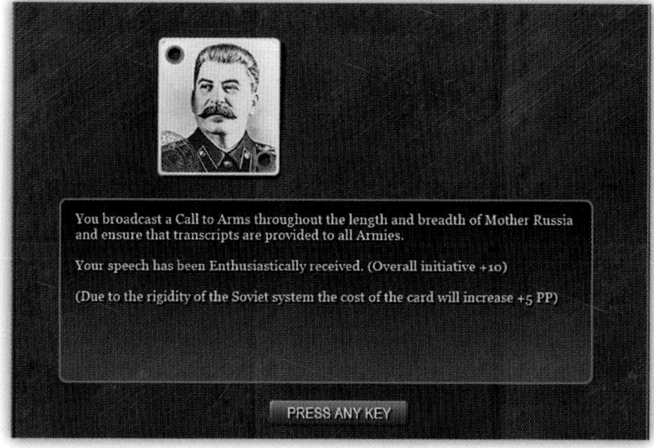
You broadcast a Call to Arms throughout the length and breadth of Mother Russia and ensure that transcripts are provided to all Armies.
Your speech has been Enthusiastically received. (Overall initiative +10)
(Due to the rigidity of the Soviet system the cost of the card will increase +5 PP)
PRESS ANY KEY

A Soviet card has been played with immediate effect (no pop-up selector window) and the confirmation message informs you of what's happened

Cards have a cost in Political Points (PP) to play. Their costs can vary as a result of decisions, your relations (see 4.8.1.3 Action Card Costs or the rigidity of the Soviet system (see 6.2.5.1 Rigidity of the Soviet system). If you have insufficient PP to pay for card it will still be visible, but the 'Play Card' button will be greyed out, and the card will be unable to be played. Certain cards are 'Free' and have no cost.

Whenever a card requires you to select a unit, or a hex, a pop-up 'Selector' window will appear enabling you to choose. For both cases the same window will appear and the process is identical.

The game will automatically determine which units or hexes are allowed to be selected and will prevent you from choosing illegal options. Any valid selection will be visible with a grey outline (units as above) or grey shading (hexes as below).

Once a valid selection has been made (you've clicked on the unit or the hex) the 'Play Card'

Unit selector. Valid units that can be chosen are highlighted with a grey outline, in this case Army HQ's

Hex selector. Valid hexes have grey shading such as the one currently under the cursor (red line). It's a Fortification card and they can't be built in Cities and swamps which you can see in the window as not having grey shading

button will become visible (red line). Click on this to implement the card and receive a confirmation message as above. At any time prior you can change your mind and press 'Cancel'. There will be no effect, or Political Points deducted.

Officer cards work the same way but are found attached to individual Officers. For the Germans this is because the Army, or Panzergruppe, has been given 'Command Focus' (see 6.1.1 Command Focus) whereas for the Soviets it's due to the presence of a Troubleshooter (see 6.2.4 Troubleshooters).

Available cards are shown in the Unit Info display. You can click on them to view larger versions

See 6.1.5 German Cards and 6.2.5 Soviet Cards.

3.9.2. OFFICER CARDS

These work the same as normal Action cards but, rather than being found in the Action Card tab (top right), are found at the bottom of the screen next to the portrait of a commander (which is why they are referred to as 'Officer cards').

They appear as a result of special circumstances. Only certain commanders (and their HQ) will receive Officer cards at any one time. Like Action cards, Officer cards can involve a cost in Political Points (PP) to play, although some can be free.

Unit counters (HQ's only) show a visual representation of small cards to indicate that the HQ, and its commander, have Officer cards available. Click on the HQ unit to see the cards (bottom right).

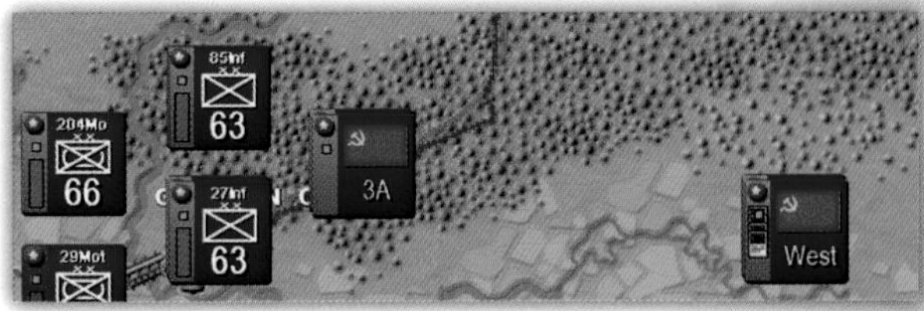

The Western District HQ (right) has Officer cards available, but the 3rd Army HQ (centre left) doesn't

The German Player receives Officer cards as a result of an Army, or Panzergruppe, receiving Command Focus (see 6.1.1 Command focus) and the cards provide a range of tactical options that can provide various bonuses to the formation's subordinate Divisions.

For more information refer to 6.1.5.8 Officer Cards.

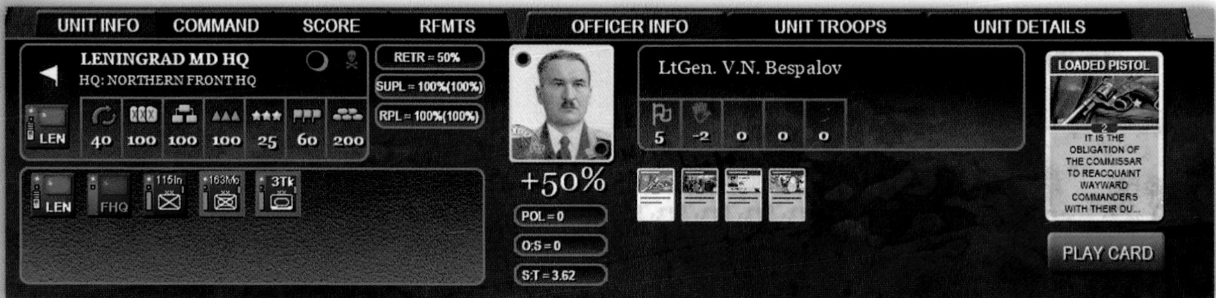

The Soviet Player receives Officer cards when an HQ (Army or Front) is visited by one of his troubleshooters. Different sets of cards are available depending on the troubleshooter and the level of the HQ.

For more information refer to 6.2.4 Troubleshooters.

4. KEY CONCEPTS

4.1. WEATHER ▶

The game generates detailed, randomised, weather patterns within the framework of an accurate, climatic model which is itself based upon Soviet meteorological data. Weather conditions impact most game mechanics and are very important.

4.1.1. RUSSIAN CLIMATE

The summer months (June, July, August) can, on occasion, warm sufficiently to cause heat exhaustion to troops and dust damage to engines. Localised summer rains are a distinct possibility, especially in July.

DESIGNER NOTE

June is assumed to be fine, no matter what. It would be unfair on the German Player to be halted, right at the start, by poor ground conditions. Summer rain events, sufficient to cause mud, only ever last for one turn.

Autumn is a period of transition. August and September are predominately fine and form the best window of opportunity for the Germans. Late October brings the onset of Rasputitsa, the mud season, where it rains more or less continuously and heavy, sticky mud becomes the norm.

November sees the rain easing and brings the possibility of early snow.

Mud to the West, Snow to East

Winters are harsh. From mid December through to mid January, the cold can reach extreme levels.

4.1.2. CLIMATIC MODEL

The map is divided into 3 separate climatic zones, dry & semi-arid, continental and boreal. It's further divided into over one hundred 'micro-zones'. Detailed climate parameters from eight different points within Russia are used to derive a weather pattern, for each micro-zone, every four days. Weather data is available for each individual hex and reflects the individual micro-zone that the hex is within.

The model is built to provide a reasonable amount of variability within accurate climatic parameters. At the end of the game you'll receive a report summarising the weather you've experienced.

There is a 'Mild Winter' option (prior to starting the game) available that ensures that the extreme conditions of late December, early January, don't arrive.

4.1.3. FROZEN LAKES AND RIVERS

Once the cold weather arrives you can expect lakes and rivers to freeze over. Not all of them. The further north they are the greater the likelihood of freezing.

The freezing over will happen progressively with smaller, northern rivers being the first to freeze over and larger, southern rivers, the last.

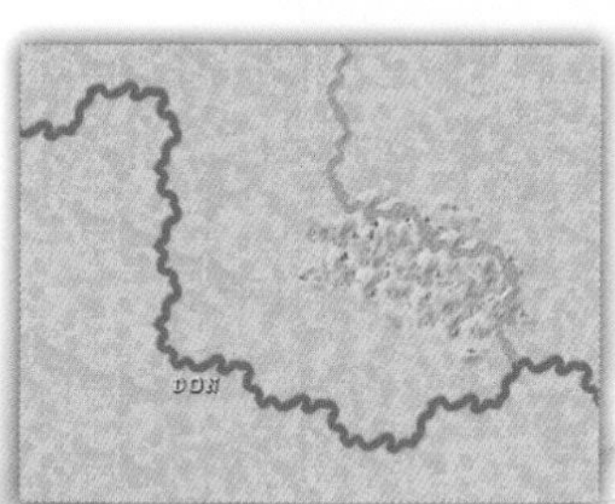

Once frozen, lakes and rivers can be crossed by individual Divisions.

The mighty Don is still flowing but its smaller tributaries are beginning to freeze over

4.1.4. WEATHER REPORTS

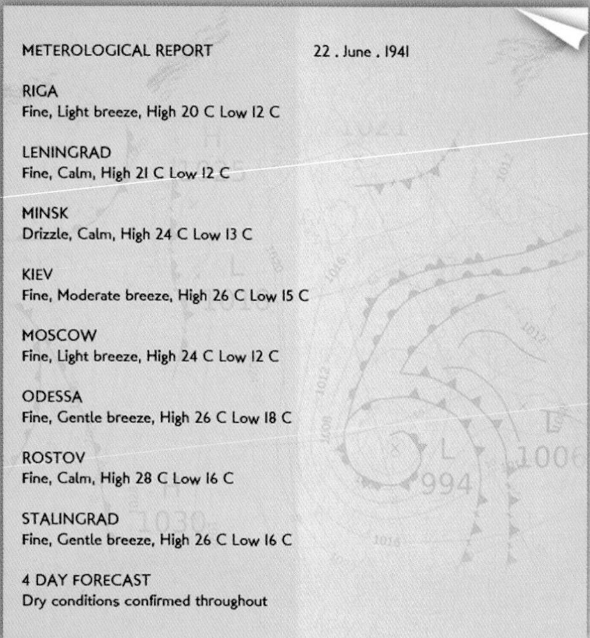

METEROLOGICAL REPORT 22 . June . 1941

RIGA
Fine, Light breeze, High 20 C Low 12 C

LENINGRAD
Fine, Calm, High 21 C Low 12 C

MINSK
Drizzle, Calm, High 24 C Low 13 C

KIEV
Fine, Moderate breeze, High 26 C Low 15 C

MOSCOW
Fine, Light breeze, High 24 C Low 12 C

ODESSA
Fine, Gentle breeze, High 26 C Low 18 C

ROSTOV
Fine, Calm, High 28 C Low 16 C

STALINGRAD
Fine, Gentle breeze, High 26 C Low 16 C

4 DAY FORECAST
Dry conditions confirmed throughout

The main source of weather information is the meteorological report that can be found at the top of the report tab, each turn. It provides accurate information on the weather in 8 different cities throughout Russia.

The report may also include a forecast for the following four day period. Because the Germans had limited sources of meteorological data from within Russia, this can vary in usefulness. When a solid forecast is available, it can be relied upon.

Whenever you find yourself talking to one of your commanders, or request a status report from a division, the weather at their location will be displayed next to their portrait.

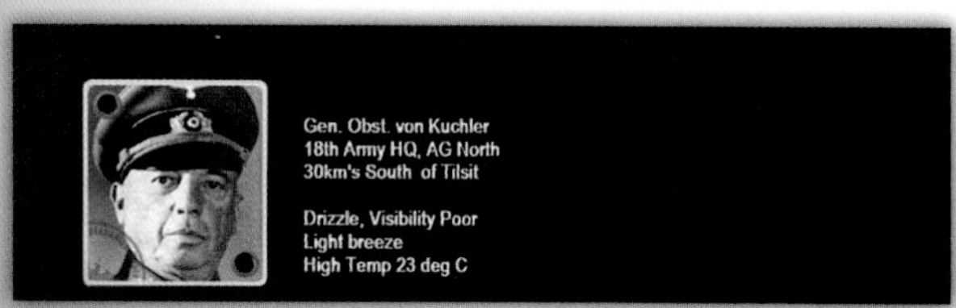

Kuchler's 18th Army are making the most of the warm, slightly wet, conditions

4.1.5. WEATHER EFFECTS

Adverse weather has a direct effect on individual Divisions, the operational tempo of the Luftwaffe, rail conversion Battalions, logistical pipelines, mechanical reliability and combat.

4.1.5.1. Hot Weather Effects

During summer months hot weather is possible. The key factor is the high temperature which can be aggravated by a hot, dry wind that kicks up dust, damages engines (especially gearboxes) and parches men's throats.

Hot weather effects, when present, will reduce the AP of both men and machines. You will receive notification of the effect, and the impact, in your Daily Logs, Unit modification reports and whenever a relevant unit is asked to Report Status!

4.1.5.2. Wet Weather Effects

Mud affects Divisions by making movement difficult, if not impossible in the case of wheeled transport (trucks). Tracked vehicles fair better and infantry can still slog their way through. Divisions with trucks can only move if they have access to all weather, sealed, roads.

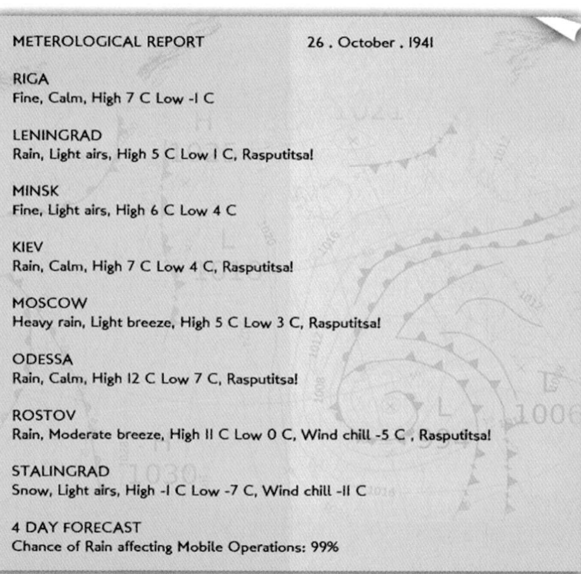

METEROLOGICAL REPORT 26 . October . 1941

RIGA
Fine, Calm, High 7 C Low -1 C

LENINGRAD
Rain, Light airs, High 5 C Low 1 C, Rasputitsa!

MINSK
Fine, Light airs, High 6 C Low 4 C

KIEV
Rain, Calm, High 7 C Low 4 C, Rasputitsa!

MOSCOW
Heavy rain, Light breeze, High 5 C Low 3 C, Rasputitsa!

ODESSA
Rain, Calm, High 12 C Low 7 C, Rasputitsa!

ROSTOV
Rain, Moderate breeze, High 11 C Low 0 C, Wind chill -5 C , Rasputitsa!

STALINGRAD
Snow, Light airs, High -1 C Low -7 C, Wind chill -11 C

4 DAY FORECAST
Chance of Rain affecting Mobile Operations: 99%

Snowing in Stalingrad, sunshine in Riga and Minsk, rain and mud everywhere else

You can expect mechanical wear and tear to increase at three times the normal rate every time a Panzer Division attempts to move through mud.

Mud, and rain, will severely impact the ability of the Luftwaffe to fly missions. The weather at both the airfield and the target hex are taken into account.

Rasputitsa on the weather report indicates that you are in the mud season and can expect periods of continuous rain.

The terrain display (top center) will give a visual indication of Mud conditions in addition to the colouring of the hex.

4.1.5.3. Cold Weather Effects

The game calculates the effect of cold, for slow Divisions (infantry) by taking the Wind chill factor, any frostbite and generating a cold weather index. This is reduced by the level of winter preparations, of the Division, and a net effect on both AP and Morale arrived at.

IN DETAIL

The lowest of the Low and the Windchill temperatures (in Celcius) is divided by 3 and any Frostbite level added to generate the Severe Weather Index (it's reduced by '1' as the baseline default is '1'). The level of Cold Weather preparations is subtracted to give the Adjusted index. This is used to apply the Cold Weather effects with the AP reduction being 10 x Adjusted Index and the Morale reduction being 5 x Adjusted Index. Fast Divisions ignore the effect of Windchill as they are assumed to be sheltered within their transports and tanks.

Soviet units are immune to the morale effects of cold weather and start the game with a high level of cold weather preparations.

German units commence with no cold weather clothing or equipment. There is a series of Decisions that enable the German Player to achieve higher levels of protection, given sufficient determination (Hitler was against the idea). For further information see 11.2 Winter Decisions.

DESIGNER NOTE

Cold Weather is a gamble for the German Player. His forces are woefully prepared and will suffer grievously in the event of being caught in severe conditions. There are options for him to counter the effects but this requires a solid investment of Political capital which could be better spent elsewhere. It comes down to an all-out determination to win the war prior to the worst of the winter (the historical approach) or being willing to hedge his bets and play the long game.

COLD WEATHER PREPARATIONS AT GAME START	
German units	Level 0 (none)
Soviet units	Level 4
Finnish units	Level 5
Siberian units	Level 6

METEROLOGICAL REPORT 30 . December . 1941

RIGA
Light Snow, Gentle breeze, High -14 C Low -22 C, Wind chill -32 C , Frostbite!

LENINGRAD
Snow, Light breeze, High -16 C Low -19 C, Wind chill -25 C

MINSK
Heavy Snow, Light airs, High -14 C Low -21 C, Wind chill -28 C

KIEV
Snow, Calm, High -10 C Low -20 C

MOSCOW
Heavy Snow, Gentle breeze, High -13 C Low -24 C, Wind chill -34 C , Frostbite!

ODESSA
Light Snow, Fresh breeze, High -8 C Low -20 C, Wind chill -33 C , Frostbite!

ROSTOV
Heavy Snow, Light breeze, High -10 C Low -19 C, Wind chill -25 C

STALINGRAD
Snow, Moderate breeze, High -15 C Low -22 C, Wind chill -32 C , Frostbite!

Severe conditions! Rug up

Contrast the travails of Schoenhaerl's 167th with the 10th Infantry Division, way up north on the Finnish front.

GenLt. Schoenhaerl's 167th Infantry Division are in blizzard conditions and badly hurting. Note that the total lack of perparations have ensured that the full effect of the severe weather are being felt by all. The Division can barely move and all his men want to do is go home

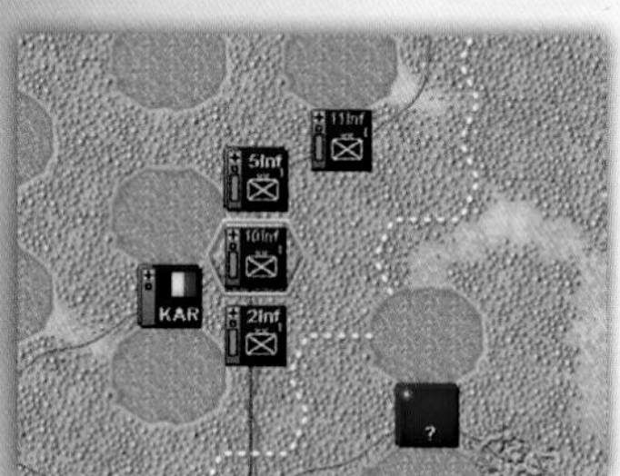

In amongst the land of a thousand, frozen, lakes

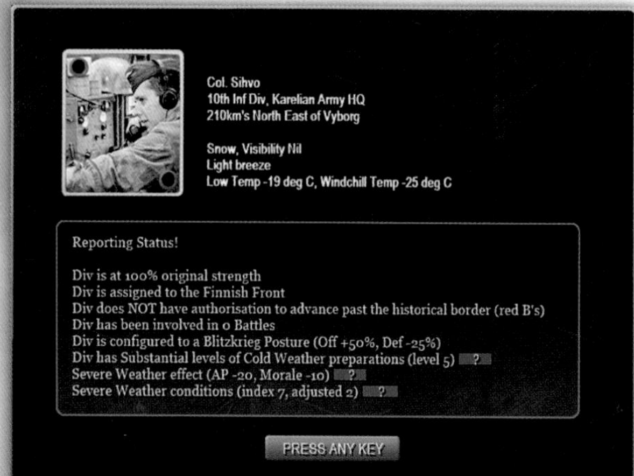

Col. Sihvo
10th Inf Div, Karelian Army HQ
210km's North East of Vyborg
Snow, Visibility Nil
Light breeze
Low Temp -19 deg C, Windchill Temp -25 deg C
Reporting Status!
Div is at 100% original strength
Div is assigned to the Finnish Front
Div does NOT have authorisation to advance past the historical border (red B's)
Div has been involved in 0 Battles
Div is configured to a Blitzkrieg Posture (Off +50%, Def -25%)
Div has Substantial levels of Cold Weather preparations (level 5)
Severe Weather effect (AP -20, Morale -10)
Severe Weather conditions (index 7, adjusted 2)
PRESS ANY KEY

Col. Sihvo's 10th Infantry are travelling well, despite an almost equivalent level of severe weather to GenLt. Schoenhaerl's 167th Infantry Division. Because of their level 5 preparations the weather effects are minimal and the 10th Infantry can be considered fully operational

4.1.6. WEATHER QUESTIONS

Why is there a bubble of good weather around Moscow in Winter?

There is a mini-climatic zone surrounding Moscow that allows it to maintain slightly higher temperatures than the surrounding regions and ensures that it freezes later.

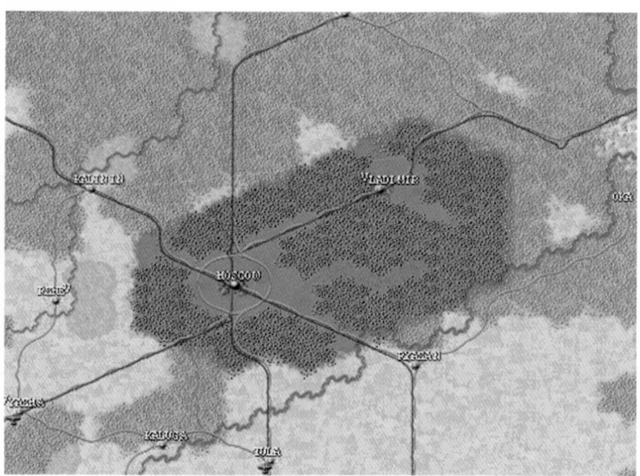

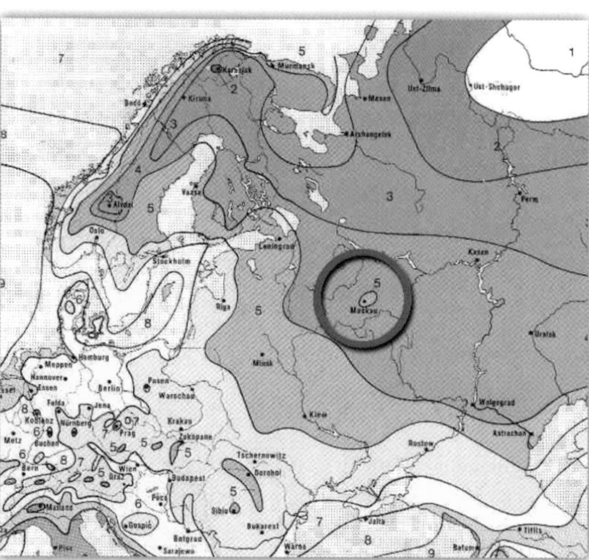

Underlying climate zone model used in the game © www.backyardgardener.com/zone/europe1zone.html

Why do the summer rains vary so much?

This is a factor of the randomisation built into the climatic model. Summer rains last only one

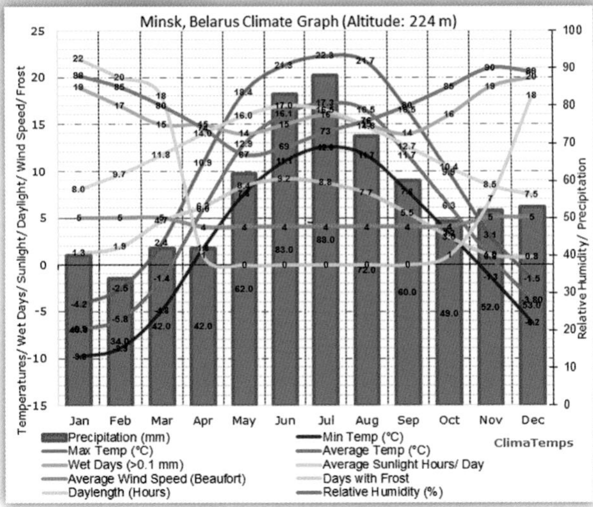

July has the highest frequency of summer rain
© www.climatemps.com

turn but they can varying in location and intensity. Without this the game would become predictable.

Keep in mind that the randomisation is corralled within a historically correct meteorological framework and that you'll receive a report at game end of the weather you have experienced.

SUMMARY

- Mud slows Divisions, especially those with Trucks.
- Cold weather can severely affect German Divisions with no cold weather equipment or clothing.
- There is a series of Decisions enabling you to receive adequate equipment and clothing.

See also

6.1.3 The Air War for the effect that weather has on Luftwaffe operations.

6.1.6 Logistics for the effect that weather has on Logistical pipelines.

6.1.8 Rail Conversion for the effect that weather has on Rail Conversion activity.

4.2. AI ▶

4.2.1. COMBAT BONUS

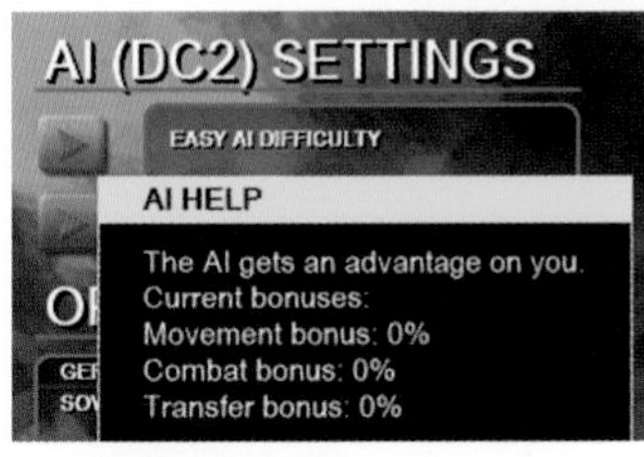

No bonuses on easy. Don't be fooled as the AI has been intensively trained up on a program of Barbarossa work outs. It's got muscles, abs and a take-no-prisoners attitude

The AI can receive a global combat bonus that applies to Offence and Defence. It can also have a global movement bonus. You can see the different levels of bonuses by the mouse over tool tips on the 'AI Settings' (start screen).

4.2.2. PENALTIES

The Soviet AI suffers initial combat penalties to reflect the normal Blitzkrieg Shock and Entrenchment penalties (see 5.2.13 Early Soviet Penalties).

The German AI suffers winter combat penalties to simulate the great difficulties they had in dealing with the extreme cold conditions.

4.2.3. FORTIFICATIONS

The Soviet AI will, at the start of the game, pre-build its full quota of garrisons on the map. It's done this way as it's easier for the AI to deal with. The locations are semi-randomised and will vary with each play through.

4.2.4. BRIDGES

The Soviet AI will attempt to blow bridges on a semi-randomised basis. Each bridge has a date after which it is tested to see if there are Germans within a certain distance. If so a random roll is made, each turn, to determine if it is destroyed.

If the German Player dawdles the AI will, sooner or later, blow a number of bridges. There is an imperative on the German Player to race forward and secure crucial bridges before this occurs, as happened historically.

4.2.5. GARRISONS

The Soviet AI will raise both conscript and major, regular, garrisons in its cities. It does so on a semi-randomised basis.

Each city has a percentage chance of having a garrison. Minor cities (grey dot) will have conscript garrisons and strategic cities (red do) major, regular, garrisons. The base chance of a city having a garrison is set an a comparable historical level. Odessa, for example, which was strongly defended by the Soviets, has a 75% chance of having a major garrison present. A typical minor, unimportant city (grey dot) would have a 25% chance of a conscript garrison being present.

The AI determines which garrisons are present at the start of the game and they are all placed on the map where appropriate. Brest-Litowsk and the three objective cities (Leningrad, Moscow and Rostov) will all have major garrisons, regardless.

The randomisation ensures that each play through will present the German Player with a different mix of garrisoned cities. There will be times when key cities are found to be undefended (this happened a lot historically due to the speed of the German's advance) and other occasions where they will have to fight their way into well defended, determinedly held cities.

4.2.6. WHAT IF? DECISIONS

The AI won't utilise What If? Decisions.

4.3. THEATRES ▶

The map is divided into three distinct theatres - North, Centre and South. These are defined by the **DASHED RED LINES** on the map. Germans call them 'Theatres' whereas the Russians refer to 'Fronts'. They are both identical.

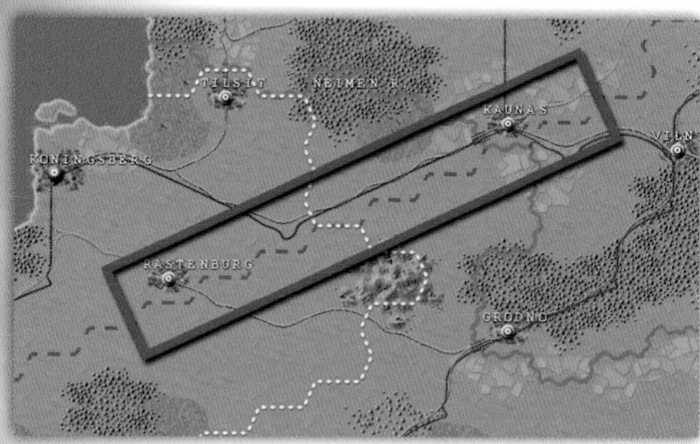

The dashed red line represents the theatre (or front) border

Theatres are fundamental to the game. Each theatre serves as its own mini-campaign and your role, as Operational Commander, is to coordinate and prioritise theatre activity and resources.

Each German theatre has its own logistical system, its own command structure, theatre artillery, specialised assets and its own supporting Luftflotte (air wing). The Russians front system is more streamlined but still adheres to separate command structures.

Refer to the designer notes for the thinking behind the theatre system (9.3.5 Theatres).

There is one section of border (between AGC and AGS) that is marked by a river, not the dashed red lines. It's done this way to reduce map clutter.

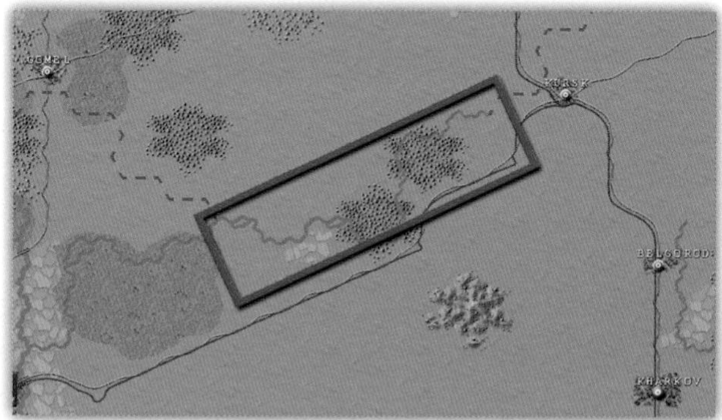

Like the Rio Grande, the theatre border follows the course of the river

4.3.1. VIOLATION PENALTIES

Armies from one theatre should avoid crossing into an adjacent theatre without authorisation. A unit that crosses a border will incur a 'violation' penalty which is expressed in political points (PP's).

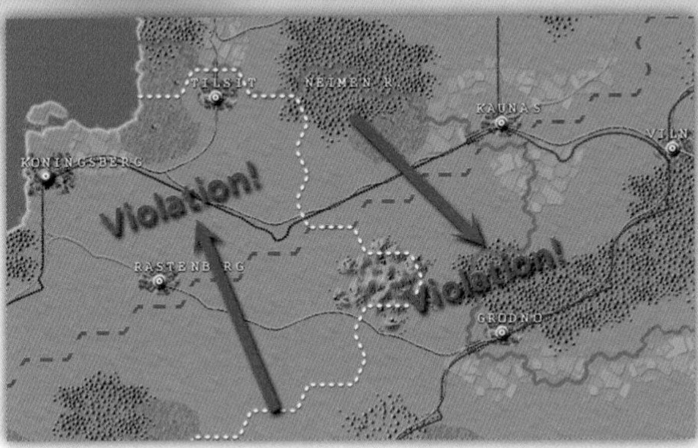

Units are required to remain within their own assigned theatre

The extent of the penalty is in proportion to how far over the border the unit has moved. Soviet units are penalised less than German ones who are expected to adhere to an historically higher level of command efficiency.

Command Übertretung!

The following Divisions have moved outside their assigned areas of operation. General Staff will find a way to accommodate the situation but the sooner it is rectified the better.

+ You incur a PP penalty for each unit that moves outside its assigned theatre to reflect the command and logistical disruption that this incurs. The further a unit crosses into another theatre, the greater the penalty

- 4th Pz Div (2nd PanzerGruppe HQ), penalty incurred -5 PP
  120km's North West of Rovno, Loc 28:46
- 10th Mot Inf Div (2nd PanzerGruppe HQ), penalty incurred -3 PP
  210km's North East of Lvov, Loc 27:45
- 297th Inf Div (6th Army HQ), penalty incurred -1 PP
  30km's South of Brest-Litowsk, Loc 25:44

The violation report appears if any of your units have transgressed operational borders. You can see three examples here of units moving 3, 2 and 1 hexes over the border along with their equivalent penalties (5 PP, the maximum / 3 PP/ 1 PP)

DESIGNER NOTE

Refer to the 9.3.5 Theatres for an explanation of the reasons behind the Theatre system.

Violation penalties will continue for as long as the unit is in the wrong theatre. Units that are cut off will not be penalised.

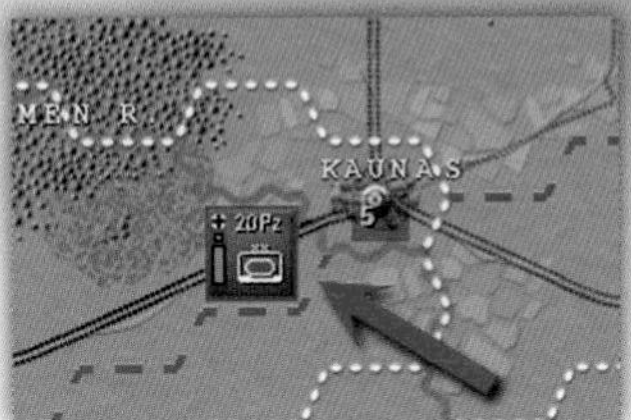

Units that violate borders are shown, at the start of the following turn, with a red highlight

Your Daily Staff Log has a summary of the effects of any violation penalties on your PP economy.

For the Russians the violation report appears only if a penalty is incurred, which will only happen if the unit moves 3 or more hexes into an adjoining Front (with a maximum penalty of only 1 PP).

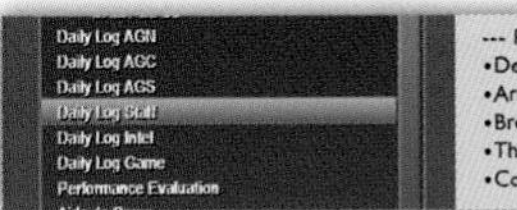

STAFF ADVICE

Violations are a serious matter for the Germans. At times it pays to deliberately incur the penalty in order to achieve a tactical outcome, especially if you are only moving a unit a single hex across the border. Large scale, Army level incursions, are not feasible. The Russians, however, have a lot more flexibility and can regularly move several hexes into an adjoining Front at no cost.

STAVKA Staff Warning!

The following Divisions have moved outside their assigned areas of operation. STAVKA Staff will find a way to accommodate the situation. Stalin will be notified. You have been warned.

+ You incur a PP penalty for each unit that moves outside its assigned theatre to reflect the command and logistical disruption that this incurs. The further a unit crosses into another theatre, the greater the penalty

- 27th Army HQ (Northern Front HQ), penalty incurred -1 PP
  60km's South West of Polotsk, Loc 34:30

The 27th Army HQ has moved a full three hexes into the adjacent Front. Anything less and it wouldn't be an issue

You can request a Status Report! Form a Division and you'll soon see if it has crossed a border.

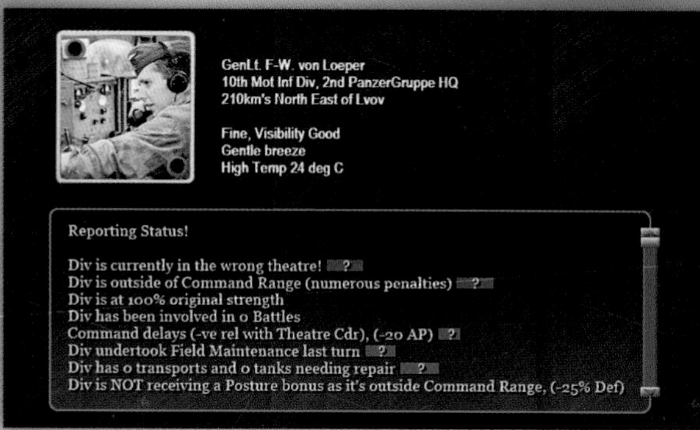

GenLt. F-W. von Loeper
10th Mot Inf Div, 2nd PanzerGruppe HQ
210km's North East of Lvov
Fine, Visibility Good
Gentle breeze
High Temp 24 deg C
Reporting Status!
Div is currently in the wrong theatre! ?
Div is outside of Command Range (numerous penalties) ?
Div is at 100% original strength
Div has been involved in 0 Battles
Command delays (-ve rel with Theatre Cdr), (-20 AP) ?
Div undertook Field Maintenance last turn ?
Div has 0 transports and 0 tanks needing repair ?
Div is NOT receiving a Posture bonus as it's outside Command Range, (-25% Def)

Not only has GenLt. Loeper's 10th Motorised Division, in the opening days of the campaign, blundered into an adjoining theatre but it is now out of Command Range. GenLt. Loeper's future prospects don't look promising

4.3.2. CHANGING THEATRES

Only German Panzergruppes can change theatres and only when approved to do so by the Führer. For more information see 6.1.2 Panzergruppes.

SUMMARY

- The map is divided up into 'Theatres' (AGN, AGC, AGS)
- The Soviets refer to them as 'Fronts' (Northern, Central, Southern)
- Theatres (or Fronts) are distinct entities with separate commands and infrastructure
- Red dashed lines mark the borders between them
- Units are required to stay within their assigned theatre (or front)
- Violation penalties (in political points) ensure if units cross borders without authorisation
- German violation penalties are stiffer than those of the Soviets
- Panzergruppes may be authorised to move into adjacent theatres but only if approved by Hitler

4.4. POSTURES ▶

Every Army, or Panzergruppe, has a posture. All subordinate Divisions assume the posture of their HQ. Postures grant various combat bonuses and penalties. Certain postures grant movement bonuses. Postures reflect major organisational configurations that dictate how an Army will move and fight. An Army will always have a posture, unless it is transitioning from one posture to another.

The possible posture types available for each regime are as follows.

GERMAN POSTURES

Posture	Effect
Blitzkrieg	+50% Offensive bonus (fast div) +40% Offensive bonus (slow div) +40 AP Blitzkrieg bonus -25% Defensive bonus (fast div) -20% Defensive bonus (slow div)
Sustained Offensive	+10% Offensive bonus -5% Defensive bonus
Defensive	-20% Offensive bonus +40% Defensive bonus
Changing posture	-20% Offensive bonus -20% Defensive bonus -40 AP

SOVIET POSTURES

Posture	Effect
Offensive	+40% Offensive bonus -20% Defensive bonus
Neutral	0% Offensive bonus 0% Defensive bonus
Defensive	-20% Offensive bonus +40% Defensive bonus
Changing posture	-20% Offensive bonus -20% Defensive bonus -40 AP

A posture, once set, remains in place until the Player wishes to change it. To change a posture you play the appropriate posture Action Card on an Army, or Panzergruppe, HQ.

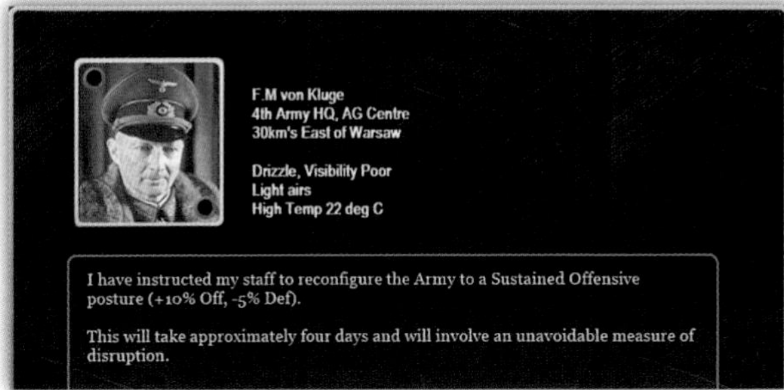

F.M von Kluge
4th Army HQ, AG Centre
30km's East of Warsaw
Drizzle, Visibility Poor
Light airs
High Temp 22 deg C
I have instructed my staff to reconfigure the Army to a Sustained Offensive posture (+10% Off, -5% Def).
This will take approximately four days and will involve an unavoidable measure of disruption.

Confirmation of a posture change

Changing from one posture to another involves a considerable amount of internal reorganisation and reconfiguring. It is no small task and is a time of vulnerability. You can expect ONE TURN of disruption while the formation realigns to the newly ordered posture. During this period all units will incur moderate combat and movement penalties as shown above in the two posture tables.

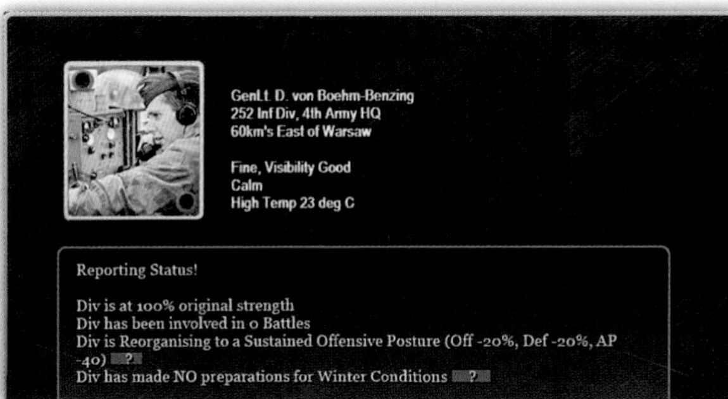

GenLt D. von Boehm-Benzing
252 Inf Div, 4th Army HQ
60km's East of Warsaw
Fine, Visibility Good
Calm
High Temp 23 deg C
Reporting Status!
Div is at 100% original strength
Div has been involved in 0 Battles
Div is Reorganising to a Sustained Offensive Posture (Off -20%, Def -20%, AP -40)
Div has made NO preparations for Winter Conditions

The 252nd Infantry are reorganising to a Sustained Offensive posture

Changing postures requires the expenditure of Political Points (PP). The cost of a Defensive posture is initially high for both sides. It took some time for both Stalin and Hitler to acknowledge the need to defend.

Soviet forces, at the beginning of Barbarossa, had a doctrine of offence with little consideration given to defending. It was anticipated that the Red Army, if attacked, would quickly sweep through Hungary and southern Poland, enveloping the advancing the Germans. Once they were destroyed it would only be a matter of time before Berlin was threatened.

All German Armies commence the game with a Blitzkrieg posture. Soviet Armies start with an Offensive posture with the exception of Armies on the Finnish Front. Soviet reinforcement Armies arrive in a Neutral posture.

Information on postures can be found in many places - Unit Modifiers report, individual Division status reports and special icons next to the unit name (bottom left).

4.4.1. BLITZKRIEG FUEL USE

German Panzergruppes receive special bonuses when set to Blitzkrieg posture as can be seen above. Because of this they use more fuel than they would normally. Panzers don't advance in a straight line and an additional fuel expenditure is required to cover the fast flowing tactical maneuvers that a rapid advance entails.

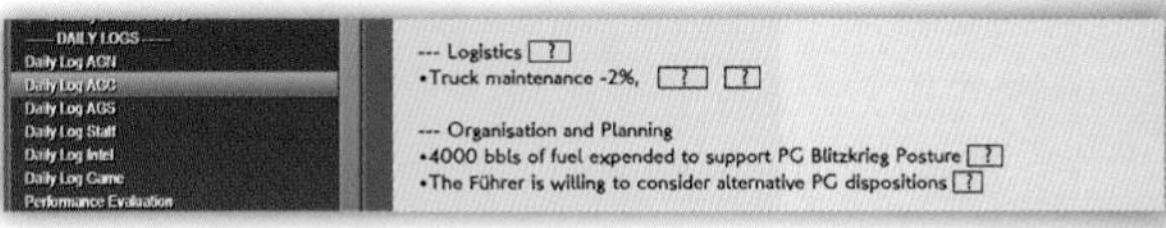

The Daily Theatre Logs detail the extra fuel use

If this additional fuel isn't available your Panzergruppes will lose their Blitzkrieg bonus. Once sufficient fuel has been found the Blitzkrieg bonuses will automatically return.

LOGISTICS REPORT - AGC

22 . June . 1941 [?]

--- Main Depot: Warsaw [?] (loc 19:42)
FUEL (start): 0 bbls IN (ZI): 13250 bbls OUT (Trains): 13250 bbls
FUEL (remaining): 0 bbls
Trains per day: 38 (requires 0 trains, distance 0 km's) [?]

--- Forward Supply Base (FSB): Warsaw [?] (loc 19:42)
FUEL (start): 0 bbls IN (Depot): 13250 bbls OUT (Trucks): 13250 bbls
FUEL (remaining): 0 bbls
Truck columns: 212 (requires 1 truck column [?], distance 150 km's)

--- Field HQ: 2nd Panzergruppe HQ (loc 21:43), 3rd PG HQ (21:35) [?]
FUEL (start): 7000 bbls IN (FSB): 13250
FUEL AVAILABLE: 20250 bbls (less 4000 bbls for Blitzkrieg Op's [?])

NET FUEL: 16250 bbls [?] (maximum allowed 55000 bbls [?])

There are two Panzergruppes in AGC hence the additional fuel is doubled

There is a decision 'Unexpected Fuel Use' that always occurs early in the campaign that requires the German Player to determine a fuel use doctrine. This will affect the Blitzkrieg bonuses as follows.

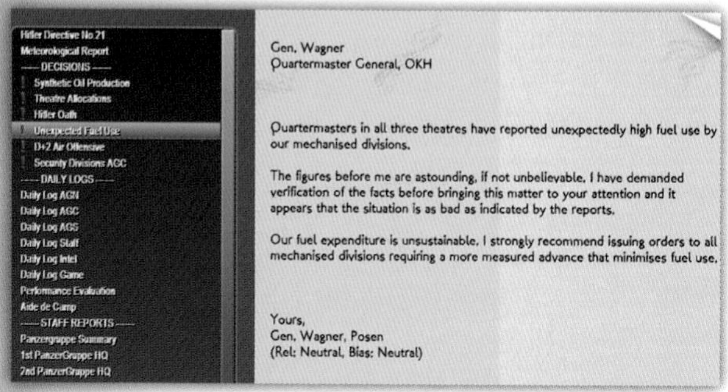
Hitler Directive No 21
Meteorological Report
---- DECISIONS ----
Synthetic Oil Production
Theatre Allocations
Hitler Oath
Unexpected Fuel Use
D+2 Air Offensive
Security Divisions AGC
---- DAILY LOGS ----
Daily Log AGN
Daily Log AGC
Daily Log AGS
Daily Log Staff
Daily Log Intel
Daily Log Game
Performance Evaluation
Aide de Camp
---- STAFF REPORTS ----
Panzergruppe Summary
1st PanzerGruppe HQ
2nd PanzerGruppe HQ

Gen. Wagner
Quartermaster General, OKH

Quartermasters in all three theatres have reported unexpectedly high fuel use by our mechanised divisions.

The figures before me are astounding, if not unbelievable. I have demanded verification of the facts before bringing this matter to your attention and it appears that the situation is as bad as indicated by the reports.

Our fuel expenditure is unsustainable. I strongly recommend issuing orders to all mechanised divisions requiring a more measured advance that minimises fuel use.

Yours,
Gen. Wagner, Posen
(Rel: Neutral, Bias: Neutral)

GERMAN FUEL EXPENDITURE

Posture	Effect
Blitzkrieg Posture (start of the campaign)	2000 bbls extra per Panzergruppe (+50% Off, -25% Def, +40 AP)
Unexpected Fuel Use decision – Full throttle	+500 bbls extra per Panzergruppe (2500 bbls) (+50% Off, -25% Def, +40 AP)
Unexpected Fuel Use decision – Avoid excessive maneuver	No change to fuel expenditure (2000 bbls) (+40% Off, -20% Def, +30 AP)
Unexpected Fuel Use decision – Fuel efficiency	-500 bbls less per Panzergruppe (1500 bbls) (+30% Off, -15% Def, +20 AP)

Maintain Offensive Momentum — Full throttle, all the way. — 3PP
Avoid Excessive Maneuvering — Keep pushing but keep the mileage down — 4PP
Fuel Efficiency is the key — Adopt a fuel efficient Offensive doctrine — 4PP
Do Nothing — Why change a winning plan? — 0PP

Unexpected Fuel use decision options that are referred to in the table above

German planners were completely taken aback by the difference in expected fuel use and actual use in Russia. Previous campaigns in the west, replete with highly developed road networks, had led them to grossly underestimate the amount of fuel needed for Operation Barbarossa. A standard load of fuel was expected to last for 100 km's (65 miles). In reality only 40 to 48 km's (25-30 miles) was achieved. Poor roads, even worse weather and the vast distances all contributed to heavy wear and tear on engines and machinery.

4.4.2. BLITZKRIEG FATIGUE

German slow Divisions (infantry on foot) accumulate Fatigue while ever they are set to a Blitzkrieg posture. Fatigue accumulates and can only be removed by ordering a Rest. Changing to a different posture will not remove fatigue but it will no longer increase. See 6.1.7.2 Fatigue.

SUMMARY

- Every Army, or Panzergruppe, has a posture.
- Soviet postures differ from German ones.
- Postures, once set, continue automatically unless you wish to change them
- You set postures by selecting an HQ. Divisions automatically assume their HQ's posture.
- Changing a posture involves a one turn period of reorganisation and vulnerability
- The German Blitzkrieg posture causes Panzergruppes to expend additional fuel
- The German Blitzkrieg posture causes slow Divisions (no transport) to accumulate Fatigue
- The German 'Unexpected Fuel Use' decision can change the fuel use and Blitzkrieg bonuses

4.5. DIFFICULTY ▶

Is a numerical rating with a base value of 100. Various factors can raise or lower the difficulty rating (higher the number, the harder the game). Its purpose is to give you an idea of the level of challenge and it also is very important in determining your Victory Points (see 4.6.2 Victory Points).

FACTORS AFFECTING DIFFICULTY		
Influencing Factor	Effect	Regime
Prior Relationships	Net tally/5 (+/-)	German
Option – Mild Winter ON	Moderate -	German
Option – Decisions LIMITED	Moderate -	German
Option – Decisions OFF	Severe -	German
Option – Easy Mode	Major -	German
Option – Fog of War OFF	Major -	Both
Option – Hide AI Moves OFF	No effect	Both
Option – Geneva Convention ON	Moderate + (Minor + with Decisions Limited)	German
Option – Plots OFF	Minor -	German
Option – Past History OFF	No effect	German
AI Difficulty – Easy	Moderate -	Both
AI Difficulty – Normal	No effect	Both
AI Difficulty – Hard	Moderate +	Both
AI Difficulty – Very Hard	Major +	Both
AI Difficulty – Super Hard	Severe +	Both
Helpers – German (Trucks/Trains/PP/Fuel)	Moderate + (each instance)	German
Helpers – Soviet (Activation)	Minor + (each instance)	Soviet

Difficulty is a zero sum game. What affects one side has an opposite affect on the other. You can see the current difficulty ratings, for both sides, in the special 'Score' tab (bottom centre).

Your difficulty rating directly affects your score in the following manner.

Score = Adjusted Victory Points x Difficulty rating

Dynamic tool tips within the leader portraits will provide a breakdown.

The sum of both sides difficulty ratings will always add up to 200

The Daily Game Log also provides details of difficulty ratings.

GERMAN SCORE
Score = Victory Points x Difficulty/100
--- Difficulty (112)
Base difficulty 100
Geneva Convention Option OFF +10
Mild Winter Option selected -10
Past Relationships +12
--- Victory Points (0)
VP's from Cities 0
VP's from Decisions 0

Most of the difficulty options revolve around choices made by the German Player but they are all reflected in equal and opposite amounts for the Soviet Player.

--- Difficulty
- Overall Difficulty Rating 112 [?]
- Geneva Convention Option OFF +10
- Mild Winter Option selected -10
- Past Relationships +12

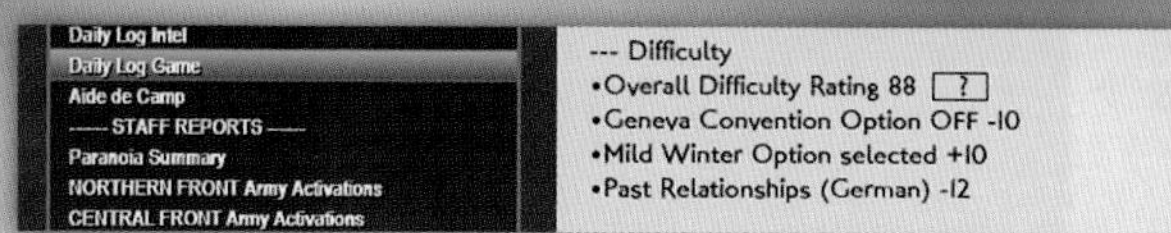
Daily Log Intel
Daily Log Game
Aide de Camp
—— STAFF REPORTS ——
Paranoia Summary
NORTHERN FRONT Army Activations
CENTRAL FRONT Army Activations

--- Difficulty
•Overall Difficulty Rating 88 [?]
•Geneva Convention Option OFF -10
•Mild Winter Option selected +10
•Past Relationships (German) -12

Past Relations (Germans), which are randomly generated at the start of the game (see 4.8.1.6 Past Relationships affect the difficulty rating by taking the sum of all relationships, adding the sum of biases (multiplied by 2) and dividing the total by 5 (there is some rounding involved).

Most of the time this will be a small number but on the occasions when you start with strongly defined relationships, good or bad, it can be significant. Whatever the result you aren't penalised as your history is taken into account by the difficulty rating.

You can choose to play without a past history by selecting the Past History OFF option at game start.

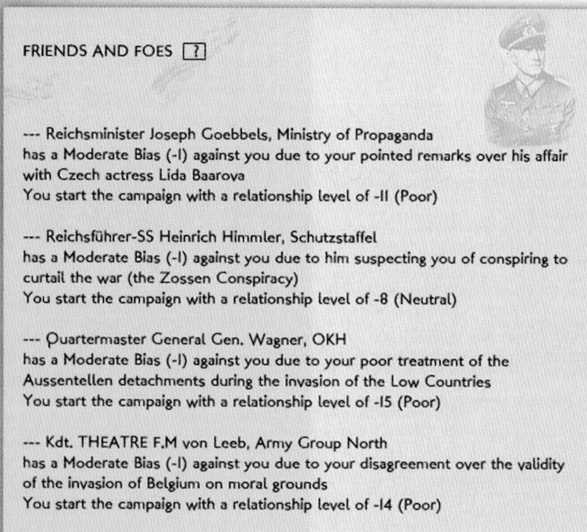
FRIENDS AND FOES [?]

--- Reichsminister Joseph Goebbels, Ministry of Propaganda
has a Moderate Bias (-1) against you due to your pointed remarks over his affair with Czech actress Lida Baarova
You start the campaign with a relationship level of -11 (Poor)

--- Reichsführer-SS Heinrich Himmler, Schutzstaffel
has a Moderate Bias (-1) against you due to him suspecting you of conspiring to curtail the war (the Zossen Conspiracy)
You start the campaign with a relationship level of -8 (Neutral)

--- Quartermaster General Gen. Wagner, OKH
has a Moderate Bias (-1) against you due to your poor treatment of the Aussentellen detachments during the invasion of the Low Countries
You start the campaign with a relationship level of -15 (Poor)

--- Kdt. THEATRE F.M von Leeb, Army Group North
has a Moderate Bias (-1) against you due to your disagreement over the validity of the invasion of Belgium on moral grounds
You start the campaign with a relationship level of -14 (Poor)

4.5.1. HELPERS

A series of buttons (bottom bar , left of centre) that provide a 'get out of jail' card. They enable you to obtain instant bonuses in return for a lowering of your difficulty rating (and a raising of your opponents).

You can use Helpers at any time, however each time you do so your difficulty rating will be adjusted. Excessive use can find you in an unwinnable situation.

DESIGNER NOTE

Helpers aren't cheats. There are times when, as a Commander, you need to yell out for assistance. Each time you do, however, the bar for victory inches higher. Helpers can be very handy when you are learning the game.

To use a Helper, press the appropriate button. You will receive a message and the button will change colour. To put the Helper into effect you need to press the button a second time.

The Train helper has been pressed but not yet activated. It will automatically reset the following turn so you are free to press any of the Helpers, without consequence, once.

ASK YOUR STAFF

Why the double press? It's a fail safe. You don't want to accidentally initiate a launch sequence.

TYPES OF HELPERS	
Button	Regime
More Trucks (20 extra Truck Columns for each theatre)	German
More Trains (2 extra trains/day for each theatre)	German
More Political Points (40 PP)	German
More Fuel (2000 bbls to each theatre sent directly to the PG HQ's and ready to use)	German
Activation (next turn ALL armies fully activate)	Soviet

German Helper buttons will take some turns to appear (surely you don't need help at the very start of the campaign?) and the single Soviet button will only show once the Luftwaffe is no longer disrupting the entire front.

NORTHERN FRONT Army Activations 30 . June . 1941

--- INITIATIVE Modifier
Luftwaffe disruption to command and control [?], (Overall) -15
Marshal Voroshilov, APPARATCHIK, Northern Front Cdr, Init -8
TOTAL Modifier -23 [?]

You can check your Activation reports to see whether the Luftwaffe is still causing chaos

Your opponent is fully informed every time you place your hand in the cookie jar

Every time you use a Helper a note is made in the Difficulty section of your Daily Game Log and your opponent also gains reciprocal information. Unlike What If? Decisions if you use a Helper your opponent will know exactly which Helpers you've availed yourself of.

--- Difficulty
•Overall Difficulty Rating 92 [?]
•Geneva Convention Option OFF +10
•Mild Winter Option selected -10
•Past Relationships +12
•Player requests Help (PP's) -10
•Player requests Help (Trains) -10

PP's and Trains. The situation is still manageable, because of your Past Relations but it wouldn't be wise to use more

SUMMARY

- Difficulty ratings start at 100. Higher values indicate a tougher game.
- Difficulty directly affects your Score
- Check your Daily Game Log or the Score Tab (bottom) for your difficulty status
- Helpers provide immediate benefits at the cost of lowered difficulty
- Helpers require a double press to activate.

4.6. WINNING THE GAME ▶

In order to win the game you are required to capture your objective (German Player), or prevent this (Soviet). There are various sudden death conditions that result in an immediate conclusion.

The objectives, and associated victory conditions, depend on what strategy you have chosen (German Player). The game will always end on round 57, the 28th January, 1942, regardless.

At any point in the game you have a score. This fluctuates as the tide of war ebbs and flows. When the game finishes, either timed out or because victory conditions have been achieved, your score plays a large part in determining the degree of victory, or defeat, that you have attained.

You can, at any point, choose to surrender and end the game.

Once the game finishes, you'll be presented with a wide range of reports and evaluations of your progress throughout the campaign.

4.6.1. CHOOSING A STRATEGY

The special Pre-Start turn (round 1) enables both sides to determine a strategy. This is a critical decision for the German Player as it sets the criteria for winning the game. The Soviet Player can't change this but they can choose an objective that will, depending on whether they hold it or not, decide the level of victory.

The German Player has a choice of three strategies, each with their own objectives.

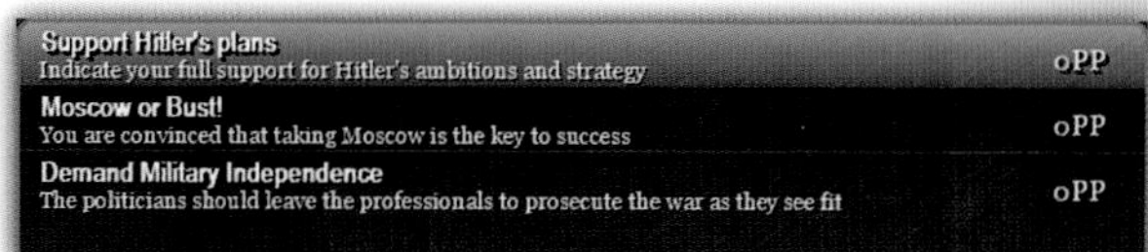

The three possible German strategies

Each strategy has an associated objective and criteria as shown below.

GERMAN STRATEGIES	
Strategy	Condition
Support Hitler	Capture Hitler's current Objective and hold to end of Jan '42
Moscow or Bust!	Capture Moscow and hold till end of Jan '42
Military Independence	Capture objective of your choice and hold for One Month

There are a pool of three possible objectives, one for each theatre. You can see, above, that the middle strategy has a fixed objective, Moscow, but the other two are variable. The top one involves the Player aligning themselves with the wishes of the Führer and the bottom one allows them to choose their own. Whatever strategy is chosen, the Player will be required to capture a single objective from the possible pool of three.

The three possible objectives are as follows.

OBJECTIVES

Objective	Criteria
Leningrad, AGN	capture
Moscow, AGC	capture
Rostov, AGS	Capture + capture either Kharkov OR Sevastopol

Note that Rostov, in AGS, requires the capture of an additional city

The Soviet Player has the more straightforward decision and can choose an objective that must be held at all costs.

STAFF ADVICE

Choose which Front you think you have the best chance of holding or chose the Front you think will be the lowest priority for your opponent.

These correspond to the objective cities in each of the three Fronts

The Victory Matrix determines how the choices of both Players interact.

VICTORY MATRIX

German Strategy	German Yes Soviet Yes	German Yes Soviet No	German No Soviet Yes	German No Soviet No
Support Hitler	Minor Win	Decisive Win	Decisive Loss	Draw
Moscow or Bust	Minor Win	Decisive Win	Decisive Loss	Draw
Military Independence	Minor Win	Decisive Win	Decisive Loss	Draw
Conditions	N/A	Germans must have a higher score (>=) with German score halved for comparison purposes	Soviets must have a higher score (>=) with German score halved for comparison purposes	Higher score has the advantage with the German score halved for comparison purposes

On the left can be seen the three possible German strategies. The columns across the top are in terms of either Player achieving their objectives, or not. For instance, if the German Player had a 'Moscow or Bust' strategy, he would be required to take Moscow. Let's say the Soviet Player chose Leningrad as his objective to hold.

If the German Player took both Moscow but failed to take Leningrad (German Yes, Soviet Yes), the German Player would achieve a Minor Win. However if the German Player took both cities (German Yes, Soviet No) then this would be upgraded to a Decisive Win. Note that there is also an additional score criteria that must be met for the Decisive Win to be achieved.

With the German Player failing in their objective they can still achieve a Draw provided they manage to take the Soviet Player's objective (German No, Soviet No).

4.6.1.1. Sudden Death

If any of these conditions apply the game will end at the completion of the current round.

GERMAN SUDDEN DEATH WIN CONDITIONS	
Condition	Criteria
1	Capture all three objectives (Leningrad+ Moscow+Rostov + Kharkov/Sevastopol

The Soviets have more scope for an instant win but they aren't easily attained.

SOVIET SUDDEN DEATH WIN CONDITIONS	
Condition	Criteria
1	Soviets capture a city across the Border – Konningsberg, Warsaw, Krakau or Bucharest
2	German Player is fired by Hitler
3	Soviets destroy any Theatre HQ (AGN, AGC, AGS)

4.6.1.2. German Strategy

The first decision in the Pre-Start turn allows the German Player to determine a strategy.

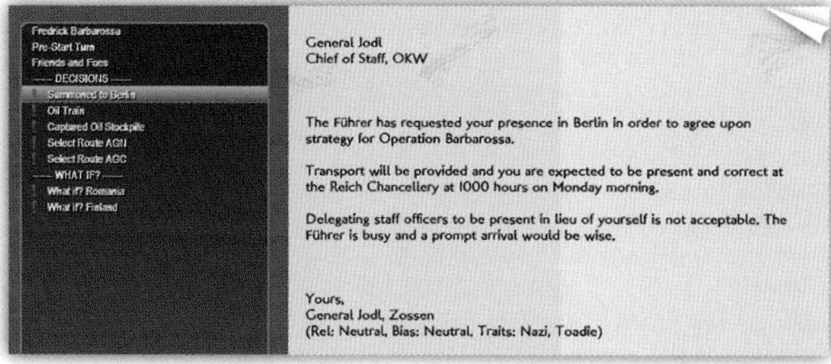
Fredrick Barbarossa
Pre-Start Turn
Friends and Foes
— DECISIONS —
Summoned to Berlin
Oil Train
Captured Oil Stockpile
Select Route AGN
Select Route AGC
— WHAT IF? —
What if? Romania
What if? Finland
General Jodl
Chief of Staff, OKW
The Führer has requested your presence in Berlin in order to agree upon strategy for Operation Barbarossa.
Transport will be provided and you are expected to be present and correct at the Reich Chancellery at 1000 hours on Monday morning.
Delegating staff officers to be present in lieu of yourself is not acceptable. The Führer is busy and a prompt arrival would be wise.
Yours,
General Jodl, Zossen
(Rel: Neutral, Bias: Neutral, Traits: Nazi, Toadie)

'Support Hitler' provides the Player with the most help in the form of Political Points and assistance throughout the campaign. It also puts the Player on an initial good footing with the Führer, something not to be underestimated.

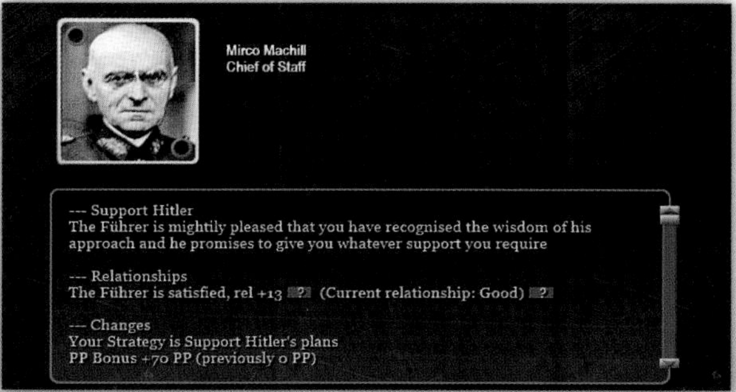
Mirco Machill
Chief of Staff
--- Support Hitler
The Führer is mightily pleased that you have recognised the wisdom of his approach and he promises to give you whatever support you require
--- Relationships
The Führer is satisfied, rel +13 (Current relationship: Good)
--- Changes
Your Strategy is Support Hitler's plans
PP Bonus +70 PP (previously 0 PP)

STAFF ADVICE

This is the easiest strategy of the three. You will have plenty of PP to make decisions with and you'll gain help along the way.

The downside is that you can expect Hitler's micromanagement tendencies to come to the fore and you will have to put up with a measure of interference (see). Your objective is that of Hitlers and this can change over time as Hitler was 'a man of whims' (see).

'Moscow or Bust' provides a clearly defined objective. Hitler won't be as impressed but will still provide a reasonable amount of PP. He will still interfere but to a lesser degree. It is to the Player's advantage to have Hitler consider Moscow as the main objective. Whenever Hitler calls a conference the Player has the opportunity to persuade him to switch to a Moscow first strategy. F.M Von Brauchitsch (High Command) and F.M Keitel (Hitler's Chief of Staff) are potential allies that will help if you have positive relations with them.

Moscow was the preferred strategy of the majority of the military leadership but Hitler, having studied Napoleon's campaign of 1812, considered it a 'fools errand'.

'Military Independence' is the hardest road to follow. You are standing up to the Führer and demanding to be able to prosecute the war as you see fit. Hitler will provide you with the bare minimum of PP and refuse to deal with you personally. Needless to say, your relationship with him won't start well.

He will not interfere but there is a risk that, if your relationship with him deteriorates too much, he will fire you (game over). F.M Von Brauchitsch (High Command), your immediate boss, is all that stands between you and the door if you upset the Führer excessively. Aim to at least keep F.M Von Brauchitsch onside (maintain a positive relationship).

The advantage of a Military Advantage strategy is that all three possible objectives are viable. Capture anyone of them, hold it for a month and you have won the game.

Whenever Hitler calls a conference you will, as Operational Commander of the Ostfront, be summonsed to attend. How you respond to this will determine how the men you command view you.

You can see your strategy and your objective in the Daily Game Log under 'Victory Conditions'.

--- Victory Conditions [?]
- Moscow or Bust
- All other objectives are secondary to the capture of Moscow
- You must taken and hold Moscow through to the end of January '42

4.6.1.3. Soviet Strategy

The 'Stalin Decides' decision in the Pre-Start turn allows the Soviet Player to choose an objective. Holding this objective enables the Soviet Player to downgrade a German Win or turn a Soviet Minor Win into a Decisive one. There is no game effect of holding, or losing, the chosen objective other than determining the extent of the level of Victory for either side.

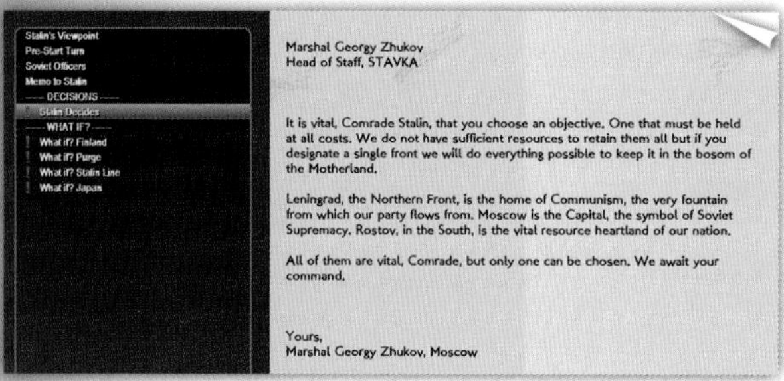

The Pre-Start turn is the only time the Soviet Player is presented with decisions

The Player's choice will be acknowledged and can be seen, at any time, in their special 'Score' tab (bottom centre).

4.6.1.4. Delegated Strategy

If the Player ignores, or deliberately delegates the 'Summonsed to Berlin'(German) or 'Stalin Decides' (Soviet) decision then their Chief of Staff resolve the matter for them.

The German Player will be assigned the 'Support Hitler's Plans' strategy and the Soviet will be given Moscow as an objective to hold at all costs.

4.6.1.5. AI Strategy

The German AI will always choose a strategy of 'Military Independence' which gives it maximum flexibility to take any of the three possible objectives. Having taken an objective, it will have to hold it for a month as would a Player.

The Soviet AI will randomly choose an objective. It has a 50% chance of choosing Moscow and a 25% of choosing either Leningrad or Rostov.

4.6.2. VICTORY POINTS

There are a fixed number of Victory Points (VP) on the map. Every city has a VP value.

VICTORY POINTS	
Location	VP
Russian Objective Cities (Leningrad, Moscow, Rostov)	10
Russian Major Cities (Red dot)	5
Russian Minor Cities (Grey dot)	1

There are a total of 129 VP available within the campaign area. While there are numerous other cities on the map that have associated VP, they will always be with one regime, or another and don't play a role. Berlin, for example, isn't likely to be captured in the course of a game representing Barbarossa in '41.

What if? Decisions can affect VP either way. These are zero sum so that a gain for the Germans would translate as a loss for the Soviets and vice versa.

At the start of the game the Soviets have ownership of all cities within the campaign area (you don't need

June 22, 1941. It's looking good for the Soviets. Hope nobody invades

to worry about what this is as every city you capture is taken into account), have an overwhelming score and the full 129 VP from cities.

4.6.3. SCORE

Each player has a score that is dynamically adjusted each turn. A visual representation of your score can be seen in the 'Score' tab (bottom centre).

A player's score provides useful feedback on their progress. Its main role, however, is in determining Victory conditions.

If the game is a Draw, for example, the Player with the higher score is given the 'advantage' as in, 'Draw, advantage Germany'. For any outcome other than a Draw, the score determines whether it is a 'Minor' or 'Decisive' victory or defeat.

A Player's score is derived from the following formula.

Score = Adjusted Victory Points x Difficulty rating

Victory points are derived from capturing cities. See 4.6.2 Victory Points.

They are 'adjusted' due to any What If? Decisions that the Player, or their opponent, may have made. See 4.10.7.4 What If? Decisions. Refer to 4.5 Difficulty for information on how the difficulty rating is calculated.

At the start of the game the Soviet Player will have a substantial score and the German none. As the Germans march eastwards the pendulum will gradually swing back the other way until the Germans will control most of the cities in the campaign area and will have the biggest score.

At game completion the German score is halved and it's this value, the 'Adjusted Score', that is used to determine the level of victory.

ASK YOUR STAFF

Why is the score halved? It would be unfair on the Soviet Player if it wasn't. At the completion of the game the Germans can reasonably expect to have captured most of the cities and have the majority of VP. Halving their scores allows the Soviet Player to compete on an equal footing.

4.6.4. HITLER CONFERENCES

Hitler has strategic goals. There are four possible goals and they are presented from the point of view of the importance Hitler grants them. The number one priority is Hitler's prime strategic goal that he is focused upon. Number two is a fall back, secondary objective. Number three is of little interest. Number four, the last, is one that he is actively opposed to.

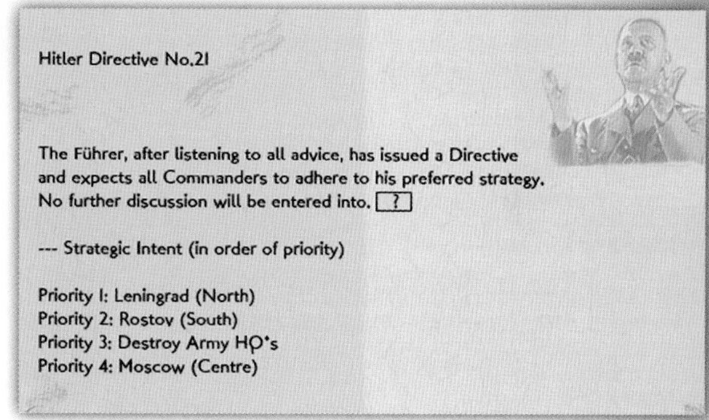

Hitler Directive No.21

The Führer, after listening to all advice, has issued a Directive and expects all Commanders to adhere to his preferred strategy. No further discussion will be entered into. [?]

--- Strategic Intent (in order of priority)

Priority 1: Leningrad (North)
Priority 2: Rostov (South)
Priority 3: Destroy Army HQ's
Priority 4: Moscow (Centre)

Hitler will always call a conference at the start of the game and issue Directive No.21. In subsequent months - early August, early September, early October - he MAY (better than even odds) call a conference which could result in a change of his priorities. The four possible goals will remain the same but the priority in which Hitler views them can change.

Hitler Directive No.21
Meteorological Report
—— DECISIONS ——
Theatre Allocations
Hitler Oath
D+2 Air Offensive
Führer Conference
Security Divisions AGC
Security Divisions AGS

Conferences are spaced at least a month apart. The above is an artificially contrived situation to highlight both a Directive and a notification for a Conference

Hitler will, regardless of what has happened previously, call a final conference in early/mid November.

Hitler called numerous conferences and regularly changed his mind over the strategic direction of the campaign, often in direct conflict with the considered advice of his commanders. It has been strongly argued that this constant flip-flopping, and consequent changes in dispositions, deprived the Wehrmacht of a consistent clear goal and was a major contributor to the failure of Barbarossa.

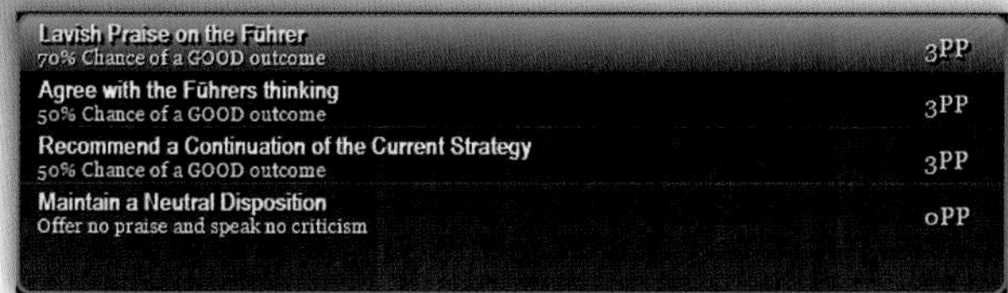

Certain options will only appear if you have the support, eg. Positive relationship, of particular characters. F.M Keitel and F.M Von Brauchitsch are potential allies in your efforts to persuade the Führer

A Führer Directive (numbered) will be issued at the completion of each conference showing Hitler's priorities. This can be referenced at any time in the Daily Game Log. What priority Hitler gives to a particular goal determines the amount of Political Points the German Player will receive from activities that support the goal and the cost of any decisions that relate to the goal.

If the Player is following a strategy of 'Support Hitler', the number one priority will be his objective for determining victory. As Hitler's top priority can change as the result of a conference this may involve a rapid adjustment. Keep in mind that once the final conference has been called in early November, the objective will be fixed.

When following either of the other two strategies, 'Moscow or Bust' or 'Military Independence', Hitler's number one priority has no impact but don't forget it still influences the PP that can be gained from capturing cities, etc. and the cost of decisions. See 4.10.3.6 Option Costs.

DESIGNER NOTE

The game design has chosen to make the 'whim of the Führer' a feature but in a manner that doesn't completely nobble the Player.

The four possible goals are randomly determined at each conference (there is a good chance that they won't change) but the randomisation is constrained within a reasonable historical framework.

At each conference the Player is presented with options that vary depending on the strategy he has chosen. There is scope for influencing the views of the Führer and steering him in a desired direction.

Whenever you capture a city, or destroy a Soviet Army HQ, you gain a number of PP determined by how well this complies with Hitler's goals.

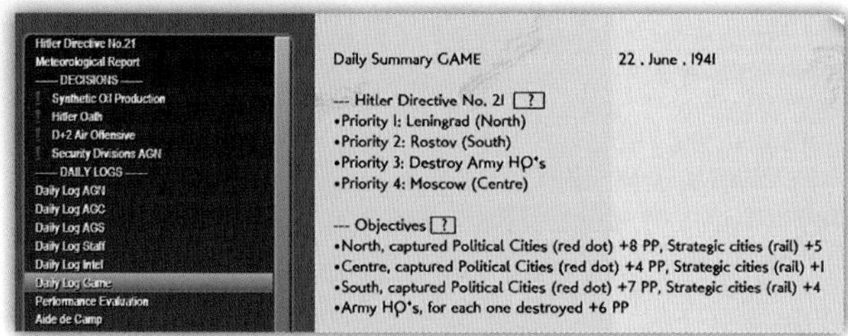

Capturing cities in AGC, which Hitler has little interest in, reaps few rewards. Taking cities up north in AGN is much more lucrative

STAFF ADVICE

Directives, historically, were to be followed to the letter, no excuses, and they were considered to above all other laws. The game does not impose these restrictions and there is no direct penalty for ignoring them. However some astute manoeuvring, both military and political, would be advised if you choose to forge your own path.

4.6.5. GAME OVER ANALYSIS

At the completion of the game you'll be provided with an unsolicited evaluation by High Command (if German) or STAVKA (Soviet). This is independent of the game outcome and is aimed at your performance as a Commander, rather than the straight military result.

You will also receive extensive information and various benchmarks of what has transpired during the campaign. If you are playing as the Germans you may be required to appear before the War Crimes Tribunal (not if you have selected the 'Geneva Convention' option at game start) and answer for your actions depending on your war crimes score.

SUMMARY

- You choose a strategy in the Pre-Start Turn (or delegate)
- Your strategy determines your objective (German Player)
- Sudden death outcomes are possible if you, or your opponent, drop the ball
- The Soviet strategy influences the degree of victory
- VP are gained from capturing cities
- Score = VP x difficulty
- There is a minimum score threshold to cross in order to attain a Decisive Win.
- The German Player's score is halved ('adjusted score') when determining victory criteria
- Hitler calls conferences at game start, early Aug/Sep/Oct (maybe) and a final one in early/mid Nov
- At a conference Hitler's priorities may change
- Priorities determine the VP the German Player gains from capturing cities and destroying HQ's
- Priorities determine decision option costs
- A 'Support Hitler' strategy requires the Player to capture Hitler's number one priority.

4.7. COMMAND STRUCTURE ▶

The command structure for both sides are similar but with a few differences. The Germans have an additional level of hierarchy with the Player expected to operate from within the structure whereas the Soviet Player is situated at the very apex.

Each element in the command structure has a character and, mostly, a Headquarters unit where that character resides. For example, Armeegruppe North is commanded by F.M Von Leeb. If you click on the AGN counter you'll see a portrait of Von Leeb.

The entire Soviet command structure is represented by on-map HQ counters. Most of the German command structure is on-map but there are parts of their hierarchy that are represented by characters only. Hitler, for example, is assumed to be in Berlin and isn't shown as part of an on-map HQ counter.

4.7.1. GERMAN COMMAND STRUCTURE

As can be seen below the Player sits midway in the structure, in command of the OKH. Above him is OKW, or 'High Command' in the game. The Führer is assumed to be one level higher in supreme political command.

DESIGNER NOTE

The German command structure, portrayed in the game, is a slightly truncated version of the real thing. This has been done for purposes of clarity and game play but, given the moving target that was reality, there is little to be gained from a higher fidelity model.

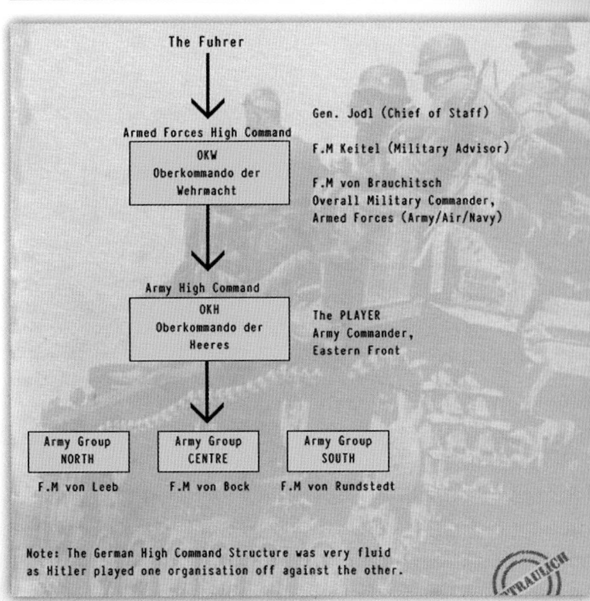

Actual German Command Structure showing the Player's position in the hierarchy

The equivalent, game, version would be as follows.

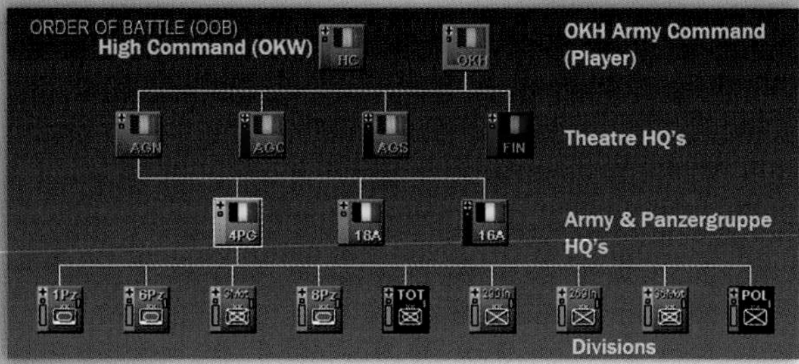

By the later stages of the time period represented by the game, Hitler had compressed the command structure even further by removing F.M von Brauchitsch and assuming direct, personal, command of the OKW which gave him total authority over all matters military.

You can see the Player's position at OKH where he has Operational Command of the entire Eastern Front. Beneath him are the three Threatre HQ's, each with their own subordinate Army and Panzergruppe HQ's that, in turn, have a collection of individual Divisions.

Note that Army and Panzergruppe HQ's are equivalent, the former comprising slow Divisions and the latter predominately fast Divisions.

The Finnish command is placed under OKH, once again for game play purposes, but in reality was a very independent organisation that went its own way and who 'took note' of German requests and demands.

All other allied axis nations (Italians, Hungarians, Romanians, Spanish, Slovakian) that sent forces to assist in Barbarossa are assumed to be under the command of a Theatre HQ, typically that of AGS.

In practical game terms, the Player sits in the middle with a two layer command structure beneath him (Theatre and Army HQ's)and a two layer structure above (High Command and the Führer).

All of the above Headquarter units are represented by an historically correct character. When referring to a particular Headquarters, or character, they are considered one and the same. There are other parts of the hierarchy that come into play, for example the Luftwaffe, but these are dealt with in an abstract manner. The only, on-map, Headquarters are those shown above.

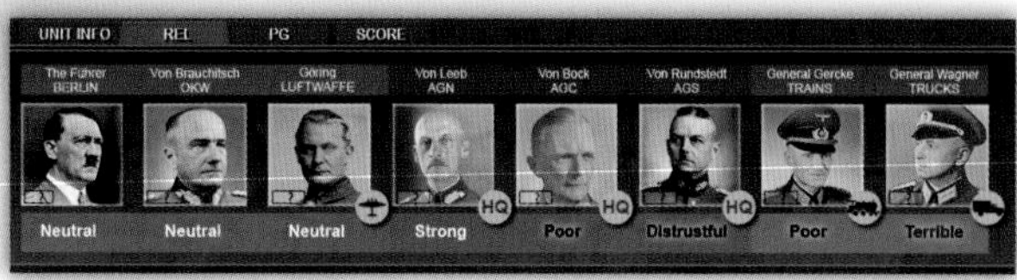

Here are the handful of characters with whom you have regular dealings with. You can see Hitler and Göring despite them not being represented on the map with an Headquarters unit. Generals Wagner and Gercke are the same. Von Brauchitsch is your boss at High Command (or OKW) and your three Theatre Commanders - Leeb, Bock and Rundstedt, are present and accounted for, all of them holding down an HQ position.

If you are uncertain of how this ties together the easiest way is to fire up the game and click on the various Headquarter units to see exactly who is where. It all falls into place quite quickly.

The Army and Panzergruppe HQ's represent individual armies and they are your main units of manoeuvre. All the other on-map HQ's are static. Their main game functions are to provide links in the supply chains and to act as central points to which units have to be able to trace a path back to in order to pass certain tests. They also provide a physical representation of the command structure and enable you to visually determine which character is where.

Refer also to 4.8.1 German Characters.

4.7.2. SOVIET COMMAND STRUCTURE

The Soviet structure is straightforward. The Player's role is that of Stalin who is assumed to be in charge

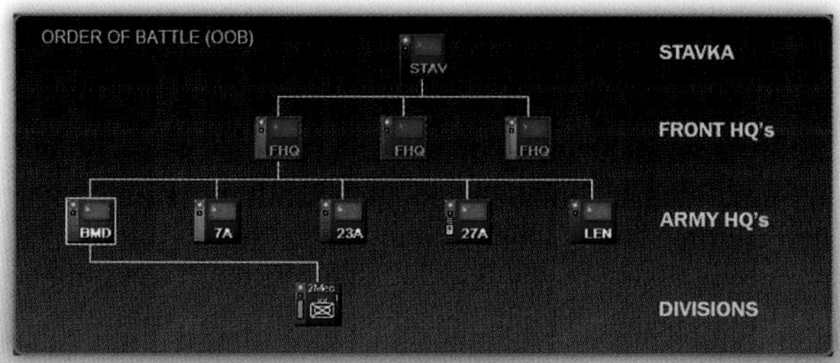

of STAVKA, the highest level HQ available. All other HQ's are subordinate to him.

There are three Front HQ's which are the equivalent of a German Theatre HQ. They command the North, Centre and Southern fronts which have identical boundaries to the German AGN/AGC/AGS theatres.

Unlike the Germans with their dual Army and Panzergruppe HQ's, the Soviets have only Army HQ's.

STAVKA and Front HQ's are unable to be moved by the Player. Army HQ's, along with their associated Divisions, constitute the manoeuvre elements of the Red Army.

The 'Command' tab (bottom centre) displays the key characters for the Soviet Player. There is Stalin, the Player himself, his three Front commanders and his two troubleshooters.

The Front commanders can, unlike the Germans, be changed during the game as a result of the Player's actions. He may choose to have one fired for incompetence, for example. A replacement Marshal would automatically arrive and the relevant portraits and statistics would be updated.

Marshal Timoshenko, Central Front, has been replaced with Marshal Rokossovsky. As both are extremely competent the logic for doing so is dubious. I would be replacing Marshal Budenny first as the size of his moustache is indirectly proportional to his military competence

The two trouble shooters, Marshal Zhukov and Commissar Khrushchev don't have on-map representation. They do, however, show up as icons next to the name of the commander of which ever Headquarters that they are currently at.

They are available to be moved around the map, from one Headquarters to another, where the need is greatest. Their formal position within the Soviet Command structure would be directly under Stalin. You can think of them as special envoys who have authority over all concerned and who answer only to Stalin.

You can order them to move to a particular HQ and carry out specific tasks (they have their own sets of Officer Cards). They cannot be changed and possess total loyalty to Stalin.

Refer also to 4.8.2 Soviet Characters.

4.7.3. HQ CALAMITIES - GERMAN

If any of the Theatre HQ's are lost you will be fired for incompetence. It's Germany invading Russia here, not the other way around.

The loss of an Army, or Panzergruppe, HQ will see it automatically reconstituted and returning the following turn as a reinforcement (Action Card). Notifications of this will be in your relevant Daily Log and your Aide de Camp report.

An Army, or Panzergruppe, that finds itself cut off (surrounded) has the option of voluntarily disbanding (Action Card 'Evacuate HQ') and reforming the following turn as a reinforcement (Action Card). Key personnel are assumed to be evacuated by air out of their encirclement whereupon they will reconstitute in a safer location. Unfortunately this option is only available for HQ's, not entire Divisions.

Emergency situations require emergency measures. The card will automatically appear in the 'Command' category whenever it is required

DESIGNER NOTE

In marked contrast to the Soviet command structure of '41, the Germans were able to adapt and innovate in the face of adversity. The loss of a Soviet Army HQ is permanent whereas an equivalent German loss is merely a temporary hiccup.

4.7.4. HQ CALAMITIES - SOVIET

The two Soviet trouble shooters can never die. If an HQ they are located at is over run and destroyed they will be picked up by the last plane out and transported back to STAVKA.

Soviet Front HQ's and STAVA will automatically relocate to a safer location in the event of threatening enemy moves. If they are destroyed they will be automatically reconstituted and immediately returned to a safe location.

DESIGNER NOTE

Originally the Player was given control of the Front HQ's and allowed to move them around at will. This worked O.K as nobody willing marched their Front HQ's under the tracks of advancing Panzers. But because they form a vital link in the command chain there were times where the Player inadvertently placed them in a situation that resulted in an entire Front's worth of Armies suddenly being out of command. To avoid this the Front HQ's were automated.

Soviet Army HQ's, once destroyed, are gone forever. Their subordinate units have a chance, each turn, of being automatically reassigned to the nearest, valid, HQ. This is only possible if the unit isn't cut-off and represents the inflexibility of Soviet Command and Control in '41 to deal with unexpected eventualities.

For every lost Army HQ, the German Player receives a bounty of Political Points.

A Soviet HQ, having lost all of its subordinate Divisions, will be automatically disbanded. If this happens the German Player will receive half their normal allocation of Political Points. A newly arrived reinforcement Army HQ cannot be automatically disbanded until five turns after its arrival (to allow for any late arriving Divisions).

DESIGNER NOTE

Having stray HQ's hanging around does little for the game play. The Soviets ruthlessly reinvented failed HQ's, typically disbanding and then reforming them with a complete new set of personnel and conscript Divisions.

4.7.5. ARMIES AND DIVISIONS

Armies are individual entities that form the building blocks of the game. They are considered integrated formations that fight and manoeuvre as one. Each Army has an HQ and a number of subordinate Divisions.

A German Panzergruppe is an Army equivalent.

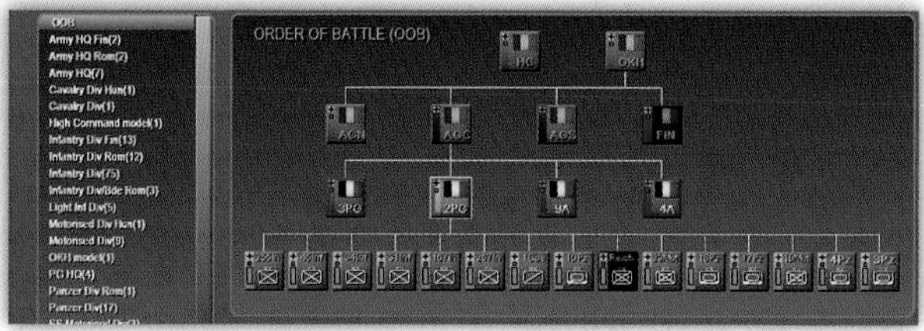

The 2nd Panzergruppe is an Army level formation under the command of the AGC theatre HQ. It has a large number of subordinate Divisions

The concept of 'Command Range' acts to bind Divisions to their HQ's (see 4.13 Command Range). Any Division that ends its turn more than five hexes from its parent HQ will suffer steep penalties.

For the German Player theatre artillery assets, tactical air support and command focus are all assigned on an army basis. Every army in the game has a posture. Reports are on an army basis.

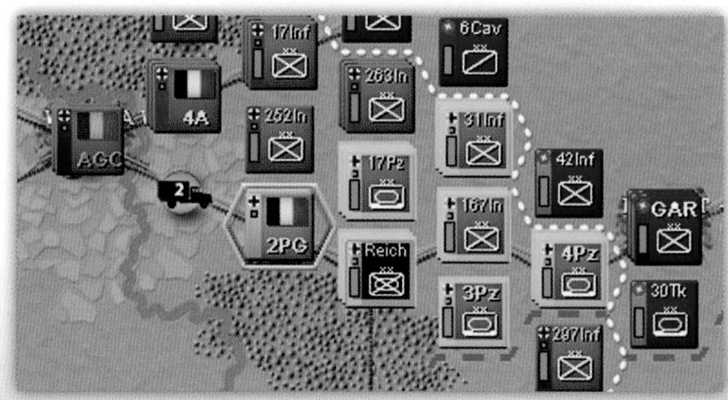

Clicking on 2nd Panzergruppe HQ will highlight all its subordinate Divisions on the map

STAFF ADVICE

Each theatre has a small number of armies available and a lot of individual Divisions. Think in terms of armies, not individual Divisions. You want to position the 9th Army over *there*, push the 3rd Panzergruppe through that gap *here*. Once you've made the big picture army level decisions you can then deal with their tactical implementation on a Division by Division basis.

4.7.5.1. Division Types

Divisions (both sides) are either 'Fast' or 'Slow'.

Fast Divisions have vehicles - tanks, trucks or half tracks. They require fuel to move. Slow Divisions have no vehicles, are mostly infantry and can move without needing a supply of fuel.

Fast Divisions suffer mechanical breakdowns. Slow Divisions suffer fatigue.

4.7.5.2. Attached Units

A number of Divisions have smaller formations attached to them. Only the Germans have attached units.

DESIGNER NOTE

A big effort has been made to retain Divisions as the lowest level unit on the map. It would have been possible to model regiments but this would have raised the counter density significantly and added nothing that couldn't have been handled by either tweaking the composition of a Division or adding an attached unit.

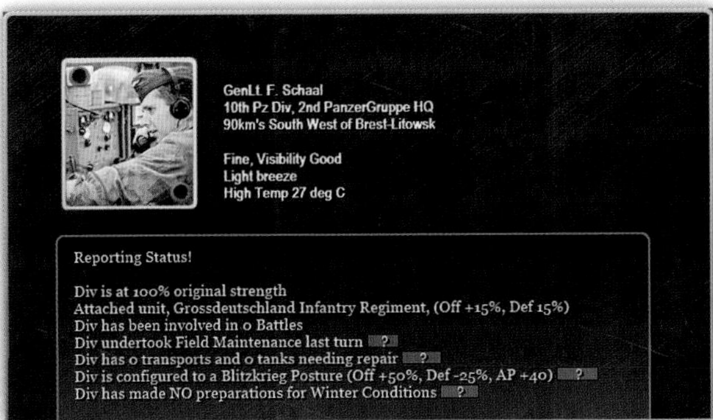
GenLt. F. Schaal
10th Pz Div, 2nd PanzerGruppe HQ
90km's South West of Brest-Litowsk
Fine, Visibility Good
Light breeze
High Temp 27 deg C
Reporting Status!
Div is at 100% original strength
Attached unit, Grossdeutschland Infantry Regiment, (Off +15%, Def 15%)
Div has been involved in 0 Battles
Div undertook Field Maintenance last turn ?
Div has 0 transports and 0 tanks needing repair ?
Div is configured to a Blitzkrieg Posture (Off +50%, Def -25%, AP +40) ?
Div has made NO preparations for Winter Conditions ?

GenLt. Schaal's 10th Panzer Division benefits from having the renowned Grossdeutschland Regiment attached (there were, surprisingly, questions raised in '41 about the Grossdeutschland's performance)

Attached units serve to provide permanent combat bonuses and can be viewed in the 'Unit Modifiers' reports or when a Division is asked to Report Status!

STAFF ADVICE

Attached units serve to make their host Divisions more powerful than normal. They provide their combat bonuses regardless of the status of the host Division. Use them wisely.

Attached units are permanent and can't be 'unattached'. If their host Division is lost they are similarly lost. Attached units can't be transferred to another Division.

--- 10th Pz Div (loc 22:44)
Army committed to a Blitzkrieg posture, +50% Off, -25% Def, +40 AP ?
Grossdeutschland Infantry Regiment attached, +15% Off, +15% Def

Unit Modifiers report for the 2nd Panzergruppe

SUMMARY

- The German Player has superiors and subordinates.
- The Soviet Player has only subordinates
- Army and Panzergruppe HQ units are the only ones you can move.
- German Army, or Panzergruppe HQ's, once lost, return as reinforcements.
- German Army, or Panzergruppe HQ's can be evacuated by air, if cut off.
- The loss of a German Theatre HQ is considered an instant win for the Soviets.
- Soviet Front HQ's and Stavka are automatically relocated if threatened.
- Soviet Army HQ's, once lost, are gone forever.
- Soviet Divisions, without an HQ, may be automatically reassigned.
- German Divisions only may have an attached unit which provides permanent combat bonuses
- Fast Divisions have vehicles (tanks, trucks or half tracks) and require fuel to move.
- Slow Divisions have NO vehicles (mainly infantry) and can move without fuel

See also 4.8 Characters and 3.9.1 Action Cards.

4.8. CHARACTERS ▶

Military endeavours aren't dry, statistical, activities where you are commanding a set of numbers. People play just as an important role as Armies and Divisions.

People, or characters, are present in the game and represent individuals within a military hierarchy. How you interact with characters differs depending on what side (regime) you are playing.

Refer also to 4.7 Command Structure for an overview of the relevant hierarchies.

4.8.1. GERMAN CHARACTERS

There are a number of characters that you will engage with when playing as the Germans. A number of them have guest appearances, lurking in the background, and you'll see them only as names attached to reports.

Others have in-game effects and they all have a relationship level (how they relate to you). All of them can be found in the various Relationship reports - Superiors, Unclear, Subordinates.

The important ones, who you'll have the most dealings with and who all have clearly defined in-game effects, are shown in the Relationship Tab (bottom centre).

4.8.1.1. Type of Relationship

Characters come in three flavours.

- Superiors (you answer to them)
- Unclear (its murky)
- Subordinates (they answer to you)

All characters work the same way but which category a character sits within provides general guidelines as to how you approach them.

You issue orders to your Subordinates. They'll carry them out although if you have negative relations they may find ways of obstructing and obfuscating your expressed intentions.

Characters are in the 'Unclear' category when your authority over them is exactly that. The two logistical Generals, Gercke and Wagner, are good examples of this. Nominally you are their superiors but they both have roles that straddle OKW & OKH (your headquarters and that of your superiors). In practise it's not as clear cut.

Superiors are different. With them you are making requests, not demands.

Superiors

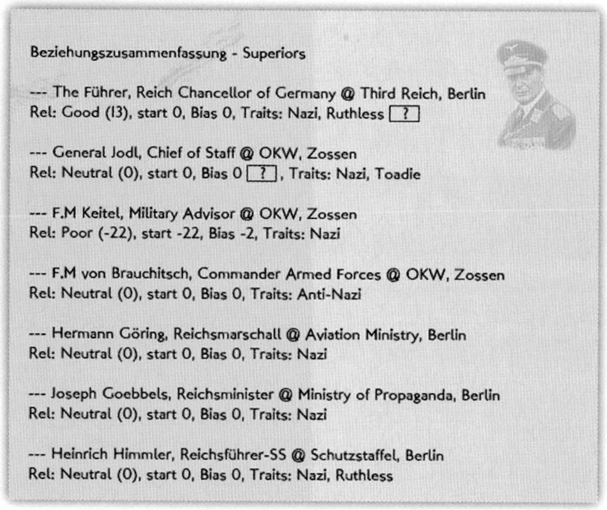

Beziehungszusammenfassung - Superiors

--- The Führer, Reich Chancellor of Germany @ Third Reich, Berlin
Rel: Good (13), start 0, Bias 0, Traits: Nazi, Ruthless [?]

--- General Jodl, Chief of Staff @ OKW, Zossen
Rel: Neutral (0), start 0, Bias 0 [?], Traits: Nazi, Toadie

--- F.M Keitel, Military Advisor @ OKW, Zossen
Rel: Poor (-22), start -22, Bias -2, Traits: Nazi

--- F.M von Brauchitsch, Commander Armed Forces @ OKW, Zossen
Rel: Neutral (0), start 0, Bias 0, Traits: Anti-Nazi

--- Hermann Göring, Reichsmarschall @ Aviation Ministry, Berlin
Rel: Neutral (0), start 0, Bias 0, Traits: Nazi

--- Joseph Goebbels, Reichsminister @ Ministry of Propaganda, Berlin
Rel: Neutral (0), start 0, Bias 0, Traits: Nazi

--- Heinrich Himmler, Reichsführer-SS @ Schutzstaffel, Berlin
Rel: Neutral (0), start 0, Bias 0, Traits: Nazi, Ruthless

Hitler (The Führer). A difficult, and important, relationship. Gambled everything on Barbarossa and lost. Assumed to have committed suicide in the Führer bunker in '45. See 4.8.1.7 Führer.

General Jodl is the gatekeeper to Hitler. Think of him as Hitler's secretary. A sycophant. Issued orders that all enemy commando's were to be shot on sight if caught behind enemy lines. Prisoners of war who were unable to walk were also shot on his orders. He signed Germany's surrender in 1945. Subsequently hung.

F.M Keitel, Hitler's personal military advisor. The man whispering in Hitler's ear. A lackey. Militarily incompetent although he predicted that Barbarossa would be a failure. He was greatly disliked by Commanders who went out of their way to ignore his orders. Hung at the end of the war.

F.M Von Brauchitsch, Commander Armed Forces, your immediate boss. Heavily in debt to Hitler, overwhelmed by his personality, he failed to stand up to him when needed. With ongoing heart problems he was unable to act as a restraining influence of Hitler's whims and wild plans. After the failure to capture Moscow he was made a scapegoat and fired.

Reichmarschall Göring, head of the Luftwaffe. A recipient of the Blue Max in WW1, by the time of WW2 he had become a corpulent cross dresser with extravagant tastes. After the Luftwaffe's abject failure at Stalingrad, he lost Hitler's confidence. He retired from public appearances and concentrated on accumulating artworks and property. Sentenced to be hung at the end of the war he took cyanide and committed suicide.

Reichsminister Goebbels, Reichs Ministry of Public Enlightenment and Propaganda. A bank clerk in his early days, he used his highly developed public speaking skills and his genius for propaganda to advance the cause of the Nazi party. He abused his position as Propaganda Minister and was known as the 'Babelsberg Stud' due to his use of the 'casting couch'. He and his wife committed suicide in the Führer bunker after killing their six children.

Reichsführer-SS Himmler. He was responsible for the internal security of the Third Reich as well as other unsavoury matters such as the Einsatzgruppen (death squads). Under Himmler the SS expanded rapidly and SS men wishing to marry had to produce family trees proving Arayan descent, going back 150 years and produce a minimum of four children. He would have failed to meet his own exacting standards and when placed in actual military command he was capable of producing only 'incoherent' reports. Himmler committed suicide while in British custody.

DESIGNER NOTE

This is, without a doubt, a collection of very unsavoury characters. The intention is not to make a political statement or pass judgement. History is what it is. The game is about Operational Command.

Unclear

General Gercke, Wehrmachttransportchief, head of Trains. He had authority over wartime transport by rail or inland waterways. His authority didn't extend to either the navy or the airforce and the best he

Beziehungszusammenfassung - Unclear

--- Gen. Gercke, Wehrmachttransportchief @ OKW, Zossen
Rel: Distrustful (-26), start 0, Bias 0

--- Gen. Wagner, Quartermaster General @ OKH, Posen
Rel: Neutral (0), start 0, Bias 0 [?]

--- F.M Antonescu, Head of State @ Rumania, Bucharest
Rel: Neutral (0), start 0, Bias 0

--- Marshal Mannerheim, Chief of Defence @ Finnish Army, Finland
Rel: Neutral (0), start 0, Bias 0

--- Gen. Masse, Comandante @ Italian Army Corps, Ostfront
Rel: Neutral (0), start 0, Bias 0

could do was to ask them to put transport capacity at his disposal. Unfortunately he also didn't have control over motor transport (Gen. Wagner) which meant that he controlled the middle of the logistical pipeline but neither of its ends.

General Wagner, Quartermaster General. He controlled motor transportation and was responsible for the supplies to be transported. While he controlled the supply depots he had no authority over the railways (Gen. Gercke) which left him controlling the ends of the logistical pipeline but not the middle.

F.M Antonescu, Head of State, Romania. Has an influence of certain decisions, otherwise can be ignored. As can Marshal Mannerheim, Chief of Defence, Finland and General Masse, Commandante, Italian Army Corps.

Subordinates

F.M Von Leeb, Theatre Commander, AGN. A Bavarian who served in China during the Boxer Rebellion. Hitler disliked the aristocratic Leeb and retired him

Beziehungszusammenfassung - Subordinates

--- F.M von Leeb, Kdt. THEATRE @ Army Group North, Ostfront
Rel: Neutral (8), start 8, Bias +1, Traits: Anti-Nazi [?]
Chance of AP Bonus 8% [?]

--- F.M von Bock, Kdt. THEATRE @ Army Group Centre, Ostfront
Rel: Neutral (1), start 1, Bias 0 [?], Traits: Anti-Nazi
Chance of AP Bonus 1%

--- F.M von Rundstedt, Kdt. THEATRE @ Army Group South, Ostfront
Rel: Neutral (1), start 1, Bias 0, Traits: Anti-Nazi
Chance of AP Bonus 1%

from the army in '38. Recalled to active duty he was given command of AGN. Hitler, frustrated at AGN's inability to capture Leningrad, commented that Von Leeb was 'obviously senile, had lost his nerve, and like a true Catholic he wants to pray but not to fight.'

F.M Von Bock, Theatre Commander, AGC. A Prussian aristocrat, he was described as being arrogant, ambitious and opinionated. Thin on theory but big on determination. He was extremely outspoken on military matters and had a habit of phoning Hitler directly from the field telling him what was what, something that Hitler tolerated only because of his success in battle. He frequently lectured his troops about the honour of dying for Germany and was nicknamed 'the Dier'. A British fighter bomber killed Bock, his wife and their only daughter as they travelled by car towards Hamburg in '45.

F.M Von Rundstedt, Theatre Commander, AGS. Another Prussian from a Saxon family with a long military tradition. He was described as an 'outstandingly able officer'. Aged 64 when WW2 began, he was recalled to active duty and eventually given command of AGS. His encirclement of Kiev was one of the greatest German successes of the war. In Nov '41, his armies exhausted, he demanded that his armies be allowed to form a defensive line and dig in for the coming winter. Hitler refused and ordered him to advance. A long time heavy smoker, he suffered a heart attack at this point. After capturing Rostov, Von Rundstedt ordered a withdrawal in the face of a Soviet counterattack and was dismissed by Hitler as a result.

Army Commanders

You have no direct interaction with your Army, and Panzergruppe, Commanders as it is the role of your subordinate theatre commanders to deal with them.

You can, however, ask your theatre commanders to 'Focus' their staff, logistical and specialist battalion resources on a particular Army, or Panzergruppe, HQ which will provide the relevant commander with a set of Officer Action Cards as a result. See 6.1.1 Command Focus.

4.8.1.2. Relationship Levels

Each character that you interact with has a relationship level expressed both as a number and a descriptor.

RELATIONSHIP LEVELS	
Level	Descriptor
-50, or below	Terrible
-25	Distrustful
-10	Poor
0	Neutral
+10	Good
+25	Strong
+50, or above	Superb

There can be pre-existing relationship levels due to 'Past Relationships'. See 4.8.1.6 Past Relationships.

Relationship levels change as whenever you choose a decision option that involves that character. Some options can change multiple relationship levels. See 4.10 Decisions.

4.8.1.3. Relationship Effects

Relationship levels can affect the cost of decision options and many other game mechanics. To see what effect your current relationship with a particular character (the important ones) has, mouse over the relevant tool tip in the special 'Relationship' Tab (bottom, centre).

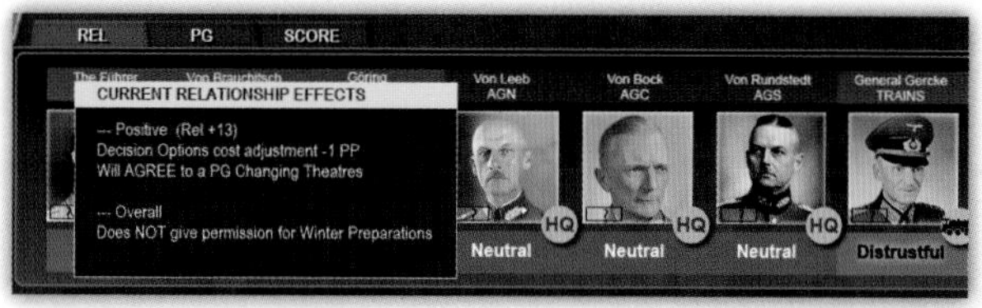

Hitler

You need a positive relationship with Hitler in order to obtain permission to reassign a Panzergruppe to an adjoining theatre. See 6.1.2.1 Changing Theatres.

You can be fired if your relationship deteriorates with both Hitler and F.M

Von Brauchitsch and you are following a strategy of 'Military Independence'. See 4.6.1 Choosing a Strategy.

Various special Hitler related decisions can trigger at different relationship levels. Different strategies generate different decisions. If the Hitler tool tip in the 'Relationship' tab (bottom centre) indicates a certain decision is possible there is no guarantee that it will occur.

F.M Von Brauchitsch

As your immediate superior this is a key relationship. Where ever possible you F.M Von Brauchitsch on side but there may be times when you have to take a stand and disagree.

A number of special decisions are possible at various relationship levels. Generally the more extreme your relationship, the more likely you are to get a decision. As with Hitler, just because the tool tip in the 'Relationship' tab indicates a certain decision is possible it's not guaranteed to show.

Reichsmarschall Göring

The prime effect of your relationship with Göring is that if it's negative, 'poor'(<-9) or worse, the cost, in PP, of all Luftwaffe Action Cards will increase. The worse your relationship, the greater the cost increase.

Resupply and TAC cards are affected.

A positive relationship has no effect and all Luftwaffe cards will be at their standard costs. Be warned that the Reichsmarschall is a nasty political infighter if you infringe on his territory.

Theatre Commanders

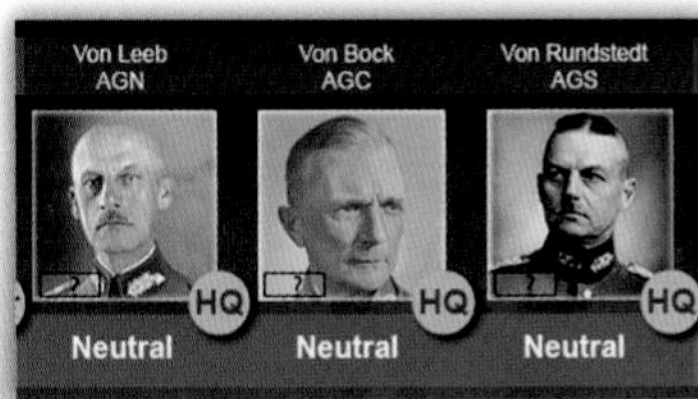

Theatre Commanders can have three specific effects as a result of your relationship with them.

- Action Card costs (can affect the PP cost of all theatre related actions cards)
- Command Effect (can experience AP bonus or penalties to Armies, and Panzergruppes, under their command)
- Command Focus (will only give Focus to a Panzergruppe if you have a positive relationship)

Action Card Costs

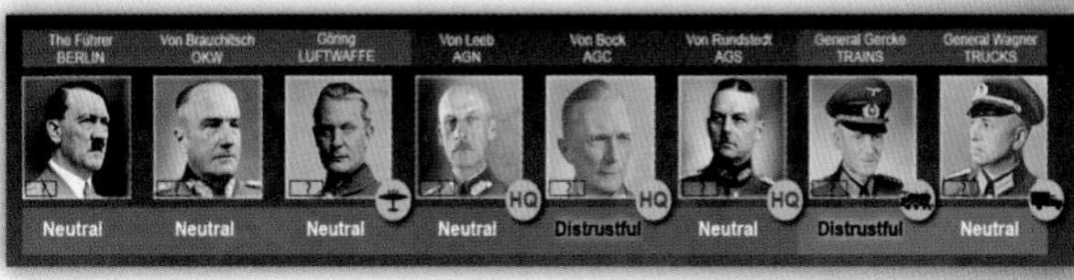

Like Göring, if your relationship becomes negative ('poor' or worse) then the cost of all theatre related Action Cards will increase. Worse the relationship, higher the cost.

This is evaluated separately for each theatre. In the example above you have a neutral relationship with all three of your theatre commanders so there will be no cost increase but if, Von Bock in AGC has a dim view of you then all AGC related cards will increase in cost.

Posture cards, Artillery cards, and Focus cards are all affected.

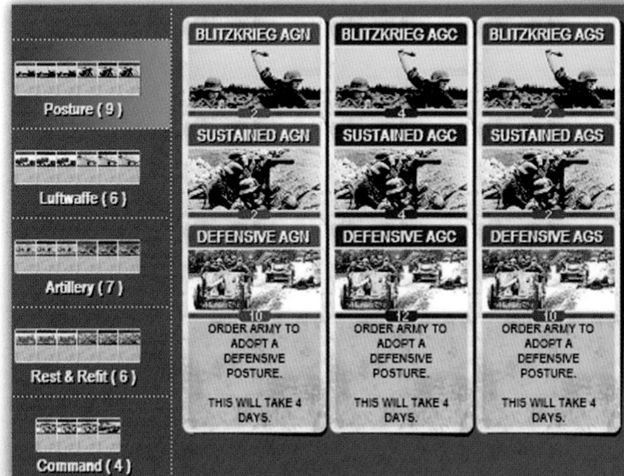

Relations with F.M Von Bock are 'Distrustful'. Note the PP cost all AGC related cards have increased

Command Effect

Your relationship level with each theatre commander determines the percentage chance of your commander going the extra mile, if positive, and facilitating excellent staff work that allows some of the Armies, or Panzergruppes, under his command to obtain bonus Action Points (AP).

With a negative relationship level your theatre commander may struggle to stay on top of the situation (or perhaps he isn't willing to give it his full attention) and there is a chance of Armies, or Panzergruppes, under his command experiencing an AP penalty.

Your Daily Theatre Logs will keep you informed as will the dynamic tool tips in the 'Relationship' tab.

Daily Summary AG CENTRE 22 . June . 1941

--- Command
•F.M von Bock, AGC, retains his old school thinking (Rel -ve) [?]
•F.M von Bock currently has not determined a Command Focus [?]
•A Distrustful (-30) relationship with F.M von Bock, Kdt. THEATRE, has I subordinate HQ experiencing Command Penalties [?] [?]

Things aren't going well in AGC. F.M Von Bock is dragging his feet. The dynamic tool tip (not shown) indicates that F.M Von Kluge's 4th Army is suffering AP penalties as a result

4th Army HQ - 30km's East of Warsaw

--- 7th Inf Div (loc 20:42)
Army committed to a Blitzkrieg posture, +50% Off, -25% Def
Negative relations incur command delays, -20 AP

--- 23rd Inf Div (loc 20:42)
Army committed to a Blitzkrieg posture, +50% Off, -25% Def
Negative relations incur command delays, -20 AP

--- 258th Inf Div (loc 21:41)
Army committed to a Blitzkrieg posture, +50% Off, -25% Def
Negative relations incur command delays, -20 AP

The Unit Modifier report for the 4th Army highlights the problem.

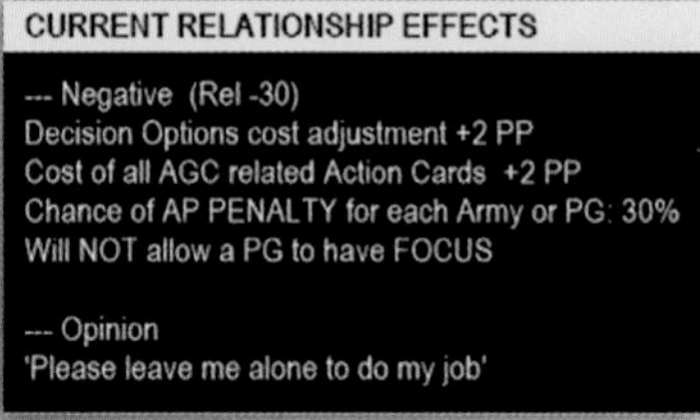
CURRENT RELATIONSHIP EFFECTS

--- Negative (Rel -30)
Decision Options cost adjustment +2 PP
Cost of all AGC related Action Cards +2 PP
Chance of AP PENALTY for each Army or PG: 30%
Will NOT allow a PG to have FOCUS

--- Opinion
'Please leave me alone to do my job'

Your relationship with F.M Von Bock is -30 giving each Army, or Panzergruppe, within AGC a 30% chance of being effected by, because it's a negative relationship level, a command Penalty

The chance of an Army, or Panzergruppe, within a theatre being affected by a Command bonus or penalty, due to your relationship with the theatre commander, is equal the absolute value of your relationship level with them.

Command Focus

Within each theatre you can choose a single Army, or Panzergruppe, to receive preferential staff, resource, logistical and specialist battalion allocations.

You can instruct your theatre commander's to Focus on a particular Army or Panzergruppe. A theatre commander will always be willing to apply their command Focus on to an Army under their command but will only do so for a Panzergruppe if you have a positive relationship with them.

DESIGNER NOTE

Historically there was an ongoing conflict between the new school Panzergruppe commanders and the old school, WW1, infantry-centric commanders. When you issue a 'Command Focus' order you are asking your subordinate, the theatre commander, to carry out your instructions. He will do so but if you have a negative relationship level with him he'll find ways to NOT provide the required support to a Panzergruppe due to his reluctance to have a hot headed Panzergruppe commander charge off and extend the flanks that he, the theatre commander, is responsible for. Subordinates are good at finding creative ways of not carrying out your orders if they don't want to.

To do so you play a 'Focus' Action Card onto the relevant HQ within the theatre.

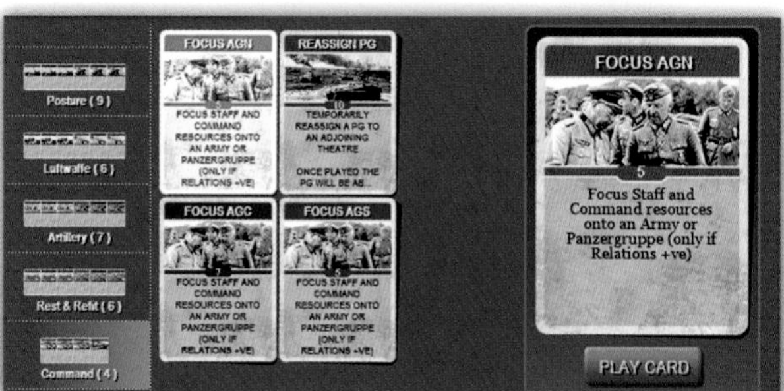

You've got a good relationship with F.M Von Leeb in AGN and he is willing to Focus on any Army or Panzergruppe within his command

By focusing on a particular Army, or Panzergruppe, within a theatre a set of Officer Action cards will become available for the HQ that has focus providing enhanced tactical options. See 6.1.5.8 Officer Cards.

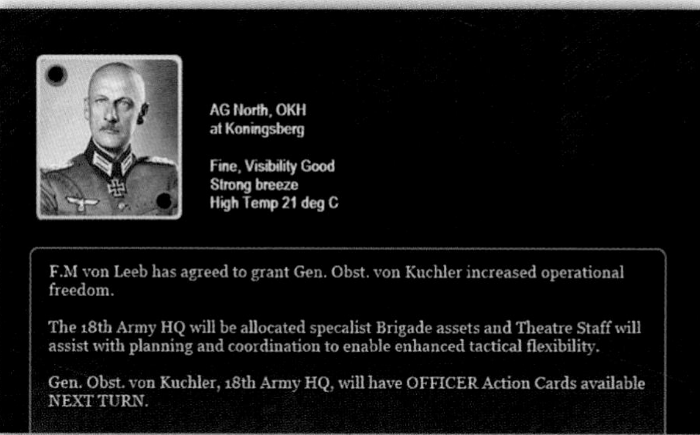

AG North, OKH
at Koningsberg
Fine, Visibility Good
Strong breeze
High Temp 21 deg C
F.M von Leeb has agreed to grant Gen. Obst. von Kuchler increased operational freedom.
The 18th Army HQ will be allocated specalist Brigade assets and Theatre Staff will assist with planning and coordination to enable enhanced tactical flexibility.
Gen. Obst. von Kuchler, 18th Army HQ, will have OFFICER Action Cards available NEXT TURN.

Gen.Obst. Von Kuchler's 18th Army has benefited from your theatre commander's focus

If you have ordered your theatre commander to focus on a Panzergruppe he will automatically withdraw his focus if your relationship turns negative (goes below zero).

STAFF ADVICE

Your Panzergruppes are the tip of the spear. Where possible you want your theatre commanders to focus on them so that your Panzergruppe commanders can access the benefits of the Officer cards. You'll need good relations with your theatre commanders and, once they are focused on a Panzergruppe, you'll need to keep them positive.

See 6.1.1 Command Focus for further information.

Logistic Generals

Your relationship with General's Gercke and Wagner can be a difficult one to manage. They are both required for the smooth operation of your logistics but they have different agendas. Often what works for one doesn't work for the other.

The system of having two people with split authority over logistical matters was a uniquely German institution that virtually guaranteed there would be ongoing problems.

General Gercke

In charge of trains. If your relationship with him is 'Poor', or worse, the incidence of adverse train events ('Inefficient Loading Practices', 'Transfer Chokepoints' and 'Lack of Cooperation') will increase. This is a global effect that extends across all theatres and reflects General Gercke unwillingness to pay attention to detail and minimise such problems when he has a dim view of yourself.

Siege Artillery is rail borne. It relocates via the rail system. Whenever it is ordered to move from one location to another there is a chance it will be delayed. The worse your relationship is with General Gercke, the less willing he is to prioritise the movement of your siege train throughout his rail network and the greater the chance of it being delayed.

CURRENT RELATIONSHIP EFFECTS

--- Negative (Rel -26)
Decision Options cost adjustment +2 PP
Chance of Hijack/Scheduling/Chokepoint problems +10%
Siege Artillery Delay chance +26%

Your relationship with General Gercke has broken down with consequences for the reliability of your rail network and the strong chance of delays in relocating your siege artillery

General Wagner

In charge of Truck columns and supply depots. If your relationship with him is

'Poor', or worse, your ability to stockpile fuel at your Panzergruppe HQ depots (the point at where it is used) is adversely affected.

The worse your relationship, the less fuel you will be able to stockpile. This is a global effect that applies to all theatres.

LOGISTICS REPORT - AGN

22 . June . 1941 [?]

--- Main Depot: Koningsberg [?] (loc 17:33)
FUEL (start): 0 bbls IN (ZI): 5000 bbls OUT (Trains): 5000 bbls
FUEL (remaining): 0 bbls
Trains per day: 24 (requires 0 trains, distance 0 km's) [?]

--- Forward Supply Base (FSB): Koningsberg [?] (loc 17:33)
FUEL (start): 0 bbls IN (Depot): 5000 bbls OUT (Trucks): 5000 bbls
FUEL (remaining): 0 bbls
Truck columns: 125 (requires 1 truck column [?], distance 90 km's)

--- Field HQ: 4th Panzergruppe HQ (loc 20:34) [?]
FUEL (start): 6000 bbls IN (FSB): 5000
FUEL AVAILABLE: 11000 bbls (less 2000 bbls for Blitzkrieg Op's [?])

NET FUEL: 9000 bbls [?] (maximum allowed 35000 bbls [?])

You can see, at the bottom of the report, the maximum amount of fuel you can stockpile at the Field HQ depot

Any excess fuel that arrives at your Field HQ is lost.

--- Logistics [?]
- Quartermaster: Warsaw FSB fully operational and ready to move [?]
- Bridge rebuilding (Loc 25:36) underway (repair 20%, roll 32), +5% next turn
- Truck maintenance +3%, [?] [?]
- PG HQ Fuel Stockpile has exceeded maximum size (9713 bbls lost) [?]
- Construction Bn's unable to convert rail (Soviet owned!) [?]

There it goes...

ASK YOUR STAFF

How can my fuel be lost? It's been dumped somewhere by mistake or omission. Entire supply trains were 'lost' during Barbarossa.

CURRENT RELATIONSHIP EFFECTS

--- Negative (Rel -39)
Decision Options cost adjustment +2 PP
Maximum Fuel stockpile size (PG HQ's) less 20000 bbls

--- Opinion
'I am sorry that it has come to this but you no longer have my support'

As your relationship has taken a turn for the worst, not only have you lost the support of your Quartermaster General, but your ability to stockpile fuel in your Field HQ's is 20,000 bbls less than what it normally would be

If you are playing with the 'Decisions OFF' or 'Easy Mode' options, this doesn't apply.

4.8.1.4. Traits

Certain characters possess a trait such as 'Nazi' or 'Ruthless'. Hitler has both of these. Traits affect the cost of decision options involving characters with traits. If you have an identical trait as the character, eg. You are 'Ruthless' when dealing with Hitler, then all your Hitler related option costs will be -1 PP cheaper. Alternatively if you are the opposite they will be +1 PP dearer.

DESIGNER NOTE

Traits represent belief systems. We prefer to be with people who have the same beliefs as we do.

The Player begins the game with no traits and a neutral disposition on all. There is no option cost involved.

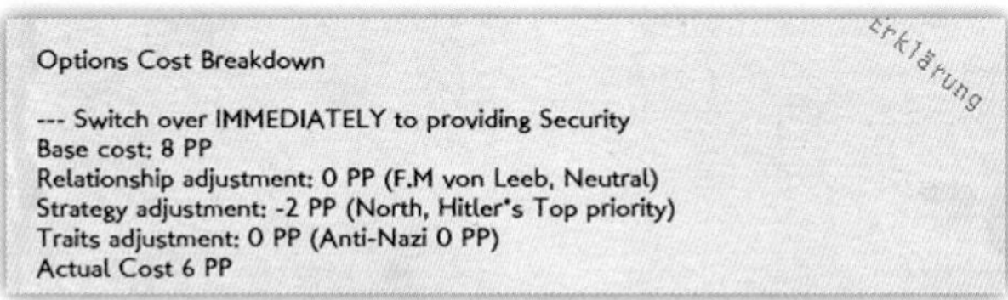

Options Cost Breakdown

--- Switch over IMMEDIATELY to providing Security
Base cost: 8 PP
Relationship adjustment: 0 PP (F.M von Leeb, Neutral)
Strategy adjustment: -2 PP (North, Hitler's Top priority)
Traits adjustment: 0 PP (Anti-Nazi 0 PP)
Actual Cost 6 PP

As the Player is neither a Nazi, or Anti-Nazi, there is no adjustment to the cost of the option

Fence sitting isn't possible for long as decisions arise that force the Player to take a position. The prime example is the 'Hitler Oath' decision.

Every officer in the Wehrmacht was required to take an oath of loyalty to the Führer

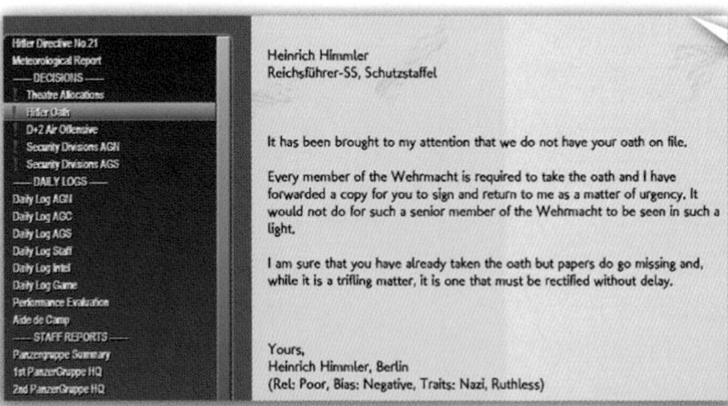

Heinrich Himmler
Reichsführer-SS, Schutzstaffel

It has been brought to my attention that we do not have your oath on file.

Every member of the Wehrmacht is required to take the oath and I have forwarded a copy for you to sign and return to me as a matter of urgency. It would not do for such a senior member of the Wehrmacht to be seen in such a light.

I am sure that you have already taken the oath but papers do go missing and, while it is a trifling matter, it is one that must be rectified without delay.

Yours,
Heinrich Himmler, Berlin
(Rel: Poor, Bias: Negative, Traits: Nazi, Ruthless)

Here the Player is given the opportunity of not only taking the oath but of joining the Nazi party. The cast of German characters can be divided into two groups - the Nazi party member, predominately the political appointees and the professional officer corps who paid lip service to the party. Siding with one side will cause friction and PP costs with the other.

Thousands of officers avoided the oath by claiming to be sick but were forced to do so after returning to duty. By swearing loyalty to Hitler, rather than the nation or the constitution, the men of the Wehrmacht found themselves honour bound to obey him, even after Hitler had declared war and ordered the Wehrmacht to commit war crimes.

ASK YOUR STAFF

Why do I have to take the oath? Not taking the oath had severe consequences such as forced retirement, forced relocation, execution by firing squad, hanging and beheading.

Take the Oath and join the Party
You wish to align yourself with the Führer and the Party power brokers — oPP

Take the Oath, nothing more
You decline the invitation to join the Nazi Party — oPP

DESIGNER NOTE

This was included because it was a dominate aspect of the internal workings of the German command. As an interesting exercise try a play through where you join the party.

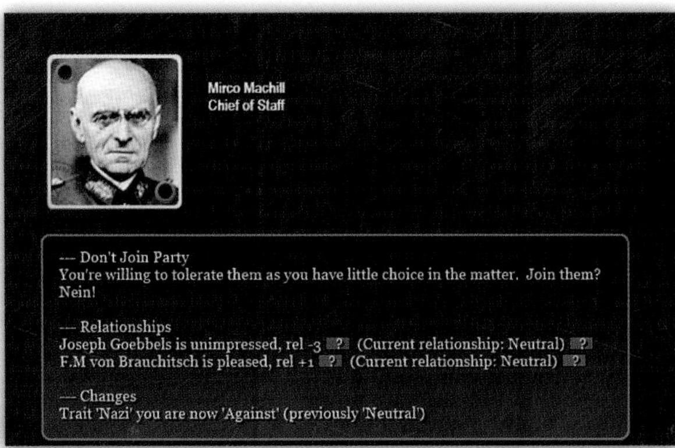
Mirco Machill
Chief of Staff
--- Don't Join Party
You're willing to tolerate them as you have little choice in the matter. Join them? Nein!
--- Relationships
Joseph Goebbels is unimpressed, rel -3 (Current relationship: Neutral)
F.M von Brauchitsch is pleased, rel +1 (Current relationship: Neutral)
--- Changes
Trait 'Nazi' you are now 'Against' (previously 'Neutral')

With an eye to a future War Crimes Tribunal, the Player has declined to join

The Nazi party (the National Socialist German Worker's Party) had a platform of anti-big business, anti-bourgeois, a belief in racial supremacy, extreme anti-semitism and anti-capitalistic. At the conclusion of the war the party was abolished and declared illegal by the Allied occupying powers, as it is to this day

Once a position has been taken all future decision options involving characters with that trait will involve an additional penalty or benefit.

Options Cost Breakdown

--- Agree to be Filmed
Base cost: 8 PP
Relationship adjustment: +1 PP (F.M Keitel, Poor)
Strategy adjustment: not applicable
Traits adjustment: +1 PP (Nazi +1 PP)
Actual Cost 10 PP

4.8.1.5. Bias

As a result of your Past History certain characters can have a 'Bias' towards you. This can be both positive and negative and represents their natural tendency to view you in such a light.

A character with a positive bias will have an inherently good opinion of you that will be unchanged by the vicissitudes of your day to day relations. A bias, once set, doesn't change. Biases can be moderate (+/-1) or strong (+/-2).

IN DETAIL

Whenever a decision option is taken that results in a change in relationship with a character is taken, at least one ten sided die is rolled internally to determine the extent of the change. Bias acts as a modifier to each roll. For example if you chose an option that seriously upset Hitler perhaps two ten sided dice would be rolled to determine the negative shift in your relationship level. If Hitler had a strong bias against you (didn't like the set of your eyes) of -2 then a roll of double 5's would result in a -14 relationship shift (-5 + -2 + -5 + -2). Over the course of the game biases add up.

4.8.1.6. Past Relationships

At the beginning of the game you are given a past history. You may find yourself with good or bad relations with certain characters as a result of historical incidents that are assumed to have occurred prior to the campaign.

DESIGNER NOTE

The war was an ongoing enterprise. Generals and politicians didn't turn up on the day not knowing each other. You can reasonably expect to have made friends and enemies amongst them.

Your past relationships will be different every play through. At times you will have no past relationships, on other occasions you'll have a long list of them. They are randomly generated but there a sensible constraints on the randomisation based on how the characters interacted historically. There is room, however, for a-historical outcomes in the interests of game play.

ASK YOUR STAFF

Won't I be penalised for starting the game with a set of bad relationships? No, your past relationships are automatically taken into account by the game's difficulty rating.

You can, if you wish, commence the game in a relationship vacuum where you begin with a neutral relationship with every character by selecting the 'Past History OFF' option.

Characters can, as a result of your past history, have a bias towards you, good or bad. See 4.8.1.5 Bias.

4.8.1.7. Führer

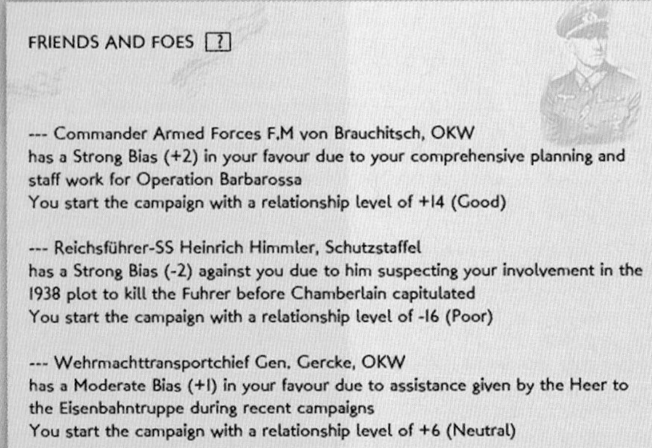

FRIENDS AND FOES ?
--- Commander Armed Forces F.M von Brauchitsch, OKW
has a Strong Bias (+2) in your favour due to your comprehensive planning and staff work for Operation Barbarossa
You start the campaign with a relationship level of +14 (Good)
--- Reichsführer-SS Heinrich Himmler, Schutzstaffel
has a Strong Bias (-2) against you due to him suspecting your involvement in the 1938 plot to kill the Fuhrer before Chamberlain capitulated
You start the campaign with a relationship level of -16 (Poor)
--- Wehrmachttransportchief Gen. Gercke, OKW
has a Moderate Bias (+1) in your favour due to assistance given by the Heer to the Eisenbahntruppe during recent campaigns
You start the campaign with a relationship level of +6 (Neutral)

F.M Von Brauchitsch is a strong ally whereas the Reichsführer-SS, Himmler, is one to keep a very close eye on.

Hitler, nominally the political leader, was an over bearing presence who strongly influenced military matters. This manifests itself in four ways.

- Hitler has his own objectives for Barbarossa, separate to that of the Player.
- Hitler can, depending on the Player's strategy, interfere with the operation of the Panzergruppes
- The cost of Action Cards to switch to a Defensive Posture is set at a higher level to reflect Hitler's aversion to anything other than an all out lunge.
- Your ability to move Panzergruppes into adjoining theatres is dependant on your relationship with Hitler.

Hitler's Objectives

Hitler has strategic objectives. There are four possible objectives (or goals) and they are presented from the point of view of the importance Hitler grants them. The number one priority is Hitler's prime strategic goal that he is focused on. Number two is a fall back, secondary objective. Number three is of little interest. Number four, the last, is one that he is actively opposed to.

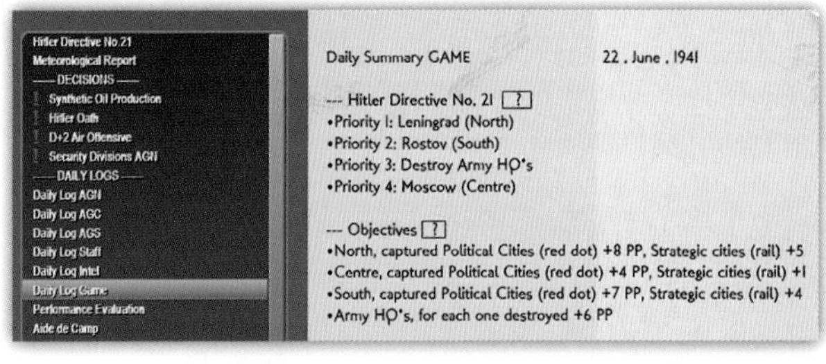

The ranking of Hitler's objectives determines the Political Points that are gained when capturing cities or destroying enemy HQ's. It also influences the cost of any decision options that are associated with a particular objective. As an example AGC, Moscow, is Hitler's last priority above. Any decision option that involves assisting AGC will not be viewed favourably and will incur a higher PP cost.

See 4.6.4 Hitler Conference for more information.

Hitler Interference

From time to time Hitler will take an interest in day to day military operations. He will bypass the chain of command and directly contact your Panzergruppe Commanders with personal orders of his own. The confusion that results from this unwanted interference manifests itself in a loss of momentum (less Action Points for all units in the affected Panzergruppe).

The chance of this occurring depends upon the strategy you have chosen. It is 3% with 'Moscow or Bust' and double that for a 'Support Hitler' strategy. Hitler will not interference if you are following a 'Military Independence' strategy. For information on strategies see 4.6.1.2 German Strategy.

Interference lasts one turn only and can be seen in the relevant Daily Theatre Logs.

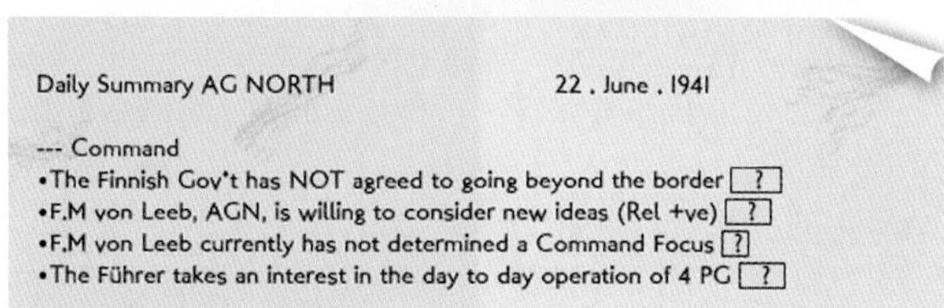

Col. Hoepner's 4th PG is the focus of the Führer's attention today

Hitler was a terrible micro manager and involved himself with even minor tactical matters on a regular basis to the great frustration of his commanders

At any time if you ask a unit to report its status, interference and its effect, will be noted.

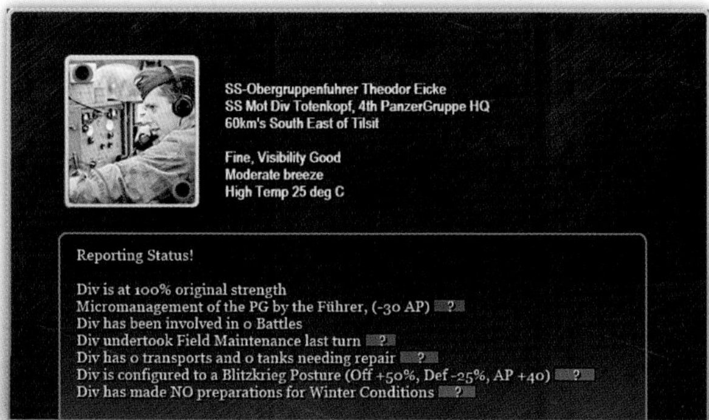

DESIGNER NOTE

Hitler's constant meddling was a stand out feature of the campaign but how to implement it in the game without placing undue restrictions on the Player has been a challenge. By focusing on the Panzergruppes, the Player's main offensive punch, there is enough of an impact to be noticed but not so much that it's restrictive. It also serves to further differentiate the three strategies.

Hitler Authorisation

It is possible to reassign Panzergruppes to adjoining theatres but you need the approval of the Führer in order to do so. See 6.1.2.1 Changing Theatres for more information.

--- Organisation and Planning
•2000 bbls of fuel expended to support PG Blitzkrieg Posture ?
•The Führer is willing to consider alternative PG dispositions ?

SUMMARY

- Past Relationships allow you to start the game with a preset group of friends and enemies
- Relationship levels can affect a wide range of game mechanics.
- Relationship levels change as a result of decision options.
- Dynamic tool tips on the character portraits in the 'Relationship' tab list all current effects.
- Bias exerts a small, but permanent influence on every decision option outcome involving the character.
- Traits involve a change to decision option costs if you have the same, or opposing trait.

4.8.2. SOVIET CHARACTERS

Unlike the German Player, you don't have relationships with various characters. As Stalin, everybody is your subordinate. You have plenty of tools (some terminal) at your disposal to bring

wayward commanders into line and as a result, a 'relationship' is irrelevant. If you ask for something to be done, it will happen.

The only constraints on your actions are the poor state of Soviet Command and Control, the low quality of your officer corps and your rising sense of paranoia.

4.8.2.1. Stalin

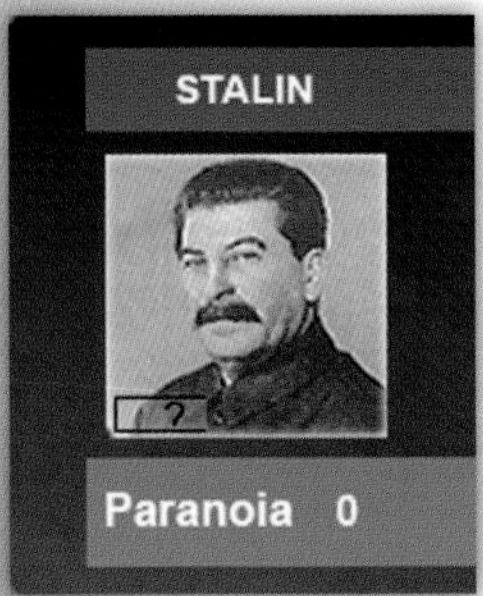

You are playing as Stalin. You are stepping into the shoes or a ruthless, paranoid, dictator. Your mental state, the 'paranoia' level, is of key interest. At a level of zero it is under control. If it creeps too high you may find yourself suffering a 'paranoid episode'.

See 6.2.3 Paranoia.

4.8.2.2. Front Commanders

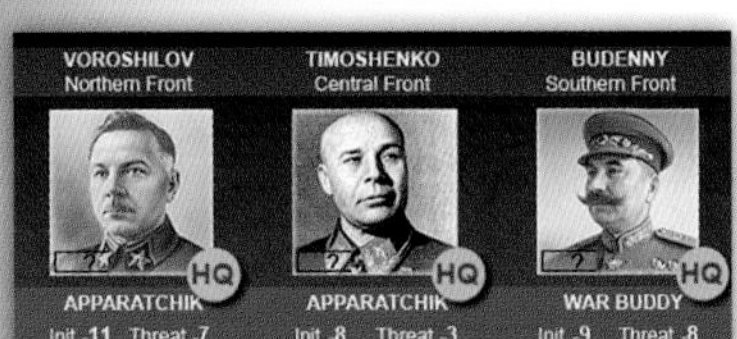

There are three Fronts, each commanded by a Marshal of the Soviet Union. Unlike the German theatre commanders, your Marshals can change over time. You can fire one, replace one with a Tsarist or simply take one out the back and have him shot.

Whenever there is a change it will be reflected in the 'Command' tab. Each Marshal has the traits of 'Initiative' and 'Threat'. The former affects the chances of Armies within their Front activating. See 6.2.2 Activation. The latter contribute to Stalin's sense of paranoia. See 6.2.3 Paranoia.

SOUTHERN FRONT

--- Fully activated
None

--- Partially activated
None

--- Didn't activate
SouthWestern HQ, at Tarnopol
5th Army HQ, 90km's South West of Rovno
6th Army HQ, 30km's North West of Lvov
12th Army HQ, 90km's North West of Czernowitz
Southern HQ, 120km's North West of Odessa
9th Army HQ, 30km's West of Kishinev
26th Army HQ, at Lvov

The dynamic tool tips in the Marshal portraits provide a quick summary of activations, within their Front, this turn.

4.8.2.3. Troubleshooters

Stalin would dispatch trusted 'envoys' to resolve whatever crisis was the most pressing.

They are available to be moved around the map, from one Headquarters to another, where the need is greatest. Their formal position within the Soviet Command structure would be directly under Stalin. They have authority over all concerned and answer only to Stalin.

You can order them to move to a particular HQ and carry out specific tasks (they have their own sets of Officer Cards). They cannot be changed and possess total loyalty to Stalin.

See 6.2.4 Troubleshooters.

4.8.2.4. Army Commanders

Every Army Commander has the dual traits of 'Initiative' and 'Threat'. The first helps determine whether their HQ will activate. See 6.2.2 Activation. The latter contributes to Stalin's sense of paranoia. See 6.2.3 Paranoia.

SUMMARY

- Stalin doesn't have relationship levels with his characters. They do as they are told, or else.
- Stalin has a paranoia level. If it gets too high he is likely to suffer an 'paranoid episode'
- Front and Army commanders have both 'Initiative' (affects activation chances) and 'Threat' (affects Stalin's paranoia)
- Troubleshooters are special envoys who answer only to Stalin. You move them around to solve crisis.
- Troubleshooters have their own special set of Officer cards (not when at STAVKA)

4.9. POLITICAL POINTS ▶

These represent an amalgamation of staff resources, goodwill and personal time allocation. It is a numerical measure of your ability to get things done.

Political Points (PP) are expended to resolve Decisions and are needed to play Action Cards. You gain PP from various sources, depending on what side you are playing.

STAFF ADVICE

PP represent your Command Authority. Without them you cannot make things happen. Aim, where ever possible, to keep some in reserve.

You can see how many PP you have, at a glance, by viewing the top bar (far left).

Your Daily Staff Log provides a breakdown of the PP economy.

DESIGNER NOTE

The German Player, with the multifaceted demands of Operational Command, runs the larger PP economy. The Soviet Player has fewer PP to reflect the difficulty in promulgating orders throughout a rigid command structure.

The German Player receives a variable Command Allowance, each turn, equal to 2 PP per Decision. If there are three Decisions generated, for example, he will receive 6 PP. He gains further PP from attaining objectives, destroying enemy HQ's and as a result of various decisions. Each decision that he delegates to his Chief of Staff will cost 1 PP and a range of other activities, such as a unit violating a theatre boundary, can result in PP penalties.

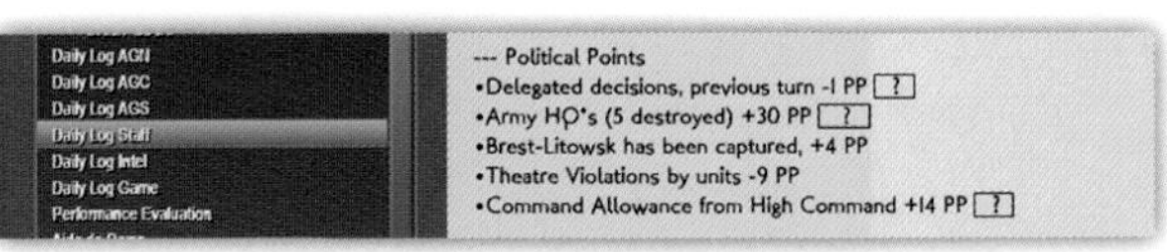

The Daily Game Log allows the German Player to view a list of current objectives (as determined by the Führer) with their associated gains in PP. Refer to 4.8.1.7.1 Hitler's Objectives for more information.

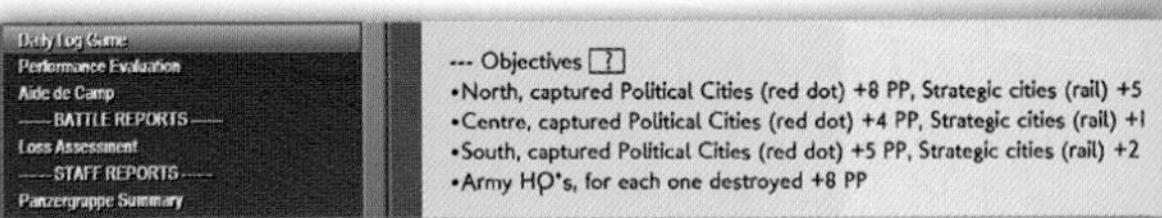

The Soviet Player receives a fixed Command Allowance each turn. This can be increased by taking certain actions. See 6.2.5 Soviet Cards. He gains further PP from destroying German units (Divisions or HQ's). Violation incursions, while more lenient for the Soviets, can still incur a penalty.

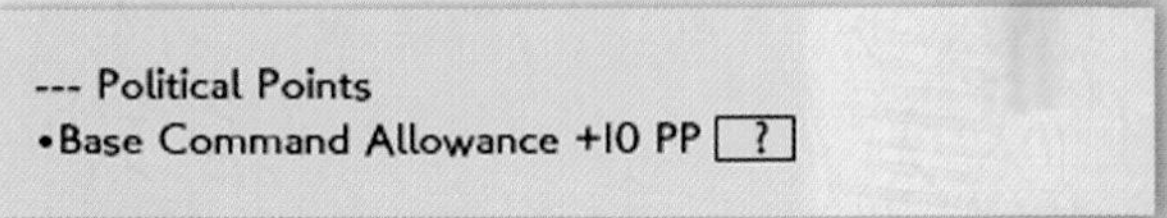

Every time you consider a Decision your current Political Points are shown above the Report Bundle. This is handy as you are able to weigh the cost of various options against the size of your current pool of PP.

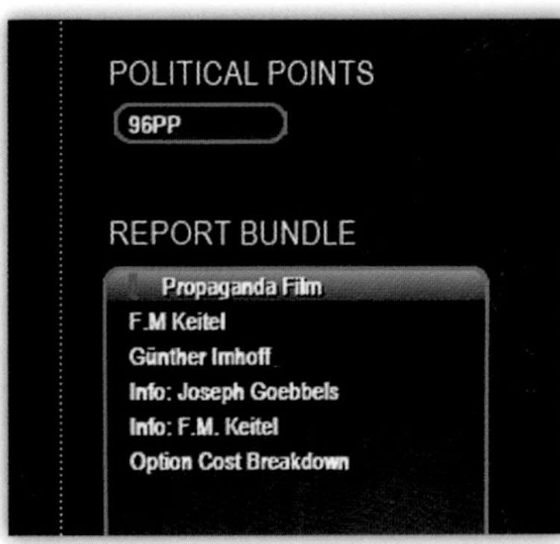

4.10. DECISIONS ▶

Are unique to the German side. The Soviets have access to decisions only in the special pre-start turn.

Decisions cover a broad range of topics. Operational Command requires you to be on top of a diverse range of subjects. It is assumed that your staff have dealt with the lower level decisions. What's left are the curly ones.

Decisions can be resolved via a range of options, each with a cost in Political Points. If you run short of PP you are severely restricted in the actions you can take.

You are not required to resolve every decision. Decisions that you ignore will be automatically delegated to your Chief of Staff who will choose an option on your behalf.

DESIGNER NOTE

Decisions are not puzzles to be solved. There is no correct answer waiting to be found for each decision. What works on one occasion might not do so well the next. It all depends on the situation, your relationships and what you are trying to achieve.

4.10.1. RANDOMISATION

The game ships with a set pool of decisions. Not every decision will appear in a given play through. The same decisions will appear at different times (within preset parameters) due to randomisation in their triggering criteria.

Certain decisions only appear as a result of previously chosen options, or specific on-map game states. Within a decision certain options may only appear if you have good, or better, relations with a particular character.

A decision option may well have a different PP cost each time it occurs due to differing relationship levels, Führer priorities, etc.

DESIGNER NOTE

Each time you play you can expect to see the same general set of decisions. As the Operational Commander of the entire Ostfront you can realistically expect to know, before the campaign starts, what kind of issues you will have to deal with. You can expect, for example, to have a 'Rail Infrastructure, AGN' decision each game. Russia is a big country, rail matters are bound to arise. What you can't know in advance, however, is when that decision will occur and what the cost of the various options will be. The big picture is known but the details are highly variable.

4.10.2. CHARACTERS

Decisions don't function in a vacuum. They involve people, the various characters within the command structure. Every time you choose an option to resolve a decision you may alter, for better or worse, your relationship with one or more characters. How a character views you will affect the cost of any related decision options.

DESIGNER NOTE

Think of decisions as resolving issues with people. There are always going to be somebody wanting to go one way and another person wanting the opposite. There is a problem, you're in charge, it's on you to make the call.

4.10.3. DECISION INTERFACE

There are different types of decisions but they all have an identical interface and operate in the same manner.

4.10.3.1. Notification

At the start of each turn the German Player receives their 'Aide de Camp' report. Down the bottom it lists how many decisions are pending that turn.

--- Other
•2 Div's Deployed, 3 Div's Failed to deploy, 1 Div Pending deployment [?]
•9 Decisions outstanding requiring your attention [?]

Once the turn begins proper, the Report Tab contains, among others, all the available decisions.

Clicking on the tab will display the decisions at the top of the list of reports.

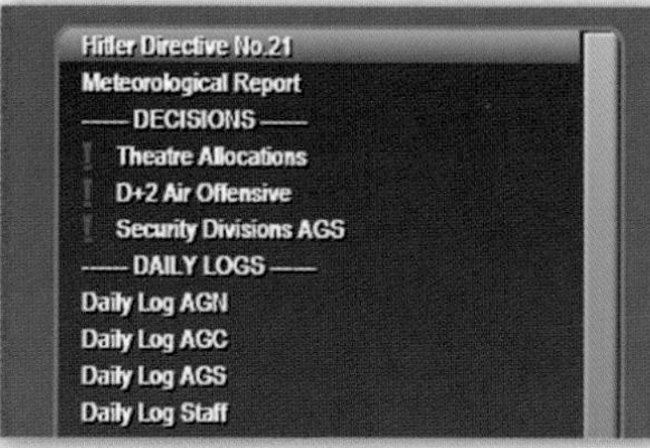

Note that the decisions are shown with a red exclamation mark beside them. This indicates that they are unresolved. Th red changes to a green tick once they have been dealt with.

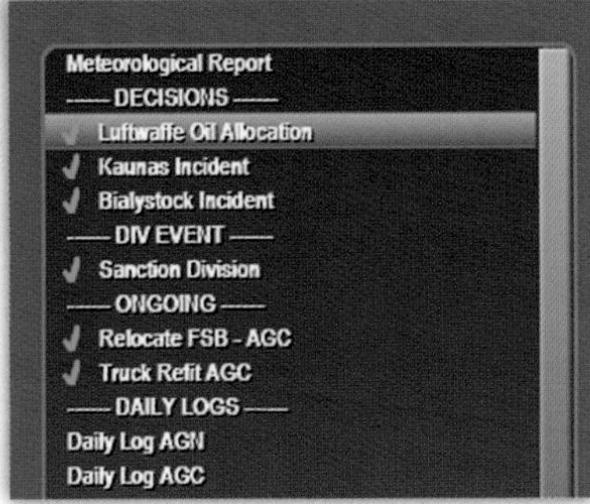

There are different types of decisions that are conveniently grouped under categories

If you complete your turn and there are any unresolved decisions you will receive a reminder but you are free to ignore this. It is a valid option to leave decisions unresolved. Left over decisions will be automatically delegated to your Chief of Staff who will take care of them.

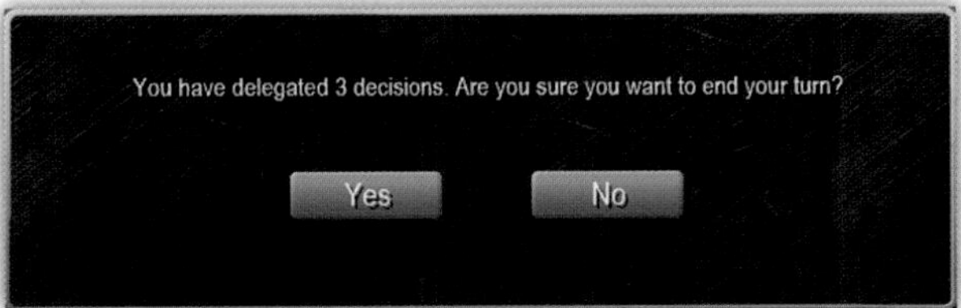

4.10.3.2. Primary Message

Each decisions has a primary message which you can view directly.

DESIGNER NOTE

Imagine yourself sitting at your desk at the OKH Headquarters. There is pile of bundled papers in front of you. Each bundle represents a decision and contains all the message, reports and other information associated with that decision. The primary message means only that it's the piece of paper displayed at the top of the bundle.

The primary message provides an idea of the what's involved with this particular decision. It may be all you need to know in order to decide to delegate it (ignore) to your Chief of Staff.

Or you, if you think further investigation is warranted, you can press the 'Make Decision' button, down the bottom of the report tab, and examine the matter further.

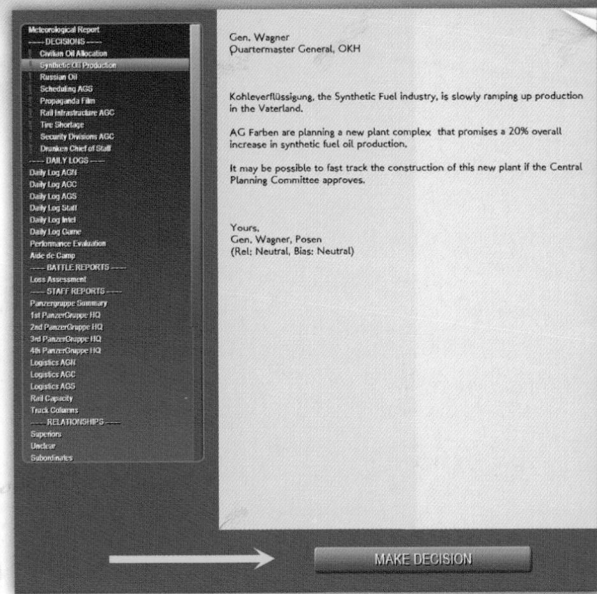

4.10.3.3. Inside a Decisions

Opening a decision presents a standard interface that is consistent across all decisions. See options overleaf.

There are a range of options that you can choose to resolve the decision (1). Once an option has been selected you press the 'Decide' button (2) to execute the decision.

Once you have finished with the decision you can press the 'Close' button (3) and exit back to the report tab. You can do this regardless of whether you have chosen an option or not. The Report Bundle (4)

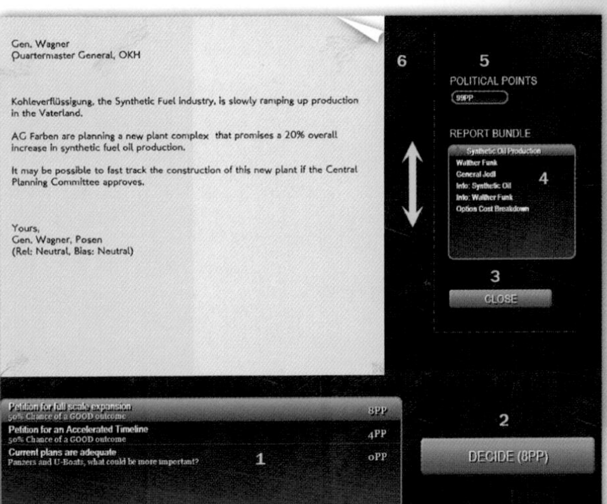

contains all the associated messages and reports for this decision.

Press the UP and DOWN arrow keys to quickly move through the bundle. Or Left Click directly onto the one you want.

There is a handy Political Points tally (5) and the report interface (6) that displays whatever report, in the bundle, that you are currently viewing.

DESIGNER NOTE

Pressing the 'Make Decision' button is the equivalent of putting down your cup of coffee, reaching over and undoing the bundle of papers. Swearing is optional and highly dependant on who is giving you trouble. General Wagner, your Quartermaster General above, is a solid sort and any issue he raises are probably worth a look.

4.10.3.4. Reports

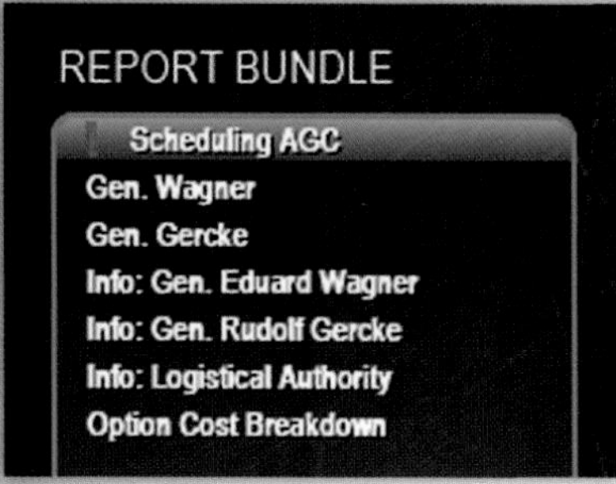

Note the red exclamation mark beside the primary message which indicates that this decision hasn't been resolved. A green tick indicates the opposite

You can find various types of messages and reports within the report bundle. There is little difference between the two, other than their purpose.

At the top of the bundle there will always be a minimum of two messages. A message is always sent to you from a character. It's worth noting who that is.

F.M von Bock
Kdt. THEATRE, Army Group Centre

Yes, our fuel deliveries are, once again, being put at risk by frivolous people who are clearly not qualified to be in charge of a Tante-Emma-Laden, let alone an important logistical organisation.

Do these imbeciles understand the ramifications of their actions? Are we dealing with adults or children?

If I am required to advance into Russland it is vital that our Panzergruppes have sufficient fuel to do so. Gottverdammt! Bang heads together man. Sort it out.

Yours,
F.M von Bock, Ostfront
(Rel: Neutral, Bias: Negative, Traits: Anti-Nazi)

In this instance you can see, from the top, that it's from F.M von Bock, your AGC Theatre commander. Down the bottom is a short summary of your current relationship (neutral), his bias towards you (negative) and any traits that he possesses (Anti-Nazi). All three will impact the cost of any options that involve F.M von Bock.

It's a standard format, person up the top, details down the bottom. The message in the middle is the meat and its content and tone will give you a good idea of the sender's position on the topic in question. F.M von Bock clearly isn't happy.

As there are always at least two messages it's a given that the second one will be from another character and that they have a different opinion. In this case there are two other messages, one from General Gercke and the following from General Wagner.

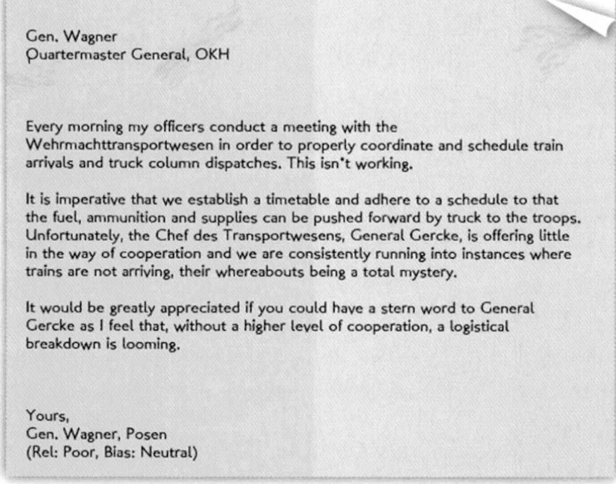
Gen. Wagner
Quartermaster General, OKH

Every morning my officers conduct a meeting with the Wehrmachttransportwesen in order to properly coordinate and schedule train arrivals and truck column dispatches. This isn't working.

It is imperative that we establish a timetable and adhere to a schedule to that the fuel, ammunition and supplies can be pushed forward by truck to the troops. Unfortunately, the Chef des Transportwesens, General Gercke, is offering little in the way of cooperation and we are consistently running into instances where trains are not arriving, their whereabouts being a total mystery.

It would be greatly appreciated if you could have a stern word to General Gercke as I feel that, without a higher level of cooperation, a logistical breakdown is looming.

Yours,
Gen. Wagner, Posen
(Rel: Poor, Bias: Neutral)

Your relationship with General Wagner isn't the best

General Gercke is equally frustrated and demanding.

F.M von Bock has raised this matter with you because the logistical system isn't working at full efficiency. The two characters in charge of the Logistics - Gercke (Rail) and Wagner (Truck Columns)- are busy blaming each other for the problem.

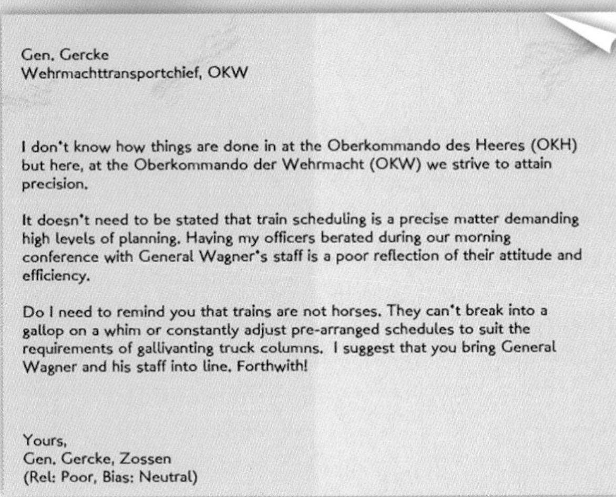

Gen. Gercke
Wehrmachttransportchief, OKW

I don't know how things are done in at the Oberkommando des Heeres (OKH) but here, at the Oberkommando der Wehrmacht (OKW) we strive to attain precision.

It doesn't need to be stated that train scheduling is a precise matter demanding high levels of planning. Having my officers berated during our morning conference with General Wagner's staff is a poor reflection of their attitude and efficiency.

Do I need to remind you that trains are not horses. They can't break into a gallop on a whim or constantly adjust pre-arranged schedules to suit the requirements of gallivanting truck columns. I suggest that you bring General Wagner and his staff into line. Forthwith!

Yours,
Gen. Gercke, Zossen
(Rel: Poor, Bias: Neutral)

The German command structure was unique in that it divided the responsibility for logistical matters between two Generals, each being in charge of one link in the logistical chain. As both had different requirements this led to endless bickering.

Decisions typically involve characters with diametrically opposed views. As nobody is willing to give ground, the matter has been shunted up the hierarchy until it lands on your desk. It's up to you to arbitrate.

Apart from messages sent from characters there will be various supporting documents in the report bundle to help you in making an informed judgement. You are not required to read any of this, or any of the messages, but the more involved you become in the process, the better informed you will be.

DESIGNER NOTE

The decisions deliberately don't spell out the consequences of taking various options. As Operational Commander you can't be expected to be spoon fed, nor can you expect to have perfect information of future outcomes. There is enough information provided, within each report bundle, for you to accurately judge the implications of exercising the options available. The game does not set out to ambush you.

4.10.3.5. Options

Every decision has at least two options to choose from.

Request von Brauchitsch deal with it 80% Chance of a BAD outcome	7PP
Ask Wagner to Cooperate 30% Chance of a BAD outcome	11PP
Ask Gercke to Cooperate 30% Chance of a BAD outcome	11PP
Call a Meeting 55% Chance of a BAD outcome	10PP
It'll resolve itself They'll figure it out. Eventually.	0PP

You can choose to flick it upstairs, hammer into one of your two Logistical Generals, get everybody together and try and to get them to cooperate or bin the whole decision and ignore it

Each option has a PP cost that must be paid to exercise the option. If you don't have enough PP you will be unable to choose that option.

Certain options involve a random roll to determine the outcome. In these cases the percentage chance of a good or bad outcome will be shown. In the Scheduling decision shown above all of the outcomes, bar the last, have a chance of bad outcome. You are in the position of having to choose the least worst option.

Note that the individual percentages don't add up to 100 as they refer to individual options which are independent of each other. For example if you choose the first one, there is a strong likelihood (80%) of it failing. Your immediate superior, F.M von Brauchitsch, won't take kindly to you passing the buck to him. He will, rightly, consider it a matter that you should resolve yourself, hence the high chance of an adverse outcome.

Exactly what a Bad outcome involves isn't spelt out. You'll have to gauge this from the messages you have received from the characters involved. As feelings are running high a bad outcome with any of the options is likely to involve, at the least, a deterioration in your relationship with the character.

The last option is always the default and the one that your Chief of Staff will choose if you ignore the decision or consciously choose to delegate it to him (which is the same thing).

ASK YOUR STAFF

Why would you choose the first option when there is an 80% chance of a bad outcome? You may have good relations with F.M von Brauchistch and can afford to burn up some goodwill. Passing the buck upstairs also avoids you having to take sides with your two logistical Generals, Gercke and Wagner. Perhaps you only have enough PP remaining to choose the first option and it's probably still going to be a better option than doing nothing (the last option) which is bound to further upset an already seriously agitated F.M von Bock.

4.10.3.6. Option Costs

At the end of every report bundle is an 'Option Cost' report which gives a breakdown on how each option's PP cost has been derived.

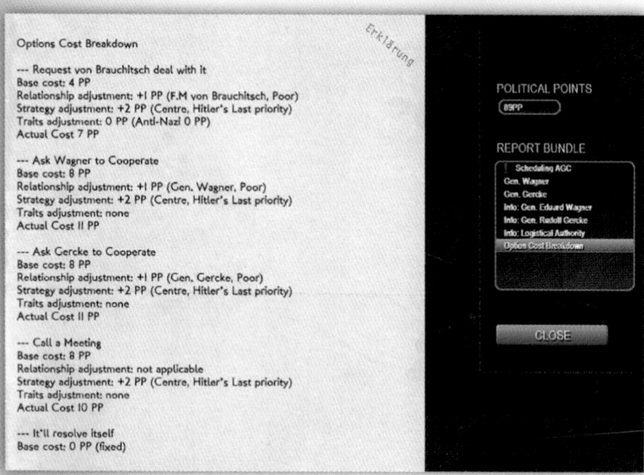

Each option has a base PP cost which is set at a level commensurate with its magnitude and the command resources required to exercise it. You can see above that the easiest option to exercise would be to handball the matter to your immediate superior (base cost 4 PP) whereas having to take the time to deal with the matter personally (Wagner, Gercke or a Meeting) have a higher base cost (8 PP).

If the option involves a character having to do something then your relationship with that character will affect the PP cost. If you have a positive relationship the character, they will be more inclined to help you and the cost will go down. If it's a negative relationship then you'll need to exert more authority and persuasion in order to get them to do as you ask.

In the example above you have poor relationships with all three characters (the top three options) and hence the cost of their options have increased. The fourth option, Call a Meeting, is a more general option that doesn't involve a specific character hence there is no Relationship adjustment.

Option costs are further modified by how they align to the Führer's current objectives. As all of the options involve attempting to improve train scheduling in AGC, and the Central theatre is currently his last priority, there is an additional cost.

Refer to 4.8.1.7.1 Hitler's Objectives for a more detailed explanation but there are always four objectives, ranked in order of Hitler's current priorities.

--- Hitler Directive No. 21 [?]
•Priority 1: Rostov (South)
•Priority 2: Leningrad (North)
•Priority 3: Destroy Army HQ's
•Priority 4: Moscow (Centre)

Moscow, AGC, is at the bottom

If one of the options involved improving the situation in AGS, which is currently Hitler's top priority, there would be a lowering of the option PP cost.

Finally there is an adjustment involving traits. This only applies to the first option, above, where your immediate superior, F.M von Brauchtisch, has the trait of being 'Anti-Nazi'. As the Player hasn't yet taken a position on this, one way or another, it's a neutral outcome.

If the Player was a Nazi party supporter this would adversely affect F.M von Brauchitsch's view of them and the cost of that option would increase. Conversely if he had a similar 'Anti-Nazi' trait there would be a sense of solidarity and the cost would decrease.

You can see, from the first option, that the adjustments add up. The base cost (4 PP) has almost doubled (7 PP). If the Player had a good relationship with F.M von Brauchitsch, the option was better aligned with Hitler's priorities and he was against the Nazi party, the cost would be around 1 PP instead of 7 PP.

STAFF ADVICE

The biggest impact on option costs are your relationship with the character. The more extreme your relationship, good or bad, the greater the effect.

The final, default, option is always free and is unaffected by adjustments.

4.10.3.7. Deciding

Choose an option and press the 'Decide' button.

DESIGNER NOTE

This is the equivalent of issuing orders. How you let your staff know what you would like to happen is up to you. You could politely press the 'Decided' button or you could slam down hard on the mouse and really bark those orders out!

Petition for full scale expansion 50% Chance of a GOOD outcome	8PP
Petition for an Accelerated Timeline 50% Chance of a GOOD outcome	4PP
Current plans are adequate Panzers and U-Boats, what could be more important?	0PP

A pop-up message will inform you of the outcome.

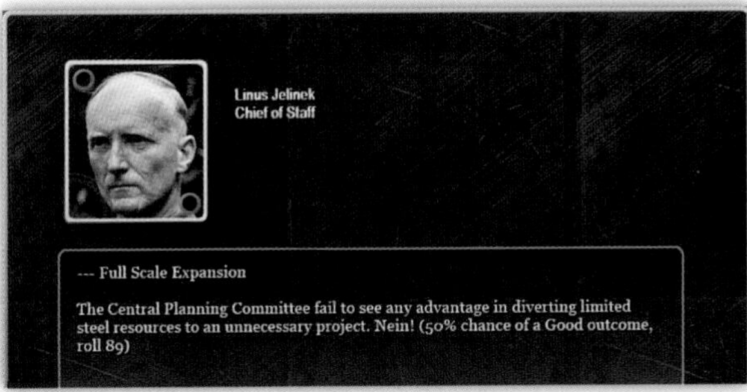

A decision, once made, is final. You will have the option of reviewing the decision at any time but this will only show the option that you chose.

REVIEW DECISION

STAFF ADVICE

Once a decision has been reached and orders issued it is a failure of leadership to change your mind five minutes later.

4.10.4. DELAYED OUTCOMES

Not all decisions have immediate effects. The Player is presented with a range of decisions that feature delayed outcomes.

DESIGNER NOTE

Operational Command involves longer term planning just as much as resolving immediate issues.

Delayed outcomes are not specifically flagged but the message contents should enable the Player to judge whether this is the case. Take the following example.

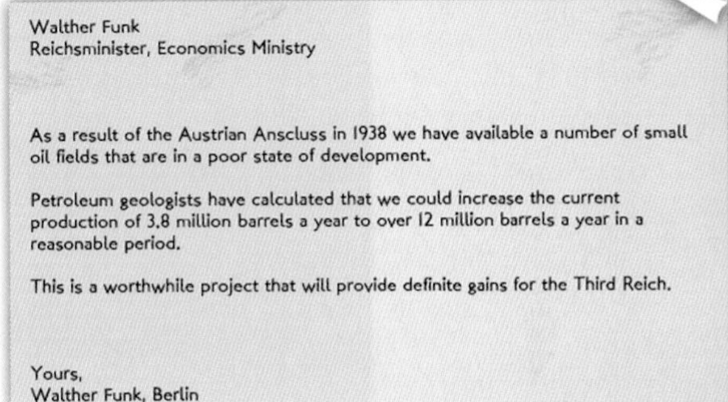

Walther Funk
Reichsminister, Economics Ministry

As a result of the Austrian Ansclus in 1938 we have available a number of small oil fields that are in a poor state of development.

Petroleum geologists have calculated that we could increase the current production of 3.8 million barrels a year to over 12 million barrels a year in a reasonable period.

This is a worthwhile project that will provide definite gains for the Third Reich.

Yours,
Walther Funk, Berlin

Developing an oil field is not something that happens overnight

The nature of the delay will be highlighted in the pop-up message once a decision has been made.

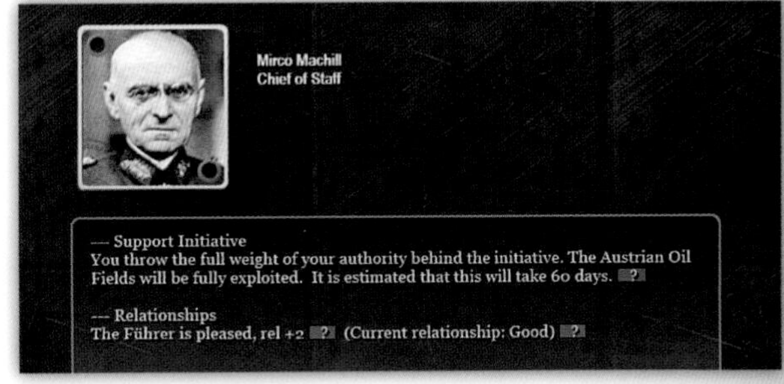

Estimates can be relied upon to be accurate

The Daily Staff Log will highlight when any delayed decisions come into affect. They will continue to do so for as long as the decision exerts a game effect.

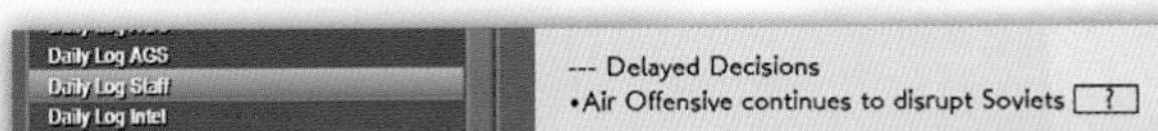

4.10.5. DELEGATION

You are NOT required to make a choice for every decision. Your Chief of Staff will take care of any unresolved decisions on your behalf. This may be a matter of preference or forced upon you as you don't have enough Political Points to do everything you want.

DESIGNER NOTE

It is easy to fall into the trap of thinking that certain decisions are irrelevant. This isn't the case and they all have a meaningful impact on the game. Perhaps not immediately but, one way or another, they matter.

Your Chief of Staff will automatically choose the last available, default, option in any decision. Generally this is the 'do nothing' option. His choice, and the outcome, will be shown in the Daily Staff Log the following turn.

You are charged 1 PP for every decision you delegate in this manner (it's still taking up staff resources) but there is no cost if you have insufficient PP remaining.

STAFF ADVICE

Knowing which decisions to delegate and which to handle yourself is an important part of effective leadership.

Your Chief of Staff has a handicap (shown in the Daily Staff Log under 'Delegated Decisions'). This applies whenever you have delegated a decision to him that involves a random roll to determine the outcome. His handicap acts as a negative influence on the roll as he is considered less capable than you.

DESIGNER NOTE

Your Chief of Staff isn't running the war. You are. His grasp of Operational Command is at a level, or two, below yours.

Each time you play the game you will be randomly assigned a Chief of Staff from a possible pool of ten. Some are better at the job than others. If you aren't playing with the 'Plots OFF' option you may receive a series of decisions revolving around your Chief of Staff. Refer to 4.10.5.2 Chief of Staff for more information.

Immediately below your Chief of Staff's handicap is a measure of your headquarters overall staff efficiency. This is set at a base of 100. This can affect the cost of decision options (like your relationship with a character) and is discussed in 4.10.6 Staff Efficiency

4.10.5.1. Delegation Example

You've chosen to delegate two decisions this turn, 'Tire shortage' and 'Security Divisions AGS'.

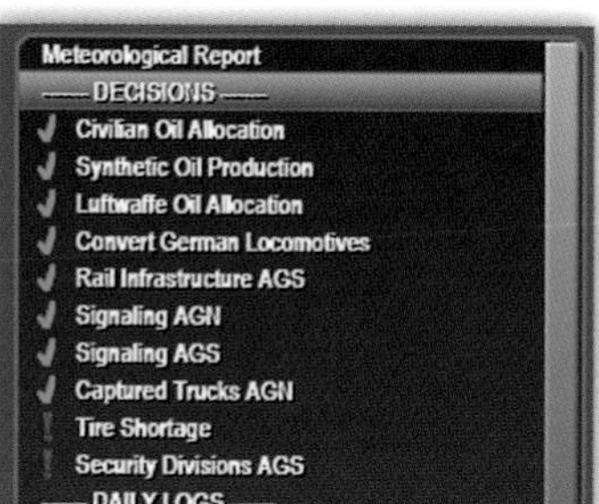

Taking a look at the Tire decision you can see that the default option (always the last) involves a random outcome. A judgement call is required and your Chief of Staff's handicap will come into play here.

Allocate Tires to AGN
This will be at the expense of the other two theatres 2PP
Allocate Tires to AGC
This will be at the expense of the other two theatres 6PP
Allocate Tires to AGS
This will be at the expense of the other two theatres 5PP
Don't bother me about Tires
75% Chance of a BAD outcome 0PP

Whereas the 'Security Divisions AGS' has a straight forward default option that can be easily resolved without your Chief of Staff having to make a decision (no handicap involved).

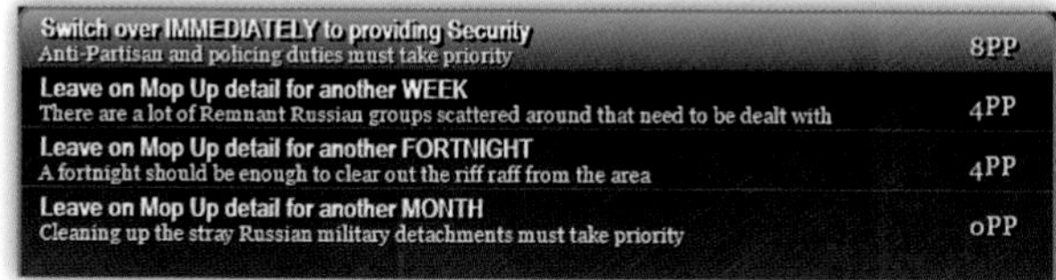

Because you have delegated two decisions you'll receive a warning prompt at turn completion. Press YES and proceed.

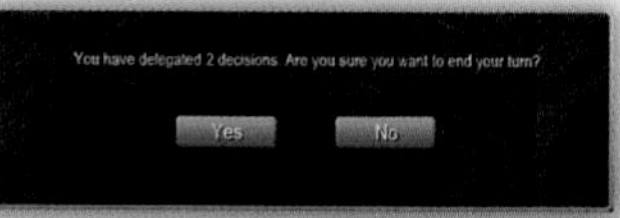

On the following turn you inspect your Daily Staff Log where

your Chief of Staff, Mirco Machill, will keep you up to date on what has transpired.

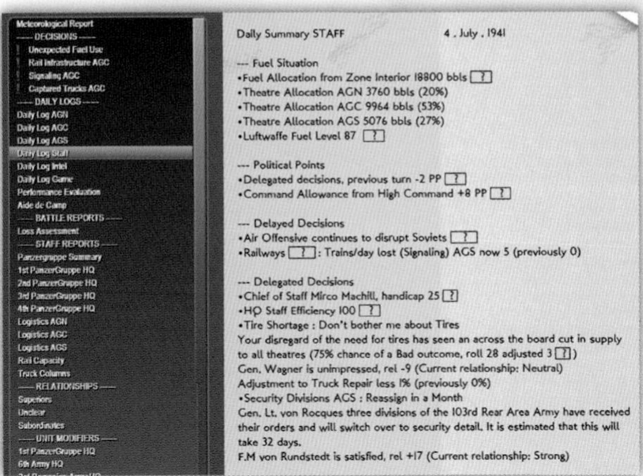

Examining the report you see that Mirco has a handicap of 25. This acts as a negative modifier to any random rolls and represents the gap between Mirco's abilities and your own.

--- Delegated Decisions
•Chief of Staff Mirco Machill, handicap 25 [?]
•HQ Staff Efficiency 100 [?]

There were two decisions that you delegated to Mirco. Examining the first one you can see that it involved a random roll. There was a 75% chance of a bad outcome (probably not a good decision to delegate), the roll (percentile, 1d100, die) was 28 which was subsequently dropped to 3 because of Mirco's handicap (28 - 25 = 3).

Unfortunately a bad outcome has occurred (with Mirco's handicap and the odds involved this was inevitable - he can't be blamed as you've overloaded poor Micro with responsibilities beyond his capability).

•Tire Shortage : Don't bother me about Tires
Your disregard of the need for tires has seen an across the board cut in supply to all theatres (75% chance of a Bad outcome, roll 28 adjusted 3 [?])
Gen. Wagner is unimpressed, rel -9 (Current relationship: Neutral)
Adjustment to Truck Repair less 1% (previously 0%)

As a result of Micro's ineffectual attempt at dealing with the great Tire crisis of '41, there is a reduction in supply (Truck repair rates have fallen although as they are already at 0% this won't have any effect) and General Wagner (your Quartermaster General who is in charge of Truck Columns) has taken offence (relationship level -9 points).

General Wagner, it's worth noting, is upset with you, not Mirco. General Wagner brought the matter to your attention as a matter of urgency and, from his point of view, your lack of interest and subsequent delegation of the matter to the bumbling Mirco is indicative of your disregard for all things Truck. You have an unhappy Quartermaster General on your hands. You can see that the situation isn't yet terminal as your current relationship level is 'neutral' but it's one to watch. Perhaps next time a decision involving Trucks arises you might want to pay it a bit more attention.

The second decision you delegated, AGS Security Divisions, had a better outcome. Mirco has done you proud.

•Security Divisions AGS : Reassign in a Month
Gen. Lt. von Rocques three divisions of the 103rd Rear Area Army have received their orders and will switch over to security detail. It is estimated that this will take 32 days.
F.M von Rundstedt is satisfied, rel +17 (Current relationship: Strong)

The difference between the two decisions is that this one didn't involve a variable outcome (random roll) that required Mirco to make a judgement call. This one is straightforward 'process' and Mirco, despite his faults, is competent enough to take care of it.

STAFF ADVICE

Avoid delegating decisions where the default option (the last in the list) involves a chance of a good or bad outcome.

4.10.5.2. Chief of Staff

Every time you play as the Germans you are assigned a Chief of Staff. He is the head of your headquarters staff at OKH and your right hand man. Whenever you delegate a decision he will personally take care of it.

Each Chief of Staff has a handicap which reflects the fact that he is, no matter how competent, worse at making decisions than yourself. The handicap acts as a negative modifier to any delegated decisions that involve a random roll to determine the outcome. See 4.10.5.1 Delegation Example.

Each play through there is a possibility of your Chief of Staff generating his own decisions as a result of a particular characteristic. These decisions can be switched off at game start via the 'Plots OFF' option.

DESIGNER NOTE

The Chief of Staff decisions are included to provide a more nuanced view of Operational Command. You are not only running a war but you're also running a staff and there bound to be personnel matters that arise requiring your attention.

CHIEF OF STAFF POOL

Name	Handicap	Special Decision Series
Jörn Markus	5	Corrupt
Günther Imhoff	10	Nazi Sympathiser
Eugen Erb	15	Convalescing Officer
Ralf Rau	20	Corrupt
Mirco Machill	25	Nazi Sympathiser
Ullrich Urbach	5	Convalescing Officer
Linus Jelinek	10	Corrupt
Marlon Körber	15	Nazi Sympathiser
Jonas Roschka	20	Convalescing Officer
Dietmar Knauf	25	Corrupt

The higher their handicap, the less competent they are. With Jörn Markus onboard you could freely delegate but with Mirco or Dietmar you'd want to be careful not to 'overburden' them.

There is a generic pool of Chief of Staff decisions that apply to all and a 75% chance (determined at game start) that the noted 'Special Decision Series' will kick in for that individual. Eg. Mirco Machill has a better than even chance of being a Nazi sympathiser.

It is possible, via certain decisions, to fire your Chief of Staff but there is no guarantee that his replacement will be any better.

4.10.6. STAFF EFFICIENCY

Your headquarters staff are an entity in their own right. You may have a highly competent Chief of Staff but if he isn't supported by efficient work done by the mass of staffers at your headquarters then matters may not proceed as smoothly as they should.

Staff efficiency is represented by an number with a base of 100. As a result of various decisions, usually involving your Chief of Staff, this may rise or fall. Whenever it goes above or below a 15% threshold (>115 or <85) the cost of all decision options will be affected.

--- Delegated Decisions
•Chief of Staff Dietmar Knauf, handicap 25 [?]
•HQ Staff Efficiency 120 [?]

Dietmar is a dud but he's backed up by excellent staff

There is a global 1 PP cost reduction, in the case of good staff work, or increase (poor staff work) which you can see in the decision option costs.

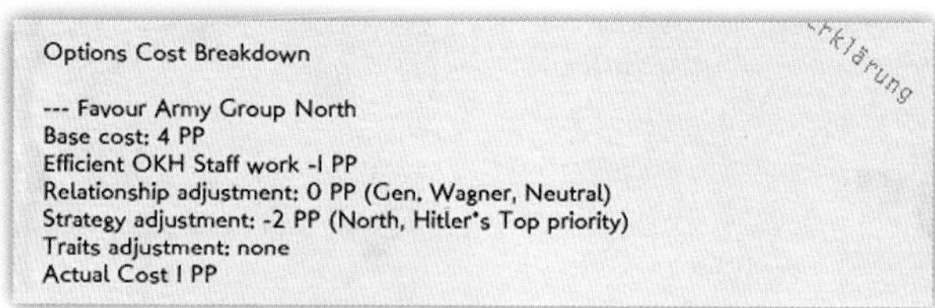

Options Cost Breakdown
--- Favour Army Group North
Base cost: 4 PP
Efficient OKH Staff work -1 PP
Relationship adjustment: 0 PP (Gen. Wagner, Neutral)
Strategy adjustment: -2 PP (North, Hitler's Top priority)
Traits adjustment: none
Actual Cost 1 PP

OKH staff have matters well in hand

4.10.7. TYPES OF DECISIONS

While there are different categories of decisions, they all work the same way and use the same interface.

4.10.7.1. First Turn Decisions

Both sides get access to decisions in the special Pre-Start Turn. There are What If? Decisions, various logistical decisions for the German Player and a Strategy decision for each.

The Strategy decision can be delegated, as can the rest, but it is a very important one and should be made by the Player.

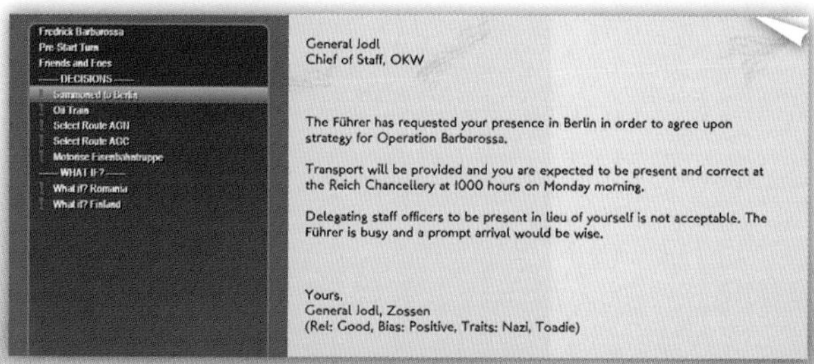

The German Player can determine his Victory conditions and objective.

The Soviet Player can choose an objective that will influence the level of victory for whatever side triumphs, if any.

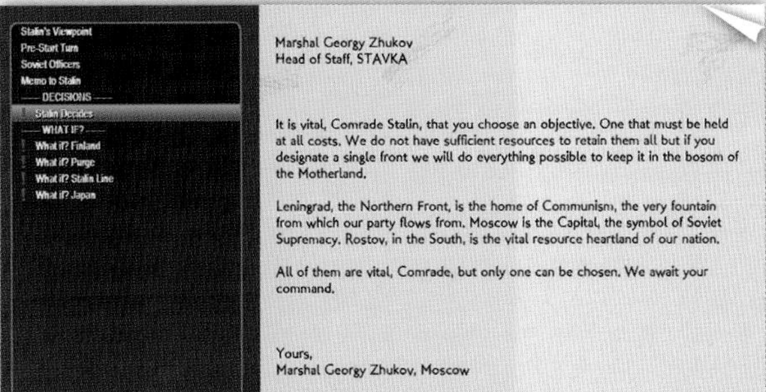

Refer to 4.6.1 Choosing a Strategy

4.10.7.2. Ongoing Decisions

These are normal decisions that appear on a regular basis. Relocating your Forward Supply Bases or Airfields would fall under this category, as would a lot of Truck related decisions.

The only difference is that, if you ignore them, there is no cost to delegate (normally 1 PP) and your Chief of Staff is under strict instructions not to do anything rash. You won't find your AGN FSB relocating to Luga without your permission, for example.

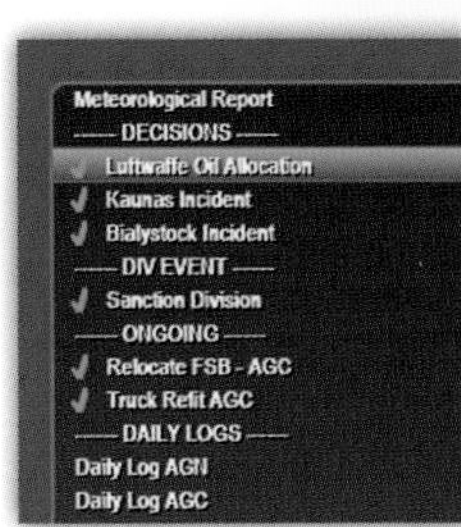

4.10.7.3. Division Events

These decisions that are dynamically generated from the Battle Reports which in turn are a result of the actions taken by the Player. For more information on Battle Reports see 5.3.5 Battle Reports.

IN DETAIL

The game engine attempts to dole out events in equal proportions of positive and negative and to provide a mix of types but this isn't always possible due to various triggering criteria having to be met.

There is a maximum of one Division Event presented per turn and there are nine possible events. Each decision affects a single Division.

DESIGNER NOTE

Division Events are there to provide a link between units under your command. Rather than simply being a counter on a map, certain of them will generate decisions, tell a story and become memorable.

The following table lists all possible events along with their triggering criteria. Just because a triggering criteria has been met it doesn't mean that an event will occur. The relevant Theatre Commander, who reads the Battle Reports just like you, is required to take an interest and it is he who will raise the matter with you.

DIVISION EVENTS

Division Event	Triggering Event
Sanction	A German unit retreated for any reason other than running out of AP during an assault
Commendation	As a result of an assault at least one Soviet unit panicked (and destroyed), broke or died.
Loss of a Senior Officer	Moderate casualties suffered when attacked by Soviet forces
Heroic Deed	Moderate casualties suffered when attacked by Soviet forces
Court Martial	Moderate casualties suffered when attacked by Soviet forces
Dsyfunctional	Moderate casualties suffered when attacked by Soviet forces
Atrocities	Moderate casualties suffered when attacked by Soviet forces
Propaganda	Moderate casualties suffered when attacked by Soviet forces
Cultural Difficulties	Must be a non-German, non-Finnish unit (Romanian, Italian, Hungarian, Spanish)

You can tell that an event has occurred by the yellow tool tip indicator in a Battle Report.

Once an event has occurred the relevant Division will have a provisional status attached to it. This is

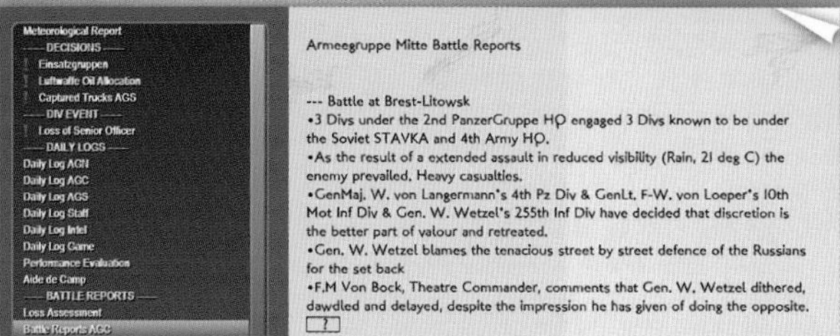

General Wetzel, Cdr of the 255th Inf Div, is in trouble!

noted if you ask the Division to Report Status! but provisional effects have no game effect.

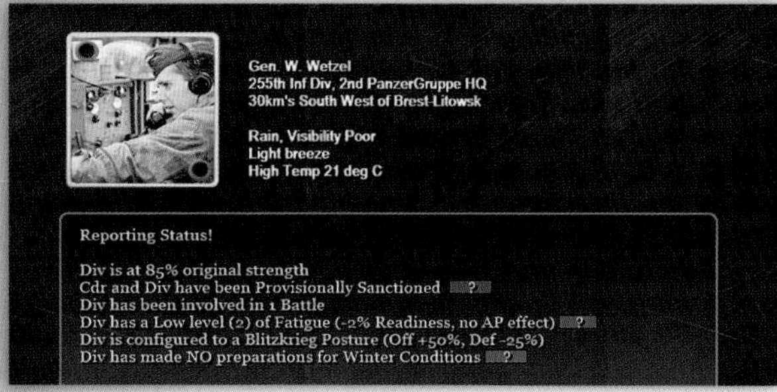

Poor old Gen. Wetzel and his 255th Inf Div have the threat of a Sanction hanging over them

The Wehrmacht bureaucracy can be slow to wind it's way through the backlog of cases before it (other times it can be surprisingly quick) but eventually a decision will be generated that requires your attention.

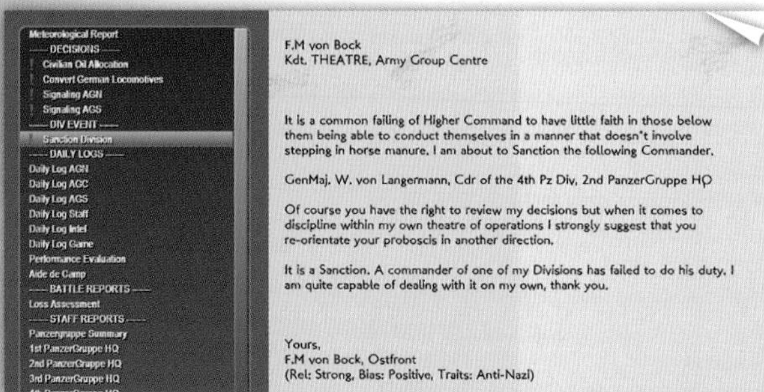

F.M Von Bock has high standards and perceives yet another Division has failed him

Decision events only ever have two options and they are set at a low base cost (4 PP). The actual cost of the options can vary depending on your relationship with the Theatre Commander, for example.

The second report in the Bundle is always an extract of the actual Battle, retrieved from the headquarter files by your Chief of Staff. These are actual battles that have occurred in the game.

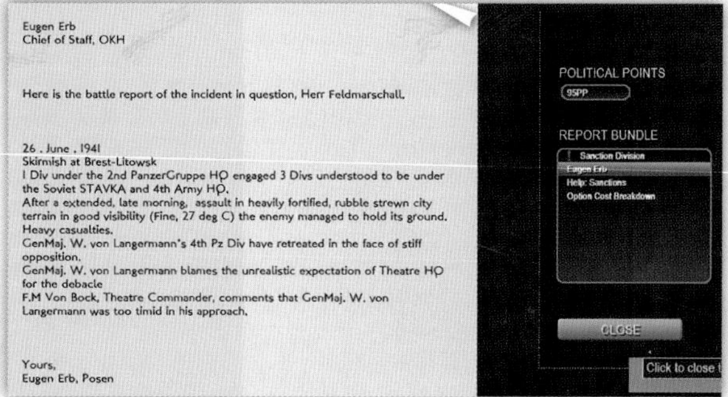

Timid Commanders aren't viewed favourably in the Heer

Division events can result in a bonus or penalty for the Division, or neither depending on the option you choose.

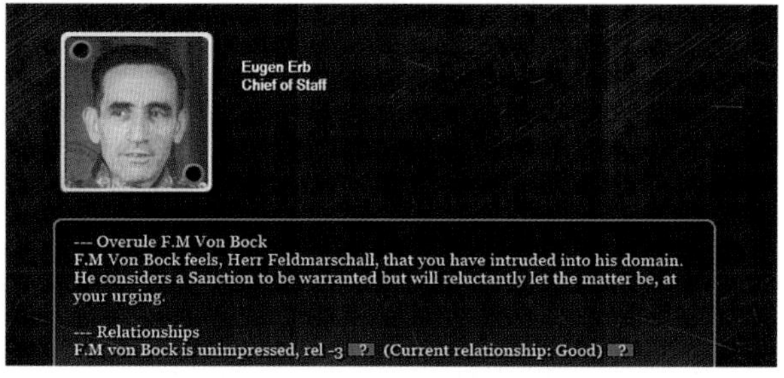

F.M Von Bock agrees to drop the Sanction but you've trodden on his toes

If you choose to exercise the provisional effect through a decision option you'll receive notification from your Chief of Staff, as per normal.

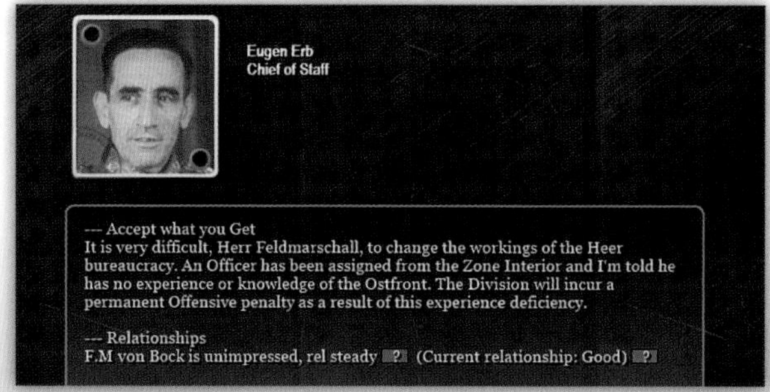

A new, unsatisfactory, senior officer has been assigned to the Division and they incur a permanent penalty

The Division reports will show the effect as will the relevant Unit Modifier report.

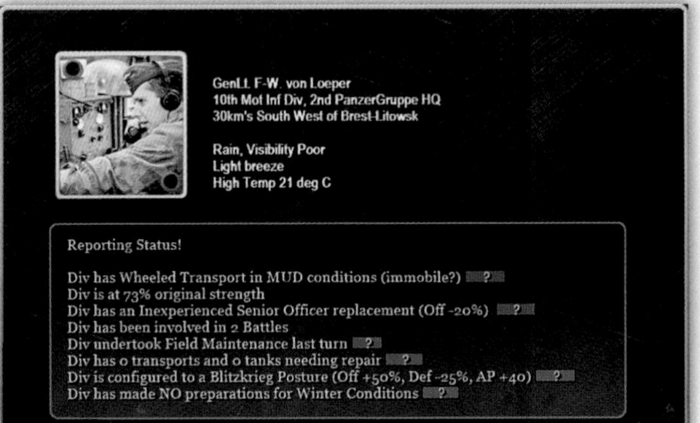
GenLt. F-W. von Loeper
10th Mot Inf Div, 2nd PanzerGruppe HQ
30km's South West of Brest-Litowsk
Rain, Visibility Poor
Light breeze
High Temp 21 deg C
Reporting Status!
Div has Wheeled Transport in MUD conditions (immobile?) ?
Div is at 73% original strength
Div has an Inexperienced Senior Officer replacement (Off -20%) ?
Div has been involved in 2 Battles
Div undertook Field Maintenance last turn ?
Div has 0 transports and 0 tanks needing repair ?
Div is configured to a Blitzkrieg Posture (Off +50%, Def -25%, AP +40) ?
Div has made NO preparations for Winter Conditions ?

GenLt. Loeper's 10th Motorised Division will have to fight the rest of the campaign with one hand tied behind their back due to a lack of experience in a key commander

4.10.7.4. What If? Decisions

These are plausible, what if, historical scenarios that can be taken advantage of at the cost of raising the bar needed for victory. They are entirely optional decisions that can be ignored.

DESIGNER NOTE

What If? decisions allow you to gamble a certain amount of Victory Points (VP) against an advantage gained (or lost).

Any VP gain, or loss, is effectively doubled as your opponent will gain or lose an equivalent number of VP's (it's a zero sum game). For example if an option costs -3 VP, your opponent will gain +3 VP making a net difference of 6 VP.

Victory points affect your game score and can make the difference between a decisive win and, lesser, minor one. As a guide to relative values, the three objectives (Moscow/Leningrad/Rostov) are worth 10 VP each and there are a total of 129 VP worth of cities (including the objectives).

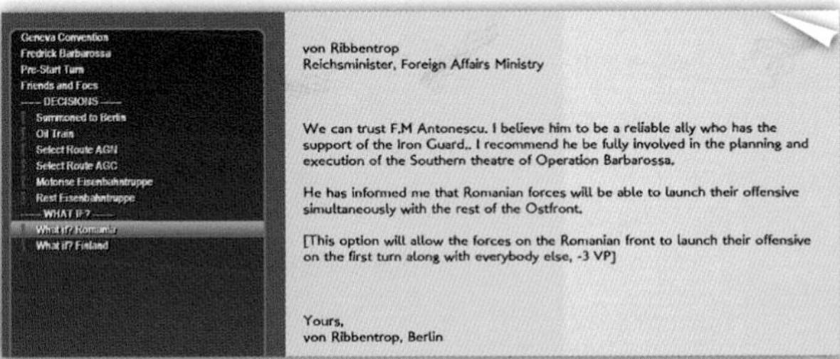
Geneva Convention
Fredrick Barbarossa
Pre-Start Turn
Friends and Foes
—— DECISIONS ——
Summoned to Berlin
Oil Train
Select Route AGN
Select Route AGC
Motorise Eisenbahntruppe
Rest Eisenbahntruppe
—— WHAT IF? ——
What if? Romania
What if? Finland
von Ribbentrop
Reichsminister, Foreign Affairs Ministry
We can trust F.M Antonescu. I believe him to be a reliable ally who has the support of the Iron Guard.. I recommend he be fully involved in the planning and execution of the Southern theatre of Operation Barbarossa.
He has informed me that Romanian forces will be able to launch their offensive simultaneously with the rest of the Ostfront.
[This option will allow the forces on the Romanian front to launch their offensive on the first turn along with everybody else, -3 VP]
Yours,
von Ribbentrop, Berlin

Refer to 4.6 Winning the Game for more information on VP. As an example, you decide to activate the Romanian front.

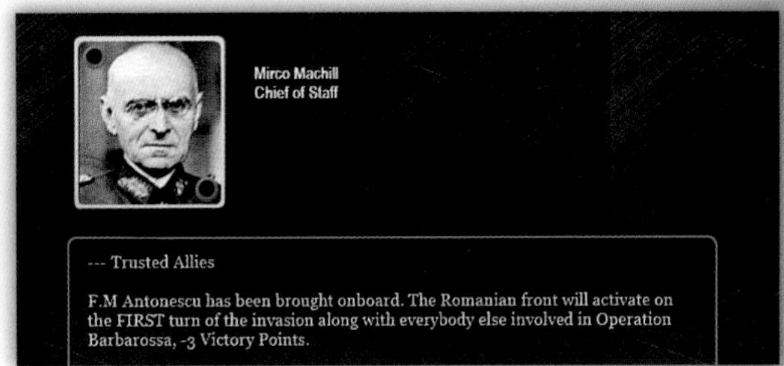
Mirco Machill
Chief of Staff
--- Trusted Allies
F.M Antonescu has been brought onboard. The Romanian front will activate on the FIRST turn of the invasion along with everybody else involved in Operation Barbarossa, -3 Victory Points.

In all subsequent turns you will be able to view your Daily Game Log and see the influence that this, and any other, What If? decisions have on your VP's.

--- What If?
•Romanians are trusted Allies (early start), -3 VP
•Total VP adjustment from What If? decisions -3 VP [?]

You can also view a summary of What If? decision in the dynamic tool tip for the Score tab (bottom centre).

UNIT INFO
REL
GERMAN SCORE
Score = Victory Points x Difficulty/100
--- Difficulty (99)
Base difficulty 100
Geneva Convention Option OFF +10
Past Relationships -11
--- Victory Points (0)
VP's from Cities 0
VP's from Decisions -3
German Objective
Leningrad
Adjusted Score 0
Soviet Objective
?
133
Soviet Difficulty 101

Both sides have access to What If? decisions in the special Pre-Game turn. You will be able to see that your opponent has made a What If? Decision but not which ones. Continuing with our example, the Soviet Player would see the following in his Daily Game Log.

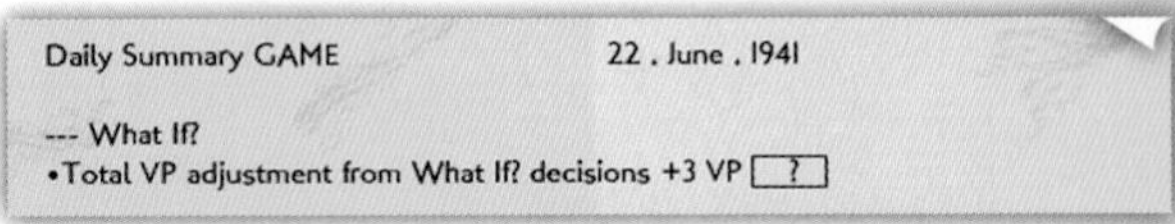
Daily Summary GAME 22 . June . 1941
--- What If?
•Total VP adjustment from What If? decisions +3 VP [?]

With a similar tool tip in his Score tab.

UNIT INFO
COMMAND
SCORE
RFMTS
SOVIET SCORE
Score = Victory Points x Difficulty/100
--- Difficulty (101)
Base difficulty 100
Geneva Convention Option OFF -10
Past Relationships (German) +11
--- Victory Points (132)
VP's from Cities +129
VP's from Decisions +3
German Objective
German Score 0
Adjusted Score 0
?
German Difficulty 99
Soviet Score 133

SUMMARY

- Apart from the special Pre-Start Turn, only the German Player receives decisions.
- Decisions are 'opt in'. Ignore any you don't want to deal with. Your Chief of Staff will take care of them for you.
- Your Chief of Staff will always choose the last, default, option. If this involves a random outcome then his handicap acts as a negative modifier.
- Any decision you delegate will cost 1 PP, but are free if you have insufficient PP to pay.
- You can see the outcome of any delegated decisions in the following turns Daily Staff Log.
- Ongoing decisions cost nothing to delegate, or ignore.
- What If? Decisions are optional and can be ignored.
- Division Events are dynamically generated decisions directly from Battle Reports
- Staff Efficiency (normally 100) can affect the cost of all decision options if >115 or <85

UP and DOWN arrows allow you to cycle through the Report Bundle

ASK YOUR STAFF

- Why do Decisions bunch?
  Because of the randomisation factors built into their triggering criteria. Sometimes it rains, sometimes it pours.
- I don't have enough Political Points to resolve all my Decisions
  It's designed that way. Part of being an Operational Commander is in figuring out which Decisions to take care of yourself and which ones to delegate.

4.11. FORTIFICATIONS ▶

These are constructed by the Soviet Player at locations of his choosing by the use of an 'Operations' Action card (see 6.2.5.3 Fortification). The Soviet AI will pre-build a range of fortifications in semi-randomised areas at the start of the game.

Fortifications provide an entrenchment bonus (helps with defence) for the Soviet units in the same hex. Once captured they are removed from the map (there is a one turn grace period to allow for recapture).

Fortifications have a number of 'Structural Points' which are shown visually (terrain windown, top centre). If they go below zero then the fortification is immediately destroyed and removed. Each turn the local garrison will automatically restore a certain number of points allowing fortification to repair their damage.

Adjacent German units receiving Direct Fire Artillery support will automatically reduce a Fortification's structural points (Engineers are assumed to be doing this under the cover of the artillery fire) each turn. See 6.1.13 Fortifications.

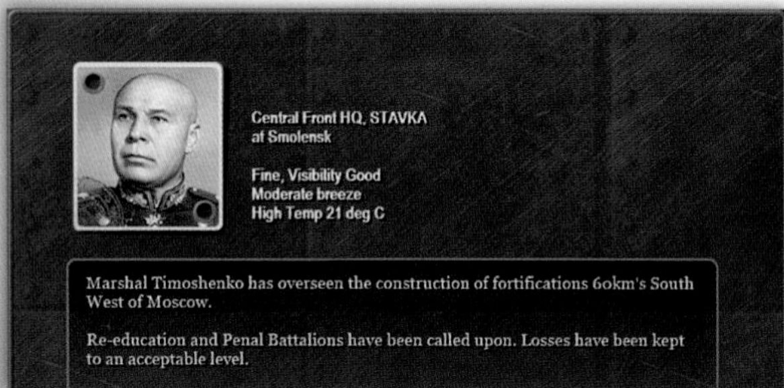

Central Front HQ, STAVKA
at Smolensk
Fine, Visibility Good
Moderate breeze
High Temp 21 deg C
Marshal Timoshenko has overseen the construction of fortifications 60km's South West of Moscow.
Re-education and Penal Battalions have been called upon. Losses have been kept to an acceptable level.

Barring the gate. Timoshenko has commenced building a ring of fortifications on the approaches to Moscow

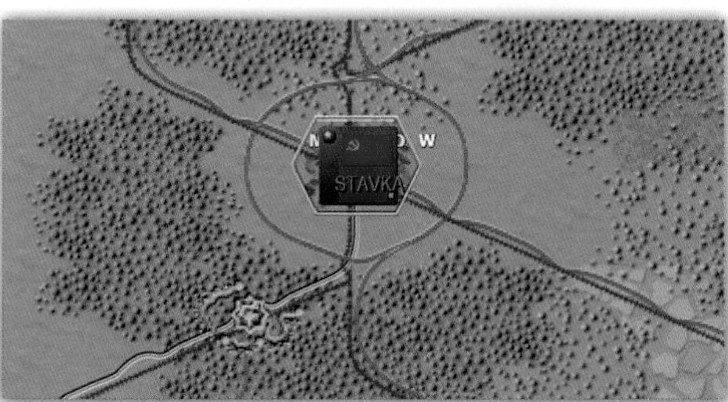

The above, newly constructed, fortification can be seen south west of Moscow on the main Moscow - Minsk - Warsaw highway

4.12. GARRISONS ▶

DESIGNER NOTE

Hitler forbade his generals from assaulting fortified cities (red dot) with Panzer Divisions. The loss in tanks was too high. Rather than impose this restriction upon the Player I've allowed them to make that decision themselves. The presence of large numbers of dug in, high quality, ATG's (76mm) ensures that the Panzer Divisions will bleed tanks in doing so. On the other hand having to bypass such a city and wait till the Infantry arrive can dangerously slow the momentum of the advance and put a wrench in the logistics (the city is inevitably going to be sitting on a major rail link). It can be a tough call.

There are two types of Soviet garrisons. Conscript garrisons, that can be raised in minor cities (grey dot) and major, regular, garrisons that can only be raised in strategic cities (red dot).

Both types can be raised by the use of Action cards (see 6.2.5 Soviet Cards). They provide garrisons which are immobile, fully entrenched, configured to a defensive posture and set to fight to the death (retreat percentage set to 100%).

They, unique among all other units, draw supplies from the cities they are in (provided they are located in the city hex) which allows them to be isolated and continue to remain fully supplied.

Conscript garrisons are understrength, under-equipped Divisions with poor quality troops.

STAFF ADVICE

Siege artillery is the most effective way of dealing with a major garrison. It will remove the substantial entrenchment bonus of any units in the city and prep the ground for a full, concentric, assault. See 6.1.4.3 Siege Artillery.

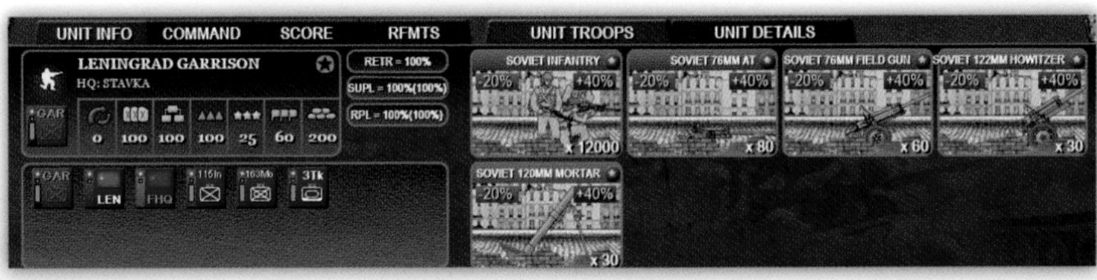

Note the presence of the 76mm ATG. This, technically, wasn't available till the later part of '41 but it represents the additional physical anti-tank defences that a fortified city would have

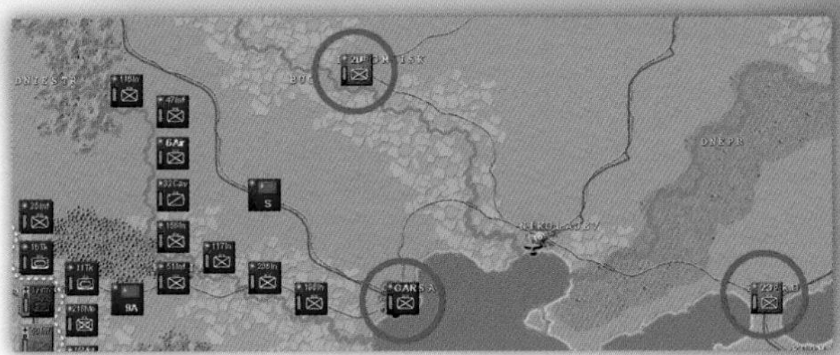

The two types of garrisons. The major, regular, garrison in Odessa (bottom centre) and several conscript garrisons, one at the top and the other to the far right. They are easy to tell apart because the conscript garrisons are brown and the major, regular, garrisons are dark red (identical colour schemes to the Conscript and Regular Soviet Divisions)

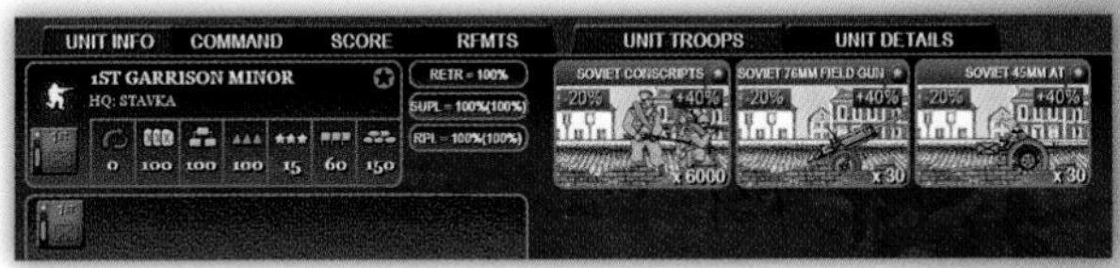

Better than nothing...

Major, regular, garrisons are over-strength and exceedingly well equipped. They are formidable obstacles and represent the fortification of the city upon the orders of Stalin.

Kiev fell on the 24th September '41. Because of the losses sustained, particularly in armour, Hitler forbade any more attacks on large Soviet cities. The experience of Kiev influenced his decision to not force an assault on Leningrad and instead he ordered it besieged.

There can only ever be a single garrison in a city, of either type. In the event that a city has been recaptured by the Soviets they will be unable to raise another garrison there.

Brest-Litowsk always commences with a major garrison as it was, historically, fortified at the commencement of the campaign.

4.13. COMMAND RANGE ▶

The central point of an Army is its Headquarters (HQ) unit. An Army, or Panzergruppe, coordinates is subordinate Divisions to achieve its goals. It has its own organic transport capabilities to ensure its Divisions remain supplied with fuel and ammunition. There is a distinct limit to how far the influence of an HQ can extend. This is a set distance of 5 hexes and applies to both the Germans and Soviets.

Armies manoeuvre and operate as integrated formations. Their subordinate Divisions can move independently but if they stray too far from their HQ they will be deemed 'outside of Command Range'.

A Division outside of Command Range will experience a range of penalties depending on their parent formation. All Divisions will lose any benefit from their posture setting and suffer Action Point (AP) penalties.

STAFF ADVICE

Avoid ending your turn with Divisions outside of Command Range. The penalties are severe and it can leave a Division exposed and vulnerable. There are times, however, when it can be necessary to have a Division take up a lonely outpost, well away from the security of it's parent formation. Judging when it is safe to do so can be a fine art.

German Divisions, who are currently suffering ammunition shortages, will have them upgraded in severity. They will additionally not receive any benefit from Artillery or TAC bonuses or Luftwaffe resupply missions.

Command range applies to Divisions only. HQ's are exempt from any requirements to be within set distances of higher level HQ's.

A unit can be out of Command Range at any time but it is *only* at the start of a turn that they are penalised for being so. You can freely move units out of command range *during* their turn and provided they don't finish their movement more than 5 hexes away there will be no penalties.

To visually see the extent of Command Ranges turn on the 'HQ Power Range' option and click on an HQ to get a coloured overlay.

The 'Preferences' tab

This has a three colour shading to represent the different levels of combat bonuses that Divisions receive from their HQ (the further away they are from their HQ the less the bonus) and represents the ability of their HQ to coordinate the bigger picture in a more effective manner than an individual Divisional commander could.

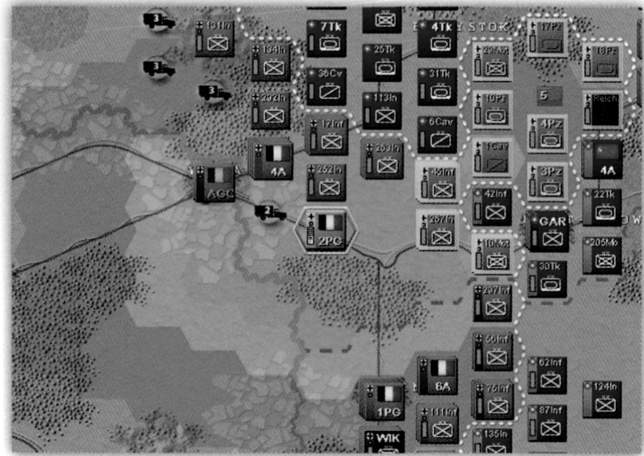

The Command Range extends out 5 hexes in all directions but not into enemy held territory. Clicking on the HQ also highlights its subordinate Divisions so that it's easy to tell which ones are outside of Command Range

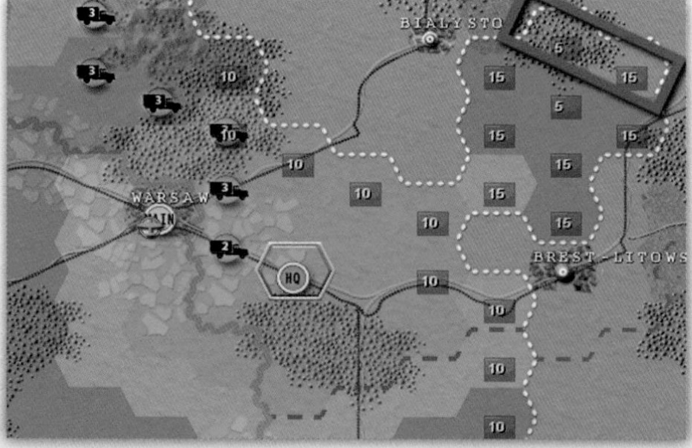

You can see from this that there are two Divisions outside of Command Range (top right), the 18th Panzer Division being one of them. Provided the 2nd Panzergruppe HQ moves forward to support the initial breakthrough they should soon be back within range

GenMaj. Nehring's 18th Panzer Division at the start of the following turn. The 2nd Panzergruppe HQ failed to follow through and the 18th Panzer Division have been caught out. Note the red faced icon of a man yelling (next to the red Blitzkrieg posture icon). This indicates that the unit has been heavily penalised (that's why the man is yelling) for being outside of command range

Press '0' (switches off the unit display, press '2' to revert back)to view a clearer picture of the extent of an HQ's Command Range.

If you request a Division to Report Status! it will indicate whether it is within range or not.

A Division will have a status icon next to its unit name (bottom centre) to indicate that it's 'Out of Command Range'. This will only happen if it is more than 5 hexes from its HQ at the *start of the turn*.

You can inspect the 'Unit Modifier' report to see the full extent of the problems facing a unit outside of Command Range.

A Fast Division will receive higher Action Point penalties (-70 AP) than a slow Division (-30 AP) to reflect the inability of its HQ to get enough fuel to

--- 18th Pz Div (loc 26:40)
Outside the fuel resupply range of HQ, -70 AP [?]
No Offensive bonus as Division is outside of Command Range
Army committed to a Blitzkrieg posture, +0% Off, -25% Def

The 18th Panzer Division is in a serious dilemma. You can see, from the pic above, that it's lost all its combat bonuses and most of it's AP

it using the HQ's organic truck capability. Infantry, even outside of Command Range, can still march but vehicles without insufficient fuel won't be going far.

STAFF ADVICE

The Soviet Player should keep a close eye out for any over enthusiastic German Divisions that may have advanced beyond their Command Range. Panzer Divisions, with their Blitzkrieg movement bonus, are prone to do so. If you can identify a Division in this situation (not easy when you may not know where its HQ is due to the Fog of War), don't hesitate. Throw everything you've got at it. Vulnerable Divisions like this are the equivalent of an animal that's sprinted to far ahead of the safety of the herd and has tripped and fallen.

For a further discussion on Command Range see 6.1.6.18 Command Range.

SUMMARY

- Command range extends five hexes outwards from an HQ
- There is an option in the Preferences tab that lets you see this visually (HQ Power Range)
- Divisions which are outside of Command Range at the START OF A TURN incur a lot of penalties
- Divisions can move outside range *during* a turn with no penalty
- Fast Divisions incur greater Action Point (AP) penalties than slow Divisions (insufficient fuel)
- The 'Red Faced Yelling Man' status icon (next to the units name) indicates Command Range penalties

4.14. SUPPLY ▶

Each unit in the game receives an allotment of supply each turn. This originates from a central supply source (eg. Berlin or Gorki) which must be able to trace a route directly to the unit (intervening HQ's aren't used for this purpose).

A unit is able to store a certain amount of supply (around 2 or 3 turns worth). Supply is consumed each turn to recover readiness (which is lost due to movement and combat). The more movement and combat that a unit engages in the more supply it will need to recover its readiness. Without supply the unit's readiness will automatically drop .

Low readiness will lower the allotment of Action points that the unit receives each turn and will adversely affect its combat performance.

Supply is separate to the German's logistical pipelines which are all about getting fuel to their Fast Divisions.

Supply affects a unit's readiness only. With adequate supply a unit can continue to move and fight. Without supply a unit will quickly become combat ineffective.

4.14.1. SUPPLY CONSUMPTION

A unit will consume supplies each turn in order to recover its readiness. The rate at which it consumes supply is shown by the supply consumption statistic.

Supply consumption. Full recovery at 100

Provided this is sitting at 100% the unit has consumed enough supply (either in stock or recently arrived) to achieve full readiness recovery (see 5.2.1 Readiness). Once the level drops below 100% the amount of readiness recovery available will drop in proportion.

STAFF ADVICE

Keep in mind that even though a unit may not have received any supply this turn, it could still have enough supply on hand (stocks) to keep its supply consumption level at 100%. You only have to worry once the supply consumption level drops below 100 as the unit will incur significant combat penalties.

At levels below 100 the unit will suffer combat penalties that increase in severity in proportion to the amount below the optimum 100 level. The maximum possible penalty (at a supply consumption level of 0) is -75% (both attack points and hit points) which, in effect, means the unit is fighting at 16 times worse than it normally would.

4.14.2. UNIT SUPPLY STATS

SUPPLY STATS	
Setting	**Explanation**
Supply Stock	The amount of supply carried by the unit (2 turns worth of basic supply unless Division belongs to a Panzergruppe – 3 turns)
Rounds of Stock	How many turns the Supply Stock will last given the current operational tempo (movement and combat)
Stockpile	x/y (z) Ammunition Stockpile (used for artillery barrages) x – Current ammunition stockpile y – Maximum ammunition stockpile z - Enough present for this number of combat rounds
Supply In Req	How much the unit is requesting this turn (this will increase as the unit's readiness drops below 100)
Supply In	How much supply arrived at the unit at the start of the turn (turn on the supply layer to get an idea of what % of their request will arrive)
Supply Lost	Not applicable to DC3 (supply lost to interdiction)

4.14.3. HOW MUCH SUPPLY DOES A UNIT NEED?

The amount of supply needed by a unit depends on their readiness. Units with low readiness need more supply. Half of a basic level of supply is needed to maintain a unit's readiness. Up to 150% more is needed to actually regain a unit's readiness. This reflects the cost in supply of a higher operational tempo (combat and movement act to lower readiness).

Supply information is found under the 'Basic Details' tab

Example 1

Unit X has a basic supply of 200 points and can store up to 400 points. It has a readiness of 100. It has 0 in storage and will therefore request full basic supply of 200 points. Half of its basic supply is needed to maintain its readiness (it's sitting on the full 100% level) so the remaining 100 points of newly arrived supply will go into its supply stock.

Example 2

Unit Y has a basic supply of 200 points and can store 400 points. If has 350 points in storage and its readiness is 90. It will therefore request its full basic supply ration of 200 points. It then uses all of its newly arrived 200 points of supply to recover readiness (half of basic supply is needed to maintain readiness and the other half to actually recover a reasonable amount. If its readiness was 47, for example, it would need the maximum 350 points of supply and would use all 200 newly arrived points and drain the rest (150) from its own supply stock).

Indicative levels of 'basic supply' for typical Divisions is as follows. Note that all Divisions can carry 2 turns worth of supply stockpile but German Panzergruppe Divisions (Fast and Slow) can carry 3.

BASIC SUPPLY		
Unit	Basic Supply level	Maximum Supply Stock
German Infantry Division	68	136 (2 turns)
German Infantry Div (PG)	68	204 (3 turns)
German Panzer Division	89	266 (3 turns)
German Motorised Division	77	232 (3 turns)
Romanian Infantry Division	48	96 (2 turns)
Soviet Regular Rifle Division	63	126 (2 turns)
Soviet Regular Tank Division	30	60 (2 turns)
Soviet Regular Cavalary Div	38	76 (2 turns)
Soviet Regular Motorised Div	61	122 (2 turns)

4.14.4. HOW MUCH SUPPLY IS ARRIVING?

Each turn units will automatically request a certain amount of supply. The lower the readiness level is the more they will request (extra supply is needed to recover readiness).

How much supply arrives depends on how far the Division is away from the source of supply. This isn't straight geographical distance between the source

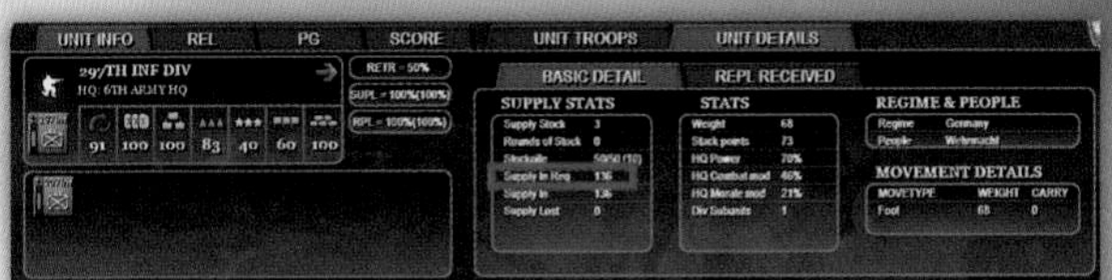

You can rely on the Quartermaster of each Division to calculate what's needed

and Division but instead the 'effort' required. If the supply can travel along rail and roads then the effort will be small compared to what is required to traverse mountains and marsh.

You can see the actual effort (in Action Points) for each type of terrain and road under the 'Supply' column in the tables found at 5.1.14 Movement Tables. Note that supply movement rates are different to normal movement rates (they are, as a whole, a lot more generous).

The Supply layer button found on the bottom button bar

Supply can travel a maximum of 250 AP from its source to the Division. Click on the Supply button to activate the supply layer.

Once activated you can click on any unit and a line of red arrows will highlight the path taken by the supply in order to get to the unit. The path is automatically optimised to be the most efficient route possible.

Supply delivery, past a certain point, becomes less effective. This is shown visually by different supply

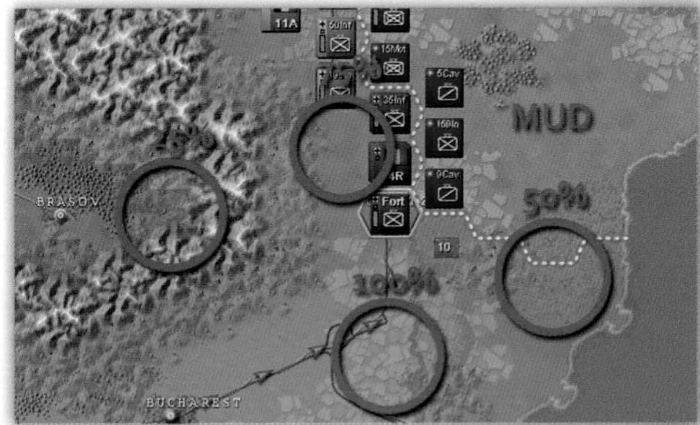

Supply overlay colours and how much of a Divisions requested supply will be delivered. The border provides a neat limit to the extent of German supply coverage (supply can't travel through enemy territory)

overlay colours and numerically in the table below. The more AP that is expended to get to the unit the less supply that will be delivered.

SUPPLY OVERLAY		
Overlay Colour	Amount of Requested Supply that can be delivered	Action Points for supply threshold
Light Green	100%	0 to 99
Dark Green	75%	100 to 149
Light Brown	50%	150 to 199
Dark Brown	25%	200 to 250

As an example if the 297th Infantry Division (in the example pic above) requested its 136 points of supply and it was located in a hex covered by the light green overlay it would receive 100% of its requested supply (136). If it was in a hex covered by the Light Brown overlay it would receive only half that (50% of 136). If it isn't covered by the overlay at all (any colour) then it would receive no supply (which happens when the unit is cut-off).

While the Supply Overlay is on click on a hex and it will tell you how many AP have been expended for supply to travel from the Highest Level HQ to the unit

ASK YOUR STAFF

My Division is within the supply coverage (dark green colour) yet it says that it received no supply ('Supply In 0'). How can this be? It's possible that the supply path to the Division was interrupted by the movement an enemy unit during its turn (it might be O.K now but if an enemy unit blocked a key rail unit it would stop supply). You could see this in the history playback. The supply system has been tried and tested over five different games and is rock solid so it's fair to say that whatever it is telling you is accurate.

Each Division has a small box at the top left of its counter that allows you to quickly see what percentage of requested supply arrived at the unit at the beginning of each turn. The colour changes depending on the

Visual indication of how much supply has arrived

situation. Green is all OK. Yellow indicates some problems but nothing severe. Blue signals major problems and Red flags a critical situation where little, or no, supply arrived this turn.

Don't forget that even though no supply might have arrived the unit may still have enough of a stockpile to meet its requirements. Its supply consumption level will only start dropping below 100% once it can't meet its requirements, each turn, from either newly arrived supply or its internal stockpile.

STAFF ADVICE

Supply is more of an issue for the Germans than the Soviets. Once lines begin to extend and bad weather hits the supply situation can become problematic for Divisions that find themselves too far from the transport grid (rail or road).

4.14.5. SUPPLY SETTING

You can set an individual Division to receive less than full supply (the default is for all units to receive 100%).

At 100% the unit will ask for all the supply it needs. At 50% (of basic supply) it will receive enough to maintain its readiness only (there won't be enough to recover readiness).

The setting is a combination of the unit and the settings of its HQ's (Army and Theatre).

ASK YOUR STAFF

Why should I ever order a Division to receive less supply? You'd only do this if there was a shortage of supply and you won't to channel it to where it was needed most. In DC3 there are generally adequate levels of supply all around and you can safely ignore this setting. There may be some specific situations where it could come in handy but it's unlikely.

4.14.6. OUT OF SUPPLY

A unit that is out of supply (not covered by the supply overlay, see 3.6.1.10 Supply) will find its readiness automatically dropping by 40% every turn. This is the only affect of being out of supply.

Whatever supply it has on hand will be used to recover readiness (see 5.2.1 Readiness). With no supply remaining the units readiness will spiral downhill. Every time it moves or fights it will drop further, in addition to the flat 40% per turn reduction penalty.

Low readiness lowers the units Action Point allowance and adversely affects its combat performance.

Note that it's possible to be out of supply but *not* cut-off, especially if in difficult terrain in mud conditions.

STAFF ADVICE

A Division that is out of supply will degrade rapidly. Do whatever it takes to rectify the situation. Provided the unit isn't cut-off the best course of action is to move it closer to the transport grid (rail or road) where supply has a better chance of arriving. Once there rest the unit to allow it to firstly recover the unit's readiness and, once this is done, to rebuild its stockpile.

For a more detailed discussion on why units that are out of supply deteriorate so quickly see 6.2.5.3 Breakout!

4.14.7. AMMUNITION STOCKPILES

To better simulate the effect of the need to prepare for offensives, stockpiling of artillery ammunition is modelled. This only applies to units with artillery (field guns, infantry guns, howitzers).

The numbers represent, in order, the ammunition stockpile on hand (50), the maximum possible stockpile (50, after the slash) and the number of combat rounds of use that this will provide (10). The ammunitions stockpile uses the same general supply but it is stored separately (so each Division has, in effect, two stockpiles of supply - the normal and the artillery one).

Each time a unit with artillery engages in combat its artillery stockpile will decrease by 5 points per round.

As an example the 263rd Infantry Division attacks the 113rd Soviet Rifle Division and uses its artillery (automatically) to bombard them.

The big number in the centre shows how many combat rounds have elapsed

As the attack lasted 11 combat rounds the entire stockpile has been expended and there are zero rounds of artillery barrage currently available (it's dynamic and updates immediately).

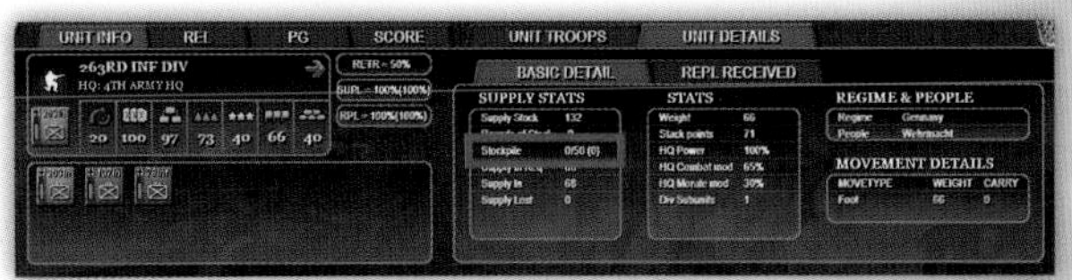

What happens during an attack if your artillery has run out of ammunition? They still fire (it's assumed there are still shells on hand but they only have enough for an harassing barrage) but operate at 25% effectiveness.

A unit's ammunition stockpile will gradually recover depending on the general supply situation.

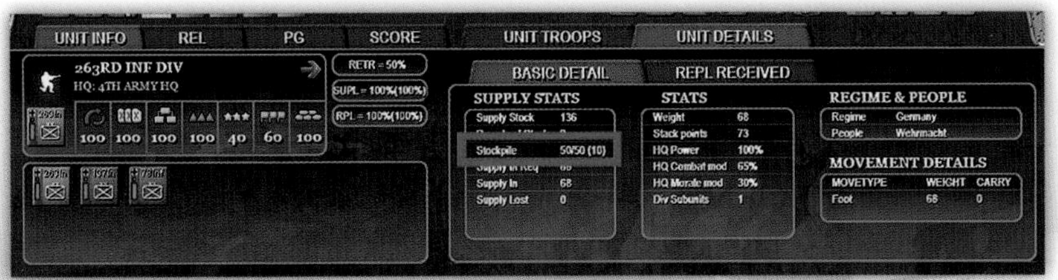

Ammunition stockpiles have no effect other than providing a means of making the effect of artillery more brutal when fully stocked (represents the devastating effects of an opening barrage).

STAFF ADVICE

For those that like to get into the nitty gritty, in order to maximise the offensive capability of a Division try and time critical attacks when it has a full ammunition stockpile and can deliver a lethal barrage.

4.14.8. SUPPLY EXAMPLE - THE SAGA OF THE 297TH

LtGen. Max Pfeffer has had a rush of blood to the head and has ordered his 297th Infantry Division across the Polish border into Russia, prior to the start of the invasion.

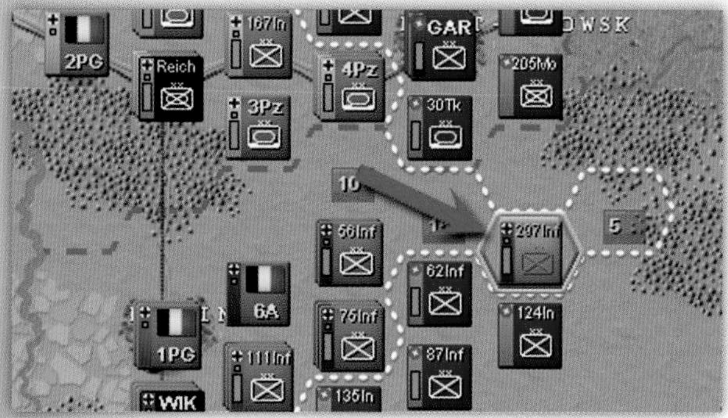

Nobody is quite sure what is going on. The 297th sent a radio report indicating nothing out of the ordinary.

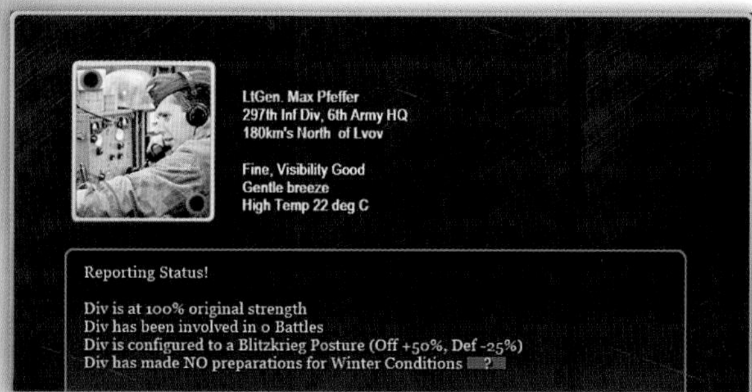

The 297th commenced their one Division campaign with a full quota of supply (2 turns of basic level supply). Note below that the 297th has requested the basic supply quota (68 supply points) in order to maintain its readiness ('Supply in Req') and this has been delivered ('Supply In') at the start of turn, prior to them crossing the border.

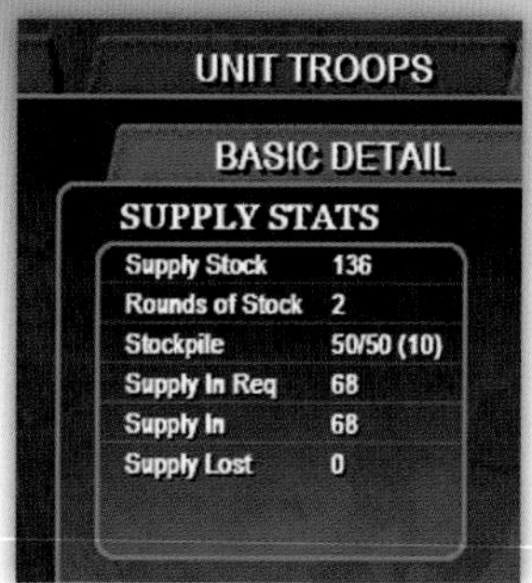

Two turns worth of the basic supply quota is the maximum that a normal Infantry Division can carry

At the end of Max's foolish foray into Mother Russia the 297th's readiness has dropped to 76 (due to the movement). While his supply status is still the same (no change in their stockpile) the 'Rounds of Stock' have dropped to below one (0.9).

'Rounds of Stock' is calculated dynamically and because the 297th is now functioning at a higher operational tempo the same amount of supply (136 Supply Stock) isn't going to stretch as far (less than one turn if Max keeps ordering them forward).

During the Soviet turn the 30th Tank Division swings neatly in behind the, now isolated, 297th Infantry Division.

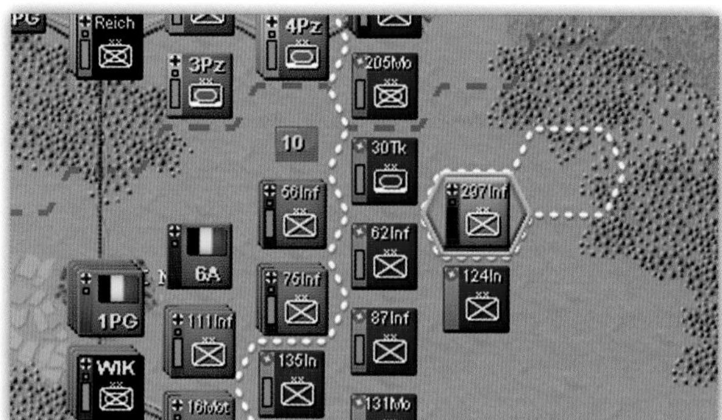

Max's quest for glory has got him into trouble

At the start of the following German turn the 297th's supply situation isn't looking so rosy.

Their readiness has recovered to 100 then dropped back to 99 due to 1 point of fatigue (movement last turn). In order to achieve this additional supply, above and beyond the basic quota, is required. As none has arrived (due to being cut-off) ('Supply In') the 297th has had to draw down on its own supply stockpile which now has only ('Supply Stock') 4 points remaining (it was 136 last turn).

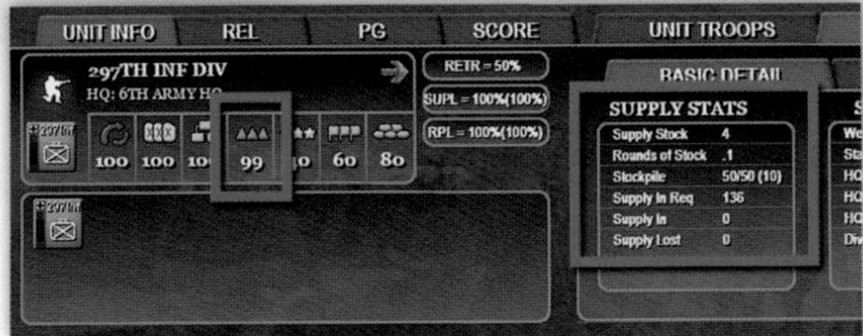

Because stocks have crashed the Division automatically requests a top-up back to its normal level (the two turn buffer of basic supply level), that being 136 ('Supply in Req'). The Divisional Quartermaster has reported to Max that the situation is grim ('Rounds of Stock' 0.1).

Contacted for comment on the radio, LtGen. Pfeffer isn't so sanguine. Theatre HQ order him to dig in and await developments.

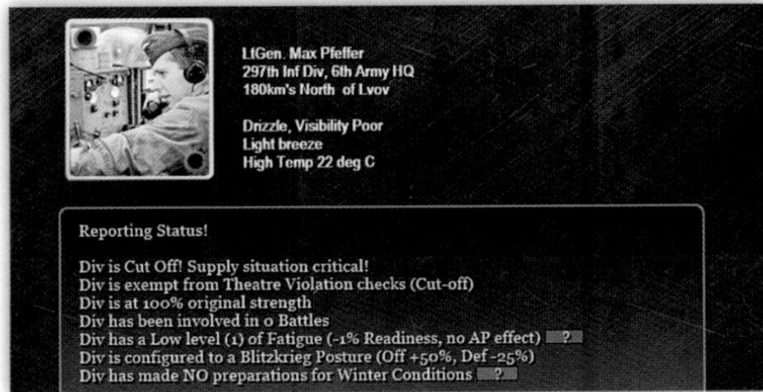
LtGen. Max Pfeffer
297th Inf Div, 6th Army HQ
180km's North of Lvov
Drizzle, Visibility Poor
Light breeze
High Temp 22 deg C
Reporting Status!
Div is Cut Off! Supply situation critical!
Div is exempt from Theatre Violation checks (Cut-off)
Div is at 100% original strength
Div has been involved in 0 Battles
Div has a Low level (1) of Fatigue (-1% Readiness, no AP effect)
Div is configured to a Blitzkrieg Posture (Off +50%, Def -25%)
Div has made NO preparations for Winter Conditions

With the Division dug in and preparing defences against an attack in any direction, their supply situation, one the following turn, has worsened.

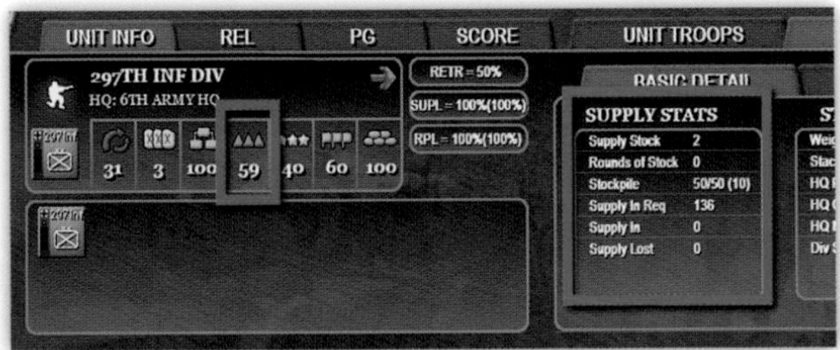

The readiness level of the 297th has dropped to 59 despite the fact that they didn't move or fight the previous turn. This is because they are cut-off and no longer receiving supply. We can switch on the supply layer (see 3.6.1.10 Supply and see this visually).

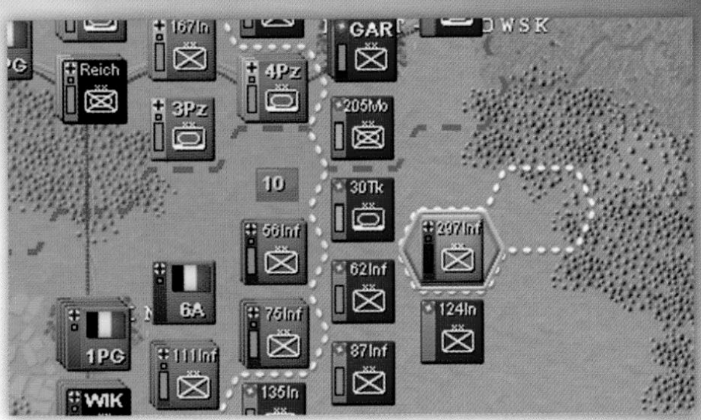

Below: Max is on the wrong side of the border and outside of the supply overlay. If you're not within a colour shading, you aren't receiving supply

When a Division is cut-off it suffers an automatic 40% drop in readiness (which takes it from the previous level of 99 down to 59). This happens each turn. Low readiness affects combat and Action point allocation. You can see that the 297th has commenced this turn, not with the 100 AP as you'd expect but, instead, only 31 AP.

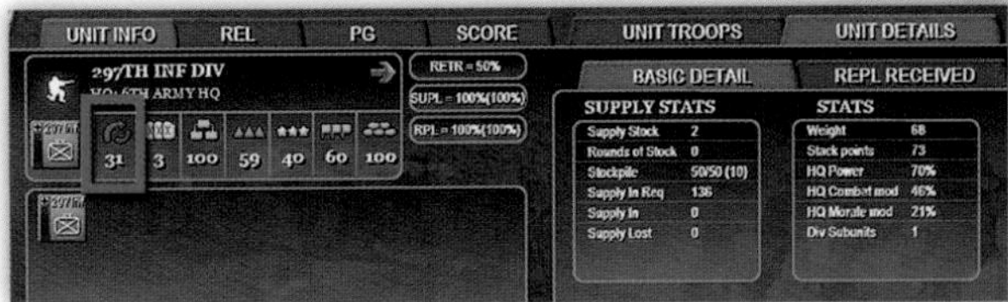

The 297th aren't going anywhere

You can also see that their Supply Consumption has crashed from the normal 100% level. This is because they are needing a full replenishment of supply (to recover their readiness) and there is none on hand (they used half of their meagre 4 supply points and there are 2 left). If Max ordered the 297th

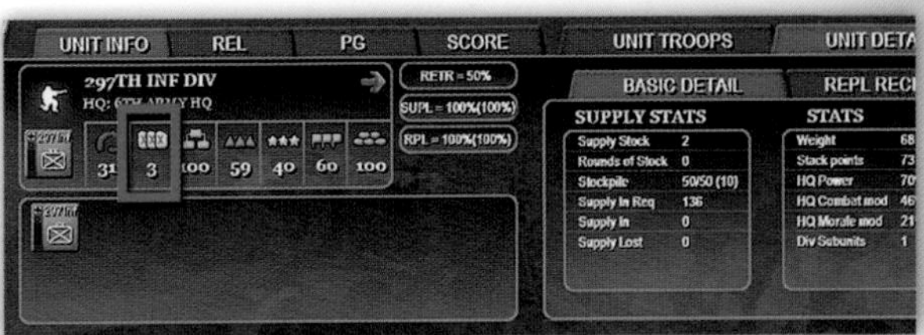

The Divisional Quartermaster is still vainly requesting supply but nothing, unsurprisingly, is turning up

to fight their way out they would be slaughtered given the steep low readiness, low supply consumption combat penalties that they would face.

FeldMarschall Von Rundstedt, AGS theatre Commander, decides that enough is enough and orders the 6th Army to rescue the 297th from their muddy grave.

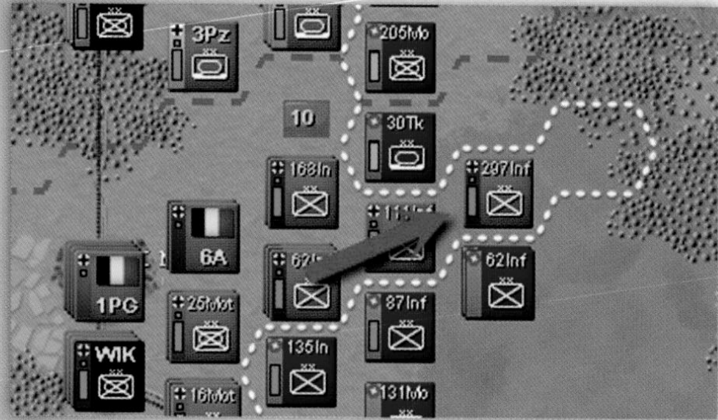

Unlike Von Paulus at Stalingrad, Max gets to live and fight another day

With supply trucks now able to reach the beleaguered 297th their situation has improved.

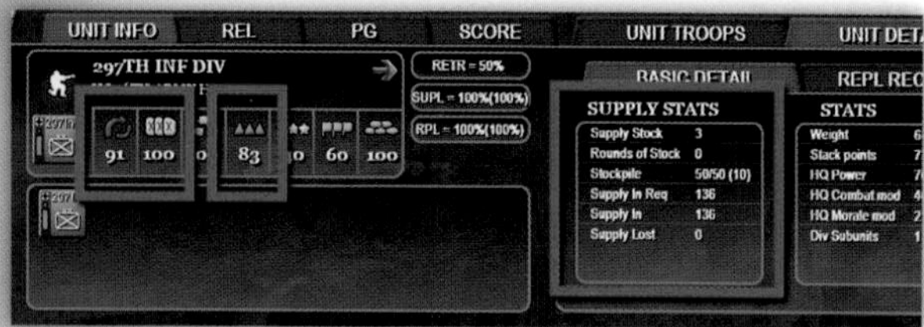

Supply stocks have barely shifted but you can see that the Quartermasters request ('Supply in Req') has been met in full ('Supply In'). All of the supply (bar a single point) has been used to recover readiness back up to 83 (there is a maximum of 40 points recovery per turn and it would have gone down even further prior to the supply arriving).

With readiness much improved the 297th have a 91 Action Point allowance (left box) and their Supply consumption has lifted back to 100%. They are on the mend.

Two turns later finds the 297th back on its feet.

They are receiving their full AP allowance (100), Supply Consumption is sitting on the normal 100

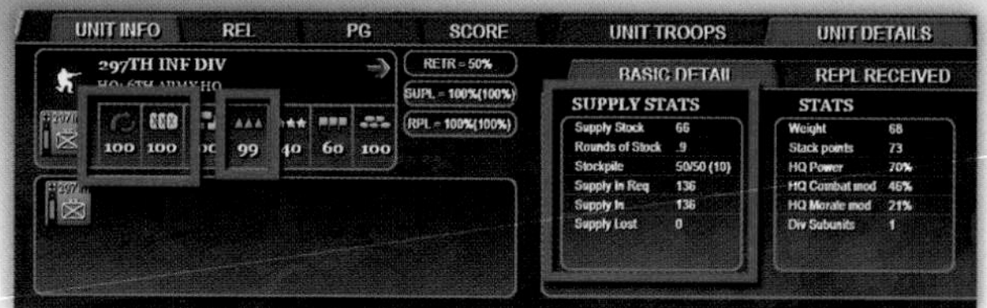

level as well and Readiness is at the maximum of 99 (normally 100 but don't forget about the 1 point of fatigue that the 297th is carrying). Because their readiness no longer needs to recover their stockpile is beginning to accumulate ('Supply Stock' 66).

One more turn of sitting idle will see the 297th with a full stockpile. Once this happens their 'Supply in Req' will drop back to the basic supply level of 68 (what it was when they first started).

Note that the Artillery ammunition stockpile ('50/50 (10)') hasn't changed throughout because at no stage did the 297th engage in combat. Their stockpile of ammunition is still intact (10 combat rounds worth) and is ready for use.

Max? He's currently explaining himself to Von Rundstedt at AGS theatre HQ. It isn't going well.

SUMMARY

- Supply applies to all units
- It is separate from the Logistical Pipelines which are for getting Fuel to German Panzergruppes
- Supply allows a unit to maintain and recover its Readiness. Supply has no other effect.
- Readiness drops every turn as a result of movement and combat
- Units can store two or three turns of supply in an internal stockpile
- Units receive a supply delivery at the start of each turn
- Supply comes travels from the source direct to the unit
- Press the Supply button (bottom bar) to view the Supply layer
- Different coloured supply overlays provide different levels of supply (light green is best)
- Units that cannot receive supply (out of range or cut-off) suffer a large readiness drop each turn and are soon rendered combat ineffective
- There is a special internal Ammunition stockpile that is used to maximise artillery barrages

4.15. RECONNAISSANCE ▶

All your units exert reconnaissance points up to 4 hexes away. If your recon is high enough you can see enemy units. There are three levels of recon but these differ between regimes as the German command of the air gave them a far superior reconnaissance ability than that of the Soviets.

Click on any hex and you can see the total recon value you have there (not much in this case)

If Fog of War isn't on (start game option) then you automatically have full reconnaissance on all enemy units.

RECONNAISSANCE LEVELS

Recon Level in hex	German Recon points	Soviet Recon points
None – you can't tell if any units are present	0 to 39	0 to 99
Low – you know a unit is there but have no information on it	> 40	> 100
Medium – partial information	40 to 400	100 to 400
High – full information	> 400	> 400

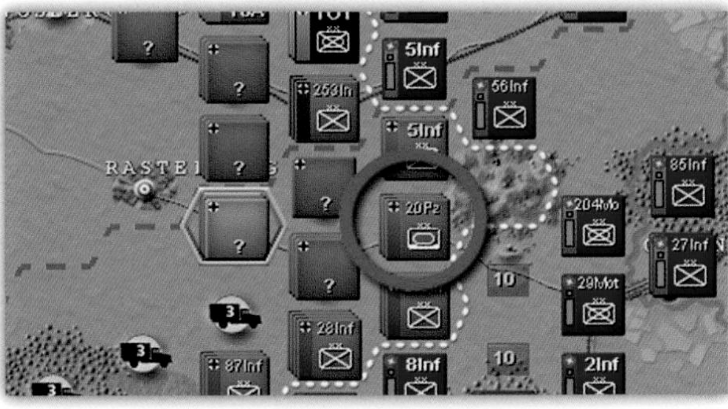

The Soviets have partial information on the 20th Panzer Division. Note that the integrity bar isn't shown on the counter. The units with '?' on them, further out, are in hexes with low levels of recon

Each Division has 1 point of recon for every infantry, gun and tank model within. The recon values of all nearby units are tallied to provide a total recon value for each hex up to four hexes distance (there is a distance penalty that increases as you get further away). Provided the total recon in a hex meets one of the threshold values in the table above you'll gain information on the enemy units.

A unit, such as the 20th Panzer above, that you have partial information on will show certain details but not all.

Among others you can't see the combat modifiers (blue and red boxes) on the unit pics although you can see the status icon for 'Blitzkrieg Posture'

For units where all you can see on the map is their counter with a question mark (low recon), there's not much to see.

Could be anyone...

5. COUNTER SHUFFLING

5.1. MOVEMENT ▶

Moving units costs Action Points (AP). The cost of movement depends on the movement type of the unit and the terrain (landscape type) that the unit is entering. The cost of moving can be increased by entering enemy terrain, enemy Zone of Control (ZOC) points, battle delay points or unbridged rivers. Roads enable faster movement, especially through difficult terrain.

When a unit moves, it does so with the range of the slowest troop type it contains. The range of the slowest troop type can be increased if the unit contains enough transport elements, eg. trucks, halftracks, capable of carrying the slower troops. The cost, in AP, of entering a hex is a combination of movement type, terrain and any penalties on hex due to enemy ZOC, ownership or previous combat.

When the available fuel reaches zero, or close to it, fast Divisions (motorised or mechanised) will be unable to move.

5.1.1. HOW TO MOVE

Select a unit on the map. Either press 'M' (move individual unit) or 'G' (move a group of units). Alternatively click on one of the two move buttons (bottom left) that correspond to the key shortcuts.

Move a single unit on the left, Group move on the right

Once you've activated movement mode a light yellow shading will appear in every hex that the unit can legally move into.

You can mouse over every shaded hex and receive a readout of the movement cost (this is the total cost to move to the hex) and, in the case of Fast Divisions, the fuel cost, prior to committing yourself to the move (see below).

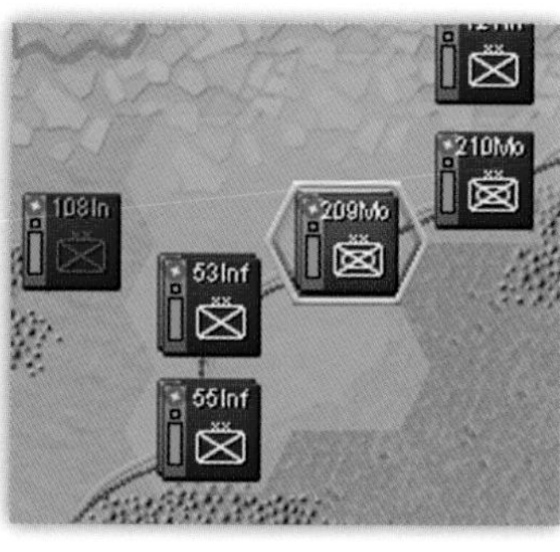

To commit to a move click on anyone of the shaded hexes and the unit will immediately change position. Action Points (AP) and Fuel, if applicable, will be expended.

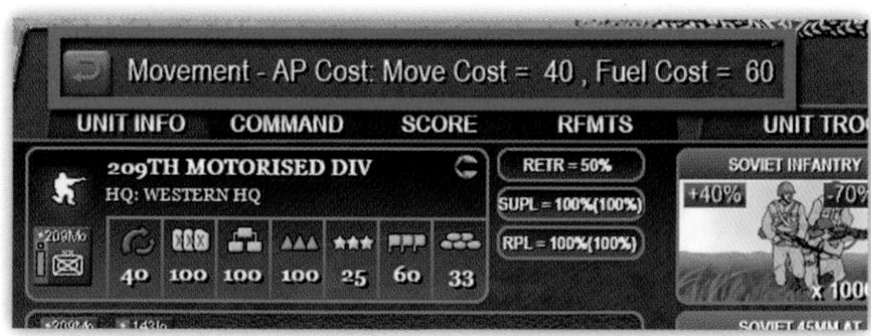

To back out of a potential move (you've changed your mind) either press ESC, Space, or the 'Revert' button to the left of the movement tool tip in the pic above.

Don't forget that a unit's movement potential is directly related to how many Action Points it has.

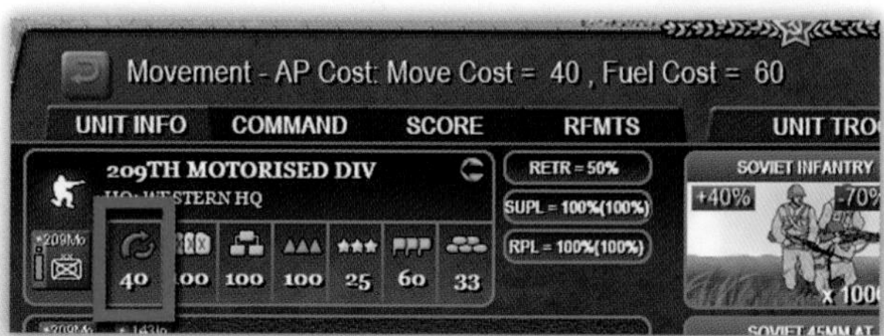

The 209th Motorised Division has failed to activate and has the minimum movement amount

Movement can be done in stages. Move a unit here. Move another unit there. Come back and move the first again. The only limitation is having sufficient AP remaining to move.

You can always ask the unit to Report Status! (see 3.6.1.4 Report Status!) to ascertain any factors that may be influencing its movement capability.

5.1.2. MOVEMENT AND THEATRES

When you move a unit a shading scheme will appear to highlight theatre boundaries. Yellow shading indicates valid moves within the units assigned theatre or front.

Reddish brown shading indicates that movement to these hexes will be into a different theatre and may well incur a theatre violation penalty (see 4.3 Theatres).

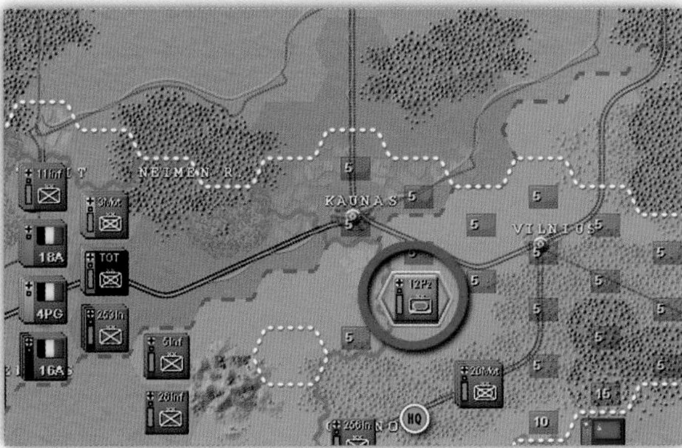

The 12th Panzer Division is assigned to AGC. Movement north across the theatre border to Kaunas will result in a violation penalty

5.1.3. MOVEMENT AND TERRAIN

Refer to the 5.1.14 Movement Tables. To see a comprehensive breakdown of all costs for a hex hover your mouse over the terrain image, top centre. This will also give the cost of any dynamic factors that apply to the hex.

Terrain display - mouseover for more information

WOODS (29,31) SOVIET UNION

ROADS PRESENT: RAIL SOVIET 2X SEALED(N,S)
LANDSCAPE: WOODS

TROOPTYPE	ATT-MOD	DEF-MOD	A-ENTR	MX-ENTR	CROSS-RIV
INFANTRY	100%	100%	150	150	-
GUNS	30%	60%	150	150	-
MOTORIZED	50%	50%	0	0	-
LIGHT TANKS	50%	50%	0	0	-
MEDIUM TANKS	50%	50%	0	0	-
HEAVY TANKS	50%	50%	0	0	-

MOVETYPE	AP COST	ROAD	RIVER
FOOT	30	20	-
MOTORIZED	30	10	-
CAVALRY	25	20	-
RAIL	NA	3	-
TRACKED	30	10	-
SUPPLY MOVE	25	2	-
IMMOBILE	NA	0	-
RAIL_CAP	NA	3	-

COVER: 20

ENEMY TERRAIN PENALTY IN AP = 5

Roads and rivers at the top, combat effects, movement costs and any hex specific costs down the bottom

5.1.4. ROADS AND RAIL

Rail is used by the logistical part of the game. It has no impact on the movement of units.

Roads, on the other hand, do affect the movement of units. There are two types - sealed and normal. Sealed roads (all weather) are shown visually on the map whereas normal roads are assumed to be present where ever there is a rail line (and the absence of a sealed road).

Sealed roads are found only in the Baltic States (AGN) and on the main Warsaw - Minsk - Moscow highway.

Movement *along* roads provides bonuses and enables certain units to enter otherwise impassable terrain (for example armour through marsh).

Once mud conditions arrive movement is severely affected. Normal roads rapidly breakdown and turn into a boggy mush. For Motorised Divisions (with wheeled, truck based, transport) the only way forward is along a sealed, all weather, road.

For more information on roads see 5.1.14.2 Road costs.

5.1.5. UNEXPECTED ENCOUNTERS

It is possible, due to the Fog of War, that you might inadvertently move into an enemy occupied hex without realising beforehand. In this case any units you have moved will be ambushed and surprise combat initiated. Suffice to say they will be at a disadvantage.

5.1.6. RIVER CROSSINGS

There is an additional cost incurred to cross rivers where a bridge isn't present. The cost varies by the size of the river (there are four) and by season (frozen or non-frozen). Refer to the 5.1.14 Movement Tables for a precise cost.

Rivers presented few obstacles for individual Divisions. The Germans were very adept at bridging rivers on a temporary basis whereas the Soviets knew where all the crossing points were. Erecting semi-permanent structures that could take a 60t truck column was more challenging, hence the high supply costs. Heavy German locomotives, running regular services, were restricted to permanent bridges (marked bridges on the map).

5.1.7. ENEMY OWNERSHIP

Moving into a hex that was occupied by the enemy at the start of the turn costs an extra 5 AP.

DESIGNER NOTE

Entering enemy territory requires a higher level of caution and awareness.

5.1.8. ENEMY ZONE OF CONTROL (ZOC)

Moving *into* a hex adjacent to an enemy unit costs 10 extra AP. If doing so while crossing a river, it costs 20 extra AP (double).

Enemy units that are hidden by the Fog of War do not exert a ZOC (no movement penalty) in order not to give their presence away.

Units that are out of supply exert no ZOC.

5.1.9. EFFECT OF BATTLES

DESIGNER NOTE

Battle delays simulate the efforts of an effective defence in slowing down the attacker

Whenever a battle has been fought in the hex a penalty may be incurred for any units trying to move into, or through, the newly opened hex. The penalty kicks in if a battle took more AP to win than it took the units that participated in the battle to move into the hex.

5.1.10. FREE MOVEMENT

If you have won a battle, your units will be able to freely move into the hex in which you battled without spending any additional action points. This is because the AP to move in was already spent in battle.

This doesn't apply if the combat was a surprise engagement (you ran into unexpected units).

5.1.11. EFFECT OF WEATHER

In general, mud places severe restrictions on movement while snow can make previously difficult terrain easier to traverse.

During Rasputitsa, the mud season, tracked vehicles can still move but wheeled ones can only do so on 'Sealed', all-weather, roads.

Normal roads were useless in mud as they quickly turned into a boggy morass. In 1941 the term 'road', in Russia, meant the equivalent of a track requiring four wheel drive to traverse, on a good day.

In Winter, rivers and lakes progressively freeze over. Once frozen they can be safely crossed. Marshes become easier to move through in winter.

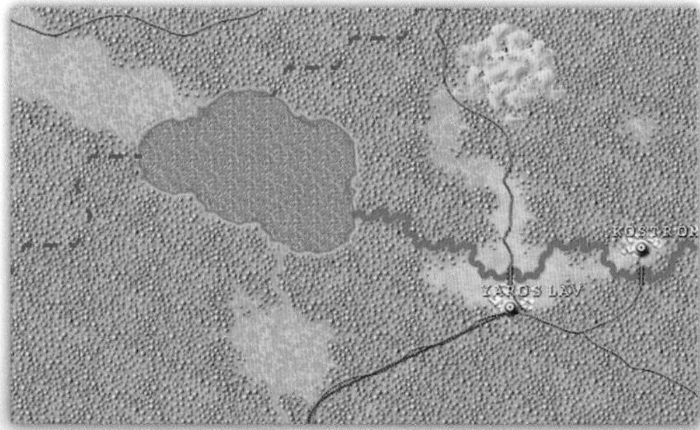

A frozen northern lake. Note the frozen river running out the south and the larger river running east which is yet to be frozen (the larger the river, the longer it takes to freeze)

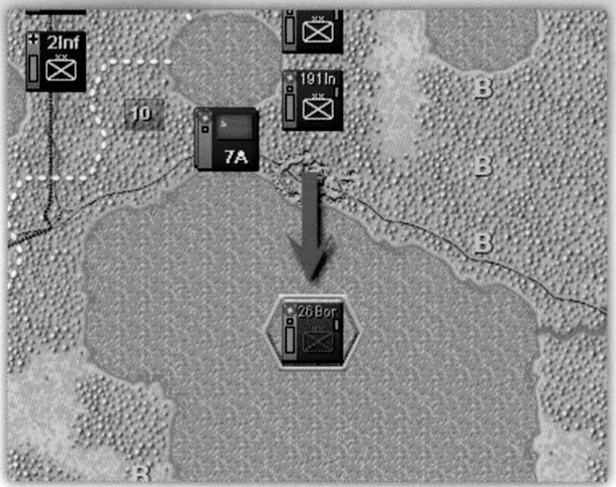

Frozen lakes can be safely moved across

5.1.12. MOVEMENT AND FUEL

Fast Divisions (ones with motorised or mechanised elements) expend fuel each time they move. Without fuel they are unable to move or initiate combat. If attacked they fight at 2/3 normal strength.

To determine how much fuel is available, select a unit and the fuel gauge (top bar, right of centre) will display the available fuel for the current theatre, or front. Each time you move a fast Division you'll see the amount of fuel going down. Combat also uses fuel.

STAFF ADVICE

German fast Divisions (motorised or Panzer) depend heavily on fuel. The entire logistical sub-game is dedicated to ensuring enough fuel is there to keep them moving. Intermittent fuel shortages are a fact of life for the German Player.

The Soviets have many mixed units with some trucks, tanks and lots of infantry. Because of shorter supply lines and decent stockpiles, the Soviets rarely have to worry about fuel.

Dynamic Fuel gauge. Click on any hex and it will provide the amount of fuel available, in bbls, for the chosen theatre, or front

5.1.13. TRANSPORT CAPACITY

In the game there are both trucks and half tracks which are capable of transporting infantry, artillery and anti-tank guns at a faster movement rate than they would normally travel at.

If you inspect the Unit Details tab (bottom, right of centre), you can see the amount of transport capacity ('Carry') and how much is required for the Infantry and Guns that are present ('Weight'). Provided the 'Carry' is greater, or equal, to the 'Weight', the unit will move at the speed of the transports which is faster than 'foot' movement.

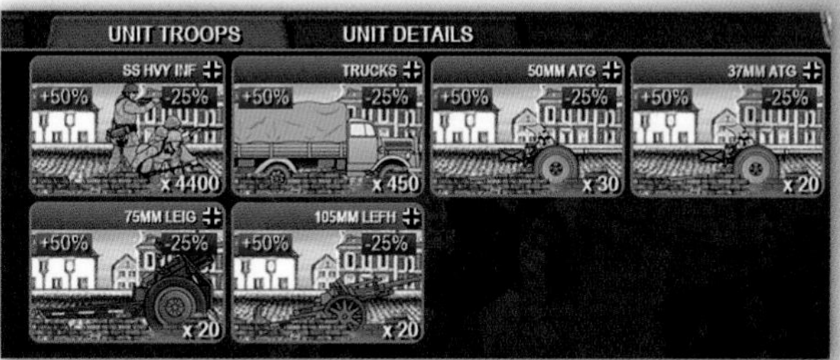

The Division has trucks which can transport the infantry and guns

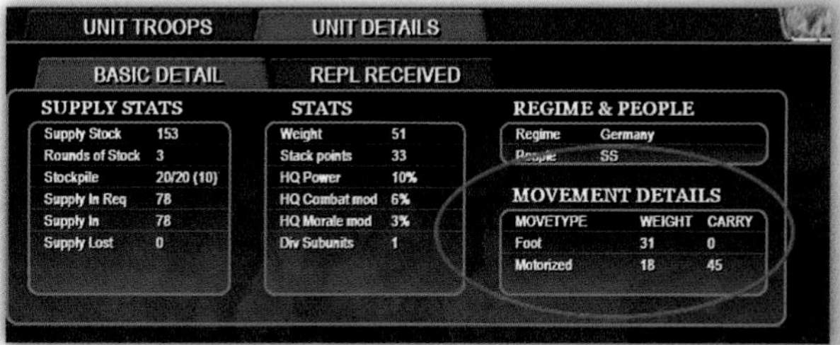

The 'Motorised' trucks have a 'Carry' (transport) capacity of 45 which is more than enough to transport the 'Foot' Infantry and guns with their 'Weight' of 31.

5.1.14. MOVEMENT TABLES

5.1.14.1. Terrain Costs

MOVEMENT COSTS BY TERRAIN					
Terrain	Infantry & Artillery (foot)	Cavalry (horse)	Trucks (wheeled)	Tanks & Halftracks (tracked)	Supply
Plains and Fields	25	20	15	15	10
Forest and Woods	30	25	30	30	25
Marsh	35	30	n.a	n.a	35
Urban	25	20	15	15	1
Low Mountains	30	25	50	50	30
Forested Low Mountains	30	25	50	50	40
High Mountains	n.a	n.a	n.a	n.a	60
MUD Plains and Fields	40	40	n.a	40	15
MUD Forest and Woods	40	40	n.a	40	45
MUD Marsh	45	40	n.a	n.a	50
MUD Urban	25	20	15	15	40
MUD Low Mountains	40	35	n.a	60	60
MUD Forested Low Mountains	40	35	n.a	60	50
MUD High Mountains	n.a	n.a	n.a	n.a	n.a
SNOW Plains and Fields	25	20	15	15	10
SNOW Forest and Woods	30	25	30	30	25
SNOW Marsh	25	20	n.a	n.a	15
SNOW Urban	25	20	15	15	1
SNOW Low Mountains	30	25	50	50	30
SNOW Forested Low Mountains	30	25	50	50	40
SNOW High Mountains	n.a	n.a	n.a	n.a	n.a

Artillery is assumed to be horse drawn in the absence of motorised transport.

Mountains are assumed to be high and inaccessible

5.1.14.2. Road Costs

MOVEMENT COSTS BY ROAD (AP)				
Terrain	Infantry & Artillery (foot)	Cavalry (horse)	Motorised (wheeled)	Tanks & Halftracks (tracked)
Sealed Road	20	20	10	10
Sealed Road MUD	20	20	10	10
Sealed Road SNOW	20	20	10	10
Road	25	20	10	10
Road MUD	40	40	Immobile	40
Road SNOW	25	20	10	10

If a road is leading *into* the hex to which you're moving, the road AP costs apply, not the terrain.

The only roads shown on the map are 'Sealed', all weather, roads. Where ever there is rail (single or double tracked, Soviet or German) shown on its own, a 'Road' is assumed to be present.

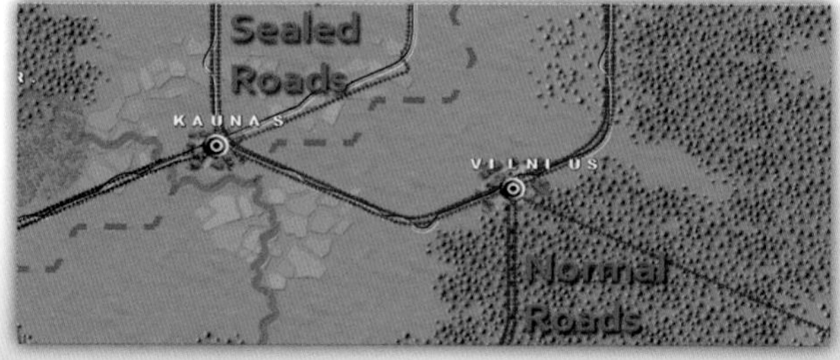

These are all 'Sealed' roads with exception of the two normal 'Roads' running south, and south east, of Vilnius (they are straight rail)

The terrain mouse over tool tips also let you know if a road is sealed.

PLAINS (24,51) SOVIET UNION
ROADS PRESENT: RAIL GERMAN 2: SEALED(,SE,SW)
LANDSCAPE: PLAINS

Sealed roads exist in the Baltic States (AGN) and on the main Warsaw - Minsk - Moscow highway. All the rest are normal roads.

STAFF ADVICE

Both types of road operate almost identically except in Mud conditions when sealed roads allow Motorised Divisions to keep going. Normal roads (the majority), in Mud, will bring a Motorised Division to a dead stop (they are bogged). All other Divisions will find the going tougher in Mud conditions unless they are on a sealed, all weather, road. There is a reason the Germans advanced straight up the main, sealed, highway to Moscow.

5.1.14.3. River Costs

MOVEMENT COSTS TO CROSS A RIVER (NO BRIDGE)

Terrain	Infantry & Artillery (foot)	Cavalry (horse)	Trucks (wheeled)	Tanks & Halftracks (tracked)	Supply
Volga	+40	+40	+70	+70	+150
Major River	+30	+30	+50	+50	+100
Medium River	+20	+20	+30	+30	+75
Minor River	+10	+10	+15	+15	+50
Frozen Volga	Free	Free	Free	Free	Free
Frozen Major	Free	Free	Free	Free	Free
Frozen Medium	Free	Free	Free	Free	Free
Frozen Minor	Free	Free	Free	Free	Free

Supply costs are higher as it involves semi-permanent facilities, not one-off crossing events.

5.1.15. MOVEMENT EXAMPLES

5.1.15.1. SS Totenkopf

Start of the campaign. SS Totenkopf Motorised Division, 4th Panzergruppe. With its blitzkrieg posture Action Point (AP) bonus it has 140 AP (the normal allowance for all units is 100 AP per turn).

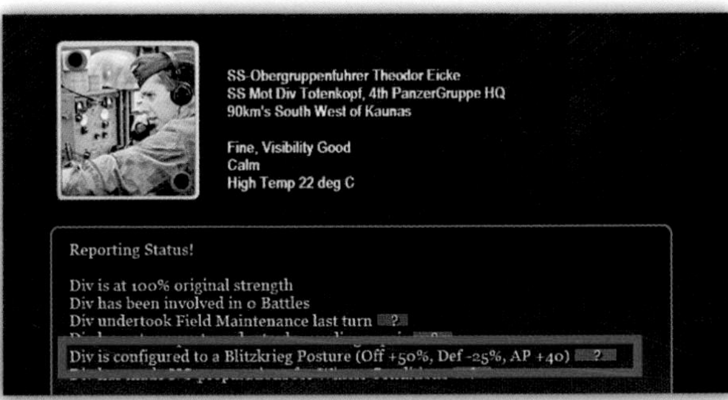
SS-Obergruppenfuhrer Theodor Eicke
SS Mot Div Totenkopf, 4th PanzerGruppe HQ
90km's South West of Kaunas
Fine, Visibility Good
Calm
High Temp 22 deg C
Reporting Status!
Div is at 100% original strength
Div has been involved in 0 Battles
Div undertook Field Maintenance last turn
Div is configured to a Blitzkrieg Posture (Off +50%, Def -25%, AP +40)

SS Obergruppenfuhrer Theodor Eicke has the Totenkopf Division ready to roll

Morale is high and it's an experienced unit that's fully supplied.

UNIT INFO
REL
PG
SS MOT DIV TOTENKOPF
140
100
100
50
70
60

Orders have been issued and the Totenkopf Division join a coordinated attack on the Soviet 5th Rifle Division which is guarding the border.

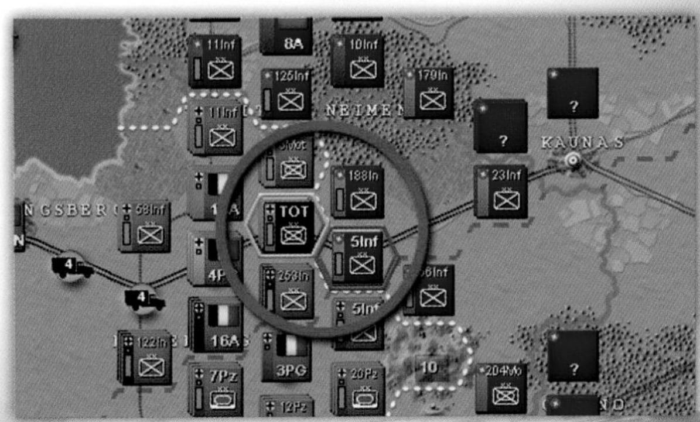
KAUNAS
TOT
5Inf

The 5th Rifle Division is routed and retreats back up the highway to Kaunas. As the combat was short and brutal (every round of combat costs AP) the Totenkopf still have a sizable amount of Action Points remaining.

Obergruppenfuhrer Eicke has pulled rank and his Totenkopf Division will have the honour of being the first across the border. He will move into the recently vacated hex to the south west. Note that there is an additional 15 AP cost (transparent box with the '15'), above and beyond the terrain cost.

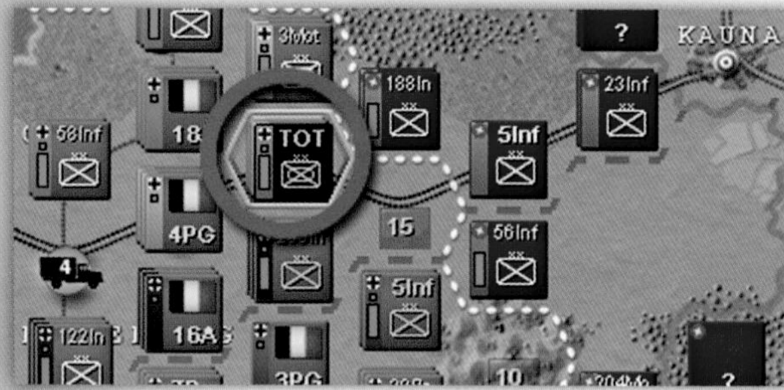

Immediately after combat

But as combat was successful and the enemy retreated, all participants receive a free move into the vacated hex so the Totenkopf will rush across the Polish border, and enter the Baltic States, at no cost.

The Totenkopf take ground!

Checking the Unit display we can see that they still have the same Action Points as at the end of combat. The free movement only applies as a result of combat that had the enemy leave the hex and it doesn't extend beyond that hex.

With the aid of other units, the Totenkopf continue to assault the beleaguered Soviet 5th Rifle Division, which again retreats back up the highway to Kaunas.

Morale is sky high! The War will be over by Christmas(blue flags - 96)

Combat lasted three rounds and the Totenkopf are down to 90 Action Points. Obergruppenfuhrer Eicke orders the Totenkopf to continue pursuit and they move into the recently vacated hex.

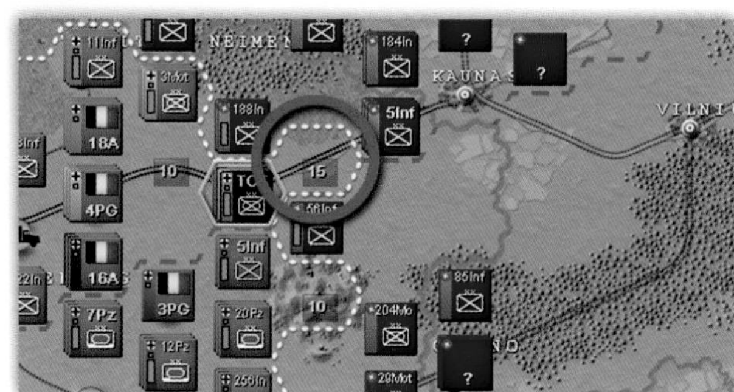

There is another additional 15 AP 'cost to enter' box showing in the hex. If we examine the mouse over tool tip for the terrain window (top centre) we can see that the 15 AP is due to enemy Zone of Control and the hex being in enemy territory.

```
REGULAR BATTLESTACK = 422
ZOC PENALTY IN AP = 10
ENEMY TERRAIN PENALTY IN AP = 5
```

None of this applies as, like above, there is a free move after a successful combat.

When you're got 'em on the run you keep chasing. Obergruppenfuhrer Eicke leads the Totenkopf into battle for the third time this turn. The Soviet 5th Rifle Division has found support from two other fresh 11th Army Divisions and it's a tougher fight.

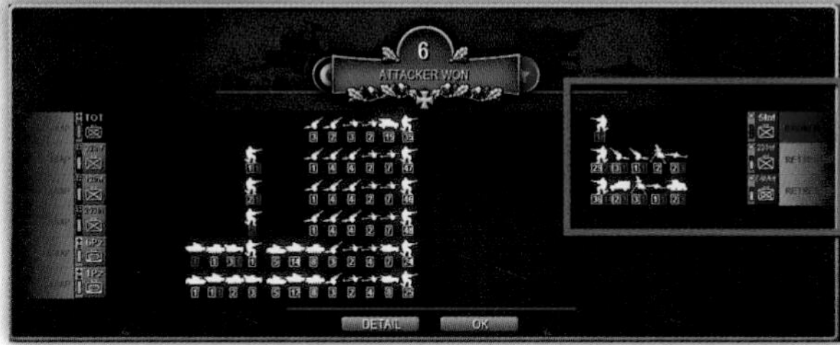

Combat lasted 6 rounds this time. The two, newly encountered, Soviet Divisions retreated and the 5th Rifle finally went under

The vacated hex has a 30 AP additional movement cost (transparent box).

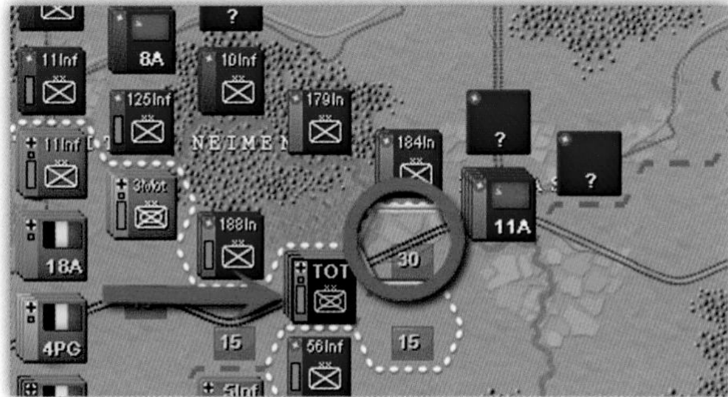

If we check the terrain window tool tip we can see that this is due to the recently fought battle. The smaller battles didn't cause any AP costs but the most recent one involved a lot of Divisions and lasted for longer.

```
REGULAR BATTLESTACK = 420
BATTLE PENALTY IN AP = 15
ZOC PENALTY IN AP = 10
ENEMY TERRAIN PENALTY IN AP = 5
```

Note the 15 AP 'Battle Penalty'. The 5th Rifle Division didn't die in vain

The Totenkopf are now jubilant (morale is at the 100 maximum) and they still have 60 AP remaining. SS-Obergruppenfuhrer Eicke sniffs glory in the air.

Moving into the vacated hex (for free, yet again), Obergruppenfuhrer Eicke assesses the situation.

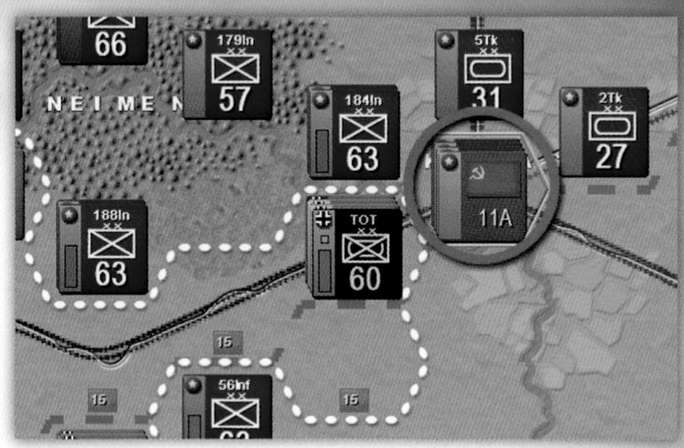

Kaunas. On the other side of the Neimen river

Holed up in the city is the 11th Army HQ and three supporting Divisions. Two of them are licking their wounds from the last encounter.

The Totenkopf would have to force a crossing over a bridge (50% combat penalty) under enemy fire with the support of only 2 Panzer Divisions. Where are the infantry Divisions when you need them?

Uncertain, SS-Obergruppenfuhrer Eicke looks at the intel on the 11th Army. Commanded by LtGen. Morozov. The Abwehr consider him to be more of threat to Russia than Germany.

Convinced that Kaunus is his, Eicke, lacking air support, organises a hasty artillery barrage from the sparse Divisional assets and orders the pioneer company to rush the bridge and disable any demolition charges before it's too late.

Fortune favours the brave. At the cost of an excessive number of Panzers, Kaunas falls!

Taking advantage of the free movement after a successful combat, the Totenkopf march into Kaunas. Obergruppenfuhrer Eicke radios in his success in capturing a vital river crossing intact. As combat lasted 8 rounds (tough fight) the Totenkopf

10 AP isn't enough to instigate combat with. Turn over. Amazingly, after four successive battles, the Totenkopf are still at 98% integrity (red outline to the right). While many of the supporting Divisions have taken casualties, especially in the last battle, the Totenkopf have sailed through almost unscathed.

have expended almost all their Action points and hunker down in Kaunas. Eicke is poised, next turn, to break out into open country and lunge for either Dunaberg or Riga.

5.1.15.2. 16th Motorised Division

AGS. Summer rains have turned the area around Lvov into a quagmire.

Let's have a quick look at the 16th Motorised Div.

Note the movement type icon, top left. It's a truck to indicate that its 'motorised' movement (wheeled rather than tracked). That's because the unit has trucks present. It wouldn't matter if it only had only a dozen trucks remaining (it's got 750 of them) it'd still be classified as 'motorised' (as well as being a 'Fast Division') as the vehicle movement type takes precedence over 'foot'.

Well that's not entirely accurate as the moment the number of trucks falls below what is required to effectively transport (see 3.6.3.7 Movement details) all the troops and guns (using its 'carry capacity') the unit would revert to 'foot' movement type as it always moves at the pace of the slowest element.

Back to the muddy ground surrounding Lvov.

The movement cost for 'Motorised' in the current, plains, mud hex is 'NA' (Not applicable). The 16th are well and truly bogged to the axles in the mud and slush.

Here the 16th Motorised Division is located on the double tracked German gauge lines, which for the purposes of unit movement, is irrelevant.

The counter has been removed to show the underlying terrain

MOVETYPE	AP COST	ROAD
MOTORIZED	NA	-
RAIL	NA	-
TRACKED	40	-
SUPPLY MOVE	15	-
IMMOBILE	NA	-
RAIL_CAP	NA	-

The 16th isn't going anywhere

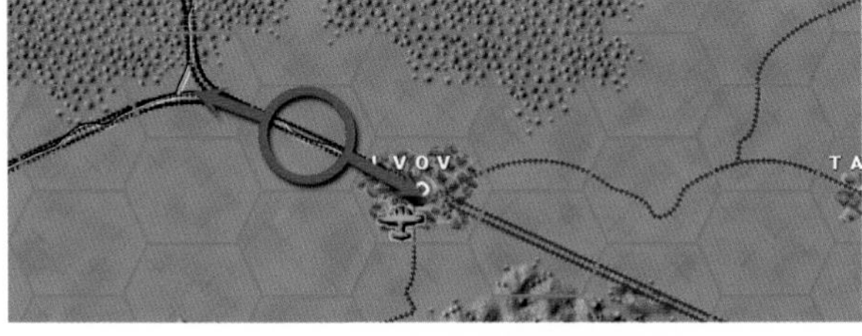

MOVETYPE	AP COST	ROAD
MOTORIZED	NA	10
RAIL	NA	1
TRACKED	40	10
SUPPLY MOVE	15	1
IMMOBILE	NA	0
RAIL_CAP	NA	1

terrain window mouse over tool tip[/image]

All that matters is that there is a road visible in the hex. As the only roads on the map are sealed, all weather, ones that's what it must be.

It's a muddy plains hex so the unit still can't move ('NA') but there is a road present with a movement rate of 10 AP. The 16th can travel along the road quite a distance, even in the mud, as it's 'sealed'. Note that it can enter Lvov but can't go any further in a south easterly or easterly direction because the sealed road finishes.

We can tell that because there is only a double and single tracked Soviet gauge rail lines present, beyond Lvov, but no road. Anytime there is rail (single or double tracked) with no road visible it's assumed that there is a 'normal' road present. Normal roads turn to mush in the mud. This might not be normal in today's developed countries but in '41, in Russia, the presence of a road that *didn't* turn to mush when it rained was abnormal.

MOVETYPE	AP COST	ROAD
MOTORIZED	NA	NA
RAIL	NA	6
TRACKED	40	40
SUPPLY MOVE	15	4
IMMOBILE	NA	0
RAIL_CAP	NA	6

The movement rate for a 'normal' road in mud is 'NA' (impassable)

Finally what would happen if the 16th was south of the sealed road? Could it move onto the road and then along it as in the example above?

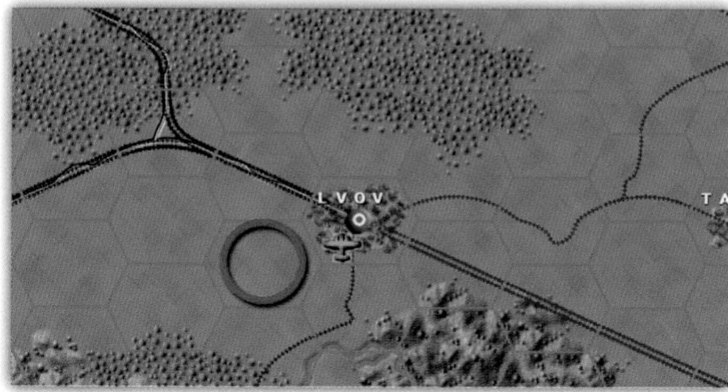

No. Road (and rail) movement rates only apply if you are moving *along* the road/rail not *onto* it. As the 16th is in a normal plains mud hex it would be bogged and immobile, exactly as in the first example given.

SUMMARY

- Movement costs Action Points (AP)
- Select the unit, press 'M' to move to any highlighted hex
- Select the stack, press 'G' to move the group (slowest unit determines movement)
- If you remove units (press '0') you'll see numbers in small squares which are additional movement costs in AP's for that hex
- Hover the mouse over the Terrain Picture (top centre) to get a detailed movement cost breakdown

DON'T FORGET

- Action points are a general pool that are used for both Movement and Combat.
- The normal allocation for each unit is 100 AP per turn but there are lots of reasons why it may have more, or less. Use the Report Status! Button to find out why.
- Roads are assumed to be where rail lines are. The only roads shown on the map are surfaced, all weather ones.
- Units with Trucks can't move in mud except on all weather roads.
- Units need to stay within their theatres, or fronts.

ASK YOUR STAFF

- Why can't my unit move?
  Check the unit display and see if it has any AP's available. It may have been involved in a battle and has expended all its AP's. Otherwise, ask the unit to Report Status! (quick Action button) to determine why it hasn't got any AP's.
  If there are AP's available, but very few, check that it has the minimum required to move into a nearby hex as it may not.
  With plenty of AP's a prime cause of being unable to move is the unit having wheeled transport (Trucks) in Mud terrain. Trucks can only move in Mud in cities or on all weather roads.
  If it is a Fast Division and has lots of AP's, check the fuel gauge, top bar, right of centre. Tanks and transports will be immobilised without fuel.
- Why is my Fast Division no longer Fast?
  Check that you still have enough transport capacity remaining in order to move your slower Infantry and Artillery and ATG elements at the higher speed. See 4.11 Transport Capacity.

5.2. COMBAT RELATED DETAILS ▶

5.2.1. READINESS

Readiness is the units ability to respond.

Readiness affects the amount of Action Points (AP) that a unit receives and influences a unit's combat strength. It is important to understand that low readiness is more of a penalty for attacking units (max 100% penalty) than a defending unit (max 50% penalty).

Movement (per 10 AP expended) and combat (per combat round) both lower a unit's readiness.

It then receives its supply allocation which raises its readiness. Readiness will improve a maximum of 40 points per turn if the unit is in full supply. Levels of supply less than full (100) will result in proportionally less readiness recovery.

A unit without supply will not recover readiness. At the beginning of each turn, where the unit is out of supply, its readiness will automatically drop by 40%.

STAFF ADVICE

Being out of supply results in a rapid decline in the units readiness which affects both movement and combat.

Supply is a combination of new supply arriving each turn and what supply stocks the unit has on hand. You can quickly tell if the unit has enough supply by looking at its 'Supply Consumption' (see 4.14 Supply). At a value of 100 it has enough supply for full readiness recovery (+40 points). At any value under 100 its ability to recover readiness will be affected.

Supply consumption. Full recovery at 100

For German Slow Divisions high levels of Fatigue (see 6.1.7 Wear and Tear) lower readiness. The effects of fatigue occur *after* the automatic drop and supply recover processes and act as an *additional* readiness penalty.

STAFF ADVICE

Throwing exhausted Infantry Divisions into an attack will only result in excessive casualties. Pull them out of the line and rest them (Action card).

5.2.1.1. Readiness Example

GenMaj. Berthold's 31st Infantry Division has been ordered to punch a whole through the Red Army border defences to let the Panzer Divisions through

It's the start of the campaign and the 31st Infantry are fully rested and ready to go

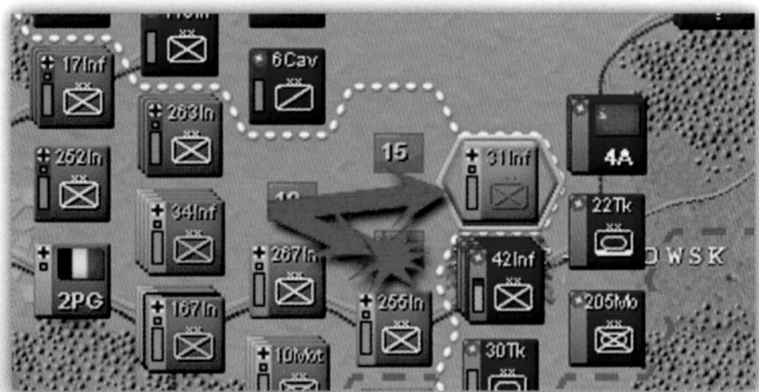

The 31st launch into an attack to the south east and dislodge a Soviet 42nd Rifle Division before moving east to flank Brest-Litowsk

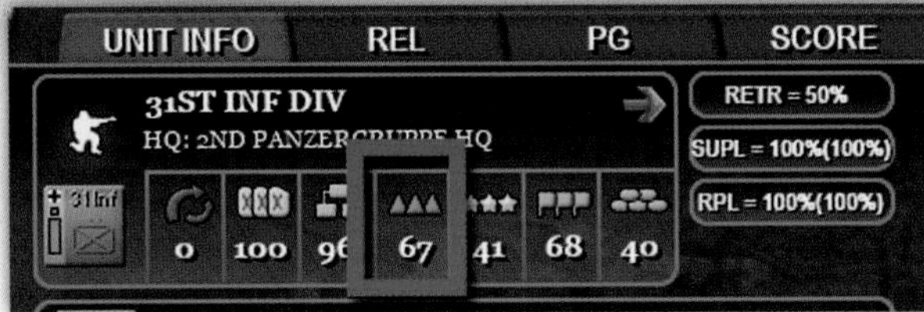
UNIT INFO
REL
PG
SCORE
31ST INF DIV
RETR = 50%
SUPL = 100%(100%)
RPL = 100%(100%)
0
100
67
41
68
40

At the end of the turn their readiness has dropped from 100 to 67 as a result of both combat and movement

UNIT INFO
REL
PG
SCORE
31ST INF DIV
HQ: 2ND PANZERGRUPPE HQ
RETR = 50%
SUPL = 100%(100%)
RPL = 100%(100%)
100
100
98
68
80

It's the beginning of the next turn and the 31st have recovered to 98 readiness points

Why have the 31st only got 98 readiness points? The dropped to 67 due to their activity the previous turn but they are in full supply so would expect to get the full +40 readiness recovery which would boost them up to 100 (actually 107 but it can't go above 100).

It's because they are fatigued after both moving and being engaged in combat the previous turn. They have accumulated one point of fatigue for both and this is taken from the units readiness *after* the recovery due to supply (100 less 2 gives 98).

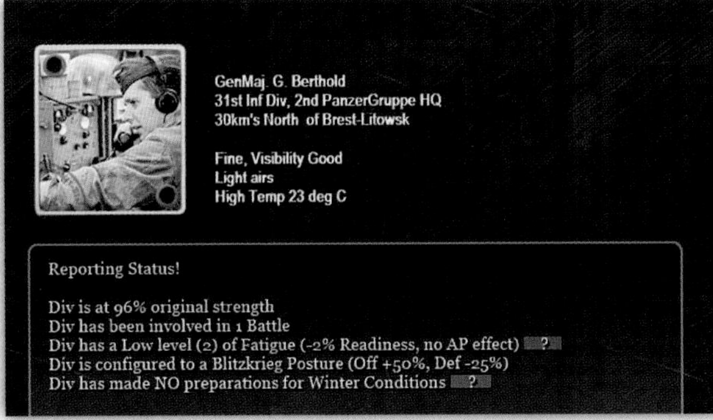
GenMaj. G. Berthold
31st Inf Div, 2nd PanzerGruppe HQ
30km's North of Brest-Litowsk
Fine, Visibility Good
Light airs
High Temp 23 deg C
Reporting Status!
Div is at 96% original strength
Div has been involved in 1 Battle
Div has a Low level (2) of Fatigue (-2% Readiness, no AP effect)
Div is configured to a Blitzkrieg Posture (Off +50%, Def -25%)
Div has made NO preparations for Winter Conditions

GenMaj. Berthold's boys are starting to work up a sweat

For a further example of how readiness and supply interact see 4.14.8 Supply Example.

SUMMARY

- Readiness determines the units Action Point allowance
- Readiness, if low, gives combat penalties, especially if attacking
- Movement and combat lower a unit's readiness
- Readiness will recover +40 each turn if the unit is in Full supply
- Fatigue affects are deducted *after* the recovery from supply
- A unit out of supply will have its readiness drop 40% per turn automatically
- If a unit's supply consumption is less than 100 its ability to recover readiness is affected

5.2.2. INTEGRITY

This shows how much of the units original Order of Battle are still present and it influences the chance of a unit breaking in combat.

It has no direct combat effect other than triggering the chance to break below the threshold shown in the tool tip. Low morale can aggravate the situation and combine to increase the chance of breaking.

The tool tip will show the level at which the unit is prone to breaking at. This varies. Normal Wehrmacht units will break at below 50% whereas for SS units it will be 30%. Romanian units, for example, can break at 60% or below. Refer to the table overleaf.

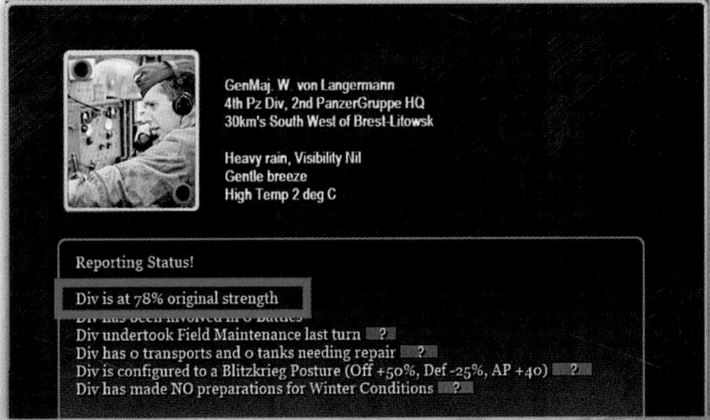
GenMaj. W. von Langermann
4th Pz Div, 2nd PanzerGruppe HQ
30km's South West of Brest-Litowsk
Heavy rain, Visibility Nil
Gentle breeze
High Temp 2 deg C
Reporting Status!
Div is at 78% original strength
Div undertook Field Maintenance last turn
Div has 0 transports and 0 tanks needing repair
Div is configured to a Blitzkrieg Posture (Off +50%, Def -25%, AP +40)
Div has made NO preparations for Winter Conditions

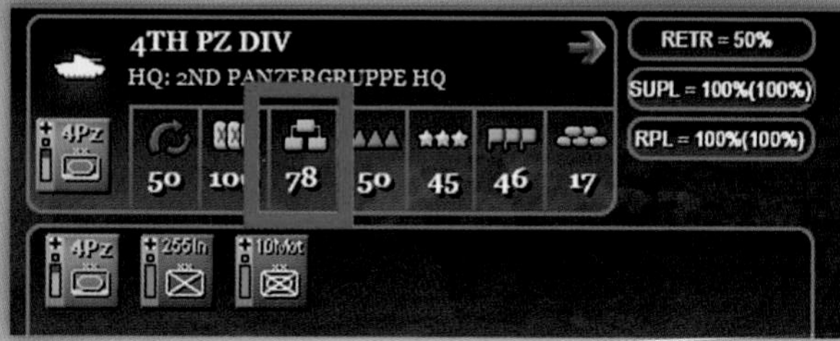

The units reported strength (previous page) corresponds directly with the unit strength (this may vary a little due to how replacements are taken account of).

BREAKING POINTS	
People	May Break if Integrity drop below this %
Wehrmacht (German)	50
SS (German)	30
Finnish	45
Romanian	60
Hungarian	60
Italian	65
Soviet Regulars	40
Soviet Conscripts	40
Siberians	30

Note that the Soviets have relatively low breaking points. While they may have low levels of training and ability (Conscripts) they are defending their homeland and can be expected to fight hard. Likewise they have a high level of morale.

5.2.3. MORALE

Morale is a measure of how well a unit will fight. Morale determines how many casualties a unit can stand before losing cohesion and panicking. A Morale level of 50 means that the unit *may* panic once it has lost 50% of its troops. An even lower Morale level of 25 means that it only has to lose 25% of its troops before it *may* panic. Panic is never certain and even low morale troops can sometimes hold out while taking severe losses.

Different types of units start the campaign with different morale levels. An elite German SS Division is going to have less chance of panicking than a Hungarian Division that has been 'volunteered' by its government to help.

BASE MORALE	
People	Base (starting) Morale
Wehrmacht (German)	60
SS (German)	70
Finnish	60
Romanian	50
Hungarian	50
Italian	50
Soviet Regulars	60
Soviet Conscripts	60
Siberians	70

5.2.3.1. Morale Changes

Units lose morale if they retreat or panic. If they retreat in an orderly manner they lose less than if they panic (automatic 50% drop in morale).

Units gain 10 to 20% morale by successfully taking an enemy hex. The more combat rounds involved the greater the gain (up to a maximum of 20%). Units lose 5 to 10% in morale from taking casualties.

Extreme cold weather can adversely affect morale (see 4.1.5 Weather effects).

5.2.3.2. Morale Recovery

Morale will recover automatically each turn at an amount that is a percentage (5%) of the unit's base

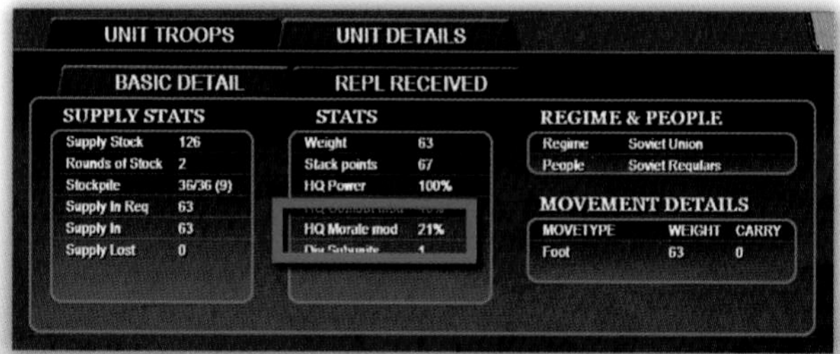

The 'HQ Morale Mod' increases the units morale recovery

morale (see previous table). If its readiness is less than 100 recovery will be slower

Recovery is increased by being within command range and as close as possible to the unit's HQ.

Morale can never increase beyond 100.

The German Officer card 'Inspire' can boost the amount of morale increase per turn (see 6.1.5.8 Officer Cards).

5.2.4. RETREAT STANDING ORDERS

Each unit has a set of standing orders that specify at what point, when engaged in combat, it should consider making an orderly withdrawal (retreat), if it takes more than this level of casualties.

The setting is found in the Unit Information Panel (bottom centre) and you can click on it to toggle through the range of options (25/50/75/100).

The default setting for all units is to retreat once losses exceed 50%.

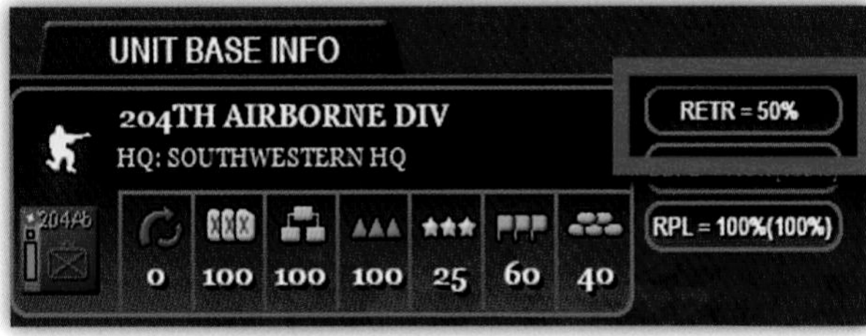

5.2.5. FALLING BACK

There are two possible ways for a unit to fall back in combat. An orderly retreat or a panicked retreat. The former represents a controlled military manoeuvre, the latter an uncontrolled event that can result in excessive casualties.

Both forms of retreat can, under the right circumstances, result in the unit breaking and surrendering.

5.2.6. EXPERIENCE

Is a major combat strength multiplier. The more experience a unit has the better it will fight. A unit with 100% experience will fight 4 times as well in battle as a unit with no experience (0%).

FALLING BACK	
Condition	Criteria and notes
Orderly Retreat	Casualty % drops below Retreat Standing Order threshold Only possible if a viable retreat location is available
Panicked Retreat	Casualty % drops below Morale – 50% chance of Panic If no viable retreat path Morale is doubled for the above If panicked higher losses are suffered in combat
Break & Surrender	Integrity lower than tool tip threshold – chance of surrendering Break test is only made if unit attempting to retreat or panicked Chance of surrender is % > morale If Readiness < 50 then a 25% chance of surrender

5.2.6.1. Eastern Front Academy

Free experience can be earned by green troops that have less than 30 experience (all Soviet units with the exception of the Siberians). They will receive one free experience point per turn as a result of the rapid learning curve forced upon them by the Darwinian environment of 'learn fast or die faster'.

5.2.6.2. Combat Experience

Every time the unit engages in combat its experience can increase. The higher a unit's experience the slower its rate of progression. Less experienced troops tend to benefit faster than veterans.

5.2.7. ENTRENCHMENT

Entrenchment is a combination of how well a unit is dug in and what level of defensive preparations they have made.

Entrenchment levels are calculated at the beginning of the

turn. Moving a unit will see it lose any entrenchment level (it's on the move, not dug in). Keeping a unit in place is the only way to gain this bonus.

Different unit types entrench at different speeds. Infantry can, as you'd expect, dig in relatively fast but not armour.

Each troop type has an allowance of entrenchment points ('entrenchment power' - 40). At the start of each turn these will be spent to entrench the unit further, up to the maximum limit available which is determined by the terrain.

ENTRENCHING

Terrain	Auto Entrench Infantry	Auto Entrench Armour	Maximum Entrench level
Plains	40	0	100
Fields	50	0	100
Woods	60	0	150
Forest	70	0	150
Marsh	40	0	100
Minor City (grey dot)	70	0	150
Major City (red dot)	100	0	200
Low Mountains	85	0	175
Forested Low Mountains	100	0	200
High Mountains	NA	NA	NA
Fortifications	+60	+30	+100
(+60 Armour)			
Snow Conditions	(extra +20)		

Each terrain type has an 'Auto Entrench' value that acts a minimum amount of entrenchment (if the units entrenchment power is less than this the 'auto entrench' value will be used instead, *unless* it is zero in which case the unit can't entrench, e.g Armour, except in a fortified hex).

5.2.7.1. Combat Effect of Entrenchment

Each point of Entrenchment gives a +1% Defensive combat bonus (+44% for the pic of the 17th Panzer Div, above). Different terrain types allow greater or lesser levels of entrenchment.

5.2.7.2. Poor Defensive Preparations

The Soviets had extensive fortifications right along the border at the commencement of the campaign. On the day of the invasion the Germans found a lot of them unmanned, undermanned, or not properly set up and they were easily overcome, presenting little obstacle.

To reflect the Soviet's lack of preparation they incur a 'Defensive Preparations' penalty which affects all units and gradually tapers off after the first turn of the campaign. It serves to lower the entrenchment values of Soviet units.

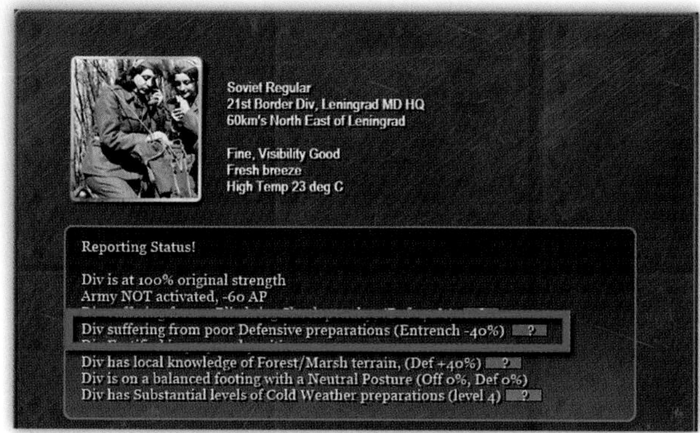

Soviet unit situated in a city are exempt from this penalty (are formidable given their 150 points of entrenchment). Even unprepared, a city offers ample defensive capability to a Division.

5.2.7.3. Fortifications

Fortifications are purpose built infrastructure (bunkers, mines, wire, moats, tank traps etc) with coordinated fire plans and defensive zones that provide significant defensive benefits.

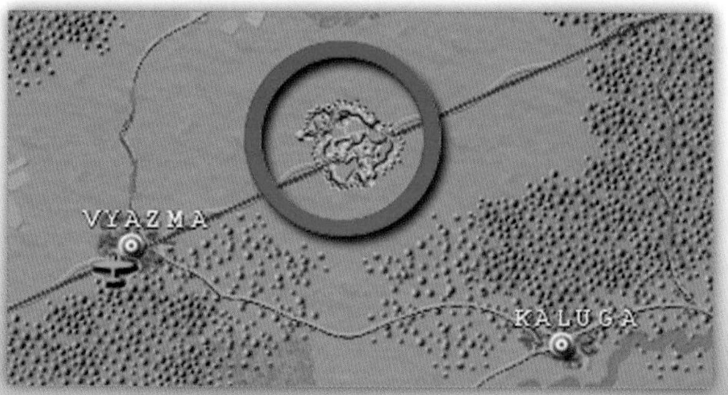

The maximum entrenchment level of any hex with a fortification is increased by +100 points.

Only the Soviets have fortifications and they have freedom to place them in any plains, fields, or forest hex.

For further information see 6.2.5.3 Fortifications.

STAFF ADVICE

A Fortification in forest terrain is a formidable obstacle. Positioned behind a river makes it even stronger.

5.2.7.4. Entrenching Example

The 18th Panzer Division starts the campaign fully entrenched in a plains hex.

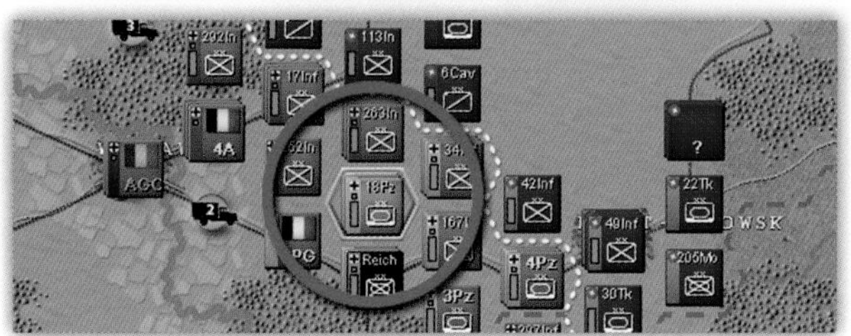

It's entrenchment level is 44. This is an *average* of all the individual troop type entrenchment levels.

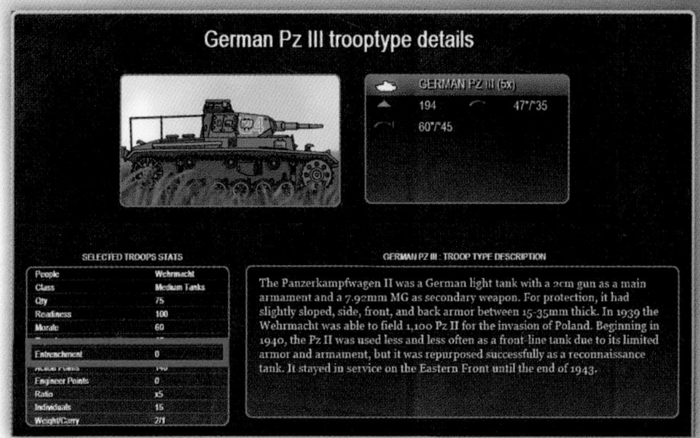

If we clicked on the 'Heavy Infantry' pic (top left in Unit Troops tab) we get a pop-up that tells us that they are fully entrenched at a level of 100 which is the maximum possible for infantry in a plains hex.

Clicking on the 'Panzer Mk III' pic (we could do the same for any of the tanks) has them not entrenched at all (level 0). This is typical of armour.

IN DETAIL

Guns (ATG and artillery) are classed as infantry for entrenchment purposes and any vehicle (tanks, trucks, half tracks) as 'armour'

It's the cumulative average of all the troop types that provides us with the, rather low, 44 Entrenchment level for the Division.

The 18th Panzer fires up and moves deep into enemy territory.

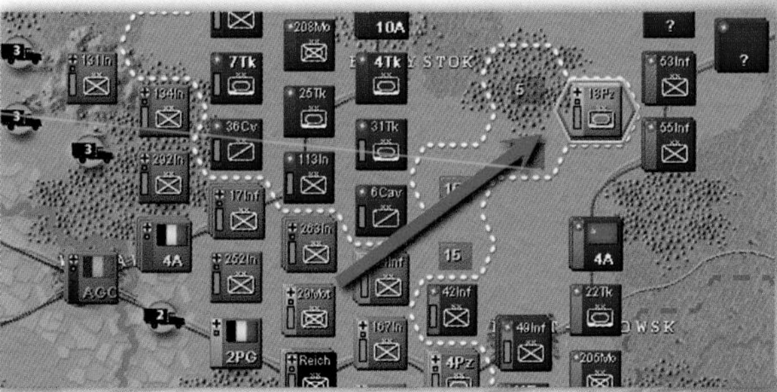

It's entrenchment statistics immediately update.

Its entrenchment level has dropped from 44 to 17. Remember once you move you lose any existing entrenchment level. It's dropped to zero but each troop type has an 'auto-entrench power' of 40 which is put towards digging into its destination hex.

To save on space I've highlighted the entrenchment level of each individual troop type (see above). All the 'infantry' are sitting on 40 which is the value of their 'entrenchment power'. The destination terrain type is 'plains'. This has an auto entrench value (for infantry) of 40 which is used as a minimum level of entrenching (unless it's zero in the case of the armour in which case the troop type can't entrench). If the infantry only had 20 points of entrenching power they would still get the full 40 points worth because of the 'auto entrench' value of the terrain.

The Divisions 17 points of entrenchment is the average of all the individual troop type entrenchment levels.

If the 18th Panzer Division rested for a turn its entrenchment level would increase as all the infantry would add another +40 points (making 80 in total, still below the maximum entrenchment cap for plains of 100). The armour would remain on zero points (can't entrench).

Sit around for a second turn and the 18th Panzer would be fully entrenched. Infantry would be have hit the cap of 100 for plains and armour would still be at zero. Division entrenchment level would be 44 as at the start.

The hex status always shows the amount of ZOC that you are exerting on the hex, not your enemy

SUMMARY

- Entrenchment is the units ability to dig in and prepare defensive positions
- Each point of entrenchment adds +1% defensive bonus in combat
- Units will progressively entrench if they remain stationary
- Each terrain type has a maximum level of entrenchment which can't be exceeded
- Armour can't entrench
- The Soviets get hit with a special entrenchment penalty at the very start (but not if in a city)

5.2.8. ZONES OF CONTROL

ZOC simulates the ability of a unit to exert a degree of control beyond the hex that they are currently in. Each unit has ZOC points proportional to its size. The amount of ZOC points that you are exerting on a hex will be a total of all nearby friendly units (within a 1 hex radius), similarly for the enemy.

You can see the number of ZOC points you have on a hex by clicking on it and inspecting the hex status information (top right).

If you have four times (4X) as many ZOC points on an enemy hex as your enemy, and the enemy has no units in the hex, ownership will change and the border will automatically adjust to show that it is now under your control.

Moving *into* a hex under an enemy zone of control will incur additional movement penalties (10 Action Points, 20 AP if crossing a river at the same time). These are shown on the map in the small transparent boxes.

Enemy units that are hidden by the Fog of War do not exert a ZOC (no movement penalty) in order not to give their presence away.

Units that are out of supply exert no ZOC.

5.2.8.1. Zone of Control Example

It's the start of the campaign and there is an unoccupied, contested, hex in AGC 180 km's east of Bialystok.

The Germans are exerting 340 ZOC points on the hex from all the units within a one hex radius (it's a number's game - the more units the better).

If we hide the units (press '0', press '2' to return) we can see that a number of German controlled hexes have a 10 AP penalty due to adjacent enemy units exerting a Zone of Control over the hexes. This penalty only applies to units that move *into* the hex.

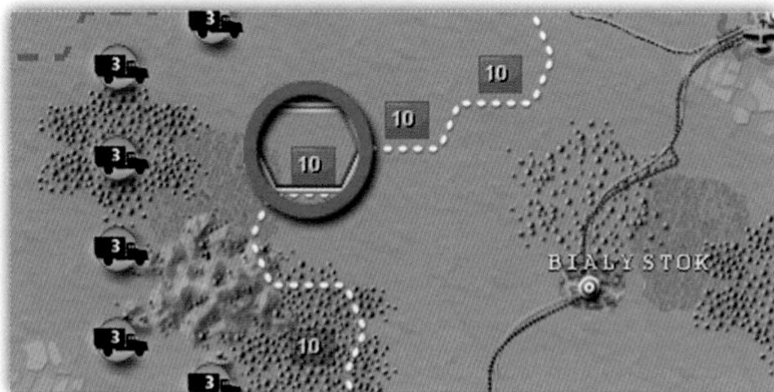

Note that the low mountains hex directly east of the contested hex doesn't have any movement penalty (no transparent box). That's because zone of control only extends one hex from units and there are no enemy units within range

Swapping over to Soviet side we can see that they are exerting 93 ZOC points on the contested, vacant, hex. This is a fair bit less than the Germans but because the Germans haven't got more than four times the Soviet's total the hex remains Soviet controlled.

If the Germans had 500 ZOC points, rather than their 340, they would have the required 4X, or better, and the hex would have flipped to German, at the start of the turn, and the regime border (dotted yellow lines) would have adjusted to reflect this.

Removing the units, again, this time during the Soviet Player's turn, we can see that all the Soviet units have a 10 AP Zone of Control penalty because of the presence of adjacent German units. Note that the contested, vacant, hex also has a 10 AP penalty because there are German units within a one hex radius exerting ZOC over it.

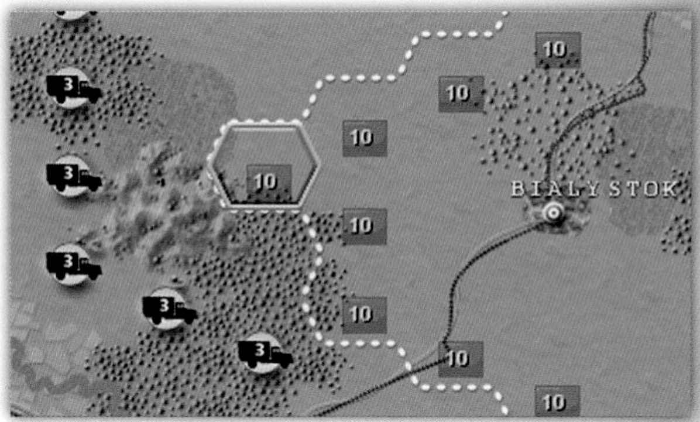

You can mouse over the terrain window, at any time, to determine what's causing the movement penalties (small transparent boxes). Currently it's only due to ZOC but there could be a range of other factors influencing it.

PLAINS (20,38) GERMANY

LANDSCAPE: PLAINS

TROOPTYPE	ATT-MOD	DEF-MOD	A-ENTR	MX-ENTR	CROSS-RIV
INFANTRY	100%	100%	100	100	-
GUNS	100%	100%	100	100	-
MOTORIZED	100%	100%	0	0	-
LIGHT TANKS	100%	100%	0	0	-
MEDIUM TANKS	100%	100%	0	0	-
HEAVY TANKS	100%	100%	0	0	-

MOVETYPE	AP COST	ROAD	RIVER
FOOT	25	-	-
MOTORIZED	15	-	-
CAVALRY	20	-	-
RAIL	NA	-	-
TRACKED	15	-	-
SUPPLY MOVE	10	-	-
IMMOBILE	NA	-	-
RAIL_CAP	NA	-	-

COVER: 0

ZOC PENALTY IN AP = 10

The explanation for movement penalties is always down the bottom of the tool tip

SUMMARY

- Units exert a Zone of Control into adjacent hexes
- The bigger the unit the greater effect it has
- All friendly, adjacent, units combine to exert ZOC over adjacent hexes
- Enemy units do the same and cause a 10 Action Point (AP) penalty (small transparent boxes)
- Crossing a river causes the ZOC penalty to double (20 AP)
- The penalty only applies if a friendly unit moves *into* the hex
- There may be other reasons for the penalty. The terrain window (top centre) mouse over tool tip provides an explanation (down the bottom of the tool tip)
- To gain control ('flip') of an enemy hex it needs to be vacant and you need 4X times the enemy ZOC points
- Enemy units hidden by Fog of War don't exert any ZOC
- Units out of supply can't exert a ZOC

5.2.9. STACKING

There is a limit to how many units can be in a hex together before the benefits of how a higher troop density is outweighed by an over concentration of forces.

If you over stack your troops will be more vulnerable and be less effective in combat. It's possible to over stack both when attacking and defending. Over stacking allows you to apply more combat power but at the cost of a higher casualty rate.

You can see the number of 'Stack Points' you have in a hex by inspecting the hex status (top right).

Stacking points are a function of unit size. The bigger the unit the more stacking points it has. As a rule of thumb the German Divisions are around 70 stacking points each. The Soviets, being weaker, are less.

Stack points spent in a failed attack (in the current turn) carry over for any further attacks in the same hex. These are called 'Battlestack' points (same thing, just named differently to allow them to be easily identified).

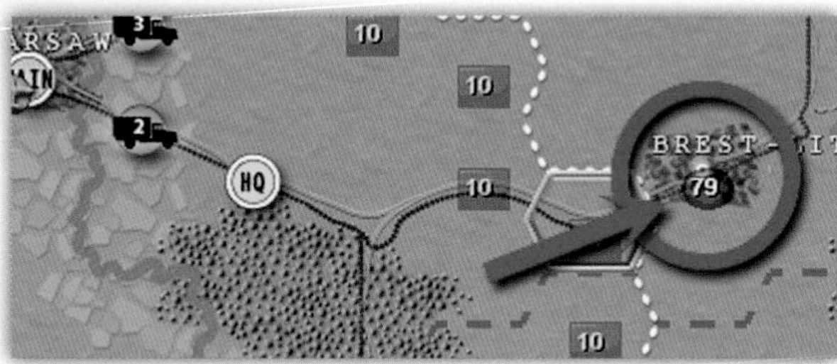

The 4th Panzer (79 stacking points)unwisely attacked Brest-Litowsk and was forced to fall back. The '79' in the black circle is a reminder that any further attacks on Brest-Litowsk are going to have to carry over the previous 79 stacking points and may result in over stacking penalties

Battlestack points are the carry over stacking points from previous battles within the hex. If, for example, you first attacked with 100 stack points of units and lose (irrelevant if you win 'cause you capture the hex). Launching a second attack (same hex) with 75 stack points will result in you having 175 stacking points (the 75 for this attack and the 100 for the previous).

DESIGNER NOTE

Multiple battles can occur in the same hex during a turn. While specific battles have a finite duration and could be accommodated within the games 4 day a turn scale, it's the pre-battle manoeuvring and positioning that multiple battles infer which creates bottlenecks of men and machines in the immediate vicinity. There needs to be some way of reflecting the resultant crowding, hence stacking points carry over.

Over stacking penalties affect combat. The more you over stack the greater the penalty (it's exponential, not linear - watch out!). The following table shows the stacking limits, after which a penalty is incurred.

STACKING LIMITS

Situation	Stacking Limit
Defender	200
Attacking from 2 sides, or less, of the hex	200
Attacking from 3 sides	300
Attacking from 4 sides	400
Attacking from 5 sides	500
Attacking from 6 sides	600

STAFF ADVICE

The more different sides of the target hex you are attacking from, the greater your stacking allowance and the more forces you can effectively use. Attacking from multiple sides has an additional 'Concentric attack' bonus (flanking bonus). Where ever possible aim to attack a hex from as many sides as possible.

Battle stack penalties can be viewed in the terrain window mouse over tool tip.

BREST-LITOWSK (25,43) SOVIET UNION

ROADS PRESENT: HIGHWAY GERMAN (ALL WEATHER)(SW), HIGHWAY RUSSIAN (ALL WEATHER)(NE)
LOCATION PRESENT: MAJOR CITY
LANDSCAPE: URBAN

TROOPTYPE	ATT-MOD	DEF-MOD	A-ENTR	MX-ENTR	CROSS-RIV
INFANTRY	100%	100%	200	200	-
GUNS	20%	60%	200	200	-
MOTORIZED	50%	75%	0	0	-
LIGHT TANKS	50%	75%	0	0	-
MEDIUM TANKS	50%	75%	0	0	-
HEAVY TANKS	50%	75%	0	0	-

MOVETYPE	AP COST	ROAD	RIVER
FOOT	25	20/20	-
MOTORIZED	15	10/10	-
CAVALRY	20	20/20	-
RAIL	NA	1/3	-
TRACKED	15	10/10	-
SUPPLY MOVE	1	1/1	-
IMMOBILE	NA	NA/NA	-
RAIL_CAP	NA	1/3	-

COVER: 50
STRUCTURAL POINTS: 1946 OF 2000, AUTO RECOVER POINTS: 250

REGULAR BATTLESTACK = 79
BATTLE PENALTY IN AP = 8
ZOC PENALTY IN AP = 10
ENEMY TERRAIN PENALTY IN AP = 5

Not only does a battle in a hex carry over stacking points it also creates an additional AP penalty. Successive battles, during the current turn, will only increase this

When initiating an attack you can view the stacking situation in the Unit information display (bottom).

In the example below you can see that Brest-Litowsk is being attacked with 4 Divisions (as a rule of thumb work on no more than 3 per hex). The 377 stacking points includes the 'Battlestack' carryover of 129 points from two previous battles, as can be seen below.

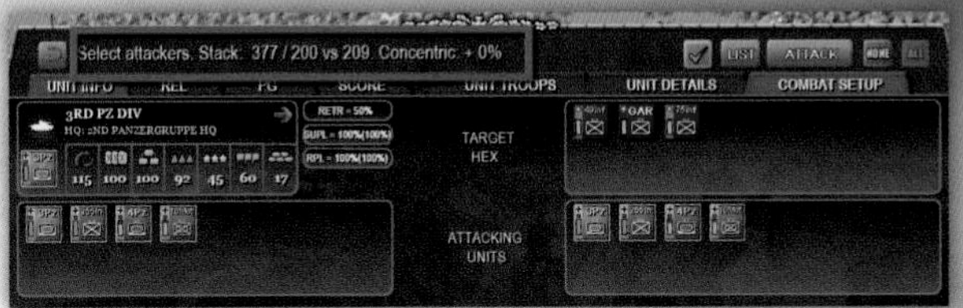

'377/200' tells you that you've got 377 stacking points and your allowance is only 200 (attacking from a single hex) so you can expect over stacking penalties to apply. The Defender is also over stacked (209 versus a universal defensive limit of 200) but only marginally

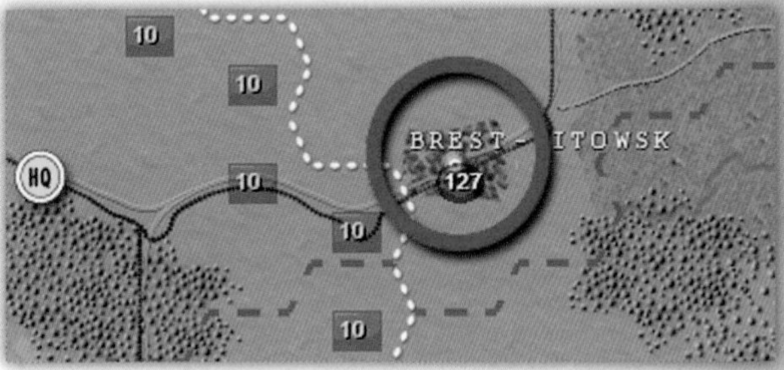

The Battlestack indicator will update after every battle. Compare this to the example given earlier in the topic when only one battle had been fought in Brest-Litowsk

SUMMARY

- Stacking represents the amount of crowding in a hex
- To see how many 'stack points' you have in a hex view the hex status info (top right)
- The bigger the unit the more stack points it will have
- There is a limit to how many units you can launch an attack with (a 'stack of doom' won't work)
- The limit varies depending on the number of hex sides you are attacking from (the more the better)
- Exceeding the stacking limit results in exponential over stacking penalties in combat and higher casualties
- Every time you fight a battle in a hex (and lose) your stacking points carry over to any further battles in the same hex, during the current turn.
- Carry over stacking points are called 'Battle stack points' and are shown visually by a small black circle in the hex
- When launching an attack you can see a summary of the stacking situation in the Unit Display (bottom)

5.2.10. CONCENTRIC ATTACKS

Attacking from multiple hex sides provides combat bonuses. The more directions that a defender is forced to deal with the easier they are to overcome.

Concentric bonuses are halved when units from different HQ's are involved.

CONCENTRIC ATTACK BONUS	
Hex sides attacking from	Offensive Combat bonus
2 sides (adjacent to each other)	10%
2 sides (one hex gap between them)	20%
2 sides (opposite sides)	40%
3 sides (adjacent to each other)	60%
4 sides (adjacent to each other)	80%
4 sides (all other cases)	100%
5 sides	150%
6 sides (unit surrounded)	200%

STAFF ADVICE

Having units from different armies launch simultaneous attacks on the same location is fraught with peril. Coordination and communication can suffer. Aim to have your armies move and fight as a integrated whole as there are significant advantages to be had for doing so.

5.2.11. SURPRISE COMBAT

This happens when you move a unit into a hex containing an unseen enemy unit (you don't have the minimum level of reconnaissance on the hex - see 4.15 Reconnaissance).

STAFF ADVICE

Know your terrain. Send armour into wood or forest only when it's absolutely necessary as they are 50% less combat effective in these circumstances. Soviet forces gain an additional bonus here which only aggravates the situation. If you have no choice but to order your Panzer Divisions into the dark depths of the forest aim to do it along a road (or rail) where the Soviet adverse terrain bonus is halved.

Be very wary of sending armour down roads through marshlands. The Soviet player should be alert for Panzer Divisions attempting to force their way through the Pripet Marshes. There is only one way in and one way out for armour. It's a tank trap

5.2.12. TERRAIN EFFECTS OF COMBAT

The table highlights the combat modifier, due to terrain, on a units when attacking or defending. A modifier of 100% infers no effect (infantry in all conditions) and anything below this reduces the units capability.

TERRAIN COMBAT EFFECTS (%)				
Terrain	Infantry (attack/ defend)	Guns (attack/ defend)	Motorised (attack/ defend)	Armour (attack/ defend)
Plains & Fields	100/100	100/100	100/100	100/100
Woods	100/100	30/60	50/50	60/60
Forest	100/100	30/60	50/50	50/50
Marsh	100/100	60/80	50/50	50/50
Low Mountains	100/100	30/60	50/75	50/75
Minor City (grey dot)	100/100	40/70	50/75	50/75
Major City (red dot)	100/100	20/60	50/75	50/75

The following table applies a flat penalty to units that are attacking directly across a river. The larger the river, the bigger the penalty.

RIVER CROSSING EFFECTS (%)				
River Size	Infantry	Guns (ATG/ Artillery)	Motorised (trucks/ halftracks)	Armour (light/med/ heavy)
Minor river	-20	-30	-30	-30/-35/-40
Medium river	-30	-45	-45	-45/-50/-55
Major river	-40	-60	-60	-60/-65/-70
Volga	-50	-75	-75	-75/-80/-85

Fighting your way over a bridge incurs a flat 50% offensive combat penalty.

STAFF ADVICE

Forcing a crossing over a river is a perilous operation that is bound to result in excessive casualties. On the Eastern front both sides did this as a last resort and would attempt, where ever possible, to find a place to cross that was unopposed.

Soviet forces gain an 'Adverse Terrain' defensive bonus (+40%) when positioned in forest, woods or swamp hexes. The bonus is halved (+20%) if there is a road present (eg. Any rail line) as the Germans were adept at fighting their way up road, even if they were deficient in both doctrine and experience in dealing with difficult terrain.

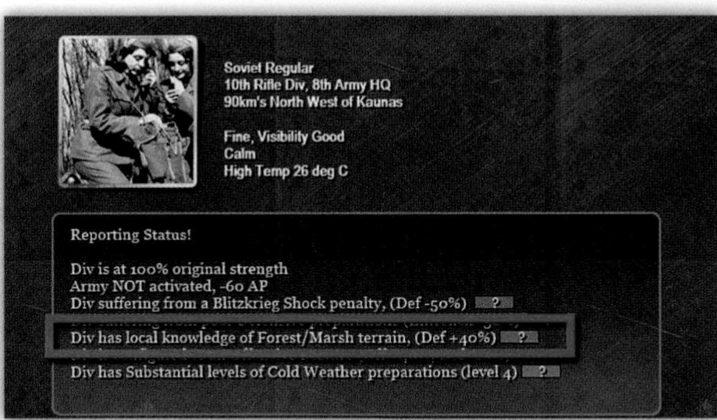

5.2.13. EARLY SOVIET PENALTIES

The Soviets incur two penalties at the start of the campaign - a Blitzkrieg Shock penalty and an Entrenchment (poor defensive preparations) penalty.

Both penalties decrease each turn, after the first, until they are gone.

Soviet units situated within a city (at the start of their turn) are exempt from both penalties.

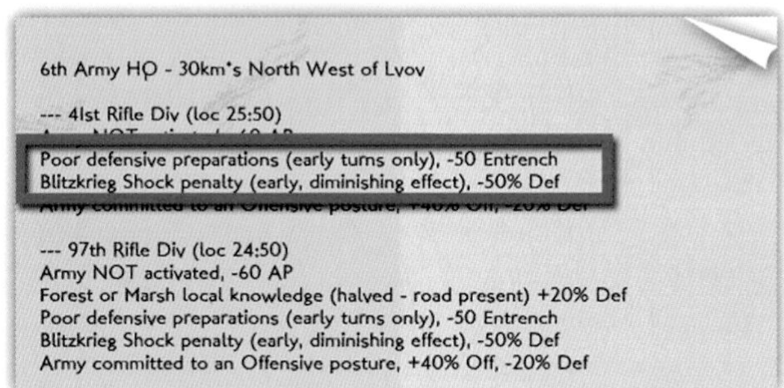

First turn disaster. Nobody was anticipating the invasion. Nobody was prepared (there were a few isolated exceptions)

The AI has a different set of combat penalties (different mechanics) but the overall effect is the same.

EARLY SOVIET PENALTIES		
Turn	Blitzkrieg Shock Penalty (defensive combat penalty)	Entrenchment Penalty (entrenchment level)
First turn of Campaign (round 2)	-50%	-50
Second	-40%	-40
Third	-30%	-30
Fourth	-20%	-20
Fifth	-10%	-10

5.2.14. HQ COMBAT MOD

All Divisions, provided they are within Command Range of their HQ (see 4.13 Command range), gain a combat benefit as a result of their headquarters staff being able to effectively coordinate their individual battles within the bigger picture.

The 'HQ Combat Mod' can be found in the 'Basic Details' tab of the Unit display (bottom right). The size of the modifier (it acts as a bonus) decreases as the Division moves further away from its HQ (like all HQ bonuses, the closer you are, the better).

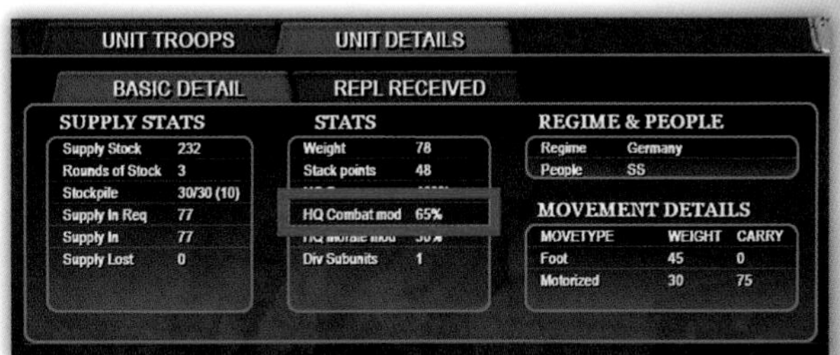

5.3. COMBAT MECHANICS ▶

5.3.1. HOW TO ATTACK

The Attack button appears as soon as you've clicked on an enemy unit

Click on the enemy unit/s that you wish to attack and press the 'Attack' button.

Keyboard Shortcut 'A'

As soon as you do this the unit display (bottom) will change to the 'Combat Setup' and the 'attack unit selection process' will start (you'll need to choose which units will attack).

The 'Defenders' box holds all enemy units within the selected hex. This is who you are attacking and it can't be changed.

To cancel an attack, at any time prior to launching it, either press ESC or the 'Revert' button (top left).

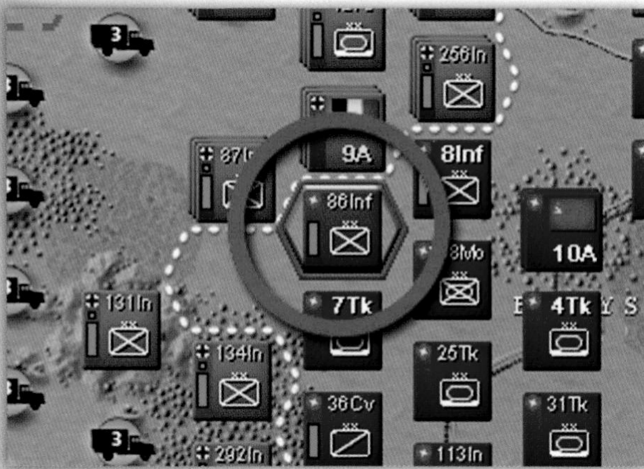

Once you start an attack the target enemy hex is highlighted in red. The attack unit selection process will take over and you won't be able to do anything else, on the map, until the attack is resolved or you cancel it. If you aren't sure if the attack selection process is still happening look for the red highlight. If it's there, it is

Before the attack can proceed you'll need to select at least one friendly unit who will be attacking. These will show up in the 'Attacking Units' box to clearly highlight who will be involved in the combat.

Up on the top left you can see information on stacking and concentric attack bonuses. This will update as you assign units to the assault and is worth keeping an eye on in order to avoid any over stacking penalty (see 5.2.9 Stacking and to maximise the concentric attack bonus see 5.2.10 Concentric attack).

On the bottom left you can click on any of the enemy units to obtain information on them, appropriate to your level of knowledge (see 4.15 Reconnaissance). You can also click on the 'Unit Troops' tab (partially covered in the pic above, it's directly under the red 'Info') to view the unit's composition.

STAFF ADVICE

Don't rush your attacks. What level of entrenchment do the enemy have? What shape are they in? What troops do they have? Throwing too many units into an attack is just as bad as not enough. Apart from the over stacking penalties that may occur, combat burns up action points, lowers readiness and increases fatigue. You want to retain enough units with sufficient movement capability to exploit any gap in the enemy lines that may result.

To add friendly units to the attack, click on any adjacent (it has to be adjacent as there is no ranged combat in DC3 due to its 30km hex scale) friendly hex. The combat setup display will change slightly and your units in the hex will appear down the bottom left (where the defenders were when you had selected their hex).

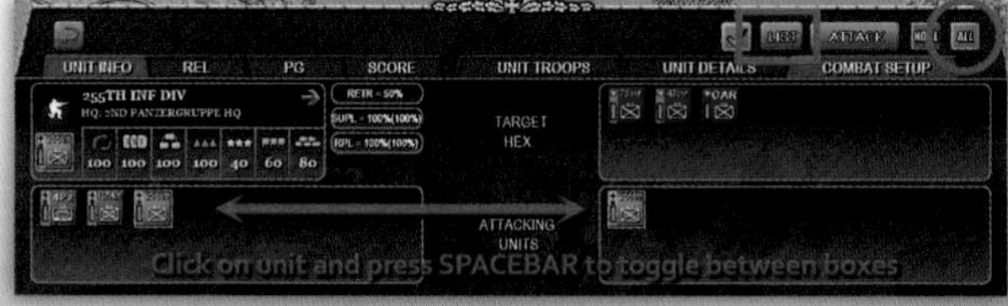

Click on a friendly unit and press SPACEBAR to toggle them in or out of the 'Attacking Units' box on the right. To select units in other hexes do the same. To quickly select every available friendly unit press the 'ALL' button, top right.

Alternatively you could press the 'LIST' button (top right) and a pop-up will appear containing all possible friendly units (from all available adjacent hexes) who are eligible (have enough AP) to join the assault. For big, multi-hex, attacks this is probably the quickest way to do it.

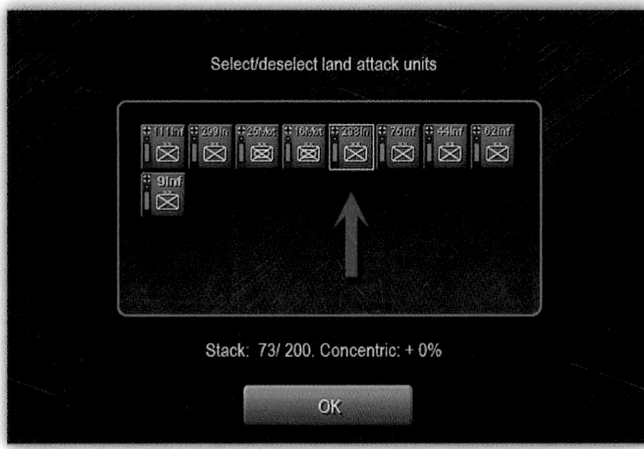

Click on the units you want and press 'OK'(or press SPACEBAR). You can toggle units on or off by clicking on them. In the pic above the only unit that has been selected is the 293rd Infantry (arrowed). Note the white highlight around the counter

A further advantage of the list box is that each unit has a handy mouse over tool tip and a dynamic summary of your stacking situation and concentric bonuses is present.

10th Mot Inf Div

7000x German Hvy Infantry, 750x German Trucks, 20x German 37mm ATG, 30x German 50mm ATG, 20x German 75mm LeIG, 30x German 105mm LeFH
Average Readiness: 100

Once you're happy with you selections, either press the 'Attack' button or press SPACEBAR to initiate the attack.

The point of no return. The assault has been ordered and will now be carried out

STAFF ADVICE

Launching an attack is pretty easy. Select an enemy hex and press 'A'. From here on in a few clicks and liberal use of the SPACEBAR will sort it out and launch the attack. For big attacks use the 'List' button. For a 'don't bother me' approach, press 'All'. Remember you can always press ESC to cancel the attack if needed.

5.3.2. COMBAT RESOLUTION

Once an attack is launched the Combat Screen will appear.

There is a fair bit of information here. At the top is the number of combat rounds the battle has taken. The longer the duration of combat (number of rounds) the more the effects on both sides.

While these varying and affect a wide range of game mechanics, common sense is the best guide. Imagine yourself amid the stress of a combat environment. The longer you spend in this environment the more ammunition you'll expend, the more worn out you'll be and the less likely it is that you'll have the energy to do much else at the end of it.

The Overall Result is also shown at the top. Did the attack succeed or fail? In the case above the result was inconclusive because the attackers spent fifteen combat rounds (about the maximum) and ran out of action points before a decision was reached.

Individual unit outcomes can be see next to each unit counter. These are coloured coded with a general scheme of green (good) - yellow - orange - red (bad).

The Attackers are always on the left, the Defenders on the Right. In the example above all three Soviet defenders stood their ground (green). Of the two German attackers the first held position but the second retreated. The colours will have a text overlay to indicate what occurred (like the 'Retreated' over the yellow bar on the left). Enemy units may not give out full information due to Fog of War but the casualties and outcomes will always be correct.

The small icons show all the troop types in an individual unit. The totals, at the start of combat, are shown in the white boxes and the casualties incurred, in the red boxes. The highlighted example, above, has the first German unit with 44 Infantry troop types (to make the numbers legible the internal, engine, numbers of troop types are used, not the more realistic game numbers which are much larger) at the start has suffered 6 Infantry casualties.

Note the separate section here. The red boxes are casualties and the white boxes are individuals that have retreated. In the above, the top Soviet 75th Rifle Division had 42 Infantry at the start of combat, lost 2 (red box) of them and had 6 retreat (white box)

IN DETAIL

Internally each unit has a number of troop types, eg. 44 Infantry. These are multiplied by a set ratio to produce the game numbers that you see displayed in various reports and screens. For infantry the ratio is 200 which means the 44 internal infantry troop types would translate to 8800 actual infantry. It's the internal numbers that are used for combat, and all other, game calculations. You can see what ratio is used by each troop type by clicking on their picture in the unit display and having a look at the stats in the left of the window that pops up. Ratio is third from the bottom.

The Combat Screen display the troop types as icons rather than numbers and that's controlled via the Preferences tab. Toggle 'Combat Numbers' on or off.

To get a more detailed (extremely!) picture of the internal workings of the combat process, press the 'Detail' button on the Combat Screen. Another

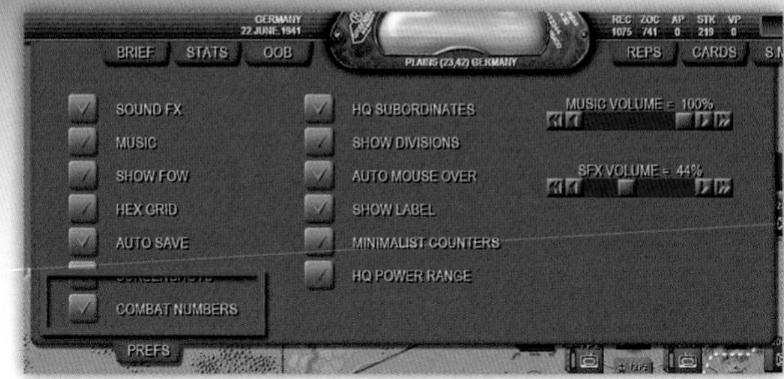

window will appear and by clicking on various pieces of information you can drill right down into the nitty gritty world of combat. Don't forget to duck.

5.3.3. HOW COMBAT WORKS

Once combat commences all troop types are treated as individuals (see the 'in detail' explanation of this in 5.3.2 Combat Resolution).

The individual troop types fight it out over a number of combat rounds (think of a boxing match) with each round costing Action Points. Once an attacking unit runs out of AP, it ceases combat.

IN DETAIL

Each combat round costs 10 AP. The minimal total cost of a battle is the cost to move into the hex.

STAFF ADVICE

The more Action points a unit has prior to combat the more effective it is likely to be and the greater chance of it carrying the day (all other considerations being equal).

Mechanically each attacker (individual troop type) has an attack score and this is compared to the defenders (once again an individual troop type) hit point score. If they are equal there is a 50% chance for the attacker to score a hit. The probability of a hit scales up or down in proportion to the difference between the attacker's 'attack score' and the defenders 'hit points'. If the attacker has twice as big a score then there is a 75% chance to hit, if half the defender's hit points then it would be only a 25% chance.

The 'attack score' depends on which troop type is attacking what other troop type. Armour, for example, have different scores versus infantry compared to other armour. Both attack scores and hit points are modified by a whole range of factors. For further information on individual factors refer to the relevant section in the manual.

COMBAT MODIFIERS

Modifier	Attacker (attack score)	Defender (attack score)	Attacker Hit points	Defender Hit points	Who does it affect
Over Stacking	Yes (small effect)	Yes (small effect)	Yes (big effect)	Yes (big effect)	Everybody either attacking or defending
Concentric Bonus	Yes				Everybody attacking
Low Readiness	Yes (big effect)	Yes (small effect)	Yes (small effect)	Yes (small effect)	Specific Unit
Low Supply Consumption	Yes	Yes	Yes	Yes	Specific Unit
Experience	Yes	Yes	Yes	Yes	Specific Unit
AI Combat bonus	Yes	Yes	Yes	Yes	All AI units either attacking or defending
Terrain	Yes	Yes			Specific Unit
HQ Combat Mod	Yes	Yes			Everybody either attacking or defending
Ttoop type Modifiers (red & blue boxes on pictures)	Yes	Yes			Specific Unit
Surprise Combat		Yes			Everybody either attacking or defending
Entrenchment				Yes	Specific Unit

STAFF ADVICE

There are a lot of potential modifiers but the important ones are the modifiers that affect both the attack score and the hit points at the same time. These have the greatest influence.

Combat proceeds with individual attackers hammering into individual defenders at which point the defenders counter attack the attackers (using the Defenders 'attack score' and the Attackers 'hit points'). A round of combat has all eligible troop types attacking and all eligible defender troop types counter attacking and continues on until the individuals (and units) run out of Action points or a result is reached.

Results are variations of one side, or the other, falling back or being destroyed.

There are two possible ways for a unit to fall back in combat. An orderly retreat or a panicked retreat. The former represents a controlled military manoeuvre, the latter an uncontrolled event that can result in excessive casualties.

Both forms of retreat can, under the right circumstances, result in the unit breaking and surrendering.

FALLING BACK	
Condition	Criteria and notes
Orderly Retreat	Casualty % drops below Retreat Standing Order threshold Only possible if a viable retreat location is available
Panicked Retreat	Casualty % drops below Morale – 50% chance of Panic If no viable retreat path Morale is doubled for the above If panicked higher losses are suffered in combat
Break & Surrender	Integrity lower than tool tip threshold – chance of surrendering Break test is only made if unit attempting to retreat or panicked Chance of surrender is % > morale If Readiness < 50 then a 25% chance of surrender

STAFF ADVICE

Be careful to avoid placing a unit where it doesn't have a viable retreat path as any 'fall back' result, in this situation, will result in the loss of the unit. Remember that armour can only enter, or leave, a marsh hex via a road. Conversely, to ensure the destruction of a unit, surround it as it will have nowhere to retreat to.

5.3.4. COMBAT DETAILS

For those that would like to peer under the hood this section provides a quick run down on the Combat Detail display (press the 'Detail Tab' on the Combat Screen). It's entirely optional and can be safely ignored unless you have a need to know.

As befits the 'down-in-the-trenches' viewpoint, the Combat Details screen makes no attempt at offering you a comfortable chair and a biscuit. You're on your own, sloshing around in the mud and snow.

Press 'Back', or ESC, to exit when you've had enough

5.3.4.1. Combat Rounds

Combat lasts for a number of combat rounds. Here (top left) you can select which combat round you'd like to view.

5.3.4.2. Units Box

Multiple units can fight in combat. Here (left centre) you can select a unit and see what happened to it during the chosen combat round.

5.3.4.3. Unit Reports Box

Here all the things that happened to the selected unit, in the selected combat round, is shown. You can chose which report you would like information on.

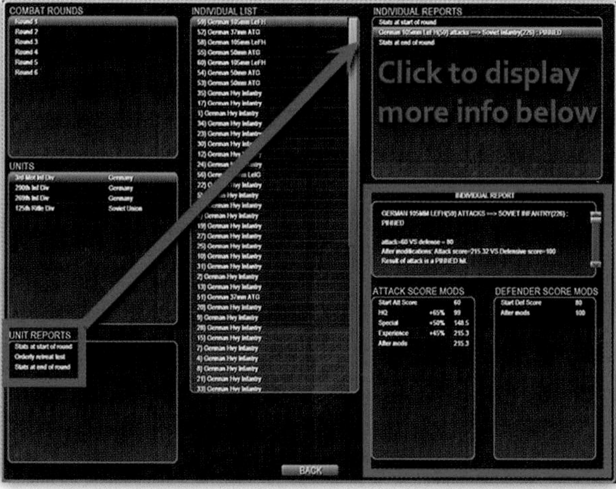

Having clicked on a general report (bottom left) you can then select any item in the Individual Reports section (top right) by clicking on it. Depending on what report you've chosen the screen below (bottom right) will change to display the relevant information.

5.3.4.4. Individual List Box

You've selected a unit ('Units' box, left centre) and all the individual troop types are displayed in the List box. Click on any of them and you'll receive an updated list of reports in the 'Individual Reports' box (top right) which, in turn, can be clicked on to display dynamic information (bottom right).

5.3.4.5. Individual Reports Box

Click on any of these to get dynamic information in the bottom right screen area. The display of information will vary depending on the type of report you've selected.

5.3.4.6. Enemy Units

If Fog of War has been selected the information you receive on enemy units will be filtered accordingly.

5.3.5. BATTLE REPORTS

Every time you authorise an assault (instigate an attack) or are attacked by the enemy, a battle report is generated the following turn based on what happened at the time.

Battle reports are shown for the German Player only. The Soviets are too busy coping with a rampant invader to worry about keeping their paperwork up to date.

The information presented is an accurate representation of the battle and very little of it is randomly generated. Many different factors are taken into account. The reports occur as a direct result of actions that you have initiated.

As an example, the Das Reich Motorised Divison, 2nd Panzergruppe, will be ordered to assault the fortified city of Brest-Litowsk, along the main highway, in mud conditions.

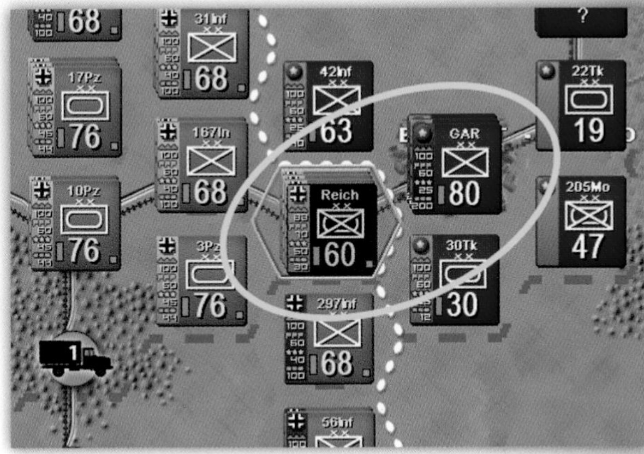

The battle, as you'd expect, was an exercise in futility with SS-Obergruppenfuhrer Paul Hausser having to contend with heavy rain, mud and nil visibility.

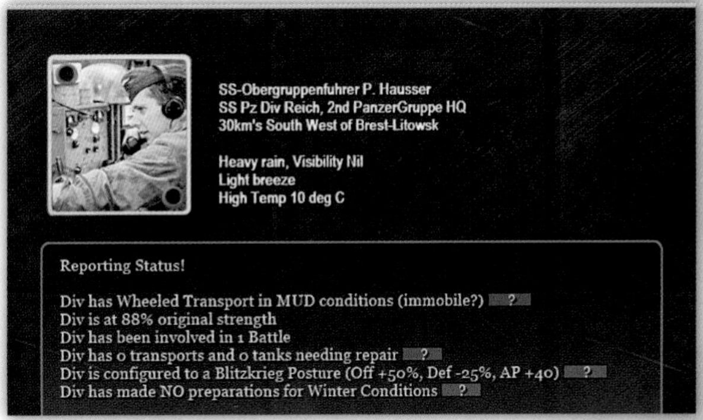

Repulsed with heavy losses

By the following turn your staff will have collated battle reports from all three theatres.

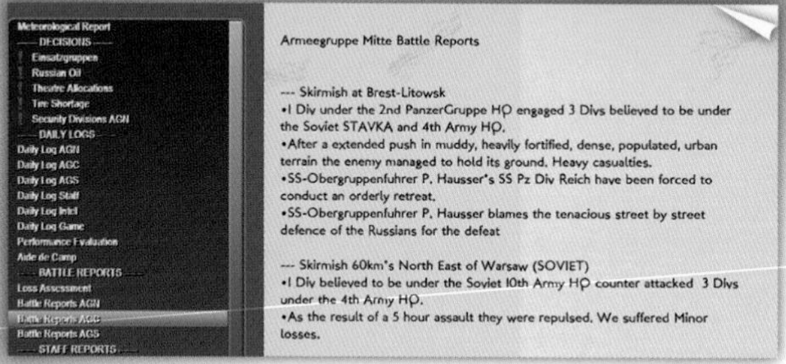

You can see that Obergruppenfuhrer Hausser has had the good grace not to blame higher authority for such a foolish order. Other commanders may be more forthright.

DESIGNER NOTE

Each time there is a failed assault the commander in question will point their finger at what they consider to be the cause. Commanders vary in how they approach this but their reason will always be appropriate to the situation.

The other report was for a minor skirmish (if it's only a single unit involved on your side it's considered a skirmish, more than one and it's a battle) nearby where the enemy counter attacked. You can tell that it was an attack launched in the enemy turn by the 'SOVIET' tag in the header.

Battle reports are there for purposes of immersion. Your Theatre Commanders are also reading the reports, prior to them being sent to your headquarters, and on occasion will add a note to the bottom of a report indicating that an issue has arisen.

These can be easily seen by the yellow tool tips within the reports and, at some point in the future, a Division Event will be generated where you will be required to resolve whatever issue it is involving the Division in question.

For more information see 4.10.7.3 Division Events.

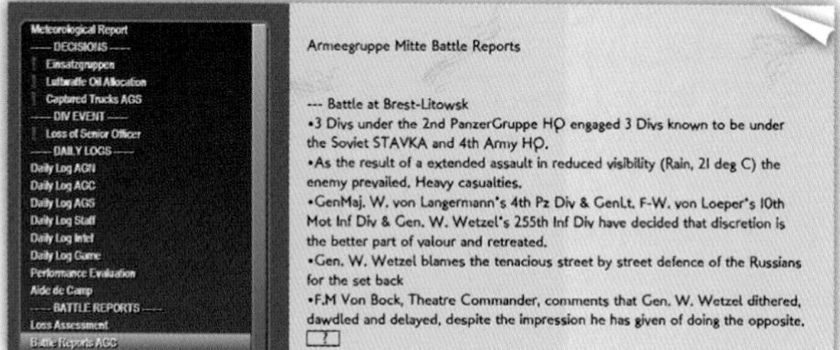

F.M Von Bock, the Theatre Commander, has appended a note to the report (indicated by the yellow tool tip)

6. COMMAND

6.1. GERMAN COMMAND ▶

6.1.1. COMMAND FOCUS

Within each theatre you can choose a single Army, or Panzergruppe, to receive preferential staff, resource, logistical and specialist battalion allocations.

You can instruct your theatre commander's to Focus on a particular Army or Panzergruppe. A theatre commander will always be willing to apply their command Focus on to an Army under their command but will only do so for a Panzergruppe if you have a positive relationship with them.

DESIGNER NOTE

Historically there was an ongoing conflict between the new school Panzergruppe commanders and the old school, WW1, infantry-centric commanders. When you issue a 'Command Focus' order you are asking your subordinate, the theatre commander, to carry out your instructions. He will do so but if you have a negative relationship level with him he'll find ways to NOT provide the required support to a Panzergruppe due to his reluctance to have a hot headed Panzergruppe commander charge off and extend the flanks that he, the theatre commander, is responsible for. Subordinates are good at finding creative ways of not carrying out your orders if they don't want to.

Daily Summary AG NORTH 22 . June . 1941

--- Command
•The Finnish Gov't has NOT agreed to going beyond the border [?]
•F.M von Leeb, AGN, is willing to consider new ideas (Rel +ve) [?]
•F.M von Leeb currently has not determined a Command Focus [?]
•A Superb (+50) relationship with F.M von Leeb, Kdt. THEATRE, has 1 subordinate HQ experiencing Command Bonuses [?] [?]

F.M Von Leeb has a good relationship with you and is willing to consider new fangled ideas

Your Daily Theatre Logs will highlight whether your theatre commander is willing to consider a Panzergruppe.

Daily Summary AG CENTRE 22 . June . 1941

--- Command
•F.M von Bock, AGC, retains his old school thinking (Rel -ve) [?]
•F.M von Bock currently has not determined a Command Focus [?]
•A Terrible (-50) relationship with F.M von Bock, Kdt. THEATRE, has 3 subordinate HQ's experiencing Command Penalties [?] [?]

F.M Von Bock isn't being so accommodating. He'd prefer to stick to the old ways, thank you very much

Your Aide de Camp report will remind you if it's possible to apply focus and you haven't already done so.

--- Focus
•AGN: You need to decide who has Command Focus (Card) [?]
•AGC: You need to decide who has Command Focus (Card)
•AGS: You need to decide who has Command Focus (Card)

It's the start of the campaign and it's to your advantage to apply focus

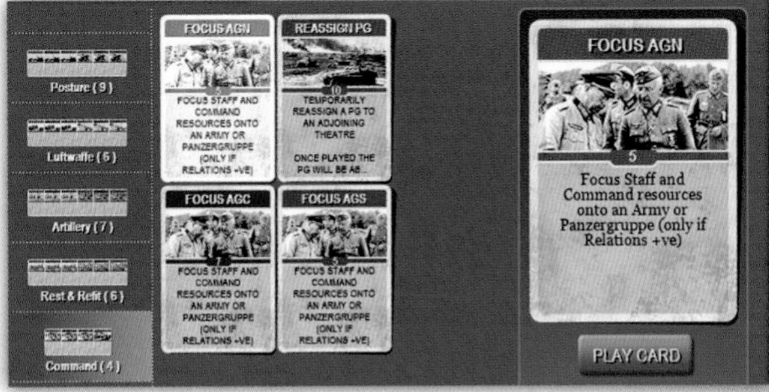

The cards have dynamic text and will highlight if anybody already has focus. In this case it's the start of the campaign and it's a clean slate

To order your theatre commander to apply their Focus, play a 'Focus' Action Card onto the relevant HQ within the theatre.

By focusing on a particular Army, or Panzergruppe, within a theatre a set of Officer Action cards will become available for the HQ that has focus providing enhanced tactical options.

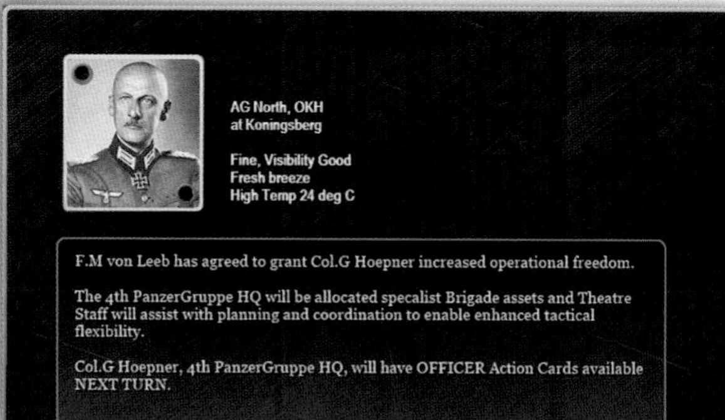

AG North, OKH
at Koningsberg
Fine, Visibility Good
Fresh breeze
High Temp 24 deg C
F.M von Leeb has agreed to grant Col.G Hoepner increased operational freedom.
The 4th PanzerGruppe HQ will be allocated specalist Brigade assets and Theatre Staff will assist with planning and coordination to enable enhanced tactical flexibility.
Col.G Hoepner, 4th PanzerGruppe HQ, will have OFFICER Action Cards available NEXT TURN.

Col.G Hoepner's 4th Panzergruppe has benefited from F.M Von Leebs willingness to focus staff and specialist resources on them

The following turn after focus has been granted you can click on the relevant HQ and make use of the provided Officer Cards. See 6.1.5.8 Officer Cards but the short version is only that one card can be in use at a time and, once played, it remains in place automatically until you change it. The traits of the HQ commander influence the effectiveness of the card.

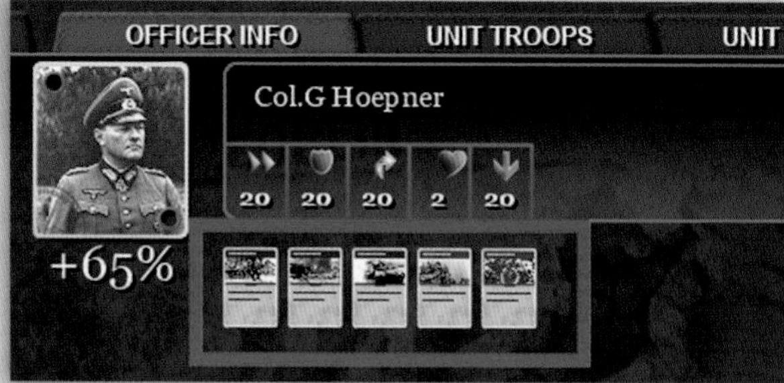

The posture of the HQ determines the type of cards that will be available for use

If you have ordered your theatre commander to focus on a Panzergruppe he will automatically withdraw his focus if your relationship turns negative (goes below zero). You'll receive notification of this in your Daily Theatre Log and your Aide de Camp report.

--- Focus
•AGS: You need to decide who has Command Focus (Card) [?]
•AGN 4th PanzerGruppe HQ, AGC 9th Army HQ [?]

Your Aide de Camp will keep you up to date with your Command Focus status

STAFF ADVICE

Your Panzergruppes are the tip of the spear. Where possible you want your theatre commanders to focus on them so that your Panzergruppe commanders can access the benefits of the Officer cards. You'll need good relations with your theatre commanders and, once they are focused on a Panzergruppe, you'll need to keep them positive.

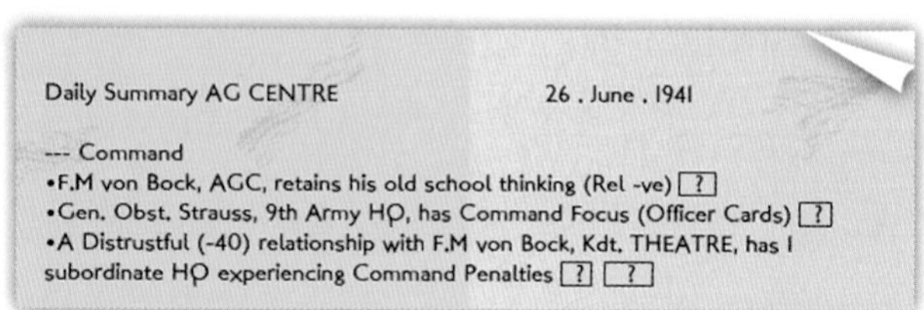
Daily Summary AG CENTRE 26 . June . 1941

--- Command
•F.M von Bock, AGC, retains his old school thinking (Rel -ve) [?]
•Gen. Obst. Strauss, 9th Army HQ, has Command Focus (Officer Cards) [?]
•A Distrustful (-40) relationship with F.M von Bock, Kdt. THEATRE, has I subordinate HQ experiencing Command Penalties [?] [?]

With F.M Von Bock it's currently Infantry, Infantry, Infantry. He's assisting Gen.Obst. Strauss's 9th Army and making it clear that you can forget about him favouring a Panzergruppe until such times as your relationship improves

COMMAND FOCUS

Icon	Focus?	Relationship with Theatre Commander
UP arrow	Panzergruppe currently HAS FOCUS	Positive
SIDE arrow	Not applicable	Not applicable
DOWN arrow	Panzergruppe COULD have focus but currently doesn't.	Positive
CROSS	Panzergruppe CAN'T have focus	Negative

There are a number of ways, apart from your Daily Theatre Logs, to quickly stay on top of your Command Focus status. The special 'Relationship'

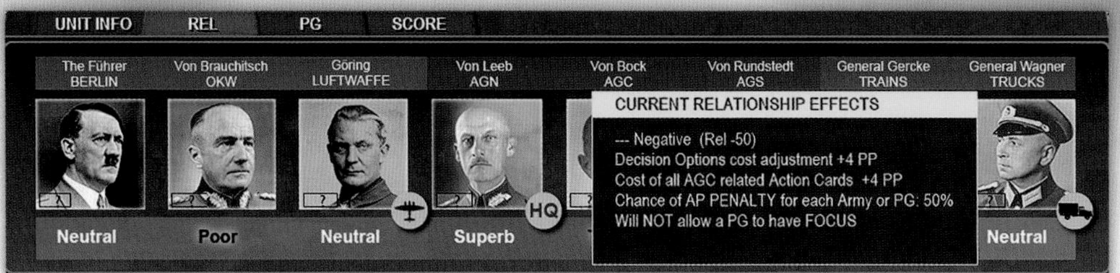

F.M Von Leeb has a superb relationship with you and will happily do as you ask but F.M Von Bock (the highlighted tool tip) is very angry. Guderian' 2nd & Hoth's 3rd Panzergruppes, in AGC, will have to do without the benefits of command focus for the foreseeable future

tab (bottom centre) will let you determine if a theatre commander is willing to provide focus to your Panzergruppes, or not.

The special 'Panzergruppe' tab (bottom centre) will give an 'at a glance' indication based on the following criteria ('Command Focus' table, above, and the example, below).

ASK YOUR STAFF

- Why weren't arrangements in place for Command Focus right from the start of the campaign?'
  The initial invasion (first couple of days) required the use of most of the specialist battalion resources and staff time that were available to theatre commands. You are able to issue orders for their reassignment to a particular Army, or Panzergruppe, on the first turn but it will take a little time (one turn) before they are released from their invasion obligations and are able to comply. Don't forget they are contributing to the 'Blitzkrieg Shock Penalty' (see 5.2.13 Early Soviet Penalties) that affects all Soviet forces, especially on turn one.

SUMMARY

- Focus directs staff and specialist resources at an HQ
- An HQ with Focus is able to access a set of Officer Cards that provide bonuses
- Only one Army or Panzergruppe within each theatre can have Focus at a time
- Once granted, it remains in place automatically.
- It takes a turn for Focus to come into effect (Officer cards appear the turn after you order Focus)
- A theatre commander will consider giving Focus to a Panzergruppe only if you have a positive relationship.
- If a Panzergruppe has Focus you must retain a positive relationship with your theatre commander otherwise your Panzergruppe will lose their Focus.
- Your Daily Theatre Logs, Aide de Camp report and the Relationship & Panzergruppe special tabs all provide information on your Command Focus status.

See also 6.1.5.8 Officer Cards and 4.8.1 German Characters.

This is a rather grim situation. Both theatre commanders in AGS and AGC are firmly against giving focus to a Panzergruppe. Only Colonel G. Hoepner's 4th Panzergruppe in AGN has any hope (Down Arrow - Command Focus possible).

6.1.2. PANZERGRUPPES

These were army level commands that consisted of two or three corps. They were made up of Panzer and motorised infantry Divisions (both termed 'Fast' Divisions compared to the 'Slow' Infantry only Divisions). Prior to Operation Barbarossa the Germans made a significant effort to have their Panzergruppes fully motorised but there weren't enough trucks, or half tracks, to do so fully and they had normal infantry Divisions as part of their formations.

A Panzergruppe HQ is the equivalent of an Army HQ.

There are four Panzergruppes (all theatres have one but AGC has two) and they form the hard hitting 'punch' of the Wehrmacht.

Panzer and Motorised 'Fast' Divisions are *only* found in Panzergruppes. Fast Divisions require fuel and the main aim of each theatre's logistical pipeline is to get sufficient fuel (via train and truck columns) from the Main Depots (back in Poland) to the Panzergruppe HQ's where it can be used.

Panzergruppes can benefit from High Octane Fuel (Action cards) as a result of a decision (see 6.1.3.8 High Octane fuel).

Hitler can, depending on your chosen strategy, interfere with the day to day operations of the Panzergruppes (see 4.8.1.7 Hitler Interference).

Panzergruppes have their own tab (bottom centre) which provides a detailed status summary of all four Panzergruppes (see 3.6.2.1 Panzergruppe). This provides the most up-to-date information. Dynamic tool tips (found on the commander portraits) provide even more information.

The Panzergruppe summary report is compiled by your staff at the beginning of each turn and provides an overview of Panzergruppe and fuel status.

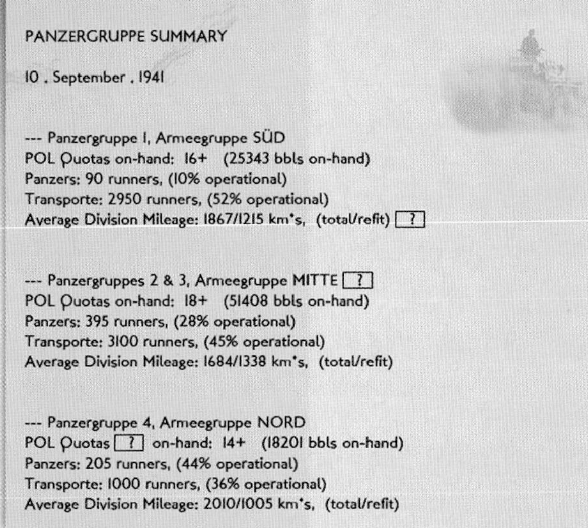
PANZERGRUPPE SUMMARY

10 . September . 1941

--- Panzergruppe I, Armeegruppe SÜD
POL Quotas on-hand: 16+ (25343 bbls on-hand)
Panzers: 90 runners, (10% operational)
Transporte: 2950 runners, (52% operational)
Average Division Mileage: 1867/1215 km's, (total/refit) [?]

--- Panzergruppes 2 & 3, Armeegruppe MITTE [?]
POL Quotas on-hand: 18+ (51408 bbls on-hand)
Panzers: 395 runners, (28% operational)
Transporte: 3100 runners, (45% operational)
Average Division Mileage: 1684/1338 km's, (total/refit)

--- Panzergruppe 4, Armeegruppe NORD
POL Quotas [?] on-hand: 14+ (18201 bbls on-hand)
Panzers: 205 runners, (44% operational)
Transporte: 1000 runners, (36% operational)
Average Division Mileage: 2010/1005 km's, (total/refit)

Mileage is accumulating. A refit beckons

STAFF ADVICE

Panzer Divisions, the tip of the spear, will gradually lose tanks over time. You can arrest their decline, to an extent, by ordering refits to recover broken down vehicles but the number of active 'runners' within a Division will inevitably fall. Directly assaulting cities, especially fortified cities, can be costly in tanks.

As the German Player you have to take the long view and aim to preserve your diminishing pool of armour for as long as possible. Replacements won't be enough. Reckless use of your Panzer Divisions will find you at the gates of Moscow with a blunt and broken spear.

6.1.2.1. Changing Theatres

Panzergruppes can be reassigned to an adjacent theatre. Only one Panzergruppe can be reassigned at a time. Armies can't be reassigned, only Panzergruppes.

A Panzergruppe can be reassigned only if the Führer authorises it which he will do provided your relationship with him is positive.

It's well into the campaign and there is a severe shortage of Panzers

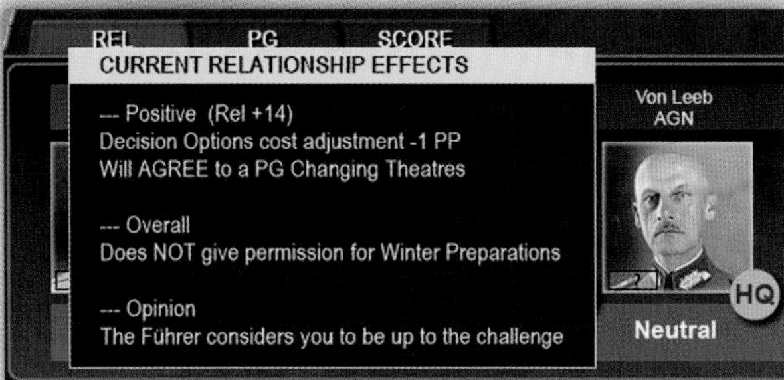

The tool tip for Hitler in the Relationship tab (bottom centre)will let you know his views on a Panzergruppe being able to change theatres

--- Organisation and Planning
• 2000 bbls of fuel expended to support PG Blitzkrieg Posture [?]
• The Führer is willing to consider alternative PG dispositions [?]

The Daily Theatre Logs, under the 'Organisation and Planning' section, also keep you informed

Reassignment is straightforward. Play the 'Reassign PG' Action card on any of the four Panzergruppes. The card will only be available if your relationship with Hitler is positive.

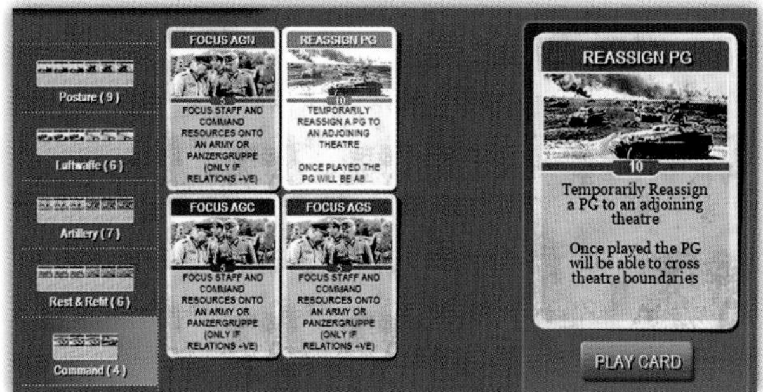

The card is found in the 'Command' category

Once played a confirmation message from the Panzergruppe Commander will display to indicate that your orders have been received and understood.

Once authorised, all subordinate Divisions will be free to cross borders and will not incur a violation penalty. They will show this when asked to Report Status!

A Panzergruppe, once reassigned, has no obligation to move into an adjacent theatre. No penalty will be incurred if the reassignment isn't used. There is no limit on how long a Panzergruppe can be reassigned but, as only one Panzergruppe can have this at a time, no other Panzergruppe will be able to obtain authorisation while another already has it.

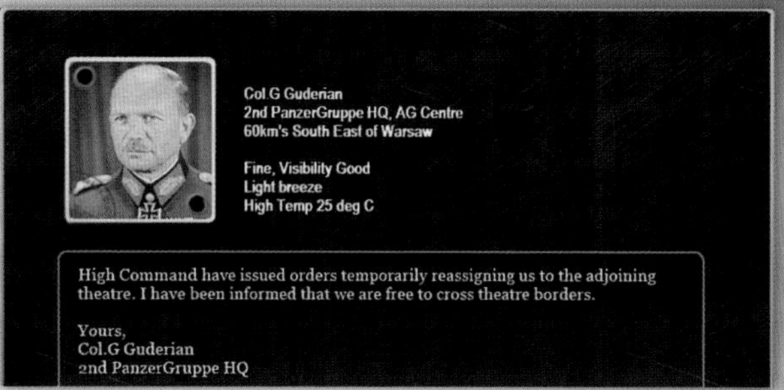

A Panzergruppe, once reassigned, can cross ANY theatre border, not just the nearest

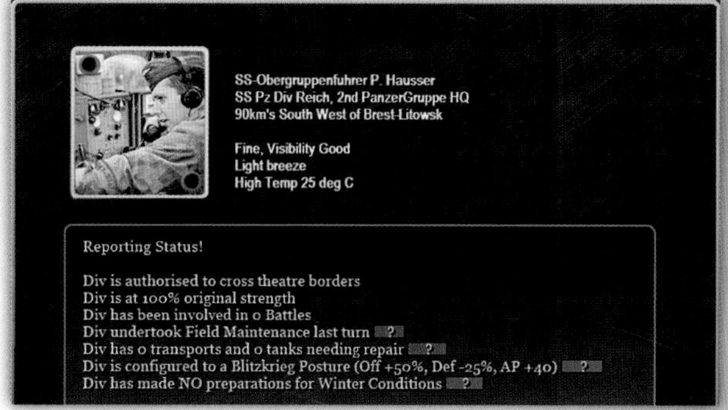

The invasion has barely commenced and Paul Hausser's SS Reich Panzer Division has been authorised to cross borders as has the rest of Guderian's 2nd Panzergruppe. Marshal Budenny, the Soviet Southern Front commander, is in for a shock

As authorisation is dependant on the Führer, if your relationship with him turns negative (<0) he will withdraw his support for any reassignment. If you currently have a Panzergruppe reassigned you will incur Political Point penalties each turn until it is 'Released'. This will happen regardless of whether the Panzergruppe is in its correct theatre or not. It's the authorisation that is upsetting the Führer, not their location.

The Political Point loss per turn is proportional to the extent of your bad relationship with Hitler. The worse it is the more you'll lose although a minor hiccup (the penalty is calculated at your relationship level divided by 5 with a minimum of 1) in your, otherwise good relationship, will only result in a small penalty.

Despite the Führer's lack of faith in your judgement you are free to maintain the reassignment and no theatre violation penalties will be incurred by the Panzergruppe Divisions although you'll still be hit with the PP penalty mentioned above (the worse your relationship the bigger the penalty).

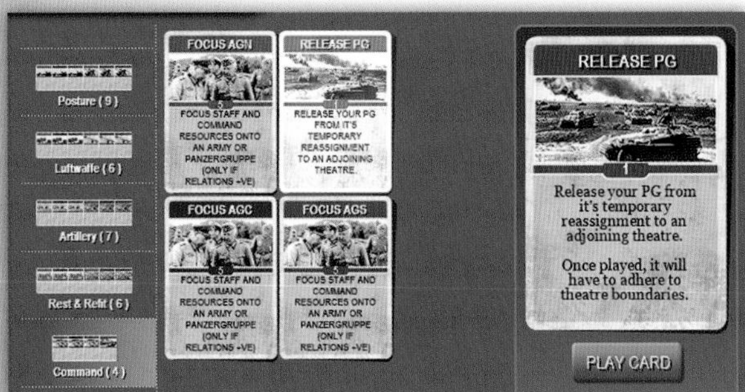

The Release PG card automatically appears in the Command category once you've played the 'Reassign PG' Action card

You can, at any time, order your reassigned Panzergruppe to be 'Released' from their temporary reassignment. Once this is done the Führer will no longer penalise you as a result of a bad relationship. After the card is played your Divisions will, on the following turn, begin incurring theatre violation penalties as normal.

STAFF ADVICE

Move your Panzergruppe back to its original theatre prior to playing the 'Release PG' Action card to avoid a rash of theatre violation penalties.

ASK YOUR STAFF

Why do I need to release a Panzergruppe? The reassignment is at the discretion of the Führer. He will agree to your request but if your relationship with him sours he will lose faith in your judgement and demand that the Panzergruppe be returned to their original theatre (if they are already there he'll still demand that you rescind their authorisation to cross theatre boundaries). Failure to heed his demands will see you incurring ongoing Political Point penalties. The 'Release PG' Action card allows you to avoid these in the event of poor relations.

After your Panzergruppe has been released you'll be able to 'Reassign' another Panzergruppe (even the same one) as the card will appear the following turn, provided your relationship with the Führer is positive.

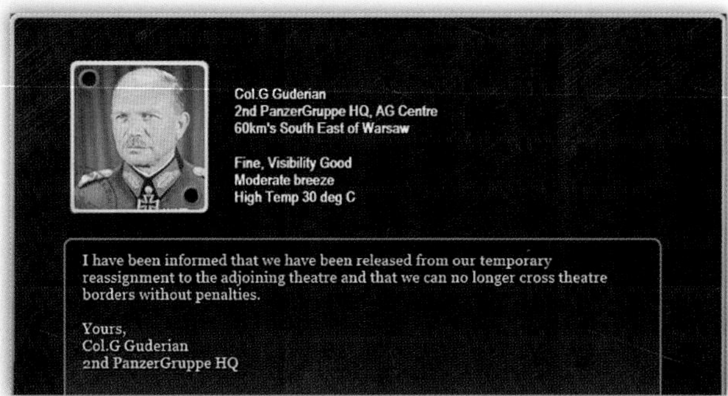

A staff snafu that has been untangled. Guderian's 2nd Panzergruppe has had its reassignment rescinded and Marshal Budenny can breath easy.

For information on the logistical implications of reassigning a Panzergruppe see 6.1.6.16 Reassigning Panzergruppes.

STAFF ADVICE

Reassigning a Panzergruppe is a powerful tool in your arsenal. Avoid doing so unless you've got a good, or better, relationship with the Führer as you don't want to get caught out with a Panzergruppe deep in an adjacent theatre with an angry Führer on your back. Advance planning is needed to handle the logistical aspects as once a Panzergruppe moves fully into an adjacent theatre it will be drawing directly from that theatre's fuel pool.

Is there going to be enough there? Should you have changed you fuel allocations before hand? Ideally you want a specific goal in mind to enable your Panzergruppe to thrust over the border, for maximum surprise, achieve its goal and return. Often this involves coordinating the actions of the existing Panzergruppe that is already in the theatre.

AGC already has two Panzergruppes. Adding a third will likely overload the capacity of its logistical pipeline to move enough fuel forward for all. Unless, of course, you've already built up a stockpile, enough to support a concerted attack on Moscow. Swinging one of the AGC Panzergruppes into an adjoining theatre can, especially in the case of AGS, enable massive encirclements. If you're planning on doing this aim to avoid having the remaining AGC Panzergruppes being too far away in order to keep your logistical situation under control (remember that the logistics in AGC are an average of the two Panzergruppes so the less distance you can keep between them the better).

For information how the logistical system handles Panzergruppes changing theatres see 6.1.6.16 Reassigning Panzergruppes.

DESIGNER NOTE

Theatres assignments are a fundamental part of the design. As the discussion in the designer notes (9.3.5 Theatres) states, it's the individual theaters that have you thinking as a true operational commander. Deciding how much freedom to allow the Player to be able to have their armies cross from one theatre to another took a lot of thought and iteration.

Minor transgressions are allowed and are handled by the theatre violations system. Moving a Division, or two, a hex over the boundaries in order to achieve a tactical outcome is quite feasible and incurs only a minor penalty. Moving an entire army across is another matter altogether. It's a major logistical undertaking that requires a lot of high level staff work and coordination.

In the end it was decided that only Panzergruppes could cross borders and then only one at a time. This provides enough scope for the Player to pivot sufficient force from one theatre to another to make a difference without breaking the operational imperative of the theatre system.

Historically this would have been a big deal. There were many heated arguments between the Führer and his Field Marshals over objectives and Panzergruppes dispositions (the two went hand in hand). F.M Franz Halder (who the Player represents) did not have the authority to unilaterally reassign Panzergruppes on his own. Nobody did without the approval of the Führer. Hence the ability to reassign a Panzergruppe is keyed off the Player's relationship with Hitler.

It's an interesting mechanic that plays the military aspect off against political one. It serves to highlight the, often neglected, fact that operational command doesn't operate in a vacuum where Generals huddle together and decide everything amongst themselves. Politics intervene. Always.

SUMMARY

- Only Panzergruppes can be authorised to cross theatre borders
- Only one Panzergruppe can be 'Reassigned' at a time
- Reassignment is only available if you have Positive relations (>0) with Hitler
- Play the 'Reassign PG' Action card on any of the four Panzergruppes
- All Divisions in a reassigned Panzergruppes can cross theatre borders without incurring violation penalties
- A reassigned Panzergruppe can cross ANY border and has no obligation to do so (it can stay in its original theatre with no penalty)
- There is no time limit to a reassignment but if your relationship with Hitler sours (goes negative) he will withdraw his authorisation and you will incur a Political Point (PP) penalty each turn until you 'Release' the Panzergruppe (Action card) or improve your relationship (>0).
- Playing the 'Release PG' Action card will remove authorisation and means that any Divisions will incur theatre violation penalties as they would normally.
- Once a Panzergruppe has been 'Released' another can be Reassigned (provided you have positive relations with Hitler)

6.1.3. LUFTWAFFE

The air war of Russia in '41 has been abstracted. There are no counters representing air squadrons, no reports indicating how many Be109's are still operational at Riga. The extremely one sided nature of the air war doesn't lend itself to a standard simulation approach.

DESIGNER NOTE

By the end of '41, the Luftwaffe was down to 30 to 40% of their original strength. They lost as many planes to the weather as they did to combat. The operational arc of the Luftwaffe, portrayed by the game, is about the effective management of a highly professional air arm in decline.

Instead there are airfields that need to be moved forward, a range of air missions that can be ordered and a number of meaningful decisions that determine the effectiveness of your air support. The key factors of the air war in '41 are all present and accounted for. In detail and without the need to micromanage.

The Luftwaffe, in Russia, was a finely honed, tactical, short range, force with a nonexistent strategic bombing capability. After achieving overwhelming air superiority early on it was free to focus on providing tactical ground support and flying resupply missions.

Each theatre has its on Luftflotte (air fleet). Each theatre has a single airfield that represents the focal point of effort. The ability to project air power (as tactical support or resupply missions) is a combination of airfield quality and overall Luftwaffe fuel level.

Air missions are executed by playing Luftwaffe Action Cards.

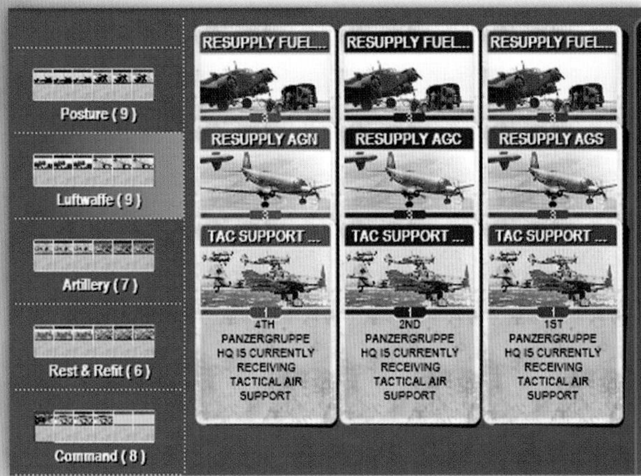

Airfields are relocated by means of ongoing decisions.

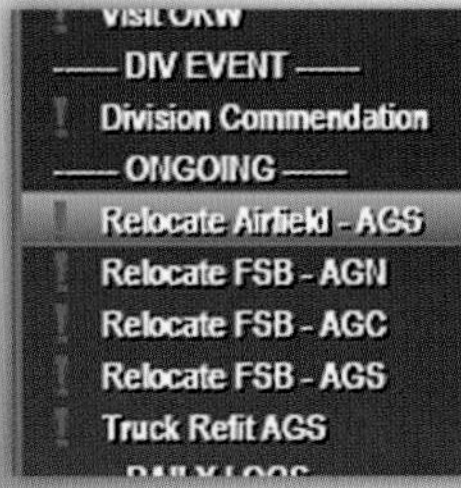

Information on the status of the Luftwaffe is found in your Daily Theatre Logs.

For an in depth discussion on the thinking behind the design of the air war component of the game refer to 11.3 Air War.

6.1.3.1. Luftwaffe Effort

This is tracked by theatre. It represents your ability to project air power within a given theatre. There are two main components, Airfield Quality and the overall Luftwaffe Oil Level.

Your NET, usable, EFFORT is taken as the airfield quality. The Luftwaffe fuel level acts as a limiting cap on airfield quality. For example if your airfield quality was 105 and your fuel level was only 95 then your net effort would be 95 as the quality of 105 would be 'capped' by fuel level.

--- Luftwaffe
- Main Airfield at Tilsit, Quality 120 (Fine, 0 upgrade) [?]
- Luftwaffe Fuel Level 100 [?]
- Net Effort (Action cards) 100 [?]

Airfield Quality has been capped by an insufficient fuel

Your Net Effort is what is used whenever you order Air missions. The higher the effort the more effective are your missions. Note that Tactical Air Support missions, once ordered, continue automatically until such times as you wish to reallocate them.

There are several special factors that can influence your Net Effort but these will be clearly highlighted when they occur. Examples are penalties that occur when your airfield is overrun, or cut off. Certain decisions can also have an impact such as allocating air support to protect your Baltic convoys.

Airfield Quality

Airfield QUALITY represents the standard of its runways (surfaced or dirt?) and the level of facilities on hand (maintenance workshops, air crew accommodation, hangers etc). The Quality of an airfield will improve each turn, provided the weather is FINE (engineers are assumed to be upgrading runways, improving facilities while damaged planes are being repaired and being put back into service).

--- Luftwaffe
- Main Airfield at Lvov, Quality 96 (Fine, +3 upgrade) [?]
- Luftwaffe Fuel Level 100 [?]
- Net Effort (Action cards) 96 [?]

Fine weather has enabled Lvov airfield to be improved. May the sun keep shining.

Bad weather (non-fine) will lower the airfield quality to reflect the decreased ability to put planes into the air in adverse conditions.

A Quality of 100 indicates an airfield capable of maintaining a normal operational temp. Quality is capped at 120.

DESIGNER NOTE

The base quality of airfields (the starting value before improvements) is at it highest at the commencing airfields on the Polish side of the border which benefited from significant level of preparation. The further you push your airfields into Russia, the lower their quality.

Luftwaffe Oil Level

There is a minimum level of fuel required to maintain standard operational tempo. This is set at a base level of 100.

The Luftwaffe Oil level applies to all theatres (it's the same level across the board) and applies as a MAXIMUM CAP to all air activity. There may well be plenty of planes ready to fly out of a well equipped airfield but if there isn't enough fuel available only a portion of them will be able to get airborne.

--- Luftwaffe
•Main Airfield at Vyazma, Quality 89 (Temp -1 C, Quality -1) [?]
•Luftwaffe Fuel Level 92 [?]
•Net Effort (Action cards) 89 [?]

The Airfield quality of Vyazma (89) isn't affected here as there is plenty of fuel available (92)

--- Luftwaffe
•Main Airfield at Tilsit, Quality 120 (Fine, +1 upgrade) [?]
•Luftwaffe Fuel Level 100 [?]
•Net Effort (Action cards) 100 [?]

Tilsit is an excellent airfield with a quality of 120 but there is insufficient fuel and the effort is capped at 100

Luftwaffe Oil levels can fluctuate as a result of decisions. The high octane fuel used by the Luftwaffe can be utilised by your Panzer Divisions to obtain superior battlefield performance (increased Action Points).

6.1.3.2. Luftwaffe Missions

There are three types of missions - Tactical Air Support, Fuel Resupply and Ammo Resupply. They are all executed by means of the appropriate Action Cards found under the Luftwaffe category.

The cost of the cards will increase if you have poor relations with Reichsmarschall Göring. See 4.8.1.3 Reichsmarschall Göring.

You can order a mission by playing the relevant card on an Army, or Panzergruppe, HQ. Tactical Air Support (TAC), once played, continues indefinitely until you decide to reassign it to another HQ. Resupply missions are one off occurrences.

For a mission to be possible the HQ must be within range of its theatre airfield. This is set at a maximum of 15 hexes (450 km's) although distances over 10 hexes incur an exponential penalty.

You can quickly check the distance of your Panzergruppes from their airfields by viewing the special PG tab above. The higher the 'Luftwaffe' arrow is pointing up the (see 'Airfield Range' table).

Kliest's 1st PG and Hoepner's 4th PG are both within acceptable range of their airfields. Guderian's 2nd PG is struggling and Hoth's 3rd PG is beyond the range of the AGC 2nd Luftflotte

Resupply missions can't be ordered if you have previously ordered a Tactical Support Mission within the theatre on the same turn (the Resupply Action Cards are removed). If you are going to order a resupply mission, do it first. Resupply missions were major undertakings and only one can be ordered, per turn, within a theatre.

ASK YOUR STAFF

Why can't I order a resupply mission AFTER assigning TAC? Transports were vulnerable and enemy fighters, normally ineffective, would likely pounce and devastate them without the presence of friendly fighter cover. By first ordering TAC you are allocating your available fighters to support ground operations and suppress any enemy fighter activity. There would be insufficient fighters available to protect a large scale resupply mission. Note that this restriction only applies if you have ordered TAC THIS TURN.

Missions are theatre based. They apply to the Army, or Panzergruppe, originally assigned to the theatre. A Panzergruppe could, feasibly, be temporarily reassigned to an adjacent theatre but its original theatre is responsible for flying any air missions to it. If the 2nd Panzergruppe (commences in AGC), for example, is reassigned to AGS then you will need to order AGC to fly the missions, not AGS.

Tactical Air Support

The Luftwaffe, in Barbarossa, was highly tuned to provide lethally effective ground support. There was effective coordination between ground liaison Officers and air crews facilitated by high quality radio equipment.

TAC isn't immediately available as the Luftwaffe is busy destroying the VVS. The 'D+2 Air Offence' decision allows you to decide whether it will continue to disrupt Soviet Command and Control or switch over to providing air support. As soon as it is released from its interdiction mission, TAC Action Cards will be available, one for each theatre. There'll also be a reminder in your Aide de Camp log.

--- Luftwaffe
•The Luftwaffe is currently fully occupied obtaining air superiority [?]

Aide de Camp log, Luftwaffe is busy, TAC not yet available

--- Luftwaffe
•You need to assign Tactical Air Support in all three Theatres (Card) [?]

Aide de Camp log, Luftwaffe freed up, TAC Action Cards ready for use

--- Luftwaffe
•AGN: You need to assign Tactical Air Support (Card) [?]
•AGS: You need to assign Tactical Air Support (Card)
•AGC 3rd PanzerGruppe HQ [?]

Aide de Camp log, Luftwaffe twiddling their thumbs, becoming impatient

Once TAC is available play the theatre Action Card on any Army, or Panzergruppe, within range (it's automatically calculated. You'll be unable to select HQ's that aren't in range (15 hexes from the airfield).

STAFF ADVICE

Tactical Air Support can be assigned to any Army but it was designed, and doctrinally intended, to support the fast moving Panzergruppes as a form of 'mobile artillery'.

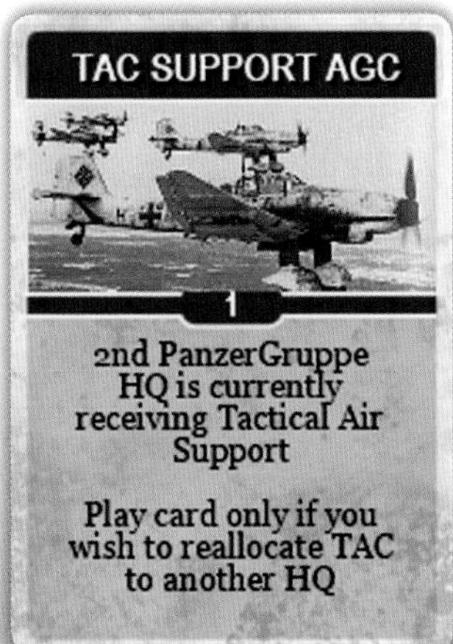

TAC SUPPORT AGC
1
2nd PanzerGruppe HQ is currently receiving Tactical Air Support
Play card only if you wish to reallocate TAC to another HQ

If you are assigning TAC for the first time (within each theatre) it will be available immediately. Beyond this there is a one turn delay as liaison officers are embedded

The dynamic text on the TAC cards lets you know who, if anyone, is currently assigned to

and protocols established. Once assigned, you can forget about it as it'll continue automatically.

The confirmation message will detail the effect of TAC. It's recalculated at the beginning of each turn as both weather and range are liable to change.

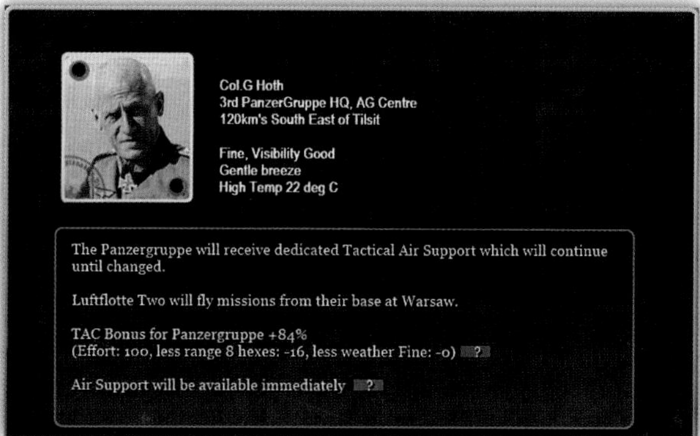
Col.G Hoth
3rd PanzerGruppe HQ, AG Centre
120km's South East of Tilsit

Fine, Visibility Good
Gentle breeze
High Temp 22 deg C

The Panzergruppe will receive dedicated Tactical Air Support which will continue until changed.

Luftflotte Two will fly missions from their base at Warsaw.

TAC Bonus for Panzergruppe +84%
(Effort: 100, less range 8 hexes: -16, less weather Fine: -0) ?

Air Support will be available immediately ?

Luftflotte Two has Col.G Hoth's 3rd Panzergruppe's back. Range is good, weather is good. TAC can be powerful

If your HQ ever moves out of range (>15 hexes) TAC will cease but will automatically pick up and continue when the HQ moves back in range (or, more likely, you relocate your airfield forward).

AIDE DE CAMP 24 . July . 1941

--- Relationships
•AGC: A Strong relationship with F.M von Bock gives Bonuses ? ?

--- Focus
•AGN 16th Army HQ, AGC 2nd PanzerGruppe HQ, AGS 17th Army HQ ?

--- Theatre Artillery
•AGN 16th Army HQ, AGC 9th Army HQ, AGS 17th Army HQ ?

--- Luftwaffe
•AGN 4th PanzerGruppe HQ, AGC 2nd PanzerGruppe HQ, AGS 1st PanzerGruppe HQ ?

--- Other
•1 Div Deployed, 12 Div's Failed to deploy, 2 Div's Pending deployment ?
•1 Div Withdrawn ?
•1 Army HQ is awaiting deployment (Card) ?
•14 Decisions outstanding requiring your attention ?

Your Aide de Camp report provides a quick overview of who is receiving TAC

Once an Army, or Panzergruppe, is receiving TAC the relevant Daily Theatre Log will highlight the effect.

--- Operations
•3rd PanzerGruppe HQ TAC Air Support bonus +84% (Start 100, Range 8 hexes: -16, Weather Fine: 0), flying from Warsaw Airfield ?

Daily Theatre Log for AGC. In AGC you can't assign TAC to both 2nd and 3rd PG's. It's one or the other

The Unit Modifier reports list TAC effects and any Division that you ask to Report Status! will do the same. The effect applies to all subordinate Divisions in the Army, or Panzergruppe.

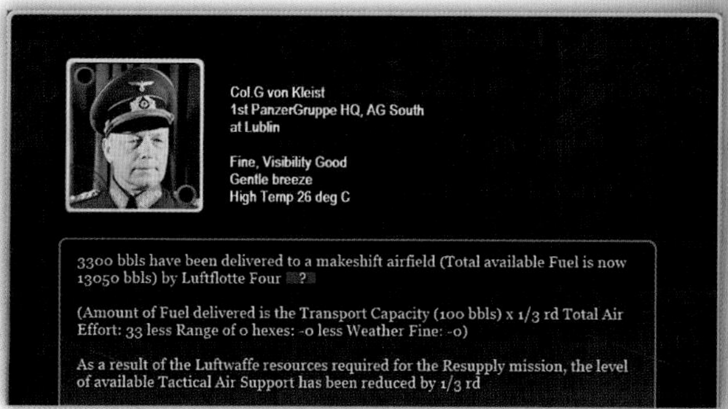
Col.G von Kleist
1st PanzerGruppe HQ, AG South
at Lublin

Fine, Visibility Good
Gentle breeze
High Temp 26 deg C

3300 bbls have been delivered to a makeshift airfield (Total available Fuel is now 13050 bbls) by Luftflotte Four ?

(Amount of Fuel delivered is the Transport Capacity (100 bbls) x 1/3 rd Total Air Effort: 33 less Range of 0 hexes: -0 less Weather Fine: -0)

As a result of the Luftwaffe resources required for the Resupply mission, the level of available Tactical Air Support has been reduced by 1/3 rd

GenMaj. Cruewell's hard fighting 11th Panzer has made it to Zhitomyr with the aid of TAC. Note the Provisional Commendation

If you have already ordered the Luftwaffe to fly a Resupply mission in the theatre then the available effort will be reduced by one third but only for the current turn.

Later in the game the Soviet Player has the ability to designate a strategic city (red dot) to receive concentrated air defences (fighter squadrons and flak battalions) which will reduce the TAC level of any Division within 3 hexes.

Resupply Fuel

Ordering this mission allows you to supply fuel

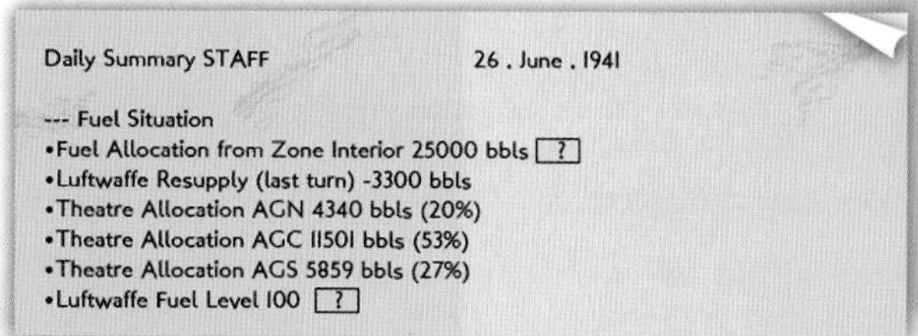
Daily Summary STAFF 26 . June . 1941

--- Fuel Situation
•Fuel Allocation from Zone Interior 25000 bbls ?
•Luftwaffe Resupply (last turn) -3300 bbls
•Theatre Allocation AGN 4340 bbls (20%)
•Theatre Allocation AGC 11501 bbls (53%)
•Theatre Allocation AGS 5859 bbls (27%)
•Luftwaffe Fuel Level 100 ?

Your Daily Staff Log highlights the consequences of any Fuel Resupply missions

directly to a Panzergruppe HQ (Army HQ's don't have vehicles or a need for fuel).

Fuel that is delivered is immediately usable but it isn't free. It's deducted from next turn's quota from Zone Interior (see above).

The amount of fuel delivered is dependant on both range and weather. One third of total Air Effort is always used as a base for the calculations.

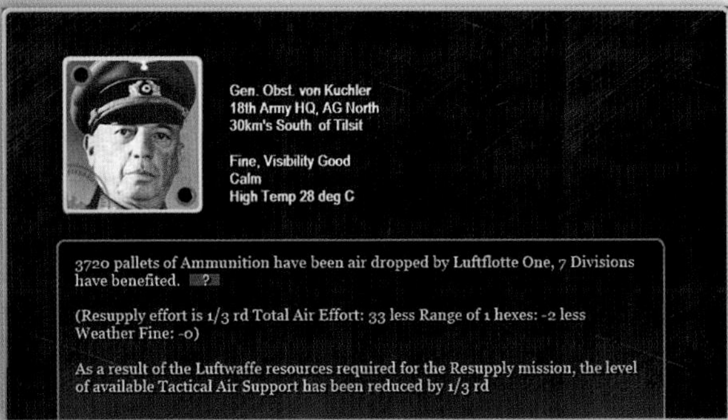

It's the start of the campaign and Col.G Von Kleist's 1st Panzergruppe has ordered a resupply even though they are right on top of the airfield (range 0). With ideal weather they have received the maximum possible resupply. They shouldn't expect anywhere near this once they start rolling eastwards

STAFF ADVICE

Ordering an emergency fuel drop won't ever provide enough fuel to keep an entire Panzergruppe on the move (notwithstanding the 'perfect world' example above) but it will provide enough to get you out of a crisis situation. Resupplies aren't cheap (in PP) but they are especially useful to cover any shortfalls when you are relocating your theatre Forward Supply Base and fuel stocks run low.

Resupply Ammo

Ammunition Resupply missions can be ordered for any HQ, Army or Panzergruppe, provided they are in range. They use, as for a Fuel Resupply, an identical one third of total Air Effort.

Ammunition (or supplies) that's delivered is parcelled out evenly among all the subordinate Divisions, including the HQ. Any Divisions outside of Command Range will miss out. See 4.13 Command

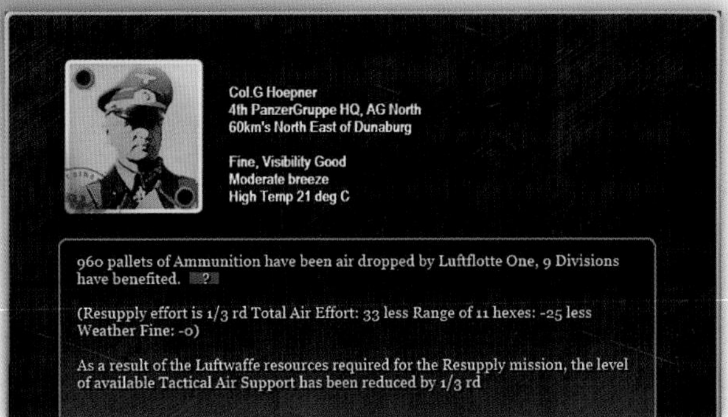

Col.G Hoepner's 4th Panzergruppe, running low on ammunition has requested the same. Distance is a problem

Range. Unlike a Fuel Resupply mission, Ammunition delivered is free supply, above and beyond the normal allocation. It's an emergency, they've found extra. There's always extra ammunition hidden away in a depot, somewhere.

Mission Effectiveness

All three mission types work the same. The Air Effort (in the case of a Resupply mission is one third of the Air Effort that's used) is modified to take into account both weather and distance.

It's possible for weather and distance penalties to exceed the available Air Effort. In this case the mission is aborted and you're notified of such. Any Political Points (PP) that you've expended to order the mission (play the Action Card) will be refunded.

ASK YOUR STAFF

Why aren't you told beforehand whether a mission will be successful or not? It's quite possible to order a mission, have it take off and, by the time the aircraft arrive over target, to find that the weather has closed in. Time and effort has still been expended and you'll be prevented from attempting another Resupply that turn. An eye on the weather report, a rough idea of the distance and an idea of the available Air Effort from your Daily Theatre Log should enable you to make an informed judgement. As a rule of thumb, unless there is bad weather involved or excessive distances, it'll be O.K.

Effect of Weather

Weather is taken into account twice. Firstly at the originating airfield. Bad weather here will lower the Airfield Quality and result in a lower net air effort.

Weather at the target HQ (Army or Panzergruppe) is allowed for in the mission calculations as seen in the mission examples. Visibility is the key factor. Nil visibility, from either rain or snow, has the steepest penalty but still allows a mission to be flown because it's assumed that there will be small windows of opportunity within a turn's four day window.

The weather effect in the mission confirmation dialogue is a result of the visibility at the intended destination. You can visually see the likely weather by viewing the map. If the HQ is experiencing mud or snow conditions then it's likely there will be problems.

Effect of Distance

Distance is calculated, as the crow flies, from the originating airfield to the destination HQ. The subordinate Divisions could well be further (up to five hexes away and still be in Command Range) but they will still gain the benefit.

ASK YOUR STAFF

Why not calculate each Division's distance separately? It's doable technically but a very poor game mechanic. When ordering a mission you'd have to take into account up to a dozen individual Divisional distances and weather situations. Not worth the effort and verging on micromanagement. Much better to have a single, clearly identified, distance calculation and have any Division within Command Range benefit.

AIRFIELD RANGE

Icon	Range to Theatre Airfield	Distance Penalty
UP arrow	Close range (<=5 hexes)	<= 10
SIDE arrow	Medium range (>5 and <=10 hexes)	>10 and <=20
DOWN arrow	Long range (>10 hexes)	>20
CROSS	Out of range (>15 hexes away)	Out of range

Distance is to the HQ, not the individual divisions. Provided the HQ is in range, all is O.K.

Effect of Command Range

You order Tactical Air Support, or Resupply missions to a specific HQ. All subordinate Divisions belonging to that HQ benefit from the mission provided they are within Command Range (5 hexes). A Division that's outside of Command Range will miss out.

Divisions outside of Command Range at the time of an Ammunition Resupply mission will miss out permanently. With a Fuel Resupply mission the delivered fuel goes into the pool and they can still access it although, being out of Command Range, they will be suffering Action Point penalties.

Tactical Air Support is only available to Divisions within Command Range at the start of a turn but if they subsequently move back into range the TAC bonus will, once again, apply.

See 4.13 Command Range.

6.1.3.3. Relocating Airfields

Each theatre has an airfield. As your forces advance there is a need to relocate the airfields to more forward locations otherwise excessive flying distances would preclude air support.

STAFF ADVICE

There is an underlying tension between staying put at an airfield (it's quality will gradually improve) and the need to keep pushing your airfields forward in order to stay within range of your advancing Panzergruppes. A small amount of Tactical Air Support is better than none.

The map highlights the current airfield sites and possible future airfield locations within each theatre. To avoid cluttering the map alternative airfields are shown only if they are enemy controlled (you have the option of relocating to an airfield in your rear but these aren't shown directly on the map).

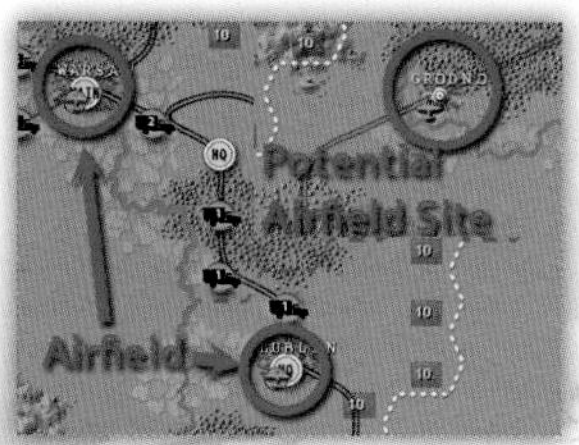

Relocation is done via a decision. These automatically occur, every three turns, if there are viable alternatives available. Each theatre rotates so AGN, for instance, will have a relocation decision on turn 'n', AGC on turn 'n+1' and AGS on turn 'n+2' to ensure that every theatre has the option of relocating at a minimum of every three turns. No decision will be generated for a theatre if there aren't any alternative airfields available.

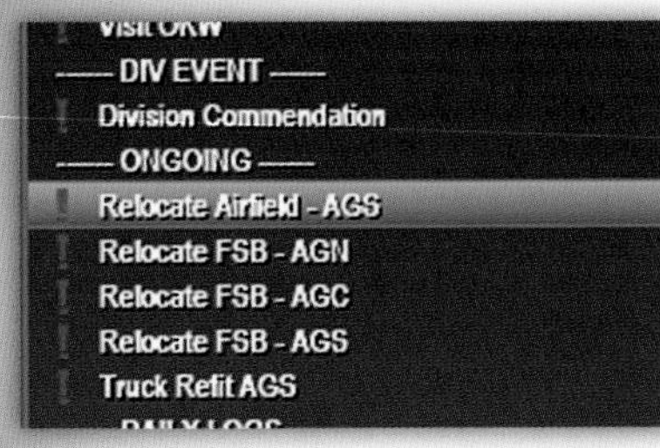

Relocation decisions are classified as 'Ongoing' and can be ignored if you don't wish to deal with them. You Chief of Staff understands not to take matters into his own hands and you won't be charged the standard 1 PP for a delegated decision

ASK YOUR STAFF

Why am I restricted in where I can relocate my theatre airfields? The answer, in short, would be partly for game play reasons and partly to reflect the restrictions that the Germans faced. Theatre airfields are, to an extent, an abstraction. In reality there would be numerous smaller airfields scattered throughout a theatre. Simulating this would only add a high degree of micromanagement (which airfield am I flying a mission out of? Do they each have an individual quality rating?) and add little. With a single airfield in each theatre representing the main effort there needs to be a few restrictions on where that can be otherwise the decisions involved become meaningless and you'd be constantly relocating. It's not that far removed from what happened in '41 as large airfields needed to be on the main rail routes and not every location had the associated logistical infrastructure that was required.

Relocation, once authorised, happens quickly. Your new airfield site will be available at the start of the following turn. An advance party is assumed to have matters in hand and all that is required is for you to issue the order.

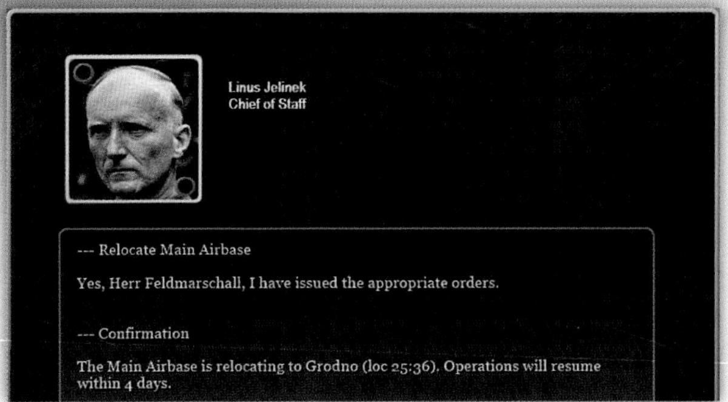

The game automatically determines if there are any viable alternatives and presents the top four choices (in terms of distance from the current airfield) as options. In the southern theatre it's possible to have more than four alternative airfield sites available but only the top four will be shown as your staff consider the more distant options to be impractical. If you are determined to move your airfield to a more distant location then you'll have to leapfrog your way there using another airfield as an interim step.

A potential airfield site must be able to trace an unbroken rail route back to OKH headquarters in order to be considered

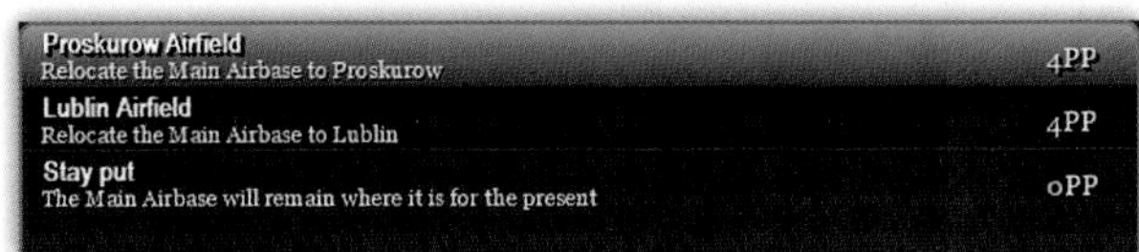

Your relationship with Reichsmarschall Gòring affects the PP cost of the options

The primary report message will highlight the option that your staff consider the best available.

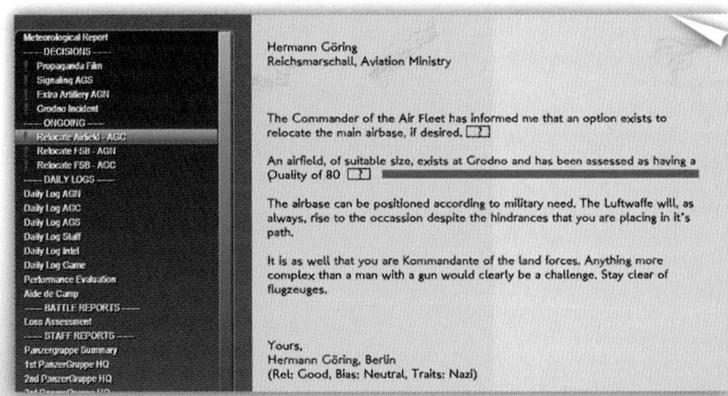

Your staff will indicate the location and Airfield Quality of their recommended choice

Within the report bundle will always be a rather terse report from Reichsmarschall Göring highlighting the details of the current airfield (location and quality) which can serve as a useful benchmark when assessing alternatives.

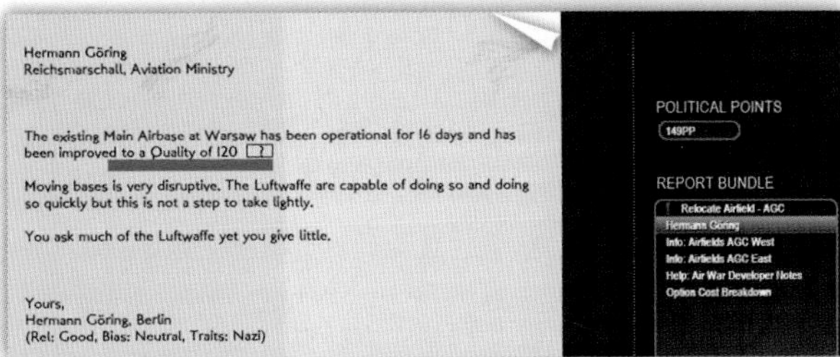
Hermann Göring
Reichsmarschall, Aviation Ministry

The existing Main Airbase at Warsaw has been operational for 16 days and has been improved to a Quality of 120

Moving bases is very disruptive. The Luftwaffe are capable of doing so and doing so quickly but this is not a step to take lightly.

You ask much of the Luftwaffe yet you give little.

Yours,
Hermann Göring, Berlin
(Rel: Good, Bias: Neutral, Traits: Nazi)

Each report bundle also contains maps of the relevant theatre displaying all the alternative airfield locations as well as the vital rail links.

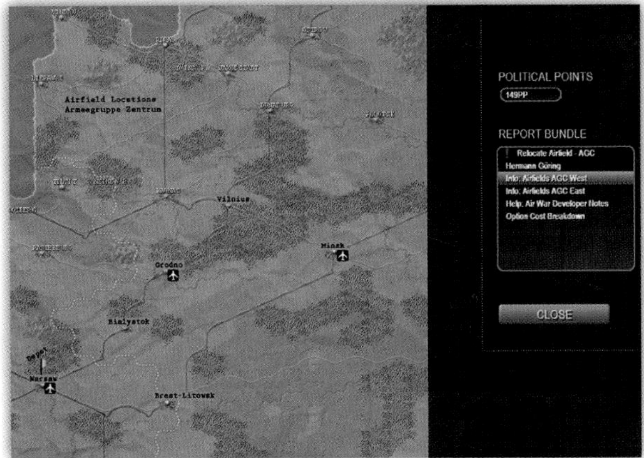

STAFF ADVICE

Airfield quality gets worse the further east you go. This is inevitable. The Soviets did their best to disable their airfields as they retreated. Facilities, at the best of times, were not up to German standards. The main consideration shouldn't be airfield quality, but being able to keep your planes within reach of where they are needed.

Decisions Off

There are no relocation decisions if this option (game start) has been chosen. Instead the German Player has three Action cards in order to move the main theatre airfields, when required.

In order to prevent unnecessarily using the cards they indicate whether there are viable alternative airfield locations available in their text (as above). A potential airfield must be able to trace an uninterrupted rail route back to Berlin in order to qualify (it needs to be able receive fuel and supplies).

6.1.3.4. D+2 Air Offensive

During the first operational turn of the game (round 2, 22nd June 1941) you are presented with the D+2 Air Offensive decision. As the opening day, overwhelming, air offensive was a forgone conclusion the destruction of the VVS is taken as a given.

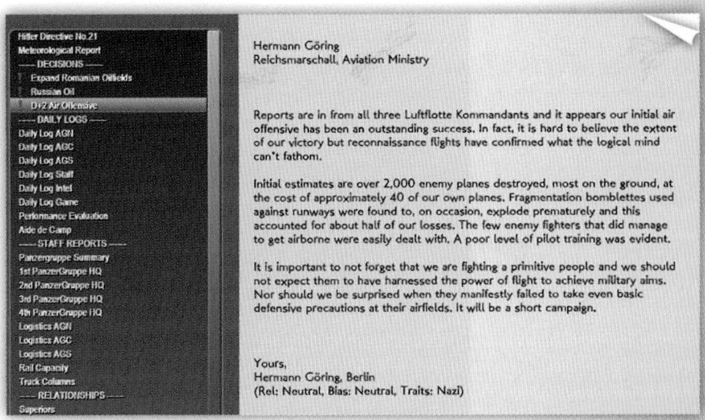
Hermann Göring
Reichsmarschall, Aviation Ministry

Reports are in from all three Luftflotte Kommandants and it appears our initial air offensive has been an outstanding success. In fact, it is hard to believe the extent of our victory but reconnaissance flights have confirmed what the logical mind can't fathom.

Initial estimates are over 2,000 enemy planes destroyed, most on the ground, at the cost of approximately 40 of our own planes. Fragmentation bomblettes used against runways were found to, on occasion, explode prematurely and this accounted for about half of our losses. The few enemy fighters that did manage to get airborne were easily dealt with. A poor level of pilot training was evident.

It is important to not forget that we are fighting a primitive people and we should not expect them to have harnessed the power of flight to achieve military aims. Nor should we be surprised when they manifestly failed to take even basic defensive precautions at their airfields. It will be a short campaign.

Yours,
Hermann Göring, Berlin
(Rel: Neutral, Bias: Neutral, Traits: Nazi)

The Luftwaffe achieved air superiority at the start of the campaign and largely retained it for the duration of '41. By the end of the year the Soviets were beginning to kick back hard but, apart from isolated, local, occurrences, the air war in '41 was predominately a one sided event.

The D+2 Air Offensive decision present the German Player with the option of maintaining the bulk of the Luftwaffe on interdicting the Soviet

Command and Control (bombing headquarters, key road and rail junctions, communication links & massed formations) or swinging them straight over to providing Tactical Air Support.

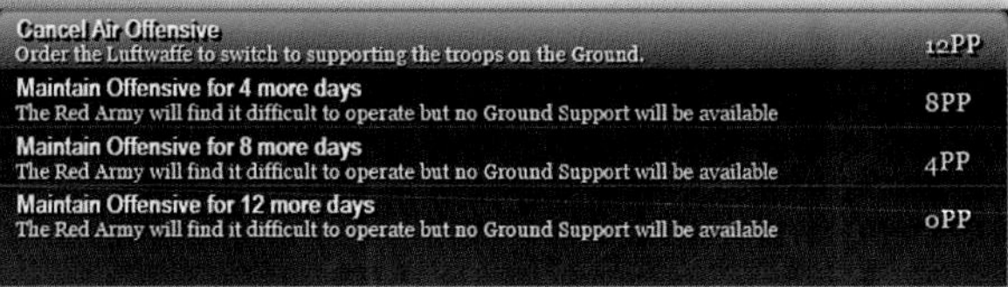

Cancel Air Offensive
Order the Luftwaffe to switch to supporting the troops on the Ground.
12PP
Maintain Offensive for 4 more days
The Red Army will find it difficult to operate but no Ground Support will be available
8PP
Maintain Offensive for 8 more days
The Red Army will find it difficult to operate but no Ground Support will be available
4PP
Maintain Offensive for 12 more days
The Red Army will find it difficult to operate but no Ground Support will be available
0PP

The effect of maintaining the Air Offensive is hidden from the German Player. It causes a global activation penalty for the Soviets. All Armies, across the length and breadth of the front, will have great difficulty in achieving full activation. See 6.2.2 Activation. It serves to help 'freeze' the Soviet Armies during the critical initial days of the campaign when the shock of the Blitzkrieg offensive is at its greatest.

NORTHERN FRONT Army Activations 22 . June . 1941

--- INITIATIVE Modifier
Luftwaffe disruption to command and control [?], (Overall) -32
Marshal Voroshilov, WAR BUDDY, Northern Front Cdr, Init -9
TOTAL Modifier -41 [?]

The Soviet Player can see the full impact of the Luftwaffe's interdiction in his activation reports

IN DETAIL

The global activation penalty is calculated, each turn, by taking a random 1d100 and dividing by 3 with a minimum floor of 5. This gives a possible range of -5 to -33 which applies to all Armies. The Soviet AI handles it differently and each individual Division is tested to see if it incurs an additional AP penalty.

While ever the Luftwaffe is interdicting Soviet Command and Control Tactical Air Support (Action Cards) will not be available. Once the interdiction is over the German Player will receive notification that TAC is available. See 6.1.3.2 Tactical Air Support.

Additionally the Soviet Helper button that allows them to request full activation for all Armies (at a cost) will be disabled until interdiction ceases'.

6.1.3.5. Soviet Air Defences

Later in the campaign the Soviets have the ability to designate a strategic city (red dot) which will be defended, in depth, by fighter squadrons and flak battalions. Any German Divisions within 3 hexes of the city, that are receiving Tactical Air Support, will suffer a reduction in their TAC level depending on their distance from the city (the closer they are, the greater the effect. No effect beyond 3 hexes from the city).

It's possible for the TAC supported Divisions to suffer a higher penalty than they receive from their own Tactical Air Support. This is allowed and represents the Soviet VVS harassing the German forces in the absence of adequate German air cover.

Weather has no effect on the Soviet air defence efforts (unlike the Germans) as the VVS are assumed to be operating from heated airfields and, additionally, because of the Soviet's familiarity with the adverse conditions.

6.1.3.6. Airfield Being Overrun

It's unlikely that this would happen without warning. The Luftwaffe were, after all, the prime source of reconnaissance intelligence.

If the enemy overrun an airfields current location it is automatically relocated to the nearest valid alternative within the theatre. No delays are incurred although the airfield that has been overrun takes a hit on its quality rating (so when you recapture the location and reuse it, once again, it will be in a poorer state than before). There will also be an 'Emergency Airfield Relocation' penalty (-10) to reflect the disruption.

6.1.3.7. Airfield Cut Off

Airfields were heavy consumers of fuel and supply. Maintaining an operational tempo required significant quantities of both.

Each turn the airfields are checked to see if they can trace a rail link back to OKH. If this isn't possible they suffer an 'Airfield Isolated' penalty of -50 to their effort.

6.1.3.8. High Octane Fuel

As a result of the decision, 'Luftwaffe Oil Allocation', the German Player can gain access to High Octane fuel (highly refined, premium fuel).

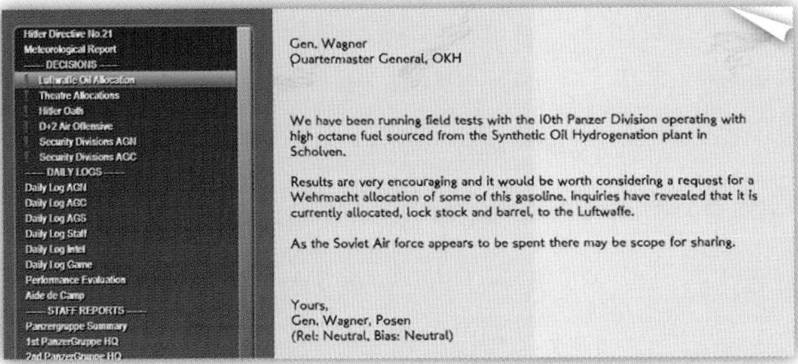

Gen. Wagner
Quartermaster General, OKH

We have been running field tests with the 10th Panzer Division operating with high octane fuel sourced from the Synthetic Oil Hydrogenation plant in Scholven.

Results are very encouraging and it would be worth considering a request for a Wehrmacht allocation of some of this gasoline. Inquiries have revealed that it is currently allocated, lock stock and barrel, to the Luftwaffe.

As the Soviet Air force appears to be spent there may be scope for sharing.

Yours,
Gen. Wagner, Posen
(Rel: Neutral, Bias: Neutral)

Why should the Luftwaffe have it all?

The decision allows you to obtain enough fuel to supply one, or two, Panzergruppes. Provided one of these options has been chosen a 'High Octane' Action card will appear in the 'Command' category the following turn.

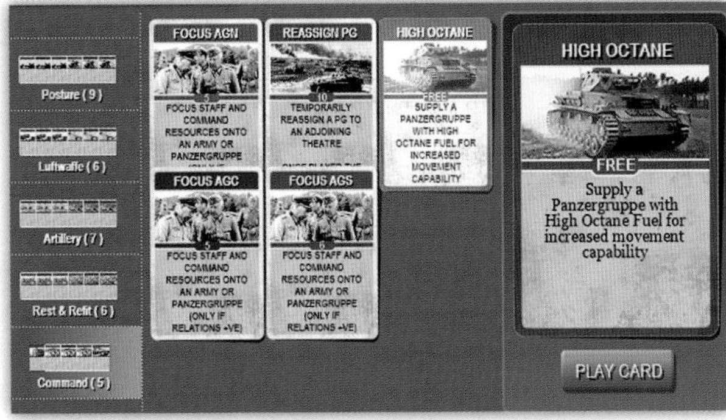

The card will remain until used. If you chose 'enough for two', you'll be able to play the card twice

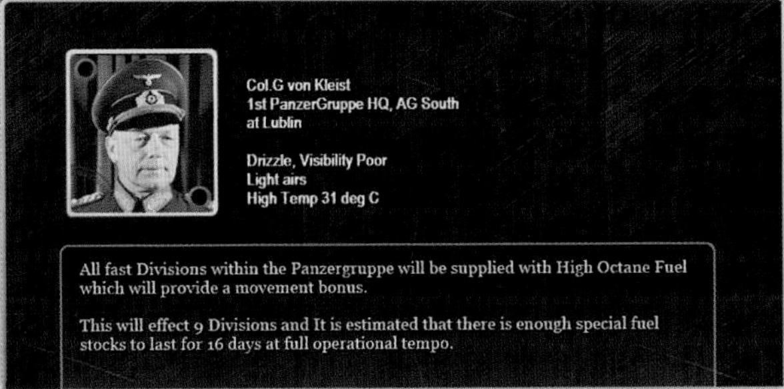

Col.G Von Kleist's 1st Panzergruppe has been turbo-charged!

The card can be played on any Panzergruppe and will provide a movement bonus (+30 AP), to all subordinate Divisions, for the next 4 turns, commencing the following turn.

Unit reports and the 1st Panzergruppe 'Unit Modifiers' report higlight the benefit.

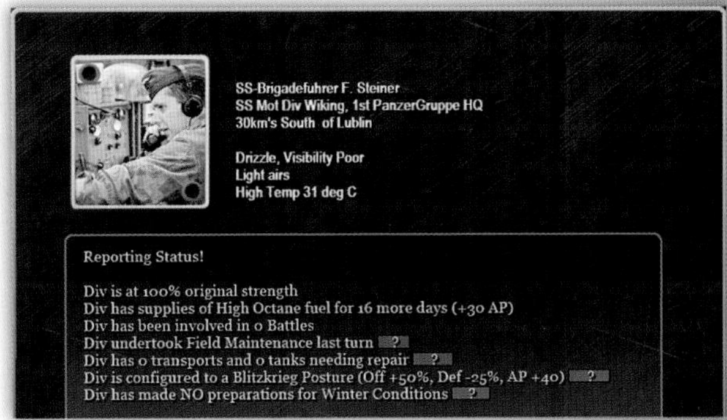

STAFF ADVICE

High Octane fuel can be a powerful boost to a Panzergruppe and allow it to push that bit further every turn. Once the card/s become available they don't have to be played immediately and you can horde them for when a better opportunity arises. Be warned that Reichsmarschall Göring (head of the Luftwaffe) doesn't take kindly to having his precious fuel 'stolen'.

1st PanzerGruppe HQ - at Lublin

--- 13th Pz Div (loc 22:47)
Army committed to a Blitzkrieg posture, +50% Off, -25% Def, +40 AP ?
High Octane fuel provides enhanced movement, +30 AP

--- 25th Mot Inf Div (loc 23:47)
Army committed to a Blitzkrieg posture, +50% Off, -25% Def, +40 AP ?
High Octane fuel provides enhanced movement, +30 AP

Unit Modifiers report

6.1.3.9. Summary

SUMMARY

- Each theatre has its own airfield and Luftflotte (air fleet)
- Airfields have a quality rating and can be relocated through decisions
- The Luftwaffe fuel level acts as a limiting cap on airfield quality

- The result is the Net Air Effort (ability to project air power)
- Net Air effort is used to determine the effectiveness of TAC and missions
- Air missions are affected by both Range and Weather
- Range is limited to 15 hexes with exponential penalties over 10 hexes
- Visibility over the airfield and target determine the weather effect
- Once Tactical Air Suppport (TAC) is assigned it continues automatically
- The first time you assign TAC in a theatre the effect is immediate
- Only one Army, or Panzergruppe, in a theatre can have TAC
- Resupply (Fuel or Ammo) cards must be played before a TAC card
- Fuel Resupply is only for Panzergruppes (fuel used isn't free)
- Ammo Resupply is for everybody
- You can only fly one Resupply mission per theatre, per turn
- Resupply missions consume one third of available Air Effort
- TAC cards are available after the D+2 Air Offence decision (depends on option)
- Airfield relocation decisions are on a rotating 3 turn schedule and can be ignored
- Cut off Airfields suffer a big penalty to their Net Air Effort
- Airfields that are over run are automatically relocated
- The Soviets can designate a city to have air defences later in the game.

6.1.4. ARTILLERY

There are three types of artillery present in the game. Divisional artillery is built into the individual units. You can see a mix of artillery types in unit display (bottom right).

To avoid unnecessary micromanagement, Corps level artillery not modelled but is instead built into the combat factors of the individual Divisions and forms part of the Theatre artillery effect.

Theatre level artillery are present in the form a Action Cards that allow you to assign them to an Army (NOT a Panzergruppe as they moved too fast for the tractor and horse drawn artillery to keep up), or to concentrate them behind an individual Division (at a cost in effectiveness). Theatre artillery can be be ordered to provide Direct Fire support (offensive bonus) or Counter Battery fire (defensive bonus).

Finally there is a Siege Artillery which is a specialised, rail borne, super heavy artillery force that can be assigned, via Action Cards, anywhere on the Ostfront provided there is a valid rail connection. A physical unit is present on the map whenever Siege Artillery is at a location. There is only one Siege Artillery force and once lost, it is gone for the duration.

6.1.4.1. Divisional Artillery

While there were a range of different calibres and guns present the game has standardised on three specific types.

The 75mm LeIG light Infantry field gun, the 10.5cm heavy field gun and the 150mm Heavy Howitzer. You can see these in the unit displays (bottom right) and click on the gun pictures for more information.

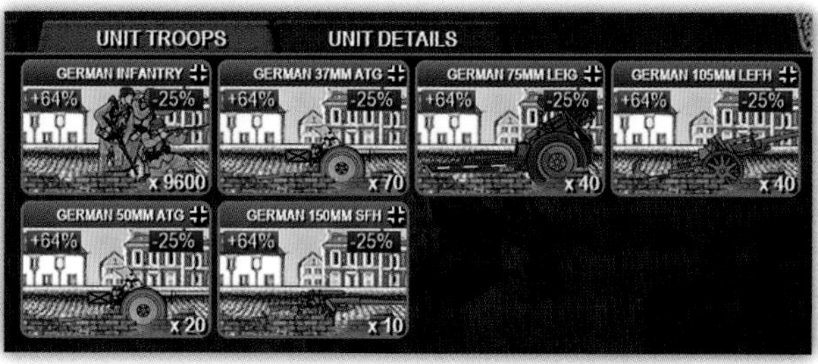

Each Division type has its own mix of artillery according to its TOE

German artillery technology was a considerable distance behind the newer Soviet models. Heavy, bulky and lacking range they were, as a whole, outgunned. Superior communications from well trained forward observers and a combined arms doctrine allowed the Germans to dominate while ever the front was fluid. Once static lines developed the Soviet superiority in artillery, and numbers, made itself felt.

6.1.4.2. Theatre Artillery

Theatre based artillery is handled by Action Cards. There are two cards for each theatre - Direct Fire and Counter Battery - plus a Siege Artillery card.

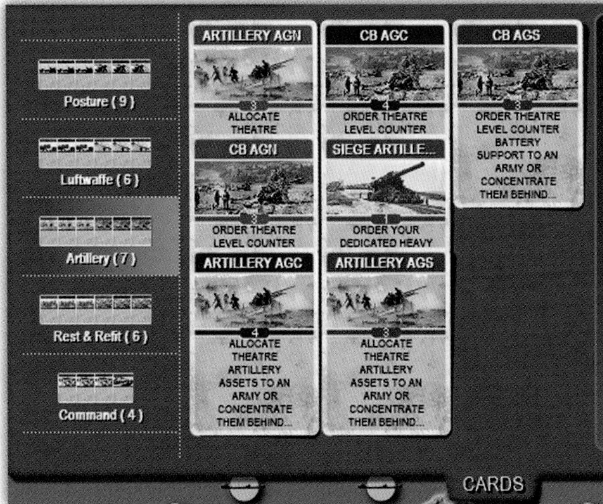

Note that the cost of AGC cards are higher than the other theatres. This is due to your poor, or worse, relationship with the theatre commander, F.M Von Bock. See 4.8.1.3.4 Theatre Commanders

Ammunition Level

Each theatre has an 'Ammunition Stockpile level' expressed numerically. A value of '100' is used to indicate a normal ammunition level. Values below one hundred indicate shortages and value over, a temporary surplus.

Each turn there is a resupply that arrives via the logistical pipelines. Unlike fuel and supply, Ammunition Stockpiles don't carry over from one turn to the next. Artillery ammunition of all calibres was in chronic short supply. As the ammunition stockpile is for use by theatre based artillery it's assumed that any left over ammunition would be quickly syphoned off and consumed by Divisional artillery Battalions.

Artillery fire exceeded all previous Wehrmacht campaigns by a huge margin. Artillery ammunition was the single biggest logistical commodity on the Eastern Front.

Your Daily Theatre Logs, under the 'Theatre Artillery' category, detail stockpile levels.

--- Theatre Artillery
- Expected resupply this turn +100 [?]
- Current Ammunition stockpile level 100 [?]
- Siege Artillery at Warsaw [?]

Your Artillery Resupply *may* affect the size of your Ammunition Stockpile if it is below 100. This is a direct consequence of the number of Truck columns you have assigned, within the theatre, to 'Infantry & Artillery use'.

IN DETAIL

With a Resupply level < 100, for example 60, a random % roll is made. If it's higher then the difference is subtracted from your Ammunition Stockpile level. If the roll was 85 the difference would be 25 (85 - 60) and this would be deducted from the base level of 100 to give an actual Ammunition Stockpile level of 75 (100 - 25). While it isn't necessary to understand this you should be aware that the lower the number of trucks columns dedicated to Infantry & Artillery use, the higher the probability that your Ammunition Stockpile level will fall. The more it falls, the less effective your artillery support will be.

TRUCK COLUMNS	30 . June . 1941		
	AGN	AGC	AGS
	---	---	---
Truck columns (Theatre & Captured)	300	400	300
- Maintenance (awaiting repair) [?]	-36	-68	-51
- Losses (permanent) [?]	-0	-0	-0
- Infantry & Artillery use [?]	-100	-100	-100
Available Truck Columns	164	232	149

All three theatres have the standard assignment of Truck columns allocated to Infantry and Artillery use

Certain decisions give you the option of changing your Truck column allocations and others allow you to raise the base Ammunition Stockpile level above 100.

ASK YOUR STAFF

Why would I want to take Truck columns away from Artillery resupply? The Wehrmacht commenced the campaign with a severe shortage of trucks. Wear and tear only served to aggravate the problem. It comes down to priorities. You may decide that the only way you can keep your Panzergruppes supplied with fuel is to 'borrow' Truck columns from other sources. You'll always be given the option of 'returning' them later.

Ammunition Related Decisions

The Truck Secondment decision (one for each theatre) allows you to reallocate truck columns from 'Infantry & Artillery use' to the general pool that is used to keep your Panzergruppes resupplied with fuel.

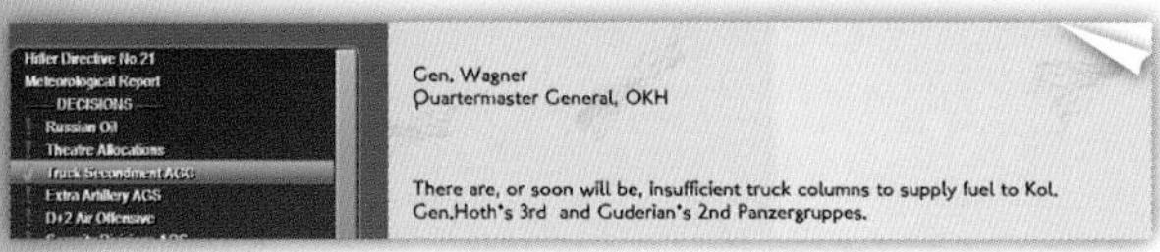

These decisions have a chance of dynamically occurring whenever you are running short on Truck columns. It's the equivalent of your Chief of Staff nudging you in the ribs and highlighting pools of trucks that you might be able to put to better use.

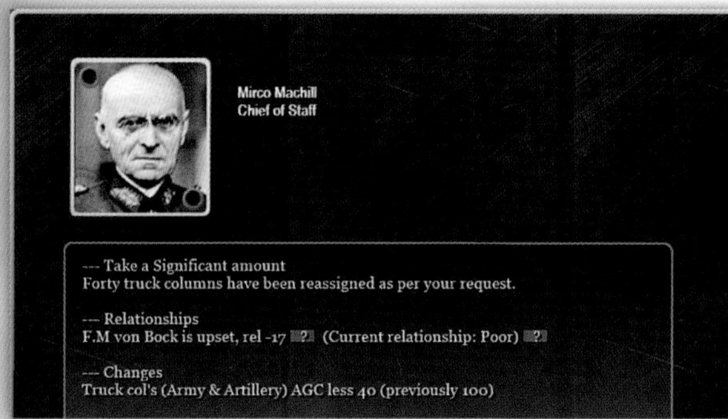

You are given various options of how many Truck columns you want to 'borrow'. Quite a few, this time.

There is a further series of theatre decisions, 'Extra Artillery', that allows you to raise the base Ammunition Stockpile level (eg. From 100 to a higher number which will increase the effect of your artillery support).

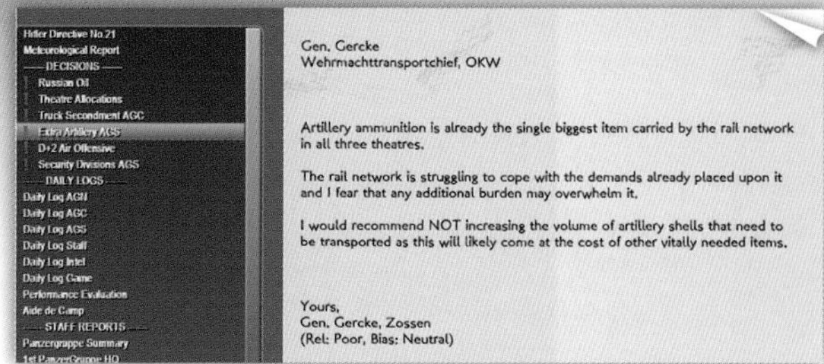

Doing so comes at the cost of having to dedicate a certain number of trains per day to the task.

STAFF ADVICE

If you have trains to spare then it's a good option, otherwise you'd need to weigh up the benefits of fuel (how much have you got stockpiled at the HQ? How great is your need likely to be?) versus increased artillery support.

Authorise a MODERATE increase in Ammunition Supplies This will use 8 trains daily but it is worth it	10PP
Authorise a SMALL increase in Ammunition Supplies This will only use an additional 4 trains daily which is neither here nor there	6PP
Don't risk overloading the Rail Network Are there that many spare trains that we can afford to give them away?	0PP

Additional ammunition requires a commitment of trains per day

Effect of Theatre Based Artillery

The size of the Ammunition Stockpile determines the affect theatre artillery has as a combat modifier for your Divisions. All Divisions within an Army, receive the same benefit. If you assign your artillery to an Army that had, for example, ten Divisions it would be spread evenly across them all.

With an Ammunition Stockpile level of 100 that would give a combat bonus of 10% to each Division. If your Ammunition Stockpile was only 60 then each Division would receive a bonus of 6% (eg. 60 divided by 10, rather than 100 divided by 10).

With the same Ammunition Stockpile level of 60, if theatre based artillery was concentrated behind a single Division it would receive a benefit of 30 (half of the 60 total) due to the law of diminishing returns (there are only so many guns you can place behind a Divisional frontage).

A Division that is out of Command Range will receive no benefit from artillery. See 4.13 Command Range.

STAFF ADVICE

Normally an Army based assignment allows for an optimum use of artillery but there are times when you need to punch through a defensive line, assault a heavily defended city or rapidly degrade a fortification when it's useful to concentrate.

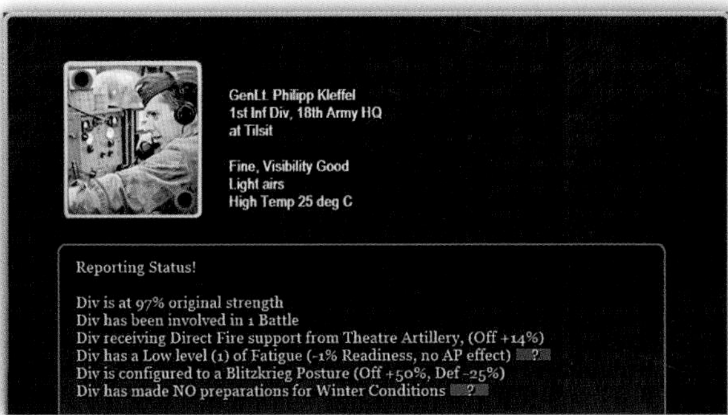

GenLt. Philipp Kleffel
1st Inf Div, 18th Army HQ
at Tilsit
Fine, Visibility Good
Light airs
High Temp 25 deg C
Reporting Status!
Div is at 97% original strength
Div has been involved in 1 Battle
Div receiving Direct Fire support from Theatre Artillery, (Off +14%)
Div has a Low level (1) of Fatigue (-1% Readiness, no AP effect) ?
Div is configured to a Blitzkrieg Posture (Off +50%, Def -25%)
Div has made NO preparations for Winter Conditions ?

GenLt. Kleffel's 1st Infantry Division, 18th Army, is benefiting from Direct Fire support from their theatre based artillery. Each Division within the 18th Army would be gaining the same +14% Offensive bonus, provided they are in Command Range

Assigning Theatre Artillery

Theatre based artillery is assigned to either Armies (not Panzergruppes) or a single Division by the use of the appropriate Action Card.

ASK YOUR STAFF

Why can't I assign theatre artillery on the first turn and have it ready immediately? The Germans gain significant bonuses during the opening days of the campaign. Part of this is due to the shock of the unexpected assault, part due to the lack of preparation by the Soviets and part due to a comprehensive and coordinated artillery barrage. Theatre based artillery assets were heavily involved in the latter which contributes to the benefit that all units receive (see 5.2.13 Early Soviet Penalties). On the first turn you can issue orders for artillery assignments but, as they are busy providing you with a major benefit (Blitzkrieg Shock Penalty), it takes a little time for them to reconfigure and implement your orders.

Within each theater a single ARMY (not PG) can be benefit from theatre based artillery. You can order the artillery to provide two types of support - Direct Fire and Counter Battery Fire. They provide offensive and defensive bonuses respectively.

ARTILLERY AGN
3
Allocate Theatre Artillery Assets to an Army or concentrate them behind a Division
(Play on an HQ or a Division)

Direct Fire Support, AGN. The card text is dynamic and will indicate who, if any, is currently receiving artillery support of this kind within the theatre

You can only have one in play so if the 9th Army in AGC, for instance, is currently receiving Direct Fire support and you reassign your theatre artillery to provide Counter Battery fire support to the 4th Army then the 9th Armies support will cease.

To prevent avoidable snafu's your staff will automatically remove the remaining theatre artillery card once you play the other (eg. If you assign Direct Fire in AGS then Counter Battery card in AGS will be removed). Both will return the following turn.

CB AGC
4
Order Theatre level Counter Battery support to an Army or concentrate them behind a Division
(Play on an HQ or a Division)

Counter Battery Support, AGC

ASK YOUR STAFF

Why the distinction between Direct Fire and Counter Battery Support? There was a large difference between the two. Direct Fire was all about communication with Forward Observers, coordinated barrages and targets of opportunity. Counter Battery was a game of cat and mouse involving sound ranging, triangulation, flash spotting and aerial reconnaissance. One was an offensive mission, the other defensive.

Whenever artillery is assigned you'll receive a confirmation message. It'll take 4 days (one turn) for the new assignment to take effect. The existing assignment, if any, will continue to provide a benefit for the remainder of the current turn so you can freely reassign at any point in a turn without incurring penalties.

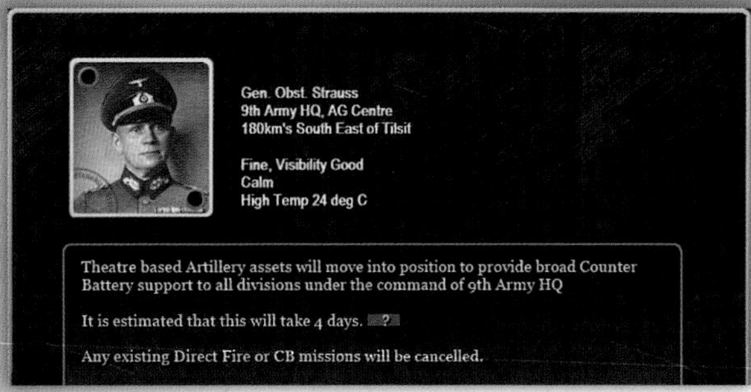

Gen. Obst. Strauss
9th Army HQ, AG Centre
180km's South East of Tilsit
Fine, Visibility Good
Calm
High Temp 24 deg C
Theatre based Artillery assets will move into position to provide broad Counter Battery support to all divisions under the command of 9th Army HQ
It is estimated that this will take 4 days.
Any existing Direct Fire or CB missions will be cancelled.

Gen.Obst. Strauss's 9th Army has been assigned CB support in order to help cope with an unexpected Soviet Offensive. Given the position of the front line the war isn't going well

Artillery Status

Your Aide de Camp report, at campaign start, reminds you that you need to assign your theatre artillery. Leaving your valuable artillery assets idle is frowned upon by High Command and your Chief of Staff does his best to prod you into action.

--- Theatre Artillery
•Your Siege Artillery is sitting idle in Warsaw (Card) [?]
•AGN: You need to assign Theatre Artillery Support (Cards) [?]
•AGC: You need to assign Theatre Artillery Support (Cards)
•AGS: You need to assign Theatre Artillery Support (Cards)

Once you've matters in hand it will keep you up to date on theater assignments.

--- Theatre Artillery
•Your Siege Artillery is sitting idle in Warsaw (Card) [?]
•AGN 18th Army HQ, AGC 9th Army HQ, AGS 17th Army HQ [?]

Whenever you ask a Division to Report Status! it will notify you of any benefits that it's receiving from theatre based artillery.

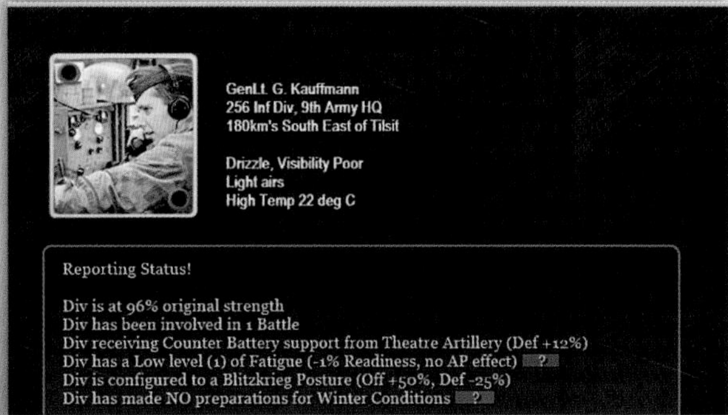

Your Army based 'Unit Modifier' reports will highlight the same.

18th Army HQ - 30km's South of Tilsit

--- 291st Inf Div (loc 20:32)
Theatre Artillery Direct Fire support, +14% Off
Army committed to a Blitzkrieg posture, +50% Off, -25% Def
Accumulated Fatigue, -1% Readiness

Your Daily Theater Logs will provide the big picture.

--- Operations
•7 Divisions are receiving Direct Fire Artillery support (+Off) [?]

The Unit display (bottom left) will show icons next to the name of the Division indicating the type of artillery support it is receiving (Direct Fire or Counter Battery).

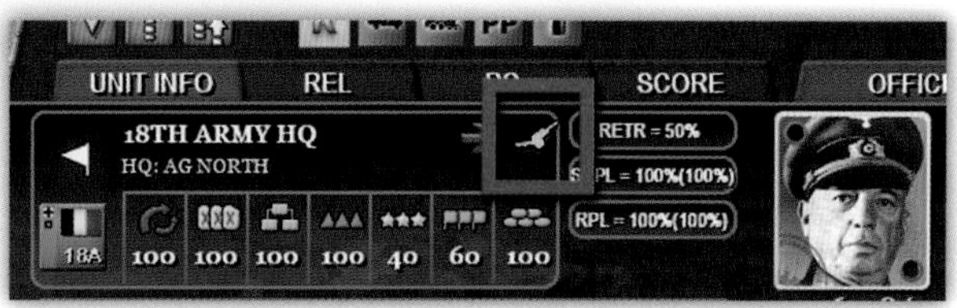

SUMMARY

- Theatre based artillery can be assigned to a single ARMY (not PG) within each theatre.
- Once assigned it automatically continues unless you wish to reassign it elsewhere.
- Assignment is done via Action Cards under the 'Artillery' category.
- Assignments come into effect the FOLLOWING turn. Any existing assignment will continue to provide benefits for the current turn.
- Artillery can be ordered to provide 'Direct Fire' (offensive bonus) or 'Counter Battery Fire (defensive bonus).
- The effectiveness of the Artillery is based on your theatre 'Ammunition Stockpile'
- This has a base level of 100 and is determined by your Resupply level each turn.
- If your Resupply level is < 100 then there is a chance of your stockpile level falling.
- There is NO carry over of unused ammunition between turns.

- Resupply levels are equal to the number of Truck Columns assigned to 'Infantry & Artillery use'
- Theatre based artillery can be concentrated behind a single Division but its effectiveness is HALVED.
- Divisions outside of Command Range receive no benefit from Theatre base artillery.

6.1.4.3. Siege Artillery

The Schwerer Gustav, an extreme example of Siege artillery. An 80cm barrel fired seven ton shells up to forty seven kilometres away. Used in the siege of Sevastopol.

Rail borne, super heavy calibre, 'knock 'em flat' artillery. There is only one set of Siege artillery available for the entire Eastern Front. It isn't represented on the map but there is a special detachment dedicated to support and protect the Siege artillery that is present.

The unit assigned to protect the Siege Artillery

STAFF ADVICE

It's always a good idea to have a friendly Division in the same location to provide additional security as the 'Siege' detachment is weak and vulnerable.

If the 'Siege' detachment unit is over run by the enemy and destroyed, your Siege Artillery is lost. This is permanent.

Siege artillery starts the campaign in Warsaw. You can order to anywhere on the map via an Action Card provided that the following conditions are met;

- The chosen location can trace a valid route, via rail, back to the Siege Artillery's current location.
- It is a friendly city (owned by the Germans)
- Alternatively it is on a rail line adjacent to an enemy held city and a friendly Division is present (Siege artillery can't be ordered to an unprotected location adjacent to enemy forces).

STAFF ADVICE

There are two scenarios with the Siege artillery. Either move it to a friendly city so it is out of harms way or use it to crack open fortified cities (move it adjacent to an enemy city, as above).

Your staff will automatically present you with a choice of valid locations that meet the above criteria. In this case there is a friendly held hex adjacent to a Soviet City (Brest-Litowsk) and Lublin, a German held city

Once orders have been issued the Siege train will make its way to the new location. The special 'Siege'

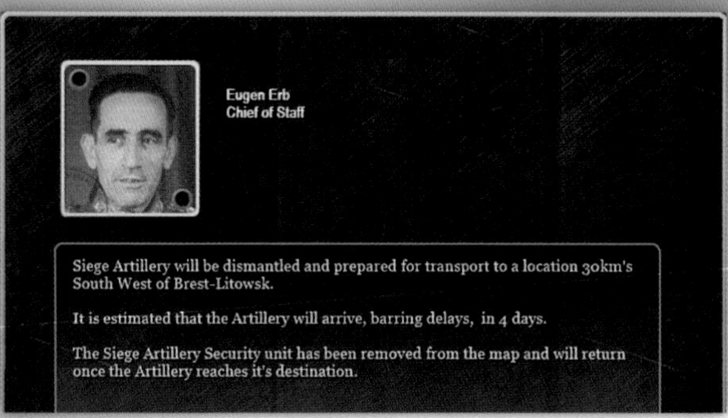

Eugen Erb
Chief of Staff
Siege Artillery will be dismantled and prepared for transport to a location 30km's South West of Brest-Litowsk.
It is estimated that the Artillery will arrive, barring delays, in 4 days.
The Siege Artillery Security unit has been removed from the map and will return once the Artillery reaches it's destination.

On its way!

detachment will be removed from the map and will return once the Siege train has arrived.

SIEGE ARTILLERY
1
Order your dedicated heavy Siege Artillery to invest a Location
(Requires a Division adjacent to the city on a rail line connected to the current Siege Artillery location)

Travelling through the rail network involves a considerable amount of ad hoc rescheduling of existing services. The time required to transit from point A to point B is determined by the distance travelled (by rail, not as the crow flies). It is possible that the Siege train may also experience unexpected delays due to congestion and scheduling issues.

If your relationship with General Gercke (Head of Trains) is negative it will increase the chance of delays. There is a low base chance of delay and any negative relationship you have with General Gercke will be added directly to the base (20%) when calculating the chance of delay. If your relationship is -21, as below, then the probability would be the base chance + 21% giving a total chance of a delay of 41%.

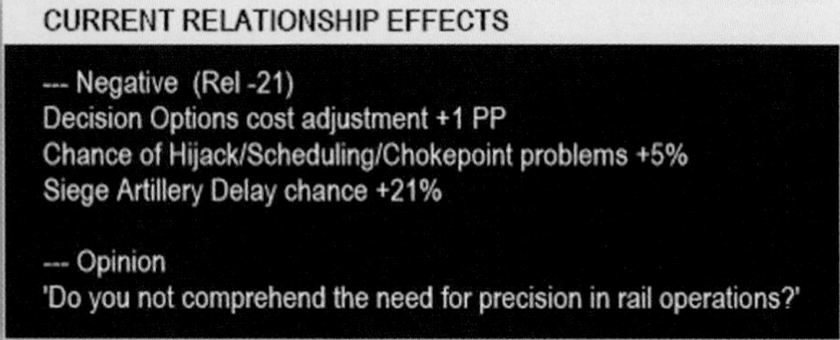

CURRENT RELATIONSHIP EFFECTS
--- Negative (Rel -21)
Decision Options cost adjustment +1 PP
Chance of Hijack/Scheduling/Chokepoint problems +5%
Siege Artillery Delay chance +21%
--- Opinion
'Do you not comprehend the need for precision in rail operations?'

The dynamic tool tip for General Gercke in the special Relationship tab (bottom centre) will let you know how much effect he has on the chance of delay.

If a delay occurs you'll receive notification in the relevant Daily Theatre Log along with a dynamic tool tip that provides a detailed breakdown of the calculations and random roll.

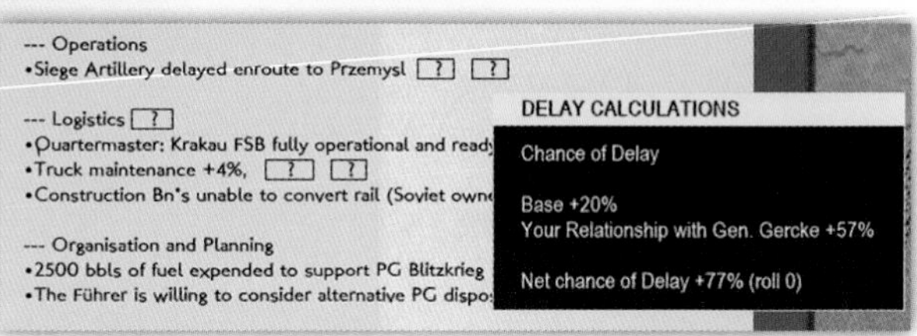

Your relationship with General Gercke have since fallen off a cliff (-57, 'Terrible'). Don't expect him to make any effort to facilitate the progress of the Siege artillery through his rail network

Once adjacent to an enemy city, your Siege artillery will commence bombardment the *following* turn. The effect is always to reduce the entrenchment level of all enemy units within the city to zero. Enemy units themselves aren't damaged but with a zero entrenchment level they are easy pickings for an all-out assault by friendly forces.

Bombardment is automatic and will continue until the city is captured or the Siege artillery relocated. While ever the artillery is bombarding the city the forces within will be unable to restore their entrenchment levels above zero.

--- Operations
•Siege Artillery investing Brest-Litowsk
•City of Brest-Litowsk suffers damage. Light civilian casualties.

The relevant Daily Theatre Log, under 'Operations', will keep you fully informed of what's happening

Civilian casualties can occur as a result of the high calibre shelling of the city and this can, if heavy enough, adversely affect your War Crimes score.

At any time you are able to issue it with new orders using the same 'Siege Artillery' Action Card.

SIEGE ARTILLERY
1
Order Artillery to break off bombardment of Brest-Litowsk and relocate

Currently bombarding the Brest-Litowsk fortress

SIEGE ARTILLERY
1
Siege Artillery ordered to 180km's South West of Lublin (in transit)
Play to change orders

Orders can be changed even when the Siege artillery is travelling from one location to the next

STAFF ADVICE

Siege artillery is critical for overcoming fortified cities. Aim to leapfrog it forward in order to keep delays to a minimum (good relations with General Gercke help) but avoid ordering it anywhere that may result in it being lost.

ASK YOUR STAFF

If I change the destination for the Siege Artillery to a closer location while it is travelling why does it take so long to get there? As mentioned there is a lot of rescheduling involved with having a large, non-standard, train move through the network. If you change your mind midway through the process General Gercke's staff will have to frantically reschedule an already disrupted network to accommodate your wishes. I wouldn't be expecting miracles.

SUMMARY

- You only have one force of Siege Artillery.
- It commences the campaign in Warsaw.
- Siege artillery isn't represented on the map
- A special 'Siege' detachment is present whenever the artillery is at a location ('Siege' unit)
- If the 'Siege' unit is over run your Siege artillery is lost. This is permanent.
- Siege artillery can be ordered to a new location via the 'Siege Artillery' Action Card
- You can change its orders at anytime by playing the same card again
- Siege artillery can be ordered to a friendly city.
- Siege artillery can be ordered to a hex adjacent to an enemy city in order to bombard it.
- A friendly Division must be present in the hex at the time of your order (no need for it remain)
- Siege artillery travels by the rail network and must be able to trace a route from A to B
- When travelling, Siege artillery can incur delays.
- If you have a NEGATIVE relationship with General Gercke the chance of delays will increase.
- Siege artillery will automatically bombard an adjacent enemy city each turn
- Bombardment results in a lowering of the Entrenchment levels, of all forces in the city, to zero.
- Bombardment results in Civilian casualties.
- Heavy Civilian casualties will adversely impact your War Crimes Score.
- The relevant Daily Theatre Log keeps you informed of all Siege artillery activity.

6.1.5. GERMAN CARDS

The German Player has a range of Action Cards that enable him to issue specific orders. The Decisions that appear in the report tab require him to deal with specific matters whereas the Action cards provide the turn by turn functionality that an Operational Commander requires.

These can be found in the Action tab (top right of centre) and are separated into different categories.

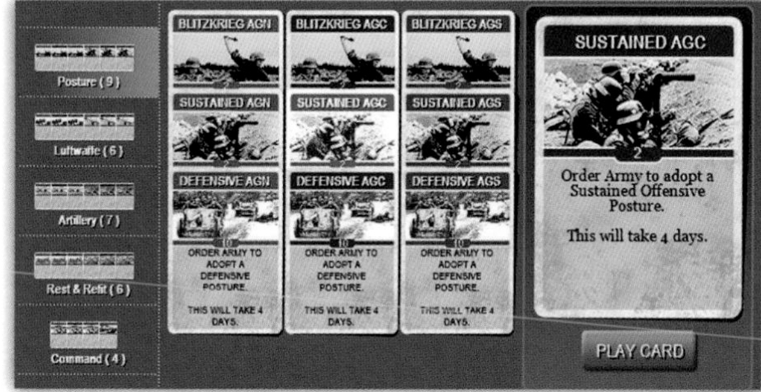

There are five 'categories' of German Action Cards (which are different to the Soviet categories). The numbers in brackets indicate how many cards are present in each category

There are also special 'Officer' cards that the Army, or Panzergruppe, commanders have access to while ever they are benefiting from Command Focus (see 6.1.1 Command Focus).

Officer cards are found next to the Commander's portrait (bottom centre) rather than up in the Action card tab at the top

6.1.5.1. First Turn

ASK YOUR STAFF

- Why can't I have my Artillery and Command Focus ready to go right from the start?
  The Germans get a very substantial first turn bonus (blitzkrieg shock penalty that is applied as a negative to all Soviet unit combat factors). This is right across the whole front. It's highest on the first turn and tails off after that.
  It represents the application of specialist battalions and resources as well as the extensive use of all available artillery assets to support the initial invasion.
  Theatre based artillery assets (artillery cards) are involved with this as well as the Focus cards (specialist resources) which is why they aren't available the first turn. They're fully occupied generating a greater effect than anything they would do if individually assigned. Once the first days of the invasion are over they are available for reassignment and the shock penalty effect begins to tail off as they are allocated to Armies and Panzergruppes.
  Tactical Air Support is available immediately (only for the first time it is assigned) as Air assets don't need to physically catch up with advancing Armies.

6.1.5.2. Card Costs

Your relationship with your three theatre commanders (F.M von Leeb, F.M von Bock & F.M von Rundstedt) can affect the cost of any theatre related Action cards (any card that is specific to a theatre, for example changing postures or assigning artillery).

Each card has a base cost, in Political Points, and this can increase if your relationship with the relevant theatre commander (if it's an AGN card then it'd be your relationship level with F.M von Leeb) is Poor, or worse. See 4.8.1.3 Action Card Costs for more information.

6.1.5.3. Posture Cards

Play these cards on any Army, or Panzergruppe, to have them reconfigure to a different posture. There is a one turn period of disruption involved when changing postures, as seen in the table below.

GERMAN POSTURES

Posture	Effect
Blitzkrieg	+50% Offensive bonus (fast div) +40% Offensive bonus (slow div) +40 AP Blitzkrieg bonus -25% Defensive bonus (fast div) -20% Defensive bonus (slow div)
Sustained Offensive	+10% Offensive bonus -5% Defensive bonus
Defensive	-20% Offensive bonus +40% Defensive bonus
Changing posture	-20% Offensive bonus -20% Defensive bonus -40 AP

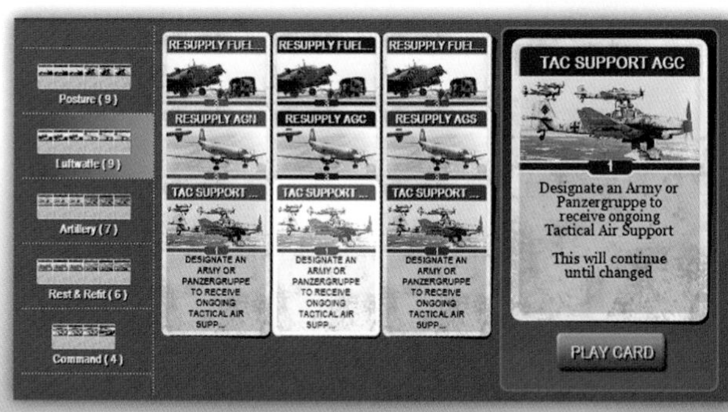

When set to a Blitzkrieg posture, Panzergruppes expend additional fuel and slow Divisions (infantry) accumulate fatigue.

For more information see 4.4 Postures.

6.1.5.4. Luftwaffe Cards

Each theatre has its own, dedicated, Luftflotte (air fleet)which operates out of the main theatre airfield.

Tactical air support (TAC) cards are only available after the Luftwaffe finishes suppressing the Soviet Command and Control (this depends on the option you choose in the first turn, 'D+2 Air Offensive' decision).

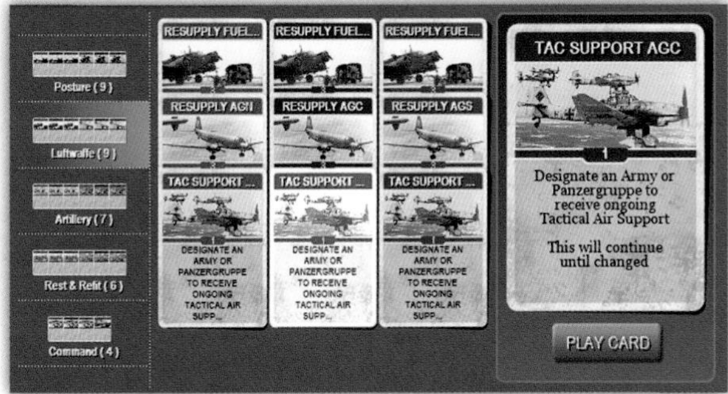

TAC, once assigned, continues automatically until you wish to reassign it. There is no need to keep replaying the cards every turn.

Resupply missions (fuel and ammo) provide a once off benefit. Flying resupply missions reduces your available air effort by one third (your TAC has one third less impact for the turn).

All Luftwaffe missions (including TAC) are distance based. The further the target Army, or Panzergruppe, HQ is from the theatre airfield, the less effective the mission will be. The maximum possible range for a mission to be flown is fifteen hexes from the airfield to the HQ.

For more information see 6.1.3.2 Luftwaffe Missions.

6.1.5.5. Artillery Cards

Theatre artillery is assigned to a single Army (Panzergruppes move too fast for the Artillery to keep up) within each theatre. It can, if you wish, be concentrated behind a single Division (with reduced effect).

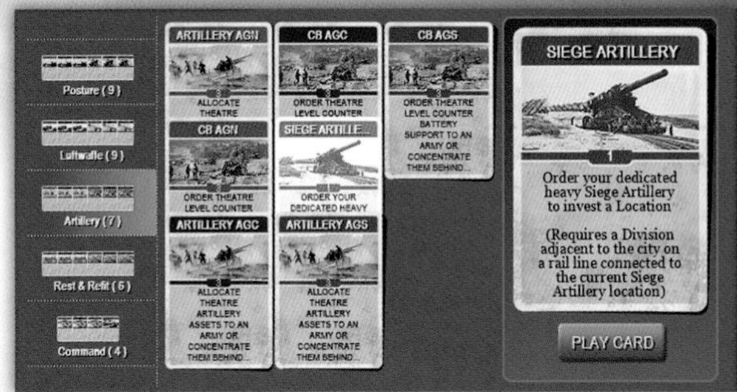

Theatre artillery, once assigned, continues automatically until you decide to reassign it.

All units who have theatre artillery assigned to them will receive a combat bonus depending on the how the artillery is configured. Artillery set to provide Direct Fire support will give an offensive bonus and while Counter Battery Fire will provide a defensive bonus. It takes a turn to change configurations or assignments.

For more information see 6.1.4.2 Assigning Theatre Artillery.

Siege artillery is a single, specialised, force that aids in reducing fortified cities. Playing the siege card enables you to order the unit to move from one location to another via the rail network.

For more information see 6.1.4.3 Siege Artillery.

6.1.5.6. Rest & Refit Cards

Tanks breakdown and men eventually collapse, exhausted from accumulated fatigue. At some point you will need to rest your men and allow your fast Divisions to stand down for a mechanical refit.

Rest & Refit cards can be played on an Army, or Panzergruppe, or on an individual Division. Once a

formation has been ordered to stand down (it takes effect the *following* turn, not immediately the card is played) it will become immobile and vulnerable for the duration of its recovery which can take several turns.

For more information see 6.1.7 Wear and Tear.

6.1.5.7. Command Cards

Focus directs staff and specialist resources at an Army, or Panzergruppe, HQ. An HQ with focus is able to access a set of Officer Cards that provide bonuses. Only one Army, or Panzergruppe, within each theatre can have focus at a time.

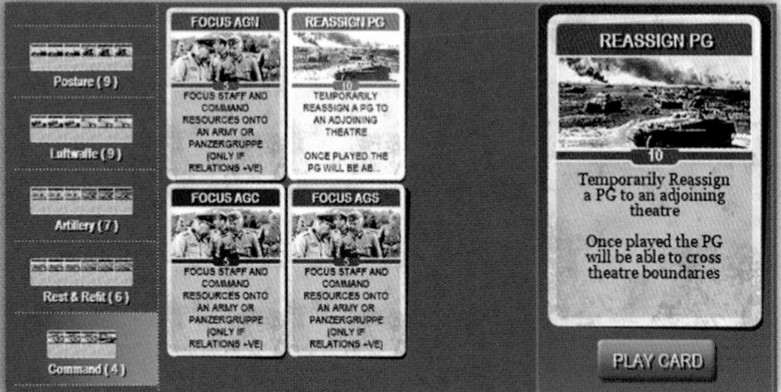

Once focus has been granted, it remains in place automatically until you wish to reassign it. It takes one turn for Focus to come into effect at which point Officer cards (6.1.5.8 Officer Cards) appear and can be played to provide tactical bonuses to the formation.

A theatre commander will consider a giving Focus to a Panzergruppe only if you have a positive relationship.

For more information see 6.1.1 Command Focus.

Panzergruppes can be reassigned to an adjacent theatre provided you have positive relations with the Führer.

For more information see 6.1.2 Panzergruppes.

Whenever an HQ finds itself cut off (isolated) the following card will appear in the command tab and provide the option of evacuating the

HQ to a safe area where it will return, the following turn, as a reinforcement (Action card)

For more information see 4.7.3 HQ Calamaties.

Reinforcements (HQ's only) will appear in the 'Command' category when they become available.

For more information see 6.1.14 Reinforcements.

As a result of certain decisions involving the Luftwaffe it is possible to obtain quantities of high octane fuel for use by your Panzergruppes. The card, below, will appear only when stocks of high octane fuel are on hand.

For more information see 6.1.3.8 High Octane Fuel.

6.1.5.8. Officer Cards

Armies, or Panzergruppes, benefiting from Command Focus (see 6.1.1 Command Focus), gain a set of Officer cards that can be used to provide their subordinate Divisions with various bonuses.

The cards appear in the unit display of the HQ & Commander who are receiving Command Focus. They are a type of action card referred to as 'Officer' cards as they are attached to a particular officer (and his HQ).

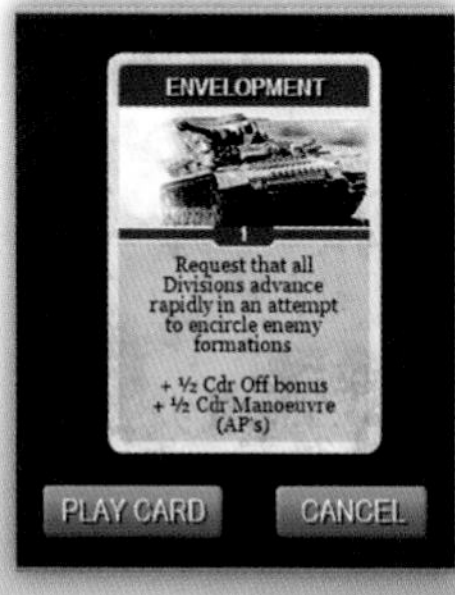

Officer cards can viewed at their normal size by use of the 'View Card' button (bottom right). The card pop-up allows you to play the card, if desired.

Only one card can be played per turn and, once

played, it will remain in effect automatically until you decide to change (there is no need to keep playing the same card every turn). The posture of the Army, or Panzergruppe, receiving Command Focus, determines the mix of cards that are provided. There are three possible 'sets', one for each posture. An Army, for example, configured to a Blitzkrieg posture will receive the Blitzkrieg cards whereas a Panzergruppe (identical to an Army for this purpose) set to a Defensive posture receives the Defensive cards.

A formation (Army or Panzergruppe) will *always* receive the 'Sustained Offensive' set of cards. If it was currently set to the Sustained Offensive posture, that's all it would receive. With any other posture (Blitzkrieg or Defensive), it will receive the set appropriate to its posture *plus* the Sustained Offensive set.

COMMAND FOCUS OFFICER CARDS			
Card	Effect	Posture	Cost (PP)
Tactical Advance	Issue orders to all Divisions allowing increased Tactical Flexibility (+Cdr Offence bonus)	Blitzkrieg	1
Flank Protection	Order all Divisions to take care to protect their flanks while advancing (+1/2 Cdr Offence bonus, +1/2 Cdr Defence bonus)	Blitzkrieg	1
Envelopment	Request that all Divisions advance rapidly in an attempt to encircle enemy formations (+1/2 Cdr Offence bonus,+1/2 Cdr Manoeuvre bonus)	Blitzkrieg	1
Manoeuvre Warfare	All Divisions are requested to adhere to Manoeuvre Warfare guidelines (+Cdr Manoeuvre bonus)	Sustained Offensive	1
Inspire	Commence a series of Divisional inspections aimed at raising morale (+Cdr Inspire bonus)	Sustained Offensive	1
Dig In!	Order all Divisions to dig in and hold their ground (+Cdr Entrench bonus)	Defensive	1
Elastic	Authorise Divisions to conduct an Elastic Defence (+Cdr Defence bonus)	Defensive	1
In Depth	Order all Divisions to adopt a Defence in Depth (+1/2 Cdr Defence bonus, +1/2 Cdr Entrench bonus)	Defensive	1

Officer Qualities

Each card provides a benefit that is directly tied into the commander's qualities. These can be found in the 'Officer Information' display to the right of the commander's portrait. There are five qualities for each commander.

Offence is the ability to prepare and execute a strong plan of attack.

Defence is being able to hold ground in the face of adversity.

F.M Von Kluge, commander of the 4th Army, AGC, is poor on the offence but extremely strong with rapidly forming a defensive position (entrenching) as befits his WW1 experience

Col.G Guderian, commander of the 2nd Panzergruppe, AGC, has very strong offence and manoeuvre qualities as you'd expect from one of the leading exponents of mobile warfare

Gen. Obst. Strauss, commander of the 9th Army, AGC, is another WW1 Infantry commander used to the trenches

Manoeuvre is the ability to keep a formation moving on the battlefield. To overcome the natural tendencies of inertia and self preservation.

Col.G Hoth, commander of the 3rd Panzergruppe, AGC, is an all rounder who can be relied upon to keep pushing ahead

Inspire is all about raising morale when the going gets tough. Most senior commanders know what to do when it is required.

Entrench. Dig in. Fast. Before the barrage starts and the shells start landing.

DESIGNER NOTE

Officer qualities are the only way that different German Army level Commanders are distinguished from each other. There was a deliberate decision to keep this aspect of the game streamlined. Each commander has 5 qualities and they only come into play once their formation has Command Focus. Only one formation per theatre can have focus. As the card effects remain in play, once used, the system provides a decent range of options and generates a small number of interesting decision points.

The individual commanders could easily have had a whole range abilities and cards but this would have added a significant amount of 'busy work' and a whole lot of low level decisions that would have detracted from the game's operational focus and 'micromanagement free' ethos.

Gen. Obst. Von Kuchler, commander of the 18th Army, AGN. Another strong entrencher. There is a reason these gentlemen haven't been placed in charge of a Panzergruppe

F.M Von Reichenau, commander of the 6th Army, AGS. Poor at everything, even entrenching. At one point Hitler blamed the Army Group South's poor situation on "that egoist von Reichenau". F.M Von Halder had an equally dim view of the man

Officer Card Effects

Each possible officer card utilises one, or more, officer qualities to determine its effect on all the Divisions within the formation. These apply directly (e.g if the quality is 5 then the effect is 5).

COMMANDER QUALITIES

Quality	Each quality translates directly to the effect shown below
Offence	(increased) Offensive Combat bonus
Defence	(increased) Defensive Combat bonus
Manoeuvre	(increased) Action Points
Inspire	(increased) Morale
Entrench	(increased) Entrenchment level

The Envelopment card, for example provides half the commander's offence quality. If this was applied to Guderian's 2nd Panzergruppe (Offence of 30) then it would translate to a +15% Offensive combat bonus (half of 30).

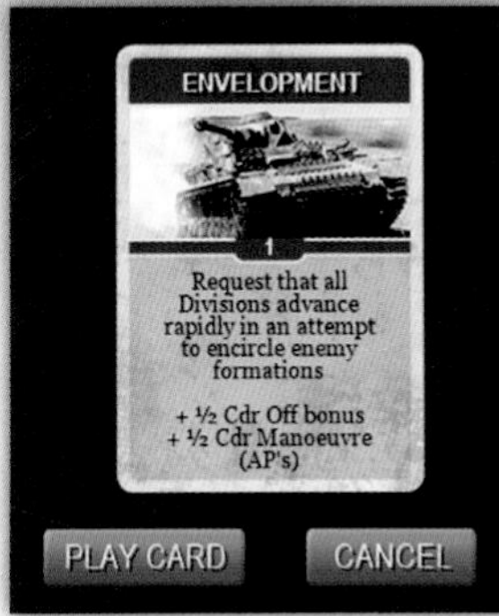
ENVELOPMENT
1
Request that all Divisions advance rapidly in an attempt to encircle enemy formations
+ ½ Cdr Off bonus
+ ½ Cdr Manoeuvre (AP's)
PLAY CARD
CANCEL

There is an additional half of the commanders maneouvre quality (30) which would give a +15 AP bonus. As Guderian has very strong qualities in both areas, 'Envelopment' would be an ideal card to play. 'Tactical Advance' would be another. As this utilises the commanders full offence quality there would be a large +30% offensive combat bonus for all Divisions within the 2nd Panzergruppe.

STAFF ADVICE

Proper utilisation of Command Focus and officer cards can make a big difference. There is a synergy between Command Focus and postures. At the start of the campaign you want to optimise the offensive punch and range of your Panzergruppes. Keep them on their Blitzkrieg postures as long as possible (until fuel stocks start to run dry) and aim to Focus on them with cards the emphasise these qualities.

Later on, when bad weather hits, consider changing Focus to an Army (with a competent commander) and take advantage of the strong defensive cards that are available when the Army is configured to a, likewise, defensive posture. An Army with focus, the correct posture and the right officer card can hold down a long exposed flank in the face of overwhelming odds and allow you to concentrate the bulk of your forces where they are needed.

The same card played on Hoth (3rd Panzergruppe) would provide a, still substantial, +20% offensive combat bonus. But have a look at the three infantry commanders shown previously. All of them have an offence quality of only 10. That's only a +10% offensive combat bonus. Their manoeuvre qualities are equally as bad. But they know how to entrench. Play the 'Dig In!' card.

STAFF ADVICE

Don't ignore the 'Inspire' card. Morale can plummet in extreme cold.

Command Range

Divisions within the formation will only receive their appropriate bonuses if they are within Command Range (5 hexes - see 4.13 Command Range).

Divisions that are cut off, regardless of being in command range or not, won't receive any benefit either (Theatre HQ is assumed to be supplying specialist Battalions to assist and this can't happen in the Divisions can't trace a route back to the theatre HQ).

Officer Card Example

FOCUS AGN
5
4th PanzerGruppe HQ is currently benefiting from Theatre HQ Focus
Play card only if you wish to reassign Focus

The card has already been played hence the text

June 22, 1941. Start of the campaign. Armeegruppe Nòrd. Our relationship with the theatre commander, F.M Von Leeb, is positive and he is willing to provide Command Focus to Hoepner's 4th Panzergruppe.

F.M Von Leeb chimes in to inform us that he has complied with our wishes.

The following turn Col.G Hoepner has a combined set of Blitzkrieg (cause of his posture, note the red arrow status icon next to the unit name) and Sustained Offensive (you always get these, regardless) officer cards. We can choose one.

Before we do this we inspect Hoepner's commander qualities. A solid, all-round performer

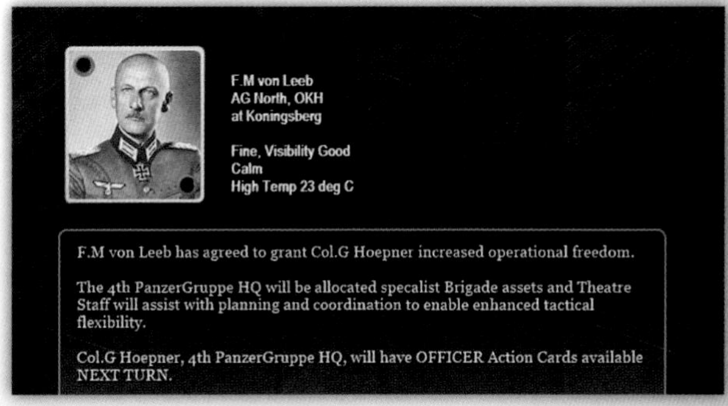
F.M von Leeb
AG North, OKH
at Koningsberg
Fine, Visibility Good
Calm
High Temp 23 deg C
F.M von Leeb has agreed to grant Col.G Hoepner increased operational freedom.
The 4th PanzerGruppe HQ will be allocated specialist Brigade assets and Theatre Staff will assist with planning and coordination to enable enhanced tactical flexibility.
Col.G Hoepner, 4th PanzerGruppe HQ, will have OFFICER Action Cards available NEXT TURN.

Von Leeb was regarded as overly cautious so we are taking advantage of our good relations with him to push him out of his comfort zone and assist the 4th Panzergruppe

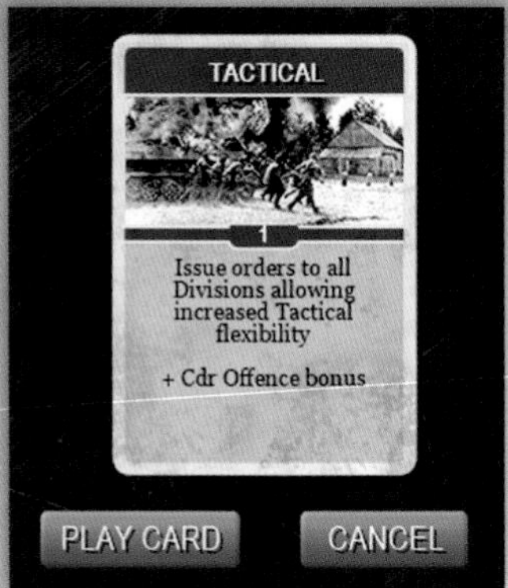

We opt to take advantage of his offence and provide the Panzers with extra punch

with the emphasis on offence, defense and manoeuvre (20 for each). He can inspire with the best of them (2). Useless with a shovel but that's O.K when you are a commander of Panzer Divisions.

Remember that once we've played the officer card it's fire and forget. We can leave Hoepner to his own devices confident that he will continue to provide increased tactical flexibility to his Divisions without any further intervention from us.

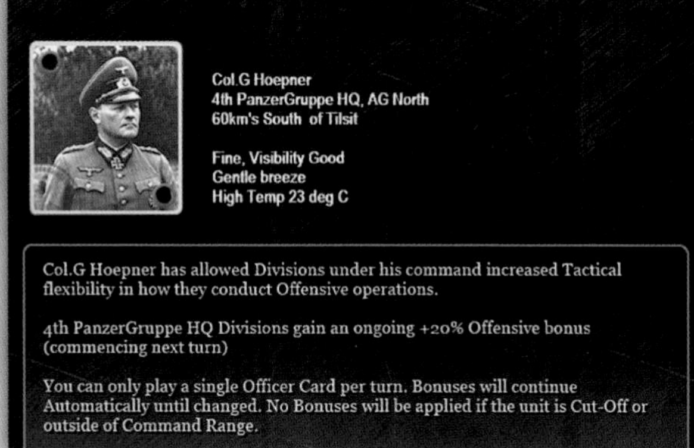

Col.G Hoepner
4th PanzerGruppe HQ, AG North
60km's South of Tilsit
Fine, Visibility Good
Gentle breeze
High Temp 23 deg C
Col.G Hoepner has allowed Divisions under his command increased Tactical flexibility in how they conduct Offensive operations.
4th PanzerGruppe HQ Divisions gain an ongoing +20% Offensive bonus (commencing next turn)
You can only play a single Officer Card per turn. Bonuses will continue Automatically until changed. No Bonuses will be applied if the unit is Cut-Off or outside of Command Range.

Nobody gets a bonus if they are cut off. As it is the 4th Panzergruppe who will be doing the encircling it shouldn't be an issue

Having played the officer card the effect is immediate. Note the big offensive combat bonus (red box on the subformations showing +70%) which is a combination of the Blitzkrieg bonus and the enhanced tactical freedom allowed.

All Divisions within the 4th Panzergruppe are receiving the bonus (provided they are within Command Range and aren't cut off) and will report as such.

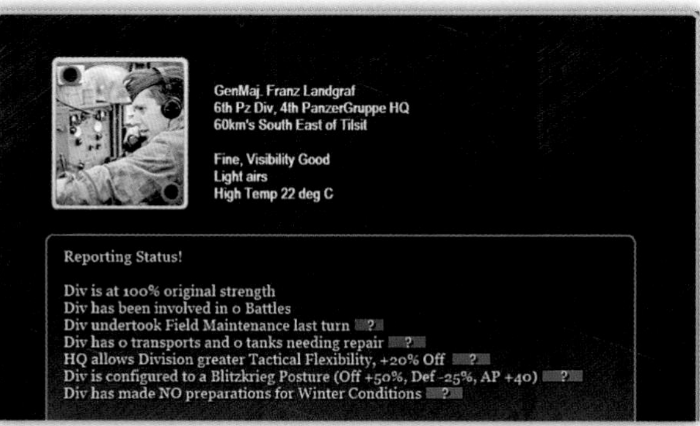

GenMaj. Franz Landgraf
6th Pz Div, 4th PanzerGruppe HQ
60km's South East of Tilsit
Fine, Visibility Good
Light airs
High Temp 22 deg C
Reporting Status!
Div is at 100% original strength
Div has been involved in 0 Battles
Div undertook Field Maintenance last turn
Div has 0 transports and 0 tanks needing repair
HQ allows Division greater Tactical Flexibility, +20% Off
Div is configured to a Blitzkrieg Posture (Off +50%, Def -25%, AP +40)
Div has made NO preparations for Winter Conditions

Excellent weather. GenMaj. Landgraf's 6th Panzer is poised, cobra like, ready to strike

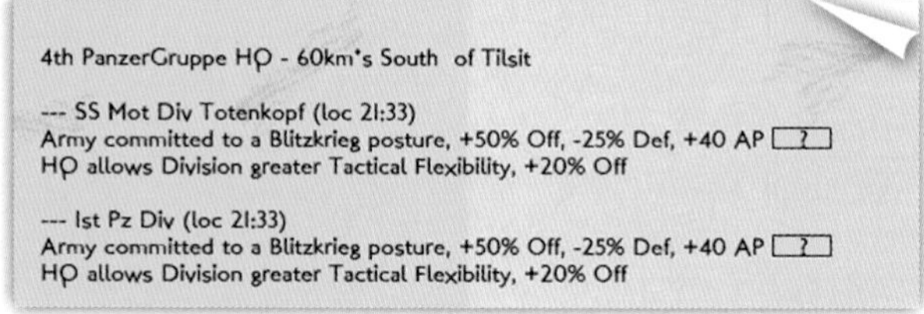
4th PanzerGruppe HQ - 60km's South of Tilsit

--- SS Mot Div Totenkopf (loc 21:33)
Army committed to a Blitzkrieg posture, +50% Off, -25% Def, +40 AP
HQ allows Division greater Tactical Flexibility, +20% Off

--- Ist Pz Div (loc 21:33)
Army committed to a Blitzkrieg posture, +50% Off, -25% Def, +40 AP
HQ allows Division greater Tactical Flexibility, +20% Off

Remember that the Unit Modifiers report, like all reports in the report tab, show the situation at the start of the turn. Once the officer card is played it won't reflect this until the following turn whereas the Report Status! is instantly updated. With the former you're reading reports compiled by your staff and with the latter you are getting up-to-date information direct from the source

You can see, next to the red Blitkrieg status icon, a double blue arrow indicating that the 6th Panzer Division is benefiting from the 'Tactical' officer card

The Unit Modifiers report for 4th Panzergruppe highlights the benefits as well. Consider what a powerhouse the 4th Panzergruppe will be once Tactical Air Support becomes available.

SUMMARY

- Officer cards are only available to an Army, or Panzergruppe, with Command Focus
- Officer cards are found in the unit display next to the Commander portrait (bottom right)
- The type of cards available depend on the posture of the Army or Panzergruppe
- One card can be played per turn
- Once played, the card remains in effect until you decide to change it (fire and forget)
- Each card utilises Commander qualities to provide bonuses to the Divisions within the formation
- Only Divisions within Command Range receive a benefit
- The unit display of each Division shows a status icon highlighting the benefit.

6.1.6. LOGISTICS

6.1.6.1. Supply and Fuel

There are two logistical related systems in the game. General Supply and Fuel.

Supply applies to both sides and to all units. Whenever units move or fight they expend readiness (see 5.2.1 Readiness). Supply is what enables them to recover their readiness. Without adequate supply a unit will automatically loose readiness and eventually become combat ineffective.

For further information see 4.14 Supply.

Fuel is required by Fast Divisions (those with vehicles). Both sides have these. Every time a Fast Division moves or fights it expends fuel, without which it can't do either.

DESIGNER NOTE

As the Soviets are falling back on interior lines and have adequate fuel reserves, it's been made into a mechanic that quietly hums away in the background. The Soviet Player need not concern himself about fuel.

The Soviets have a very simple fuel allocation, every turn, to each front that is enough to cover their requirements on most occasions. For them fuel is something that arrives automatically and is rarely a problem.

The Germans face a different situation. They are advancing deep into enemy territory with ever stretching logistical 'pipelines' (rail and truck column links that combine to transport the fuel) that struggle to get enough of their limited fuel stocks to where it is needed. It was a major factor in the campaign and the game models it in detail.

Which it does, it's worth pointing out, without any micromanagement involved. There is no 'fiddliness' or 'busy work', just big picture decisions that have an impact. The engine handles all the details and provides ample feedback on what's happening.

DESIGNER NOTE

While the logistical system is one where the Player pulls the big levers only it's also one where it is very easy to make a mess of it. This is deliberate. The game's logistical model is a fair bit more forgiving than it was on the day but inattention and disregard of the fundamentals can still bring the German advance to a grinding halt halfway to Moscow. It was a vitally important aspect that underpinned the whole campaign and the German Player is required to assume a measure of responsibility for its operation.

While the nature of the campaign has the German Player constantly struggling to keep a creaky logistical system from springing leaks, a big effort has gone into making it a fun experience. Watching your trains and truck columns slowly creep across the map, knowing that you've managing to keep the fuel flowing in the face of adversity, is very satisfying and gives you a strong appreciation of just how much of a challenge it is to invade a geographically vast country such as Russia.

The German logistical pipelines (shown visually on the map) are there for getting fuel to the Fast Divisions which are all concentrated in the Panzergruppes. All the logistical decisions that appear revolve around these three (one for each theatre) pipelines that keep the Panzergruppes in fuel.

For those that would prefer a more streamlined experience there is the 'Decisions OFF' option (game start).

SUMMARY

- All units require general supply so they can recover readiness.
- Fast Divisions (those with vehicles) require fuel to move and fight.
- The Soviets get their fuel automatically and it's not a concern.
- The Germans need to transport their fuel through three logistical pipelines (one for each theatre) before it can be used by their Panzergruppes (where their Fast Divisions are)
- There is an 'Decisions OFF' option (game start) that provides a more streamlined logistical system

6.1.6.2. Quotas

Tanks and transports require fuel. Technically they require POL (petrol, oil and lubricants) but for simplicities sake this is all referred to as 'fuel'.

There needs to be a means of easily determining if your Panzergruppes have enough fuel. As the number of vehicles within each Panzergruppe is constantly changing due to battle casualties, breakdowns, refits and replacements, knowing that there is, for example, 5,000 bbls (barrels) of fuel available in AGS for Kleist's 1st Panzergruppe isn't much use.

If the 1st PG had a lot of 'runners' (working vehicles) then 5,000 bbls might not be enough for a full turns movement. If they have only half of their starting complement of vehicles remaining then that same amount of fuel may well be in excess of what they require.

A Player could feasibly work out that they have 'x' number of vehicles as 'runners' and that they could then calculate their an expected fuel usage but this would be extremely tedious and the numbers involved would be changing from turn to turn.

The German High Command had the same problem and they used a system of *quotas* to ensure that they could easily know how much fuel was on hand, relative to what was required.

A quota is enough fuel for 4 days (one turn) for the entire Panzergruppe to operate at maximum tempo (all Fast Divisions expending 100 AP - Slow Divisions don't have vehicles and don't use fuel so they aren't counted). A Player's staff automatically calculates vehicles and fuel usage for each Panzergruppe each turn and presents the information in the form of quotas.

Knowing that there is one full quota available for a Panzergruppe is enough for a Player to be confident that he can freely move all Divisions without being concerned with running out of fuel. If there are two or more quotas then he knows that he has a buffer on hand. Three quotas, for example, would give him three turns of fuel at full usage and probably a lot more at anything other than full tempo.

With less than one quota on hand then the Player needs to keep an eye on the available fuel as there may not be enough to do all that is intended.

The Panzergruppe Summary report shows fuel quotas as well as actual fuel amounts.

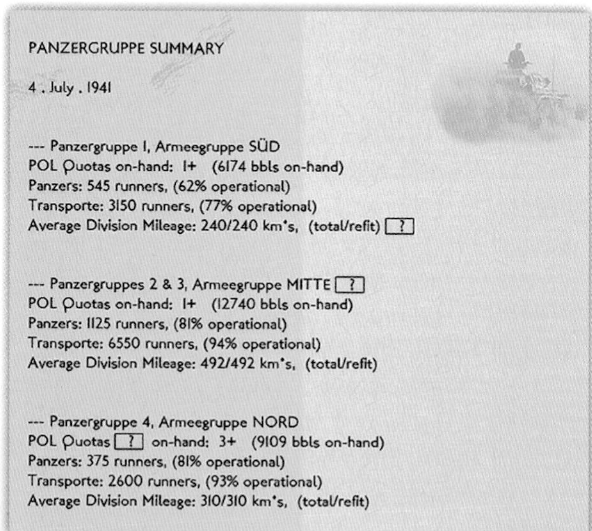

PANZERGRUPPE SUMMARY
4 . July . 1941
--- Panzergruppe I, Armeegruppe SÜD
POL Quotas on-hand: 1+ (6174 bbls on-hand)
Panzers: 545 runners, (62% operational)
Transporte: 3150 runners, (77% operational)
Average Division Mileage: 240/240 km's, (total/refit) ?
--- Panzergruppes 2 & 3, Armeegruppe MITTE ?
POL Quotas on-hand: 1+ (12740 bbls on-hand)
Panzers: 1125 runners, (81% operational)
Transporte: 6550 runners, (94% operational)
Average Division Mileage: 492/492 km's, (total/refit)
--- Panzergruppe 4, Armeegruppe NORD
POL Quotas ? on-hand: 3+ (9109 bbls on-hand)
Panzers: 375 runners, (81% operational)
Transporte: 2600 runners, (93% operational)
Average Division Mileage: 310/310 km's, (total/refit)

There is enough fuel for AGS & AGC to not be worried and AGN has an abundance

The Panzergruppe tab (bottom centre) has an indicator dial for each Panzergruppe that provides a quick visual indication of the quotas on hand.

STAFF ADVICE

Know how many quotas you have for each theatre (The quota for AGC is total for both PG 2 & 3). If you've got less than one quota (the down arrow on the Panzergruppe tab) it's time to pay attention to your logistical situation or consider ordering the Luftwaffe to fly an emergency fuel resupply mission. You'll start the campaign with extra fuel stocks on hand but the rapid early thrusts can deplete stocks quickly.

Quota calculations don't take into account combat (difficult to predict in advance). Intensive combat operations can burn through more fuel than movement.

FUEL

Icon	Quotas on hand	Effect
UP arrow	Two, or more, Quotas (>=2)	Plenty of fuel. All OK.
SIDE arrow	Between One (>=1) and Two Quotas (<2)	Adequate fuel. All OK.
DOWN arrow	Less than One Quota (<1)	Fuel Rationing needed.
CROSS	No Fuel on hand	Out of Fuel!

SUMMARY

- A Quota is enough fuel for a Panzergruppe to operate at full tempo (expend 100 AP) for one turn
- It's dynamically calculated for each Panzergruppe at the beginning of each turn
- The Quota for AGC includes both PG 2 & PG 3 (it's the only theatre with two Panzergruppes)
- A Quota is a shorthand way of quickly knowing if you have enough fuel on hand
- Aim to think in terms of Quotas rather then fixed fuel amounts

6.1.6.3. Logistical Overview

Each of the three theatres has its own logistical pipeline that consists of trains and truck columns that combine to transport the fuel to where it is needed.

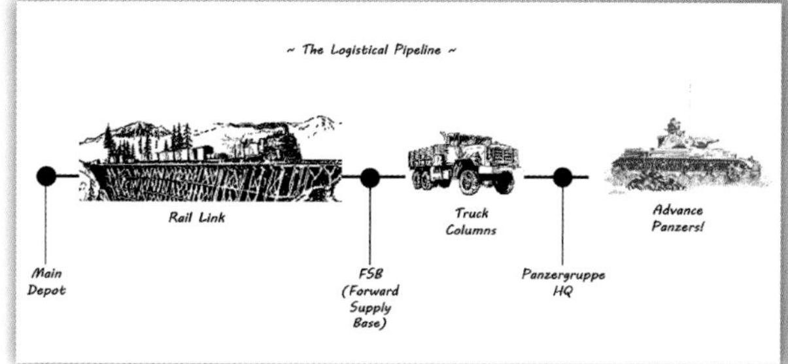

Pipelines all work the same way. There is a main depot at a fixed location on the Polish side of the border. Trains moves the fuel between the depot and the Forward Supply Base (FSB). From here truck columns transport the fuel to the Panzergruppe HQ's where it becomes available for use.

They are called 'pipelines' because they are long and skinny and can spring leaks. Like a plumber's pipe they can go around corners. The pipelines can be seen visually as a series of train and truck icons connecting up three different types of bases (Main Depot, FSB, PG HQ).

You can see, in the pic below, the Main Depot at Koningsberg. This is a fixed location that doesn't ever move. The fuel allocated, each turn, to Armeegruppe Nörd (AGN) arrives here.

There is a train link (see the train icons with 'N' on them to represent AGN) that transports the fuel to the Forward Supply Base (FSB) at Kaunas.

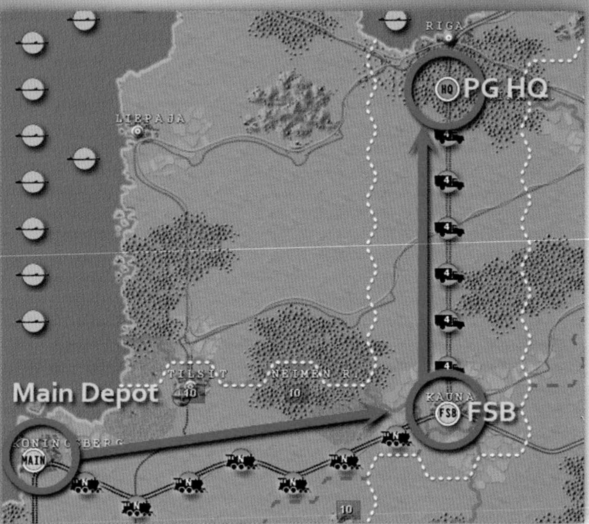

AGN Pipeline in action. The colours of the icons let you know how things are going. Green is good, red is bad

The FSB changes location, during the game, at the discretion of the Player. Knowing when to leapfrog your FSB forward is a key decision.

From the FSB truck columns (notice the icons have changed to trucks with '4' on them to represent Panzergruppe 4) move the fuel up to where ever the 4th Panzergruppe HQ is. Once here it can be used.

You can see up on the top bar how much fuel is available at the PG HQ.

'10k' is shorthand for 10,000 bbls (barrels) of fuel. That's a fair bit

ASK YOUR STAFF

Why are there only Fast Divisions in the 4th PG? What about the other Divisions in AGN, don't they need fuel too? No. Only Fast Divisions need fuel and, in the German Order of Battle, the Fast Divisions were all concentrated in the Panzergruppes. Each theatre has a Panzergruppe (AGC has two) making a total of four. When we are talking about logistical pipelines we are talking about getting enough fuel to the Panzergruppes, within each theatre, so that their individual Fast Divisions can move and fight.

Every time you move, or engage in combat with, a Fast Division from the 4th Panzergruppe the fuel 'gauge' will go down to reflect the fuel consumed.

That's pretty much it. Each turn 'x' amount of fuel arrives (from the Zone Interior) at your Main Depot. If everything is working as intended then it will be automatically transported through your pipeline and turn up at your PG HQ, ready for use and reflected in the updated fuel gauge.

As the game progresses you'll move the 4th Panzergruppe HQ further into Russia and, at some point, will have to order the FSB to leapfrog forward to a new city in order to stay in touch. If the FSB and the HQ get too far apart your truck fleet will have to work too hard (there's a limit to how far they can go) and will start blowing black smoke out their exhaust.

There are three areas where the German Player has input into the process. The first is how he moves his Panzergruppe HQ. As mentioned above there is a limit to how far the truck columns can effectively travel between the FSB and the HQ. Charging the Panzergruppe deep into Russia while leaving your FSB far behind isn't going to be a winning plan. The location of the FSB puts a limit on how far the Panzergruppe HQ (the HQ unit, not the individual Divisions) can realistically move.

DESIGNER NOTE

A good way to think about this is by visualising a bungie cord (the ones the adrenalin nuts use to strap to their ankles before leaping headfirst off a bridge into the looming chasm below) tied to a fixed point (that's your Main depot). The cord leads directly to the FSB. As it's sponsored by the department of trains there is a fair bit of stretch in this bungie cord. Your FSB can move a long way and still be accommodated by the bungie cord's elasticity.

Your FSB, attached to the main depot, itself has a bungie cord running out to the Panzergruppe HQ. But this one isn't commercial standard. It's provided by the trucker's union and it's shorter and less stretchy than the other. It can snap completely. You want everybody connected to everybody. If something snaps it'll break the link and no fuel will get through.

When and where to relocate your FSB is the second major point of Player input. You've got to move it forward to prevent the distance between the FSB and the Panzergruppe HQ becoming excessive.

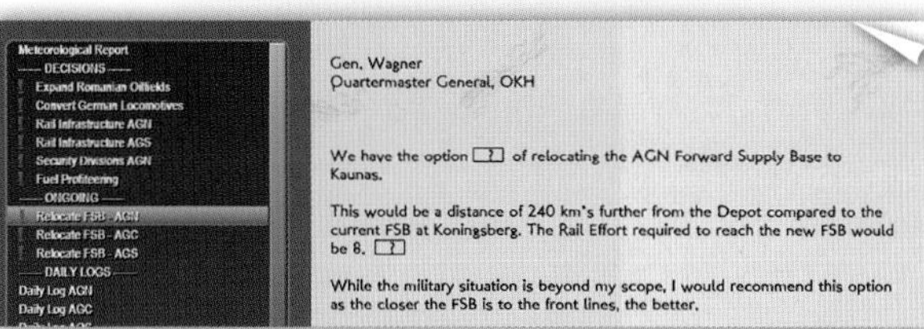

Relocating your FSB is done via a Decision and costs Political Points

ASK YOUR STAFF

Why wouldn't I automatically move it forward whenever the opportunity arises? Because there is a catch. When you relocate your Forward Supply Base there is a lot of internal disruption. No fuel will make it through the pipeline until the relocation is complete. That can take a couple of turns. If you haven't built up a stockpile it might not be an opportune moment to run short.

The final area of Player input is in a wide range of decisions that are brought to your attention. Each of them deal with some aspect of the pipeline. You make a judgement call on these, or delegate to your Chief of Staff, and something happens that makes it easier, or harder, for the fuel to move through the pipeline.

LOGISTICS REPORT - AGN

30 . June . 1941 [?]

--- Main Depot: Koningsberg [?] (loc 17:33)
FUEL (start): 0 bbls IN (ZI): 3840 bbls OUT (Trains): 0 bbls
FUEL (remaining): 3840 bbls
Trains per day: 0 (requires 0 trains, distance 240 km's) [?]

--- Forward Supply Base: RELOCATING to Kaunas, 4 days (loc 25:32)
FUEL (start): 0 bbls IN (Depot): 0 bbls OUT (Trucks): 0 bbls
FUEL (remaining): 0 bbls
Truck columns: 0 (requires 0 truck columns, distance 210 km's)

--- Field HQ: 4th Panzergruppe HQ (loc 25:25) [?]
FUEL (start): 7259 bbls IN (FSB): 0
FUEL AVAILABLE: 7259 bbls (less 2000 bbls for Blitzkrieg Op's [?])

NET FUEL: 5259 bbls [?] (maximum allowed 55000 bbls [?])

The Logistics Report for AGN.

There are a number of different reports that keep you informed of what's happening.

They are there to show the inner workings of the logistical system and can be handy to troubleshoot problems on occasion but you can ignore them if you wish. The logistical icons on the map (all those little train and truck ones) are colour coded and are designed such that you can stay on top of your logistics by them alone.

SUMMARY

- Each theatre has its own logistical pipeline
- Pipelines consist of bases (Main depot, FSB, PG HQ) connected by train and truck column links
- Fuel automatically travels through the pipelines from one end to the other (where it can be used)
- The Main Depots are fixed and don't move. Each turn fuel allocations arrive here.
- The Forward Supply Bases (FSB) can be relocated to another city via a Decision
- Whenever you relocate an FSB the pipeline shuts down and no fuel arrives for a couple of turns
- The transport links (train and truck) automatically extend as you move your FSB's and PG HQ's
- The truck column link to from the FSB to the Panzergruppe HQ has limits on how far it can stretch
- The bases and transport links are shown visually on the map by colour coded icons
- There are a lot of decisions that arise about the operation of various components of the pipeline.

6.1.6.4. AGC Logistics

This differs from the other two theatres in that it has two, not one, Panzergruppes.

The Panzergruppes share a common Main Depot and a common Forwards Supply Base but have separate truck columns transporting fuel to each from the FSB.

They share a common pool of fuel and their truck column situations are AVERAGED in all the internal logistical calculations.

For further information see 6.1.6.18 Compromises.

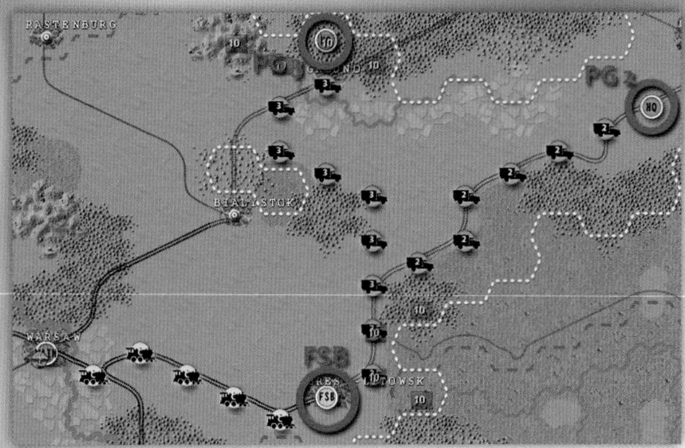

Note that the truck column icons have a number on them - '3' indicates Hoth's 3rd Panzergruppe and '2' Guderian's 2nd Panzergruppe

6.1.6.5. Logistical Icons

The logistical icons that depict the pipelines are colour coded. It's worth understanding how this works as it enables you to see what is happening with your pipelines at a glance.

There are two types of icons - bases (Main, FSB & HQ) and transport links (trains and truck columns).

Base icons show how much fuel is currently present at the base. Transport links show the *capacity* of the link as in how much fuel it can transport in a turn.

All icons are current for the start of the turn. They will update between turns, ready for the next.

LOGISTICAL ICON COLOUR CODING		
Colour	Transport Link	Base
Green	Enough to move 2+ Quotas	2+ Quotas on hand
Yellow	Only enough to move between 1 & 2 Quotas	Between 1 & 2 Quotas on hand
Red	Only enough to move less than 1 Quota	Less than 1 Quota on hand
Grey	Insufficient transport to move anything	No fuel on hand

Viewing the Icons

It can be difficult to get a clear picture of what's going on with your logistics when the map is cluttered with units.

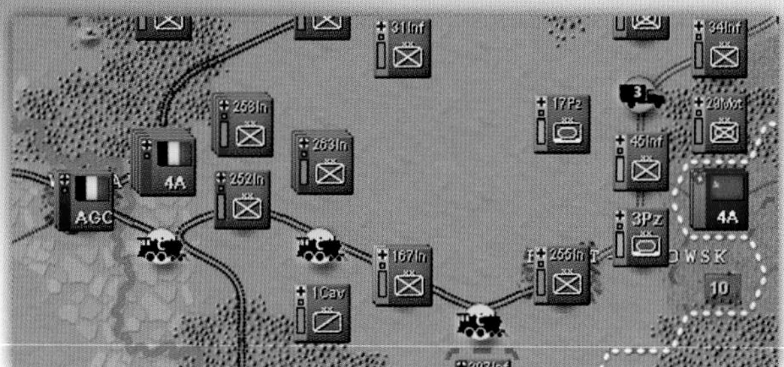

What's going on here?

To obtain a clear view of the icons turn off the unit display.

Click this button to toggle through the three unit display options (NATO counters/silhouettes/counters OFF)

Keyboard shortcuts '2', '1' & '0'

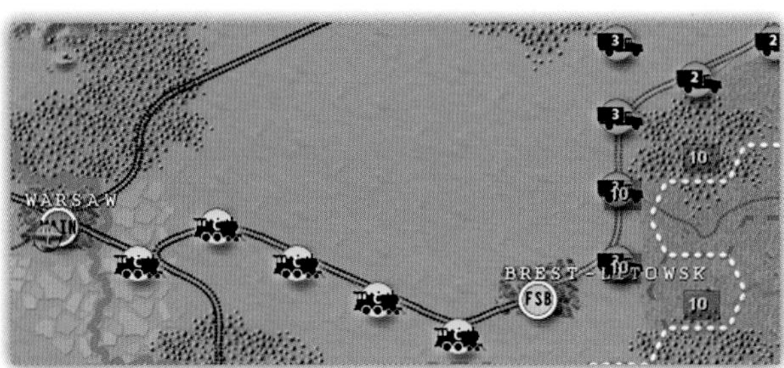

With the counters removed it's a lot easier to see what's happening

If you don't see anything it's probably because the 'Extra Hex Information' has been toggled off.

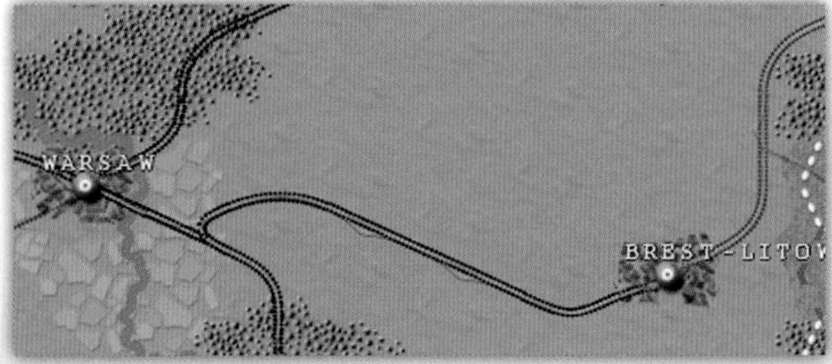

An empty map. No counters and no icons

You can do this via the button down the bottom. Keyboard shortcut '4'

No counters showing (on the left) and no icons (on the right). Press '4' to return the icons and '2' to return the counters

6.1.6.6. Starting Logistics

At the commencement of the campaign there are no Forward Supply Bases on the map. That's because they are still at the Main Depot. There are also no trains as movement from the Main Depot to the FSB is instantaneous if they are at the same location.

The FSB is at the Main Depot until you relocate it forward

STAFF ADVICE

There is a temptation to forget about your logistics in the early stages of the campaign. Before you know it your truck columns will be over-extended (beyond their 10 hex limit) and, if you're not careful, will start suffering high rates of mechanical failure well before they should. Take the first opportunity that arises to relocate your Forward Supply Base from its starting position at the Main Depot. It's important that you get your train transport link up and running and take the weight of your truck columns.

6.1.6.7. Trains

DESIGNER NOTE

Truck columns are represented as the number of truck columns actually present. Trains are shown as 'trains per day' which is a measure of throughput, not actual numbers. It's done this way as it's irrelevant (it's assumed you've always got a minimum number) how many trains you have on hand. If you've got one hundred trains on hand and only sixteen make it through, in a given time period, then for practical purposes you've only got sixteen trains that are doing anything useful. The other eighty four are sitting idle because of various restrictions in track and infrastructure that are preventing them from being used.

The train transport links, in the pipelines, connect the Main Depots to the Forward Supply Bases.

Trains are expressed in terms of the 'number of trains per day'.

Each theatre has an ideal number of trains per day that are assumed to transit the rail network. These figures are close to historical reality (tweaked a bit for balance) and are taken as the starting point for how many trains are operating.

From this 'ideal' number, trains are added or subtracted depending on circumstances to provide a net 'actual number of trains per day' that made it through. The only time you can realistically expect to achieve an ideal throughput of trains is right at the start of the campaign when the track distance is short and everything is working as it should.

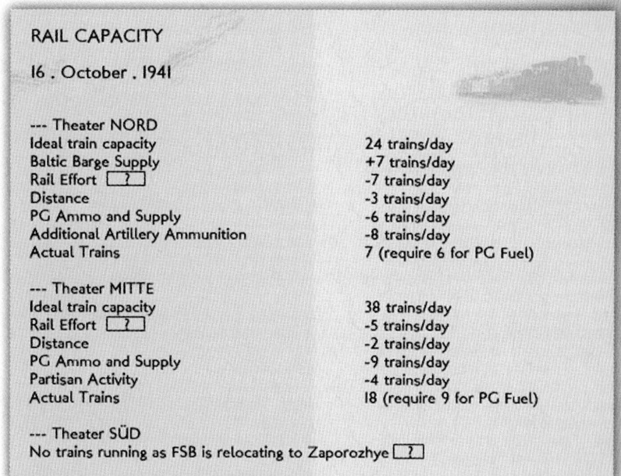

RAIL CAPACITY

16 . October . 1941

--- Theater NORD	
Ideal train capacity	24 trains/day
Baltic Barge Supply	+7 trains/day
Rail Effort [?]	-7 trains/day
Distance	-3 trains/day
PG Ammo and Supply	-6 trains/day
Additional Artillery Ammunition	-8 trains/day
Actual Trains	7 (require 6 for PG Fuel)
--- Theater MITTE	
Ideal train capacity	38 trains/day
Rail Effort [?]	-5 trains/day
Distance	-2 trains/day
PG Ammo and Supply	-9 trains/day
Partisan Activity	-4 trains/day
Actual Trains	18 (require 9 for PG Fuel)

--- Theater SÜD

No trains running as FSB is relocating to Zaporozhye [?]

Mid October. Plenty of problems but enough trains are still getting through

General Gercke is in charge of all Train related matters.

Rail Capacity Report

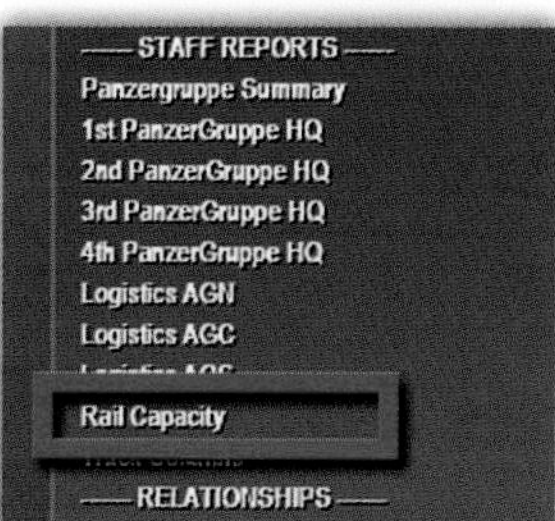

This provides a detailed breakdown of all train activity. It's found in the report tab under 'Staff Reports'

As each theatre runs its own separate train system the report details train activity by theatre. At the top of each theatre section is the ideal number of trains that would occur if there were no problems. This amount can change during the game as a result of decisions.

ASK YOUR STAFF

- **Why is the picture on the train icon of an older, pre-war model?**
  The modern (1941) German locomotives were found to be too heavy to be used on the Eastern Front. Soviet loco's were smaller and consequently the track foundations were lighter. When the track was changed over to the German gauge the foundations weren't sturdy enough to support the heavier German locomotives. Nor were most of the bridges. Consequently the Germans were forced to use their much older locomotive stock, even bringing a number out of retirement. The 'cow catcher' was fitted to a lot of the trains to deal with fallen trees, and other obstacles, that were a 'feature' of Russian rail.

  The trains used in '41 weren't like the icon example but they weren't that far removed. The icon picture has the additional requirement of having to be clearly identifiable, at a glance, as a train.

RAIL CAPACITY

16 . October . 1941

--- Theater NORD	
Ideal train capacity	24 trains/day
Rail Effort [?]	-7 trains/day
Distance	-3 trains/day
PG Ammo and Supply	-6 trains/day
Additional Artillery Ammunition	-8 trains/day
Actual Trains	7 (require 6 for PG Fuel)

--- Theater MITTE	
Ideal train capacity	38 trains/day
Rail Effort [?]	-5 trains/day
Distance	-2 trains/day
PG Ammo and Supply	-9 trains/day
Partisan Activity	-4 trains/day
Actual Trains	18 (require 9 for PG Fuel)

--- Theater SÜD

No trains running as FSB is relocating to Zaporozhye [?]

Under the ideal number are any factors that are influencing train operations, within the theatre, good or bad. These can vary considerably from turn to turn and are based on physical constraints ('Rail Effort' and 'Distance') or as a consequence of decisions taken.

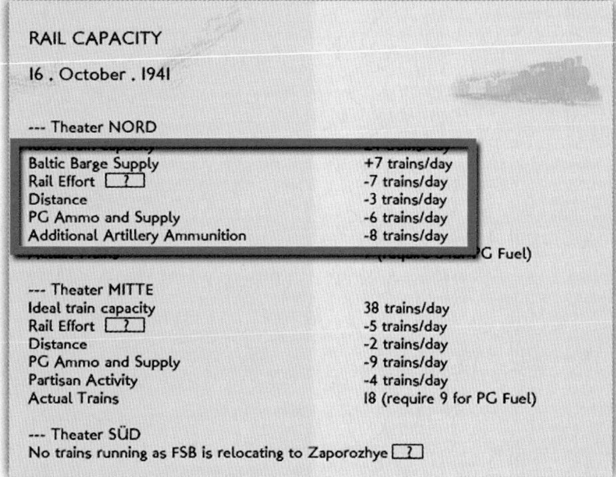

RAIL CAPACITY

16 . October . 1941

--- Theater NORD	
Baltic Barge Supply	+7 trains/day
Rail Effort [?]	-7 trains/day
Distance	-3 trains/day
PG Ammo and Supply	-6 trains/day
Additional Artillery Ammunition	-8 trains/day

--- Theater MITTE	
Ideal train capacity	38 trains/day
Rail Effort [?]	-5 trains/day
Distance	-2 trains/day
PG Ammo and Supply	-9 trains/day
Partisan Activity	-4 trains/day
Actual Trains	18 (require 9 for PG Fuel)

--- Theater SÜD

No trains running as FSB is relocating to Zaporozhye [?]

All the various factors (such as above) are tallied up and subtracted from the ideal to give an 'actual' number of trains running per day. This is the number that counts and represents what's happening on the ground.

RAIL CAPACITY

16 . October . 1941

--- Theater NORD	
Ideal train capacity	24 trains/day
Baltic Barge Supply	+7 trains/day
Rail Effort [?]	-7 trains/day
Distance	-3 trains/day
PG Ammo and Supply	-6 trains/day
Actual Trains	7 (require 6 for PG Fuel)

--- Theater MITTE	
Ideal train capacity	38 trains/day
Rail Effort [?]	-5 trains/day
Distance	-2 trains/day
PG Ammo and Supply	-9 trains/day
Partisan Activity	-4 trains/day
Actual Trains	18 (require 9 for PG Fuel)

--- Theater SÜD

No trains running as FSB is relocating to Zaporozhye [?]

'Require 6 for PG Fuel' is the number of trains needed to transport one full quota

Whenever a Forward Supply Base (FSB) is relocated the entire logistical pipeline shuts down and this is reflected in the report.

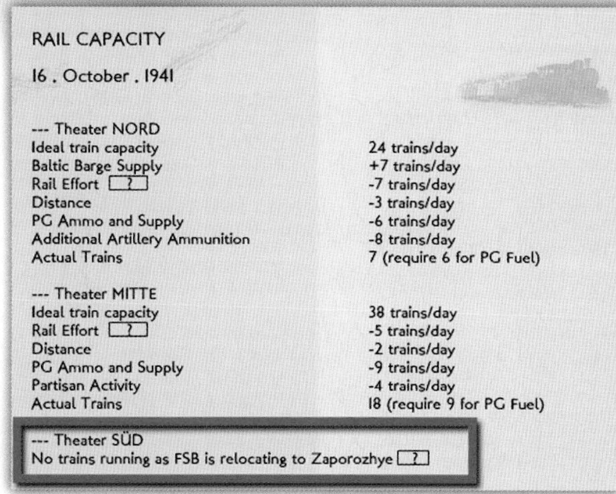

RAIL CAPACITY

16 . October . 1941

--- Theater NORD	
Ideal train capacity	24 trains/day
Baltic Barge Supply	+7 trains/day
Rail Effort [?]	-7 trains/day
Distance	-3 trains/day
PG Ammo and Supply	-6 trains/day
Additional Artillery Ammunition	-8 trains/day
Actual Trains	7 (require 6 for PG Fuel)
--- Theater MITTE	
Ideal train capacity	38 trains/day
Rail Effort [?]	-5 trains/day
Distance	-2 trains/day
PG Ammo and Supply	-9 trains/day
Partisan Activity	-4 trains/day
Actual Trains	18 (require 9 for PG Fuel)

--- Theater SÜD
No trains running as FSB is relocating to Zaporozhye [?]

Rail Network

Single track running north west (to the top left)

There are two types of rail in the game, single and double tracked. These are shown visually.

There are two types of rail gauge, Soviet and German. Soviet is shown (as above) as dark red and German as black.

Trains can run on both. The engine internally calculates the 'Rail Effort', hex by hex. It's easier to run trains down a double tracked line than a single. It's also easier to run trains down a proper German gauge line than a Soviet gauge.

DESIGN NOTE

The different gauges ensure that German trains can only operate on German gauge rail. Captured Soviet locomotives and rolling stock are needed to run on Soviet gauge and the overall efficiency of doing this is lower than the German gauge and train combination.

The Einsenbahntruppe (rail construction battalions) will progressively convert double tracked Soviet rail to German as the campaign progresses (see 6.1.8 Rail Conversion).

Rail Calculations

In the Rail Capacity Report there are always (once rail is being used) two items, 'Rail Effort' and 'Distance'.

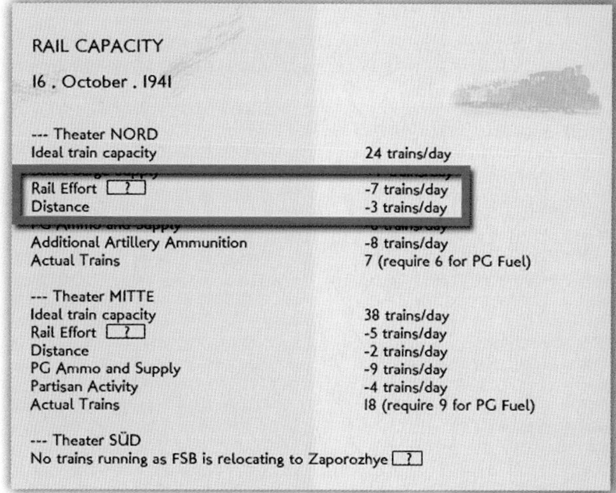

RAIL CAPACITY

16 . October . 1941

--- Theater NORD	
Ideal train capacity	24 trains/day
Rail Effort [?]	-7 trains/day
Distance	-3 trains/day
Additional Artillery Ammunition	-8 trains/day
Actual Trains	7 (require 6 for PG Fuel)
--- Theater MITTE	
Ideal train capacity	38 trains/day
Rail Effort [?]	-5 trains/day
Distance	-2 trains/day
PG Ammo and Supply	-9 trains/day
Partisan Activity	-4 trains/day
Actual Trains	18 (require 9 for PG Fuel)

--- Theater SÜD
No trains running as FSB is relocating to Zaporozhye [?]

These both act as restrictions on the number of trains able to be utilised. Distance is straight forward. The longer the length of track travelled, the larger the impact. The further that trains have to travel, the less of them that will make the trip in a given period of time.

Rail Effort is a measure of the 'difficulty' involved in the trains travelling from A to B. Running down a double tracked line is always going to be easier than a single tracked one where trains are forced to pull over and let others through.

As mentioned previously the German gauge rail is going to be more efficient than the Soviet. The engine calculates all these factors, for every hex traversed by the rail link, and comes up with a 'Rail Effort' figure that reflects this.

STAFF ADVICE

You can tell, from the table below that double tracked is always going to better than single. Soviet single tracked is horrendous in mud conditions and you'll see your Rail Effort spike if you are using it. German gauge is also better and there is a noticeable pay off in converting the key sections of double tracked line.

The following table is used internally in the calculations and is useful in that it provides a relative value of the effort involved in using different types of track (lower the number, the easier it is for trains to use).

RAIL CAPACITY			
Terrain	Rail Capacity Normal	Rail Capacity MUD	Rail Capacity SNOW
German Double Tracked Sealed	1	1	1
Soviet Double Tracked Sealed	3	3	3
German Double Tracked	1	2	1
Soviet Double Tracked	3	6	3
German Single Tracked	2	4	2
Soviet Single Tracked	6	20	6

ASK YOUR STAFF

Do I have any control over what route is used? Not directly. The game will automatically calculate the optimum route for you (it's very good at doing so). What does have an impact is the positioning of your FSB's and your choice of rail conversion routes. Ideally you want both to be running straight along your main invasion routes but this isn't always possible given enemy activity and overarching strategic plans. Capturing key cities and rail sections plays a big role in ensuring your use of the rail network is optimised.

Train Examples

Icons Example

To show the interaction between the number of trains per day and the train icons we'll use the previous train report of 16th October '41.

Armeegruppe Nörd (AGN) has 7 actual trains running. It requires 6 to supply a full quota to the 4th Panzergruppe. As the actual ('7') is greater than the requirement ('6') there is at least enough capacity to transport at least one full quota but not much more (there would have to be 12 trains to move 2 full quotas).

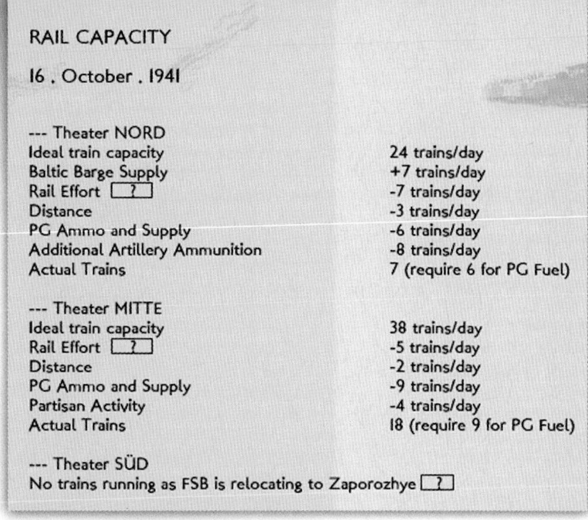

RAIL CAPACITY

16 . October . 1941

--- Theater NORD

Ideal train capacity	24 trains/day
Baltic Barge Supply	+7 trains/day
Rail Effort [?]	-7 trains/day
Distance	-3 trains/day
PG Ammo and Supply	-6 trains/day
Additional Artillery Ammunition	-8 trains/day
Actual Trains	7 (require 6 for PG Fuel)

--- Theater MITTE

Ideal train capacity	38 trains/day
Rail Effort [?]	-5 trains/day
Distance	-2 trains/day
PG Ammo and Supply	-9 trains/day
Partisan Activity	-4 trains/day
Actual Trains	18 (require 9 for PG Fuel)

--- Theater SÜD

No trains running as FSB is relocating to Zaporozhye [?]

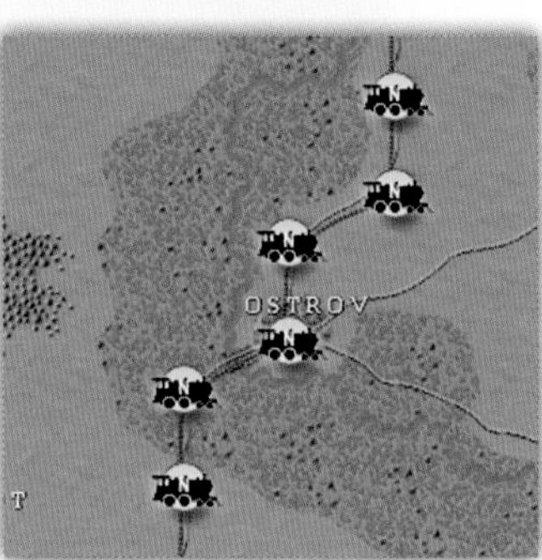

The 'N' indicates AGN trains. Yellow shows between 1 and 2 quotas capacity which is what we'd expect from the numbers

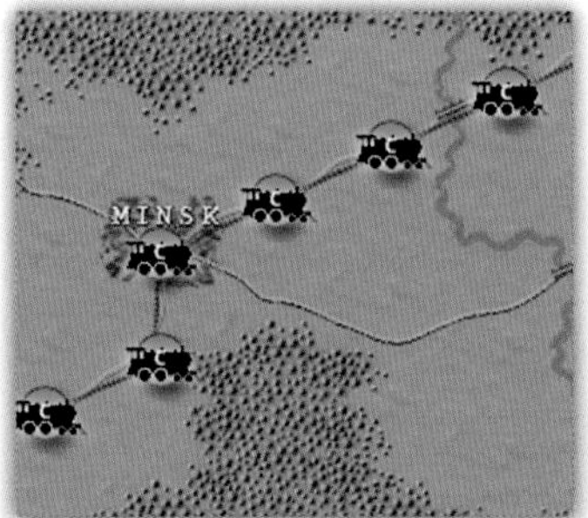

The 'C' represents AGC trains and the green colour shows that there is enough capacity to move 2, or more, quotas by train, through this link of the AGC logistical pipeline

Armeegruppe Mitte (AGC) has 18 actual trains and requires 9 to supply a full quota to the 2nd and 3rd Panzergruppes (remember AGC has two Panzergruppes, not one like the others). If 9 trains per day is enough to transport one quota then 18 is enough for two.

Armeegruppe Süd is currently relocating and no trains are running. What colour should the icon be here? That's easy - with no trains running it'll be grey (the same way that a base that has no fuel on hand is grey).

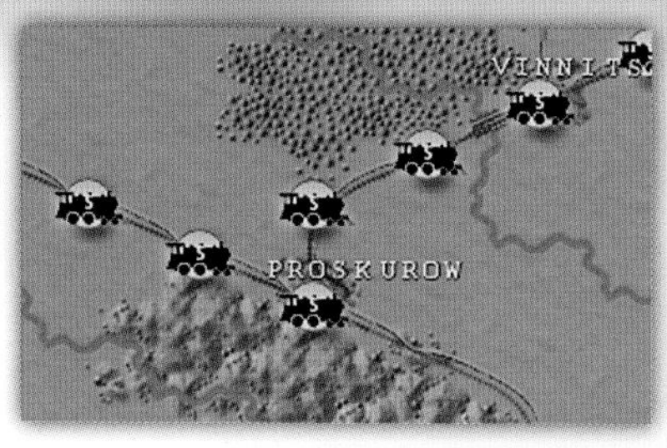

The AGS train link is shut down while the FSB is relocating

The Long Way Around

Early campaign once more. AGC. Warsaw Main Depot. Bialystok FSB.

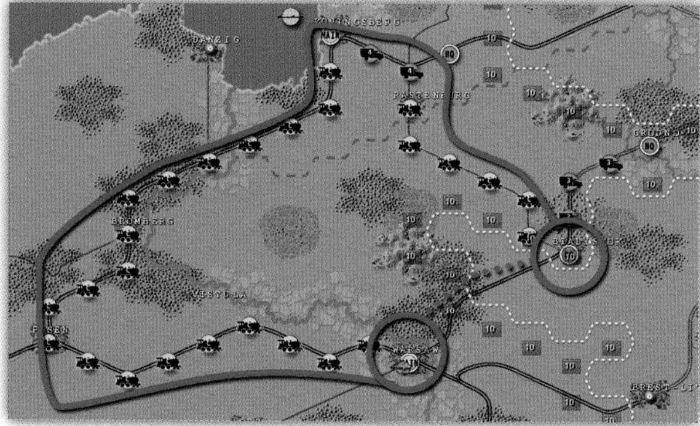

The direct link to Bialystok (dotted land) is still in Soviet hands necessitating a long loop around to the north on decent double track German gauge and from there south east through Rastenburg on a single track line.

The Rail Capacity report sums it up.

RAIL CAPACITY

12 . July . 1941

--- Theater NORD	
Ideal train capacity	24 trains/day
Actual Trains	24 (require 0 for PG Fuel)
--- Theater MITTE	
Rail Effort [?]	-7 trains/day
Distance	-3 trains/day
Actual Trains	14 (require 14 for PG Fuel)
--- Theater SÜD	
Ideal train capacity	32 trains/day
Lack of Infrastructure	-1 trains/day
Actual Trains	32 (require 0 for PG Fuel)

The distance component is creeping up (less 3 trains per day) but the rail effort is now a sizable amount (less 7 trains per day). Once you start using single track line it makes a difference. If it was Soviet gauge single track it'd be worse.

Once the summer rains hit the situation actually does get worse.

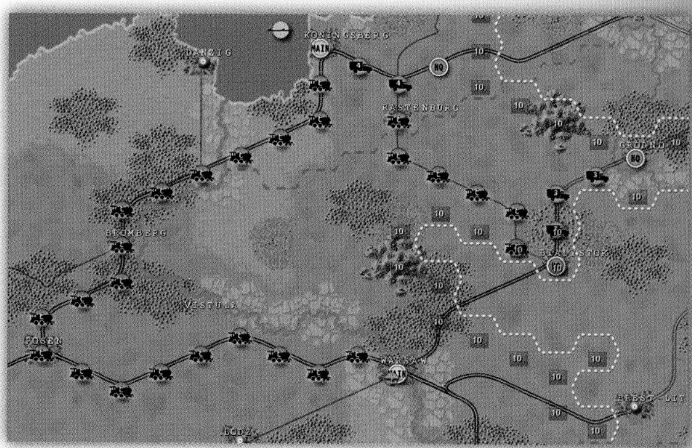

Code red

The combination of the big rail effort and the distance has caused the number of trains per day to drop below the one quota capacity threshold (red icons) and not all the fuel is being transported up the pipeline. Some of it is being stockpiled at the main depot.

RAIL CAPACITY

16 . July . 1941

--- Theater NORD	
Ideal train capacity	24 trains/day
Lack of Infrastructure	-1 trains/day
Lack of Signaling Equipment	-2 trains/day
Actual Trains	24 (require 0 for PG Fuel)
--- Theater MITTE	
Rail Effort [?]	-10 trains/day
Distance	-3 trains/day
Actual Trains	11 (require 14 for PG Fuel)
--- Theater SÜD	
Ideal train capacity	32 trains/day
Actual Trains	32 (require 0 for PG Fuel)

As a comparison here's how it looks with the direct shot from Warsaw to Bialystok (dotted line) along a short length of German gauge double track.

--- Theater MITTE	
Rail Effort [?]	-2 trains/day

STAFF ADVICE

Examine your anticipated route of advance. Look at the rail network and figure out which sections you're going to need to control in order for your Panzergruppes to keep receiving fuel. Historically the German planners, prior to the invasion, realised that the only viable routes into Russia were those that followed the main rail routes.

There's no distance component and the effort is minimal (less 2 trains per day).

6.1.6.8. Naval Operations

Baltic Convoys

Once the Germans capture certain Baltic sea ports (up the top of the map, AGN) they are presented with Decisions (within a couple of turns of the city being captured) allowing them the option of running barge convoys up the Baltic sea.

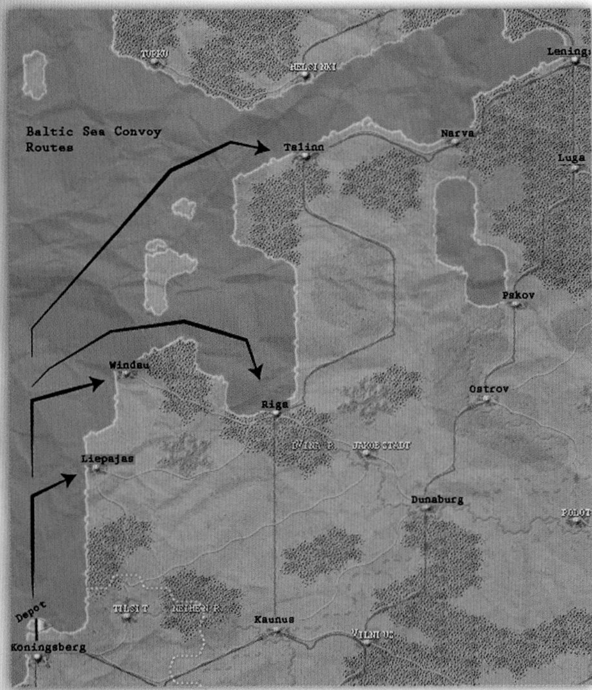

The four possible convoy ports are Leipajas, Windau, Riga and Talinn

All convoys originate out of Koningsberg and are shown visually (with green or yellow icons) once activated.

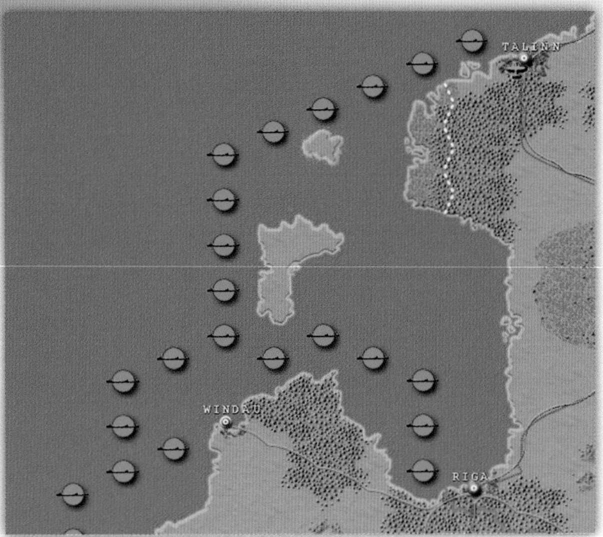

Convoys are running to all four ports

The convoys serve to increase the number of trains per day for AGN. In effect they provide train equivalents that can't be affected by all the various land based rail problems.

The Daily AGN Theatre Log provides convoy details as well as the Rail Capacity Report.

--- Logistics [?]
- Quartermaster: 4 days needed to consolidate the new FSB at Leningrad [?]
- Barge convoy to Liepaja equivalent to +1 trains/day [?]
- Barge convoy to Windau equivalent to +1 trains/day [?]
- Barge convoy to Riga equivalent to +2 trains/day [?]
- Barge convoy to Talinn equivalent to +3 trains/day [?]
- Trains allocated for additional Artillery ammunition
- Truck maintenance -1%, [?] [?]

The maximum possible 7 trains per day equivalent from the Baltic convoys

A convoy to a port won't provide any benefit (even though it's showing as green icons) if a rail route can't be traced between the port and the AGN Forward Supply Base. Whatever arrives by convoy has to have a valid means of actually getting to the FSB otherwise it's assumed to be stockpiled at the port. You'll receive a message in your Daily AGN Theatre Log if there is an interruption.

The Talinn convoy decision requires the allocation of Luftwaffe resources (it's close to the Soviet Baltic Fleet base at Leningrad) in order to receive the full effect (3 trains/day).

DESIGNER NOTE

The convoys served as a useful supplement to the standard logistical pipeline in AGN. They transported large amounts of fuel and supplies. By having them represent extra train services the system is kept streamlined and there is no need for additional reports or special mechanics.

Black Sea

The Soviets had a sizable Black Sea (down the bottom of the map, AGS) Fleet and air bases in the Crimea that were capable of naval interdiction. For the duration of '41 the Germans (who had minimal naval assets in the region) kept a low profile and naval activity was not a big enough factor to be modelled in the game.

6.1.6.9. Truck Columns

The truck column links, in the pipelines, connect the Forward Supply Bases to the Panzergruppe HQ's.

Truck columns are expressed in numbers (you have 'x' number of truck columns).

TRUCK COLUMNS	16 . October . 1941		
	AGN	AGC	AGS
	---	---	---
Truck columns (Theatre & Captured)	337	411	345
- Maintenance (awaiting repair) [?]	-124	-143	-100
- Losses (permanent) [?]	-0	-2	-3
- Infantry & Artillery use [?]	-90	-100	-90
Available Truck Columns	123	166	152
Panzergruppe Truck columns	123	166	•
- PG Supply and Ammo [?]	-0	-15	•
- Distance penalty [?]	-0	-18	•
- Route difficulty [?]	-0	-6	•
Surplus Truck columns	123	127	•
Required (PG Fuel) [?]	0	15	•
Distance, FSB to HQ (km's) [?]	0	360	•
Accumulated Mileage (km's) [?]	360	6720	•

• Black Dots indicate that truck columns are busy relocating your FSB.

Mid October. Still coping. AGC due for a refit as mileage is excessive

Truck columns can be permanently lost and are prone to breakdowns. It's quite possible to run critically short of trucks columns and find that no fuel is getting through as a result.

STAFF ADVICE

Truck columns are the weak link in the logistical pipelines. The Germans were critically short of trucks, tyres and spare parts. The quickest way to bring your invasion of Russia to a grinding halt is to run your truck columns into the ground.

Trains can efficiently transport fuel and ammunition over long distances. Truck columns, however, have a finite limit as to how far they can operate. At distances over 300 km's (ten hexes)the use of truck columns becomes impractical as they use excessive amounts of fuel (their job is to deliver fuel, not use it).

DESIGNER NOTE

Barbarossa was very much a railway war. The German armies were forced to follow the few decent rail lines as the vast distances of Russia made any other form of logistical transport impractical. Truck columns were used extensively but mainly as a means of covering the relatively short distance from the rail head (in game terms the Forward Supply Base) to the troops.

Similar to trains the number of truck columns are reduced by the distance travelled and the difficulty of the route. Reductions manifest as breakdowns and, as time progresses, there will be an increasing percentage of truck columns out of action and requiring maintenance. Decisions allow you to take actions to rectify this on a planned, or emergency, basis.

The Wehrmacht fielded over two thousand different types of trucks in Barbarossa which was a maintenance and supply nightmare. There were many confiscated civilian trucks from Germany, all manner of 'liberated' French, Belgium, Dutch and Polish trucks. There were even trucks purchased from Switzerland.

General Wagner is in charge of all Truck related matters.

Truck Columns Report

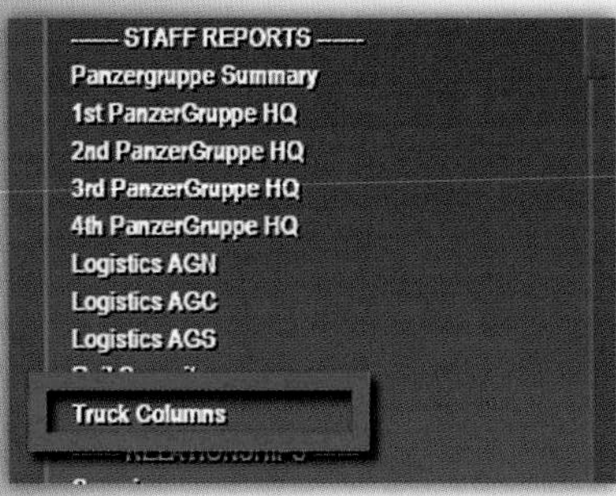

This provides a detailed breakdown of all truck column activity. It's found in the report tab under 'Staff Reports'

As each theatre runs its own separate truck column system the report details train activity by theatre.

TRUCK COLUMNS — 22 . June . 1941

	AGN	AGC	AGS
	---	---	---
Truck columns (Theatre & Captured)	300	400	300
- Maintenance (awaiting repair) [?]	-60	-80	-60
- Losses (permanent) [?]	-0	-0	-0
- Infantry & Artillery use [?]	-100	-100	-100
Available Truck Columns	140	220	140
Panzergruppe Truck columns	140	220	140
- PG Supply and Ammo [?]	-1	-1	-1
- Distance penalty [?]	-1	-2	-3
- Route difficulty [?]	-2	-13	-15
Surplus Truck columns	136	204	121
Required (PG Fuel) [?]	1	1	1
Distance, FSB to HQ (km's) [?]	90	150	210
Accumulated Mileage (km's) [?]	270	450	630

• Black Dots indicate that truck columns are busy relocating your FSB.

Truck situation at Campaign start. There are already a number of truck columns needing repair

A truck column typically consists of 20 Opel Blitz trucks with a combined carrying capacity of 60 tonne (roughly 420 bbls).

At the top of the report are the number of truck columns available in each theatre. There is a set number that each theatre commences the campaign with but this can be supplemented by captured Soviet trucks (via Decisions) as the campaign progresses.

TRUCK COLUMNS — 22 . June . 1941

	AGN	AGC	AGS
	---	---	---
Truck columns (Theatre & Captured)	300	400	300
- Maintenance (awaiting repair) [?]	-60	-80	-60
- Losses (permanent) [?]	-0	-0	-0
- Infantry & Artillery use [?]	-100	-100	-100

Captured Russian trucks (GAZ-AA) were found to be better equipped and more reliable in the atrocious conditions than the German Opels (which weren't equipped with all-wheel drive) and were greatly prized by the Germans. They could also use captured fuel stocks directly without it having to be refined (benzene needed to be added).

From the total number of truck columns available are deducted losses, those out of action and requiring maintenance and those assigned to keeping the Infantry and Artillery Divisions supplied.

This gives a net figure for the number of truck columns available to transport the fuel from your Forward Supply Base to your Panzergruppe HQ's.

TRUCK COLUMNS — 22 . June . 1941

	AGN	AGC	AGS
	---	---	---
Truck columns (Theatre & Captured)	300	400	300
- Maintenance (awaiting repair) [?]	-60	-80	-60
- Losses (permanent) [?]	-0	-0	-0
- Infantry & Artillery use [?]	-100	-100	-100
Available Truck Columns	140	220	140

There are 220 truck columns remaining for moving fuel to both the AGC Panzergruppes

The main use of the truck columns is to keep your rapidly advancing Panzergruppes supplied with fuel and ammunition. There is a fixed number ('100') of truck columns that are dedicated to keeping the regular armies supplied ('Infantry and Artillery use', see pic above). You'll have the opportunity (via

Decisions) to change these allocations, if desired. Historically there was a chronic shortage of trucks throughout the entire Eastern front and they were in great demand from all quarters.

Reducing the number of trucks assigned to the artillery and regular armies can have consequences (see 6.1.6.13 Ammunition).

Panzergruppe truck columns (a direct carry over from the above, eg. 220 for AGC) are further whittled down by a number required to keep the Panzergruppes in general supply and with adequate amounts of ammunition plus deductions for the distance travelled and the route difficulty.

Panzergruppe Truck columns	140	220	140
- PG Supply and Ammo [?]	-1	-1	-1
- Distance penalty [?]	-1	-2	-3
- Route difficulty [?]	-2	-13	-15
Surplus Truck columns	136	204	121

What's left over is the 'Surplus Truck Columns' and this is the number of truck columns actually transporting fuel from your FSB's to your HQ's.

Beneath are the number of truck columns required to transport one full quota to enable you to get an idea of whether you've got enough trucks, or not.

Surplus Truck columns	136	204	121
Required (PG Fuel) [?]	1	1	1
Distance, FSB to HQ (km's) [?]	90	150	210
Accumulated Mileage (km's) [?]	270	450	630

This corresponds directly with the Logistics report.

Down the bottom is a readout of the distance covered by the truck columns. Once distances exceed 300 km's (190 miles), the truck columns will incur exponential distance penalties. Mileage covered by the truck columns is tracked as this plays a part in maintenance calculations (the more kilometres you clock up, the greater the likelihood of mechanical problems).

Cumulative mileage will only increase if there are actually truck columns making it through to the HQ's.

LOGISTICS REPORT - AGC

22 . June . 1941 [?]

--- Main Depot: Warsaw [?] (loc 19:42)
FUEL (start): 0 bbls IN (ZI): 13250 bbls OUT (Trains): 13250 bbls
FUEL (remaining): 0 bbls
Trains per day: 38 (requires 0 trains, distance 0 km's) [?]

--- Forward Supply Base (FSB): Warsaw [?] (loc 19:42)
FUEL (start): 0 bbls IN (Depot): 13250 bbls OUT (Trucks): 13250 bbls
FUEL (remaining): 0 bbls
Truck columns: 204 (requires 1 truck column [?], distance 150 km's)

--- Field HQ: 2nd Panzergruppe HQ (loc 21:43), 3rd PG HQ (21:35) [?]
FUEL (start): 7000 bbls IN (FSB): 13250
FUEL AVAILABLE: 20250 bbls (less 4000 bbls for Blitzkrieg Op's [?])

NET FUEL: 16250 bbls [?] (maximum allowed 55000 bbls [?])

AGC has 204 truck columns available and requires 1 truck column to move the fuel which ties in with the numbers in the Truck Columns report, above

Surplus Truck columns	136	204	121
Required (PG Fuel) [?]	1	1	1
Distance, FSB to HQ (km's) [?]	90	150	210
Accumulated Mileage (km's) [?]	270	450	630

Road Network

For the movement of units there are only two types of roads in the game - sealed and normal. Sealed are shown visually and normal roads are inferred to be where ever a rail line is (provided a sealed road isn't already present).

For logistical purposes (only) the situation is more nuanced and, while the same system applies, it's more detailed. None of this is 'need to know' (it's explained in the next section for those that would like more information) as it's all handled internally by the game.

Provided you remember the basic rules of thumb that sealed roads, where available, are always going to be the best routes and that normal roads will turn to mush in the mud, you'll be fine.

Plains, fields, forest and woods hexes are all assumed to have a network of local country 'lanes' that the truck columns can utilise but they are of extremely poor quality and using them will cause a lot of wear and tear on your trucks.

Armeegruppe Mitte (AGC)

Unlike the other theatres, this has two Panzergruppes - Guderian's 2nd and Hoth's 3rd Panzergruppes.

They share a combined logistical system. For a discussion on why this is see 6.1.6.18 Compromises.

In practical terms they have individual truck columns originating form a mutual Forward Supply Base. For all logistical calculations their truck column situations are AVERAGED.

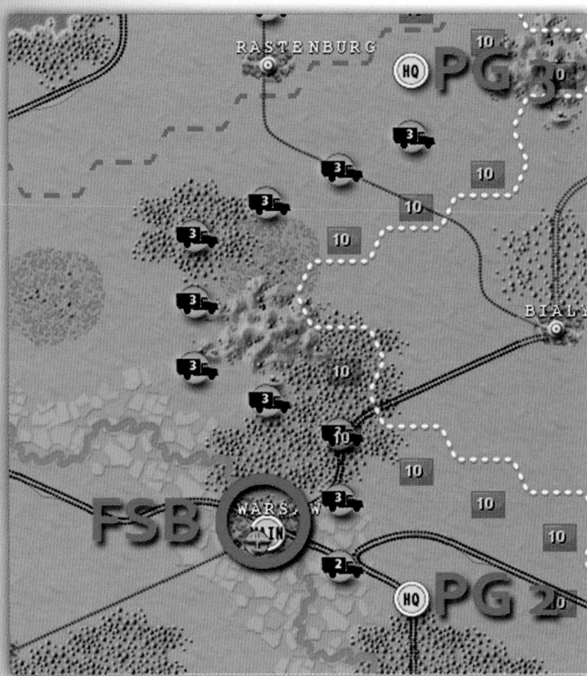

Situation at campaign start. The FSB is yet to be relocated so it's still at Warsaw, at the Main Depot

You can see from the above that Hoth's 3rd Panzergruppe (note that the truck icons have a '3') has a route extending ten hexes distance whereas Guderian's 2nd Panzergruppe is only two hexes from the FSB.

As they are averaged the game would assume that there is a single truck column route of 6 hexes distance (10 + 2 halved). It's the same when it came to calculate the 'Route difficulty'. Although in this case it wouldn't be as straightforward as each hex would have an individual cost in difficulty that varied depending on terrain and the presence of roads. Whatever the two totals were, for both Panzergruppes, it'd be averaged.

Not Enough Trucks

If you don't have enough truck columns available to move the fuel from your FSB's to your Panzergruppe HQ's a minimum amount of fuel will still arrive (the trucks are assumed to still be operating they just aren't very effective).

Truck Calculations

Panzergruppe Truck columns	140	220	140
- PG Supply and Ammo [?]	-1	-1	-1
- Distance penalty [?]	-1	-2	-3
- Route difficulty [?]	-2	-13	-15
Surplus Truck columns	136	204	121

Like trains there are two main factors - distance and route difficulty (with trains it's referred to as 'effort'). Distance is a simple A to B calculation.

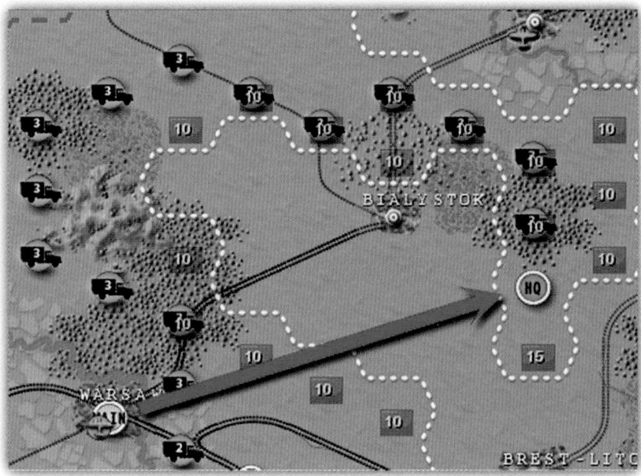

Distance is calculated based on the actual route travelled, NOT 'as the crow flies' (arrow)

Route difficulty is calculated hex by hex based. The table below provides an indication of the relative difficulty involved. Remember that rail is assumed to be 'normal' road unless there is a 'sealed' (all weather) road present.

Maintenance is calculated each turn and is shown as a percentage figure in the Daily Theatre Logs and as a number (of truck columns) in the Truck Report.

TRUCK DIFFICULTY			
Terrain	Truck Difficulty Normal	Truck Difficulty MUD	Truck Difficulty SNOW
Rail single German	6	40	6
Rail single Soviet	6	40	6
Rail single German Sealed	4	6	4
Rail single Soviet Sealed	4	6	4
Rail double German	4	20	4
Rail double Soviet	6	40	6
Rail double German Sealed	4	6	4
Rail double Soviet Sealed	4	6	4
Urban (city hex)	1	1	1
Plains & Fields	20	50	30
Forest & Woods	30	60	40
Marsh	50	100	70
Low Mountains	50	100	70
Low Mountains Forested	60	100	80

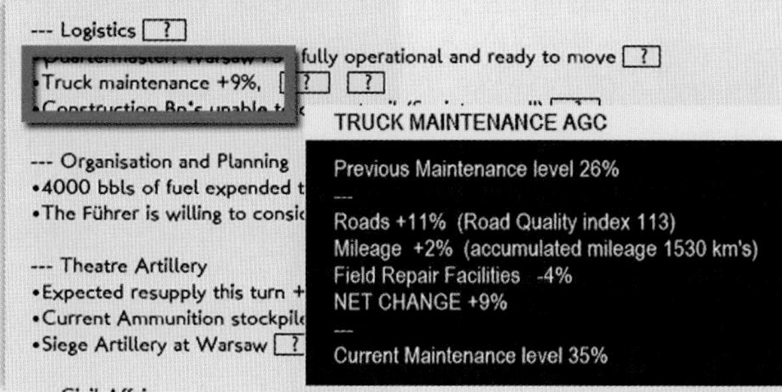

Daily Theatre Log, AGC

The dynamic tool tip, next to the maintenance entry, shows that the percentage of truck columns out of service, awaiting maintenance, has climbed 9% to a total of 35%.

This is due to the poor roads in use (+11%) and the accumulated mileage (+2%). Field repair facilities reduce this (-4%) to give a net increase of 9%.

The 'Road Quality Index' is the same as the 'Route difficulty' but expressed as a index (where zero is ideal and the higher the index, the greater the difficulty) for comparison purposes.

Mileage is in direct proportion to the accumulated mileage (which you can see in the Truck Report). The more mileage on the clock the bigger the effect. Truck refits (Decisions) will reduce the mileage.

Mileage is calculated as the number of hexes (each of 30 km's across) times a 'mileage factor' which is '3' (there and back plus the fact it's not a straight line and there will be plenty of wartime diversions).

Field Repair Facilities are always present and they do what they can to fix problems before they take a truck out of action. Certain Decisions can affect the percentage amount that they deduct every turn.

The unexpectedly poor quality of the Russian roads extracted a heavy toll on the truck columns. A month after the invasion, Armeegruppe Mitte (AGC) had lost a third of their trucks due to mechanical failures. Engine wear and tear, lube oil and fuel consumption all soared due to the heavy going. A chronic shortage of rubber for tyres only accentuated the problems.

TRUCK COLUMNS	30 . June . 1941		
	AGN	AGC	AGS
Truck columns (Theatre & Captured)	300	400	300
Maintenance (awaiting repair)	-42	-104	-81
			-0
- Infantry & Artillery use	-100	-100	-100
Available Truck Columns	158	196	119

The 104 trucks down for maintenance, for AGC, corresponds to the 26% Maintenance level in the Daily Theatre pic above. The current maintenance level (35%) will be reflected in the following turn's report

The higher the maintenance percentage climbs the less truck columns there will be to transport fuel to your Panzergruppes.

Apart from the allocations of truck columns for other purposes (supplying the regular armies, for example) the number of truck columns will be reduced by the maintenance percentage. This is tied into the route difficulty (or 'road quality index'), the theatres field repair ability, and the accumulated mileage.

The remaining truck columns are what's left to look after your Panzergruppes. Their numbers are diminished by the distance travelled and the route difficulty.

Note that the route difficulty affects your truck columns twice. It's the single most important factor.

Advice for Truckers

Truck columns travel the link between your Forward Supply Bases (FSB) and your Panzergruppe HQ's. Anything that makes this task easier will help.

Shorten the distance. Truck columns are inefficient at distances over ten hexes and suffer exponential penalties beyond this. Whenever the distance exceeds ten hexes, you've got a problem. Either move your FSB forward or shift your Panzergruppe HQ's closer to your FSB's.

Improve the route travelled. The game will automatically determine the optimum route (out of all possible ones) but you can strongly influence this by positioning your Panzergruppe HQ's on part of the road network that is directly connected to the relevant FSB location.

Having your HQ on a road (any road) is always going to be better than having it in the countryside (see the table above for the relative 'difficulty' values). A sealed road would be ideal. The 'road quality index' (see above) in the Daily Theatre Log tool tip will give you an idea of how bad the route is (the higher the index, the worse it is).

STAFF ADVICE

Think of yourself as head of a trucking company. You're tasked with moving 'x' amount of fuel in a given period of time. What's going to make that easier? A short route. Good roads. Not overdoing it. The same principles apply in the game. Don't forget mud. Would you have your truck fleet travel down narrow, muddy, country lanes once it started raining? Would you even do that when the sun was shining?

If you're going to move your Panzerguppe HQ's off into the wild blue yonder, away from a road, check your truck columns situation beforehand.

Sit tight. Pause (make sure your HQ is on a road before you do so) and let your field repair battalions do their job. Constantly pushing forward, turning your logistical pipeline into an overstretched rubber band is only going to have one outcome. Historically the Wehrmacht was forced to halt, on a number of occasions, for just this reason.

Other than this, use whatever captured trucks that you can get hold of, do what you can to improve your field repair services and order truck refits often (all done via Decisions).

Truck columns are the most vulnerable part of the entire logistical system and the most prone to problems if handled incorrectly.

6.1.6.10. Relocating Forward Supply Bases

FSB's are the middle men in the logistical pipelines. Trains bring the fuel in from the Main Depot and truck columns move it onward to the Panzergruppe HQ's. As the Panzergruppes advance further into Russia you'll need to relocate your FSB's forward as well. Failure to do so will see your truck columns being over extended and you'll soon find yourself with most of your trucks broken down, awaiting maintenance.

At the start of the campaign all three FSB's aren't shown on the map as they are still at the main depots. It's not until you order them to a location that you'll see them on the map.

FSB's are moved by Decisions. Whenever valid options are available, and the FSB is ready to move, a decision will appear in the 'ONGOING' category. These can be ignored, at no cost, until you chose to ignore them. Your Chief of Staff won't get involved with Forward Supply Base decisions. He knows to leave these matters to your discretion.

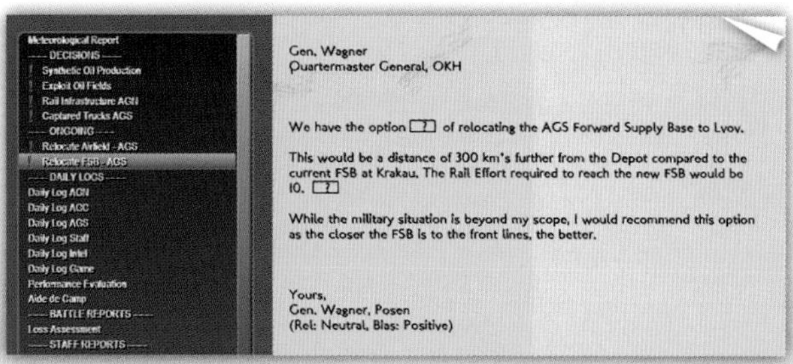

The decision will present you with whatever alternative FSB locations are available (up to four, if more then the closest four)

ASK YOUR STAFF

- **Why can't I put the FSB's where I want?**
  Relocating the main theatre forward supply base was a major undertaking that involved immense disruption and required a significant amount of forward planning. It isn't something that's done lightly and making it into a decision, with a few associated limitations (when and where), is a deliberate design decision to ensure that you are operating under similar constraints that the operational commander of the day had to deal with.

FSB locations are only found on double tracked rail routes. These were major logistical undertakings and decent throughput is essential. Not all cities on double tracked lines are potential FSB sites as adequate station, storage and sidling facilities are a requirement.

To qualify as an alternative, the potential FSB must be in German hands, be able to trace a rail route back to the main depot and there must also be a rail link between it and the current FSB location.

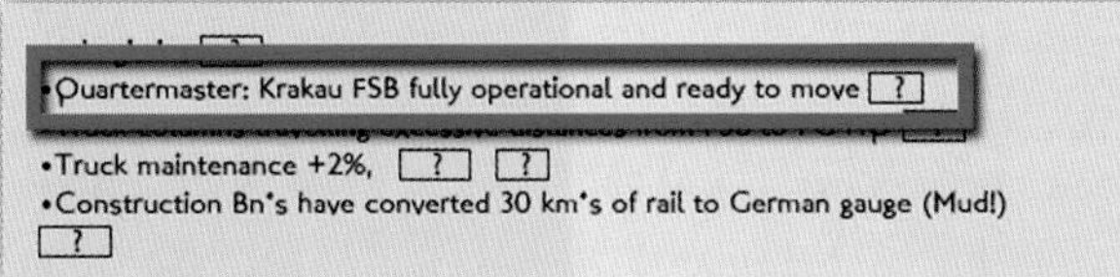

A decision will only appear if you get the 'ready to move' message in the 'Logistics' section of the Daily Theatre Log. The three theatres are on a rolling roster, so provided an FSB wsa ready to move a decision would appear, giving you the option to relocate, every three turns

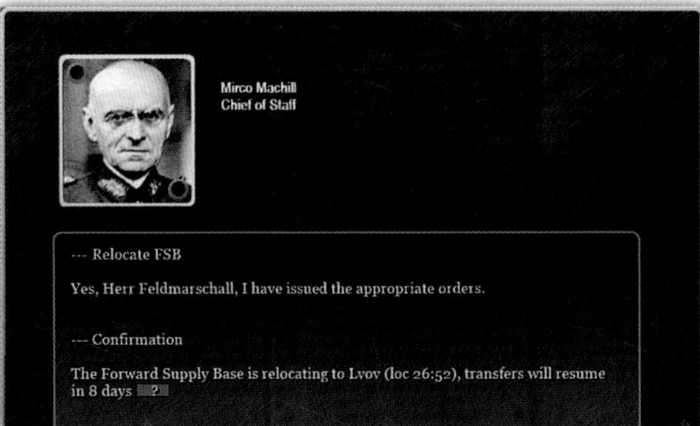

Once an option is chosen there will be a delay, usually 8 days (two turns, including the current one), while the FSB is relocated. The length of the delay is distance related. The further the new FSB site is from the currrent, the longer the delay you can expect.

No fuel will travel through the pipeline while an FSB is being relocated. Total shutdown.

STAFF ADVICE

If it all possible plan ahead. Pause your Panzergruppe for a turn to allow fuel stocks to accumulate prior to a relocation. Alternatively take the opportunity to order a refit. Another option is to have the Luftwaffe fly resupply missions to keep the fuel flowing in the interim.

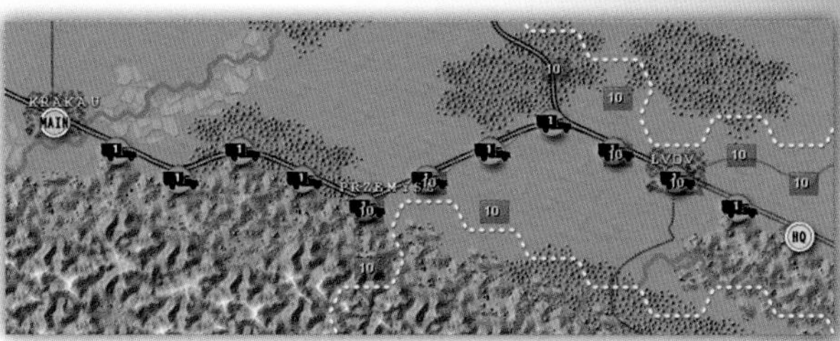

AGS. The situation immediately prior to the relocation. FSB still at the main depot at Krakau. Over extended truck columns. FSB ordered to relocate to Lvov

The following turn the relocation is underway and both the rail and truck column links are showing as grey icons as no transport is available. The main depot has gone from its normal grey colour to red as the standard fuel allocation still arrives. It's got nowhere to go so it stockpiles at the main depot.

The Daily Theatre Log lets you know the status.

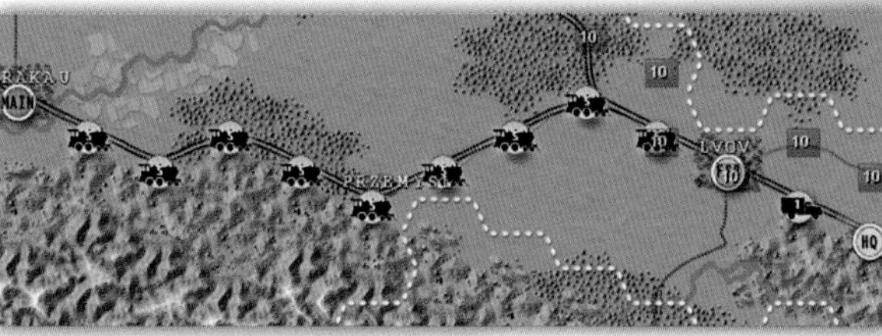

You can now see an FSB at Lvov. It's busy getting set up and has no fuel, hence the grey icon

--- Logistics [?]
•FSB relocating to Lvov, transfers resume in 4 days [?]
•Truck maintenance -1%, [?] [?]
•Construction Bn's have converted 30 km's of rail to German gauge (Mud!)

A normal FSB relocation involves a single turn of disruption as the 8 day period encompasses the turn it is ordered

The Logistics report for AGS shows the fuel accumulating at the main depot and the total absence of train and truck columns (they're busy moving stockpiles for the new FSB).

LOGISTICS REPORT - AGS

4 . July . 1941 [?]

--- Main Depot: Krakau [?] (loc 16:51)
FUEL (start): 0 bbls IN (ZI): 5076 bbls OUT (Trains): 0 bbls
FUEL (remaining): 5076 bbls
Trains per day: 0 (requires 0 trains, distance 300 km's) [?]

--- Forward Supply Base: RELOCATING to Lvov, 4 days (loc 26:52)
FUEL (start): 0 bbls IN (Depot): 0 bbls OUT (Trucks): 0 bbls
FUEL (remaining): 0 bbls
Truck columns: 0 (requires 0 truck columns, distance 60 km's)

--- Field HQ: 1st Panzergruppe HQ (loc 28:53) [?]
FUEL (start): 11573 bbls IN (FSB): 0
FUEL AVAILABLE: 11573 bbls (less 2000 bbls for Blitzkrieg Op's [?])

NET FUEL: 9573 bbls [?] (maximum allowed 55000 bbls [?])

Next turn and the FSB is up and running. As there is plenty of transport available all the stockpiled fuel at the main depot (plus this turns allocation from Zone Interior) is shunted straight up the pipeline to the Panzergruppe. Green icons all around apart from the main depot and the FSB.

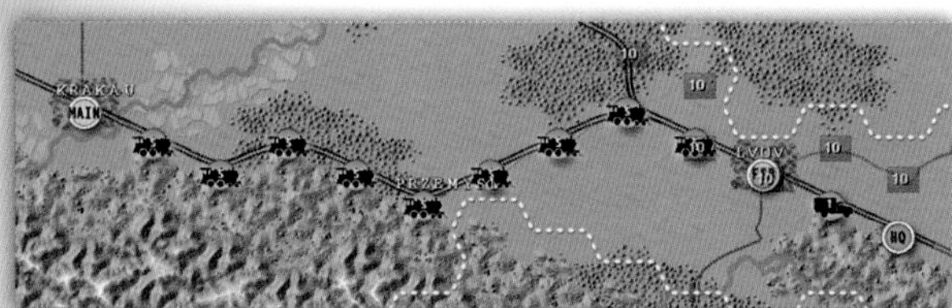

Now there are both train and truck column transport links

Moving an FSB is akin to having a kink in the garden hose. Once the kink is ironed out the build up of pressure will see the water gush out the other end.

STAFF ADVICE

The only time the icons for the main depot and the FSB will change from grey (no fuel present - it's been transported down the pipeline) is when there is a blockage (lack of transport) in the system preventing the fuel from flowing. It'll build up (stockpile) at either base (depending on where the blockage is) and their icons will no longer be grey. For the main depot and FSB you want grey icons. Anything else and you're either relocating or there's a problem.

The Daily Theatre log will tell you what you already know from the icons on the map. What's new is that every time you relocate there is going to be a period of consolidation needed before a further relocation can be considered. It takes time to establish a new FSB.

A decision, for a possible relocation, won't be generated until this consolidation period is over and the 'ready to move' message appears (see following).

SUMMARY

- FSB's start the campaign at the main depot locations.
- FSB relocate via decisions found in the 'ONGOING' category
- The FSB decisions can be safely ignored (no PP penalty, no Chief of Staff interference)
- A decision will only appear if there are viable alternative options available
- A theatre will only show a decision every three turns (there's a rolling roster)
- FSB's can only be situated at cities connected with double tracked rail
- Not all possible cities are usable as potential FSB sites (lack of suitable infrastructure)
- Up to four options will be shown in an FSB decision (if more, only the closest four)
- It takes at least one full turn to relocate (more if it's a long way apart)
- No trains or truck columns will be available during relocation (no fuel gets through!)
- Once relocated there is a two turn period of consolidation.
- Subsequent relocations can only occur after consolidation ('ready to move' message in Daily Log)

--- Logistics [?]
•The new FSB at Lvov is up and running! [?]
•Quartermaster: 8 days needed to consolidate the new FSB at Lvov [?]
•Construction Bn's have converted 30 km's of rail to German gauge (Mud!) [?]

6.1.6.11. Logistical Disasters

All disasters, interruptions and alternative route planning is handled by the game automatically. You'll receive appropriate notification in the relevant Daily Theatre Logs and the map icons will provide visual indication of the situation.

A grey icon transport link (grey train or truck column icons) means that there isn't enough transport available. The total absence of icons indicates an interruption in the service (the trains or truck columns physically can't get through).

Panzergruppe HQ being Over Run

The HQ will be automatically reconstituted (like any destroyed German Army HQ) and will arrive (NO COMMA) the following turn, at a nearby city. Any residual fuel stockpile will be lost (in the case of an AGC PG being lost only half the stockpile will go).

Forward Supply Base being Over Run

It will be automatically relocated to the nearest, safe, location (to the rear) and most of the fuel stocks (if any) that were present will be lost. Expect a period of disruption.

Main Depot Over Run

All three main depots are across the border in Poland. Consider yourself fired, effective immediately.

Interrupted Transport Link

Both rail and truck column links can be interrupted by enemy action or zones of control. The game tests for a viable transport link at the beginning of every German turn. If one isn't available then the fuel will stockpile at a base until the situation is resolved.

An interruption to the truck column link isn't normally fatal as the game will automatically reroute the truck columns to the next best available route. Trains are trickier because an alternative rail route may not be available.

A destroyed bridge (over a river) will slow down truck columns (increase the route difficulty) but will stop a train link dead in its tracks (provided an alternative rail route from the main depot to the FSB can't be found).

6.1.6.12. Logistical Examples

Ideal Conditions

Here is a pipeline operating at peak performance.

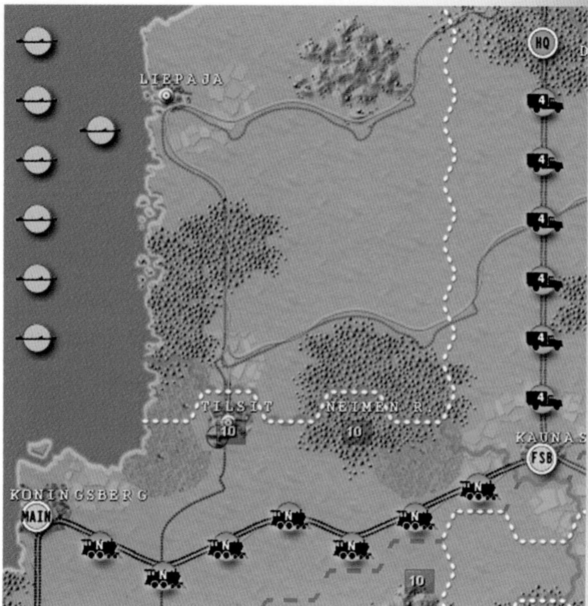

The Main Depot and the FSB are both grey indicating that there is no fuel present. The Panzergruppe HQ is green so there must be at least two full quotas present (usable by the Fast Divisions). Both transport links are showing green telling us that they have the capability to move two more quotas through the pipeline, this turn.

This is great. The allocation of fuel for the turn has arrived at the Main Depot and has been efficiently transported through the pipeline to the HQ. Throughput is the key. Fuel moves arrives at one end (Main depot) of the pipeline and travels through to the other (HQ) all in one turn.

If there was a problem with the transport links (not enough capacity) then fuel would be stockpiling somewhere in the system, either at the Main depot (not enough trains) or the FSB (not enough truck columns). A lack of transport causes a constriction in the pipeline. Fuel backs up.

Because the Main Depot and the FSB are both showing grey (no fuel present) you can see that the fuel is flowing through the pipeline (automatically) as it should. It's accumulating at the far end (the HQ). If there isn't enough demand (Fast Divisions moving or engaging in combat) it will continue to stockpile at the HQ. This isn't a problem because once the fuel reaches the HQ it becomes fuel that can be used. The more the merrier.

We can, if we want, inspect the AGN Logistics Report.

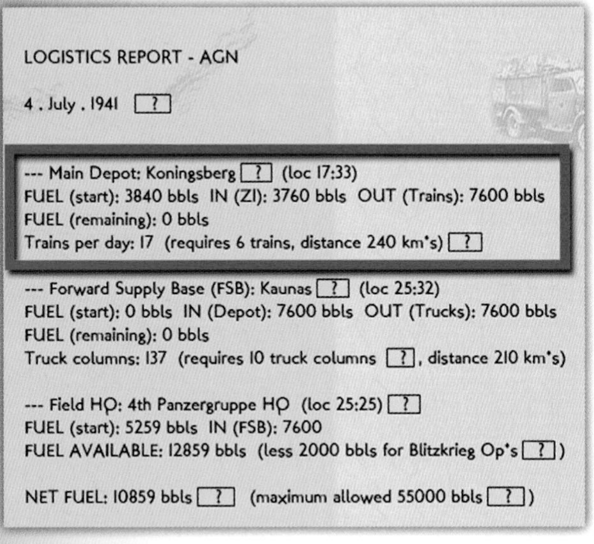

LOGISTICS REPORT - AGN

4 . July . 1941 [?]

--- Main Depot: Koningsberg [?] (loc 17:33)
FUEL (start): 3840 bbls IN (ZI): 3760 bbls OUT (Trains): 7600 bbls
FUEL (remaining): 0 bbls
Trains per day: 17 (requires 6 trains, distance 240 km's) [?]

--- Forward Supply Base (FSB): Kaunas [?] (loc 25:32)
FUEL (start): 0 bbls IN (Depot): 7600 bbls OUT (Trucks): 7600 bbls
FUEL (remaining): 0 bbls
Truck columns: 137 (requires 10 truck columns [?], distance 210 km's)

--- Field HQ: 4th Panzergruppe HQ (loc 25:25) [?]
FUEL (start): 5259 bbls IN (FSB): 7600
FUEL AVAILABLE: 12859 bbls (less 2000 bbls for Blitzkrieg Op's [?])

NET FUEL: 10859 bbls [?] (maximum allowed 55000 bbls [?])

The FSB has just finished relocating so there is a residual amount of fuel from last time (FUEL start: 3840 bbls). There is an additional amount that has arrived from the Zone Interior (IN: 3760 bbls).

There are enough trains (17 present, 6 needed) to move all the fuel (7600 bbs) to the next base in the pipeline, the Forward Supply Base (FSB).

IN DETAIL

The required number of trains and truck columns shown in the logistical report is for one quota of fuel. More than one quota would need correspondingly more transport. For the example above you'd need 12 trains to move 2 full quotas and 18 for three.

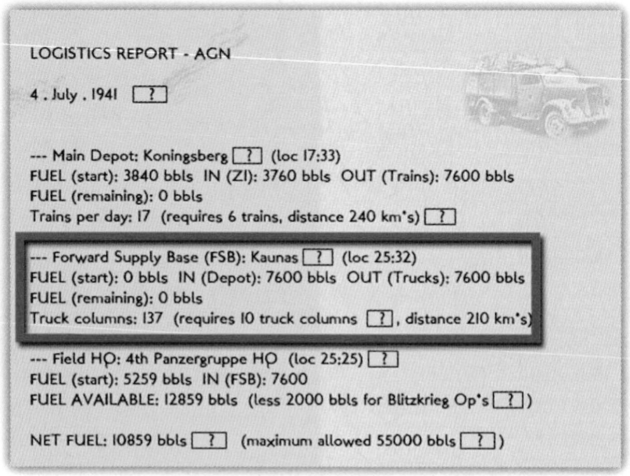

LOGISTICS REPORT - AGN

4 . July . 1941 [?]

--- Main Depot: Koningsberg [?] (loc 17:33)
FUEL (start): 3840 bbls IN (ZI): 3760 bbls OUT (Trains): 7600 bbls
FUEL (remaining): 0 bbls
Trains per day: 17 (requires 6 trains, distance 240 km's) [?]

--- Forward Supply Base (FSB): Kaunas [?] (loc 25:32)
FUEL (start): 0 bbls IN (Depot): 7600 bbls OUT (Trucks): 7600 bbls
FUEL (remaining): 0 bbls
Truck columns: 137 (requires 10 truck columns [?], distance 210 km's)

--- Field HQ: 4th Panzergruppe HQ (loc 25:25) [?]
FUEL (start): 5259 bbls IN (FSB): 7600
FUEL AVAILABLE: 12859 bbls (less 2000 bbls for Blitzkrieg Op's [?])

NET FUEL: 10859 bbls [?] (maximum allowed 55000 bbls [?])

At the FSB there wasn't any fuel from previous turns (FUEL start: 0 bbls) and, because there were enough trains, it received everything that was sent up from the Main Depot (FUEL In: 7600 bbls). There are enough truck columns (137 present, 10 needed) to move all the fuel up the next link in the pipeline to the Panzergruppe HQ.

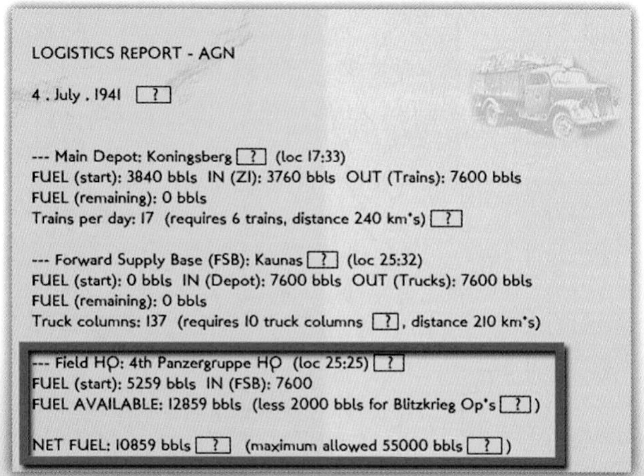

LOGISTICS REPORT - AGN

4 . July . 1941 [?]

--- Main Depot: Koningsberg [?] (loc 17:33)
FUEL (start): 3840 bbls IN (ZI): 3760 bbls OUT (Trains): 7600 bbls
FUEL (remaining): 0 bbls
Trains per day: 17 (requires 6 trains, distance 240 km's) [?]

--- Forward Supply Base (FSB): Kaunas [?] (loc 25:32)
FUEL (start): 0 bbls IN (Depot): 7600 bbls OUT (Trucks): 7600 bbls
FUEL (remaining): 0 bbls
Truck columns: 137 (requires 10 truck columns [?], distance 210 km's)

--- Field HQ: 4th Panzergruppe HQ (loc 25:25) [?]
FUEL (start): 5259 bbls IN (FSB): 7600
FUEL AVAILABLE: 12859 bbls (less 2000 bbls for Blitzkrieg Op's [?])

NET FUEL: 10859 bbls [?] (maximum allowed 55000 bbls [?])

The 4th Panzergruppe HQ already had a stockpile of fuel (FUEL Start: 5259 bbls) and has received the full amount coming through the pipeline from the Main depot (FUEL In: 7600 bbs). This gives it a total of 12,859 bbls (FUEL Start + FUEL In) but because they are configured to a Blitzkrieg posture there is an 2,000 bbl cost that must be paid to cover the additional manoeuvring and combat operations that this entails (see 4.4.1 Blitzkrieg Fuel Use).

The usable amount of fuel is therefore 10,859 bbs (12,859 less 2,000) and that's shown in the fuel gauge up the top.

Note that there is, in the last logistical pic above, a '(maximum allowed 55000 bbls)' note at the bottom right. This is the maximum size of the stockpile that can be accumulated at the 4th Panzergruppe HQ before wastage kicks in (everything above this is lost). The maximum stockpile size varies depending on your relationship with General Wagner (see 4.8.1.3 Logistical Generals).

Summer Rains

Early days. Hoth's 3rd Panzergruppe, Armeeruppe Mitte (AGC), pushing up the line towards Vilnius. The Forward Supply Base has just been moved to Bialystok. Main Depot, as usual, at Warsaw.

The train link is red. Why?

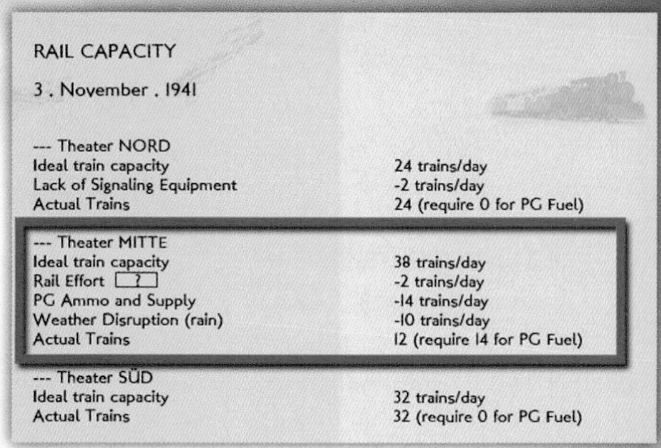

RAIL CAPACITY

3 . November . 1941

--- Theater NORD	
Ideal train capacity	24 trains/day
Lack of Signaling Equipment	-2 trains/day
Actual Trains	24 (require 0 for PG Fuel)
--- Theater MITTE	
Ideal train capacity	38 trains/day
Rail Effort [?]	-2 trains/day
PG Ammo and Supply	-14 trains/day
Weather Disruption (rain)	-10 trains/day
Actual Trains	12 (require 14 for PG Fuel)
--- Theater SÜD	
Ideal train capacity	32 trains/day
Actual Trains	32 (require 0 for PG Fuel)

Ignore the date as we played with the clock for purposes of explanation

The rail effort is at the minimum. It's double tracked German gauge line from the Main Depot to the FSB. The distance component is so small doesn't register in the report. None of these are a problem.

But the rain is. Flash flooding has washed away a section of the line and reduced its capacity by ten trains per day. This is a one turn effect (although it's possible it may happen again the following turn, just not likely) and it has dropped the actual number of trains down to 12 per day. More than this (14) are required to transport a full quota of fuel so we are in a 'only enough capacity for less then one quota' situation. Code red.

Because this is AGC there are the two Panzergruppes and they are averaged. But the

LOGISTICS REPORT - AGC

3 . November . 1941 [?]

--- Main Depot: Warsaw [?] (loc 19:42)
FUEL (start): 10176 bbls IN (ZI): 9964 bbls OUT (Trains): 8400 bbls
FUEL (remaining): 11740 bbls
Trains per day: 12 (requires 14 trains, distance 150 km's) [?]

--- Forward Supply Base (FSB): Bialystok [?] (loc 23:39)
FUEL (start): 0 bbls IN (Depot): 8400 bbls OUT (Trucks): 8400 bbls
FUEL (remaining): 0 bbls
Truck columns: 100 (requires 25 truck columns [?], distance 150 km's)

--- Field HQ: 2nd Panzergruppe HQ (loc 21:43), 3rd PG HQ (26:36) [?]
FUEL (start): 17880 bbls IN (FSB): 8400
FUEL AVAILABLE: 26280 bbls (less 4000 bbls for Blitzkrieg Op's [?])

NET FUEL: 22280 bbls [?] (maximum allowed 55000 bbls [?])

averaging only applies to the truck columns, not the single rail link that runs to the FSB.

The Logistics report shows the Main Depot carrying over fuel from the previous turn ('Fuel Start: 10176 bbls'). This is due to the FSB having just been relocated. Another allotment of fuel has arrived from the Zone Interior ('Fuel In: 9964 bbls') but only 8,400 bbls made it out.

This is because the train capacity is right down (line washed out by the rain) and that's all that can be moved this turn. The remaining fuel ('Fuel (remaining): 11740 bbls') is stockpiled at the Main Depot for possible transport the following turn. Hopefully by then the rail situation will have improved.

As there are plenty of truck columns available the small amount of fuel that arrives at the FSB is quickly and efficiently transported to the PG HQ where a nice sized stockpile is building up.

As the FSB is, as it should, acting as a relay station, it's not holding any fuel and has a grey icon (it's at Bialystock, partially obscured). The Panzergruppe HQ has ample fuel stocks (26,280 bbls) which is well and truly 'two or more quotas' so has a green icon.

TRUCK COLUMNS	22 . June . 1941		
	AGN	AGC	AGS
	---	---	---
Truck columns (Theatre & Captured)	300	400	300
- Maintenance (awaiting repair) [?]	-60	-80	-60
- Losses (permanent) [?]	-0	-0	-0
- Infantry & Artillery use [?]	-100	-100	-100
Available Truck Columns	140	220	140

'Infantry and Artillery use' always starts at 100 truck columns

6.1.6.13. Ammunition

The general supply system and the logistical pipelines providing fuel to the Panzergruppes are two separate systems.

General supply (see 4.14 Supply) affects all units (both regimes) and allows a unit to recover readiness which it loses every time it moves or fights. The logistical pipelines are all about getting enough fuel to the German Fast Divisions in order that they can move and fight (Fast Divisions require *both* supply and fuel, slow Divisions only supply).

There is one area of overlap between the two systems. The Truck Column report details the number of truck columns assigned to keep the infantry armies and the theatre based artillery in ammunition.

Certain decisions ('Truck Secondment') allow the German Player to transfer a number of these truck columns over to pool used for the transportation of Panzergruppe fuel. Doing so runs the risk that there will be ammunition shortages. This can also happen if there aren't enough truck columns available to cover the requirements of the infantry armies and artillery (see 6.1.4.2 Ammunition Level).

--- Operations
•34 Divisions have been affected by Limited Ammunition shortages [?]

IN DETAIL

With the # of truck columns < 100 a random roll is made for every Slow (infantry) division. If the roll exceeds the available truck columns (dedicated to armies) then a shortage occurs. Depending on the difference between the threshold (number of available truck columns) and the roll, the Division will suffer 'Limited' or 'Moderate' ammunition shortages. If the Division is 'Out of Command Range' the severity will go up a notch - Limited to Moderate, Moderate to Severe.

Ammunition shortages are manifested as a reduction in general supply that happens *after* all normal supply calculations. Units with lower supply have less ability to recover readiness and will move and fight at lower levels of effectiveness.

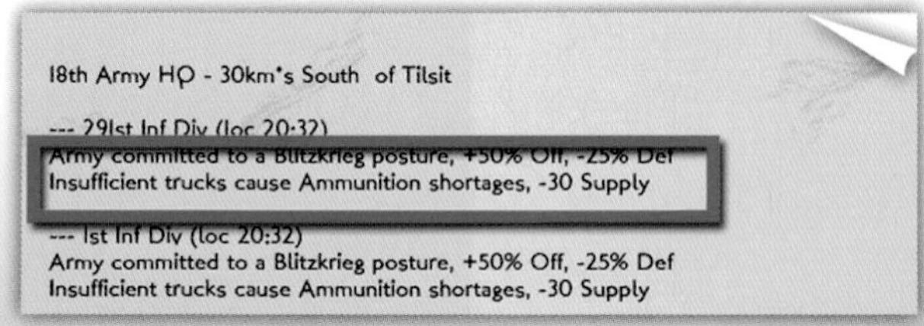

18th Army HQ - 30km's South of Tilsit
--- 291st Inf Div (loc 20:32)
Army committed to a Blitzkrieg posture, +50% Off, -25% Def
Insufficient trucks cause Ammunition shortages, -30 Supply
--- 1st Inf Div (loc 20:32)
Army committed to a Blitzkrieg posture, +50% Off, -25% Def
Insufficient trucks cause Ammunition shortages, -30 Supply

You could also ask a Division to Report Status!

A similar mechanic exists if there aren't enough truck columns available to cover the ammunition requirements of the Panzergruppes.

Panzergruppe Truck columns	140	220	140
- PG Supply and Ammo [?]	-1	-1	-1
- Distance penalty [?]	-1	-2	-3
- Route difficulty [?]	-2	-13	-15
Surplus Truck columns	136	204	121

Only 1 truck column is needed, per theatre, at the start of the campaign. This will change

STAFF ADVICE

A shortage of truck columns leads to a lack of fuel and a lack of ammunition. Look after your truck columns!

6.1.6.14. Panzergruppe Stockpiles

Your relationship with General Wagner (in charge of truck columns and depots) determines the size of the stockpile of fuel that can be built up at your Panzergruppe HQ's (the amount ready for use).

Normally this is a fixed amount (see below) but if your relationship with General Wagner deteriorates ('Poor', or worse) the amount he will be willing to let to let your stockpile amass will fall.

LOGISTICS REPORT - AGC

22 . June . 1941 [?]

--- Main Depot: Warsaw [?] (loc 19:42)
FUEL (start): 0 bbls IN (ZI): 13250 bbls OUT (Trains): 13250 bbls
FUEL (remaining): 0 bbls
Trains per day: 38 (requires 0 trains, distance 0 km's) [?]

--- Forward Supply Base (FSB): Warsaw [?] (loc 19:42)
FUEL (start): 0 bbls IN (Depot): 13250 bbls OUT (Trucks): 13250 bbls
FUEL (remaining): 0 bbls
Truck columns: 204 (requires 1 truck column [?], distance 150 km's)

--- Field HQ: 2nd Panzergruppe HQ (loc 21:43), 3rd PG HQ (21:35) [?]
FUEL (start): 7000 bbls IN (FSB): 13250
FUEL AVAILABLE: 20250 bbls (less 4000 bbls for Blitzkrieg Op's [?])

NET FUEL: 16250 bbls [?] (maximum allowed 55000 bbls [?])

No more than 55,000 bbls can be stockpiled

For more information see 4.8.1.3 General Wagner.

6.1.6.15. Logistics 101

Plan your routes of invasion. Aim to convert the key sections of double tracked rail over to German gauge. Keep your Panzergruppe HQ's on a road (any rail hex). Keep pushing your Forward Supply Bases forward.

Resist the temptation to advance your Panzergruppes too far from from your FSB's. Avoid over extending your truck columns.

Aim where possible, to stay on good terms with your two Logistical Generals (Gercke and Wagner) as bad relations will ratchet up the PP cost of all related decisions.

STAFF ADVICE

There is an inherent conflict between the military necessity of advancing as far and as fast as possible and the risk of out running your logistics. This is a conflict that the Germans failed to satisfactorily resolve. There were a number of periods of 'enforced' halts where the Panzergruppes had no choice but to wait for their logistical pipelines to catch up and start supplying them with fuel once more.

6.1.6.16. Reassigning Panzergruppes

Normally your Fast Divisions draw fuel from a pool specific to each theatre (what's shown in the fuel gauge on the top bar which reflects the amount of fuel at the Panzergruppe HQ). The state of each theatre's logistical pipeline determines how much fuel makes it through to your Panzergruppe HQ's.

A Fast Division (one with vehicles) will draw fuel from the theatre it is in (at the *start* of its movement, not during). For example the SS Totenkopf Division,

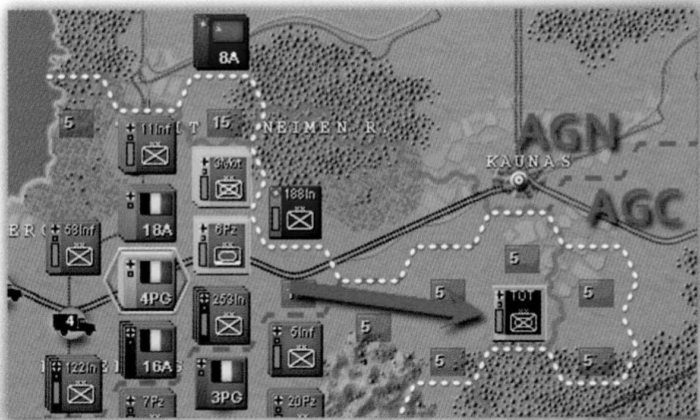

4th Panzergruppe, moves from the northern theatre (AGN) to the central one (AGC). It would draw fuel from the AGN (northern) fuel pool because it commenced its movement there. Next turn it would be drawing from the AGC pool.

If a Panzerguppe has been reassigned to an adjoining theatre then a portion of its fuel stockpile (at the HQ) will flow into the adjacent theatre's pool to help alleviate the burden on the other theatre's logistics that the additional Panzergruppe is placing upon it.

The amount of fuel that gets transferred depends on how many of a Panzergruppe's Fast Divisions are in the adjoining theatre. If all of them are present then 100% of its fuel (the amount the HQ receives each turn) will be sent to the adjoining theatre.

Importantly fuel transfers from one theatre to another will only commence once the *Panzergruppe HQ moves into the adjoining theatre*. This allows you a measure of control over how fuel is transferred between theatres and used.

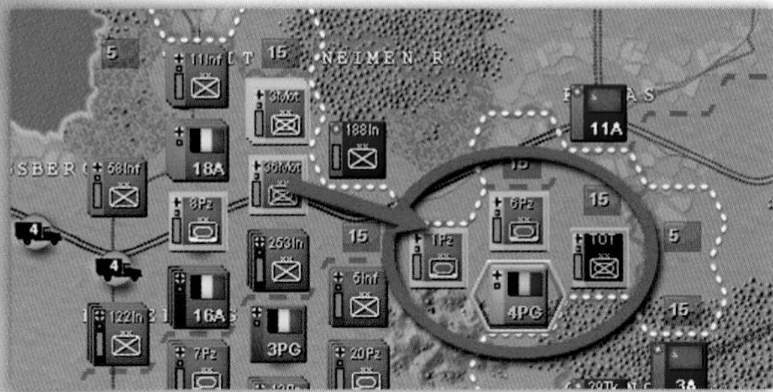

The 4th PG HQ has crossed into AGC so fuel transfers will occur

In the pic above the 4th Panzergruppe has been reassigned and has partially moved from AGN to AGC. Because it has half of its Divisions present in AGC, 50% of its fuel will flow to the AGC pool. The remainder will go the AGN pool.

If the 4th Panzergruppe HQ returns to AGN, but left its three Divisions in AGC, then no fuel would be transferred from one theatre to another as the HQ wasn't present (in AGC).

Regardless of which theatre a Panzergruppe moves into, its own or an adjoining one, it will need to manage its logistical pipeline that still derives from its original theatre.

If we take the situation shown above and run the game ahead a turn you can see that the 4th Panzergruppe HQ is still relying on a logistical pipeline originating out of the main depot in Koningsberg. This pipeline will follow it where ever it goes.

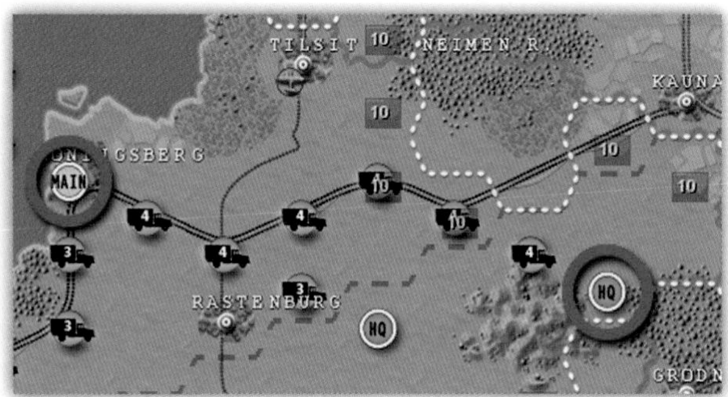

SUMMARY

- Individual Divisions draw fuel from the theatre they start their turn in
- Fuel will transfer between theatres only when your Panzergruppe HQ crosses the border.
- The logistical pipeline arrangements don't change

6.1.6.17. Decisions Off Logistics

This provides a more streamlined logistical experience that adheres to the same operational principles and still requires reasonable levels of player input.

There is no FSB but instead a direct connection between the main depot and the Panzergruppe HQ's. Removing the FSB takes away the need for having two types of transport links (there's only one and it's assumed to represent both types) and the requirement to relocate FSB's.

There are no logistical decisions to make as all decisions are switched off. Logistical icons still follow the same colouring scheme, no different.

Ammunition shortages no longer apply and Baltic convoys are handled automatically (when a port is captured additional transport capacity is added provided the port can trace a rail route back to Berlin).

ASK YOUR STAFF

- **Why is there only one transport icon?**
  As there is no Forward Supply Base there is a need only for one although it represents both trains and truck columns. Should the icon be trains which will then have to travel cross country or trucks that follow the rail? At the moment it's trains but by the time the game is released it could be trucks. Can't make up my mind.

There are no logistics, truck column or rail capacity reports. Instead the Daily Theatre Logs handle it succinctly in their 'Logistics' sections.

--- Logistics [?]
•Fuel Allocation +4400 bbls [?]
•Stockpile (Main Depot) 0 bbls [?]
•Transport Capacity 9000 bbls (distance 0, friction 0) [?]
•Fuel Delivered to HQ 4400 bbls
•Blitzkrieg Fuel Use -2000 bbls
•Carry Over (HQ) +6000 bbls [?]
•Available Fuel (HQ) 8400 bbls [?]

There's a fuel allocation each turn, as normal, and a main depot stockpile that can accumulate in the event of a blockage in the pipeline.

Transport capacity is an abstract representation of the combined capacity of your trains and truck columns (rather than having individual systems for both as per the normal game). It's your transport capacities that determines how much fuel is moved through the logistical pipelines.

--- Logistics [?]
•Fuel Allocation +4400 bbls [?]
•Transport Capacity 9000 bbls (distance 0, friction 0) [?]
•Blitzkrieg Fuel Use -2000 bbls
•Carry Over (HQ) +6000 bbls [?]
•Available Fuel (HQ) 8400 bbls [?]

Transport Capacity is reduced by Distance and Friction effects. Distance is geographical and can't be changed, other than having your Panzergruppe HQ fall back on your main depot.

Friction represents all the things that can, and do, go wrong with your trains and truck columns. This includes weather effects, partisans, collisions, wash outs, breakdowns, poor signalling, a lack of track infrastructure, etc. You can minimise its effects by keeping your Panzergruppe HQ's on roads where ever possible.

Like the normal game, the two Panzergruppes in AGC have their distance and friction affects averaged and share a common AGC fuel pool.

Transport capacity indicates how many barrels of fuel can be moved through the pipeline this turn (in the pic above it's 9,000 bbls).

Fuel Delivered is how much arrives at the other end of the pipeline at the Panzergruppe HQ. In the given example that's 4,400 bbls. Even though the transport capacity is much more at 9,000 bbls, there is only 4,400 bbls at the main depot available to transport.

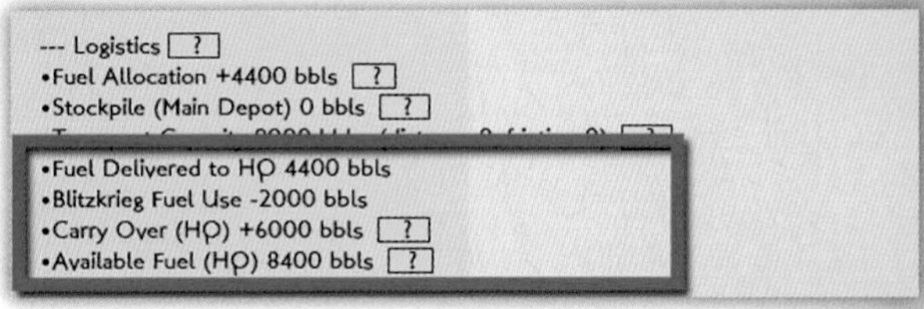
--- Logistics [?]
•Fuel Allocation +4400 bbls [?]
•Stockpile (Main Depot) 0 bbls [?]
•Fuel Delivered to HQ 4400 bbls
•Blitzkrieg Fuel Use -2000 bbls
•Carry Over (HQ) +6000 bbls [?]
•Available Fuel (HQ) 8400 bbls [?]

From this any blitzkrieg posture fuel allocation is deducted (as per the normal game), any previous (unused) fuel is added to give an 'Available fuel' amount of, in this case, 8,400 bbls. This is the amount of fuel showing in the fuel gauge (top right) and available for use by the Fast Divisions.

As the campaign progresses and the front line pushes eastwards, both distance and friction factors will reduce the transport capacity of each theatre. There are two additional Action cards provided in the 'Command' category - Logistics and Fuel. Both cards are played on a Theatre HQ (AGN/AGC/AGS).

The Logistics card represents the various decisions that you might take in the normal game to rectify assorted problems. It serves to reduce the effect of friction in the chosen theatre. It's your main tool for maintaining sufficient transport capacity (reducing friction will increase capacity) to move enough fuel through the pipeline.

The Fuel card provides additional fuel to the chosen theatre. It appears in the following turn in the Main depot stockpile, ready for transport through the pipeline.

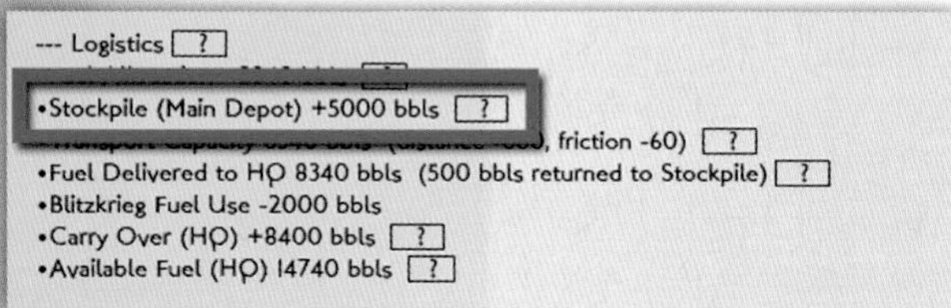

As the fuel comes from the strategic reserves there is a finite amount. Each time the card is played the amount received will diminish. Use it wisely.

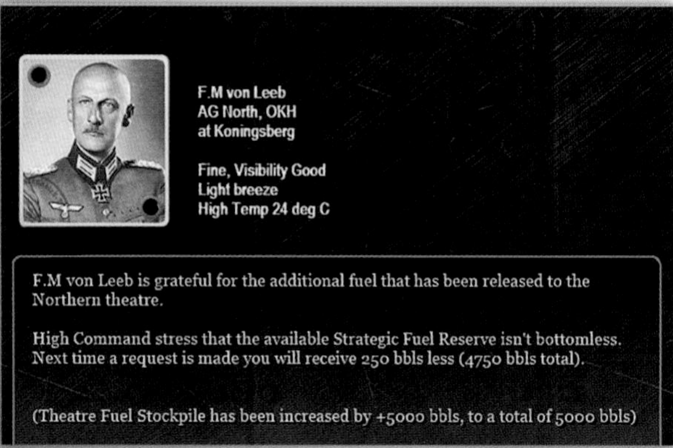

STAFF ADVICE

The flow of the logistical side of the game, with Decisions off, is in saving enough Political Points to play enough 'Logistical' cards in order to keep the friction under control and by boosting fuel supplies at critical points with the 'Fuel' card. You won't be able to do keep everything running smoothly and will have to prioritise which theatres you play the cards on.

SUMMARY

- There is a single transport link between the Main Depots and the Panzergruppe HQ's
- The transport icon used represents both trains and truck columns
- There are no Forward Supply Bases or Logistical Decisions
- 'Transport Capacity' determines how much fuel can be moved through the pipeline
- Distance and Friction both reduce this
- Distance is geographical and is based on how far the HQ's are from their main depots
- Friction represents wear and tear on trains and truck columns and increases every turn
- Aim to keep your Panzergruppe HQ's on roads where ever possible
- Friction can be reduced by playing the 'Logistics' card on a theatre HQ
- Strategic Fuel Reserves can be released by playing the 'Fuel' card on a theatre HQ but this is a diminishing resource.

6.1.6.18. Compromises

The logistical system provides a fairly accurate, realistic and detailed model of the Eastern front in '41 without burdening the Player with micromanagement.

It's inevitable that any design has to make compromises as to fully model reality would be both unworkable and unplayable.

There are two main design compromises that have been made which are worth knowing about. The first directly affects game play and the second is a matter of perception.

DESIGNER NOTE

I have included this here (rather than with the other designer notes) as it's an area that has provoked discussion during Beta testing. If you are concerned, or interested, about logistical matters, read on. Otherwise check the summary at the end and feel free to skip the rest.

Armeegruppe Mitte

How Armeegruppe Mitte (AGC) is handled is the first compromise. Unlike its adjoining theatres, AGC has two Panzergruppes, Guderian's 2nd and Hoth's 3rd.

One option would be for both to have their own logistical pipeline and individual pools of fuel which they draw from. This runs into a couple of problems. It'd make the map horribly complicated, especially AGC, having two complete pipelines snaking through the theatre and jostling each other for the use of road and rail links.

It would also require a complete new suite of reports that track the two pipelines. It's a major overhead in complexity and comprehension that isn't justified for the small gain in realism that it would provide.

Instead there is a single logistical pipeline for the theatre. From the Forward Supply Base (FSB) truck columns deliver fuel to both Panzergruppe HQ's. There are two links here rather than the normal one and they are AVERAGED for purposes of truck column efficiency and maintenance.

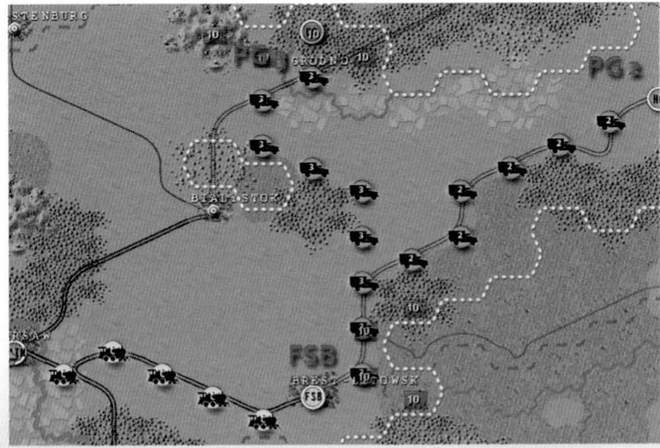

Showing the dual truck column links in the pipeline

STAFF ADVICE

You may have one PG HQ sitting on a rail link of German gauge and close to the FSB. This is great. But you might have the other PG HQ way off in the wilderness where truck columns are forced to travel long distances down poor quality country 'roads' in order to reach it. The overall logistical effect will be an average of the two (one good, one bad). When issuing orders for AGC you need to keep in mind the shared logistical situation of both Panzergruppes. If you are going to have one move into a logistically detrimental situation you should be aiming to do the opposite with the other.

The other side effect of a shared logistical pipeline is that there is a single pool of fuel in AGC (identical to the other theatres). Both Panzergruppes draw from the same AGC pool. Which provides a large degree of flexibility in times of shortages. You can prioritise one Panzergruppe over another by simply moving it first and using the bulk of the available fuel.

All compromises involve a downside and in this case if one Panzergruppe allows itself (the HQ) to be cut off, the combined logistical apparatus will undergo spasms until the situation is resolved (if one PG is out of reach no NEW fuel will arrive through the pipeline for the other).

If Hoth's 3rd Panzergruppe rashly advanced and allowed itself to become isolated then any fuel that continued to flow to Guderian's 2nd Panzergruppe would be available to Hoth's as they share the same pool. Hence the restriction.

It's not too terrible as if Hoth (or more likely Guderian give his historical propensity to push his luck) does make a misjudgement there will still be whatever is currently remaining in the theatre pool for use by Hoth to engineer a breakout. But that's it. There won't be any NEW fuel arriving until logistical links have been restored to both HQ's.

Command Range

The second compromise is, as mentioned, one of perception. The logistical system puts a lot of effort into getting fuel to where it's needed - the Panzergruppe HQ's. From the HQ to the subordinate

Divisions is assumed to be done by the organic truck capability of the Panzergruppes (they each had a large number of trucks for this purpose).

Provided the Divisions are within Command Range (5 hexes) they will receive fuel. Outside of Command Range and they will still be able to draw from the theatre pool of fuel but they are given stiff Action Point penalties to reflect the fact that their distance from their HQ will prevent them receiving their full quota of fuel.

This is fine. Works well. Keep your Fast Divisions in Command Range or expect them to have a lot less movement and combat capability. If your Panzer III is running short on fuel you aren't going to be racing off over the horizon.

Where the model falls down is that the ONLY restriction is that the Division be within the 5 hex Command Range of its HQ. There could be a major river, without a bridge in sight, separating the Division from its HQ. Doesn't matter, the trucks will still get through and the Division will get full movement because it's within 5 hexes.

Not quite. The Germans were adept at finding ways to make their 'local logistics' work. They would have put up a temporary pontoon bridge, shuttled a few trucks across the river and kept the Division going. Historically they did this in AGS and had Panzer Divisions of 1st Panzergruppe operating on both sides of a large river simultaneously.

A worse situation would be where there is an intervening swamp between the PG HQ and the Division. Trucks are unlikely to be able to penetrate a major swamp and the Division, provided there isn't any other feasible truck routes to it, should, by rights, not be receiving fuel from its HQ.

But it does because it's within Command Range. This, admittedly fairly unlikely, situation is unrealistic. There is going to be the odd occasion when you peer at the map and think 'something isn't right'.

It's the compromise. It doesn't impact game play but it can change how you perceive the underlying logistical model.

Consider the alternative. Yes, it's feasible to individually calculate the path to individual Divisions. Not easy as the algorithm would have to consider all possible routes and settle on the best. Given the possible permutations involved with a 5 hex radius this would chew up a lot of computer cycles as each Division is checked. Turn processing time would increase.

While they'd be a percentage of Players who were willing to put up with this in return for a higher fidelity model the real issue is comprehension. Take Guderian's 2nd Panzergruppe. It's got ten Fast Divisions. There will be times when a number of them will be deemed 'outside of local logistical range'. How is the Player meant to know this? There could be a status icon but you'd also have to provide detailed feedback as that's the only way the Player could know for certain what was going on.

That's a lot of reports. A lot of figuring out why this Division could move and that one couldn't. If Fast Divisions are accurately modelled why then shouldn't Slow Divisions be the same. In the same 2nd Panzergruppe there are a handful of Slow Divisions. It would be unfair if they didn't obey the same rules. What about all the Infantry Armies and their individual supply situations? More reports, more having to figure out what's going on.

How would the Player know where to position his individual Divisions each time he moved them? Certain situations would be obvious but others would be line ball. Nobody would want to deliberately move a Division where it couldn't receive fuel or supplies.

You could have a graphical overlay of the HQ's that automatically took into account all of the many variables but is the game going to have to momentarily pause and recalculate every time you move the HQ? What if you moved your Division before the HQ and found that there was no way of moving the HQ to keep that Division in range? Should you, in order to avoid getting into a pickle, be forced to move your HQ before your Divisions? What if you have to do it in increments - move your HQ forward a few hexes, shuffle your Divisions forward then repeat the process?

The dark, dangerous, depths of micromanagement beckon with a mermaid's siren call.

It's good to be deaf on occasion. There's a single, universal, easily understood, rule. If you're in Command Range, you're OK.

SUMMARY

- AGC has a shared logistical system that applies to both Panzergruppes (2nd and 3rd)
- The dual AGC Truck column link from the FSB to the PG HQ's is averaged.
- Both AGC Panzergruppes draw from the same, theatre-wide, pool of fuel.
- You can prioritise one AGC Panzergruppe over another by moving it first.
- If one AGC Panzergruppe is cut off no NEW fuel will arrive for the other.
- A Division outside of Command Range (5 hexes) will suffer Action Point (AP) penalties.

6.1.7. WEAR AND TEAR

Machines break down and men become fatigued. The more you push your forces (leave them on 'Blitzkrieg Posture') the greater the cumulative impact. Eventually you'll need to order a Rest and Refit to allow vehicles to be repaired and men to recover.

Both of these are done through identical Action Cards. The underlying rules that govern them are similar although the effects differ. A single Army, or Panzergruppe, in each theatre can be pulled out of the line and ordered to rest and refit each turn.

ASK YOUR STAFF

Why can't I Rest multiple Armies in a single turn? You're playing the game with the benefit of historical hindsight. The Germans were dealing with many unknowns and were extremely reluctant to stand down large portions of their forces at the same time. They staggered them, over time, to cover unforeseen eventualities. In the game it's possible to have multiple Armies resting at once but you'll need to order them to do so over successive turns. This also ties in with the games operational focus as there is an element of advanced planning involved.

6.1.7.1. Mechanical Reliability

Tanks, trucks and half track will all eventually suffer mechanical failure and breakdown. The more mileage your vehicles accumulate, the higher the probability that some of them will break down. Ordering a Rest and Refit (Action Card) will allow the recovery of most of your broken down vehicles. Only Fast Divisions are affected by breakdowns as they are the only ones with vehicles.

--- Operations
•10th Pz Div (28:39) has suffered mechanical failures (12% chance)
•8 Divisions are receiving Direct Fire Artillery support (+Off) [?]

You are notified in your Daily Theatre Logs of any breakdowns

The poor roads, excessive distances and adverse weather all contributed to high levels of mechanical failure during Operation Barbarossa. A lack of spare part, especially new tank engines which Hitler refused to release, accentuated the problem.

Every Division has its mileage tracked individually. TOTAL mileage is the distance traveled since the commencement of the campaign. REFIT mileage is the distance traveled since the last Rest and Refit. The flat rate traveled, eg. 1 hex = 30 km's, is multiplied by a factor of 3 to reflect the fact that vehicles don't travel in a straight line across difficult terrain in combat conditions. Mileage is tripled in mud conditions.

ASK YOUR STAFF

Why doesn't Total mileage go down after a Refit? Think of your car. It has a regular yearly service but that doesn't stop the odometer (total mileage) rolling over and eventually you'll start experiencing major problems as the mechanical components of the car age.

When calculating the chance of breakdowns the main factor is the Refit mileage. Total mileage has a smaller impact. HQ's are exempt from breakdowns as they are assumed to swap any affected vehicles with functioning ones from their Divisions.

2nd PanzerGruppe HQ [?]

4 . July . 1941

--- 3rd Pz Div, (loc 29:38) Field Maint: no [?]
Pz: 150 (97% Op) Trans: 450 (100% Op) Km's Total: 600 Km's Refit: 600

--- 4th Pz Div, (loc 29:38) Field Maint: no
Pz: 105 (68% Op) Trans: 400(89% Op) Km's Total: 540 Km's Refit: 540

--- 10th Mot Inf Div, (loc 29:38) Field Maint: no
Pz: 0 (0% Op) Trans: 450 (100% Op) Km's Total: 480 Km's Refit: 480

--- 10th Pz Div, (loc 28:39) Field Maint: no
Pz: 90 (58% Op) Trans: 450 (100% Op) Km's Total: 480 Km's Refit: 480

Your Panzergruppe reports detail mileage and Field Maintenance for each Division

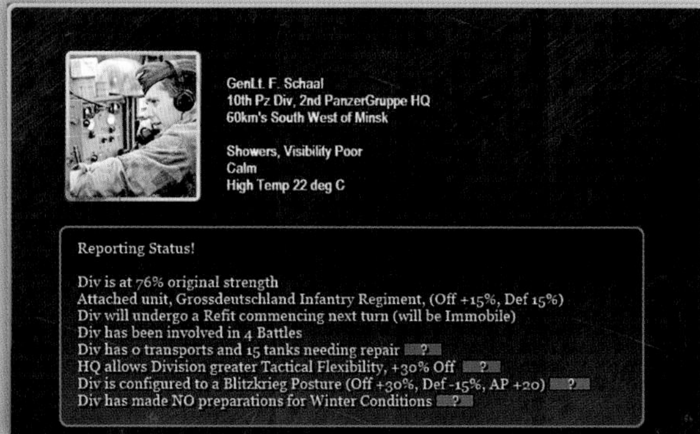

GenLt. F. Schaal
10th Pz Div, 2nd PanzerGruppe HQ
60km's South West of Minsk
Showers, Visibility Poor
Calm
High Temp 22 deg C
Reporting Status!
Div is at 76% original strength
Attached unit, Grossdeutschland Infantry Regiment, (Off +15%, Def 15%)
Div will undergo a Refit commencing next turn (will be Immobile)
Div has been involved in 4 Battles
Div has 0 transports and 15 tanks needing repair
HQ allows Division greater Tactical Flexibility, +30% Off
Div is configured to a Blitzkrieg Posture (Off +30%, Def -15%, AP +20)
Div has made NO preparations for Winter Conditions

GenLt. Schaal's 10th Panzer has 15 tanks currently broken down. Not enough to order to a Rest and Refit for but worth keeping an eye on

IN DETAIL

There is a low chance of a breakdown while ever the Refit mileage is beneath a set threshold (1000 km). Above this the probability doubles. The base chance of breakdown is adjusted by the total mileage which is divided by a fixed amount and added to the overall breakdown probability. Total mileage has a negligible effect initially but slowly increases in proportion to miles traveled. If a breakdown check is triggered, all vehicles are tested. Tanks have a higher probability of being affected than transports.

Any Fast Division that spends the turn not moving, or fighting, will have had the opportunity to undergo field maintenance and will be exempt from the following turns breakdown check. You can see whether a unit qualifies by viewing the Panzergruppe Staff report or asking the Division to Report Status! (quick button, bottom bar).

STAFF ADVICE

If you push your Fast Divisions too hard for too long they will experience high levels of breakdowns. A good time to order a Rest and Refit is when you are relocating your Forward Supply Base as the less strain you put on your fuel supplies at this time the better.

The Soviet system doesn't involve tracking mileage but is more severe as mechanical failure was a bigger problem for them than the Germans. See 6.2.7 Mechanical Reliability.

Refits

You can, at any time, order an individual Division or an entire Panzergruppe to undergo a Rest & Refit. If you order a Panzergruppe to Refit then ALL Divisions are affected. Slow Divisions will automatically take the opportunity to Rest and remove their fatigue while a Refit is underway.

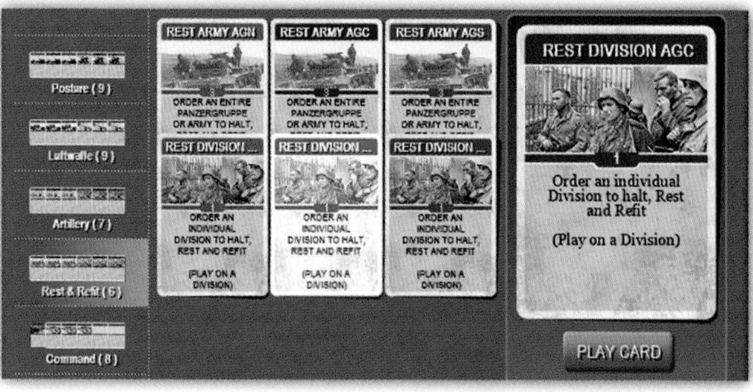

The Rest cards do dual purpose of Resting fatigued slow Divisions and Refitting fast Divisions with broken down vehicles. You don't need to worry about the distinction as it's handled automatically

In order to qualify for a Refit the following criteria must be met.

- It must have a Refit mileage > 0 (Individual Divisions)
- It must be able to trace an uninterrupted route back to its theatre HQ using wheeled transport (trucks will have to reach it with spare parts).
- Because of the above Refits can't be ordered when the unit is located in a marsh.

Once you play the card on a Division, or a Panzergruppe HQ, you have the remainder of the turn to move the unit/s to a safe location, if it isn't already.

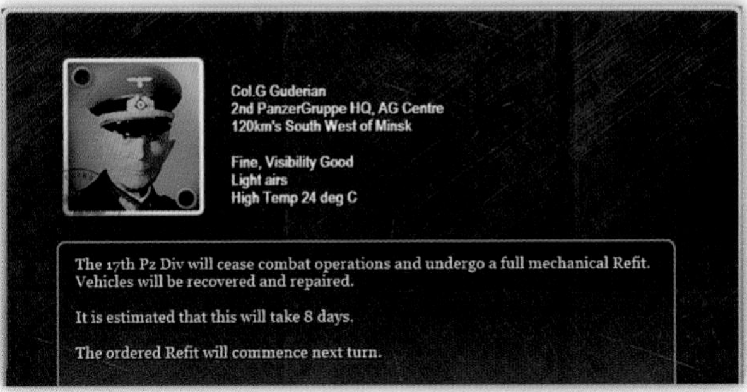
Col.G Guderian
2nd PanzerGruppe HQ, AG Centre
120km's South West of Minsk
Fine, Visibility Good
Light airs
High Temp 24 deg C
The 17th Pz Div will cease combat operations and undergo a full mechanical Refit.
Vehicles will be recovered and repaired.
It is estimated that this will take 8 days.
The ordered Refit will commence next turn.

Guderian is pulling the 17th Panzer Division out of the line for a much needed Refit

Once ordered, a Refit will commence the following turn and take 8 days (2 turns) where the Division will be immobile (0 AP) and suffer moderate penalties if involved in combat. A Refit order can't be reversed. Once the clutch and transmission has been stripped out of a tank it isn't feasible to replace it at a moments notice.

Any affected Divisions will report their current Refit status, when requested, and your Daily Theatre Logs will show a summary.

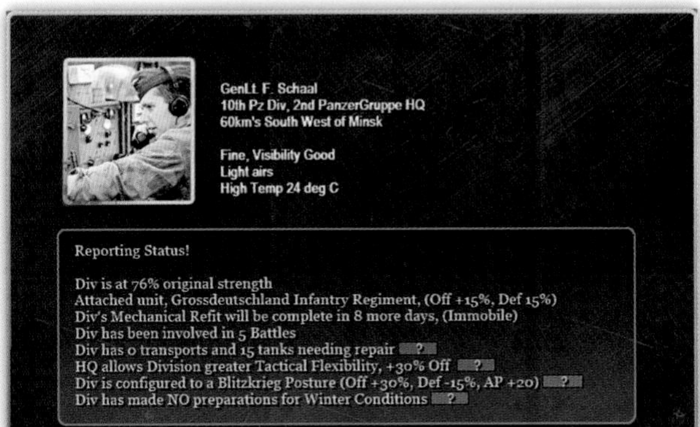
GenLt F. Schaal
10th Pz Div, 2nd PanzerGruppe HQ
60km's South West of Minsk
Fine, Visibility Good
Light airs
High Temp 24 deg C
Reporting Status!
Div is at 76% original strength
Attached unit, Grossdeutschland Infantry Regiment, (Off +15%, Def 15%)
Div's Mechanical Refit will be complete in 8 more days, (Immobile)
Div has been involved in 5 Battles
Div has 0 transports and 15 tanks needing repair ?
HQ allows Division greater Tactical Flexibility, +30% Off ?
Div is configured to a Blitzkrieg Posture (Off +30%, Def -15%, AP +20) ?
Div has made NO preparations for Winter Conditions ?

GenLt. Schaal's 10th Panzer is out of action for the next 8 days and has 15 tanks that need attention

At the completion of a Rest & Refit, all affected Divisions will have their Refit mileage reset to zero (their Total mileage will be unaffected) and a portion of broken down vehicles will be recovered. There is a high chance of recovery (85%) for each vehicle but it's not a given. Note that recovery isn't calculated until the END of the Refit as the engineers are doing their utmost right up to the last moment. Any vehicles that fail a recovery test may still be able to be recovered in a future Refit (perhaps the right part, that will fix the problem, is finally sent from Zone Interior).

Once the Refit is completed the unit/s are free to proceed normally and notification is provided in the relevant Daily Theatre Log.

--- Operations
•9 Divisions are receiving Direct Fire Artillery support (+Off) ?
•1 Fast Division is undergoing a Mechanical Refit (Immobile) ?
•Refit complete (5 Tanks and 0 Transports recovered) ?

Panzergruppe HQ report will reflect the updated Refit mileage figure (it's reset to zero ensuring that breakdowns will unlikely to be a problem for a while).

--- 10th Pz Div, (loc 31:36) Field Maint: YES
Pz: 90 (58% Op) Trans: 450 (100% Op) Km's Total: 720 Km's Refit: 0

GenLt. Schaal's 10th Panzer is out of the garage and back on the road

The Panzergruppe summary will also reflect the change in mileage.

PANZERGRUPPE SUMMARY

16 . July . 1941

--- Panzergruppe 1, Armeegruppe SÜD
POL Quotas on-hand: 3+ (11911 bbls on-hand)
Panzers: 460 runners, (53% operational)
Transporte: 4150 runners, (79% operational)
Average Division Mileage: 278/278 km's, (total/refit) ?

--- Panzergruppes 2 & 3, Armeegruppe MITTE ?
POL Quotas on-hand: 3+ (25729 bbls on-hand)
Panzers: 1035 runners, (74% operational)
Transporte: 6350 runners, (91% operational)
Average Division Mileage: 640/592 km's, (total/refit)

--- Panzergruppe 4, Armeegruppe NORD
POL Quotas ? on-hand: 5+ (12819 bbls on-hand)
Panzers: 365 runners, (78% operational)
Transporte: 2500 runners, (89% operational)
Average Division Mileage: 540/540 km's, (total/refit)

The combined Refit mileage for Armeegruppe Mitte (AGC) has lowered to reflect 10th Panzer's Refit

6.1.7.2. Fatigue

Fatigue was a huge issue for the Germans. As the campaign progressed the men of the Ostfront wore out. It didn't take long before sheer exhaustion began affecting combat capabilities. With the imperative to always keep pushing forward and the looming threat of the coming winter, there was little opportunity for rest. The acute lack of transport found the majority of the German Army marching their way across Russia.

DESIGNER NOTE

Imagine walking from the Polish border to Moscow. It's a long, hard walk. Try doing it with no rest days. Take a heavy pack. Carry a heavy rifle. Strap on grenades and load your pockets up with ammunition. Take away all decent food and force yourself to sleep many nights rough, out in the field and rain. Remember not to change your underpants for months at a time. Forget about having a wash. Infest yourself with lice. Don't forget about all those Russians trying to kill you en route. You'll have to find the energy to fight your way through. Don't stop. Keep moving. It'll be getting cold soon.

Slow Divisions (no vehicles) configured to a Blitzkrieg posture accumulate fatigue. Every turn that they move their fatigue increases by +1. Every turn that they fight their fatigue goes up +1. During mud conditions the effects are doubled. A unit that both moves and fights in a turn, in mud, will accumulate +4 fatigue. Any unit that doesn't move, or fight, during a turn will be considered to have rested and won't accumulate fatigue.

2nd PanzerGruppe HQ - 120km's South West of Minsk

--- 255th Inf Div (loc 30:38)
Army committed to a Blitzkrieg posture, +50% Off, -25% Def
Accumulated Fatigue, -4% Readiness
HQ allows Division greater Tactical Flexibility, +30% Off

GenLt. Franke's 162nd Infantry Division is slowly starting to accumulate fatigue and will continue to do so while ever configured to a Blitzkrieg posture

A unit only accumulates fatigue when set to Blitzkrieg posture but, if configured to another posture, its fatigue levels will not drop (nor will it increase). Only by ordering a Rest (Action Card) can you lower a unit's fatigue.

Fatigue manifests as a direct reduction in the unit's Readiness. See 5.2.1 Readiness. A unit with a fatigue level of 12, for example, will have its Readiness reduced by -12.

Once fatigue increases above a certain amount the unit will incur a movement penalty (less AP).

FATIGUE LEVELS

Fatigue	Level	Movement Effect
< 10	Low	none
10 - 20	Moderate	-10 AP
21 - 30	High	-20 AP
31+	Severe	-30 AP

STAFF ADVICE

Fatigue can, if not managed, completely eviscerate the combat effectiveness of your Armies. There is never a good time to pull an Army out of the line for a Rest when you are driving hard towards an objective. You are dealing with men here, not counters. You can only push them so far.

Soviet units aren't affected by fatigue as they were predominately peasant stock, used to hardship, and were fighting to defend their homeland.

Rest

You can, at any time, order an individual Division or an entire Army to undergo a Rest & Refit. If you

The Rest cards do dual purpose of Resting fatigued slow Divisions and Refitting fast Divisions with broken down vehicles. You don't need to worry about the distinction as it's handled automatically

order a Army to Rest then ALL Divisions are affected. You can order a Panzergruppe to Rest and any Fast Divisions will automatically take the opportunity to Refit and repair broken down vehicles.

In order to qualify for a Rest the following criteria must be met.

- It must have a Fatigue > 0 (Individual Divisions)
- It must be able to trace an uninterrupted route back to its theatre HQ using wheeled transport (trucks will have to reach it).
- Because of the above Rests can't be ordered when the unit is located in a marsh.

Once you play the card on a Division, or an Army HQ, you have the remainder of the turn to move the unit/s to a safe location, if it isn't already.

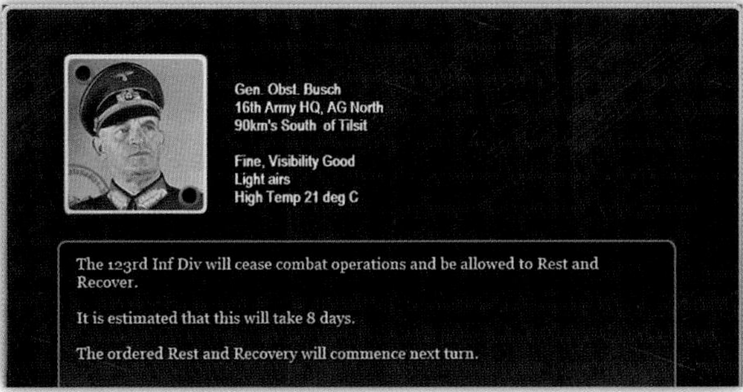
Gen. Obst. Busch
16th Army HQ, AG North
90km's South of Tilsit
Fine, Visibility Good
Light airs
High Temp 21 deg C
The 123rd Inf Div will cease combat operations and be allowed to Rest and Recover.
It is estimated that this will take 8 days.
The ordered Rest and Recovery will commence next turn.

Gen. Obst. Busch is pulling the 123rd Infantry Division out of the line to allow it to rest

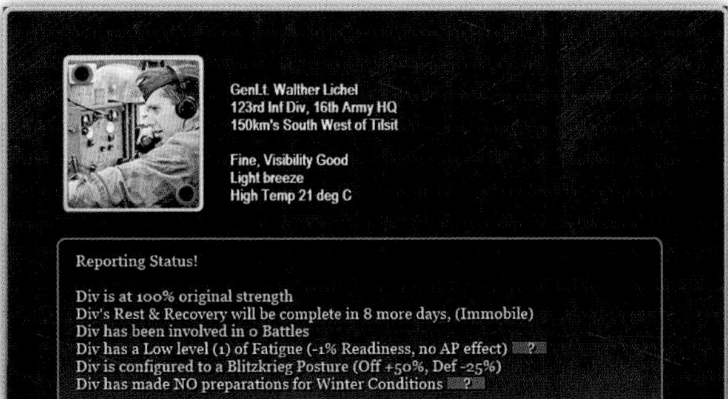
GenLt. Walther Lichel
123rd Inf Div, 16th Army HQ
150km's South West of Tilsit
Fine, Visibility Good
Light breeze
High Temp 21 deg C
Reporting Status!
Div is at 100% original strength
Div's Rest & Recovery will be complete in 8 more days, (Immobile)
Div has been involved in 0 Battles
Div has a Low level (1) of Fatigue (-1% Readiness, no AP effect) ?
Div is configured to a Blitzkrieg Posture (Off +50%, Def -25%)
Div has made NO preparations for Winter Conditions ?

GenLt. Lichel's 123rd Infantry Division can look forward to 8 days of R&R. Gen. Obst. Busch, commander of the 16th Army, who ordered the rest can start packing his bags as the 123rd is in fine shape.

Once ordered, a Rest will commence the following turn and take 8 days (2 turns) where the Division will be immobile (0 AP) and suffer moderate penalties if involved in combat. A Rest, once ordered, can't be reversed.

Any affected Divisions will report their current Rest status, when requested, and your Daily Theatre Logs will show a summary.

At the completion of a Rest, Divisions will have their Fatigue levels reset to zero and the unit, or Army, will be free to proceed normally.

6.1.8. RAIL CONVERSION

Each theatre has a force of Eisenbahntruppe (rail construction engineer battalions under the command of General Gercke) which progressively converts Soviet rail over to German. The Germans had expected to capture large numbers of Soviet locomotives and rolling stock but, when this didn't eventuate (the Soviets were adept at retaining their locomotives), they had little choice but to instigate a crash program of rail conversion.

Soviet rail was of a wider gauge (5 foot) than German rail (4'8.5"). German locomotives were unable to be easily converted to run on the wider gauge and the only practical option was too convert the track. This was time consuming and didn't solve all the problems as Soviet sleepers were wooden rather than iron, Soviet rail was lighter (per unit of length) and the overall number of sleepers in place was a third less than German practice dictated. This all combined to ensure that the much heavier, more modern, German locomotives couldn't be used and older, less efficient, German loco's had to be pushed into service instead.

The rail network was of vital importance to the Germans ability to keep their forces resupplied with fuel and ammunition. Captured, unconverted, Soviet rail can be used but this has a hefty penalty attached to it. Every time you are using Soviet rail as part of your network you are using scarce Soviet locomotives and rolling stock. As they are the only way of moving goods on Soviet rail gauge it involves unloading all cargo from a German train and reloading it onto a Soviet one at the point where the two rail gauges meet (a transport and logistical chokepoint).

It's extremely inefficient and hence the penalty for using Soviet rail links. The more of your network that you can convert to German gauge, the better.

Only double tracked rail can be converted. Single track routes are assumed to have bottlenecks of some form (unstable rail sections, bridges unable to cope with the increased weight or perhaps unsuitable stations with limited loading/unloading facilities) and any conversion would make little difference.

DESIGNER NOTE

Single track routes were converted in '41 but they were of a considerably lower priority than the critical, high volume, double tracked ones.

You can visually see the two different rail gauges on the map. German gauge is black and the wider, Soviet, gauge is a reddish brown.

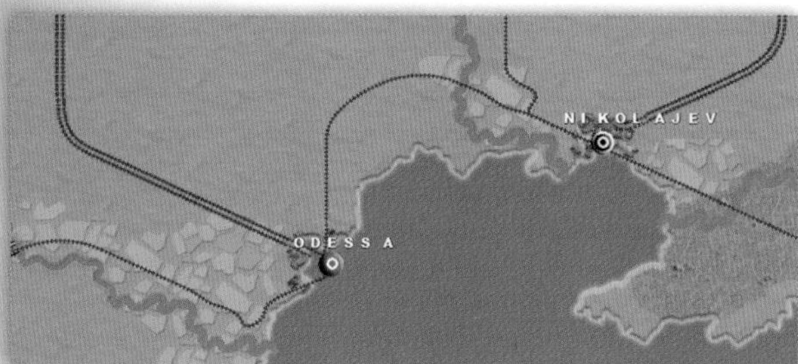

Soviet gauge showing single and double track sections

Eisenbahntruppe aren't shown on the map. However once they convert a section of rail the visual representation changes from Soviet to German gauge (red/brown to black).

At the start of the game you'll be asked to make a few decisions regarding which routes to convert. You Chief of Staff will take the default options if you delegate the matter to him although General Gercke (Head of Transport) may not pleased with your flippant approach to rail related matters.

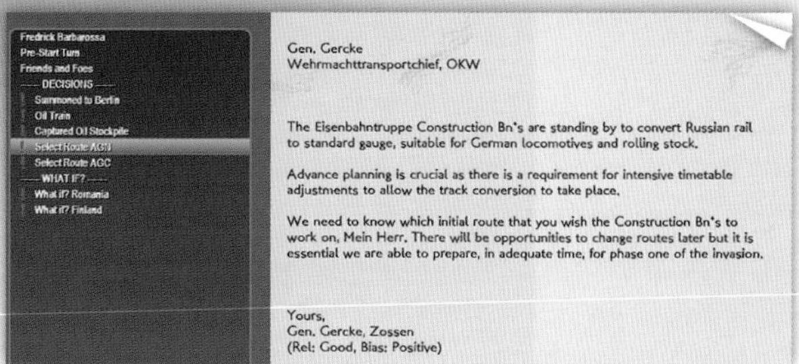

One of the rail conversion route decisions that always appear in the special, pre-start, turn

Whenever rail has been converted to an appropriate city (at the end of the chosen route) conversion will cease and another route selection decision will be generated.

Convert the Kaunas-Riga-Narva line — 1PP
Rail conversion efforts will be focused on this line initially
Convert the Kaunus-Dunaburg-Luga line — 1PP
Rail conversion efforts will be focused on this line initially
Do Nothing — 0PP
F.M Keitel is correct. This decision is beneath you.

Route decisions typically provide a choice of two options

ASK YOUR STAFF

Why can't I change my mind halfway through a route conversion? A standard double tracked rail line had, theoretically, up to 48 trains a day running along it. Track conversion involved significant disruption and rescheduling. A route was chosen, the arrangements were made and changes were contemplated only after that section of line had been done, preferably as quickly as possible.

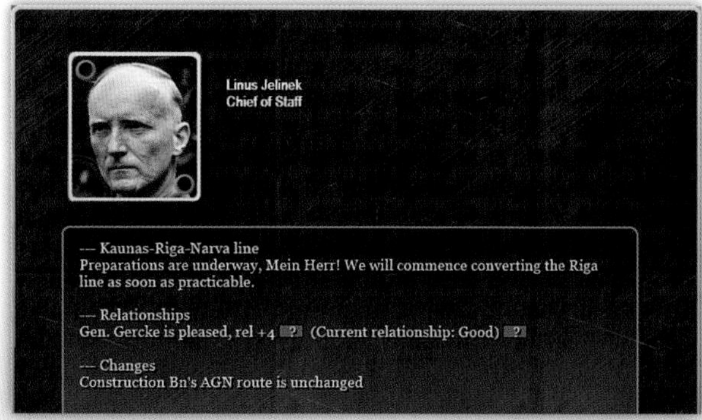

A route has been chosen for AGN. General Gercke is pleased. Conversion will start the following turn provided sections of Soviet rail have been captured

The conversion process happens automatically. It will continue across any destroyed bridges (which is considered separately) and cease only when it reaches the end of the designated route. Each turn you are notified of the Eisenbahntruppe's progress in the 'Logistics' section of your Daily Theatre Logs (as well as by the on-map change of the rail gauges).

--- Logistics [?]
•Quartermaster: Koningsberg FSB fully operational and ready to move [?]
•Truck maintenance : Static [?] [?]
•Construction Bn's have converted 30 km's of rail to German gauge [?]

Making progress. AGN Daily Theatre Log

At any time if there is no rail to convert then you'll receive a message to that effect.

--- Logistics [?]
•Quartermaster: Warsaw FSB fully operational and ready to move [?]
•Truck maintenance : Static [?] [?]
•Construction Bn's unable to convert rail (Soviet owned!) [?]

Down in AGS the Eisenbahntruppe are sitting idle

6.1.8.1. Conversion Calculations

Each theatre has an Eisenbahntruppe force. Their rail conversion 'effort' is represented numerically. Armeegruppe Nord, for example, starts the campaign with the smallest force which has an effort of 130. The number represents both men, supplies and equipment. Various related decisions can increase or decrease the effort of each theatre. Partisan activity (see 6.1.9 Partisans) can also reduce it.

The Dynamic tool tip next to the rail conversion entry in your Daily Theatre Log (see following) shows all relevant information and is updated each turn.

Rail conversion calculations are straightforward. It costs 100 points of effort to convert a single hex. With sufficient effort multiple hexes can be converted in a turn. If there is less than 100 effort to convert a hex a random roll is made and the hex will convert if the result is less than, or equal, to the available effort.

In mud conditions only one hex can be converted, regardless of the available effort. In a similar vein, if a city is reached conversion stops. Adverse weather (hot & dusty or freezing) will lower the available effort.

In order not to bring a low conversion effort to a dead stop, if the effort in a theatre is 50, or below, an unsuccessful conversion in one turn will have the effort 'carried over' to the next to ensure that conversion still continues, albeit slowly. If the Einsenbahntruppe effort is reduced to zero, from decisions, weather or partisans, conversions will cease.

RAIL CONVERSION AGN

Selected Route: Kaunas-Riga-Narva
Total Route distance 960 km's
Cold Weather preparations Level 0
Eisenbahntruppe currently 60km's North of Kaunas

Conversion effort at Campaign start 130
Effect of Eisenbahntruppe related Decisions -32
Actual Effort (manpower available) 98

Successfully converted 30 km's of rail to German gauge
Partial effort 98 to convert hex: Roll 5, Successfully converted!

The selected route and the available effort are shown in addition to the outcome

Successfully converted 30 km's of rail to German gauge
Partial effort 98 to convert hex: Roll 5, Successfully converted!

An effort of 98 is insufficient to automatically convert the hex so a random 1d100 roll is made and the result of 5 allows a successful conversion.

ASK YOUR STAFF

Why can't I reinforce my Einsenbahntruppe Battalions? The amount of Eisenbahntruppe needed, as well as the necessary equipment and supplies they required, were chronically underestimated by the German planners. In '41 the cupboard was bare.

6.1.8.2. Conversion Decisions

There are some interesting decisions associated with the Eisenbahntruppe that can benefit from careful thought. Not all decisions will appear in a given play through.

There are three possible Pre-Start Turn decisions that may appear (Motorise Eisenbahntruppe, Supply Eisenbahntruppe & Rest Eisenbahntruppe). All of them provide you with the opportunity to improve your rail conversion efforts.

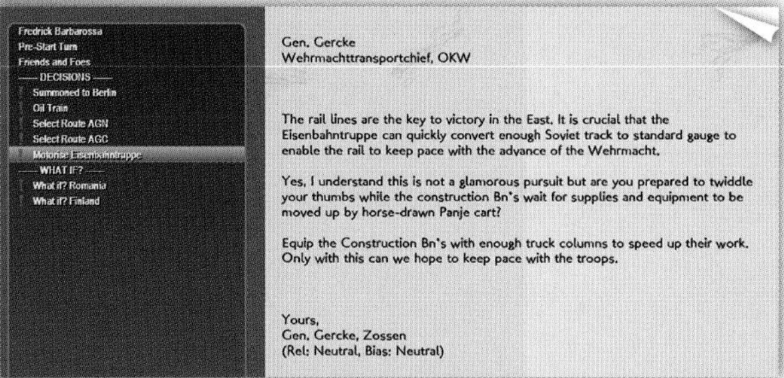

Historically formations such as the Eisenbahntruppe were stripped of their transport in order to muster enough truck columns to keep the Panzergruppes supplied. Prior to the invasion they were given limited training and supplied with enough signals and communication supplies to last for only 60 miles.

STAFF ADVICE

A stalled rail conversion effort can seriously crimp your ability to maintain an effective logistical pipeline. In a worst case scenario it can put a limit on how far your forces can advance in a given theatre.

In the early part of the campaign there will be an individual 'Eisenbahntruppe' decision, one for each theatre. This ask you to determine a basic operational doctrine. Choosing the safe option wasn't done historically.

The Eisenbahntruppe were under a lot of pressure to convert the maximum amount of track in the quickest possible time and didn't always do their job with a view to operational use. Necessary items such as workshops, engine sheds, switching yards and even double tracking were left undone in the race to push the converted track ever forward.

There are a further two individual decision series (each theatre will recieve both) that appear early on, 'Rail Infrastructure' and 'Signaling Equipment'.

A lack of appropriate rail infrastructure hindered the Germans. Soviet locomotives were larger and carried more water. Because of this the Soviet Water Stations were too far apart (many were also deliberately destroyed by both sides) for the German locomotives. Signals and communication equipment were in short supply and were typically destroyed by the retreating Soviets or, equally, by the advancing Germans. Train collisions were common.

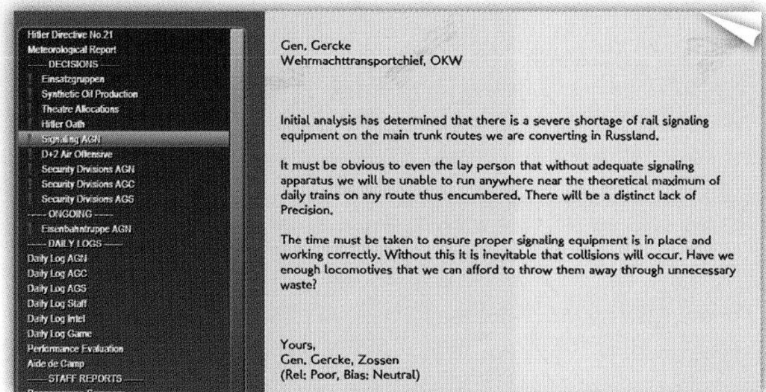

SUMMARY

- There are two types of rail gauge on the map, German (black) and Soviet (red/brown). They are incompatible.
- Eisenbahntruppe construction Battalions convert Soviet rail to German gauge.
- Only double tracked rail can be converted.
- Each theatre has its own Eisenbahntruppe force.
- Eisenbahntruppe are abstracted and aren't present on the map.
- Soviet Rail, once converted, changes to German gauge (black) on the map.
- Rail conversion effort is expressed numerically and occurs automatically.
- It takes 100 points of conversion effort to convert a single hex (30 km) of rail.
- Partial conversions (less than 100 points of effort) require a random roll
- Mud conditions limit conversions to a maximum of one hex per turn.
- If conversion fails the effort will 'carry over' to the following turn if <= 50.

- Conversion stops, that turn, once a city is reached.
- The 'Logistics' section of the Daily Theatre Logs report conversion activity.
- The dynamic tool tip next to the Daily Log entries provides full details.
- You are required to choose a route. Once a route is complete you choose another.
- Partisan activity can affect your Eisenbahntruppe.
- There are a range of decisions that affect your Eisenbahntruppe.
- Not all of the decisions will appear in a given play through.

6.1.9. PARTISANS

As the Germans advance into Russia there will be a gradual awakening of partisan resistance. Partisan levels are tracked individually by theatre. The probability of there being any noticeable partisan activity during a turn is equal to a theatre's partisan level. Eg. If the level of AGS is 10% then that's the chance of activity (10%). Partisan levels can't exceed 100%.

If partisan activity is triggered there is an equal chance of either truck columns being destroyed, rail services being interrupted or the rail conversion battalions suffering casualties. Partisan activity can affect only one of the three in a given turn and only if triggered.

A number of factors can cause the partisan level to rise. Security forces are the only way to lower the level.

Special Divisions were established in early '41 to combat partisans and provide a rear area policing force. Most of them were derived from Landwehr (militia) Divisions manned by second-line reservists. Designated as rear area support units they were poorly equipped and made up of men who were unfit for front line service. It wasn't uncommon for Ukrainian, Russian and French soldiers to be present as manpower became increasingly stretched.

In the opening phases of Barbarossa you have the option of leaving your Security Divisions to clean up remnant Russian detachments or to swing them across to anti-partisan duties. Once assigned to combating partisans they will gradually increase in effectiveness up to a maximum which is determined by the number and type of Divisions present in the theatre.

Rear area Security forces (Divisions) for each theatre are abstracted and, while present in decisions and reports, aren't represented on the map.

PARTISAN EFFECTS

Item	Effect on Partisan Level
Captured Cities	+1 per captured city
Governors	Gradually accumulates each turn once a Governor in place. Capped at 10.
Incidents	Accumulates as a result of the 'Incident' decision options that you have chosen
Partisan Bands	Cumulative effect due to the Soviets playing their 'Partisan' Action Card to disband cut off Divisions
Policies	Cumulative effect as a result of options you have chosen for various decisions
Security (lowers Partisan level)	Increases each turn depending on available security resources in each theatre (decisions). Capped at 30.

If Geneva Convention Option (see 3.1.2.2 Game Settings) is selected a lot of the factors won't apply and the Partisan threat will be minimal. There is an automatic lowering of the German Player's difficulty rating as a result.

--- Civil Affairs
- Overall Partisan level and risk of activity +10% [?]
- Increase: Conquered Cities +8, Incidents +2 [?]

Details of the partisan levels can be found in the Daily Theatre Logs

Certain cities don't have a partisan effect as they were very pro German in '41. These include most of the Baltic States (Kaunas, Riga, Dunaberg, Windau, Liepaja, Jakobstadt) and Vyborg, on the Karelian Isthmus, which was captured by the Russians in the Winter War.

ASK YOUR STAFF

If the Baltic State cities are excluded why aren't Vilnius or Talinn? The partisan effect of cities represents the surrounding region as well at the city. Both Talinn and Vilnius were on the border and there was significant partisan activity nearby.

The Soviet Player has the option of voluntarily disbanding encircled Divisions (maximum of one per turn) which contribute to the partisan level of the affected theatre.

STAFF ADVICE

Conquered cities are straightforward geography - the more land you take the greater the risk of partisan activity, but you are able to influence all the other factors, to a degree, via decisions.

--- Civil Affairs
•Overall Partisan level and risk of activity +18% [?]
•Increase: Conquered Cities +8, Incidents +10 [?]
•Decrease: No. of Sec. Div's (or equivalents) 3, Security Effect 0 [?]

Three Security Divisions have just been assigned and have yet to make an impact

Reich appointed Governors, once installed, will gradually increase their effect on the partisan level, over time (up to a cap). The Reichskommissariat Ostland covers both AGN & AGC whereas the Reichskommissariat Ukraine covers AGS.

Reichskommissariat's were an administrative office headed by a government official established in occupied countries where civilian Reichskomissars ruled them on behalf of the Führer. German settlers were brought in, German language newspapers were published, German businesses took over state enterprises, Soviet state property was confiscated and a range of policies were implemented to further the Reich. The plan was for a merging of all territories into a Greater Germanic Reich that stretched from the North Sea to the Ural mountains.

6.1.10. REMNANT RUSSIANS

The sudden, brutal, thrust of the Panzergruppes into, and through, Red Army formations ensured that there were numerous remnant formations wandering throughout the 'insecure' zone that existed between the hard charging Panzergruppes and the slowly advancing infantry.

Early on in the campaign you are given the option of what to do with your rear area Security Divisions, within each theatre.

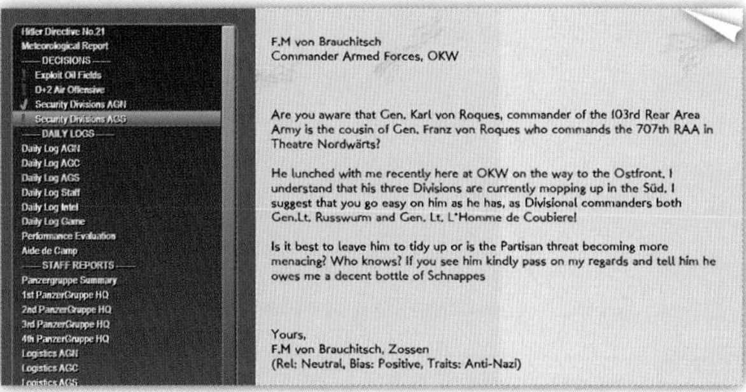

There is the possibility of swinging them over immediately to anti-partisan duties or to leave them, for a variable amount of time, on cleaning up remnant Russian forces.

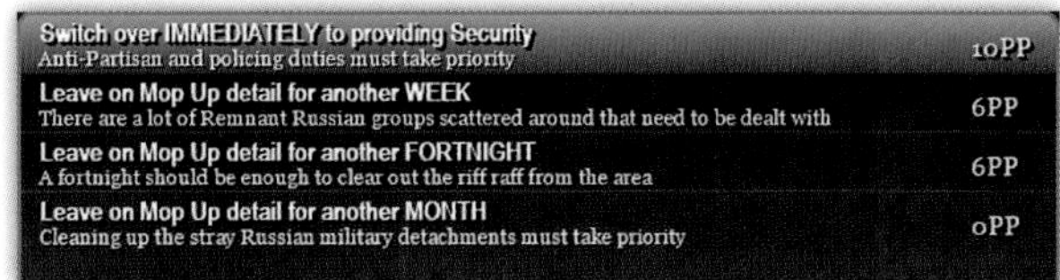

There are benefits to either approach but the downside of concentrating on anti-partisan duties (which involves predominately focusing on securing supply routes and rear area facilities) is that your forces may become delayed when they encounter stray Soviet formations.

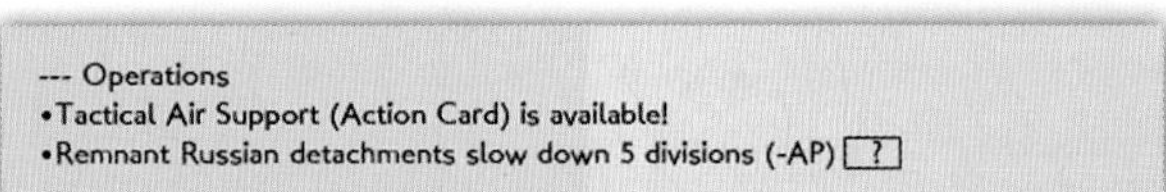

--- Operations
•Tactical Air Support (Action Card) is available!
•Remnant Russian detachments slow down 5 divisions (-AP) [?]

Your Daily Theatre Logs indicate the extent of the problem

The delays are small enough to be noticeable but no more. Any affected Division is assumed to have to make a small diversion to deal with the remnant forces. As organised resistance isn't expected the time and effort required will be minimal.

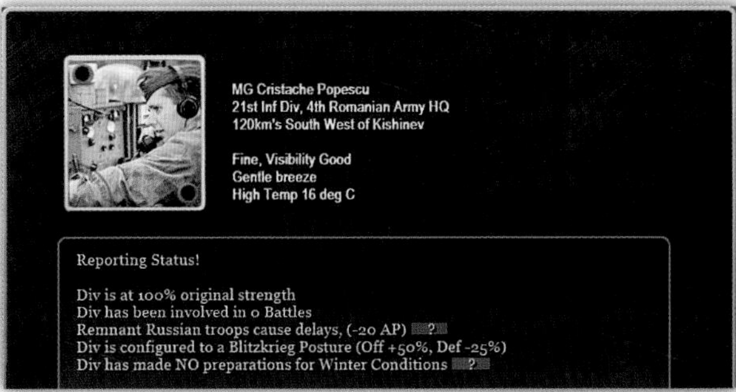

MG Cristache Popescu
21st Inf Div, 4th Romanian Army HQ
120km's South West of Kishinev
Fine, Visibility Good
Gentle breeze
High Temp 16 deg C
Reporting Status!
Div is at 100% original strength
Div has been involved in 0 Battles
Remnant Russian troops cause delays, (-20 AP)
Div is configured to a Blitzkrieg Posture (Off +50%, Def -25%)
Div has made NO preparations for Winter Conditions

MG Popescu's 21st Infantry Division has been delayed

Delays from remnant Russian forces are variable (based on a random roll) and are only possible for the first ten rounds of the campaign. Beyond this point any stray formations would be no longer capable of being anything other than a road bump.

The Unit Modifiers Army reports also highlight any Divisions affected.

4th Romanian Army HQ - 150km's South West of Kishinev

--- Guards Div (loc 36:67)
Army committed to a Blitzkrieg posture, +50% Off, -25% Def

--- 15th Inf Div (loc 36:67)
Army committed to a Blitzkrieg posture, +50% Off, -25% Def

--- 35th Inf Div (loc 36:66)
Army committed to a Blitzkrieg posture, +50% Off, -25% Def

--- Border Div (loc 35:65)
Army committed to a Blitzkrieg posture, +50% Off, -25% Def

--- 21st Inf Div (loc 36:66)
Army committed to a Blitzkrieg posture, +50% Off, -25% Def
Remnant Russian detachments cause delay, -20 AP

--- Fortress Div (loc 36:68)
Army committed to a Blitzkrieg posture, +50% Off, -25% Def

See also 6.1.9 Partisans for the effect of your decisions on theatre Partisan levels.

6.1.11. INTELLIGENCE

Each turn you receive a Daily Intelligence Summary which is a collation of reports from both Army (OKW) Intelligence, the Luftwaffe and the Abwehr. This will only be available if you have chosen the 'Fog of War ON' option at game start. There's not much point in an intelligence report if you have full knowledge of Soviet dispositions.

For the first active turn of the campaign (round 2) the report is always the same and summarises the situation as the Germans saw it in June '41. You'll notice that there is a fair amount of air space between their perception and the reality they encountered.

Daily Summary INTELLIGENCE 22 . June . 1941

--- Overall
•OKW Intel confidently estimate Russia to have no more than 213 Divisions

•154 Infantry Divisions (understrength TO&E's?)
•25 Cavalry Divisions (antiquated?)
•37 Motorised, or Mechanised, Divisions (vintage Tanks and AC's)

•Troop quality marginal. Mostly peasant conscripts.
•Officers, Mid and Low level, assessed as illiterate with little training
•Officers, Division level and above, have little combat experience. Performed poorly in Poland.

•Ability to mobilise once hostilities begin is assessed as limited due to poor organisation and counter productive Communist party ideology

•Civilian population is expected to favour our arrival, especially in the West

The Germans grossly underestimated the size of the Soviet forces that they would face. After rapid mobilisation the Soviets were able to field more than double the German estimates

Daily Summary INTELLIGENCE 4 . July . 1941

--- AGN [?]
•1 Army HQ, 12 Div's and 12 unknown formations have been identified
•Radio intercepts indicate the probable presence of another Army HQ
•Luftwaffe reconnaissance has detected 5 HQ's and 31 Div's

--- AGC
•1 Army HQ, 15 Div's and 9 unknown formations have been identified
•Radio intercepts indicate the probable presence of another Army HQ
•Luftwaffe reconnaissance has detected 1 HQ's and 10 Div's
•0 Army HQ's and 0 Div's have been destroyed recently (Total 1 HQ, 11 Div's)

--- AGS
•1 Army HQ, 33 Div's and 15 unknown formations have been identified
•Radio intercepts indicate the probable presence of another Army HQ
•Luftwaffe reconnaissance has detected 5 HQ's and 35 Div's

--- Overall
•A total of 3 Army HQ's, 60 Div's and 36 unknown formations have been identified
•Heer Intel radio intercepts indicate the presence of another 3 additional Army HQ's
•We have destroyed 1 Army HQ and 11 Div's throughout the Ostfront [?]

--- Abwehr
•Marshal Voroshilov has been seen by informants at Northern Front HQ
•Finland based aircraft have observed NO enemy formations near Leningrad

From the following turn onwards the reports become dynamic and a useful planning tool.

The prime focus of the report is an estimate of Soviet forces within each theatre.

STAFF ADVICE

Keep an eye on Soviet dispositions as it's here that you'll find clues as to the arrival of reinforcements and other useful tit bits.

There is a range of additional information that appears, on occasion, as a result of a wide range of intelligence gathering activities.

Every time the Soviet Player performs an one of the following actions there is the possibility that German intelligence will become aware of it. The probability of various activities becoming known varies but is set at a low base level given the abysmal performance of German Intelligence in '41. historically.

SOVIET ACTIVITY
Activity that could, potentially, be reported
Rail Activity (Reinforcement Armies arriving)
Troubleshooter locations (Zhukov and Khrushchev)
Construction of Fortifications
Raising of Garrisons
Destruction of Bridges
Presence of Front Commanders (name and location)
Soviet Air Defences (presence in a city)
Soviet Forces in a particular City (as a result of aerial reconnaissance)

Aerial reconnaissance can be relied up to provide more timely information although Leningrad can be problematic due to the high level of air defences that forced reconnaissances aircraft higher. There is an element of 'fuzziness' associated with all intelligence but this is only to be expected in a wartime environment.

6.1.12. BRIDGES

The Soviet Player has the ability to blow up bridges whenever Marshal Zhukov is present (see 6.2.6 Blowing Bridges). The Soviet AI will also make an attempt to destroy bridges prior to them being over run by the Germans (see 4.2.4 Bridges).

Bridges, once captured, can be repaired by the 'Pioniers' (engineers). This process is automatic and happens in the background (it's something that is taken care of at a level well below your pay grade).

The chance of a bridge being repaired is directly proportional to the size of the river required to be bridged. The larger the river, the longer it will likely take. Bridges on rivers that have frozen over can't be repaired.

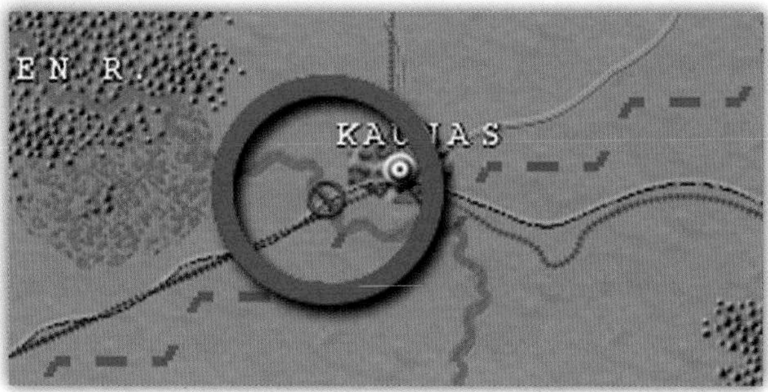

Destroyed bridge at Kaunas

Bridges straddle two hexes and you only have to capture one side in order for repairs to automatically commence. It isn't necessary for a unit to be present in order for repairs to be undertaken.

ASK YOUR STAFF

Didn't the Germans have a great ability to throw up a temporary bridge? Yes they did which is why any of your Divisions can move freely across rivers (at a cost in AP). The bridges represented on the main a key rail bridges. Once destroyed they need to be repaired to a standard sufficient to safely accommodate a fully laden train. As German locomotives were heavier than Soviet ones a lot of the bridges were inadequate, even before being blown. Repairing a bridge to the required standard was no small undertaking and very different to the temporary pontoon bridges that could be thrown up to allow truck columns to cross.

Bridges that fail to repair will carry over a portion of their work into the following turns until the bridge has been rebuilt. Your Daily Theatre Log will keep you informed.

--- Logistics [?]
•Quartermaster: Warsaw FSB fully operational and ready to move [?]
•Bridge rebuilding (Loc 25:36) underway (repair 10%, roll 73), +5% next turn
•Truck maintenance : Static [?] [?]
•Construction Bn's unable to convert rail (Soviet owned!) [?]

The bridge over the Neimen river (medium sized river), near Grodno, is down but is slowly being repaired

Wartime feats of engineering are unpredictable matters and a bridge could be rebuilt quickly or may take a while.

--- Logistics [?]
•Quartermaster: Warsaw FSB fully operational and ready to move [?]
•Bridge rebuilding (Loc 25:36) underway (repair 15%, roll 61), +5% next turn
•Changes to Truck Repair capability (Decision) -1%, now 3%
•Truck maintenance +2%, [?] [?]
•Construction Bn's unable to convert rail (Soviet owned!) [?]

One turn later the base chance of being repaired has been raised +5%.

Visually, once the bridge has been rebuilt the map will show it as such.

--- Logistics [?]
•Quartermaster: Koningsberg FSB fully operational and ready to move [?]
•Destroyed Bridge (Loc 24:33) Rebuilt (strong enough to run Trains over)
•Truck maintenance -1%, [?] [?]
•Construction Bn's have converted 30 km's of rail to German gauge [?]

A second downed bridge over the Neimen, this time near Kaunas, has been quickly restored

BRIDGE REPAIRS		
River Size	Starting Repair%	Increase each turn
Minor	15	+5
Medium	10	+5
Major	5	+5
Volga	0	+5

SUMMARY

- Bridges are repaired to a standard strong enough to take a fully laden train.
- Destroyed bridges, once captured, are automatically repaired by your engineers.
- Bridge repairs will start provided you've captured the side (hex) that it was destroyed from
- The base, starting, value of the repair effort depends on the size of the river
- Larger rivers are harder to rebuild over than smaller ones (thicker the river on the map, the harder it is)
- For a bridge to be rebuilt a random 1d100 roll must be <= repair effort.
- The repair effort increases each turn until the bridge is rebuilt.
- It isn't necessary for a unit to be present for repairs to be undertaken.
- Your Daily Theatre log keeps you fully informed

6.1.13. FORTIFICATIONS

Soviet fortifications can be reduced by the Pioneers (German Engineers). This will happen automatically whenever there are German Divisions, adjacent to a fortification, who are receiving Direct Fire Artillery support.

Fortification each have 2000 'Structural Points' (represents their integrity, think of it as a health bar). Combat and the Pioniers will reduce this until it goes below zero and the fortification is destroyed and removed from the map. Fortifications have the ability to rebuild themselves (local garrisons carrying out repair work) by +200 structural points per turn.

Only Divisions receiving Direct Fire Artillery support can reduce fortifications.

DESIGNER NOTE

Engineers are abstracted. Typically they would assault fortifications under the cover of artillery barrages and smoke. Having adjacent Divisions who receive Direct Fire Artillery support automatically reduce fortifications is a straightforward way of representing the small scale engineering battalions without getting to fiddly.

IN DETAIL

The loss in structural points is equal to a Divisions Theatre Artillery effect (eg. +8% Offensive bonus) times 20 (gives 160 structural points damage per turn). A single Division in this situation would be ineffective as the fortification would auto repair +200 points each turn so it pays to stack Divisions as their effects are cumulative. Six Divisions (similar to the first) stacked in two adjacent hexes to the fortification would reduce it by 960 points (6 x 160).

--- Operations
•Fortifications (22:41) reduced by Pioneers (-960 Structural pts) [?]
•12 Divisions are receiving Direct Fire Artillery support (+Off) [?]

The Daily Theatre Log notifies you of your engineer's activities

STAFF ADVICE

An adjacent Division does not have to assault the fortification to reduce it (provided it's receiving the DF artillery). It can sit there and allow its engineers to gradually destroy the fortification. For best results use whatever Army that has the Theatre Artillery as your 'Fortification Buster'. Stack its Divisions against fortifications for maximum effect. For a fortification in an awkward spot (a choke point such as the Kerch peninsular in the Crimea, for example) consider concentrating all your Theatre Artillery assets behind a single Division.

The green 'health' bar is indicating a fortification that is almost half destroyed

```
COVER: 0
STRUCTURAL POINTS: 1040 OF 2000, AUTO RECOVER POINTS: 200

ZOC PENALTY IN AP = 10
ENEMY TERRAIN PENALTY IN AP = 5
```

The mouse over tool tip in the terrain window (top centre) gives a numerical readout of the remaining structural points. 960 points of damage have been done but it will recover 200 during the Soviet Player's turn

6.1.14. REINFORCEMENTS

Unlike the endless waves of Soviet armies, the Germans receive few reinforcements, mostly individual Divisions.

Reinforcements arrive in two distinct stages. Firstly the Army HQ arrives. An Action card is generated and placed in the 'Command' category (which is different to the Soviet 'Reinforcements').

Once the Army HQ has arrived its subordinate Divisions will begin arriving from the following turn onward. This happens automatically. The only Player intervention required is to deploy the Army HQ on the map via the Reinforcement Action card. Divisions won't turn up until their HQ has been deployed.

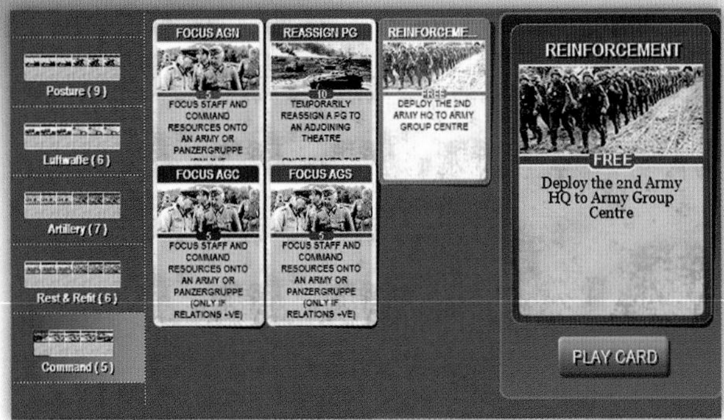

Weichs 2nd Army is ready to deploy

To place the HQ on the map play the reinforcement card and select a suitable hex within the theatre. Only hexes that aren't cut off and are connected to the transport grid will be available (the HQ arrives by train).

AGC. It's complicated.

Once the HQ is on the map any subordinate Divisions will begin arriving the following turn. Their arrival is automatic and probability based due to chaotic war time conditions (very few schedules were maintained in the face of constantly having to adapt to changing circumstances).

Notification of pending HQ arrivals and all other reinforcement related matters are found in the relevant Daily Theatre Log.

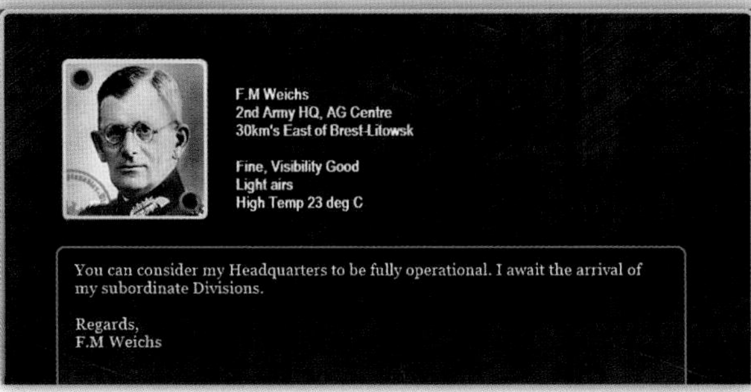
F.M Weichs
2nd Army HQ, AG Centre
30km's East of Brest-Litowsk
Fine, Visibility Good
Light airs
High Temp 23 deg C
You can consider my Headquarters to be fully operational. I await the arrival of my subordinate Divisions.
Regards,
F.M Weichs

Weichs has arrived

--- OOB [?]
- 2nd Army HQ is available for deployment (ACTION CARD)
- 31st Inf Div (2nd PanzerGruppe HQ) has been withdrawn
- 110st Inf Div (9th Army HQ) failed to deploy (25% chance, roll 98) [?]

A summary of all theatres is available via the Aide de Camp report.

--- Other
- You appear to be delegating a lot of decisions. [?] Who is running this war?
- 3 Div's Deployed, 4 Div's Failed to deploy, 1 Div Pending deployment [?]
- 1 Div Withdrawn, 1 Div Failed to withdraw [?]
- 1 Army HQ is awaiting deployment (Card) [?]
- 5 Decisions outstanding requiring your attention [?]

Aide de Camp

If an HQ card isn't played it doesn't matter. The HQ will remain ready to deploy until you do so although none of their Divisions will arrive until they are on the map.

The arrival of Divisions is, as mentioned, probability based. It's modified by the terrain that their immediate HQ is in (this could be the newly arrived HQ or an existing HQ receiving a new Division). Once the HQ has been deployed it is free to move where ever it wishes and its subordinate Divisions will arrive in that same location. As reinforcements arrive by train, if the HQ moves off the transport grid then the probability of Divisions arriving will halve as truck transport will need to be organised (debark off the train, hop in trucks, travel to the HQ) and they aren't in abundant supply.

On the other hand if the HQ moves to, or is already in, a city with its associated rail station infrastructure, the probability of Divisions arriving will double.

Newly arrived Divisions incur a -50 Action Point (AP) penalty but only for the turn that they arrive.

SUMMARY

- Reinforcements arrive in two stages - Army HQ's first followed by their Divisions
- Army HQ's are deployed on the map by the Player by use of Action Cards ('Command' category)
- Army HQ's can be deployed anywhere, within their assigned theatre, on the transport grid
- Divisions arrive automatically but only after their HQ has been deployed
- Divisions have a probability of arriving each turn
- If their HQ is not on the transport grid then this is halved
- If their HQ is in a city then it is doubled
- Divisions incur a -50 AP penalty on their turn of arrival
- The Daily Theatre Logs contain full details of all reinforcement activity

6.1.15. WITHDRAWALS

Withdrawals are unique to the Germans. There aren't many of them and they are mainly based around a number of Divisions being pulled out of other formations in order to help form the new 2nd Army that arrives in AGC.

Withdrawals are straightforward. You'll receive notification in both the Aide de Camp report and your relevant Daily Theatre Log that a certain Division has been earmarked for withdrawal. As soon as this happens the status of the Division in question will be noted.

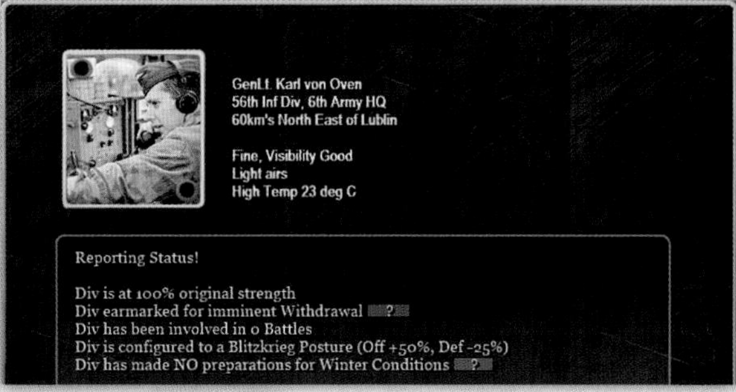
GenLt. Karl von Oven
56th Inf Div, 6th Army HQ
60km's North East of Lublin
Fine, Visibility Good
Light airs
High Temp 23 deg C
Reporting Status!
Div is at 100% original strength
Div earmarked for imminent Withdrawal ?
Div has been involved in 0 Battles
Div is configured to a Blitzkrieg Posture (Off +50%, Def -25%)
Div has made NO preparations for Winter Conditions ?

GenLt. Von Oven's 56th Infantry will be pulling out shortly

Like Reinforcements, Divisional withdrawals are probability based (to reflect the vagaries of wartime scheduling). Details can be found in the relevant Daily Theatre Log (down the bottom).

--- OOB [?]
•56th Inf Div (6th Army HQ) failed to be withdrawn (50% chance, roll 95)
[?]

The 56th will have to hang in there for a bit longer

Unlike reinforcements the terrain that the Divisions immediate HQ (or the Division itself) is situated on has no effect. It's assumed that a Division can withdrawal at will, provided transport is available.

ASK YOUR STAFF

Why can't a Division be fully engaged and unable to withdraw? In the early part of the campaign, when most withdrawals occur, the Germans dominated the battlefield. The Red Army had little capacity to hold an experienced, confident German Division to account.

Once a Division has been notified of its pending withdrawal it should be treated with care. Deliberately exposing a Division that is about to pull out to excessive casualties will result in a sharp rebuke from High Command (you will lose Political Points if the Division is handled roughly prior to its withdrawal).

SUMMARY

- Forthcoming withdrawals are notified in your Daily Logs
- Terrain effects have no impact on withdrawal probabilities
- Units earmarked for withdrawal should be pulled out of the line to avoid penalties (PP) if they take excessive damage

6.1.16. OCCUPATION DIVISIONS

Once a Soviet city is captured there is the possibility that a rear echelon, 'Occupation Division' will arrive to ensure that it remains subdued.

Strategic cities (red dot) gain an Occupation Division after being held for a certain time. Minor cities (grey dot) don't qualify for an Occupation Division.

Occupation Divisions arrive automatically and are additional Division above and beyond normal reinforcements. They are weak, poorly equipped, Divisions made up of the dregs of the army that are immobile and useful solely as a defender of the city they are in.

Referring to such a formation as a 'Division' is an exercise in optimism.

Unlike Soviet garrisons, if cut-off they do NOT draw supply from their city and will eventually wither and die like any other Division that has been isolated.

6.1.17. REPLACEMENTS

Reinforcements are complete Divisions or HQ's that arrive, ready to be deployed. Replacements are individual soldiers and tanks that are intended to replace 'gaps in the ranks' as a result of casualties. Replacements include men designated for the task and returning wounded servicemen who have completed their convalescence and are deemed fit for active duty.

Replacements arrive, from the Zone Interior, in distinct mobilisation 'waves' (as they did historically). There are five waves and they arrive on the following rounds 10, 20, 30, 40 & 50 (24th July, 2nd September, 12th October, 21st November and the 31st December).

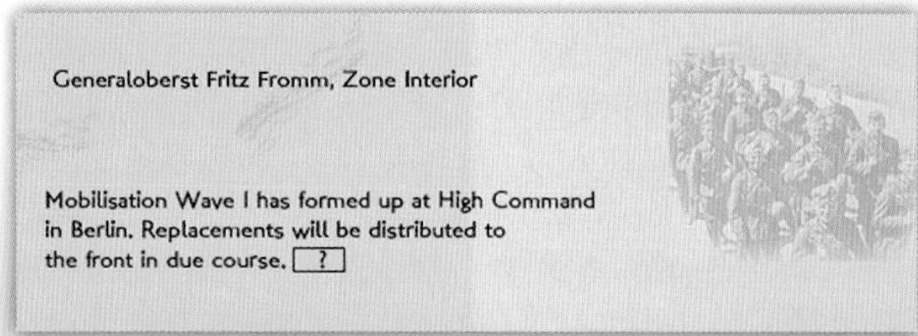

Generaloberst Fritz Fromm, Zone Interior
Mobilisation Wave I has formed up at High Command in Berlin. Replacements will be distributed to the front in due course. [?]

You'll receive notification at the start of a round whenever a 'wave' arrives

Replacement waves form up in the High Command HQ ('HC') at Berlin. Once they have arrived here they will be progressively distributed to Divisions, at the front, who have requested them. This process is automatic.

Note the white square on the 'Unit Troops' tab header. It indicates that there is more information than can fit in the space available and the clicking on the white tab will provide the full information in list form

The 'Replacements Sent Out' tab allows you to see how many have been dispatched to the front this turn. 'REQ' is the total requested by all Divisions, of that type. 'OUT' is the number sent. 'D-OUT' is the number lost due to interdiction (not applicable for this game but retained for compatibility with the previous games in the series). 'RET' is the number sent back from the front. These will be added to the pool of replacements.

Divisions will request replacements as they incur casualties. The unit information display, under the 'Unit Details' tab (bottom right) has a 'Replacements Received' tab (directly underneath).

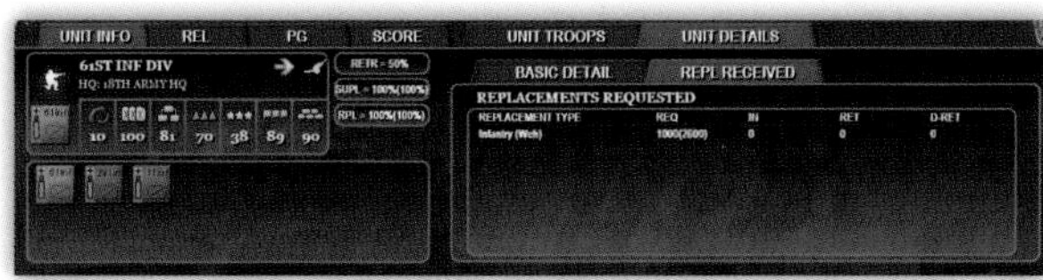

There are never enough infantry to go around

The 'REQ' column shows the number of men, guns or vehicles that have been requested. The main number (1000 in the pic above) shows what's being asked and the number in brackets (2600 shown above) highlights what would ideally be needed. It's unlikely that a Division will receive everything it wants in one go so there is a gradual process of feeding replacements into it over time that will, provided there are enough replacements on hand, gradually return it to full strength (as a rule of thumb a Division that has almost been wiped out should return to full strength in around ten turns).

The 'IN' column is straightforward and is the number of replacements that have arrived (from High Command) that turn.

The 'RET' column indicates how many have been sent back to the High Command pool. This is rare and would only happen if the unit became over strength for a reason (a Panzer Division may have undergone and Refit and recovered a lot of broken down tanks which may have resulted in having too many if it's been receiving replacements in the meantime).

D-RET refers to replacements that where attempted to be returned but where destroyed in the process by enemy interdiction of some sort. This feature has been switched off.

ASK YOUR STAFF

Why can't I voluntarily disband my units like I could in the previous Decisive Campaign games? It was an exploit. The Soviets could voluntarily disband their cut-off units and recover most of their forces and the Germans could disband their Occupation Divisions and use them to bulk up their front line Divisions.

The entire replacement system is something that happens automatically in the background. The German Player does, however, have a specific level that he can pull to influence how replacements are distributed and at what level of loss Divisions will begin requesting them.

Each unit has a 'Replacement Percentage' setting. Clicking on this will toggle through the various options. Hovering a mouse of it will provide a tool tip with a full explanation.

'RPL' refers to the Replacement Percentage Level'

REPLACEMENT PERCENTAGE LEVEL	
RPL Level	Explanation
25%	The Division will only start requesting replacements if below 25% strength
50%	The Division will only start requesting replacements if below 50% strength
75%	The Division will only start requesting replacements if below 75% strength
100%	The Division will replacements if below 100% strength
PRIORITY	Acts the same as the 100% setting but the Division will receive precedence over others

The 'RPL' setting on the unit display has two indicators. The first one shows the setting of any higher level Headquarters and the Division setting is found within the brackets.

In the pic above the 6th Panzer Division has a dual setting of 100% for both. This is the default setting that all German (and allied) units start the campaign with.

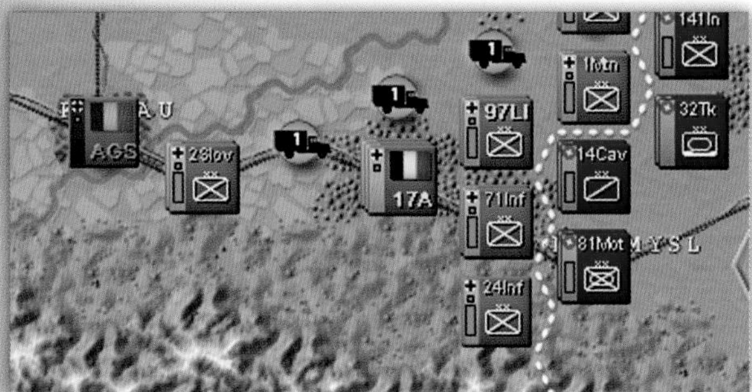

Game start. Note the 24th Infantry Division, 17th Army, AGS, bottom right

The combined settings of both Headquarters, and the Division, are used (they are averaged). To see how this works in practise we'll take a look at the 24th Infantry Division (as shown above).

The unit setting for the 24th Infantry Division is 100% (the number within the brackets). Its Headquarters setting is PRIORITY. But, as can be seen from the pic above, it has two HQ's - it's 17th Army HQ and the AGS Theatre HQ. How do these interact to provide a single 'PRIORITY' setting?

The RPL setting is 'PRIORITY (100%)'

The settings of both HQ's are averaged to provide a combined 'PRIORITY', in this case. The easiest way to see this is to start a new game, go to the first turn, and fiddle with the settings of the two strata of HQ's and the 24th Infantry Division. You'll soon see how they interact.

STAFF ADVICE

The HQ settings allow you to make some quick, broad brush changes. You could, for example, prioritise replacements for one entire theatre over the others but leaving everything as it is and only changing that theatre HQ's setting to PRIORITY. Or you could go a level lower and do the same for a particular army, or Panzergruppe. The system allows you a high degree of control over where your replacements are sent. Don't forget that the more units (or armies or theatres)that you set to PRIORITY the less impact it will have.

Certain Decisions can impact the overall replacement numbers and you can access summaries of replacements by viewing the 'Statistics' tab (top left), under the 'Regime Stats' category.

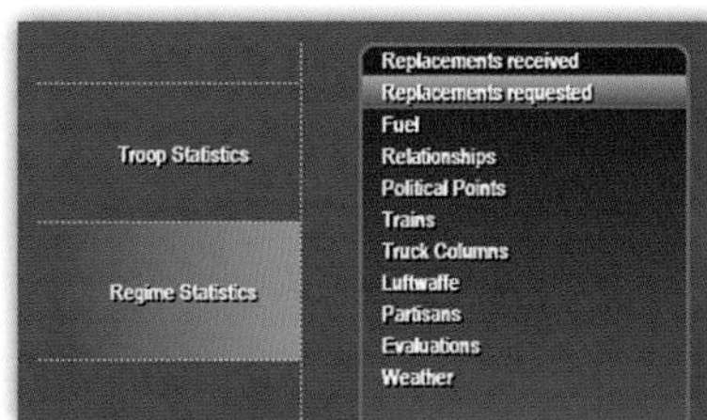

The STATS tab

SUMMARY

- **Replacements arrive in five mobilisation waves, once every ten turns**
- **Replacements, once they arrive, are visible in the High Command HQ in Berlin**
- **Replacements are automatically distributed to the front line Divisions**
- **Divisions will automatically request replacements**
- **Divisions, and HQ's, have a 'RPL' setting (bottom centre) which allows you to adjust who will receive replacements first by adjusting the level at which Divisions request replacements**

6.2. SOVIET COMMAND ▶

6.2.1. COMMANDERS

The Soviet command structure is straightforward. The Player's role is that of Stalin who is assumed to be in charge of STAVKA, the highest level HQ available. All other HQ's are subordinate to him.

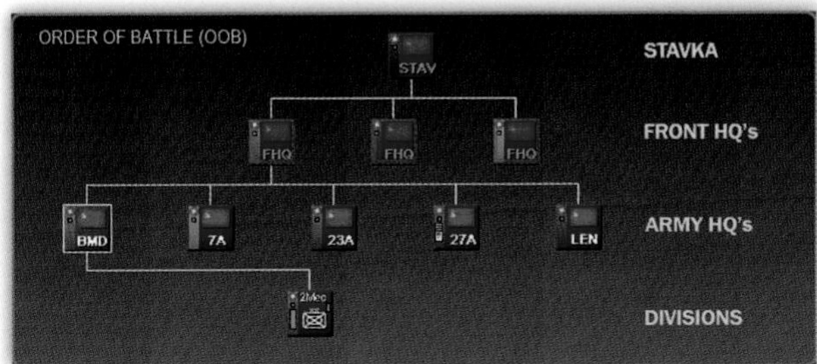

There are three Front HQ's which are the equivalent of a German Theatre HQ. They command the North, Centre and Southern fronts which have identical boundaries to the German AGN/AGC/AGS theatres. Front's are commanded by Marshals.

Unlike the Germans with their dual Army and Panzergruppe HQ's, the Soviets have only Army HQ's.

STAVKA and Front HQ's are unable to be moved by the Player (they relocate automatically if threatened). Army HQ's, along with their associated Divisions, constitute the manoeuvre elements of the Red Army.

The 'Command' tab (bottom centre) displays the key characters for the Soviet Player. There is Stalin, the Player himself, his three Front commanders and his two troubleshooters.

The Front commanders (Marshals) can, unlike the Germans, be changed during the game as a result of the Player's actions. He may choose to have one fired for incompetence, for example. A replacement Marshal would automatically arrive and the relevant portraits and statistics would be updated.

Marshal Timoshenko, Central Front, has been replaced with Marshal Rokossovsky. As both are extremely competent the logic for doing so is dubious. I would be replacing Marshal Budenny first as the size of his moustache is in direct proportion to his military competence

The two trouble shooters, Marshal Zhukov and Commissar Khrushchev don't have on-map representation. They do, however, show up as icons next to the name of the commander of which ever Headquarters that they are currently at.

They are available to be moved around the map, from one Headquarters to another, where the need is greatest. Their formal position within the Soviet Command structure would be directly under Stalin. You can think of them as special envoys who have authority over all concerned and who answer only to Stalin.

You can order them to move to a particular HQ and carry out specific tasks (they have their own sets of Officer Cards). They cannot be changed and possess total loyalty to Stalin.

Front and Army Commanders possess two qualities - an Initiative and a Threat rating. These can change during the course of the game.

Initiative on the left (blue flag), Threat on the right (red hand)

Initiative is a measure of their military competence (higher the better) and is used to determine Army Activations (how many Action Points each Army gets per turn).

Threat rating is how they are perceived by Stalin. The higher their Threat rating the more they contribute to his growing sense of paranoia.

DESIGNER NOTE

There is a basic underlying tension for the Soviet Player between having competent Commanders (high initiative ratings) and military duds (low initiative ratings). Competent Commanders typically have higher threat ratings which can result in Stalin suffering debilitating paranoid episodes. The duds, as a rule, present no threat. This models the fundamental problem faced by dictators and tyrants throughout history - do they surround themselves with useless, grovelling, sycophants or competent military commanders who are liable to take matters into their own hands?

Interestingly most dictators attained their position through ruthlessly exploiting the military route and are loathe, once they have secured power themselves, to leave the door open for somebody else to terminally topple them in the same manner. Stalin was no different and his great purges of the Officer Corps, prior to the war, were all about making sure the door was firmly locked behind him. Which is also the reason you usually start the game with such a motley collection of military duds and have such difficulty getting them to do anything.

6.2.1.1. Commander Types

All Commanders, Front and Army, are one of six possible 'types'. Marshals can arrive with their historically correct type or have a randomly generated one depending on the 'Historical' game option setting.

The Marshal traits are determined by rolling the required number of d10 dice. A TOADIE, for example, would roll 1 x ten sided dice for his Initiative rating and the outcome would be negative. He'd roll 2 x ten sided dice for his Threat rating and it would, once again, be negative.

It can be seen from the table that the, potentially, worst type of commander is the APPARATCHIK. Because of the rolls required to determine their ratings they could still end up being better than a particularly bad WAR BUDDY, for instance.

SOVIET COMMANDER TYPES - MARSHALS

Type	Initiative (1d10)	Threat (1d10)
WAR BUDDY Old Stalin war buddy. Outdated modes of thought. Poor ability.	-1	-1
APPARATCHIK Loyal Party member promoted beyond their level of ability.	-2	-2
TOADIE Curries favour with Stalin in order to work the system to his advantage.	-1	-2
LOYAL SOLDIER Competent military officer who is hindered by his desire to gain Stalin's approval.	0	0
NEW SCHOOL Young, technically trained, enthusiastic with little regard for old school thinking.	2	2
TSARIST Experienced, well trained Tsarist officer rehabilitated due to the emergency situation.	3	2

TSARISTS and NEW SCHOOL are the best commanders (high Initiative ratings) but both have, potentially, high Threat ratings and require careful management.

A LOYAL SOLDIER is fixed and always has both an Initiative and Threat rating of zero.

Army Commanders always have a randomly determined type (it's historically weighted but the probabilities can throw up some interesting combinations). Unlike the Front Marshals their type determines their Initiative and Threat ratings without the need for random rolls.

You can click on a Commanders portrait to get an overview of their type and ratings.

SOVIET COMMANDER TYPES – ARMY COMMANDERS		
Type	Initiative (fixed)	Threat (fixed)
WAR BUDDY Old Stalin war buddy. Outdated modes of thought. Poor ability.	15	-1
APPARATCHIK Loyal Party member promoted beyond their level of ability.	10	-1
TOADIE Curries favour with Stalin in order to work the system to his advantage.	5	-2
LOYAL SOLDIER Competent military officer who is hindered by his desire to gain Stalin's approval.	20	0
NEW SCHOOL Young, technically trained, enthusiastic with little regard for old school thinking.	30	1
TSARIST Experienced, well trained Tsarist officer rehabilitated due to the emergency situation.	40	2

6.2.1.2. Commander Initiative Rating

This is a direct measure of the Commander's military competence and is used to determine Army activations (see 6.2.2 Activation).

The Initiative of Front Marshals acts as a modifier to the Initiatives of all their subordinate Army Commanders for activation purposes. A Marshal with a negative Initiative rating will make it harder for his Army Commanders to activate and vice versa.

Army Commanders must, each turn, make a roll to determine their level of 'Activation' (how many Action Points their Divisions will have available for movement and combat). Their Initiative rating is modified by that of their Front Marshal's and any other relevant modifiers to determine an adjusted Initiative which, when compared to a d100 roll, determines their activation level (Full, Partial or None).

The higher an Army Commander's Initiative rating the greater the chance that they will fully activate. Army Commanders with higher Initiative ratings are considered to be more competent than those with lower ratings.

Initiative ratings can change during the course of the game. The mechanics that govern this are different for Front Marshals (only as a result of actions taken by Troubleshooters) and Army Commanders (each time they activate their initiative rating increases).

6.2.1.3. Commander Threat Ratings

Both Front Marshals and Army Commanders have a threat rating which reflects how Stalin perceives them (see 6.2.3 Paranoia).

Threat ratings work identically for both. They directly contribute to Stalin's Paranoia level. Front Marshals can, depending on their type, have a negative threat rating which acts to reduce Stalin's level of paranoia (good). Marshals with a positive threat rating increase it (bad).

Front Marshals can have their threat ratings change but only through the actions of Troubleshooters (Commissar Khrushchev). Most of the time their threat rating is fixed.

Army Commanders threat ratings will increase over time as they gain in competence (increased initiative, see 6.2.2 Activation). Over time the Army Commanders will collectively present a larger threat to Stalin's peace of mind, than any other single factor.

6.2.1.4. Commander Randomisation

The three Front Marshals will always be the same when you start a game. With the 'Historical' game option ON (see 3.1.2.2 Game Settings) they will present as historically accurate types (always the same).

With the History OFF game option (default) they will be a randomly determined type (weighted to an historical outcome). This can present the Soviet Player with a lot of variety. The typical outcome is to have three militarily incompetent Marshals who Stalin perceives as being little threat (War Buddy, Apparatchik or Toadie). Occasionally there will be a 'Loyal Soldier' who straddles the middle ground between the incompetents and the stars.

It's possible to receive New School, or even Tsarist, Marshals. This gives a very different game. Their high initiatives (better Army activations) allow the Player to be nimbler in their response to the invasion and provides scope for early spoiling manoeuvres. But their equally high threat ratings ensure that the Player has to take immediate steps (Commissar Khruschev) to manage Stalin's sense of paranoia lest it gets out of hand.

STAFF ADVICE

As the Soviet Player the first step, upon starting a new game, is to examine your three Front Marshals and formulate a strategy around these three key individuals. You'll may have an Initiative problem or a Threat problem. Perhaps a blancmange of both. The former places restrictions on your military strategy and the latter creates a combustible, volatile, Stalin.

Army Commanders, while having historically correct names and assignments, always have a randomly chosen type (within reasonable historical parameters).

DESIGNER NOTE

There are simply too many Soviet Army Commanders and information on them is very sparse, especially for the Commanders of the numerous Conscript Armies. Any attempt at being historically correct would have involved more guess work than fact.

6.2.2. ACTIVATION

Soviet Command and Control was significantly below that of the well oiled Wehrmacht. To reflect this each Army has to make a roll each turn to determine its level of Activation. Different levels provide differing amounts of Action Points (AP) for all subordinate Divisions within the Army.

The main problem confronting STAVKA wasn't the poor combat performance of their Armies. Poor communications, even poorer quality Commanders (Stalin's great purge before the war had removed most of the experience and talent), an inefficient command structure and a large dose of chaos and confusion all contributed to a Red Army that struggled to conduct even basic military actions in a coordinated, methodical manner.

A number of factors influence this and you can find a detailed breakdown in the three Front 'Activation' reports. Reorganising the command structure (see 6.2.5.4 Command Cards) is vital to improving the overall Activation chances.

6.2.2.1. Activation Levels

There are three levels, in order of priority, they are Full, Partial and None. An Army will achieve one of these levels each turn and all subordinate Divisions within the Army will have their Action Points (AP) adjusted accordingly.

ACTIVATION LEVELS

Level	AP Penalty	Criteria
Full	(full 100 AP)	Activation roll <= Cdr's Adjusted Initiative
Partial	-30 AP	Activation roll > Cdr's Adj. Initiative and <= 2 x Adj. Init.
None	-60 AP	Activation roll > 2 x Cdr's Adjusted Initiative

STAFF ADVICE

You want Commanders with high Activation levels. Their Armies will be mobile and responsive if they can gain the full 100 AP allowance each turn.

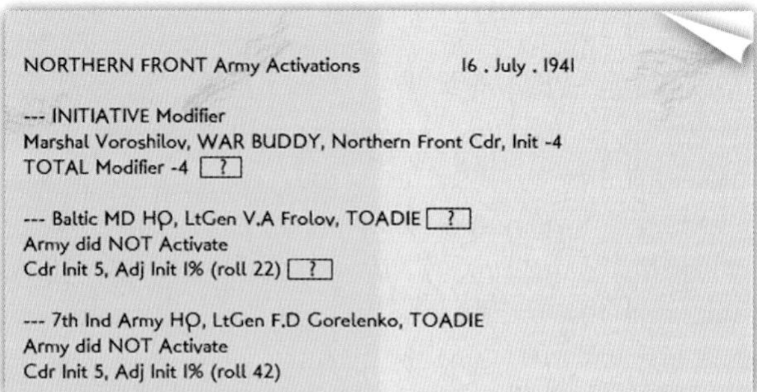
NORTHERN FRONT Army Activations
16 . July . 1941
--- INITIATIVE Modifier
Marshal Voroshilov, WAR BUDDY, Northern Front Cdr, Init -4
TOTAL Modifier -4 ?
--- Baltic MD HQ, LtGen V.A Frolov, TOADIE ?
Army did NOT Activate
Cdr Init 5, Adj Init 1% (roll 22) ?
--- 7th Ind Army HQ, LtGen F.D Gorelenko, TOADIE
Army did NOT Activate
Cdr Init 5, Adj Init 1% (roll 42)

It's in the early stages of the invasion and the Northern front is struggling

6.2.2.2. Activation Mechanics

An Armies Activation Level is determined by its Commander's Adjusted Initiative. This is calculated by taking the Commander's Initiative rating and modifying it by a range of factors including the

Front Commander's Initiative, actions taken by the Germans, actions taken by Stalin and actions taken by the two Troubleshooters.

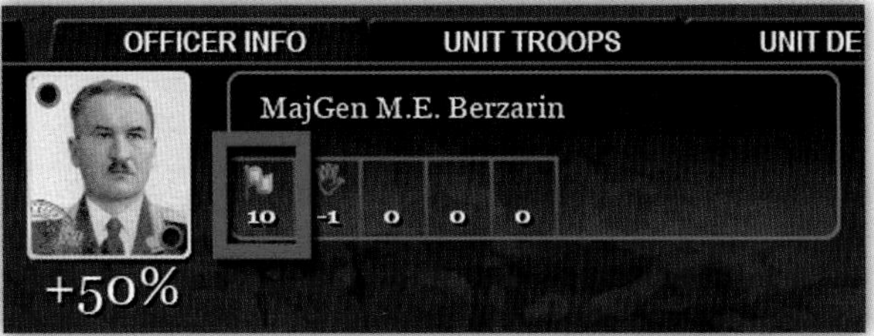

The Blue Flag is the Initiative rating of the Commander. It's a measure of their competence and the higher it is the better

An Army will Fully Activate if the Activation roll is Less than, or Equal, to its Commander's adjusted initiative. If a Commander, for example, had an adjusted initiative of 20, he will Fully Activate on any roll of 20 or less.

An Army will Partially Activate if the Activation roll is between the Commander's adjusted initiative and TWICE that. If the same Commander, for example, had an adjusted initiative of 20, he will Partially Activate on any roll between 21 and 40.

If an Army fails to either Fully or Partially Activate it is considered to have not activated (activation level of 'None').

Adjusted Initiative

The Army Commander's Initiative rating is adjusted by any 'Initiative Modifiers' that are specified in the Front Activation reports. If an item isn't mentioned in the 'Initiative Modifiers' section then it doesn't apply. All items (or influencing factors) are summed and are added to each Army Commander's Initiative in order to determine their 'Adjusted Initiative'.

STAFF ADVICE

Front Commanders are critical. A Front Commander with a poor Initiative rating will act as a drag on everybody. Consider replacing them with a Tsarist (Action Card) or send Commissar Khrushchev to 'have a quiet word' in his ear (see 6.2.4 Troubleshooters).

NORTHERN FRONT Army Activations 4 . July . 1941

--- INITIATIVE Modifier
Comrade Stalin gives a rousing Speech, (Overall) +13
Overhauled Soviet Command Structure, (Overall) +10
Marshal Voroshilov, APPARATCHIK, Northern Front Cdr, Init -14
TOTAL Modifier +9 [?]

--- Baltic MD HQ, LtGen V.A Frolov, TOADIE [?]
Army did NOT Activate
Cdr Init 19, Adj Init 28% (roll 82) [?]

--- 7th Ind Army HQ, LtGen F.D Gorelenko, WAR BUDDY
Army did NOT Activate
Cdr Init 25, Adj Init 34% (roll 70)

--- 23rd Army HQ, MajGen P.S. Pshennikov, APPARATCHIK
Army Partially activated [?]
Cdr Init 22, Adj Init 31% (roll 35) Init +2% [?]

--- 11th Army HQ, LtGen V.I. Morozov, TOADIE
Army Fully activated [?]
Marshal Georgy Zhukov's dynamic presence +60
Cdr Init 23, Adj Init 92% (roll 47) Init +4%

Part of the Northern Front report with the Initiative Modifiers up the top. There are three separate factors modifying every Army Commander's Initiative rating

The Front Commander is always a factor and his Initiative affects all Commanders within his front. There are a wide range of other possible factors but they apply only when applicable unlike the effect of the Front Commander which is a constant.

--- INITIATIVE Modifier
Comrade Stalin gives a rousing Speech, (Overall) +13
Overhauled Soviet Command Structure, (Overall) +10
Marshal Voroshilov, APPARATCHIK, Northern Front Cdr, Init -14
TOTAL Modifier +9 [?]

Marshal Voroshilov, in this instance an APPARATCHIK (it can vary on different play throughs), is a military dud and has been promoted well beyond the level of his competence

NORTHERN FRONT Army Activations 16 . July . 1941

--- INITIATIVE Modifier
Marshal Voroshilov, WAR BUDDY, Northern Front Cdr, Init -4
TOTAL Modifier -4 [?]

--- Baltic MD HQ, LtGen V.A Frolov, TOADIE [?]
Army did NOT Activate
Cdr Init 5, Adj Init 1% (roll 22) [?]

A very straightforward example. The only modifier is the Front Commander who is always present. Lt.Gen. Frolov of the Baltic Military District (MD) has an Initiative rating of 5. This is lowered by the Total of all modifiers (in this case -4 due to Marshal Voroshiliv having an Initiative of -4) to give an adjusted Initiative of 1. Lt.Gen. Frolov's Baltic MD failed to activate because his Activation roll was 22, well above his adjusted initiative of 1.

CENTRAL FRONT Army Activations 4 . July . 1941

--- INITIATIVE Modifier
Comrade Stalin gives a rousing Speech, (Overall) +13
Overhauled Soviet Command Structure, (Overall) +10
This Front has been designated a Priority by Comrade Stalin +25
Marshal Timoshenko, WAR BUDDY, Central Front Cdr, Init -8
Commissar Khrushchev's grim reaper reputation [?] -4
TOTAL Modifier +36 [?]

--- Western HQ, Col.G D.G. Pavlov, NEW SCHOOL [?]
Army Fully activated [?]
Cdr Init 46, Adj Init 82% (roll 5) Init +4% [?]
Threat +1% (rqd 40%, roll 31) [?]

A more involved example. There are multiple modifying factors but their net, total effect is +36 (excellent!). Col.G Pavlov's Western HQ has an Initiative rating of 46 which, when modified (has the +36 added to it) becomes an Adjusted Initiative of 82. Not unexpectedly, the Western HQ fully activates (an 82, or less, was needed and it rolled a 5).

--- INITIATIVE Modifier
Comrade Stalin gives a rousing Speech, (Overall) +13
Overhauled Soviet Command Structure, (Overall) +10
Marshal Voroshilov, APPARATCHIK, Northern Front Cdr, Init -14
TOTAL Modifier +9 [?]

--- Baltic MD HQ, LtGen V.A Frolov, TOADIE [?]
Army did NOT Activate
Cdr Init 19, Adj Init 28% (roll 82) [?]

--- 7th Ind Army HQ, LtGen F.D Gorelenko, WAR BUDDY
Army did NOT Activate
Cdr Init 25, Adj Init 34% (roll 70)

--- 23rd Army HQ, MajGen P.S. Pshennikov, APPARATCHIK
Army Partially activated [?]
Cdr Init 22, Adj Init 31% (roll 35) Init +2% [?]

We're back with Marshal Voroshilov the APPARTATCHIK. Stalin and Stavka are working hard to compensate for his failure to grasp basic military principles. There's a total modifier of +9. You can see all three Army Commanders have had their Initiative rating's raised by this amount. The last one, MajGen. Pshennikov's 23rd Army, has an Adjusted Initiative of 31 and rolls a 35. Because this is between his Adjusted Initiative and twice that (>31 and <=62) he achieves a Partial Activation. Neither of the other to Commanders managed this although the middle one, Lt.Gen Gorelenko's 7th Army almost did (he needed less than, or equal to 68 and got a roll of 70).

Initiative Increase

Every time an Army Commander achieves any form of activation his Initiative rating will increase. The amount of increase will be greater if he has Fully Activated (+4) than if he only Partially Activated (+2).

Initiative ratings of Army Commanders always increase whenever they achieve a Partial Activation or better.

--- Western HQ, Col.G D.G. Pavlov, NEW SCHOOL [?]
Army Fully activated [?]
Cdr Init 46, Adj Init 82% (roll 5) Init +4% [?]
Threat +1% (rqd 40%, roll 31) [?]

Col.G Pavlov's Western HQ has fully activated and, as a result, his Initiative rating increases +4% to 5.

The Initiative rating of Front Commanders (Marshals) don't increase in this manner (they're fixed) although certain Troubleshooter Action Cards can change them. See 6.2.4 Troubleshooters.

STAFF ADVICE

Soviet Army Commanders underwent a rapid learning curve. Many of them lost their Armies before they could achieve a basic level of competency. The better a Commander's Initiative rating, the faster it will improve making high Initiative Commanders very valuable.

--- 16th Army HQ, LtGen M.F. Lukin, WAR BUDDY
Army Partially activated [?]
Cdr Init 15, Adj Init 51% (roll 100) Init +2%

LtGen. Lukin's 16th Army has partially activated and his Initiative rating improves by +2 as a result

Threat Increase

Whenever an Army Commander achieves Activates (Partial or Fully) there is a chance that his Threat rating will also increase (the more competent a Commander is, the greater his popularity and the more Stalin perceives him to be a threat). Commanders that Fully Activate have a higher probability of increasing their Threat rating (40%) than those that only Partially Activate (20%).

--- 19th Army HQ, LtGen W.I. Kuznetsov, WAR BUDDY
Army Fully activated [?]
Cdr Init 15, Adj Init 51% (roll 21) Init +4%
Threat +1% (rqd 40%, roll 15)

LtGen. Kuznetsov's 19th Army has Fully activated and, as a result, LtGen. Kuzentsov's Threat rating has increased. Note that increases in Threat ratings will only show in the Activation Reports if the required rolls succeed

If a Commander's Threat rating increases it will always do so by +1.

The Threat rating of Front Commanders (Marshals) don't increase in this manner (they're fixed) although certain Troubleshooter Action Cards can change them. See 6.2.4 Troubleshooters.

See 6.2.3 Paranoia for more information on a Commander's Threat rating.

6.2.2.3. Activation Reports

Activation information can be obtained by various means.

The Aide de Camp report will always summarise the overall Activation situation at the beginning of each turn.

--- Front Summary
•NORTH: Marshal Voroshilov, APPARATCHIK, Initiative -14, Threat -10 ?
•CENTRE: Marshal Timoshenko, WAR BUDDY, Initiative -8, Threat -1
•SOUTH: Marshal Budenny, TOADIE, Initiative -3, Threat -12

•NORTH: 2 Armies Fully activated, 2 Partially, 2 Didn't ?
•CENTRE: 7 Armies Fully activated, 1 Partially, 0 Didn't
•SOUTH: 5 Armies Fully activated, 1 Partially, 1 Didn't

An 'at a glance' summary of your Front Commanders and the Armies they command. While there are other factors that can influence Activations the Front Commanders have a significant impact. It's instructive that the Northern Front, with the worst Front Commander (Marshal Voroshilov, Initiative -14) has achieved the fewest activations

The three Activation reports are your primary source of information and can be found in the Report tab.

—— STAFF REPORTS ——
Paranoia Summary
NORTHERN FRONT Army Activations
CENTRAL FRONT Army Activations
SOUTHERN FRONT Army Activations

Army 'Unit Modifier' reports will provide details of Activations and the effects of this on the individual Divisions.

7th Ind Army HQ - 210km's North East of Leningrad

--- 54th Rifle Div (loc 36:5)
Army NOT activated, -60 AP
Forest or Marsh local knowledge (halved - road present) +20% Def
Poor defensive preparations (early turns only), -20 Entrench
Blitzkrieg Shock penalty (early, diminishing effect), -20% Def
Army committed to an Offensive posture, +40% Off, -20% Def

The 54th Rifle Division, 7th Ind. Army, had better hope that the Finns don't launch an assault over the border

The special 'Command' tab (bottom centre) has dynamic tool tips for each of your three Marshals that provide a summary of activations within their Fronts.

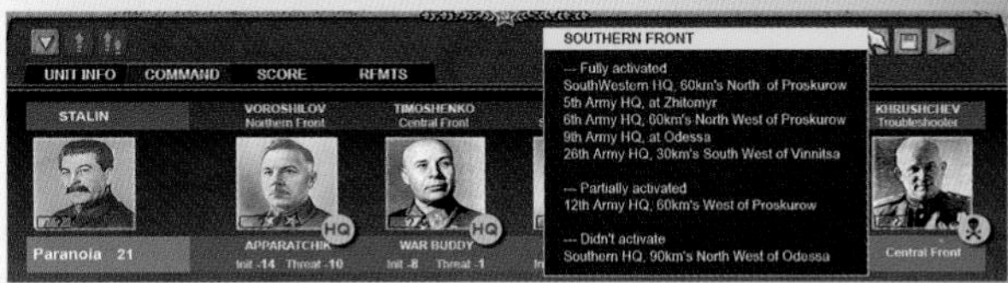

If you ask an individual Division to Report Status! they will include their level of Activation and any effect that this is having on their movement capability (Action Points).

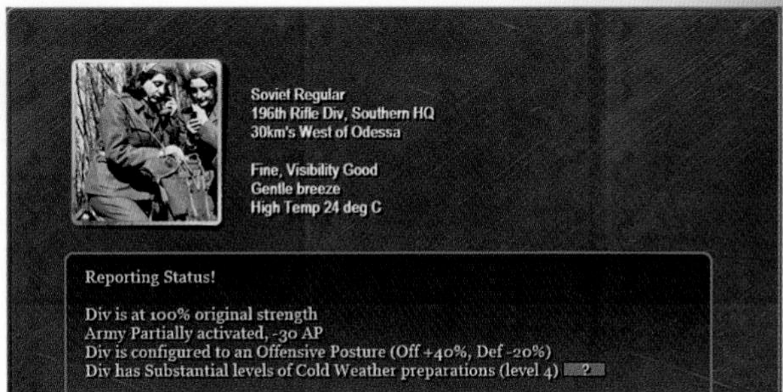

6.2.2.4. Effect of Troubleshooters

Marshal Zhukov will provide a significant activation bonus to any HQ that he is present at (no effect if at STAVKA). His presence at an Army HQ is enough to stiffen resolve and provide a +60 modifier to the Army Commander's activation chances. At Front HQ he still exerts a strong presence and will provide a +20 modifier to all subordinate Army Commander activation chances within the Front.

Marshal Zhukov can be dispatched to where ever he is needed most

Commissar Khrushchev provides no bonus and can, instead, generate an activation penalty. His reputation precedes him and Commanders are unwilling to demonstrate initiative in his presence for fear of retribution. The penalty increases depending on his actions (if he starts ordering people shot, for example, it will rise) but remains minor.

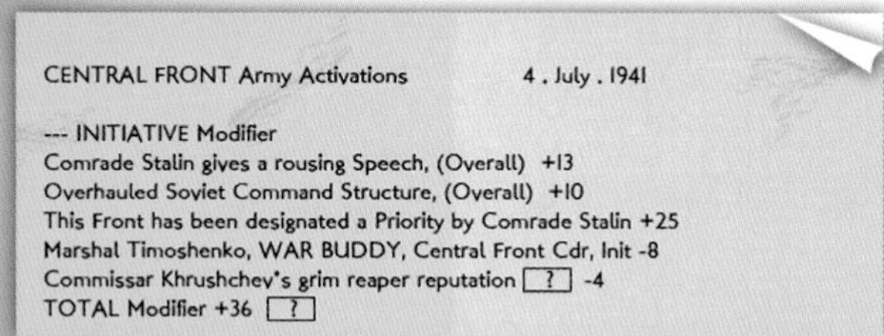
CENTRAL FRONT Army Activations 4 . July . 1941

--- INITIATIVE Modifier
Comrade Stalin gives a rousing Speech, (Overall) +13
Overhauled Soviet Command Structure, (Overall) +10
This Front has been designated a Priority by Comrade Stalin +25
Marshal Timoshenko, WAR BUDDY, Central Front Cdr, Init -8
Commissar Khrushchev's grim reaper reputation [?] -4
TOTAL Modifier +36 [?]

Word gets around. Nobody appreciates a visit from Commissar Khrushchev. Sometimes, however, it's necessary

6.2.2.5. Luftwaffe Disruption

The German Player (or AI) has the ability to order the Luftwaffe to continue to disrupt Soviet Command and Control after the initial air offensive is over. If this happens there will be a global (affects all) activation penalty that remains in force for while ever the Luftwaffe continues the mission (the length of time is determined by a decision taken by the German Player).

The effect will vary from turn to turn as factors such as weather, visibility and local targeting ensure that there is a variable outcome.

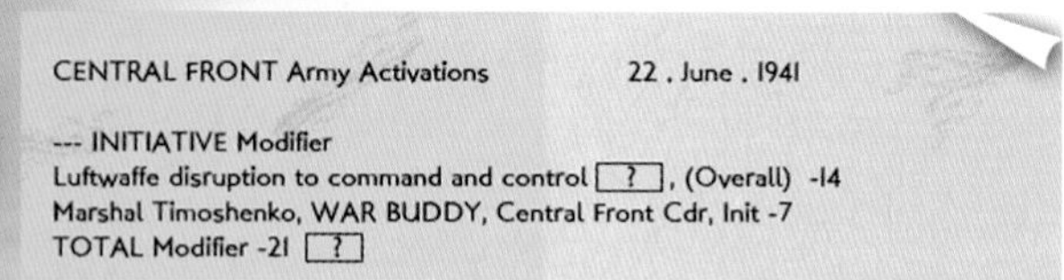
CENTRAL FRONT Army Activations 22 . June . 1941

--- INITIATIVE Modifier
Luftwaffe disruption to command and control [?], (Overall) -14
Marshal Timoshenko, WAR BUDDY, Central Front Cdr, Init -7
TOTAL Modifier -21 [?]

See 6.1.3.4 D+2 Air Offensive.

6.2.2.6. Activation Advice

There a number of ways to improve your Armies chances of activating.

Prioritise a Front (Action Card). Doing so will increase all activations, within the front, by +25.

Overhaul the Soviet Command Structure. This will give a +10 global bonus (to all) each time played. The effect is permanent.

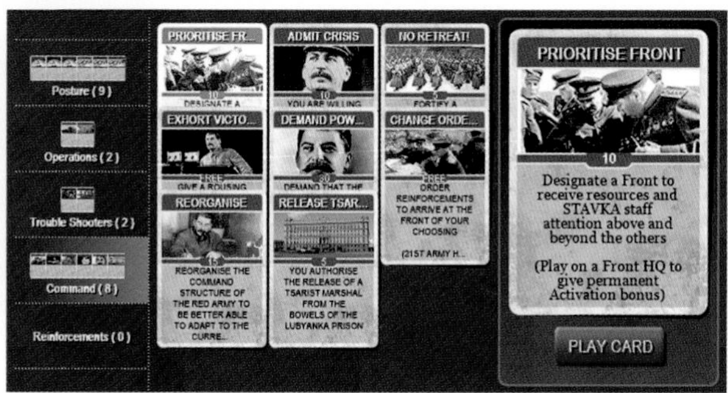

Give a speech. Everybody appreciates a rousing call to arms.

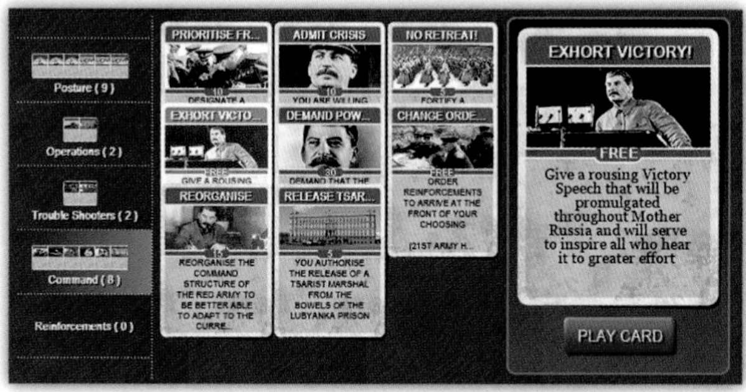

Consider replacing your worst (lowest Initiative) Front Marshal with a Tsarist Marshal released from prison. These are experienced, knowledgeable men who have been incarcerated as a result of Stalin's purge before the war.

Use Marshal Zhukov. Send him to an Army HQ to provide a massive activation bonus or ask him to visit a Front HQ to provide a smaller, but still significant, bonus to all Armies within the Front. See 6.2.2.4 Effect of Troubleshooters.

Marshal Zhukov has a number of Officer Cards which can greatly assist. Army Commanders can

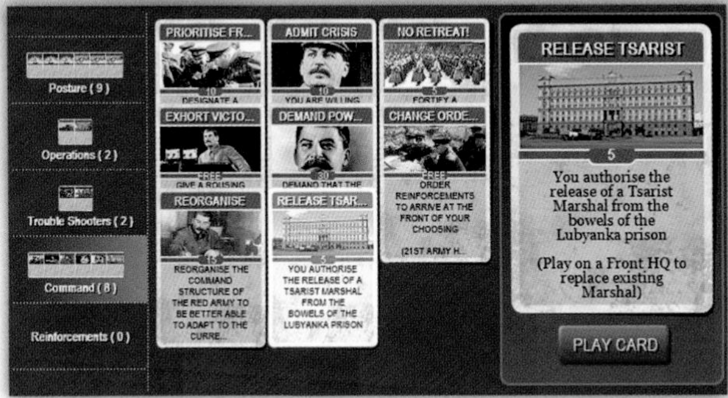

--- 27th Army HQ, MajGen M.E. Berzarin, TOADIE
Army Partially activated [?]
Marshal Georgy Zhukov's dynamic presence +60
Cdr Init 5, Adj Init 50% (roll 73) Init +2% [?]

Marshal Zhukov is a no-nonsense, get-it-done, character who has a major impact where ever he goes

be 'Granted Independence' and given a permanent activation bonus.

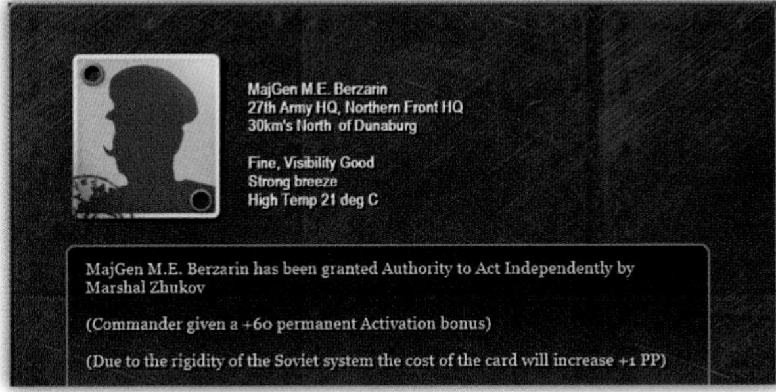

MajGen M.E. Berzarin
27th Army HQ, Northern Front HQ
30km's North of Dunaburg
Fine, Visibility Good
Strong breeze
High Temp 21 deg C
MajGen M.E. Berzarin has been granted Authority to Act Independently by Marshal Zhukov
(Commander given a +60 permanent Activation bonus)
(Due to the rigidity of the Soviet system the cost of the card will increase +1 PP)

Authority to act independently was a rare occurrence in the Red Army of '41. MajGen. Berzarin was so overcome by the honour bestowed upon him that he ducked when his official portrait was taken

They can also be 'Inspired' which will immediately raise the activation rating. Zhukov can 'Instil Backbone!' into a Front Marshal, raising their Initiative. A more drastic approach would be for him to personally 'Take Command' which will ensure all Armies within the Front activate the following turn. See 6.2.4 Troubleshooters.

INSPIRE
2
Have Zhukov give the Commander one of his 'Inspirational' talks. In a soundproof room.
(Commander Initiative significantly increased)

A quiet 'talk' can work wonders

At a last resort, in times of absolute crisis, you could use the 'Helper' button to ensure that all Armies fully activate. This comes at a cost. See 4.5.1 Helpers.

SUMMARY

- Armies make a roll each turn to determine their level of Activation.
- Without Full Activation the Army will incur Action Point penalties (AP).
- Full Activation (no penalty), Partial Activation (-30 AP), No Activation (-60 AP)
- Activation is checked each turn and is modified by a range of factors.
- Front Commanders Initiative ratings affect all Army activations under their command
- The three FRONT Activation reports detail the modifiers and the activation outcomes.
- Army Commander's Initiative will increase each time they activate
- Army Commander's Threat rating *may* increase whenever they activate

6.2.3. PARANOIA

Stalin was extremely paranoid ('an extreme and irrational fear or distrust of others') and imagined threats around every corner. The 'Paranoia Level' reflects the possibility of the Soviet Officer Corps launching a coup.

It's not an absolute threat but one that Stalin PERCEIVES exists against him. Coups didn't happen historically nor will they in the game but if the Paranoia level rises too high Stalin may well suffer a PARANOID EPISODE with adverse consequences.

Stalin was faced with a situation of total chaos, confusion and panic. He didn't have the luxury of issuing numerous orders and directives to address all his problems. He had to fight and scrabble his way through with what he had on hand. Every now and then, if he isn't careful, it will (in the game and also historically, in the very early days) all get too much for him.

DESIGNER NOTE

Stalin has absolute power but there needs (for both game play and historical reasons) to be a restriction on the exercise of this power. Even ruthless dictators have limits imposed upon them. The mechanism for doing this is the Paranoia system. For a detailed explanation of the thinking behind this see 9.3.7 Stalin.

6.2.3.1. Paranoia Mechanics

Stalin's mental state is tracked by his 'Paranoia Level'. The higher it rises, the more twitchy he becomes. His Paranoia level can never fall below zero and represents the percentage chance of a Paranoid Episode occurring each turn (with a Paranoid level of 5 there would be a 5% chance of an episode).

The Paranoia Summary Report gives a detailed description of what's happening with Stalin's mental state.

CONFIDENTIAL NKVD Paranoia Analysis 4 . July . 1941

--- Summary [?]
Paranoia Level 21 (change this turn +19 [?])
Risk of Paranoia 21% (roll 25) Unaffected, normal mental state maintained

--- Calculation [?]
Effect of Front Marshals (see below) -23
Effect of Army Commanders (see below) +4
Loss of Politically Important Cities +40 [?]
TOTAL Paranoia Level (all of the above) +21 [?]

--- Front Commands [?]
Marshal Voroshilov (Northern Front), APPARATCHIK, Threat -10
Marshal Timoshenko (Central Front), WAR BUDDY, Threat -1
Marshal Budenny (Southern Front), TOADIE, Threat -12

--- Northern Front
LtGen V.A Frolov (Baltic MD HQ), Threat -1
LtGen F.D Gorelenko (7th Ind Army HQ), Threat -1
MajGen P.S. Pshennikov (23rd Army HQ), Threat -1
LtGen V.I. Morozov (11th Army HQ), Threat -1
MajGen M.E. Berzarin (27th Army HQ), Threat -1
(Leningrad MD HQ), Threat +3

Stalin is on the edge. The pressure is building...

Breaking down the report into its component parts you can see that the Summary indicates his Paranoia level and the vitally important 'Paranoia roll'. The risk of a Paranoid episode is equal to the Paranoia level (21, below). An Episode will occur if the roll is less than, or equal, to the Risk (or Level, same thing).

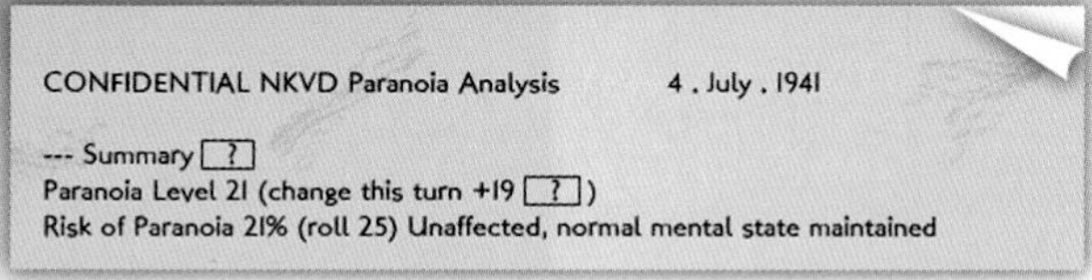

CONFIDENTIAL NKVD Paranoia Analysis 4 . July . 1941

--- Summary [?]
Paranoia Level 21 (change this turn +19 [?])
Risk of Paranoia 21% (roll 25) Unaffected, normal mental state maintained

Almost! With a Risk of 21% any roll of 21 or less and Stalin would have cooked off

The Calculation section provides a summary of how Stalin's Paranoid Level is calculated. The first two components, the effect of Front and Army Commanders, are always present. There are a lot of other possible factors that may be present but they are all situational, unlike the effect of the Commanders which are a constant.

The Paranoia Level is a straight Total of all the factors present in the 'Calculation' section. If it's not in there, it doesn't count.

--- Calculation [?]
Effect of Front Marshals (see below) -23
Effect of Army Commanders (see below) +4
Loss of Politically Important Cities +40 [?]
TOTAL Paranoia Level (all of the above) +21 [?]

Effect of Army Commanders

Each Army Commander has a Threat rating which contributes to Stalin's Paranoia level. You can see the cumulative total of all Army Commanders in the 'Calculation' section of the Paranoia Summary report.

Army Commanders, unlike Marshals, have a Threat rating that can evolve over time. Every time an Army Commander activates there is a chance that his Threat rating will increase. See 6.2.2.2 Threat Increase.

--- Northern Front
LtGen V.A Frolov (Baltic MD HQ), Threat -1
LtGen F.D Gorelenko (7th Ind Army HQ), Threat -1
MajGen P.S. Pshennikov (23rd Army HQ), Threat -1
LtGen V.I. Morozov (11th Army HQ), Threat -1
MajGen M.E. Berzarin (27th Army HQ), Threat -1
(Leningrad MD HQ), Threat +3

A section of the report showing all Army Commanders in the Northern Front. Their total contribution to Stalin's Paranoia level is -2 (-1 five times +3) and this would be added to the total from the other two Fronts to give the net effect of all Army Commanders of +4, as shown above

STAFF ADVICE

As a rule of thumb the more competent (higher Initiative rating) a Commander becomes, the higher his Threat rating will rise due to Stalin's inherent suspicion of any military commander with rising popularity.

A breakdown of Army Commanders, and their Threat ratings, is provided in Paranoia Summary, grouped by Front.

Effect of Front Marshals

Each Front Commander (they are always a Marshal) has a Threat rating which contributes to Stalin's Paranoia level. You can see the cumulative total of all Front Commanders in the 'Calculation' section of the Paranoia Summary report.

--- Calculation [?]
Effect of Front Marshals (see below) -23
Effect of Army Commanders (see below) +4
Loss of Politically Important Cities +40 [?]
TOTAL Paranoia Level (all of the above) +21 [?]

It's early in the campaign and the three Front Marshals are able to suppress the negligible level of threat emanating from the ranks of the Army Commanders

As senior leaders within the Red Army, Marshals have an important impact on Stalin's Paranoia level. Mostly they are supportive of Stalin but TSARISTS and NEW SCHOOL Marshals (the most competent) can possess dangerously independent views (they have a positive Threat rating which adversely affects Stalin).

DESIGNER NOTE

The Front Marshals are, at the start of the campaign, typically militarily incompetent (very low levels of Initiative). They are, as a rule, very supportive of Stalin and have negative Threat ratings which act to keep a lid on any discontent coming from below. This is why they have the job. Stalin's prime concern was to fill the upper echelons of the military with commanders who supported him. Military competence came a distant second.

The 'Front Commands' section of the Paranoia Summary report details the impact that each of the three Front Marshals are having. A negative Threat rating acts to reduce (good) Stalin's Paranoia level and a positive to raise it (bad).

--- Front Commands [?]
Marshal Voroshilov (Northern Front), APPARATCHIK, Threat -10
Marshal Timoshenko (Central Front), WAR BUDDY, Threat -1
Marshal Budenny (Southern Front), TOADIE, Threat -12

The sum of all three Marshal threat ratings is -23 which can be seen in the summary above

Effect of Strategic Cities

Strategic cities (ones with the Red dots) were politically important and have a significant impact on Stalin's Paranoia Level. With each successive loss of such a city the impact grows by +10 (it's capped). If Stalin suffers a Paranoid episode any residual effect from the loss of cities will disappear.

BREAKING NEWS!

Brest-Litowsk has fallen to the invading Huns!

Paranoia Increase +10

Brest-Litowsk has fallen. The effect of the next Strategic city to fall will be double this (10+10 gives 20)

In the early stages of the campaign when the German Panzers are running rampant the loss of a series of Strategic Cities can have a large impact.

If a captured Strategic city is retaken by the Soviets the Paranoia effect of losing Strategic cities is lowered by -20 (can't go below a minimum of 5) which will ensure that any future Strategic cities that are lost will have a lower impact. It's a big morale boost. The 'Recapture' bonus can only happen once per Strategic city (you can't keep recapturing and gaining the bonus).

Effect of Troubleshooters

Where Marshal Zhukov's role is to improve activations and combat performance, Commissar Khrushchev is the man who deals with 'threats'. A number of the actions he takes will decrease Stalin's Paranoia level such as ordering a Marshal to be shot, but in general the effect is small.

He has a range of useful Officer cards that can be used to lower or control commander threat ratings. See 6.2.3.5 Paranoia Advice.

Effect of Action Cards

There are a number actions that Stalin can take, via Action Cards found in the 'Command' category, which affect his Paranoia level but their impact is mostly incidental. There aren't any Action Cards that directly allow Stalin to manipulate his own Paranoia level.

Any affects are shown in the Paranoia Summary report.

A good example. Lunge for more power at a cost of increased paranoia

Tapering Effects

With the exception of the effect of Front and Army Commanders, any other effects on Stalin's Paranoia level will gradually taper over time. They don't appear one turn and are then gone the next (they can but only because they have dissipated the following turn). All non-Commander effects 'taper off' by 10 each turn until they reach zero and are no longer a consideration.

CONFIDENTIAL NKVD Paranoia Analysis 26 . June . 1941

--- Summary [?]
Paranoia Level 0 (change this turn 0 [?])
Risk of Paranoia 0% (no roll) Unaffected, normal mental state maintained

--- Calculation [?]
Effect of Front Marshals (see below) -33
Effect of Army Commanders (see below) -15
Loss of Politically Important Cities +20 [?]
TOTAL Paranoia Level (all of the above) 0 [?]

'Loss of Politically Important Cities +20'

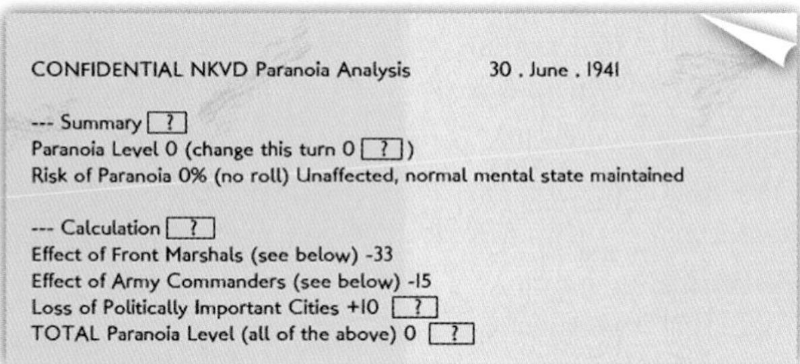

CONFIDENTIAL NKVD Paranoia Analysis 30 . June . 1941

--- Summary [?]
Paranoia Level 0 (change this turn 0 [?])
Risk of Paranoia 0% (no roll) Unaffected, normal mental state maintained

--- Calculation [?]
Effect of Front Marshals (see below) -33
Effect of Army Commanders (see below) -15
Loss of Politically Important Cities +10 [?]
TOTAL Paranoia Level (all of the above) 0 [?]

It's the following turn and the Cities effect has dropped to +10. Next turn it will drop another -10 be gone

In the above example if the Germans had captured another Strategic City between turns, because of the escalating effect (see 6.2.3.1 Effect of Strategic Cities) the 'Cities' effect would increase by +30. So it started at +20 in the first turn, tapered by -10 and went up again by +30 giving a net effect of +40.

It would then slowly taper by -10 per turn (eg. +40 to +30 to +20 etc.) until gone, provided a further Strategic City wasn't captured in the meantime.

6.2.3.2. Paranoid Episode

When Stalin fails his Paranoia roll (the random 1d100 roll is less than or equal to his Paranoia Level) he will suffer a Paranoid Episode which generates a number of adverse effects which will last for the current turn only.

The 'Command' tab (bottom centre) makes it clear that Stalin is not himself

Whenever Stalin suffers a Paranoid Episode his first reaction is to execute those Officers who pose a threat. He will shoot ONE Army Commander during his first Episode and an additional one for each subsequent episode (it's capped at a certain point to prevent a bloodbath).

The unlucky Commanders are chosen randomly but the selection process is heavily weighted towards those who have a higher Threat rating. Replacement Commanders are automatically assigned to the recently vacated posts. They are drawn from an historical pool and are assigned a random type (eg. TOADIE) with the probability of them being competent commanders increasing as the campaign progresses.

Comrade Stalin has suffered a Paranoid Episode!

Paranoia level 144, roll 94

--- Effects
•1 Army Commander will be executed [?]
•As a result of Stalin's confused state of mind the only Action Cards that can be played are Reinforcement ones
•There will be one turn of confusion in the affected Armies due to the sudden change of Commanders
•Overall Paranoia level has been reduced by -40 (next turn) as the pressure on Stalin has eased
•Comrade Stalin is in no mood for trivialities. Any saved Political Points are lost (5 PP's)
•All Army Commanders have had their Threat level reduced by -5 [?]

---Outgoing Commanders
•LtGen F.D Gorelenko, TSARIST, 7th Ind Army HQ, has been arrested and is to be shot by Firing Squad (Init +44, Threat 0)

---Incoming Commanders
•MajGen A. Sharshin, TSARIST, has assumed command of the 7th Ind Army HQ (Init +40, Threat +2)

Lots of things happen in the event of an episode

The only Action Cards available during an episode are those for Reinforcements

Paranoia effects, other than executed Commanders, include an inability to play Action Cards.

Any accumulated Political Points (PP) are lost. As compensation any PP's lost will serve to reduce the Threat rating of all Army Commanders by the same amount. As an example if Stalin had an episode and there were 5 PP in the pool then they would be lost but every Army Commander would have their Threat rating reduced by -5. No Army Commander can have their Threat rating reduced below zero as a result of this.

STAFF ADVICE

A number of Action Cards require you to accumulate enough PP before you can use them. Keep an eye on Stalin's Paranoia level and if it's getting too high consider using your PP rather than risk losing them to an episode. An alternative strategy is, when confronted by large number of Army Commanders with high Threat ratings is to deliberately build up PP's in order to 'reset' the Commander's Threat ratings back to a more manageable level.

When an episode occurs Stalin is considered to have 'blown off steam' and undergone an easing of his self induced paranoia. To reflect this 'drop in pressure' his Paranoia level will be reduced by a factor which will increase with every episode (the more episodes he has the greater the counterbalancing 'relief' that he experiences). Like other effects (excluding Commanders) this will taper off over time.

CONFIDENTIAL NKVD Paranoia Analysis 8 . July . 1941

--- Summary [?]
Paranoia Level 94 (change this turn -50 [?])
Risk of Paranoia 94% (roll 95) Unaffected, normal mental state maintained

--- Calculation [?]
Effect of Front Marshals (see below) -29
Effect of Army Commanders (see below) -17
Comrade Stalin has admitted that there is a Crisis +180
An Episode gives temporary relief to Stalin -40
TOTAL Paranoia Level (all of the above) +94 [?]

Stalin has been deliberately given the red pill (see 'Admit there is a Crisis' - it's been artificially induced) and suffered an episode. The 'temporary relief of -40' acts as a counterbalancing force to lower his paranoia

6.2.3.3. Effect of Destroyed German Units

Whenever the Soviets manage to destroy German units there is a general reduction of all Army Commander Threat ratings in proportion to the number of units destroyed. German HQ's have a bigger effect than Divisions. Morale is boosted and Stalin's sense of Paranoia eases.

No Army Commander can have their Threat rating reduced below zero as a result of this. The Soviet Player additionally gains a Political Point (PP) bonus which scales with the number of units destroyed. Notification of reductions and bonuses are shown in the Daily Front Logs.

STAFF ADVICE

The benefits of completely destroying a German unit are significant and it can be worth sacrificing units to do so. Watch out for over extended units that have advanced beyond their logistical support. Keep an eye on any German Army and Panzergruppe HQ's that you know of. The further they are positioned away from the transport grid, especially in mud conditions, the more vulnerable their Divisions will be.

Look for overly enthusiastic Divisions that have advanced beyond Command Range (5 hexes) of their HQ. Aim to fully encircle them and make a concentric attack. Consider ordering Marshal Zhukov (troubleshooter) directly to a nearby Army HQ and have him instigate an 'All out Effort'. This will ensure the Army fully activates and has combat bonuses.

6.2.3.4. Paranoia Reports

The Paranoia Summary report provides the most detailed information on Paranoia. The Aide de Camp report will highlight the main points only - the level and whether there was an episode.

--- Key Data
•Paranoia Level 21 (change this turn +19) [?]
•Central Front has Priority (Initiative +25) [?]

Aide de Camp

The 'Command' tab (bottom centre) shows Stalin's Paranoia level at a glance.

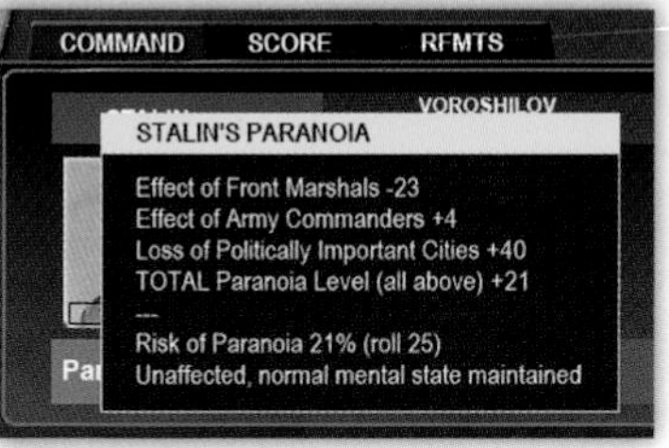

The dynamic tool tip attached to Stalin (Command tab) provides a useful summary of Paranoia status.

6.2.3.5. Paranoia Advice

At the start of the campaign you typically have two or three sycophant Front Marshals who, while militarily incompetent, serve to stamp down on any Threat emanating from the collection of Regular Army Commanders. As the Army Commanders are usually the same (militarily useless) their combined Threat rating is minimal.

As they start to gain combat experience (the more they activate the more their Initiative and Threat ratings will climb), they will become a bigger problem especially when combined with the snowballing paranoia effects from the loss of strategic cities.

With the arrival of the large number of Conscript Armies the dynamics will change as the number of Army Commanders swell. Left unchecked the threat from Army Commanders can rise rapidly. By this time you have probably replaced a Marshal, or two, with more competent versions and have lost the beneficial effects of their negative Threat ratings.

By taking a 'hands off' approach you can find yourself paralysed by multiple Paranoid episodes.

What to do about it?

Use Commissar Khrushchev. It's tempting to ignore him and leave him sitting idle in STAVKA. Put him to work as soon as possible. Stalin's sense of paranoia can't be negated but it can be managed to ensure an optimal outcome.

As soon as possible you should move Commissar Khrushchev to a Front HQ and have him 'Intimidate'.

Commissar Khrushchev's job is to deal with threatening Commanders

While not a WW2 era picture it's an apt example of Khrushchev in full intimidatory mode

This will prevent all Army Commanders, within the Front, from increasing their Threat ratings.

The randomisation of Front Marshals can entail starting the game with a NEW SCHOOL or a TSARIST Marshal on hand (see 6.2.1.1 Commander Types). This presents a different challenge. On one hand you've got an excellent Marshal who will fire up his subordinate Army Commanders and help ensure they activate but on the other hand they usually present with a positive Threat rating.

Have Commissar Khrushchev pay them a visit and 'Lay Blame'

The nature of how the Threat ratings of Army Commanders increase (see 6.2.2.2 Threat Increase) will ensure that there will be a handful, as time goes on, who stand out with much higher Threat ratings than others. This is the time to have the Commissar drop by.

If you'd prefer to handle the situation with more tact there are several alternatives the Commissar Khrushchev will pursue, if ordered.

It's always a good policy to blame others for your own failings. Stalin was a master of this

Individual Commanders aren't important. The security and safety of the Motherland is

Everybody has a secret. The Commissar knows what to do with them

The bearded gentleman wasn't present at Barbarossa but, given the opportunity, I'm sure he would have been, organising a full scale partisan uprising

Options not mentioned, but equally valid, are to order Commissar Khrushchev to remove troublesome Front and Army Commanders by more forceful means.

6.2.3.6. Summary

SUMMARY

- Stalin's mental state is represented by his Paranoia level
- This can never fall below zero
- Stalin's Paranoia level is affected by his Army and Front Commander's cumulative Threat ratings

- Commissar Khrushchev (Troubleshooter) is best placed to lower Commander threat ratings
- Loss of Strategic Cities (red dot) can increase his Paranoia level
- Stalin's own actions (taken via Action Cards) can increase the Paranoia level
- Army and Front Commanders have Threat ratings which directly contribute to Stalin's Paranoia level
- Effects, other than from Commanders, will gradually dissipate over time.
- The Risk of a Paranoid Episode, each turn, is equal to his Paranoia level
- If the Paranoia Roll (random 1d100 roll) is <= Paranoia Risk, an episode occurs
- All non-Commander Paranoia effects taper by -10 per turn until gone.
- Destroying German units lowers the Threat rating of all Army Commanders and grants PP bonuses
- Recaptured Strategic cities grant a one time bonus which lowers the Paranoia effect of losing a city
- A Paranoid Episode lasts one turn and prevents the playing of Action Cards (except Reinforcements)
- A Paranoid Episode will reset any effect from the loss of Strategic cities to zero.
- Any accumulated PP are lost during an Episode but Army Commander Threat ratings are reduced by the same amount.
- Stalin will order a number of Army Commanders executed whenever he has an Episode.

6.2.4. TROUBLESHOOTERS

Marshal Zhukov and Commissar Khrushchev are special envoys of Stalin who can be ordered to any Soviet HQ on the map. They have unique Officer cards that can be used when present at an HQ (other than STAVKA). Each has two sets of cards, one for when they are present at a Front HQ and the other for when they are present at an Army HQ.

Whenever a troubleshooter is present at an HQ there will be a set of Officer cards available which can be found in the Unit Display (bottom right)

Troubleshooters are trusted by Stalin and have no effect on his paranoia. They aren't represented on the map as counters but their location is shown in reports and tabs as well as be indicated by status icons displayed next to the name of the HQ they are currently at.

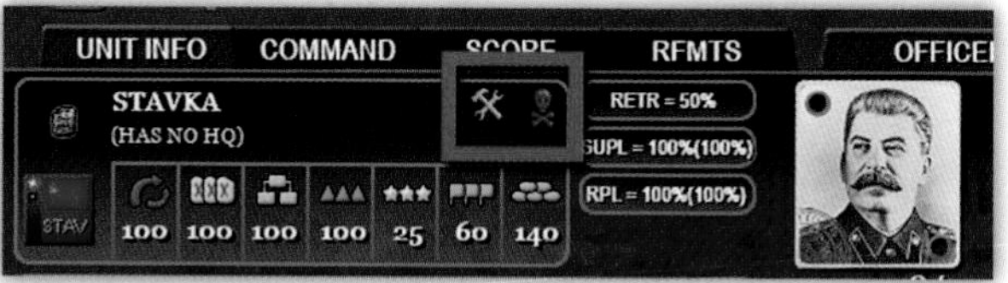

Both at STAVKA

Both troubleshooters commence the campaign at STAVKA and can be freely ordered elsewhere by the appropriate Action Card.

Troubleshooters are free to move (no PP)

6.2.4.1. Travel

Troubleshooters can move to any valid HQ, Front or Army. Once travel orders have been issued (by playing the troubleshooter Action Card) you will receive a confirmation message.

Travel always takes 4 days (1 turn) and the troubleshooter should arrive the following turn. There is a chance of delay (it's wartime) which is dependant on the distance involved. The greater the distance, the higher the chance of a delay.

Each delay results in a lost turn. The troubleshooter is still in transit but has yet to arrive. Their Action Card (allowing different travel orders

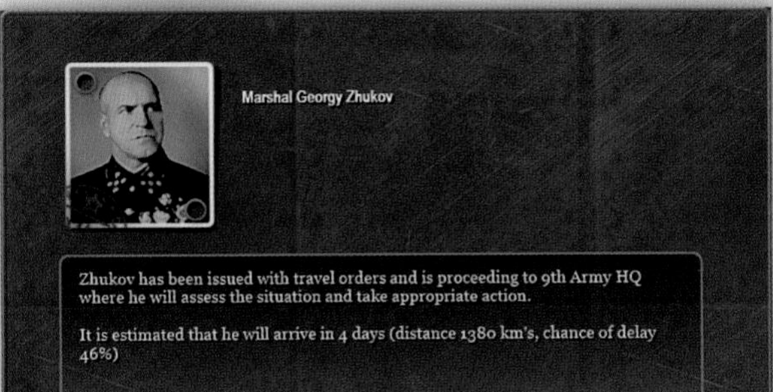

Marshal Zhukov has been asked to travel from STAVKA to the Black sea coast, a considerable distance with a high chance of him being delayed

to be issued) will only become available when they are at an HQ. It isn't possible to divert them enroute.

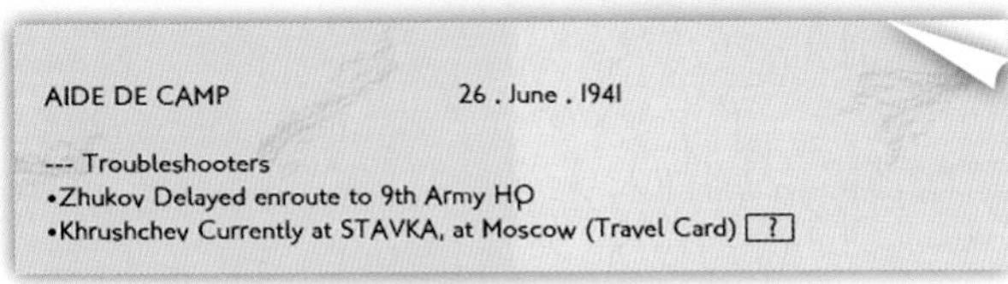

AIDE DE CAMP 26 . June . 1941
--- Troubleshooters
•Zhukov Delayed enroute to 9th Army HQ
•Khrushchev Currently at STAVKA, at Moscow (Travel Card) [?]

Aide de Camp report - Zhukov delayed

There can be multiple delays, one after the other. Unlikely, but possible. After each delay the chance of another is halved giving a decreasing probability of delay.

--- Marshal Zhukov
•Delayed enroute to 9th Army HQ (chance 46%, roll 31) [?]

--- Commissar Khrushchev
•Currently at STAVKA, at Moscow (Loc 52:25) Travel Card [?]

Daily Staff Log - Marshal Zhukov has been delayed. The chance of a second delay would be 23% (half of 46%)

STAFF ADVICE

The rule of thumb is the further you order your troubleshooter to travel, the greater the chance they will be delayed. If you require your troubleshooters to take an active role put some thought into route planning to minimise downtime from delays.

If the troubleshooter's destination HQ is overrun while they are in transit, they will be automatically diverted back to STAVKA.

If the HQ that the troubleshooter is currently at is overrun they will be, at Stalin's orders, flown out at the last minute and returned to STAVKA. The unfortunate HQ Commander will be left to the Germans.

It isn't possible for a troubleshooter to be lost.

6.2.4.2. Marshal Zhukov Cards

Zhukov has, like all both troubleshooters, two sets of cards. One for when his is at a Front HQ and the other for when he is at an Army HQ. There are no cards available if he is at STAVKA.

Marshal Zhukov's cards are focused on getting things done. Activations and combat bonuses.

MARSHAL ZHUKOV FRONT CARDS

Card	Effect	Base Cost (PP)
Instil Backbone!	Force the Marshal to grow a backbone and start acting like the decisivie leader that he should be. Permanent +10 to Marshal's Initiative	5
Take Command	Push the Marshal aside and have Zhukov take command. He'll soon straighten out the mess. Activation bonus to the entire Front.	5

MARSHAL ZHUKOV ARMY CARDS

Card	Effect	Base Cost (PP)
Grant Independence	Zhukov will authorise the Commander a greater measure of Independence. Permanent Activation bonus to Army	2
Inspire	Have Zhukov give the Commander one of his 'Inspirational' talks. In a soundproof room. Commander's Initiative increased	2
All out Effort	Order Zhukov to step in and coordinate a proper military response. Combat bonus to all Divisions in the Army for the DURATION of Zhukov's visit	2
Blow Bridge!	Ask Zhukov to ensure the job is done properly. Blows up ALL valid bridges in selected hex. A Division of the Army must be present in the hex	Free

6.2.4.3. Commissar Khrushchev Cards

Khrushcheve has, like all both troubleshooters, two sets of cards. One for when his is at a Front HQ and the other for when he is at an Army HQ. There are no cards available if he is at STAVKA.

Commissar Khrushchev's cards are focused on protecting Stalin from any perceived threat emanating from his Officer Corps.

COMMISSAR KHRUSHCHEV FRONT CARDS		
Card	Effect	Base Cost (PP)
Firing Squad!	There are times when it pays to make an example. Order the Marshal dragged outside and shot! New Marshal and a large Paranoia reduction	5
Lay Blame	It's not going well. You need a scape-goat. Make it clear who is at fault. Lowers Marshal's Threat rating	5
Dismiss Marshal	Incompetence has no place in the Red Army. Clear out the dead wood to make way for the new. New Marshal	5
Intimidate	Exert an overbearing presence on the Front HQ and all subordinate Army HQ's Prevents Army Commanders from increasing their Threat ratings while ever the Commissar is present	5

COMMISSAR KHRUSHCHEV ARMY CARDS		
Card	Effect	Base Cost (PP)
Loaded Pistol	It is the obligation of the Commissar to reacquaint wayward Commanders with their Duty to the Soviet Union. New Commander and a moderate Paranoia decrease	2
Fire!	There is no place in the Red Army for Commanders with an inflated sense of their own worth. (New Commander)	2
Investigate	Dig around and who knows what dark and dirty secrets will be revealed? Commander's Threat rating reduced to zero	2
Confidante	Let the Commander know that Comrade Stalin looks favourably upon his performance. Commander's Threat rating will NEVER increase	2

6.2.4.4. Activation Effects

Marshal Zhukov will provide a significant activation bonus to any HQ that he is present at (no effect if at STAVKA). His presence at an Army HQ is enough to stiffen resolve and provide a +60 modifier to the Army Commander's activation chances. At Front HQ he still exerts a strong presence and will provide a +20 modifier to all subordinate Army Commander activation chances within the Front.

Marshal Zhukov can be dispatched to where ever he is needed most. The mere presence of Zhukov is enough to spur Armies and Commanders into action

Commissar Khrushchev provides no bonus and can, instead, generate an activation penalty. His reputation precedes him and Commanders are unwilling to demonstrate initiative in his presence for fear of retribution. The penalty increases depending on his actions (if he starts ordering people shot, for example, it will rise) but remains minor.

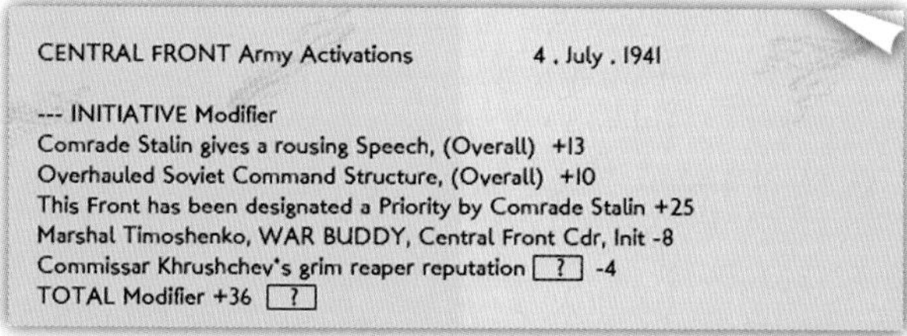
CENTRAL FRONT Army Activations 4 . July . 1941

--- INITIATIVE Modifier
Comrade Stalin gives a rousing Speech, (Overall) +13
Overhauled Soviet Command Structure, (Overall) +10
This Front has been designated a Priority by Comrade Stalin +25
Marshal Timoshenko, WAR BUDDY, Central Front Cdr, Init -8
Commissar Khrushchev's grim reaper reputation [?] -4
TOTAL Modifier +36 [?]

Word gets around. Nobody appreciates a visit from Commissar Khrushchev. Sometimes, however, it's necessary

6.2.4.5. Troubleshooter Reports

Information on troubleshooters can be found in a number of places. The most accessible source is the Command tab (bottom centre).

The Command tab provides 'at a glance' status on both troubleshooters

Dynamic tool tips provide detailed information

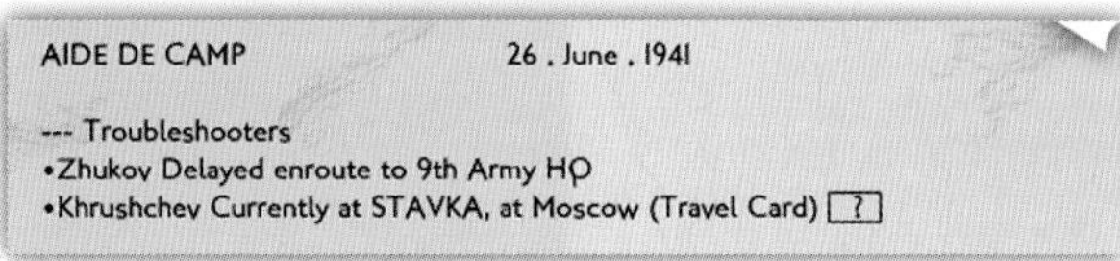

Daily Staff Log - up to date information on both troubleshooters

Aide de Camp - summary and a reminder that Khrushchev is waiting, bags packed

Several reports, the Daily Staff Log and the Aide de Camp, mention troubleshooters.

Both present at the Central Front HQ. Note the number of cards available

Don't forget that any HQ with a troubleshooter will show status icons, next to their name, highlighting this.

6.2.4.6. Summary

SUMMARY

- Troubleshooters don't affect Stalin's paranoia (he trusts them implicitly).
- Troubleshooters aren't directly represented on the map.
- Troubleshooters can't be lost. They will be automatically diverted to STAVKA if there is a problem.
- Troubleshooters can be ordered to any HQ via an Action Card ('Troubleshooters' category)
- Troubleshooters take one turn to travel to any friendly HQ (Army or Front).
- Troubleshooters can be delayed enroute. Chance of delay is proportional to distance travelled.
- Troubleshooters, when present at an HQ (not STAVKA) have access to Officer cards (bottom right)
- Troubleshooters each have two sets of Officer cards - one for Front HQ's and one for Army HQ's
- Marshal Zhukov's cards are focused on getting things done - Activations and Combat bonuses
- Marshal Zhukov's presence at an Army HQ will increase Activation chances significantly.
- Marshal Zhukov's presence at a Front HQ will increase Activation chances for all subordinate Army Commanders.
- Commissar Khrushchev's cards are focused on neutralising any perceived threat to Stalin
- Commissar Khrushchev has a minor negative effect on Activation chances where ever he is.
- The Command tab (bottom centre) provides an 'at-a-glance' status of both troubleshooters.
- The dynamic tool tips on the Command tab give more detail on troubleshooter activity.
- The Daily Staff Log provides a similar level of information and the Aide de Camp a summary.
- Status icons (next to unit name) indicate presence of troubleshooters at an HQ.

6.2.5. SOVIET CARDS

The Soviet Player exerts command through a range of Action Cards. These can be found in the Action tab (top right of centre) and are separated into different categories.

There are also special 'Officer' cards that the two troubleshooters have access to when they are present at a Front, or Army, HQ (but not when they are at STAVKA).

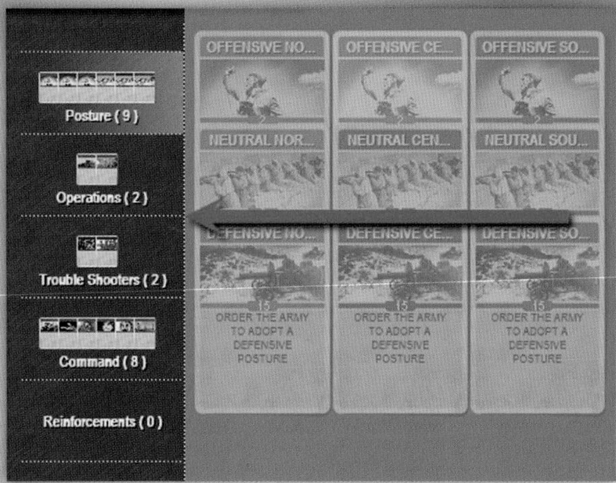

The five different categories of Soviet Action Cards. The numbers in brackets indicate how many cards are present in each category

Commissar Khrushchev has arrived at the Leningrad Military District Army HQ and a range of Officer cards (above the red line) are now available for him to use. LtGen. Besapalov is a worried man.

6.2.5.1. Rigidity of the Soviet System

A lot of the cards available to the Soviet Player will increase in cost every time they are used. This reflects the rigidity and inflexibility of the heavily centralised Soviet command structure. While it's possible for Stalin to issue many orders, having them implemented rather than being buried in the bureaucracy is another matter.

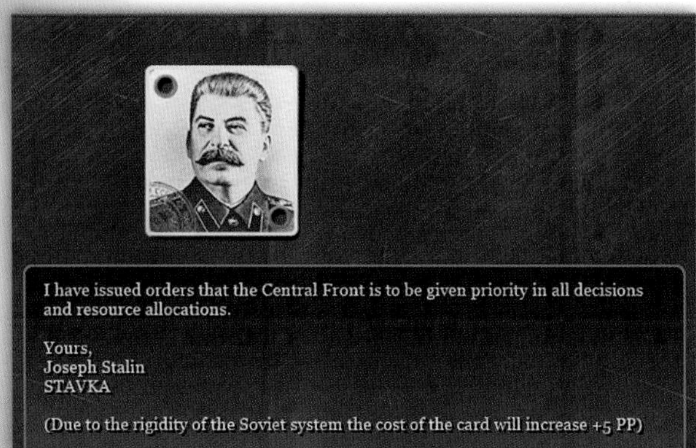

I have issued orders that the Central Front is to be given priority in all decisions and resource allocations.
Yours,
Joseph Stalin
STAVKA
(Due to the rigidity of the Soviet system the cost of the card will increase +5 PP)

Normal Action Cards will increase in cost at a faster rate than the troubleshooter Officer cards as their actions are more direct

6.2.5.2. Posture Cards

Posture cards are played on an Army HQ and allow the entire Army to be reconfigured to a different posture setting (see 4.4 Postures).

Unlike a lot of other Soviet action cards, Posture cards do NOT increase in cost every time they are used. The cost of the Defensive posture cards can DECREASE as a result of the Soviet Player utilising the 'Admit Crisis' card.

SOVIET POSTURES	
Posture	Effect
Offensive	+40% Offensive bonus -20% Defensive bonus
Neutral	0% Offensive bonus 0% Defensive bonus
Defensive	-20% Offensive bonus +40% Defensive bonus
Changing posture	-20% Offensive bonus -20% Defensive bonus -40 AP

To change an Armies posture choose the correct posture and Front card and select the HQ you want.

ASK YOUR STAFF

Why is the cost of the Defensive Posture Cards so high? Stalin, like Hitler, had an aversion to a defensive doctrine. He had delusions of rapidly overcoming a German invasion of Russia and sweeping through Eastern Europe in a grand enveloping manoeuvre that would end in the capture of Berlin. A Red Army on a defensive posture played no part in his vision. Until Stalin confronts reality ('Admit Crisis' action card) the cost will remain high.

STAFF ADVICE

Don't forget that whenever you change an Armies posture there is one turn of 'reorganisation' involved where the Army is in a vulnerable state (see the table above). If you order an Army to change posture when it is engaged with the enemy it will quickly find itself overrun.

6.2.5.3. Operations Cards

There are a number of cards that can appear in the 'Operations' category. Some appear only when certain conditions have been met and others after a certain point in time.

Central Front, Neutral posture. The pop-up will automatically highlight valid Army HQ's for you (yellow outline) and, once you click on one, will highlight all of the Armies subordinate Divisions to enable you to see who will be affected

OPERATION CARDS

Card	Effect	Base Cost (PP)
Fortifications	Order Fortification built to protect Mother Russia! (Can be built on any Plains, Fields, Woods or Forest hexes in Summer only)	Free
Garrison	Raise a Conscript Garrison in any Minor City (grey dot) currently without a Garrison and which hasn't previously raised a Garrison. (An immobile, entrenched, unit that is supplied from the City)	Free
Partisan	Have a Cut-Off Division dissolved with the intention of forming irregular Partisan bands to harass the enemy. (adds to the German Partisan level)	Free
Breakout!	Resupply a Cut-Off Army from local magazines and order it to conduct a Breakout! (Play on the Army HQ which must also be Cut-Off and located in a city)	Free
Massed Artillery	Katyusha Rockets and other Artillery are concentrated behind a single Division. (Offensive bonus for one turn, must be a Division located in a Front designated as a Priority.	2
Massed Armour	Additional Tank Brigades are assigned to achieve a critical mass for the attack. (Offensive bonus for one turn. Division must already have some Armour and be located in a Front designated as a Priority.	2
Air Defence	Assign Fighters and Flak to defend a major City. (reduces the benefit of German Tactical Air Support for any enemy Division within 3 hexes of the City. Will provide combat penalties if insufficient TAC available)	10

Fortifications

These can be freely built, one per turn. Only in Plains, Fields, Woods or Forest hexes and only during fine weather (the Soviets did construct them in mud and snow conditions but they weren't very effective). They provide an entrenchment bonus to any unit in the same hex.

Once captured by the Germans the Soviet Player has the following turn to recapture them otherwise they are considered destroyed (or more likely 'rendered

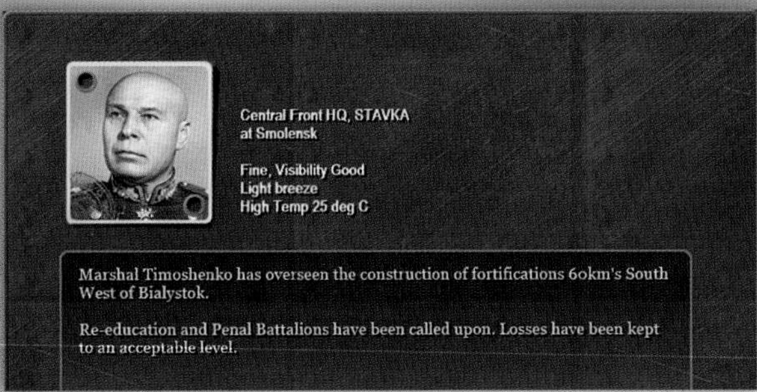

Central Front HQ, STAVKA
at Smolensk
Fine, Visibility Good
Light breeze
High Temp 25 deg C
Marshal Timoshenko has overseen the construction of fortifications 60km's South West of Bialystok.
Re-education and Penal Battalions have been called upon. Losses have been kept to an acceptable level.

Fortifications have been constructed on the border!

ineffective') and are removed from the map.

A fortification can be damaged by German Engineers to the point where it is also destroyed. Fortifications can not be rebuilt on a hex that has previously had a fortification on it.

Daily Summary CENTRE FRONT 26 . June . 1941

--- Operations
•Fortifications have been constructed 60km's South West of Bialystok
•Fortifications (22:41) damaged by the enemy (-960 Structural pts) [?]

Daily Front Log. Notification of all fortification related activity is found here

A fortification has 2000 'structural points'. Once this goes below zero it is considered destroyed. Fortifications have the ability to 'regenerate' a certain number of 'structural points' per turn (+200) automatically (repairs and rebuilding work undertaken by the local garrison). A captured Fortification will immediately drop to zero structural points and will slowly recover, provided it is immediately recovered.

The terrain window (top centre) shows a Fortification in a hex. The green bar at the top is a visual representation of the structural points. A full bar is 2000 points, empty zero.

Fortifications can be damaged by combat and also by adjacent German units who are receiving Direct Fire Artillery support (it's assumed that their engineers are at work under cover of the artillery). Fortifications will continue to provide their entrenchment bonus provided there are some structural points remaining.

PLAINS + FORTIFICATIONS (23,41)

LANDSCAPE: PLAINS

TROOPTYPE	ATT-MOD	DEF-MOD	A-ENTR	MX-ENTR	CROSS-RIV
INFANTRY	100%	100%	200	200	-
GUNS	100%	100%	200	200	-
MOTORIZED	100%	100%	50	50	-
LIGHT TANKS	100%	100%	50	50	-
MEDIUM TANKS	100%	100%	50	50	-
HEAVY TANKS	100%	100%	50	50	-

MOVETYPE	AP COST	ROAD	RIVER
FOOT	25	-	-
MOTORIZED	15	-	-
CAVALRY	20	-	-
RAIL	NA	-	-
TRACKED	15	-	-
SUPPLY MOVE	10	-	-
IMMOBILE	NA	-	-
RAIL_CAP	NA	-	-

COVER: 0
STRUCTURAL POINTS: 2000 OF 2000, AUTO RECOVER POINTS: 200

ZOC PENALTY IN AP = 10

The mouse over tool tip for the terrain window (top centre) shows, at the bottom, how many structural points the fortification has as well as a reminder of it's ability to regenerate

Once built, fortifications are visible to the Germans on the map. It's difficult to hide construction activity on such a large scale from aerial reconnaissance.

DESIGNER NOTE

Rather than provide a fixed set of historical fortifications on the map the positioning of them has been handed over to the Soviet Player and forms an interesting mini-game. With the ability to place one fortification per turn a range of strategies can be employed. Once the weather turns fortifications can no longer be built. There is a finite number available. Does the Player aim for a strategy of forward defence in order to channel the Germans in a particular direction, a traditional 'Stalin Line' to hold back the tide or would he be better to focus on building a ring of fortifications around his objective cities?

See also 6.1.13 Fortifications.

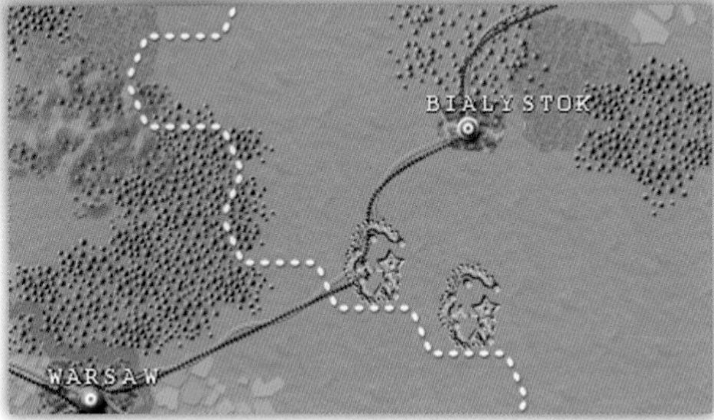

Would the Germans sit still while fortification were constructed under their noses? Unlikely.

The Polish border showing dispositions. Germans asleep. If you press '0' it will remove the units and allow you to see the fortification underneath (picture above). Press '2' to return the units

ASK YOUR STAFF

Why don't the fortifications stop the Germans? Historically they didn't except in areas where the terrain significantly added to the difficulty such as the ring of defences around Leningrad in heavily wooded, swampy ground. The German Pioniers (engineers), in coordination with their artillery, were adept at breaching anything that the Soviets put in their path. Fortifications are speed bumps, not barriers.

STAFF ADVICE

Build fortifications in difficult terrain. The perfect place would be in forested terrain directly behind a river. Any Divisions here would benefit from the 'Adverse Terrain bonus' (see 5.2.12 Terrain Effect), the penalty that attacking units suffer when having to assault across a river and the fortification entrenchment bonus.

SUMMARY

- Fortifications can be freely built once per turn while-ever the Weather is fine.
- Fortifications can only be built on Plains, Fields, Woods or Forest hexes.
- You can only build Fortifications in a hex once (can't rebuild).
- Fortifications provide an entrenchment bonus (a great help to defence) for any unit in the hex.
- Fortifications have 2000 structural points (see the green bar in the terrain window, top centre)
- When damaged by combat, or German engineers, this reduces.
- If the structural points go below zero the fortification is destroyed (removed from map)
- Fortifications will regenerate +200 structural points per turn automatically.
- If captured you will have to recapture immediately (following turn) or the fortification is destroyed.
- When you build fortifications the enemy can see this on the map (aerial reconnaissance).
- The terrain window mouse over tool tip provides information the structural points status
- Fortifications will continue to provide a benefit provided they have some structural points remaining.
- The Daily Front Logs provide details of Fortification related activity.

Garrisons

Conscript garrison can be raised to defend minor cities (grey dot). Strategic cities (red dot) are able to raise much larger, better equipped, regular garrisons by the use of the 'No Retreat' card. Both types of garrison work the same.

Conscript garrisons are immobile, set to a Defensive posture (+40% defensive combat bonus), fully entrenched and have their 'Retreat percentage' set to 100% (will fight to the last man). They will draw supplies from the city (local magazines and stockpiles) and will remain in full supply even if cut-off.

If they are forced off their city hex, as a result of combat, they will automatically disband.

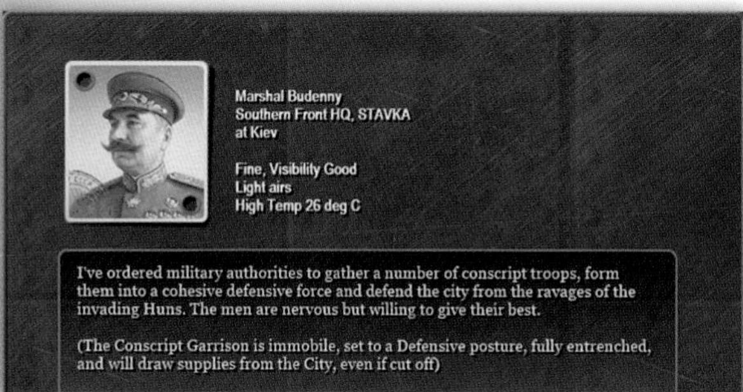

Marshal Budenny
Southern Front HQ, STAVKA
at Kiev
Fine, Visibility Good
Light airs
High Temp 26 deg C
I've ordered military authorities to gather a number of conscript troops, form them into a cohesive defensive force and defend the city from the ravages of the invading Huns. The men are nervous but willing to give their best.
(The Conscript Garrison is immobile, set to a Defensive posture, fully entrenched, and will draw supplies from the City, even if cut off)

Conscript garrisons are free to raise (no PP cost to play the Action card) and can be placed in any minor city (grey dot) provided it hasn't previously raised a garrison (only one per city) and it can trace an interrupted supply path back to STAVKA (you can't raise a garrison in a city that is cut off).

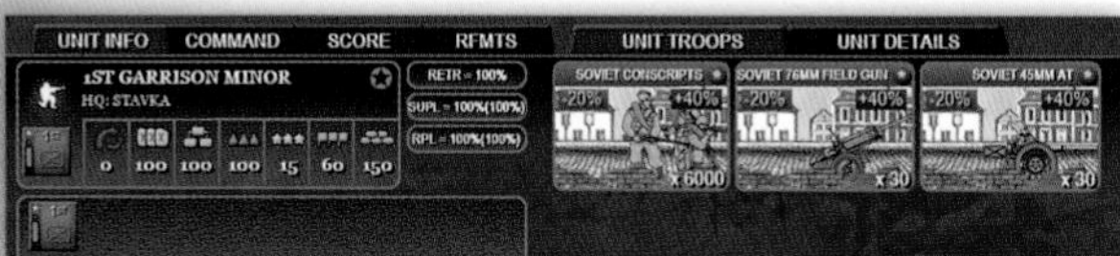

Conscript garrisons are under strength, poorly equipped, Divisions. Note the 'RETR=100%' (top centre) which represents Stalin's orders to 'Fight and die where you stand'

Partisans

Any Division that has been cut-off can be voluntarily disbanded and order to blend into the country side and continue the fight as Partisans.

PARTISANS
FREE
Have a Cut-Off Division dissolved with the intention of forming irregular Partisan bands to harass the enemy
(adds to German Partisan level)

The card is free to play (no PP cost) and will automatically appear in the 'Operations' category whenever there is at least one cut-off Division. You'll be notified in your Aide

--- Other
•PARTISAN Card can be played ("Operations")
•BREAKOUT Card can be played ("Operations")

Aide de Camp Report under 'Other', down the bottom

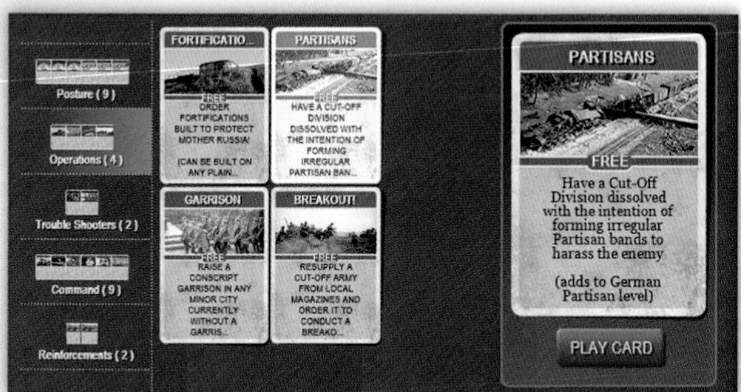

Normally the Partisan (and its related twin, Breakout!) aren't present. Keep an eye on your Aide de Camp report as they can provide useful options when they are available

de Camp report of its presence. Once a Division has been selected (you can choose any type of Division but not an HQ as they are expected to remain and continue the fight) the unit will be removed from the map and the partisan level in the relevant theatre/ front will increase by +2%.

STAFF ADVICE

While this doesn't sound like a lot it can add up. Partisans (see 6.1.9 Partisans) can hinder trains, destroy truck columns and attack rail construction Battalions. A cut-off Soviet Division is, under normal circumstances, unlikely to break out and can serve a useful role as partisans. If the Germans are making little effort to reduce the pocket it may be wise to delay dissolving any Divisions as their mere presence can cause problems.

The 86th Rifle Division will don civilian clothes and fight on

Selecting a suitable Division. Note that the 10th Army HQ can't be selected. Not only would it be inappropriate thematically it would also be an exploit enabling the Soviet Player to deliberately dissolve his surrounded HQ's in order to prevent the Germans from gaining a Political Point bonus from their capture

These are to have an Army HQ that is both isolated and situated in a city hex. Notification of the card's presence is found in the Aide de Camp report.

Playing the card on the HQ provides a supply boost to every unit within Command Range. Note that the supply will arrive immediately but it won't be until the following turn that the units will be 'perked up' in the same way you don't immediately turn into superman after eating high energy food.

The card can only be played on an HQ once and gaining extra supply doesn't mean that the Army will gain Full Activation the following turn (maximum movement). An incompetent commander, even given extra supplies, may well decide to do nothing and wait to see what develops (see 6.2.2 Activation).

Breakout!

There were times, historically, when encircled Soviet pockets came to life and vigorously attempted to break out and escape.

BREAKOUT!

FREE

Resupply a Cut-Off Army from local magazines and order it to conduct a Breakout!

(Play on HQ, must be Cut-Off and in a City)

Cut-off units will, relatively quickly, lose their military effectiveness from a lack of supplies. Without sufficient supplies units suffer from many penalties, including Action Points, and are eventually rendered immobile and barely able to defend themselves.

The Breakout! Card allows a trapped army to reinvigorate itself with supplies (assumed to be found in local magazines within a nearby city) and attempt to escape, or at least give the invaders an unexpected bloody nose.

Like the 'Partisans' card the Breakout! Card only appears when there are valid conditions for its use.

--- Other
•PARTISAN Card can be played ("Operations")
•BREAKOUT Card can be played ("Operations")

It's not always the case that both cards will appear together as there won't always be an HQ unit that's cut-off and in a city

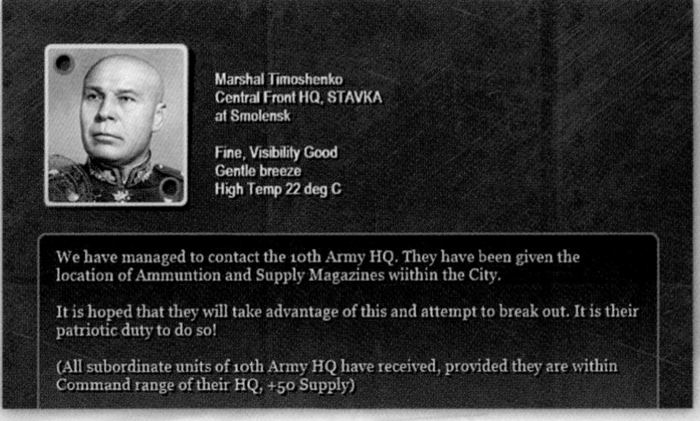

Marshal Timoshenko
Central Front HQ, STAVKA
at Smolensk
Fine, Visibility Good
Gentle breeze
High Temp 22 deg C
We have managed to contact the 10th Army HQ. They have been given the location of Ammuntion and Supply Magazines wiithin the City.
It is hoped that they will take advantage of this and attempt to break out. It is their patriotic duty to do so!
(All subordinate units of 10th Army HQ have received, provided they are within Command range of their HQ, +50 Supply)

The pressure is on the 10th Army to act decisively

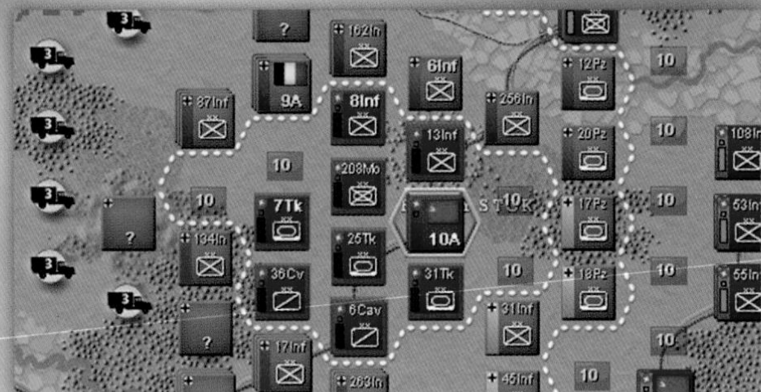

10th Army situation. There's hope

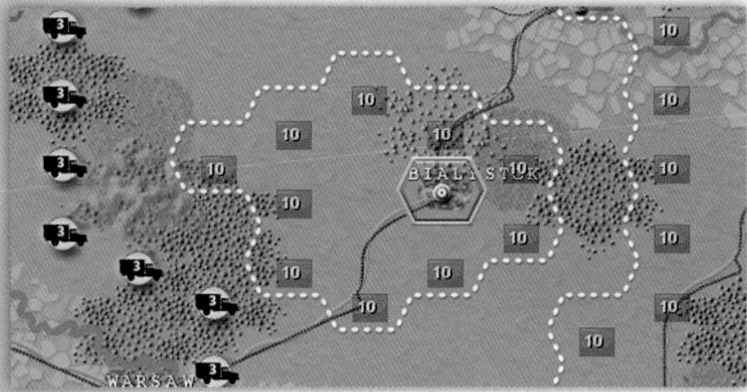

With the unit display switched off (press '0') you can see the city that the 10th Army is holed up in

DESIGNER NOTE

There are examples of encircled Soviet pockets forcefully breaking out after several weeks of being isolated. This couldn't happen in the game as the lack of supply would preclude a breakout attempt after one or two turns of isolation (depends on their supply level prior to being cut-off). While the Breakout! Card is a way of simulating this is important to keep in mind the games scale. Divisions will lose their coherency very quickly once cut-off. This is the case both in the game and in '41. Lower level formations can exist for longer and maintain a measure of military capability but not so Divisions (roughly ten thousand men) hence the fairly rapid degradation that ensures when they are cut off.

The fact that a cut-off Division losses its ability to operate as an integrated military formation able to undertake coordinated military action within a week or so of losing all forms of supply is accurate for the conditions of '41. That there would be smaller scale elements that were still functioning for much longer periods isn't in dispute but, given the game's scale, they are irrelevant.

A final point is the conditions that are required to be met for the Breakout! Card ensure that some planning is required on the part of the Soviet Player. HQ's need to be in a city. Given that they are always situated on part of the transport grid and provide excellent defensive bonuses this isn't a bad spot to have them anyway. The Breakout! Card, however, isn't meant to be a 'get out of jail for free' event. The Soviet Player won't always be able to use it or it won't provide enough of a 'bang' (no combat bonus) to allow the Army to escape.

The main purpose of the card is to create a situation where large groups of encircled Soviet units COULD breakout. They aren't something that the German Player can simply bypass and ignore. The mere threat of rear area chaos ensures that isolated pockets of Soviet units need to be dealt with. Doing so causes casualties and fatigue amongst the German Infantry Armies. It all adds up and the need to reduce the, sometimes massive, pockets was a major headache for the German Commanders.

SUMMARY

- Play on an Army HQ
- Must be Cut-off
- Must be located in a city
- All subordinate Divisions receive +50 supply the following turn
- Divisions outside of Command Range miss out

Massed Artillery

Soviet artillery was superior to that of the Germans. Once sections of the front began to stabilise during the latter part of '41 they were able to overcome their disadvantage in communications and coordination by massing artillery, and Katyusha rocket launchers, in localised areas to great effect.

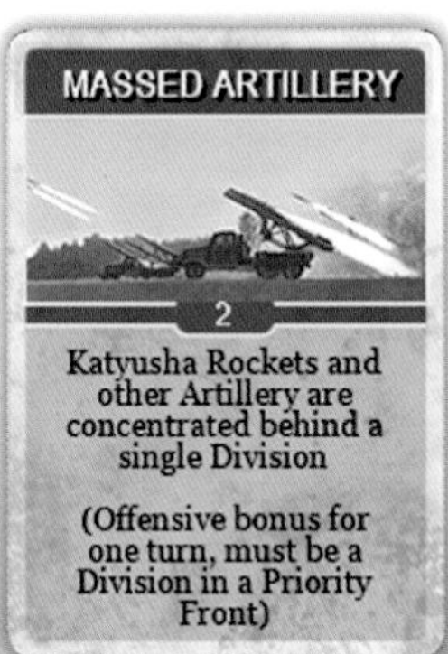

This card appears in the 'Operations' category only from round 35 (1st November) onward.

It can be played on any INFANTRY Division (no armour present) that isn't cut-off and is located in a front that currently has priority (see 6.2.5.4 Prioritise Front). The Division will receive a +40% Offensive bonus on the following turn (it last for one turn only).

SUMMARY

- The card doesn't appear till round 35 (1st November)
- Play on an Infantry Division
- Division can't be cut-off
- Division must be in a designated Priority Front
- Provides a one-off +40% Offensive combat bonus the following turn

Massed Armour

The Soviets underwent a major shift in armoured doctrine during the course of '41. Their initial 'fully armoured Divisions' changed to a system of attached tank brigades. This is reflected in the changing composition of the reinforcement Divisions (for further information see 10.4 Soviet). Once winter began the Soviets began grouping tank brigades in localised areas in order to achieve a critical mass.

This card appears in the 'Operations' category only from round 35 (1st November) onward (along with 'Massed Artillery' and 'Air Defence').

It can be played on any ARMOURED Division (must have armour present but doesn't need to be fully armoured) that isn't cut-off and is located in a front that currently has priority (see 6.2.5.4 Prioritise Front). The Division will receive a +40% Offensive bonus on the following turn (it last for one turn only).

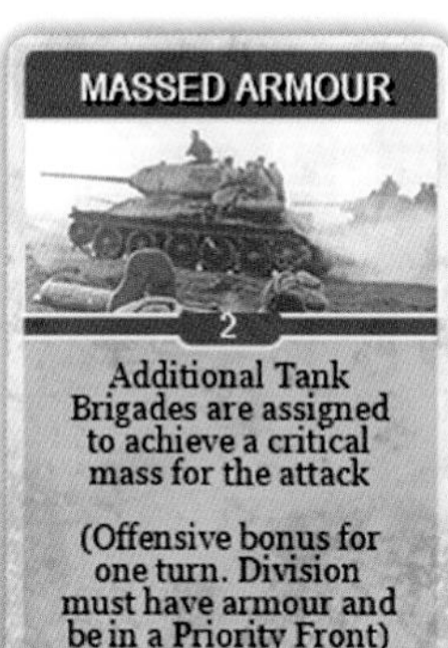

MASSED ARMOUR
2
Additional Tank Brigades are assigned to achieve a critical mass for the attack
(Offensive bonus for one turn. Division must have armour and be in a Priority Front)

SUMMARY

- The card doesn't appear till round 35 (1st November)
- Play on an Armoured Division
- Division can't be cut-off
- Division must be in a designated Priority Front
- Provides a one-off +40% Offensive combat bonus the following turn

Air Defence

The Soviet Airforce (the VVS) didn't cover itself in glory in '41 but by the end of the year they were able to mount a sustained defence of a major city with a combination of fighter squadrons and massed anti-aircraft Battalions. Leningrad is a good example.

AIR DEFENCE
10
Assign Fighters and Flak to defend a major City
(will reduce the benefit of German Tactical Air Support within 3 hexes of City)

This card appears in the 'Operations' category only from round 35 (1st November) onward (along with 'Massed Artillery' and 'Massed Armour').

It can be played on any Soviet owned, strategic city (red dot). It can be played even if the city is isolated from STAVKA (air defences are assumed to be present and fighter squadrons can fly in).

The effect of the card is to reduce the TAC bonus (see 6.1.3.2 Tactical Air Support) of any German Division within 3 hexes of the city. The closer the units are to the city, the greater the effect.

AIR DEFENCE	
Hexes distance from City	Effect on TAC bonus
1 hex	-20
2 hexes	-10
3 hexes	-5

Only one city can have Air Defences at a time (there were limited resources and the card is referring to a level of protection above and beyond what was normally expected).

Once the card has been played the effect will remain in force, automatically, until the city is either over run or the Soviet Player changes his mind and orders the defences shifted to another location.

SUMMARY

- The card doesn't appear till round 35 (1st November)
- Play on a friendly Strategic City (red dot)
- City can be cut-off
- Serves to reduce, or eliminate, any TAC bonus of nearby German Divisions (up to 3 hexes from city)
- Continuous, automatic, effect once played
- Play again to change cities

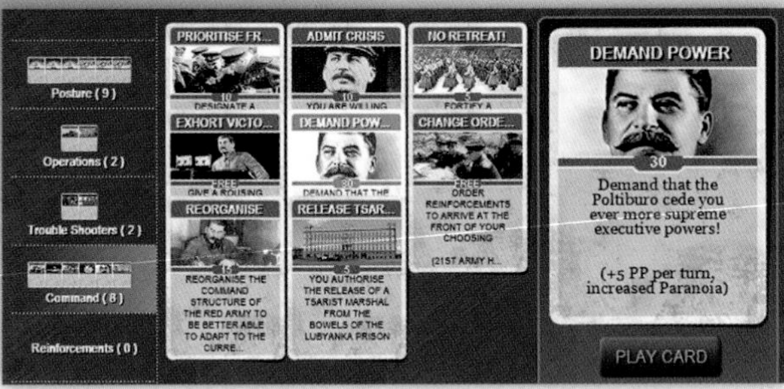

Command category

The Soviet Player exercises Command through the use of Action cards. The 'Command' category contains all the high level options available to him.

6.2.5.4. Command Cards

COMMAND CARDS

Card	Effect	Base Cost (PP)
Prioritise Front	Designate a Front to receive resources and STAVKA staff attention above and beyond the others. (Play on a Front HQ to give a permanent Activation bonus to all Army Commanders within the Front)	10
Exhort Victory	Give a rousing Victory Speech that will be promulgated throughout Mother Russia and will serve to inspire all who hear it to greater effort. (global Activation bonus)	Free
Reorganise Command	Reorganise the Command Structure of the Red Army to be better able to adapt to the current situation. (Improved Communications and a global Activation bonus)	15
Admit Crisis	You are willing to concede that, yes, we are being invaded and that, yes, it is serious. (Lowers the cost of Defensive Posture Cards. Raises Stalin's Paranoia level)	10
Demand Power	Demand that the Poltiburo cede you ever more supreme executive powers! (+5 PP allowance per turn. Raises Stalin's Paranoia level)	30
Release Tsarist	You authorise the release of a Tsarist Marshal from the bowels of the Lubyanka prison. (Play on a Front HQ to replace the existing Marshal with a new, Tsarist, one)	5
No Retreat!	Fortify a politically important, strategic (red dot) city with a major garrison. (Can be played on Brest, Minsk, Riga, Talinn, Lvov, Kiev, Odessa, Kharkov, Leningrad, Moscow, Rostov, Stalingrad)	5
Change Orders	The next Army HQ reinforcement that arrives can be deployed in the theatre of your choice. (The Army HQ and all it's subordinate Divisions will be diverted)	Free

Prioritise Front

There are three fronts - North, Central, South (corresponding to the German Theatres). Stalin can pick one and declare it a priority. Staff and military resources will be directed at it in preference to the others. Commanders on that front are made aware that it is of special interest to Stalin and that failure is not an option.

The card is played on one of the three Front HQ's. At the start of the campaign no front has priority.

Once a front has been declared a priority there will be an Activation bonus (see 6.2.2 Activation) given to all Army Commanders within the front. Certain Operational cards - 'Massed Artillery' and 'Massed Armour' - are only available to units located in the front with priority.

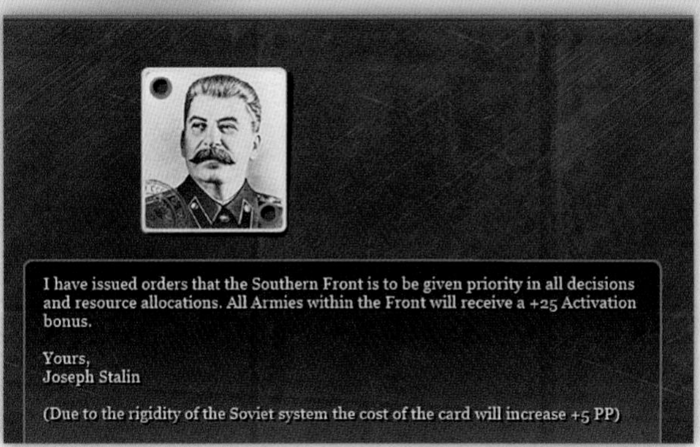

I have issued orders that the Southern Front is to be given priority in all decisions and resource allocations. All Armies within the Front will receive a +25 Activation bonus.
Yours,
Joseph Stalin
(Due to the rigidity of the Soviet system the cost of the card will increase +5 PP)

The Southern Front has been declared a priority. Marshal Buddeny had better sharpen up

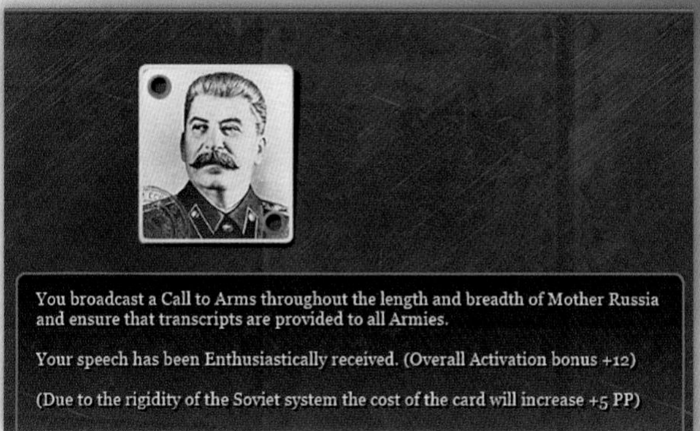

You broadcast a Call to Arms throughout the length and breadth of Mother Russia and ensure that transcripts are provided to all Armies.
Your speech has been Enthusiastically received. (Overall Activation bonus +12)
(Due to the rigidity of the Soviet system the cost of the card will increase +5 PP)

Stalin has given it his all and his speech has been well received

--- Key Data
- Paranoia Level 0 (change this turn 0) [?]
- Southern Front has Priority (Initiative +25) [?]

The Aide de Camp report highlights the Front that has priority

Only one front can have priority at a time and once declared, it will automatically remain so until Stalin (the Player) decides to change his priorities to a different front. Each time the card is played the cost, in Political Points, increases.

SOUTHERN FRONT Army Activations 30 . June . 1941

--- INITIATIVE Modifier
Luftwaffe disruption to command and control [?], (Overall) -9
This Front has been designated a Priority by Comrade Stalin +25
Marshal Budenny, APPARATCHIK, Southern Front Cdr, Init -11
TOTAL Modifier +5 [?]

The Southern Front Activation report shows the effect of the Front having Priority. It's enough to offset the useless Marshal and the Luftwaffe disruption

Exhort Victory!

There is nothing like a stirring speech to inspire those beneath you to try harder.

Stalin can give one speech per turn. The cost, in Political Points, will increase each time a speech is given (the law of diminishing returns) with the initial speech being free.

Every time Stalin gives a speech there is a global bonus to all Army Commander's activation chances throughout Russia (see 6.2.2 Activation). There is no guarantee that a speech will be as effective as the one in the example above. It's possible for Stalin to fluff his lines and have his speech fall flat.

IN DETAIL

There will always be a minimum +5 Activation bonus no matter how poor the speech. The maximum possible bonus is +15.

CENTRAL FRONT Army Activations 26 . June . 1941

--- INITIATIVE Modifier
Comrade Stalin gives a rousing Speech, (Overall) +12
Luftwaffe disruption to command and control [?], (Overall) -19
Marshal Timoshenko, TOADIE, Central Front Cdr, Init -5
TOTAL Modifier -12 [?]

All three Activation reports show the effect of the recent speech. It appears to have been drowned out by the Luftwaffe bombing raids

STAFF ADVICE

A speech is an easy way to gain a global activation bonus. The first three speeches are cost effective and you need to use them wisely.

Reorganise

The Soviet Command structure was a shambles at the start of the campaign. It underwent multiple reorganisations in '41.

A poor command structure manifests itself in the inability of Army Commanders to achieve full Activation and desultory communications between the front line and STAVKA.

The 'Reorganise' card can be played multiple times with a benefit gained with each instance. The cost of the card (in Political Points) will likewise increase each time it is used.

Reorganising provides a global (affects everybody) Activation bonus (+10) (see 6.2.2 Activation) and reduces the chances of communication breakdowns.

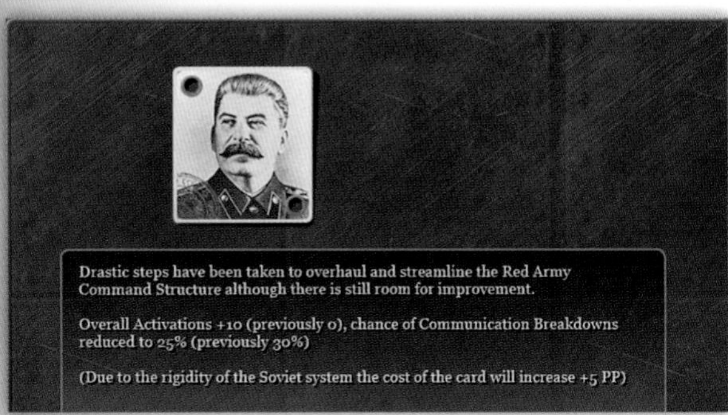

Admit Crisis

It took Stalin some time before he gave up on his delusional fantasies of repelling the invader and having the Soviet flag flying over the Reichstag before the christmas of '41.

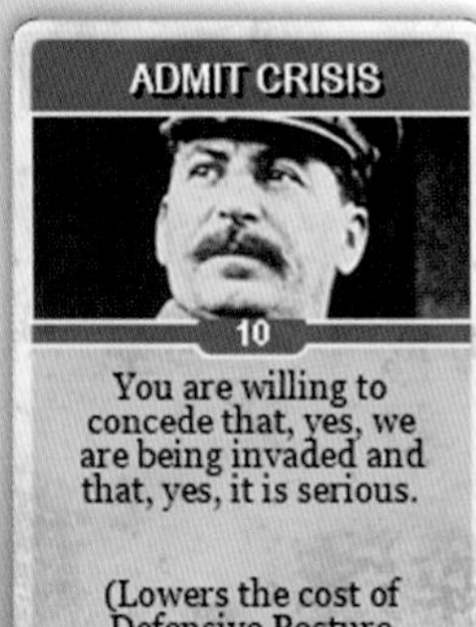

The main symptom of his reluctance to admit to the seriousness of the situation is the cost of the Defensive posture cards. Initially this is high at 15 Political Points but each time that Stalin grudgingly admits that matters aren't going well, the cost will drop by -5 PP (it can't go below zero).

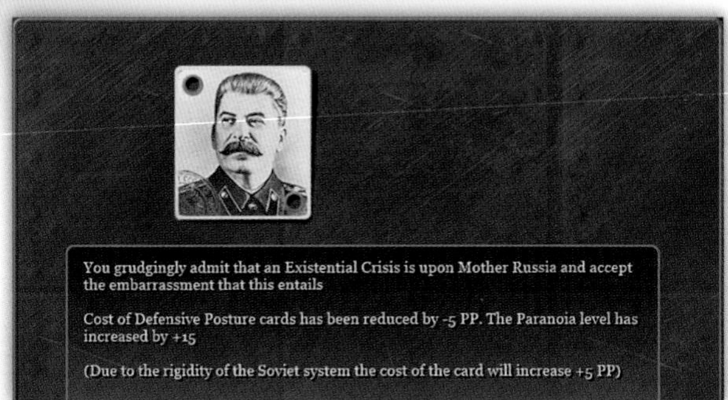

There is a cost in doing so, other than the PP's expended, of an increased Paranoia level. Dictators, as a rule, don't like to admit to making mistakes as they can be perceived as being weak and vulnerable.

STAFF ADVICE

Having your armies set to a Defensive posture makes a big difference. Most armies start configured to an Offensive posture which gives a -20% defensive combat penalty. Changing them over to a defensive posture makes this a +40% combat bonus, a difference of 60%! Soviet Divisions, dug into adverse terrain (woods & swamps) gain a further defensive combat bonus of up to +40% (see 5.2.12 Terrain Effect).

Having Admitted to a Crisis the cost of the Defensive posture cards has lowered to 10 PP. Stalin will have to make further mea culpa's before reconfiguring armies over to the defence is feasible

Demand Power

Stalin had significant levels of power but it wasn't total. He can, if he wishes, demand more.

DEMAND POWER
30
Demand that the Poltiburo cede you ever more supreme executive powers!
(+5 PP per turn, increased Paranoia)

Power is expressed in Political Points (PP). The more Stalin has the more he can do. The normal 'Command Allowance' (representing the limits of what Stalin can achieve within the 4 day time frame of a turn) of 10 is increased to 15 for the duration of the game.

Your blatant grab for ever more power has left the Poltiburo confused and bewildered but they concede to your demands
+5 PP amount per turn (total 15 PP), Paranoia +20
(This card can only be played ONCE)

The downside is that Stalin's Paranoia level will increase (+20). Grabbing more power is a once only event. The card will be removed once played.

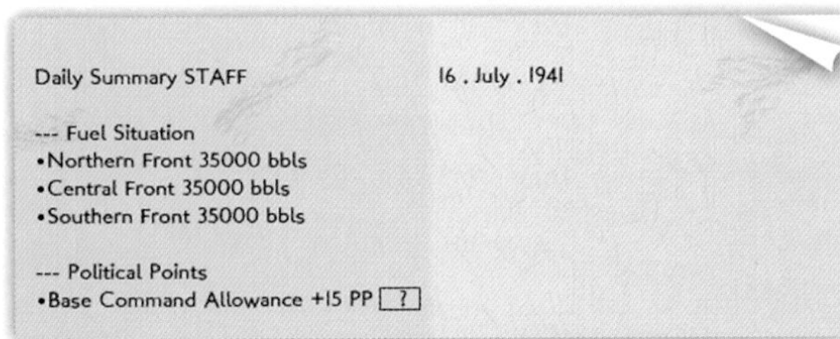
Daily Summary STAFF   16 . July . 1941

--- Fuel Situation
- Northern Front 35000 bbls
- Central Front 35000 bbls
- Southern Front 35000 bbls

--- Political Points
- Base Command Allowance +15 PP [?]

Daily Staff Log. 50% more PP per turn. That's a lot

STAFF ADVICE

If you are going to make a grab for power time it carefully. Avoid doing so when your Paranoia level is high as the +20 increase from playing the card will likely tip you over the edge.

Release Tsarist

At any time Stalin could replace a front Marshal by having Commissar Khrushchev pay them a visit and using one of his Officer cards ('Firing Squad' or 'Dismiss Marshal'). The Marshal is removed, one way or the other, and a replacement is immediately sent to take his place. The replacement, however, is of a randomly determined type (unless you're using the 'Historical' option).

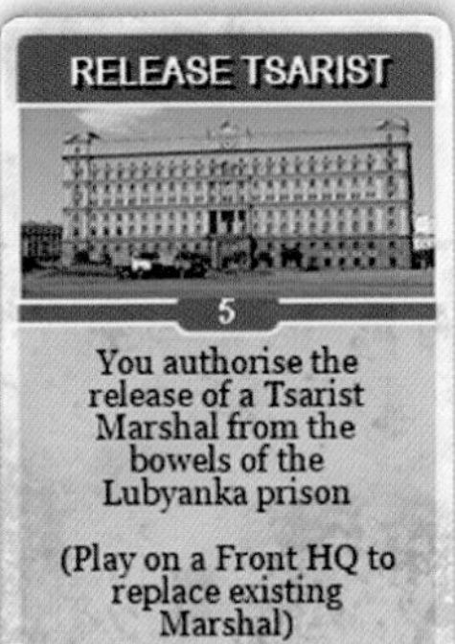

RELEASE TSARIST
5
You authorise the release of a Tsarist Marshal from the bowels of the Lubyanka prison
(Play on a Front HQ to replace existing Marshal)

The 'Release Tsarist' card allows Stalin to authorise a Tsarist (the most competent Marshal, see 6.2.1.1 Commander types) to be released from prison (where Stalin incarcerated him in the first instance during the great purges before the war).

The situation prior to playing the card. Marshal Budenny is marginally more incompetent (Initiative -8) than Marshal Voroshilov up north

Play the card on any Front HQ and the current Marshal will be replaced with a Tsarist one.

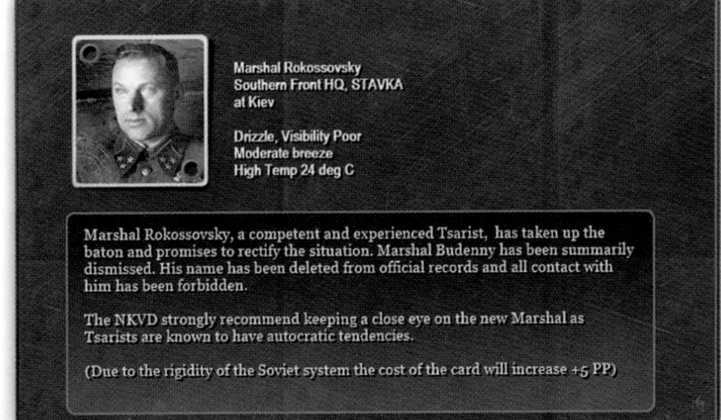

Marshal Rokossovsky
Southern Front HQ, STAVKA
at Kiev
Drizzle, Visibility Poor
Moderate breeze
High Temp 24 deg C
Marshal Rokossovsky, a competent and experienced Tsarist, has taken up the baton and promises to rectify the situation. Marshal Budenny has been summarily dismissed. His name has been deleted from official records and all contact with him has been forbidden.
The NKVD strongly recommend keeping a close eye on the new Marshal as Tsarists are known to have autocratic tendencies.
(Due to the rigidity of the Soviet system the cost of the card will increase +5 PP)

Marshal Rokossovsky has assumed command of the Southern Front. Marshal Budenny has been frog marched out the door

The Command tab (bottom centre) will be instantly updated to reflect the changes.

Stalin will have to be careful as two of his Marshals are now Tsarists. He needs to have Commissar Khurshchev pay them both a visit before his Paranoia level gets out of hand

No Retreat!

Major, regular, garrison can be raised to defend strategic cities (red dot). Minor cities (grey dot) are able to raise smaller, less well equipped, conscript garrisons by the use of the 'Garrisons' card (under the 'Operations' category). Both types of garrison work the same.

NO RETREAT!

5

Fortify a Politically Important City.

(Brest, Minsk, Riga, Talinn, Lvov, Kiev, Odessa, Kharkov, Leningrad, Moscow, Rostov, Stalingrad)

Major garrisons are immobile, set to a Defensive posture (+40% defensive combat bonus), fully entrenched and have their 'Retreat percentage' set to 100% (will fight to the last man). They will draw supplies from the city (local magazines and stockpiles) and will remain in full supply even if cut-off.

If forced out of the city they are defending they will be automatically disbanded.

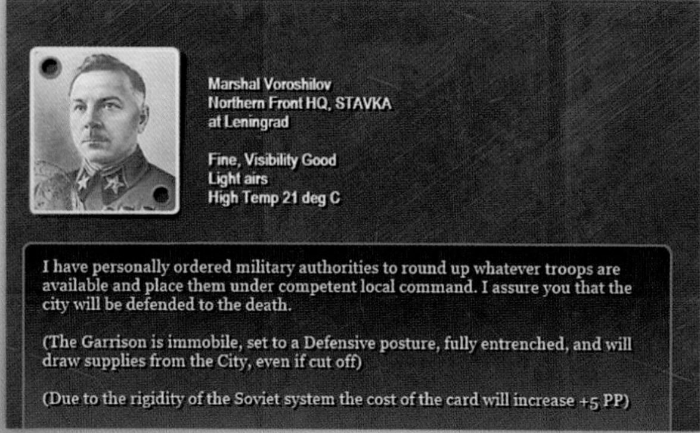

Major garrisons, unlike the conscript versions, cost Political Points to raise (the cost will increase after every garrison) and can be placed in any strategic city (red dot) provided it hasn't previously raised a garrison (only one per city) and it can trace an interrupted supply path back to STAVKA (you can't raise a garrison in a city that is cut off). Only a single major garrison can be raised per turn.

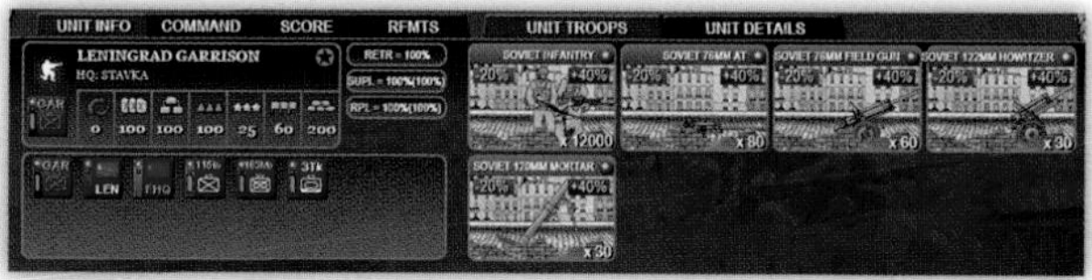

Major garrisons are over strength, extremely well equipped (note the 76mm ATG's), Divisions that represent not only men but their efforts to fully fortify the city in question , Odessa, Kiev and Leningrad being good examples of this

STAFF ADVICE

Major garrisons are significant obstacles to the Germans advance. Strategic cities often lie squarely on major transport and logistical routes and can seriously hinder the Germans advance. The escalating cost of raising major garrisons make the choice of where they are placed important. You may want to secure your objective cities first (Leningrad, especially, is on the front line once the Finns activate) or play a more forward defence strategy.

Minsk can prevent a rapid advance straight down the main highway to Moscow. Down south, major garrisons in both Kiev and Odessa can shut down both main lines of advance. Odessa, in particular, can be problematic for the Germans as they have only weak Romanian Armies in the region. An early gambit is to place a garrison in Lvov. Forcing the German Player to bypass this with Kleist's Panzergruppe 1 will result in his truck columns being worn out well before their time as they will be forced to travel long distances cross country. If you want to bring a Panzergruppe to a halt, take away their trucks.

Change Orders

The Soviets have a large number of reinforcement armies. They arrive according to a fixed schedule based on historical information. Each army is assigned to a particular front. It's possible, by the use of the 'Change Orders' card to have an army

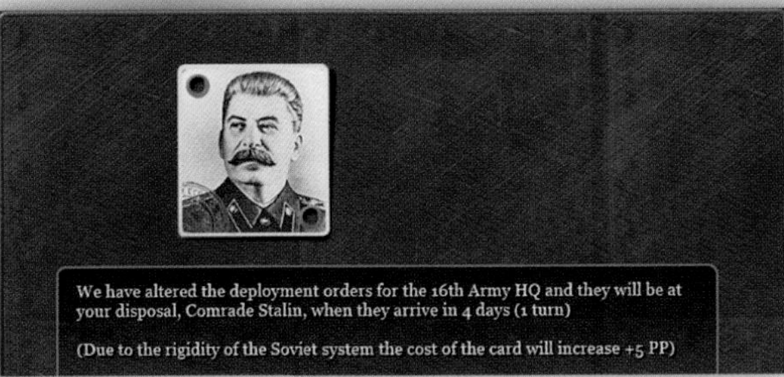

We have altered the deployment orders for the 16th Army HQ and they will be at your disposal, Comrade Stalin, when they arrive in 4 days (1 turn)
(Due to the rigidity of the Soviet system the cost of the card will increase +5 PP)

The 16th Army has been reassigned

CHANGE ORDERS
FREE
Order Reinforcements to arrive at the Front of your choosing
(16th Army HQ, Central Front, in 4 days)

The card will highlight the next available army which will be the one available for reassignment

arrive at a different front, of your choosing.

In the case of multiple armies arriving on the same turn the first available one will be chosen.

The first time the card is played it is free (no PP) but thereafter its cost increased each time it is used.

When reinforcement armies arrive their HQ's are deployed on the map via an Action card found in the Reinforcements category.

Note the card text for the 16th army. 'Deploy to ANY Front'. All the other, normal reinforcement cards, specify a front (in this case they are all going to the Central front to protect Moscow)

Playing the reinforcement card will allow you to place the newly arrived 16th Army HQ in any of the three fronts.

DESIGNER NOTE

Adhering to history is fine but there needs to be some flexibility built into the system to allow the Player to respond to changing circumstances.

6.2.5.5. Reinforcement Cards

Reinforcements arrive in two distinct stages. Firstly the Army HQ arrives. An Action card is generated and placed in the 'Reinforcements' category.

The Aide de Camp report provides notification of HQ's awaiting deployment (Action cards are available).

--- Reinforcements
•4 Div's Deployed, 83 Div's Failed to deploy, 22 Div's Pending deployment [?]
•10 Army HQ's are awaiting deployment [?]

Aide de Camp report. The important part are the HQ's. You'll need to play their reinforcement cards in order to deploy them.

The relevant Daily Front Log provides a comprehensive list of all reinforcement related activity with HQ's and their associated Action cards being highlighted at the top.

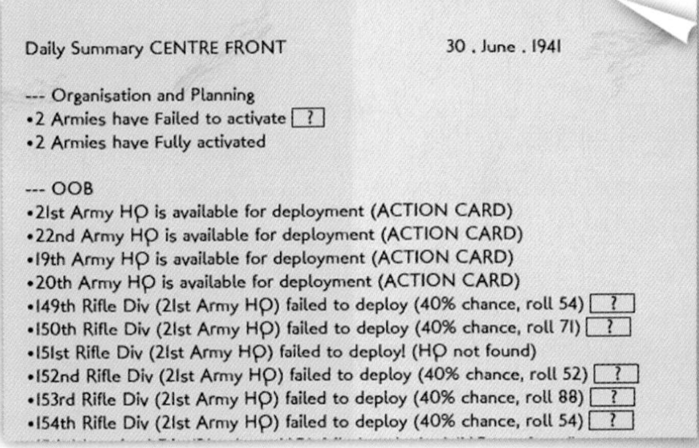

Daily Summary CENTRE FRONT 30 . June . 1941

--- Organisation and Planning
•2 Armies have Failed to activate [?]
•2 Armies have Fully activated

--- OOB
•21st Army HQ is available for deployment (ACTION CARD)
•22nd Army HQ is available for deployment (ACTION CARD)
•19th Army HQ is available for deployment (ACTION CARD)
•20th Army HQ is available for deployment (ACTION CARD)
•149th Rifle Div (21st Army HQ) failed to deploy (40% chance, roll 54) [?]
•150th Rifle Div (21st Army HQ) failed to deploy (40% chance, roll 71) [?]
•151st Rifle Div (21st Army HQ) failed to deploy! (HQ not found)
•152nd Rifle Div (21st Army HQ) failed to deploy (40% chance, roll 52) [?]
•153rd Rifle Div (21st Army HQ) failed to deploy (40% chance, roll 88) [?]
•154th Rifle Div (21st Army HQ) failed to deploy (40% chance, roll 54) [?]

The 19th Army is only one of a number of reinforcements to the Central front

Once the card is played and the army HQ is placed on the map, at a location selected by the Player, on following turns the armies subordinate Divisions will automatically begin arriving. Divisions can't arrive until their Army HQ is deployed onto the map via an Action card.

ASK YOUR STAFF

What happens if I don't deploy an HQ and let its card sit there for a few turns? Nothing other than the fact that you aren't receiving the benefit of the Army. They are sitting in a rear area awaiting your command to move to the front. They'll happily sit there until you issue the required orders.

Army HQ's can be deployed on any hex, within the specified front, provided it is on the transport grid (and isn't cut-off).

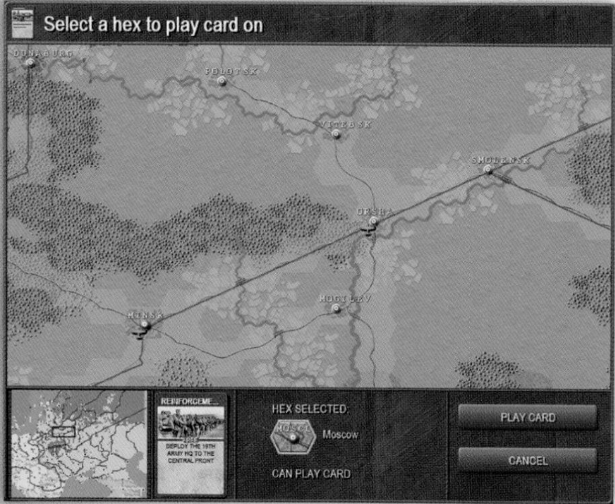

The 19th Army has a wide range of deployment options

Once deployed the HQ will make immediate preparations for the arrival of its subordinate Divisions.

STAFF ADVICE

Reinforcements arrive by train. As the HQ's arrive before their Divisions it's important to not place them in a situation where they could get over run prior to establishing themselves as a viable military formation. Subordinate Divisions will begin arriving the following turn but they won't be able to form up and move until the turn after that (it takes a while to untangle the chaos of Divisions arriving piecemeal on different trains). Plan ahead.

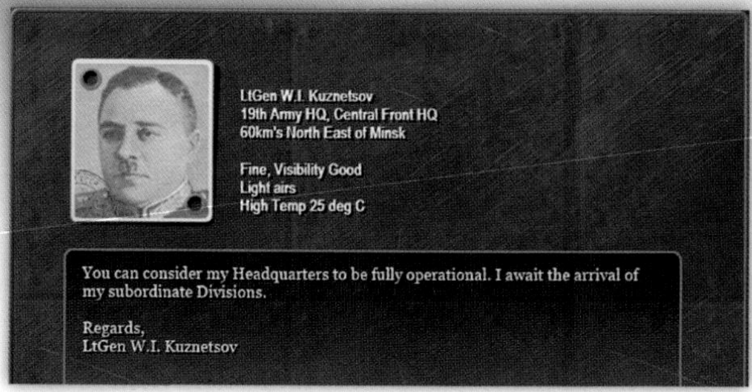

Rest easy as LtGen. Kuznetsov is here

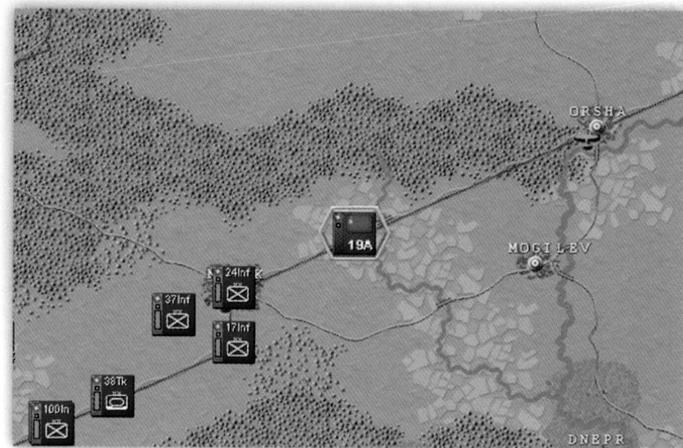

Positioned on the main Warsaw-Minsk-Moscow highway LtGen. Kuznetsov's 19th Army will be assuming a blocking role

6.2.5.6. Troubleshooter Cards

There are two types of Troubleshooter cards. The main tab, travel cards (below) which allow you to order you troubleshooters to visit any HQ on the map.

Once at an HQ (other than STAVKA) Officer cards become available (different sets for each troubleshooter and different sets again depending

on the type of HQ they are at). These are found attached to the Commander of the HQ where the troubleshooter is located.

Officer cards for the Troubleshooters work the same was Officer cards for the German Army Commanders who are benefiting from Command Focus (see 6.1.1 Command Focus).

More information can be found at 6.2.4 Troubleshooters.

Marshal Zhukov Cards

Zhukov has, like all both troubleshooters, two sets of cards. One for when his is at a Front HQ and the other for when he is at an Army HQ. There are no cards available if he is at STAVKA.

Marshal Zhukov's cards are focused on getting things done. Activations and combat bonuses.

MARSHAL ZHUKOV ARMY CARDS		
Card	Effect	Base Cost (PP)
Grant Independence	Zhukov will authorise the Commander a greater measure of Independence. Permanent Activation bonus to Army	2
Inspire	Have Zhukov give the Commander one of his 'Inspirational' talks. In a soundproof room. Commander's Initiative increased	2
All out Effort	Order Zhukov to step in and coordinate a proper military response. Combat bonus to all Divisions in the Army for the DURATION of Zhukov's visit	2
Blow Bridge!	Ask Zhukov to ensure the job is done properly. Blows up ALL valid bridges in selected hex. A Division of the Army must be present in the hex	Free

MARSHAL ZHUKOV FRONT CARDS		
Card	Effect	Base Cost (PP)
Instil Backbone!	Force the Marshal to grow a backbone and start acting like the decisivie leader that he should be. Permanent +10 to Marshal's Initiative	5
Take Command	Push the Marshal aside and have Zhukov take command. He'll soon straighten out the mess. Activation bonus to the entire Front.	5

Commissar Khrushchev Cards

Krushchev has, like both troubleshooters, two sets of cards. One for when his is at a Front HQ and the other for when he is at an Army HQ. There are no cards available if he is at STAVKA.

Commissar Khrushchev's cards are focused on protecting Stalin from any perceived threat emanating from his Officer Corps.

COMMISSAR KHRUSHCHEV FRONT CARDS		
Card	Effect	Base Cost (PP)
Firing Squad!	There are times when it pays to make an example. Order the Marshal dragged outside and shot! New Marshal and a large Paranoia reduction	5
Lay Blame	It's not going well. You need a scapegoat. Make it clear who is at fault. Lowers Marshal's Threat rating	5
Dismiss Marshal	Incompetence has no place in the Red Army. Clear out the dead wood to make way for the new. New Marshal	5
Intimidate	Exert an overbearing presence on the Front HQ and all subordinate Army HQ's Prevents Army Commanders from increasing their Threat ratings while ever the Commissar is present	5

COMMISSAR KHRUSHCHEV ARMY CARDS		
Card	Effect	Base Cost (PP)
Loaded Pistol	It is the obligation of the Commissar to reacquaint wayward Commanders with their Duty to the Soviet Union. New Commander and a moderate Paranoia decrease	2
Fire!	There is no place in the Red Army for Commanders with an inflated sense of their own worth. (New Commander)	2
Investigate	Dig around and who knows what dark and dirty secrets will be revealed? Commander's Threat rating reduced to zero	2
Confidante	Let the Commander know that Comrade Stalin looks favourably upon his performance. Commander's Threat rating will NEVER increase	2

6.2.6. BLOWING BRIDGES

BLOW BRIDGE!
FREE
Ask Zhukov to ensure the job is done properly
(Blows up ALL valid Bridges in selected hex. A Division of the Army must be present in the hex)

There is no cost (in PP) to blow a bridge

This can only be done by Marshal Zhukov (troubleshooter) being present at an Army HQ (with at least one of its Divisions in the hex with the bridge) and playing his 'Blow Bridge' card.

Once a bridge is blown it remains destroyed until the Germans repair it (see 6.1.12 Bridges). In order to be repaired the Germans must have captured the hex used to blow the bridge. Repair is handled automatically but the larger the river that is required to be bridged, the longer it will likely take. Bridges can't be repaired when iced over.

ASK YOUR STAFF

Why is it that only Zhukov can blow a bridge? Lots of people in the Red Army can blow bridges up. Historically many did. Most of the time they messed it up. The bridge was damaged but it was easily repaired by the advancing Germans. Typically Soviet Commanders, fearful of making a wrong decision, would leave the destruction of a critical bridge to the last minute, often with the result that the Germans captured it intact. With Marshal Zhukov present, it was done properly.

DESIGNER NOTE

There is an interesting game mechanic here. Requiring Zhukov to be present has been used to model the poor track record of the Soviets in this area but it also creates a nice tension between having Zhukov racing to destroy a crucial bridge when he is urgently needed elsewhere.

STAFF ADVICE

A destroyed bridge can stop the German logistics dead. Trucks columns incur large penalties to cross rivers (it's assumed over temporary pontoon bridges) and trains have to find an alternative route (if one exists). Always blow a bridge on the Soviet side of the bridge as the Germans can attempt to repair it only from the hex it was destroyed from. A bridge of note is the main bridge over the Dnepr at Dnepropetrovsk (hex 52,54). Blow this and you can seriously crimp the German's advance on Rostov. Historically the Germans failed to capture it intact and they suffered grievously as a result.

6.2.7. MECHANICAL RELIABILITY

Every time a Soviet Fast Division (includes vehicles) moves there is a chance of vehicles being lost due to mechanical breakdowns. Unlike the German system where the chance of a breakdown test being triggered is based around accumulated mileage, the Soviet's are assumed to automatically fail a breakdown test every time they move.

All vehicles within a Division have to pass a mechanical reliability check. There is only ever one check per turn regardless of how often the unit moved or fought. The check is done at the completion of the turn and comes into affect the following turn.

The Soviet Mechanised forces suffered, in '41, from a chronic lack of spare parts and competent tank crews. More tanks were lost to mechanical breakdowns than to combat. Tanks that broke down, even from easily repairable causes, were abandoned by their untrained crews.

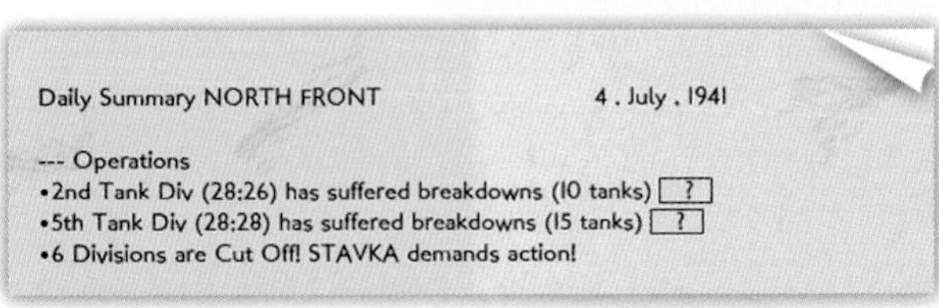

Daily Summary NORTH FRONT 4 . July . 1941

--- Operations
- 2nd Tank Div (28:26) has suffered breakdowns (10 tanks) [?]
- 5th Tank Div (28:28) has suffered breakdowns (15 tanks) [?]
- 6 Divisions are Cut Off! STAVKA demands action!

Breakdowns are reported in the relevant Daily Front Logs

Soviet vehicles that breakdown are unable to be recovered by playing a 'Refit' card as can the Germans. For the Soviets, if it breaks down, it's gone, left in the ditch at the side of the road.

IN DETAIL

The Soviet system ensures that a fully equipped Division will suffer a lot of breakdowns but, as the numbers dwindle, the breakdowns will become rarer.

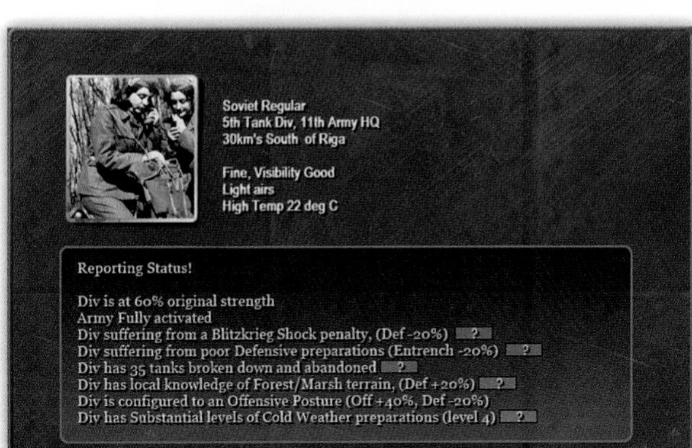

The 5th Tank Division of the 11th Army has abandoned 35 tanks, to date, due to mechanical failure. All you can do about it is curse

6.2.8. INTELLIGENCE

Each turn you receive a Daily Intelligence Summary which is a collation of reports from all available intelligence sources. This will only be available if you have chosen the 'Fog of War ON' option at game start. There's not much point in an intelligence report if you have full knowledge of German dispositions.

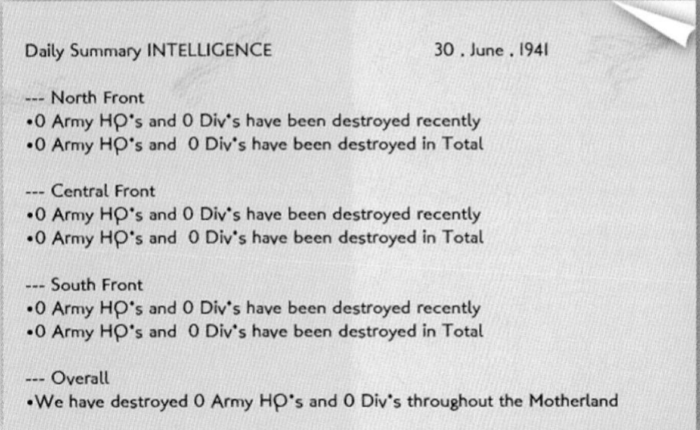

Daily Summary INTELLIGENCE 30 . June . 1941

--- North Front
- 0 Army HQ's and 0 Div's have been destroyed recently
- 0 Army HQ's and 0 Div's have been destroyed in Total

--- Central Front
- 0 Army HQ's and 0 Div's have been destroyed recently
- 0 Army HQ's and 0 Div's have been destroyed in Total

--- South Front
- 0 Army HQ's and 0 Div's have been destroyed recently
- 0 Army HQ's and 0 Div's have been destroyed in Total

--- Overall
- We have destroyed 0 Army HQ's and 0 Div's throughout the Motherland

Unlike the German Intelligence report the Soviet one is very bare bones as befits their ability to distill any information on enemy activity other than the basics. Beyond 1941 STAVKA gradually increased their intelligence capability but '41 was predominately about survival of the Motherland and a fast moving, fluid front line ensured that they had knowledge of only that which was directly in front on them.

6.2.9. REINFORCEMENTS

Reinforcements arrive according to an historical schedule. Each Army HQ has a designated front where it will be deployed by use of an Action card. It's possible to alter the front by use of the 'Change Orders' Action card (see 6.2.5.4 Change orders).

There are a number of distinct waves of reinforcements - the Regular armies being railed in

UNIT INFO COMMAND SCORE RFMTS

NORTHERN Front reinforcements	CENTRAL Front reinforcements	SOUTHERN Front reinforcements
T+4, 48th Army HQ, Conscript (early)	T+1, 16th Army HQ, Stavka Reserve	T+4, 47th Army HQ, Conscript (early)
T+9, 42nd Army HQ, Conscript (early)	T+1, 19th Army HQ, Stavka Reserve	T+5, 44th Army HQ, Conscript (early)
T+10, 52nd Army HQ, Conscript (early)	T+1, 20th Army HQ, Stavka Reserve	T+5, 45th Army HQ, Conscript (early)
T+11, 54th Army HQ, Conscript (early)	T+2, 24th Army HQ, Stavka Reserve	T+5, 46th Army HQ, Conscript (early)
T+12, 55th Army HQ, Conscript (early)	T+2, 28th Army HQ, Regular	T+9, 37th Army HQ, Conscript (early)
T+35, 59th Army HQ, Conscript (late)	T+2, 29th Army HQ, Regular	T+10, 38th Army HQ, Conscript (early)
	T+2, 30th Army HQ, Regular	T+11, 40th Army HQ, Conscript (early)
	T+3, 31st Army HQ, Regular	T+12, 51st Army HQ, Conscript (early)

T+4, for example, indicates that the Army HQ (not the complete Army, just the HQ) will be arriving in four turns from now. T+1 is the following turn. The three dots (...) at the bottom of front (Central and Southern) highlight that there are more Armies to come beyond those shown in the tab. As time passes they'll move up the list in the same manner as an airport notification board has flights moving up as they get closer to their time of departure

from other parts of Russia, the early, hastily formed, badly equipped, conscript armies, the later conscript armies with the good gear and the experienced and lethal Siberians. Refer to the designer notes for more information 10.4 Soviet.

The Reinforcement tab provides a breakdown of reinforcement arrivals. The information within is updated each turn and allows the Soviet Player to plan ahead.

Reinforcements arrive in two distinct stages. Firstly the Army HQ arrives. An Action card is generated and placed in the 'Reinforcements' category. Refer to 6.2.5.5 Reinforcement Cards for information on deploying Army HQ's.

Once the Army HQ has arrived its subordinate Divisions will begin arriving from the following turn onward. This happens automatically. The only Player intervention required is to deploy the Army HQ on the map via the Reinforcement Action card. Divisions won't turn up until their HQ has been deployed.

If the Division's HQ has been destroyed before they can deploy then they will be reassigned to another HQ, assigned to the same front, arriving shortly.

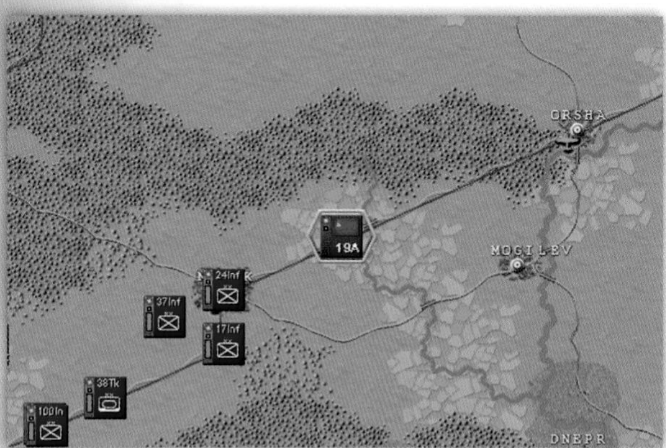

The story of LtGen. Kuznetsov's 19th Army continues. He's been deployed. He's on the map.

Divisional reinforcements have a probability of arriving. For the Soviets this is usually 40% and represents the chaos and unpredictability of having to move large numbers of men and equipment through a rail network that is struggling to cope with the demands placed on it by war time conditions. Even in the best of times the trains are unlikely to arrive when expected.

•135th Rifle Div has been deployed to 19th Army HQ (loc 35:34)
•136th Rifle Div has been deployed to 19th Army HQ (loc 35:34)
•137th Rifle Div (19th Army HQ) failed to deploy (40% chance, roll 64) [?]
•138th Rifle Div has been deployed to 19th Army HQ (loc 35:34)
•139th Rifle Div (19th Army HQ) failed to deploy (40% chance, roll 70) [?]
•140th Rifle Div (19th Army HQ) failed to deploy (40% chance, roll 66) [?]
•141st Rifle Div (19th Army HQ) failed to deploy (40% chance, roll 82) [?]
•13th Motorised Div (19th Army HQ) failed to deploy (40% chance, roll 54) [?]
•58th Tank Div (19th Army HQ) failed to deploy (40% chance, roll 84) [?]
•59th Tank Div (19th Army HQ) failed to deploy (40% chance, roll 72) [?]

The Daily Front Logs provide a full breakdown of reinforcement activity. You can see that a number of 19th Army Divisions arrived this turn and a number 'failed to deploy' and will attempt to do so on each following turn until they do

The standard 40% probability of arrival is modified by the terrain that the HQ is in. Once the HQ has been deployed it is free to move where ever it wishes and its subordinate Divisions will arrive in that same location. As reinforcements arrive by train, if the HQ moves off the transport grid then the probability of Divisions arriving will halve (down to 20%) as truck transport will need to be organised (debark off the train, hop in trucks, travel to the HQ) and they aren't in abundant supply.

•57th Tank Div (16th Army HQ) failed to deploy! (HQ not found)
•137th Rifle Div (19th Army HQ) failed to deploy (20% chance, roll 72) [?]
•139th Rifle Div has been deployed to 19th Army HQ (loc 35:33)
•140th Rifle Div (19th Army HQ) failed to deploy (20% chance, roll 32) [?]
•142nd Rifle Div (20th Army HQ) failed to deploy (40% chance, roll 93) [?]

LtGen. Kuszentsov has taken it upon himself to wander off into the countryside. Only one Division managed to catch up. The other two may take a while (20% chance of deployment). Note the entry for the 57th Tank Division at the top. It's failed to deploy because its HQ hasn't been placed on the map via an Action Card.

STAFF ADVICE

By far the best place to deploy your Army HQ's are in cities. Their subordinate Divisions will arrive quickly (80% chance per turn) and the Army can then move to where ever it is required. Cities also provide good defensive bonuses in the event that the Germans arrive unexpectedly.

On the other hand if the HQ moves to, or is already in, a city with its associated rail station infrastructure, the probability of Divisions arriving will double (up to 80%).

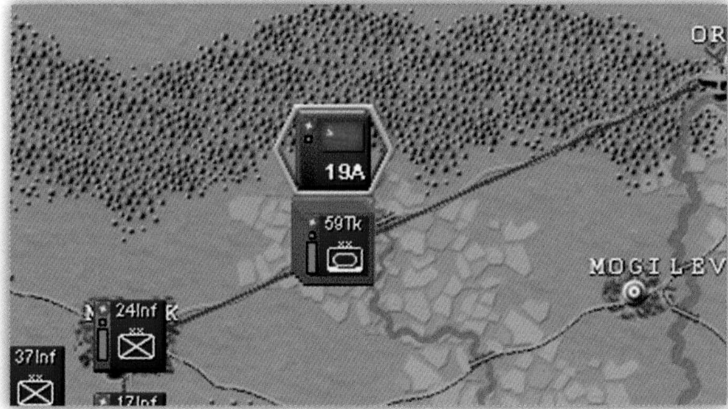

LtGen. Kuszentov heading north to the safety of the forest. What is he doing? Come back, man, come back! A stellar career in the Red Army isn't anticipated

Newly arrived Divisions incur a large Action Point penalty (-50 AP) but this only last for the turn of arrival.

LtGen. Kuznetsov's 19th Army is forming up. You can see three Divisions (on the right) that arrived the previous turn and are now fully mobile (not quite as LtGen. Kuznetsov failed to read his orders this turn and the 19th Army didn't activate so they only have 40 AP each). The four 'greyed out' Divisions arrived this turn and the combination of their 'Newly Arrived Reinforcement' penalty as well as LtGen. Kuznetsov's dilatory ways have ensured that they are immobile.

--- 139th Rifle Div (loc 35:33)
Army Partially activated, -30 AP
Newly arrived from the Interior, -50 AP

It's the following turn and LtGen. Kuznetsov is showing belated signs of action. More or less. He's achieved Partial activation which is enough for the newly arrived 139th Rifle Division to at least retain some Action Points (20 AP)

Asking a unit to Report Status! Or inspecting the Unit Modifier report will highlight the penalty.

SUMMARY

- Reinforcements arrive in two stages - Army HQ's first followed by their Divisions
- Army HQ's are deployed on the map by the Player by use of Action Cards ('Reinforcement' category)
- Army HQ's can be deployed anywhere, within their assigned front, on the transport grid
- Play the 'Change Orders' Action card to choose which front the Army HQ will deploy to
- Divisions arrive automatically but only after their HQ has been deployed
- Divisions have a probability of arriving each turn (standard 40%)
- If their HQ is not on the transport grid then this is halved (20%)
- If their HQ is in a city then it is doubled (80%)
- Divisions incur a -50 AP penalty on their turn of arrival
- The Reinforcements tab (bottom centre) provides a list of forthcoming reinforcements
- The Daily Front Logs contain full details of all reinforcement activity

6.2.10. COMMUNICATIONS

The Soviets had a severe shortage of radios. Most communications between the various components of the Red Army were conducted by fixed phone lines or telegraph. The German's invasion severely

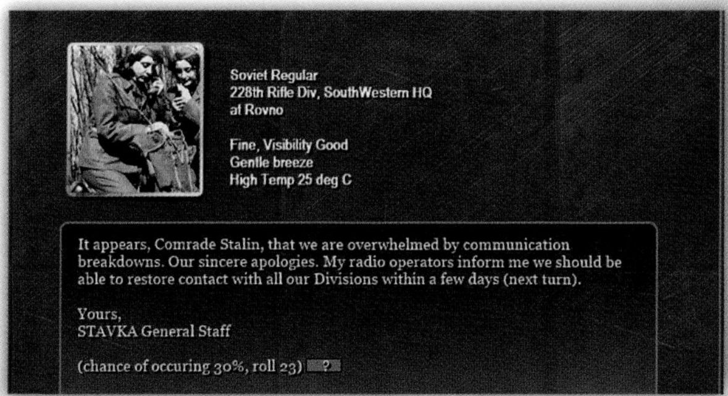

What's happening with the 228th Rifle Division? Nobody knows

disrupted both and communication between the front and STAVKA was problematic. An inflexible and complicated command structure didn't help.

Whenever the Soviet Player requests a unit to Report Status! a random roll is made and if it is less than, or equal, to the 'Communication threshold' (there is no need to remember this, it's for explanatory purposes only), the request will fail and no further units, that turn, will be able to report their status.

Unit Modifier reports for Armies can also suffer from the same malady.

26th Army HQ - at Lvov

We have been unable to contact the Army, Comrade Stalin, due to an unexplained breakdown in communications.

We are doing what we can to restore telephone and radio links. We regret to inform you that the information you have requested is currently not available.

(chance of occuring 30%, roll 23) [?]

To improve communications play the 'Reorganise' card (see 6.2.5.4 Reorganise).

6.2.11. SOVIET LOGISTICS

The Red Army were falling back onto interior lines and logistics weren't anywhere near the issue that

--- Reinforcements
•4 Div's Deployed, 83 Div's Failed to deploy, 22 Div's Pending deployment [?]
•10 Army HQ's are awaiting deployment [?]

Each time the card is played the 'Communications threshold' lowers by -5% (it starts at 30%).

it was for the Germans with their limited resources and over stretched logistical pipelines.

Each Soviet Front gets a fixed allowance of fuel per turn. There are no bases, depots or pipelines, simply a central pool of fuel for each front. They will rarely be short of fuel.

Supply works the same as for the Germans but due to the shortening distances between STAVKA and their armies it is, generally, not a concern.

There are two instances where it may be. Firstly if a unit is cut-off. Expect their supply situation to rapidly deteriorate. For more information on this and for a possible remedy see 6.2.5.3 Breakout.

There are additional sources of supply at both Leningrad and Stalingrad which act as back-ups in the event of Armies becoming isolated from STAVKA.

In summary, logistics are not a concern for the Soviet Player except in the case of adverse circumstances where you would reasonably expect there to be problems.

7. CAMPAIGN SPECIFICS

7.1. FINLAND ▶

At the commencement of the campaign the German Player can activate the Finnish forces and move into Russia. Up to the historical Finnish/Soviet border which is marked on the map with red 'B' symbols.

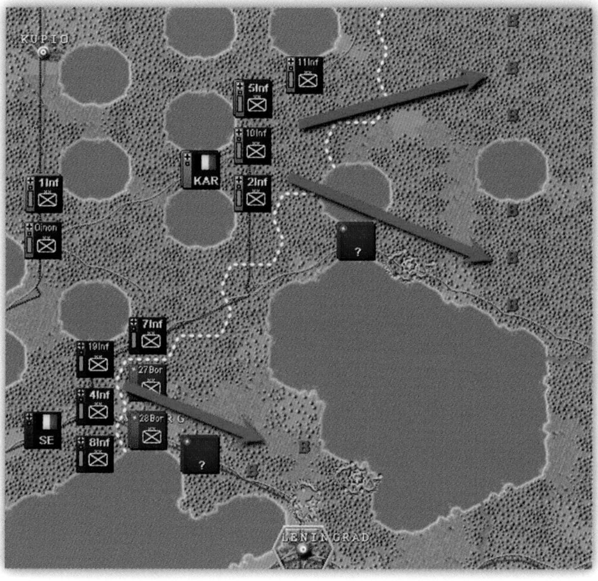

This was the official border between the two countries prior to the Winter War of 1939 - 1940. Finland felt justified in recapturing land that it had so recently ceded to Russia during peace negotiations at the conclusion of the Winter war. Going beyond this into Russia proper was another matter altogether and was tantamount to invading Russia sovereign territory

Until the Finnish government authorises a full invasion of Russia no Finnish unit can cross the border (they can move *onto* the hexes with the red 'B' but not beyond them). The Daily AGN Theatre log will let you know the current status. Individual unit reports will highlight this as well as the usual 'Unit Modifier' reports.

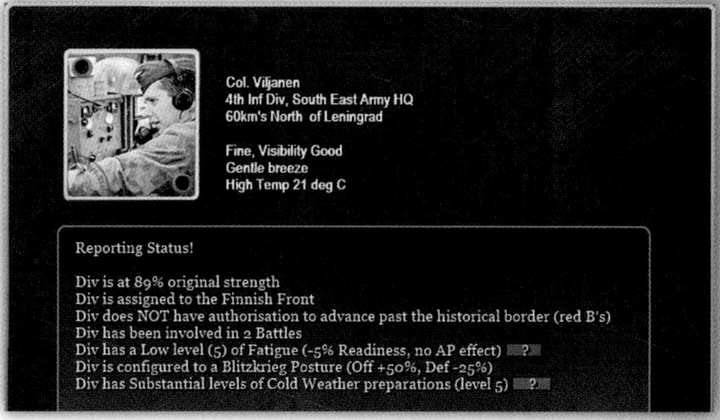

Col. Viljanen
4th Inf Div, South East Army HQ
60km's North of Leningrad
Fine, Visibility Good
Gentle breeze
High Temp 21 deg C
Reporting Status!
Div is at 89% original strength
Div is assigned to the Finnish Front
Div does NOT have authorisation to advance past the historical border (red B's)
Div has been involved in 2 Battles
Div has a Low level (5) of Fatigue (-5% Readiness, no AP effect) ?
Div is configured to a Blitzkrieg Posture (Off +50%, Def -25%)
Div has Substantial levels of Cold Weather preparations (level 5) ?

Col. Viljanen's 4th Infantry Division have fought their way across to the historic border but that's as far as they are going for the foreseeable future. Unlike the German Army, they are ready for winter

Daily Summary AG NORTH 22 . June . 1941

--- Command
- The Finnish Gov't has NOT agreed to going beyond the border [?]
- F.M von Leeb, AGN, is willing to consider new ideas (Rel +ve) [?]
- F.M von Leeb currently has not determined a Command Focus [?]

Command Übertretung!

The following Divisions have moved outside their assigned areas of operation. General Staff will find a way to accommodate the situation but the sooner it is rectified the better.

+ You incur a PP penalty for each unit that moves outside its assigned theatre to reflect the command and logistical disruption that this incurs. The further a unit crosses into another theatre, the greater the penalty

- 11th Inf Div (Karelian Army HQ), penalty incurred Finnish Unit advancing without Authorisation! -10 PP
390km's North East of Leningrad, Loc 40:1

There is a 10PP per unit penalty. Having fared badly in the recent Winter War, the Finnish government was extremely reluctant to provoke the Soviets unnecessarily

If you order any unit cross the historic border, prior to receiving authorisation, there will be fierce political consequences.

Cross border attacks (having Finnish units attack, but not move across, the red 'B' border) will likely result in a 'Cross Border Incident' with adverse consequences for the German Player. It is a very delicate political situation that must be respected.

--- Political Points
•Delegated decisions, previous turn -10 PP [?]
•Theatre Violations by units -10 PP
•Command Allowance from High Command +4 PP [?]

Mishandling the Finnish frontier can result in a dearth of Political Points

The Finnish government will consider authorising an attack into Russia proper only when they can see the Germans making significant gains. This translates, in game turns, into the capture of Luga and Narva, large population centres on the approach to Leningrad.

Each turn, after at least one of the cities has been captured, the mood of the Finnish government is polled. There is a 5% chance per turn of them agreeing to cross the historic border. If both Luga and Narva have been captured the chance is doubled (10%). The Daily AGN Theatre log provides details of the probability of the Finnish government changing their mind.

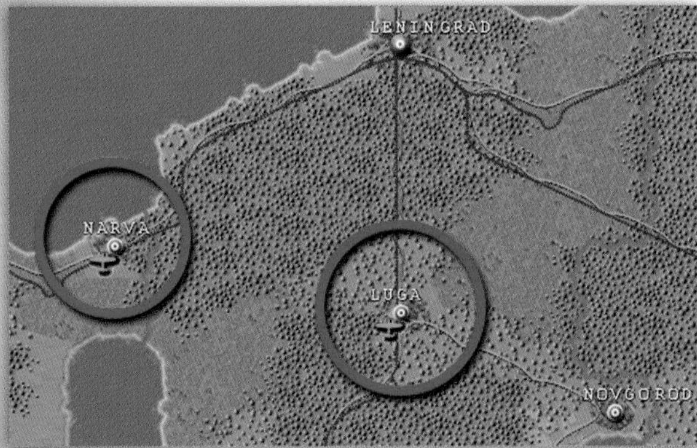

The two cities that will help convince the Finns that the Germans might be doing well

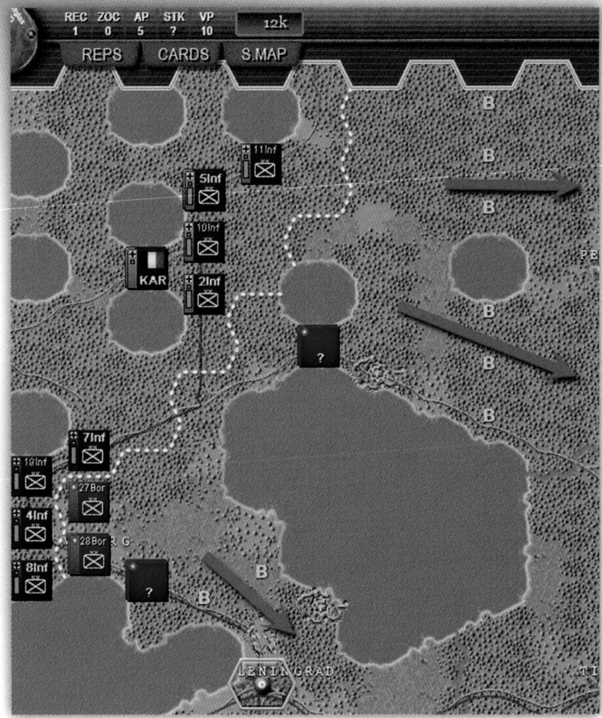

Authorisation has been given! The Finns are free to advance

Once authorisation has been given there will be prominent message, at the start of both player's turns, to highlight this. The red 'B' indicators will change to a blue 'B' (red for stop, blue for go).

ASK YOUR STAFF

- **Why can't I have more control over when Finland activates?**
  Finland was a fiercely independent country. It never signed a formal alliance between it and the German Reich, a source of great consternation to the Germans as the campaign progressed (Finland wasn't formally obligated to do anything). Among German allies, Finland was the only working democratic state and had little interest in undergoing a fascist transformation.
  Hitler placed excessive demands upon Finland during the war but the Finnish government acted, at all times, in its own best interest, always wary of not upsetting the Russian Bear to the point of

retaliation. The Finns, in the game, as well as historically, will *consider* going further into Russia only when they can see the Germans making solid progress. The Germans were unable to influence the actions of the Finnish government, beyond the point of naked self interest, and the game reflects this by having a variable Finnish entry point rather than a, 'spend 'x' amount of Political Points', type of fixed, predictable, option.

Finland AGREES to advance beyond their historic border with Russia! [?]

Notification is given to both sides of the change of status

The Daily AGN Theatre Log, as well as all the usual unit and Army reports, will highlight the freedom now granted Finnish units.

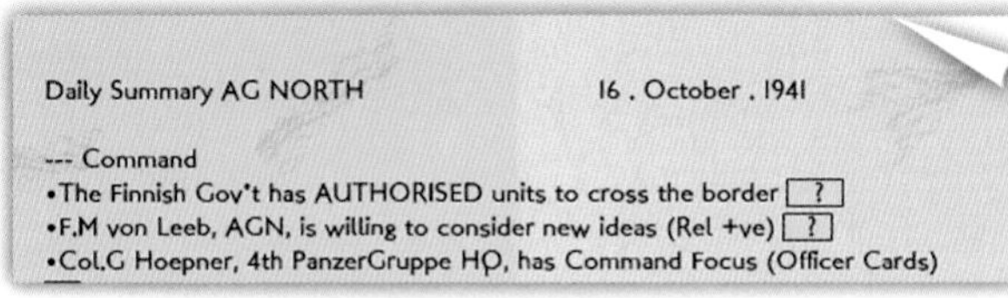
Daily Summary AG NORTH 16 . October . 1941

--- Command
- The Finnish Gov't has AUTHORISED units to cross the border [?]
- F.M von Leeb, AGN, is willing to consider new ideas (Rel +ve) [?]
- Col.G Hoepner, 4th PanzerGruppe HQ, has Command Focus (Officer Cards)

The Soviets, at wars end, extracted a heavy price from Finland in terms of territory and reparations. The Finns suffered heavy losses and had to cope with very large numbers of refugees from Karelia (captured by the Soviets). Despite all this they ended the war with their country largely intact and their army still fit for service. Finland was also Germany's only European ally that wasn't occupied.

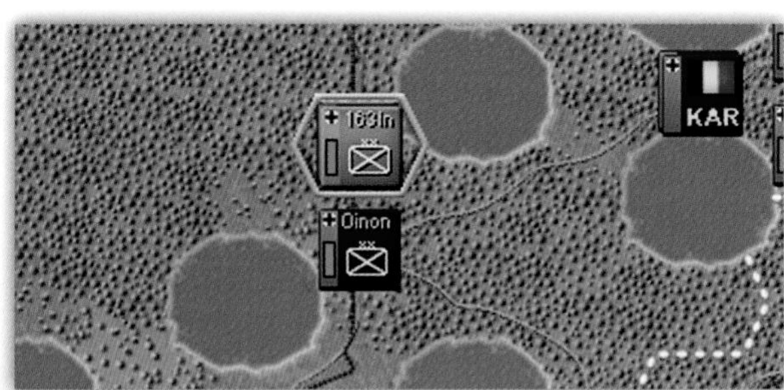

The 163rd Infantry Division was seconded to the Finnish front. It suffered heavy losses as it wasn't equipped, or trained, for the forest fighting that was a feature of the northern war

7.1.1. FINLAND WHAT IF?

Both sides have What If? Options regarding Finland during the special Pre-Start turn. Like all What If? Decisions these are entirely optional and can be safely ignored.

The Germans have the interesting option of committing the Finns to a formal military alliance.

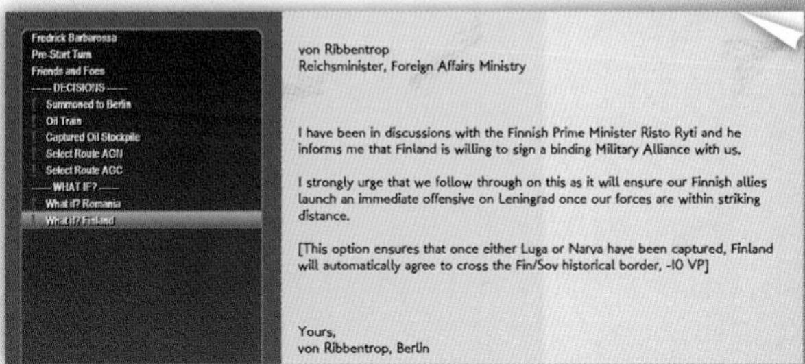

von Ribbentrop
Reichsminister, Foreign Affairs Ministry

I have been in discussions with the Finnish Prime Minister Risto Ryti and he informs me that Finland is willing to sign a binding Military Alliance with us.

I strongly urge that we follow through on this as it will ensure our Finnish allies launch an immediate offensive on Leningrad once our forces are within striking distance.

[This option ensures that once either Luga or Narva have been captured, Finland will automatically agree to cross the Fin/Sov historical border, -10 VP]

Yours,
von Ribbentrop, Berlin

An alliance will force the Finns into immediate activation once a key city is captured. It comes at a heavy cost in Victory Points but allows a twin pronged attack on the northern Soviet front and the greatest opportunity of capturing Leningrad

The Soviets have equally intriguing options. They are in a position to threaten Finland into submission.

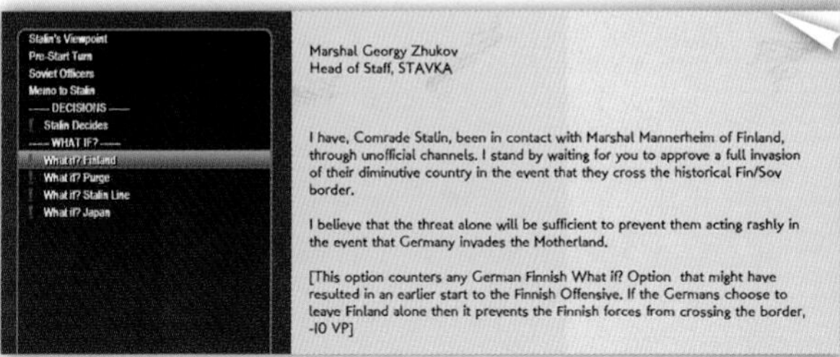

Marshal Georgy Zhukov
Head of Staff, STAVKA

I have, Comrade Stalin, been in contact with Marshal Mannerheim of Finland, through unofficial channels. I stand by waiting for you to approve a full invasion of their diminutive country in the event that they cross the historical Fin/Sov border.

I believe that the threat alone will be sufficient to prevent them acting rashly in the event that Germany invades the Motherland.

[This option counters any German Finnish What if? Option that might have resulted in an earlier start to the Finnish Offensive. If the Germans choose to leave Finland alone then it prevents the Finnish forces from crossing the border, -10 VP]

DESIGN NOTE

There is some gamesmanship involved here as neither side will be aware of what the other is doing. These two options are largely for PBEM games although they can provide some interesting alternative strategies for single play.

If they choose the first option, 'Threaten Invasion', then any military alliance that the Germans have signed with the Finns will be negated (no effect, Finnish activation works normally). If the Germans haven't instigated a military alliance then the threat of severe consequences will be enough to prevent the Finns activating for the duration of the campaign (they will be unable to cross the red 'B' border).

The AI will not utilise any Finnish What If? Decisions.

By choosing the first option the Soviet Player can neutralise the threat from Finland. This is a viable strategy if the Northern Front is chosen as the Soviet Objective

7.2. ROMANIAN FRONT ▶

The 600 kilometre Romanian front is frozen for the first full turn of the campaign. All units within are immobile. On the second turn it will activate and the German Player is free to launch an offensive across the Prut river.

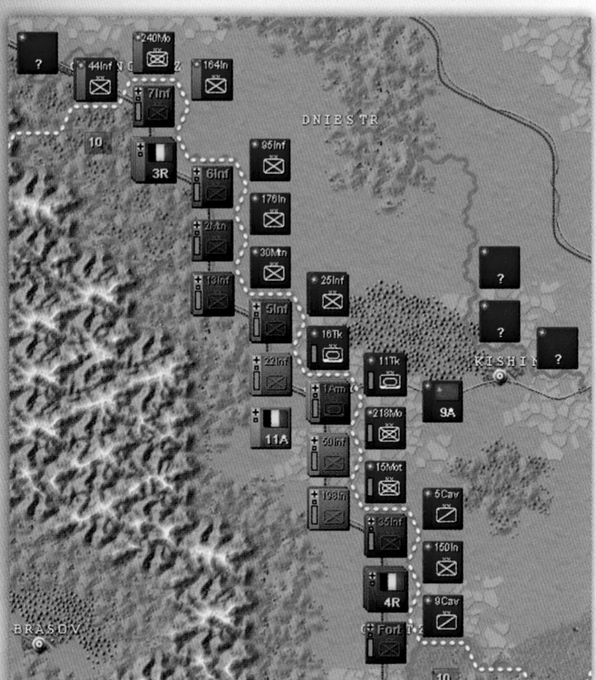

The length and breadth of the Romanian front

Asking a unit to Report Status! will highlight its immobility on the first turn.

The Romanian front activation is automatic on the second full turn of the campaign. The German Player has access to a What If? Decision in the special Pre-Start turn that enables him to activate the Romanian front a turn earlier, or later.

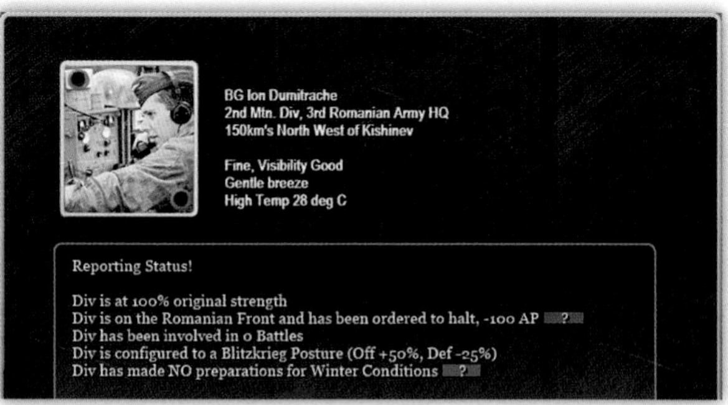

BG Ion Dumitrache's 2nd Mountain Division is awaiting word from above

Hitler was very reluctant to inform his Romanian allies of the start date for Barbarossa. Rightly or wrongly, his view of the Romanian military was that they were 'cowardly, corrupt, rotten and fit for use only when protected by broad rivers'. Marshal Antonescu, no doubt unaware of the Führer's opinion, ordered his troops to attack Russia on the same day that Barbarossa commenced with the intention of recapturing Romanian territory (Bessarabia) taken by the Soviets a year before. However very little was done until the 2nd July '41. The game takes a midline viewpoint and allows the front to activate on the 26th July '41.

7.2.1. ROMANIAN WHAT IF?

During the special Pre-Turn the German Player can, if he wishes, use this decision to activate the Romanian front a turn earlier (in line with the official commencement of Barbarossa) or a turn later (the third full turn). There are minor Victory Point implications for both options.

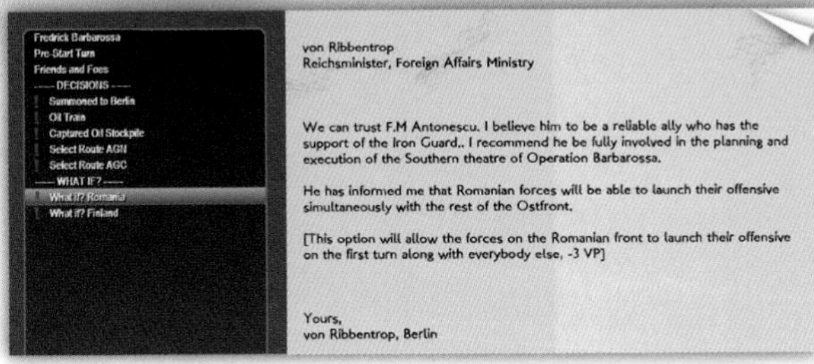

Fredrick Barbarossa
Pre-Start Turn
Friends and Foes
—— DECISIONS ——
Summoned to Berlin
Oil Train
Captured Oil Stockpile
Select Route AGN
Select Route AGC
—— WHAT IF? ——
What if? Romania
What if? Finland
von Ribbentrop
Reichsminister, Foreign Affairs Ministry
We can trust F.M Antonescu. I believe him to be a reliable ally who has the support of the Iron Guard.. I recommend he be fully involved in the planning and execution of the Southern theatre of Operation Barbarossa.
He has informed me that Romanian forces will be able to launch their offensive simultaneously with the rest of the Ostfront.
[This option will allow the forces on the Romanian front to launch their offensive on the first turn along with everybody else, -3 VP]
Yours,
von Ribbentrop, Berlin

As the campaign in the east dragged on past '41 the Romanians made significant contributions in men and blood. Relations with their neighbour, Hungary, were particularly bad

SUMMARY

- The Romanian front is frozen for the first full turn and normal thereafter
- The Finns are able to immediately advance to their historic border (red 'B' border)
- Finnish units can safely enter the hexes marked with a red 'B' but not go beyond
- To go beyond the historic border the Finns require authorisation from their government
- Violating the border will incur very steep penalties as will cross border attacks.
- Authorisation is randomly determined only once Luga or Narva have been captured by the Germans
- The probability of authorisation being granted is 5% per turn (10% if both cities have been taken)
- Once authorisation is give the red 'B' border changes to a blue 'B' border and the Finns can cross freely.
- Formal notification of the change of status is given to both sides when it occurs.
- The Germans had a seconded Division, the 163rd Infantry, on the Finnish front
- Both sides have What If? Decisions available in the special Pre-Start turn that can affect the Finnish front

8. MISCELLANEOUS

8.1. ABBREVIATIONS & TERMINOLOGY ▶

Abwehr:	German Military Intelligence organisation
AP:	Action Points (used by units for movement and combat)
Armeegruppe :	Army Group
AGN/AGC/AGS:	Army Group North/Centre/South
Bbls:	Barrels of fuel (a barrel is 159 litres or 42 US gallons)
Eisenbahntruppe:	German Rail construction battalions
Einsatzgruppen:	SS para-military death squads.
Fast Division:	A Division that has any wheeled or tracked vehicles, eg. Panzer, Motorised, Tank, etc.
Feldmarschall:	Field Marshal
Front:	There are three fronts (delineated by dashed red lines, North, Centre & South). Fronts are the Soviet equivalent of German theatres
Front Commander:	Each Soviet front has a Front Commander (Marshal) who resides in a Front HQ. Front Commanders can change throughout the game
FSB:	Forward Supply Base (see Logistics)
Führer:	Hitler
Heer:	The German Army
Hitler:	Supreme Leader of Germany, also referred to as the Führer
Logistical Pipelines:	Rail and Truck Column links that combine to transport the fuel (shown visually on the map)
Luftflotte:	German Air Fleet. There was one per theatre.
OKH:	Oberkommando des Heeres, the Supreme High Command of the German Army. F.M Von Halder was in charge during the time period of the game and which is the role that the German Player takes.
OKW:	Oberkommando der Wehrmacht, the Supreme Command of the German Armed Forces (Army, Airforce, Navy). F.M Von Brauchitsch is in command during the time period of the game
Ostfront :	Eastern front
POL:	Petrol, oil and lubricants. 'Fuel' for short.
PP:	Political Points
Panzergruppe:	A German Army consisting of predominately fast (wheeled and tracked) divisions.
Rasputitsa:	Mud Season
Regime:	Side, e.g German or Soviet
Slow Division:	A Division that has only foot or horse, eg. Infantry, Cavalry
STAVKA:	The Soviet equivalent of the German High Command (the highest level HQ's available)
TAC:	Tactical Air Support (German)
Theatre:	There are three theatres (delineated by dashed red lines, AGN, AGC, AGS). Theatres are the German equivalents of Soviet fronts

Theatre Commander: Each German theatre has a Theatre Commander (Field Marshal) who resides in a Theatre HQ. Theatre Commanders are fixed throughout the game

VP: Victory Points

VVS: Soviet Air Force (RussianВоенно-воздушные силы,'*Voyenno-Vozdushnye Sily*', literally "Military Air Forces")

ZOC: Zone of control

Zone Interior: (ZI) German homeland.

8.2. HOT KEYS ▶

8.2.1. GAME WIDE

GAME WIDE HOT KEYS	
Hot key	Effect
ESC	Exit a window or tab
SPACE	Continue to the next message Exit windows like Trooptype, officer or message pop-up Acknowledge a miscellaneous pop up screen, + Abort move / group move. Initiate combat, end turn confirmation.
RIGHT CLICK	If the 'Auto Mouse Over' preference is switched OFF you'll need to Right Click on question marks to obtain tool tips.
MOUSE WHEEL	Can be used to scroll through the report tab and decision bundles
MOUSE HOVER	Over any '?' tool tip and most interface elements will provide further information

8.2.2. MAIN SCREEN

MAIN SCREEN HOT KEYS	
Hot key	Effect
F1	Preferences tab (press again or ESC to close)
F2	Briefing tab (press again or ESC to close)
F3	Statistics tab (press again or ESC to close)
F4	OOB tab (press again or ESC to close)
F5	Reports tab (press again or ESC to close)
F6	Action Card tab (press again or ESC to close)
F7	Strategic Map (press again or ESC to close)
F8	Minimap (press again or ESC to close)
M	Move (individual unit)
G	Group Move (stack, will move at speed of the slowest unit)
A	Attack (click on unit to be attacked then press 'A')
+ / MOUSE WHEEL	Zoom in
- / MOUSE WHEEL	Zoom out
< / >	Previous unit / Next unit
← / ↑ / → / ↓	Scroll map
0	Hide units
1	Units use Silhouettes
2	Units use NATO symbols
4	Toggle extra hex info ON/OFF (logistical icons)

8.2.3. HISTORY SCREEN

HISTORY SCREEN HOT KEYS	
Hot key	Effect
P	Start or Stop Autoplay

8.3. CREDITS

8.3.1. VR DESIGNS

Game Engine
Victor Reijkersz

AI Development
Victor Reijkersz

Producer
Victor Reijkersz

Game Design
Cameron Harris

Programming
Victor Reijkersz, Cameron Harris

Manual
Cameron Harris

General Artwork
Cameron Harris

Equipment and Troop Illustrations
Nicolas Eskubi

GUI Artwork
Marc von Marial

Hex Artwork
Frederic Genot

Music
Tempest for an Angel

Beta Testers
A big thanks to all the many testers who did an excellent job of keeping the project on track and heading in the right direction. Special thanks to the following for services above and beyond the call of duty.

Pierre Roduit, Audie Radzvickas, Jose Linares, Bill Bates, Gary Gardner, Per Ostergaard, Zakblood and Nicolas Ackad

8.3.2. MATRIX GAMES

Chairman
Jd Mcneil

Development Director
Iain Mcneil

Producer
Tamas Kiss

Operations Director
Erik Rutins

Technical Director
Philip Veale

Creative Director
Richard Evans

Marketing Director
Marco A. Minoli

Public Relations Manager
Olivier Georges

Community Manager
Daniele Meneghini

Production Design
Marta Falbo

Manual Layout
Myriam Bell

Production Lead
Matthew Davies

Production Assistant
Andrew Loveridge

Administration
Dean Walker, Liz Stoltz

Customer Support Staff
Paulo Costa, Joseph Miller

Web Development
Valery Vidershpan, Andrea Nicola, Fernando Turi

9. DESIGNER NOTES – COMMAND

9.1. WHAT ARE WE TRYING TO ACHIEVE? ▶

Designer intent

If I had to summarise the design in a single word it would be COMMAND.

Specifically Operational Command in a Military context.

Imagine yourself - mid morning, a murky mug of ersatz coffee in hand, staring as junior Oberleutnants mark the latest updates on the big operational map spread across the wall of your drafty headquarters. Squinting suspiciously at the growing pile of reports on your desk.

There is another pile, equally large, full of requests. The phone rings constantly. Your staff are spiking teletype printouts from the front ever higher and Colonel Rat Face, currently in dispute with your Quartermaster General, is impatiently waiting for you next door, demanding that you intervene.

That's the game, right there.

You will have limited time and command resources. Delegation will become a necessity rather than an option.

You'll be dealing with people. Strongly defined personalities. People under pressure. They can be difficult and demanding. You aren't going to be able to please everybody.

You'll be issuing orders. Defining and shaping a strategy that will enable your forces to traverse large distances and overcome opposition in order to take and hold their objectives.

But some of those forces aren't going to want to move. Perhaps you shouldn't have delegated that particular decision?

AND CAN SOMEBODY PLEASE TELL ME WHY THE HECK MY PANZERS HAVEN'T GOT ENOUGH FUEL?

Because there is a shortage of signals on the Army Group North rail network it appears that there has been a collision. Deliveries have been delayed. Because you chose to allocate the limited Signaling supplies to F.M von Rundstedt's Rail Construction Battalions way down South several weeks ago. Because it was easier to do that than send them North when the Führer had shifted his priorities to the Ukraine. Because you have a better working relationship with F.M von Rundstedt than the overly cautious whiner who is holding down Armeegruppe Nordwärts.

Above all you are in COMMAND. It is this gnarly, gritty experience of front line, Operational Command that the game seeks to capture.

9.2. THE LAST COMMANDER I MET WAS MADE BY MATTEL ▶

Defining Command

Before going any further it's worth discussing what is meant by Command. How does it differ from Leadership and Management?

A Manager is a title given to you. It's a position within a hierarchy. A Leader, on the other hand, is a title that other people bestow upon you.Command could be defined as the exercise of authority over military forces. A Commander is a mix of both a Manager and, hopefully, a Leader.

Your rank, akin to that of a Manager, is something that is given to you. In a military context your rank alone provides a proportional measure of authority. People will do as you ask, because of your position, as to do otherwise would incur adverse consequences.

This is no different to being a Line Manager in an Company making widgets. People below you will do as you ask because you are their boss. Ignoring you risks them being fired.

Leadership is what makes the difference between an ordinary, run of the mill, Manager and an effective one. People are hard wired to go the extra mile for somebody they respect rather than a person merely going through the motions because they're either not interested or they've been promoted above their level of competence. They aren't a *Leader*.

A Military Commander has an advantage over a Line Manager in that the hierarchy he is operating within is a more strictly defined one and his subordinates have a greater likelihood of obeying his orders. But without the skills of Leadership he will still run into the same resistance and push back that a '*by the rules*' Line Manager would. His subordinates will find ways to subvert his orders just as much as the group of team leaders on the factory floor will be creative in ignoring the demands of their Line Manager boss.

Effective Command therefore infers Leadership.

A no nonsense definition of Leadership would be the art of getting people to do what you ask, willingly. A Leader brings people with him. Leaders have followers.

But enough of these Management Consultant cliches. There is a war on, you say. It's different to the world of business or bureaucracy. Resources are limited. The raw material of decisions isn't money, it's people's lives. You are playing for bigger stakes. There isn't the luxury of being able to sit down, form a committee and argue over a dot point list of future actionable items. Time is critical. Something needs to happen. NOW.

You would be correct. There are unique aspects to Military Command that aren't found elsewhere. But Command, for all its differences, still involves people.

People require Leadership.

9.3. WHERE ARE THE VITAL ORGANS? WE'LL BE OPERATING TOMORROW ▶

Which elements to Model?

Determining which elements of Command and Leadership to represent isn't easy. They are both fairly abstract concepts. How do you program into a game characters who may, or may not, be willing to follow you, the Player?

How, for example, do you portray the war induced stress and pressure that those characters are under?

You could, perhaps, have a selection of soundtracks that play on demand for a certain character. As his sense of humour progressively fades away he could be made to swear at you in an increasingly vocal and inventive manner. But would having a nebulous, computer generated character, casting aspersions on your mother and your ancestry be an enjoyable experience?

What would your wife or girlfriend say when they heard the high volume, barrack room rant of an unhappy, stressed, character? Would the crude bluntness of the language prevent you from playing the game only after your kids had gone to bed and were safely asleep behind closed doors?

Could you resist the urge to start swearing back at Colonel Rat face because he isn't snapping to attention and doing what you ask? Is your relaxing couple of hours in the evening to become a stand up, full on, swear fest as you attempt to give back as good as you are getting?

It wouldn't be long before you are being asked - more likely told - by your better half to take your computer and to go and play that *disgusting game* in the cold, poorly lit, garage.

With the dog. The dog would keep you company.

Clearly there are limitations in what can be achieved.

But if we take a step back there are a number of easily defined elements that could be modelled in a manner that didn't involve you spending quality time shivering in the cold with your dog.

There is a Chain of Command. Superiors and Subordinates. Decisions. Delegation. Resources.

There are other, subtler, aspects.

Imperfect knowledge. The fact that the people you are dealing with have their own concerns and agendas. The inevitable politics as people lobby for scarce resources. The restrictions that operating within a hierarchy might place upon you. The Dark side of the war. The uneven, stop-start nature of Command where sometimes it rains and sometimes it pours.

9.3.1. WHO IS GOING TO MAKE MY CUP OF COFFEE IN THE MORNING?

The Chain of Command

This is a little trickier than it first appears. Yes there is a Chain of Command. But where does the Player sit within it?

Most military simulation type games answer this by having you, the Player, being at the very apex of whatever Chain of Command exists. It's an easy way to do it. You are the guy in charge. You make all the decisions. There is no need to worry about the implications of a hierarchy.

There are multiple subordinates who willing carry out your wishes. They are typically portrayed as a collection of stats. Their main purpose is to apply those stats as bonuses to various game mechanics. They have no opinions or agendas of their own. Their raison d'etre is to carry out your orders as invisible, one dimensional characters, who are *there* in the same way as a mountain is *there*.

Of course not all games are like this. There are some excellent examples in other genres but they are rarely found in the world of military simulations.

Back to the topic. The game takes a dual approach to the Chain of Command. For the Germans the Player is placed within the hierarchy whereas the Soviet Player finds himself representing the man at the top, Stalin. This allows the game to present two very different Command experiences.

Traction equipment lacking: Tests now in progress to determine serviceability of French traction equipment. Only limited mobility. Will have supply vehicles, but tactical mobility cannot be achieved (no ammunition columns). Two batteries are put on self-propelled mounts, to serve as heavy tank destroyers. "Traction Bns., motorised" could be formed, but chain of command and control would be very difficult in practice.

F.M Von Halder's War Diary, 27th February, 1941

If you're Stalin, you're not going to be fussed about politics. Or opinions. You're a ruthless dictator. Anybody steps out of line and you'll have them lined up in front of a firing squad in short order. There is a directness and simplicity in being able to do exactly as you wish.

Is this then, the typical war game approach as mentioned above? No. People are still involved and while they aren't going to argue the toss they will present other challenges. Still, once you put the Player at the head of the hierarchy the people aspect becomes less important. They tend to fade into the background. There needs to be a different focus.

What that focus might be did indeed present a design challenge. The approach I settled on was to make it an internal one - Stalin's state of mind. More on this later but, for the Soviet Player, the role of the people involved, all of them subordinates, is not themselves but in what affect they have on Stalin himself.

9.3.2. ZEN AND THE ART OF KNOWING WHO TO SALUTE

Superiors and Subordinates

Once it was decided to model a Chain of Command there was a need to fill the hierarchy with people. For the Soviet side they were all subordinates but the German side involved an equal mix of superiors as well.

Subordinates are easy to deal with. You give them orders and they carry them out. Perhaps not quite how you'd like them to and perhaps with a degree of resistance but, overall, if you ask them, they'll do it.

Superiors immediately run into the problem of authority. They are your boss. You've got one at work and you've probably got one at home. Do you want another, game based, one telling you what to do?

Having an upset subordinate yelling at you might not be ideal but having the computer speakers spout forth curt, arrogant, orders from above, demanding that you do this or that, is only going to have you grumpily checking the prices of a new monitor the following day and having to explain why you've got a bandaged hand.

A key design challenge that had to be overcome was how to give a sense of being within a hierarchy while at the same time not hobbling the Player's ability to play the game as he'd like. This is, as you'd imagine, a pretty fine line. Go too far in the direction of authority and the Player ends up chaffing against unwanted restrictions. Swing back the other way and you've lost the immersion of having to answer to Superiors.

The German High Command structure helped in this. Rather than the highly efficient, well oiled machine that it is typically portrayed as it was, in reality, a dysfunctional organisation with many quirks. There were reasons for this and it deserves a detailed explanation of its own but, for the moment, we can assume that the lines of authority were, in many cases, fuzzy.

Von Paulus (on phone) about his conversation with Jodl on the command set-up in North Africa. All the Führer cares about is that Rommel should not be hampered by any superior Hq. Put over him. Jodl will send up another plan.

F.M Von Halder's War Diary, 13th May 1941

There were many cases of overlapping authorities and individual power bases. Who reported to who was clear cut only where everybody involved was a professional military officer. Higher up, where there were Party members and assorted flunkies, it was a lot vaguer.

It was greatly complicated by the micromanagement and interference of Hitler himself, the man sitting at the top of the Chain of Command. He hadn't read the book on 'How to Delegate, sit back and let your Generals Win the War'. Then again, perhaps he had and it had ended up in the rubbish bin. Hitler's interference was a doubled edged sword. There were times when his intuitive grasp of a situation was far superior to any of the professional military judgements on offer. As the campaign progressed he became more and more convinced that he knew better. Hubris be thy name.

Eventually the great gambler succumbed to the inevitable 'reversion to the mean' that applies to all mortals. Sheer force of personality and a domineering, dictatorial, manner couldn't overcome the law of averages. Like any compulsive gambler he ended up losing more than he started with.

Which is a topic well outside the scope of this book. But in terms of superiors it offers some interesting angles. The Player has the role of Operational Commander of the Eastern front - F.M Franz Halder. He had a direct superior officer, that of F.M Von Brauchitsch who was Commander in Chief of the German Army. Both are professional military men and it was a clear cut relationship.

Except it wasn't. F.M Von Brauchitsch was considered ineffectual in dealing with Hitler. Here is a superior who, on occasion, would step forward and do his job but who, most of the time, was too busy dealing with his own problems. Hitler was his personal banker. Von Brauchitsch was in heavy debt to the Fuhrer. He lacked the moral fibre to stand up to Hitler when it was necessary. By the end of 1941 he was gone. A convenient scapegoat for the failure to take Moscow and in failing health. Exit stage right.

Then there were the motley cast of Party characters who were all higher up the Chain of

Command but whose influence over the Player's assigned role varied and was, at times, murky. They were superiors but off to one side, tangential to the main game. But all of them were capable of exerting an influence when the need arose. We could consider them to be part time Superiors.

The German Command structure was unique in that authority over logistical matters was split between two people - General's Gercke and Wagner. Logistical concerns are always going to play an important part of an invasion of a country as geographically vast as Russia. Gercke and Wagner are destined to have staring roles in a game portraying Operation Barbarossa.

Which raises the question of whether they were superiors or subordinates? They were neither. Both were in the category best defined as 'unclear'. Both straddled multiple roles in dual headquarters (OKH & OKW).

This is a gift. Here are two characters dealing with the one key function. It's a little like having two separate builders work simultaneously on an extension for your house. They both have their own teams of subcontractors. They are both jointly building your extension. Yet when there is a problem who do you talk to? Is one going to blame the other? Are you going to have to take sides? How are you going to keep them both happy and maintain the momentum?

What about inter service rivalries? Naval matters were largely constrained to the bathtub. They did play a part but it was the kind of role that you'd hire somebody off the street for. They'd be instructed to say a few lines, smile at the camera and don't cause any trouble.

For the Luftwaffe, however, you'd need a competent actor, one with enough gravitas to carry the part. It's a major role. The Air war was an important aspect of the campaign. Hermann Goering, the corpulent, overdressed Reichsmarschall, competently holds down this role with his own unique style. He is both a superior in the chain of command and a character with whom the player will have a lot of contact with. He was colourful, unpleasant, eccentric and a take-no-prisoners political infighter. Perfect.

9.3.3. IT WOULD HELP IF I WASN'T SURROUNDED BY IDIOTS

Delegation

Being in Command entails making a lot of decisions. A fundamental rule is that the higher up the Chain of Command you climb the more decisions there are to make. This applies equally to the Joint Chiefs of Staff and the CEO of a Fortune 500 company.

Typically the increase in decisions required escalates in an exponential manner with each step up the hierarchy. It doesn't take long before anyone attempting to 'do-it-all' is overwhelmed by sheer volume. It's not hard to find examples of people who have reached an evolutionary dead end as a micro manager.

Delegation steps in. Commanders have staff. They have subordinates. Their job is to take care of all the lower level decisions, freeing up the Commander for the important ones.

A model of Command would be very one dimensional if it didn't incorporate delegation. You would be, once again, elevating the Player up to a God like status where Command is a mere wave of the hand.

Delegation implies tension. You're busy, you've got a lot on your plate. There isn't time to personally take care of everything, even if your staff have ensured you are only dealing with the important decisions.

Choosing which decisions to delegate is an interesting decision in itself. Having your Chief of Staff deal with a matter is likely to result in a less optimal outcome than if you tackled it yourself. His grasp of the bigger picture, his strategic understanding is at a lower level than your own. As it should be. He's not in charge, you are.

In order to make this model work there needs to be a currency of Command. A finite resource that is accumulated and spent. Which would be Political Points (PP). These are an abstract concept that encompass your personal time and energy, your political goodwill and your available staff resources.

Political Points allow decisions to be quantified. Yes, you can choose *that* option but it will require 'x' amount of PP's. Certain decision options require more PP's than others. At times you aren't going to have enough PP's to cover all the decisions. Delegation becomes necessary.

Do you keep a reserve of PP's against a rainy day when a really crucial decision might turn up or do you spend, spend, spend, moving forward on a wing and a prayer?

9.3.4. THERE ARE KNOWN UNKNOWNS AND UNKNOWN UNKNOWNS

Imperfect Knowledge

Our model of Command is shaping up. We've got a hierarchy, superiors and subordinates, decisions to be made, a currency of Command and a need to delegate. But there is one important element still missing.

There is a disconnect between a typical war game and the reality of Command. In a war game the Player makes equivalent decisions to our hypothetical real life Commander. Well, not really, but for the purposes of the discussion, close enough.

What's different about how they both decide? One is making decisions in full possession of the facts and the other is having to do so with imperfect knowledge.

Yes, there might be Fog of War and a few other game mechanics fuzzying up the picture but the level of information available to a war gamer is far greater than any Commander on the day had. The war gamer deals purely in numbers whereas the Commander is required to filter everything through the personalities above and below him. The numbers he has access to don't have nearly as much fidelity as those of the war gamer.

Imperfect knowledge, therefore, is a missing element in our Command model. But how to implement this without taking away control from the Player? Nobody would leap at the chance of making decisions when they had no idea of the consequences of the various options on offer. Blind leaps of faith don't make for good game mechanics.

Conversely, the more information you provide to the Player about possible outcomes, the further you are moving away from real life and into the realms of the God-like-knowledge. Which raises the question of whether it is even necessary to incorporate imperfect knowledge into our model of Command?

Phone talk with Greiffenberg (AGC): Fourth Army wants to start off with its centre part on 1 Dec. Theatre Command approves. Reasons:

A) According to reliable information, the enemy is withdrawing forces from this sector. Panzergruppes 3 & 4 provide covering at this front.

B) The Supreme Command insists on carrying on the offensive even if it means risking the last strength of our troops completely.

I have to tell him that this is also the view of OKH

F.M Von Halder's War Diary, 29th November 1941

The best way to answer that is to stop for a moment and consider your current list of worries. If you're like me you've probably got three things on your mind at any one time that, while they might not necessary be of concern, they are definitely an issue. Could be anything - relationships, work, finances or social events. Maybe the dog is infested with fleas.

Pick the three things uppermost on your mind and resolve to clear the decks. You're going to decide what to do about all three, right now. Do you have all the information available to you to make an informed decision? If not, can you look it up? Can Mr. Google help out? Do you know what will happen if you decide on a particular course of action?

If I use me as an example again I can say unequivocally that I don't have everything at my fingertips nor do I know exactly what will occur if I choose to do this or that. I can finesse this even further by saying if I'm dealing with objects or things the unknowns would be less than if I'm dealing with people. Until everybody comes from the planet Vulcan they are going to continue to be as predictable as tomorrow's weather forecast.

Sure, it's going to rain. The weather man says so. Eighty percent chance of precipitation. He should know given that the world's biggest computer is probably sitting in the room next door.

Most of the time that's what's going to happen. It'll rain. You'll be grateful you took an umbrella. But not all the time. When the weather man and his petaflop silicon assistant get it wrong, they really get it wrong.

People are like this. Predictable, within reason, most of the time. Completely off the reservation for the rest. How many times have you been surprised by the reaction of people to a seemingly innocuous action of your own? This is pretty much unique to people. Objects can do strange things at times but there is usually a logical reason for it.

If you lifted the bonnet of your car and spent the next hour fiddling around in the engine bay because you've decided it 'didn't look right' there is a strong likelihood that, once you've finished, it won't start. Which is probably because you've freed your spark plugs from the tyranny of their connection to that evil starting motor. Or dangled your fan belt artfully over your carburettor and wound it around the radiator like a lassoed steer in a western movie.

Your car won't start but the reasons are mechanical. Somebody with better knowledge than you can easily set things to right. They might charge you a lot of money but you'll end up with a fully functioning vehicle.

People are different. They are emotional and complex. They make decisions that aren't logical. They aren't as easily fixed when broken.

Which brings us back to our list of worries. We have only imperfect knowledge when we choose a course of action and the expected outcome is reasonably predictable. Most of the time. Which is especially the case when we are dealing with people.

Command, in war time environment, is all about dealing with people. Even if the decision involves moving beans and bullets from point A to point B, there are people involved whose cooperation is needed to carry out that function.

Imperfect knowledge could be considered a fact of life for both decision evaluation and expected outcomes. Take a moment to reflect back on your list of worries. If you knew everything there was to know about the individual issues and the outcomes were one hundred percent predictable then they would no longer be worries. In fact, if you could maintain the same level of information awareness you'd probably find yourself living a worry free existence. You'd also be bored silly.

As our model of Command involves dealing with people (superiors and subordinates) it would be worthwhile throwing imperfect knowledge into the mix. But it needs to be balanced. The Player should have enough information available to make an informed decision and the outcome should be predictable.

Most of the time.

9.3.5. COULD ONLY MANAGE A TICKET TO THE MATINEE SESSION

Theatres

Dividing the map into three operational theatres was a key decision that under pinned the rest of the design. It's the foundation that everything else is built upon.

Why are they there? An easy answer would be because that's the way it was on the day. The Germans enforced strict operational boundaries between their individual theatres for practical reasons of command and control and logistics.

Fair enough but the immediate reply from a typical Player would be that it places unnecessary restrictions upon them. The Eighteenth Army in Armeegruppe Nord should be allowed to assault Rostov, way, way down south, if that is what the Player demands.

Maybe. By the time it force marched the 1500 km's from A to B it would no longer be a functioning military force, more of a group holiday booking in the making. As this distance is as the crow flies the actual ground to be covered would likely be double that. Would they even get there before the game was over?

What about the trains? That's feasible but the rail network was extremely busy and relocating an entire army from one extremity of Russia to another was a major undertaking.

A typical war game places no restrictions on a Player's ability to shuffle their forces all over the map. There are probably requirements for individual

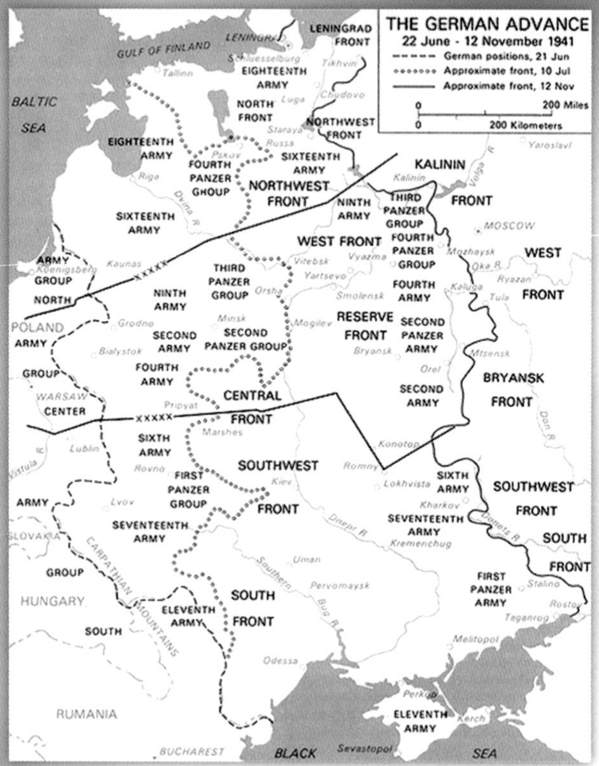

© http://www.ibiblio.org/hyperwar/USA/USA-EF-Decision/USA-EF-Decision-2.html

Divisions to maintain contact with their immediate HQ but that's usually as far as it goes. The Player is gifted a level of freedom that simply didn't exist.

Still, that's not a reason for doing otherwise. A strict adherence to historical reality can often lead you down dead end streets where there is nothing but a rundown, dirty, diner with a nicotine ravaged girl called Thelma serving greasy chips and bad coffee. Not where you want to be.

Gen. Von Greiffenberg, AGC, on the phone: Briefing on the differences between our and OKW's formulation of AGC's mission. F.M Von Bock must be informed for tomorrow's high visitors (Führer). Caution in presenting the Yelnya situation. Guderian and Hoth must be called in for the Führer conference to press demands for tank replacements.

F.M Von Halder's War Diary, 3rd August 1941

This particular game is all about Operational Command. You aren't an all seeing, all knowing, God. Instead you're somebody trying to juggle more balls in the air than you can handle. Inevitably you're going to drop some.

One of the prime ways the game creates this feeling is by splitting the map into clearly defined theatres. Each theatre has its own commander, its own hierarchy of command. Each has its own logistical system, its own air force, its own fuel allocation.

Each theatre is unique and has its own set of challenges. Your job is to allocate resources between theatres, to manage each theatre just so in order to achieve the big picture outcome that you are aiming for.

There may be, for example, an additional supply of vitally needed spare parts for trucks. But, as is typical, there is only enough for one theatre. Who do you assign them to? You might check the status of each theatres truck columns. You might consider which theatre needs to push harder or which theatre has the greatest reliance on an extended truck column umbilical cord.

You could also take into account your relationship with the three individual theatre commanders. Whichever way you jump with the spare parts, somebody is going to be pleased while the others will be the opposite. The Führer's current strategic direction plays a part as any decision you make that is in line with his goals will be an easier one to carry out (less Political Points) versus one that isn't.

It is these kinds of decisions that elevate the game into Operational Command territory. Sure, you are still the person who shuffles the counters around the map but you are also the person who has to deal with the big picture - the hard, gritty reality of having to play one theatre off against another.

Splitting the map into individual theatres creates a strong sense of individuality. It gets you thinking of the campaign in terms of theatres. AGN is stalled, AGC badly needs more fuel, AGS is rolling straight towards Kharkov but fatigue is becoming an issue. That's how an Operational Commander thinks.

There is still scope for reassigning forces between theatres. Panzergruppes can move into an adjacent theatre. But they will need to drag their logistical tail behind them. In '41 the Germans railed Hoepner's 4th Panzergruppe into Armeegruppe Mitte to form part of the assault on Moscow for Operation Typhoon. It was integrated into Armeegruppe Mitte's logistics along with Guderian and Hoth's 2 & 3 Panzergruppes.

How did that work? It didn't. The rail capacity of Armeegruppe Mitte was woefully inadequate for the task of keeping three entire Panzergruppes supplied with sufficient fuel to launch and sustain a major offensive. There simply weren't enough trains getting through. Nor was this a solvable problem in the winter of '41.

Which is why the game requires any Panzergruppe venturing into an adjoining theatre to maintain a logistical link back to their theatre of origin. It's still eminently doable but it requires some foresight and planning. As it should.

It also requires the approval of the Führer. The four Panzergruppes formed the hard hitting, offensive punch of the Wehrmacht in Russia. They were the sharp point of the spear. Hitler took a strong interest in their deployment and use.

The game won't allow you to take a major decision such as reassigning a Panzergruppe on your own. This feeds straight back into another aspect of the design - that of the player operating *within* a hierarchy of command.

Talk with Heusinger and Von Paulus: Our command function is exhausted in details, which are really the responsibility of the Theatre Hqs, where we should be giving them clear-cut mssions and the material means for independent action. In order to remedy this situation it would be necessary for ourselves to have a clear idea of what the political command regards as the prime objective of the campaign.

F.M Von Halder's War Diary, 4th August 1941

Hitler is your superior. To gain his approval you need to have positive relations. Which is reasonable. He is more likely to trust your judgement if he has a favourable view of the job your are doing. If Hitler is overheard speaking of you in terms best not mentioned in polite company then your Panzergruppes will be staying right where they are.

Which is another ball you will have to juggle. Maintaining positive relations with your superiors. That's the red ball. The hot one.

9.3.6. HITLER

Hitler was an outlier. Here was a domineering, driven, charismatic man who exerted a level of control well beyond any reasonable expectations of somebody perched at the very apex of a command pyramid. That those same personal qualities that enabled him to overpower and overshadow all those beneath him also drove him in directions best described as dark and sinister is not in dispute.

He was a most unpleasant individual but, having acknowledged this, it's his influence on the command structure that is of particular interest from a design point of view.

The German Player is firmly ensconced within the hierarchy. Hitler dominates from the top. How do you accommodate the reality of Hitler's influence without turning the Player into a wooden puppet that jerks to the string pulls of a computerised Führer? Yet the Hitler factor was so strong that to exclude it from a game modelling Operational Command would be a major oversight.

Disassociating the game from Hitler's dark side is an easy first step. That's the low hanging fruit plucked and consumed. We'll have to jump for the rest.

Hitler didn't help matters. Rather than having clearly defined goals for his invasion of Russia, he kept changing his mind. One moment he was charging towards Leningrad, the next the Ukraine. Like a child with Attention Deficit Disorder he was easily distracted and would flip flop from one objective to the next.

At the commencement of Operation Barbarossa there was a specific plan in place which was largely followed as originally laid out. But it ceased after the Battle of Smolensk. The plan anticipated that by then the Red Army would have been defeated. Indeed it suffered such horrendous casualties that, if it had been a boxer, it would have been flat on its back on the canvas. But rather than stay down for the count it staggered, bloodied and dazed, to its feet. It possessed reserves hither to unknown by the Germans. They kept punching, landing blow after blow. It reeled and stumbled but stayed upright.

The Germans must have thought they were fighting a Bolshevik Golem. No matter how hard they hit, how often they hit or where they hit, it just wouldn't die.

When Plan A succeeded tactically but failed strategically, the Germans were left in a conundrum. Tensions boiled over between Hitler and his High Command. Everybody had a different view on what to do next. There was no clarity or consensus.

It's no surprise that Hitler became fickle and changeable. He wasn't favourably disposed to taking the advice of the upper echelons of the Prussian Officer Corps at the best of times but when they failed to agree among themselves as to the best course of action he fell back onto his own devices.

Plan B was rapidly followed by Plan C which, in turn, was swept off the table to make room for Plan D.

To accommodate the 'whim of the Führer' the game has Hitler calling a conference to discuss strategy roughly once a month. There are five of these and it's not guaranteed that one will be called every month. There is a measure of uncertainty. Some will be skipped. Except the last one in early November. That's a given as it's necessary to provide certainty for the Player.

At the completion of each conference Hitler will issue a new, numbered, 'Directive' that will outline his goals in order of priority. The Player has, depending on his chosen strategy, the ability to exert a measure of influence.

Mechanically we now have a reasonably realistic facsimile of Hitler's decision making process. At irregular intervals the Player will be summonsed to a conference where upon Hitler will arbitrarily decide which objectives are to be given precedence over others. But what impact will this have on the Player? Will they be forced to comply with the fickle demands of the Führer?

Well that depends. Right at the start of the game they choose one of three over riding strategies that they will follow. The first requires them to support Hitler and take whatever is his current objective. As this is a moving target there are some obvious disadvantages. These are offset by assistance that Hitler is willing to give along the way.

At the other extreme 'Demand Military Independence' will have the Player standing up for his right to fight the war on his own terms. Without assistance and with the risk of getting fired if he fails to cover his flanks politically.

The interaction between the Player's approach and Hitler's changeable goals now becomes apparent. With one approach - Support Hitler - the outcome of a conference becomes vitally important and there is a need for the Player to be able to place himself in a position where he can exert some sway over what is decided.

With a different approach - Demand Military Independence - what Hitler decides is irrelevant as the Player has determined to tread his own path, albeit with some risk attached. Here we've got a workable mechanism that allows the Player to trade independence for ongoing assistance.

But that's not all. The Hitler factor is woven into the fabric of the game even deeper. Every decision that is taken which aligns with Hitler's current primary objective will be easier to make. It will cost less Political Points. It will be the path of least resistance.

Conversely a decision that is diametrically opposed to the stated goals of the Führer will be a harder road to tread with a Political Point premium being charged. To highlight this consider a straightforward fuel allocation decision. Perhaps you decide that you'd like Armeegruppe Mitte to have a greater share at the expense of the other two theatres. If Hitler has his heart set on Moscow then you'll receive a discount but if Moscow is sitting third or fourth on his current list of priorities then you'll be paying a premium in Political Points.

It's a subtle way of reminding the Player that, while you are free to do as you wish, the view of the Führer needs to be taken into account.

Let's not forget the fiddling. Hitler couldn't help himself. As Barbarossa progressed he inserted himself more and more into day to day operational matters that were well below his remit as supreme commander. That book on Delegation previously mentioned? In one ear and out the other.

The game models this by applying intermittent movement penalties to a randomly selected Panzergruppe as these were the 'bright, shiny, light' formations that most caught the Führer's attention. The level of interference is minor but enough be an annoyance. The frequency of the interference is keyed into the Player's chosen approach. It's assumed that if you've chosen to 'Support Hitler' then you are sufficiently inside the tent for him to meddle more often than if standing at the entrance, one foot on either side, with a 'Moscow or Bust' approach. A big advantage to the 'Demand Military Independence' approach is the total absence of interference by the Führer. He is standing off to one side, impatiently waiting for you to drop the ball.

The ability to shift a Panzergruppe from one theatre to another, as previously mentioned, requires the assent of Hitler. If the two of you aren't on speaking terms then your strategic flexibility will be constrained.

Which highlights the focus that the game has given the 'H' factor. He's there. He's important. The Player is given scope to work with him, or against him, with corresponding trade-offs but without being forced to don a straight jacket.

9.3.7. STALIN

Stalin provides a diametrically opposite command experience. This time it is the Player who dominates the command structure. There is no need to play politics when you are the alpha male, the top dog.

Which creates a new set of design challenges. How do you provide a sense of hierarchy in this situation? Where is the necessity to cooperate with other people when you can have any one of them executed at will? Does placing the Player at the top of the hierarchy completely negate the people element that we have previously identified as crucial to any model of Operational Command?

It's tricky. Take away the people and you end up with the typical God-like approach of many other war games. But if those people have no direct impact on the Player's actions they quickly morph into window decorations.

The game has taken a different approach. The people are there and they do indeed exert a strong influence but it is an internal one. Before looking at this in detail it's worth taking a step back and contrasting the two different command experiences on offer.

The German Player is part of a hierarchy. He is required to be a political player just as much as a military one. He has at his command arguably the, at the time, world's best army. The Wehrmacht was the arch typical well-oiled machine that conquered all before it. The martial tools available to the German Player are honed to a sharp edge. They are proven and are interchangeable. Everything meshes together into a synchronised whole. A world class symphonic orchestra in full flight at the peak of its power.

The Soviet Player, on the other hand, is in possession of a smartly attired but discordant, back alley rabble where half the musicians are asleep and the other half have rarely held an instrument, let alone had to play in harmony with others. The conductor is way off in the cheaps seats, well to the rear of the auditorium. The musicians have to squint to see the movement of his baton.

This has come about because the owner of the Orchestral company had, a few years previously, rounded up all the competent musicians and taken them out the back where they were summarily shot. Others he locked up in the basements of notorious prisons and threw away the key. To fill the gaps and maintain a full orchestral roster he rounded up a bunch of hanger's on and flunkies and told them that, henceforth, they were to be a violin player. Everybody got a shiny new uniform.

Anyone can pick up a violin and create sound. Just like anybody can command an Army. On a good day, when the sun is shining and the biggest potential problem is the lack of decent refreshment.

Stalin's Great Officer Purge of '37 and '38 was aimed at eliminating the last remaining threat to his power. In doing so he eviscerated the Red Army. A consistent historical motif of Dictators is the need to clear the decks of any competition once they themselves have clawed their way to the top by fair means or foul.

We are being too kind to Dictators here. None of them used fair means. A ruthless, take no prisoners, climb over the bodies, style was the norm. Anyone who had assumed power on this basis would be paranoid about others doing the same to them. He who trades in knives spends a lot of time with his back to the wall.

Stalin was no different to any of history's police line-up of successful, brutal, dictators. Paranoia be thy name.

It was the reason he instigated the purge. It was the reason he remained highly sensitive to any threat emanating from his Officer Corps. It is also a great solution to our design conundrum.

The people in the Soviet hierarchy aren't important in the sense that Stalin needs their help. It will be given, regardless, as they are ruled by fear. They are, however, important in how they affect Stalin's state of mind. His level of paranoia.

At no point did the Red Army Officer Corps have any realistic prospects of mounting a successful coup. What mattered more was Stalin's perception of the threat of this occurring. He was genuinely paranoid at the prospect of being terminally removed from his post by those beneath him.

Every subordinate presented as a potential threat. The cumulative tally of these individual threats, along with a few other factors such as the loss of politically important cities all contribute to Stalin's level of paranoia.

At certain points the pressure cooker inside his head will blow and he will suffer a Paranoid Episode. There are consequences. Army Commanders will be shot, the wheels of command will stutter and seize. The Player's freedom of action will be temporarily constrained.

Here we have a workable mechanic that allows for a top down command experience while elevating the subordinates within the hierarchy as people who have an impact on the Player's experience and who need to be taken into consideration.

It also aligns with reality of Stalin. Yes he did have Army Commanders shot for no other reason than he perceived them to be a threat. Whether he suffered paranoid episodes in the manner and frequency depicted by the game is debatable but we've already decided that game play trumps strict adherence to historical fidelity.

If we are going to sit down for a relaxing cup of coffee we'd much rather it be a Starbuck's experience than any rancid liquid concoction in a cracked, fly specked, mug likely to be served by Thelma who resides at the end of 'Relentless Full Simulation' alley.

9.3.8. THE DARK SIDE

In days of yore battles were fought by men chosen for the task in places specially selected to be well clear of everybody except the combatants. Slings were slung, spears were lunged and swords were clanged against shields with the only people getting hurt being those involved. It was a neat, contained, affair that allowed matters to be decided by force of arms alone.

It wasn't civilised. Whenever men decide to kill each other it is always going to be shades of ugliness and horror. But, and it's a big BUT, innocent bystanders didn't get harmed. The violence was constrained to the field of battle.

That's not the case nowadays. In any given conflict the single biggest casualty count will be that of civilians. If you bothered to research and chart the ratio of military personnel killed vs. Civilians over time then you'd likely end up with a graph that looked like the Stairway to Heaven. It'd be Heaven only because of the ascending nature of the graph. Other metaphors may be more appropriate but they couldn't avoid the unpleasant fact of ever increasing civilian casualties in proportion to military ones.

The reasons for this aren't hard to fathom. Battles today aren't fought on a wide, flat, field over yonder hill, far from the town. They are conducted inside the town with no consideration given to its population cowering in the basements. The lethality and reach of artillery has far surpassed that of the longbow and enabled the point of conflict to spread, amoeba like, over vast distances. Air power has brought the ability to directly target civilian centres and further smear the conflict zone into areas previously presumed safe.

The advent of smart weapons has only accentuated the trend. Once you have the ability to target *this* building in amongst a street full of them you are more likely to do so. Hope you flattened the right building. Smart weapons are only smart in a targeting sense. They don't have the ability to check every room in the building for sleeping families before leveling it in an explosive cloud of concrete and plaster dust.

That group of people milling around the courtyard in the high angle, black and white, satellite image that is being peered at by operators on the other side of the world? Are they militants or a wedding party? There is an AGM-114 Hellfire toting Predator drone doing it's best to look like a nonchalant eagle waiting on the decision.

We could keep talking about all manner of other modern day horrors that have become an integral part of armed conflict. We could, but we won't. It's enough to acknowledge that a Dark Side of war exists and that it is a significant part of modern day conflict. We aren't here to judge or take a moral or ethical stance, simply to accept the fact that it is, sadly, what it is.

Was it a factor in Operation Barbarossa? How could it not be? This was the single biggest conflict in the history of the world. The Guinness Book of Records doesn't deal in this area but it is yet to be beaten. Over twenty seven million people died. The biggest casualty count was civilian.

It was an existential war. Both sides were playing for their very survival. Negotiated peace settlements were never an option. Destroy or be destroyed. No quarter given.

You could fill pages with a list of atrocities carried out by both sides. The Dark Side of the war had a particular sinister tinge to it in Barbarossa. Two ruthless dictators throwing millions of fighting men at each other in a struggle for their countries, their beliefs and their own lives. The lady selling peace, happiness and roses was doomed to close from a lack of customers given the stakes and personalities involved.

Yes, there was a Dark Side. It was a significant factor in the War in Russia. But does it belong in our model of Operational Command?

In most war games the answer is a definitive no. It's a touchy, very political area that is best steered clear of. There are people still alive who have personal experience of the events. Besides, who wants to be confronted by the uglier aspects of a knock down, fight to the death, that was Barbarossa?

They are all good arguments. There appears to be little upside in dealing with the Dark Side.

The game isn't interested in politics. It's agnostic. It's also not the role of the game designer to take a stance, one way or another, on all the bad things that happened. It's a game, not a recreation of the worst atrocities of the twentieth century.

The core focus is of Operational Command. Juggling the balls, trying not to drop them. The Dark Side of war has become a necessary, and important, element of this. It can't be anything else. If we are going to fight wars in amongst civilians there will be a multitude of decisions, big and small, that revolve around this aspect.

It's an important part of Operational Command. A grey area that, if omitted, would be leaving a sizable void. If we are going to a lot of trouble to model all the other elements involved why leave this out?

Including the Dark Side requires walking a fine line. There are, as it turns out, quite a few fine lines involved in the design of this game but this is the most delicate of them all. Just as well my ballet shoes still fit. Which they would if they came in size 14 (Euro size 47). Good luck with that.

An essential requirement would be to keep any mention of the Dark Side as generic as possible. There is no need for specific details that might confront a Player. The literature, and media, of the conflict is sufficiently broad and well established that the Player will automatically fill in the details themselves. All we need to do is provide a broad picture outline of generic events that touched on the ugly side of the war. Along with this comes the aforementioned need to remove any hint of political statement.

There should also be the option to switch this part of the game off. In fact it is OFF by default. It's not everybody's cup of tea and that's fair enough. But for those after a more nuanced command experience, it's there.

In the time period portrayed by the game it is largely a German Player experience. It's woven into the game mechanics of relations, decisions and partisans. There are some tough decisions to be made. Scope is provided for the Player to take the line of least resistance or to assume the high morale ground.

Why would anyone not chose the best, most ethical, course of action? Why indeed? Do psychopaths play war games? Who knows? It's a reasonable assumption that, if they did, they would be an insignificant minority.

The reason why a Player may chose to take the easy way out is that the high moral ground requires a commensurate cost in Political Points. Recall the German Player's position in the hierarchy. A number of his superiors, including the man at the top, were strongly pushing an ideological position that wouldn't sit well with anybody other than those with short circuits in their neural networks.

Yes, you can oppose and protest the Dark Side but as you are going against the wishes of your superiors it will come at a cost in Political Points and relationships. To add some spice to the mix at the end of the game the Player is scored in a range of intangible areas. One of these is his likelihood of having to answer to the war crimes tribunal.

Of course the International Criminal Court will not be dispatching its minions to knock on his door in the wee small hours if he clocks in a dubiously low score. It's a piece of game chrome, nothing more.

With the focus on Operational Command the real juice of the game is in the decisions it requires of you. The tougher, more challenging that those decisions are the better the game is at generating that experience.

Deciding on fuel allocations between theatres is a decision of import. It is a straight strategic judgement call that involves winners and losers as well as a realignment of relations that will affect your ability to prosecute the war going forward.

Deciding what line to take when confronted by atrocities committed by some of the more unsavoury forces present, perhaps not under your direct command, is a matter of a different dimension. It has relationship ramifications but there is no direct on-the-map impact. It taps into another part of your brain - the part that determines what is right and wrong. The war crimes score serves to bring this into sharper focus. You are dealing with a *moral* decision.

These aren't decisions that can be easily tossed to one side. They make you think. The Political Points you will have to expend to hold a righteous line could be better spent elsewhere. It is unlikely that you've got a reservoir of spare PP's to burn. Game wise it's a cut and dried decision to go with flow. Sweep it under the carpet. Move on.

But there's that voice niggling away at the back of your head. It doesn't feel *right*. Nobody wants to do the wrong thing. Nobody wants to front a War Crimes Tribunal. Yet are you willing to burn a few bridges and a lot of Political Points when you badly need them to lobby for additional Divisions to be transferred from the West?

Welcome to Twentieth Century Operational Command.

9.3.9. MICROMANAGEMENT

A lot of people equate micromanagement with depth, detail and decisions. Fair enough, but I'd take a different point of view. The presence of micromanagement, is to me, a failure in design. It's something to be avoided at all costs. The game has all three of the aforementioned elements in spades but it is a micromanagement free zone.

There is a suburb in a city I used to work in that had council erected signposts all over. They stated, in pedantic terms, that you are entering a 'Nuclear Free Zone'. It was a comforting thought to know that nobody was going to nuke you while ever you were between the signs and that a Fukushima nuclear power plant wasn't just around the corner, slowly melting into a gooey, fizzing, blob. You could relax, knowing you were safe and confident that the red skin on your chest was a result of exposure to the sun and not an indiscriminate radiation burn.

The same council had signs on the local beach explaining that, if you swam between the flags, the lifeguards would keep an eye on you and that you were entering a 'shark free zone'. As sharks were higher up the probability scale than being nuked I got less of a warm fuzzy feeling from those signs. Of course the alternative reality dimwit in the council who authorised such bold statements had forgotten to inform the sharks. I'm also confident that they hadn't fronted the United Nations and pushed a bill through requiring all nukes to avoid detonating within 100 metres of a designated 'Nuclear Free Zone'.

Yet here I am, erecting a 'Micromanagement Free Zone' sign, to be seen by all and sundry. B*lls of steel. Not really. As I'm the designer of the small slice of virtual life that is Decisive Campaigns 3: Barbarossa all the sharks and missiles work for me. They do as they are told. Just for fun try moving an infantry division into the Black Sea. Or the hex that is the location of the current day Chernobyl Power Plant. Put your darkest shades on and stand well back.

Micromanagement does indeed provide depth, detail and decisions. But not in a good way. The depth and detail is of the fiddly, busy work, kind. The decisions are micro. Too small to matter. Next time you play a game that features micromanagement ask yourself, what is it adding to the experience?

DC3: Barbarossa eliminates micromanagement in a number of ways.

Firstly by throwing decisions at the Player. Big ones that have a meaningful impact. Take an Army. It's got plenty of subordinate Divisions but your main focus is on the Army as a whole. You can set the posture of the Army, assign Theatre based Artillery, Tactical Air Support, ask your Theatre Commander to focus his specialist resources on it, for example. Any decision you make with regards to the Army will automatically flow through to the subordinate Divisions.

Importantly, once an Army based decision has been made, it stays in place until you wish to change it. Fire and forget. The decisions matter because, if you've assigned something to an Army, all the other Armies within that theatre miss out. Changing your mind matters because there is an element of command friction and inertia involved. Armies don't, for example, reconfigure from a full-on Blitzkrieg posture to a Defensive posture overnight. Doing so is a major undertaking that involves a transitional state of vulnerability.

Secondly the unit count has been ruthlessly pruned down to the bare essentials. Which, for a game portraying Barbarossa, still is a reasonably sized number. The fewer units on the map the more important each of them become. Saturating the map with counters is just another form of micromanagement. How the unit count is minimised is discussed extensively elsewhere

Finally the elf that lives within the engine has been given the job of handling all the details. He's a busy elf who gets booted out of bed every time you fire up the game. It's his job to work flat out and handle all the numerical detail that churns away in the subterranean caverns of calculation. I pay him nothing and every time he slips up and drops a digit I make sure that his big elfy ears get tasered. Zzzzzttt! Don't feel sorry for him as he's an elf.

To give him credit he does a good job. Consider Logistics. It's detail with a capital 'D'. How fuel moves through the three separate pipelines, stage by stage, is a marvel of calculation engineering. It would be very easy to provide the Player with a range of levers to pull and buttons to push at different points in the process. You could make an entire sub-game out of the logistical mechanics by having the whole process ascend up through the clouds into micromanagement heaven.

But that would do the elf out of a job and that wouldn't be right. He deals with all the nuts and bolts and leaves the Player to make the big picture decisions that matter.

When do I relocate the Forward Supply Base forward? Should I halt my Panzergruppe for a turn to build up enough stockpile to cover the interruption? Do I keep my Panzergruppe HQ within cooee of the transport grid or spear off into the wilds, hoping that the elf can cut me some slack and keep the fuel flowing?

Don't count on it. The elf has no empathy or compassion. Probably because he keeps getting zapped. But what can you do? He's an elf.

All three approaches; meaningful decisions, streamlined unit count and having the engine take care of all the details, combine to ensure that the game can present a lot of depth without bogging the Player down in needless micromanagement.

9.3.10. INFORMATION

How information is presented is a big, topical, subject. A game can live and die by its ability to provide adequate feedback to the Player. Game mechanics that chug away in an information vacuum are no fun for anybody. If there is something going on you want to know why and how.

Being presented solely with the outcome is like finding yourself married to a woman whose personality changes every day. She's still you wife, you're still married, but why she keeps morphing into a different woman is a mystery. One day she fawns over your dog, the next she informs you that Chuckles the Chiwawa has left, in dubious company, to start a career in the restaurant trade.

The amount of information that needs to be presented to the Player is proportional to the complexity of the game. For Pacman a score and a timer readout constitute adequate feedback. For *DC3: Barbarossa*, with its multitude of game mechanics, there is a dump truck's worth of information that needs to be thrown at the Player each turn in order to convey what is going on.

Straight up there is a problem. Information overload. Drowning under an excess of data is a feeling that we all familiar with, one way or another. Nobody wishes to replicate the experience in a game. The information needs to be presented in an easily digestible format.

The primary way the game tackles this is by making the information optional. There are, if you're playing the German side, dozens of reports available in the report tab each turn. Do you need to read each and everyone of them in order to play the game? No. You can, in fact, ignore them all.

Delegate all decisions and fill your virtual wastebasket up to the brim. Of course there will be a train wreck at some point. You'll lose the game. Probably get slaughtered. But not immediately. Importantly the game will keep ticking over without any input from the Player. If all you want to do is shuffle counters across the map then you can do this. For a while. Until your fast Divisions run out of fuel and a number of other, cascading, disasters catch up with you.

The game is about Operational Command and it assumes that you are going to at least make an effort to stay on top of what is going on. It also assumes that you'll make a few decisions and read a few reports. But only a few. The rest are there to be dipped into at your leisure. The degree at which you choose to do that is up to you.

Which fits in nicely with the Operational vibe of the game. You've got a pile of reports on your desk. You can read the 'need to know' stuff and wing all the rest. Or you can be the one of those Commanders who are regarded as 'on top of their brief'. Up to you.

Which of the two archetypes would you consider to be the better Operational Commander? Probably the second. I say 'probably' because Mr 'I-don't-fight-the-war-from-behind-a-desk' might have other, equally valid, ways that enable him to keep his finger on the pulse. Which he would need to because there is no way to dodge around the fact that he would have to be on top of what is going on before he could make informed decisions. Does this mean that you've got to brew up a cup of stiff coffee and wade through endless reports each and every turn? No.

Information is presented in multiple ways and in multiple formats. You can access it textually or visually, or both. The game goes out of its way to provide you with different information channels and allows you to pick the one the suits. It also layers the information. Get the big picture and then peel away, Shrek-like, for further details.

Is it perfect? Nope. But the design has made a big effort to provide ample feedback, in a streamlined manner. Here's how it is done.

Lets start with reports. There are a heap of them. Most of them are contextual. You would reference them only if you wanted specific information, the headquarters equivalent of asking your staff to provide a detailed breakdown on such and such.

The core, important, reports are the Daily Logs. They contain all the goings on in one place. If something has happened in the game, at a level that you need to be aware of, then it'll show up in the appropriate Daily Log. They are divided into topics but, once the campaign gets underway, there can be a lot of stuff in there.

To provide a quick reference filter for the really important, need to know information there is the Aide de Camp which is essentially a distillation of all the major Daily Logs into a single, heavily condensed, report showing only the vital stuff. It'll serve to give you a gentle prod if you've forgotten to tell the Luftwaffe what to do, for example, or have Theatre Artillery assets sitting around, twiddling their thumbs.

Tool tips. They are like rabbits in a breeding frenzy. Everywhere you look there is a tool tip. Pregnant and about to drop another litter of little tool tips. A lot of them are static. They provide the same information every time you read them. They are the dull neighbours or the boring in-laws type of rabbits.

But lots of others are dynamic. They are hopping around faster than a rabbit has a right too. They are the exciting, razzle dazzle, rabbits. The Matrix versions. Their little bunny brains neurally shunted directly into the virtual construct, constantly updating.

Report Status! Originally this was an Action Card but it received pride of place as a special button. It's not happy if you aren't pressing it. Everything you need to know about a Division or an Army is right there. With tool tips.

If you're playing the Soviets you may find that the cogs of Command grind to halt at unexpected times. But that's life in the Red Army. The rabbits and buttons are all on tranquillisers. As are the channels of communications that feed STAVKA with reports from the front lines. If your playing Stalin you might want to give your entire Command Structure a decent shake. Wake everybody up. Unclog the blockages. Have all the dopey ones who haven't snapped to attention taken out back and shot.

Where ever applicable, Action Cards have dynamic text that updates after being played. If you want F.M Von Leeb, up North, to change his focus you'll be able to see who currently has it before issuing new orders.

Status icons adorn the Unit displays to indicate various conditions. Logistical icons march across the map enabling you to accurately ascertain the state of your logistics purely from their colours, without the need to read a single report.

A comprehensive mouse-over is available for every hex with dynamic information on movement costs and combat. Small icons adorn the map letting you know of any additional, non-standard movement costs as a result of recent combat, or ZOC's, for example.

Then there are the Special tabs down the bottom. Three for each regime. All of them aimed at a particular aspect of the game. All of them with extensive dynamic tool tips that serve to condense most of the information contained within the numerous related reports. One stop information shops.

9.3.11. THE MAP

This is another area where the game has stripped out all of the non-essential information and retained only what matters. There is a temptation, with maps, to go overboard with cartographic noise. Not here.

The transport network is the best example of this. Russia was, in 1941, criss crossed with rail lines. Roads were the same. If you choose a hex at random, the odds were that there would be, at the minimum, a road of some form and, possibly, a rail line. Perhaps not in the more remoter regions but in the portion of the map that the campaign is fought out on, yes.

From an Operational Command perspective, the high density transport grid meant little. Roads in Russia, in '41, were predominately goat tracks, unusable when it rained. One of the major surprises to confront the Germans was the poor quality of the roads. Having recently invaded some of the more advanced, more urbanised, countries of Europe they were dismayed at what they found.

In practical terms the roads were of less use than those of previous campaigns. The game deals with this by assuming any Plains, Field or Forest hex will have a network of local roads present. Low grade dirt roads but roads nevertheless. There is no need to portray these on the map. If you are in a Plains hex, for example, it's a given that your forces will utilise the 'roads'.

There were exceptions. Hard top, sealed, roads that were able to still function when rasputitsa hit. These are marked on the map as they are vitally important routes. Few and far between, however. The main highway running from Warsaw to Moscow, via Minsk, qualifies. As do a lot of the roads in the Baltic states. But that's it. While there were other roads which were surfaced, they were of such a poor quality that the surface quickly broke down with the passage of vehicles in wet conditions.

If you find yourself peering at the map wondering where all the roads are, that's the reason. Only the decent, all weather ones are shown. All the rest are assumed to be the equivalent of a modern day dirt track requiring a decent four wheel drive to traverse. On a good day. Once the campaigning season recommenced in '42 the Germans made a concerted effort to upgrade a number of routes but this is outside the scope of the game.

Rail? Why is there so little? Similar to the roads, most of the rail was useless from an Operational Command perspective. Standard German doctrine was for each advancing army to be supported by a double tracked rail line. If you take a quick look at Armeegruppe Mitte, you can see one double tracked line (it has lots of branch lines but essentially there is only one viable route). There are four armies, the 4th, 9th, 2nd PG & 3rd PG, that are relying on it for fuel, supplies and ammunition. Armeegruppe South has an even worse rail route to armies ratio.

The reason that a double tracked rail line was needed was that this was the only way you could achieve the 48 trains per day throughput that was necessary. That's an ideal number that's achievable only if all the supporting infrastructure is in place. Stations with decent loading/unloading platforms, shunting yards, adequate signaling, water towers, engine maintenance facilities, etc. For an advanced rail nation such as German, this was par for the course, a by product of the need to potentially have to fight a two front war.

For Russia it was a distant dream. A route that was double tracked could easily have its effective daily throughput reduced to that of a single tracked route due to a lack of basic infrastructure. So yes, there were many rail lines throughout Russia, but few of them were capable of handling the number of trains necessary to keep entire Armeegruppes on the move.

What's on the map is the usable transport grid, admittedly fudged a little for game play purposes.

9.4. DESIGN COMPROMISES ▶

9.4.1. PEOPLE

We've talked about a lot of things that are part of the design. It's worth discussing aspects that aren't. We'll start with the curliest, people.

People are a key component. Without them there is no hierarchy and no relationship system. There wouldn't be a lot of point modelling command if there weren't any people involved. Nor would it be anywhere near as interesting absent homo sapiens.

Yet there are limits to how far we can venture down this path. You want the people to be well defined and have a meaningful impact but go too far beyond this point and you end up in the realms of Role Playing Games. It's a war game we are putting together here, not Dungeons and Dragons.

How we represent people is an interesting facet of the design. Originally people were present in name only. Their opinion of you was expressed numerically. The people experience was pretty bland and nerdy.

Over time they have evolved. They now communicate their opinions in plain speak that everybody can understand, eg. Good or Poor. The numbers are still there but they take a secondary role to the descriptors. There is a command tab that explicitly displays pictures. There are faces. It's a lot easier to relate to a character when you can look them in the eye. There are dynamic tool tips that highlight, in the one spot, all the current game effects that your relationship with a character has.

Overall it's a much better experience. The people are more fleshed out and visible. You can easily tell what impact they are having.

But they still can't swear. I would have liked that. Immersion plus. Time with the dog.

Another challenge was weaving the people into the game mechanics. At the start they were plugged into the Decision system and a few other secondary mechanics. As time went on they were knitted ever closer into the fabric of the design. More and more game functions were affected by your relationship with a relevant character.

With this came greater reliance on a Player's choices over which relationships to favour and which to ignore. There are distinct factions in the cast of characters and it is very difficult to keep everybody onside. Compromises have to be made. This is good.

9.4.2. STAFF

A related idea that has evolved as the game has developed is Staff. F.M Franz Halder, in the manner of the day, dispatched staff members, typically junior officers, to the front with the purpose of returning with first hand impressions of how things were progressing.

The design called for a roster of staff members that the Player could call upon to carry out inspection missions. There would be reports on the status of varying staff members - where they were, what they were doing. Divisional and Army updates would only be available once a staff member had visited and safely returned to OKH.

This ran into a few problems. It was found to be too restrictive to only be able to get a report on a Division, or Army, once the staff member had returned. The design was tweaked to provide up to date reports while ever a staff member was present at the relevant formation. This was an improvement. Now there was an interesting resource management aspect to how and where you allocated your limited supply of staff members. It allowed for a few wrinkles like travel delays or accidents that might indispose a staff member for a period.

It was better but still not where it should be. Staff management was interesting in its own right but it was a fiddly, micromanagement heavy, game mechanic. Exactly what the design was going at great lengths elsewhere to avoid.

Besides, with an efficient communications net comprising telephones, telegraphs and radios, a Player should realistically be able to get a report on a particular Division at will.

The whole staff dispatch concept was scratched and replaced with a simple button in a prominent spot that allowed instant reports on any selected unit, be they Divisions or HQ's. The reports themselves were made more inclusive and included hard data on every modifier and game effect that applied. It was a big improvement. A quick, detailed, overview of any unit was now available with a single click.

The Staff concept wasn't abandoned. It changed direction. One more in line with the games focus.

Command infers delegation. It's part of the model. There is scope for some depth here. The Player is assigned a Chief of Staff who handles all delegated matters. Each play through a random Chief of Staff is assigned from a fixed roster of around ten possibles.

When a decision is delegated the Chief of Staff will choose the default option. Most of the time this is a do nothing, maintain the status quo option. Not always. There are default decisions that involve a random outcome. Perhaps there is a 60% chance of a good outcome occurring. An internal die roll is made and that outcome most likely happens or doesn't.

If the matter has been delegated to your Chief of Staff then his 'handicap' is factored in. The size of this varies but the effect is to lower the odds of a positive outcome. Your Chief of Staff isn't running the war, you are, and their ability to make informed decisions should be at a lower level than yours. Which feeds into the Player determining which decisions to delegate and which ones to handle themselves.

With a straight, default, do nothing option you can safely delegate confident in the outcome. With an option that is probability based then you'll be taking a long hard look at your Chief of Staff and decide whether he is up to the task. Perhaps that's a decision you should be dealing with yourself?

Staff infer management issues. If you are relying on a key individual to handle your delegated decisions then, at some point, it's possible that this individual may present challenges in their own right. Each of the ten possible candidates for Chief of Staff have a predisposition to a particular 'issue'. These range widely from recovering from post traumatic stress, being a rabid party disciple to being an inherited problem foisted upon you. There are others.

In any given play through your Chief of Staff will do his job without saying boo. On others he will present you with a sequence of decisions that revolve around his predefined 'issue'. While none of these reflect historical events they are all feasible scenarios. They are there to add a further subtle shade to the command experience.

As the commander of the entire eastern front, the Player is constantly making decisions of great import. The staff decisions aren't like this. They are minor, niggling, distractions. But they still matter and are there to remind you that your exulted position of authority isn't enough to wall you off from the day to day people problems that plague us all.

10. DESIGNER NOTES – ORDER OF BATTLE (OOB)

10.1. OVERVIEW ▶

A core design goal of the game is to maintain a streamlined approach to units. There are Divisions and multiple levels of HQ's. That's it. Everything else has been removed and dealt with in other ways. The focus of the game is NOT on having a squillion counters on the map representing a veritable kitchen sink of military formations and related organisations.

Instead the focus is firmly on the experience of Operational Command. Having a map jammed full of units, off multiple size and purpose, adds little to this experience and quite likely detracts from it. Operational Command is about making decisions, not being bogged down shuffling an excessive number of counters around a map.

Doubling the unit density on the map and differentiating units by endless minor variations doesn't add to the quotient of interesting decisions. What it does do is create a lot of busy work and micromanagement, two things the game has deliberately steered clear of.

With an Order Of Battle (OOB) anchored firmly on the Division as the basic unit of manoeuvre there are a few comprises that have had to be made. Historical fidelity has been firmly adhered to but there has been, by necessity, some fudging and shoehorning. This is unavoidable. Whatever scale was chosen - Corps, Divisional, Regimental or Brigade - there are always going to be exceptions to the rule and formations that don't neatly fit into whatever predefined organisational cut-off is chosen.

Once we've resolved to adhere to a particular formation size and set the bar on a streamlined OOB that excludes everything else, judgement calls have to made and compromises accepted.

How these are done is important. An arbitrary cut-off that eliminates everything that doesn't meet a set criteria is going to leave a lot on the floor. A butcher who decides he'll only accept the very best cuts will soon find himself knee deep in, once edible, meat that is sloshing around in a sea of blood and offal. We don't won't to see that happening with the many useful formations that don't correlate to the divisional mold.

Our aiming point is to maintain as high a level of historical fidelity as possible while meeting our stated design goal of a minimum practical unit count and a streamlined OOB that has only divisions and HQ's on the map.

How low can we limbo with our unit count? With a divisional focus that still leaves us with close to a thousand units overall. That's a lot, way more than we want, but only a portion of them are on the map at the same time. Barbarossa in '41 was a party with a lot of movement in guests coming and going. Most of those that went didn't do so voluntarily. With the benefit of hindsight they would have declined the invitation to attend.

Breaking the map into three distinct theatres goes a long way to make the unit count manageable. As each theatre can be viewed as a separate entity, the number of units you are dealing with in any one theatre is more palatable.

The games Artificial Intelligence (AI) places a hard limit on the lowering of the unit count. It requires a certain unit density to work optimally. Luckily this coincides with our Divisional focus.

What does streamlining mean in practice? The removal of all subsidiary military formations, for example Artillery and Air. Restricting on-map units to Infantry, Cavalry, Motorised and Armoured Divisions. Stripping out the fat from the Table of Organisation and Equipment (TOE).

10.1.1. NO UNNECESSARY UNITS

Removing Artillery and Air elements from the map was a big decision. A typical war game player expects to see them present. They are notable by their absence. Like the Best Man forgetting to turn up on the day of the wedding. Is it still a wedding if he isn't there to hand over the ring?

He's been abstracted. Bad luck, buddy. The effect of the Best Man is still present. The Bridegroom still gets his ring, there is still a mini hand over ceremony but not in the traditional sense of the Best Man being present.

It's a wedding. What's important is the Bride tying the knot with the Bridegroom. As long as the ring is there the Best Man is peripheral to the main event. Friends and family haven't come to see the Best Man standing up front, they've come for the wedding.

Now this isn't a perfect analogy. Of course everybody would prefer the Best Man to be present. He handles the ring, he gives a speech and offers moral support to the Bridegroom. He's an important element of the whole wedding experience.

But the church only has room for a limited number of people. It's already pretty full. If we wanted the focus to be firmly on the key couple then it makes sense to remove extraneous participants provided that the *effect* of having a Best Man isn't thrown out as well.

Which is the reason Artillery and Air units were removed from the game. They didn't add anything by being on the map apart from additional clutter. Removing them allowed the design to retain their effect and magnify the operational aspect.

Divisional artillery is incorporated into individual units. Theatre based artillery assets are above and beyond this and you assign these to an Army. One Army. The others within the theatre miss out. The decision becomes which Army do I give my theatre based Artillery too? That's an Operational Command decision. It's one that matters.

It's finessed further by your ability to specify the Artillery should be used in an offensive or defensive capacity. Once assigned, the Artillery will automatically continue to support its host Army with no further action from the Player required other than a decision to reassign.

Keep in mind that the Artillery we are talking about is the additional, theatre based, Artillery assets that are on hand to be allocated where the need is greatest and are above and beyond the standard Divisional/Corps Artillery sub formations that have been factored into the units combat statistics already.

The alternative of shuffling a bunch of artillery counters around a map to support this division or that is a *tactical* decision. It's also heavy on micromanagement and predisposes the map to counter gridlock. As Operational Commander you wouldn't be expected to worry about matters at this level. You've got subordinates who take care of this. Your job is to decide that the 9th Army will receive additional support, not the 4th.

Air units follow a similar theme although there is a lot more depth presented as this was an important aspect of the campaign. I discuss this in greater detail elsewhere but the same Operational Command approach of deciding which Panzergruppe, or Army, benefits from air support is followed. Air support has the potential to seriously empower whoever is receiving it. Those that aren't, miss out. The design has each theatre's Luftflotte being dedicated to supporting a single Army or Panzergruppe.

10.1.2. TOE

The Table of Organisation and Equipment (TOE) for the various formations involved in Operation Barbarossa is a zoo. It's a zoo that has at least one of everything. Whatever weird and wonderful animal you can think of, it's there. The two-headed polka dot Numbat is bound to be found lolloping around out back.

If you are in the business of Zoo's then having the Numbat, as well as all manner of other crazy animals, present would be a big plus. It'd attract lots of customers. Five dollars for a photo of you with the Numbat. *Sign here first, Madam. He's got sharp teeth. Known to eat fingers.*

Spamming the game with every possible type of weapon system employed on the Eastern front isn't going to enhance its appeal. Players, when they see an Infantry Division, should be confident that they are dealing with a consistent entity. Yep, it's an Infantry Division. It's got so many infantry, so many AT guns, so many artillery guns. If it's a Light Infantry Division it will have less of everything.

That's about as far as you want to go. What if the TOE of the 95th Infantry division had two battalions less of infantry than the 96th which, in turn, had an additional AT gun section to the 97th? Would it matter? From a strict historical detail perspective it might. From a game play one, no. The differences are so small that they become irrelevant in a game with a divisional perspective.

The first difference mentioned, that between an standard Infantry Division and a Light Infantry Division, is worth modelling as it's significant. One had three regiments and the other two. The second example that featured a difference in a battalion or a section isn't. Including it would only add to the background noise. The Player should be able to look at a Division and know what he is dealing with, without having to individually check each and every one to figure out the minute differences that exist between them.

The level of detail required by the design is set to cover all main differences and trends. The make up of the different types of Soviet Divisions, for example, underwent major changes which are reflected within the game. The composition of Divisions should be representative of the major components present, not actuarially accurate tallies of everything and the kitchen sink. The fact that there were 40 of this in one and 35 in another is secondary to the need to give the Player a consistent force structure that is easily understood.

There are other games out there that provide additional levels of detail in OOB and TOE. The focus here is on Operational Command. Meaningful decisions. Historical accuracy is acknowledged and adhered to up to the point where going beyond only ratchets up the background noise level.

There are no two-headed Numbats here. Your fingers are safe.

10.1.3. SPECIALIST UNITS

Special units, eg. a Nebelwerfer battalion, are handled in a different manner. Theatre Commanders can allocate specialist battalions and resources to an Army, or Panzergruppe, via the 'Focus' mechanic. A set of Officer Action Cards become available to the recipient that provide various bonuses to reflect the presence of such units.

It's a neat way of abstracting this element into the game with minimal micromanagement. It retains the effect, plays to the Operational Command focus and gets interwoven into the relationship system. Even though you may ask for a Theatre Commander to give focus to a Panzergruppe he will find ways to delay and obfuscate if you don't have a good working relationship with him.

Once an Army has focus you can play a card, receive the effect and then ignore the matter until you wish to change your mind. It's hands off. The specialist battalions have arrived and been put to use. They will continue to assist automatically.

It's another either/or decision. Only one Army, or Panzergruppe, can have focus at a time. There are only so many theatre resources available. As Operational Commander you can choose to really throw some resources behind a formation. The 2nd Panzergruppe could be assigned dedicated Luftflotte Air support as well as be given the benefit of theatre focus. You can turn them into an unstoppable powerhouse that can leap tall buildings in a single bound. Until, that is, they run out of fuel. Or suffer too many breakdowns. Or you have a disagreement with your Theatre Commander and he withdraws his focus.

This is a part of the design that has undergone major evolution. Originally the Player was to be given a shopping list of specialist battalions available in each theatre. There were all manner of interesting battalions as diverse as Bridging and 88cm Anti-aircraft units.

The idea was for the Player to cherry pick from what was available - I'll have this, this and *that* - and assign them to individual divisions within a theatre. After a set time period they would return back to the theatre reserve with appropriate delays to reflect transport and repair requirements. Some of them would have been depleted by combat and wear and tear.

It was a mess. Lots of micromanagement, multiple reports and lots of convoluted code to hold it all together with matches and glue. Edge cases abounded.

The Tank Destroyer battalion attached to the 11th Panzer Division is due to return. The 11th Panzer Division is running on empty. Should the battalion be allowed to return to Theatre reserves if its host hasn't got enough fuel to do anything other than snort and snarl? Shouldn't the 11th Panzer being drawing a larger fuel allocation if it has to support the battalion? What if it had a mine laying Pioneer Battalion instead? How are they supposed to keep up with the fast moving Panzer Div when their main form of transport was horses?

Worst of all it didn't add anything other than a series of repeating, low level, decisions that had little impact. Busy work.

Giving a bonus to this Division *here* and that Division *there* was also pointless. As Operational Commander you don't spread your limited resources all over the map like a madman with a butter knife. You concentrate them where it matters.

Abstracting them into Officer Cards gave the required effect in a manner appropriate to the games prime focus. It also allowed scope for individual Army/Panzergruppe Commanders to have an impact as well as the formations current posture setting.

The decision of who to give focus to is meaningful. The decision of what use to put that focus to, via the cards, is also interesting. The fact that it's set and forget and restricted to a single formation in each theatre makes it easily manageable.

On their own these decisions, while important, aren't big deals. But they are another set of balls. The Player, with his Commander's hat firmly jammed on, already has a number that he is having to juggle. It's adding up.

10.1.4. BRIGADES

Specialist Brigades and Regiments deserve a mention of their own. All participants attached, on occasion, Brigades and Regiments, to their Divisions. A lot of these can be factored into the make up and combat stats of the Divisions themselves but there are others that are more notable and worthy of special treatment.

The GrossDeutschland Regiment is a good example. To small to be a Division and to important to be left out. Cases like these are handled by making them an attachment to a Division. They act to buff the combat stats in proportion to their capability.

The Axis have a number of these. Not a lot, but enough to cater for all the situations where it was considered better to include them as individual units.

We are bending our rules here. Making Divisions unique. Accommodating subsidiary formations. While a strict set of guidelines are an admirable thing they can become very arbitrary at times. People with knowledge of the Eastern Front expect to see the GrossDeutschland Regiment present and accounted for, regardless of the scale of the game. Flexibility overrides rigid adherence. We'd be in trouble if it didn't.

The Soviets are a different matter. They had numerous attached brigades. There is a threshold test here. Does the fact that the 202nd Mechanised Division, in the 12th Mechanised Corps of the 8th Army, had the 10th Motorcycle Regiment attached make a difference? Given the qualitative difference that existed between German and Soviet Divisions the answer is probably, no, it doesn't.

The Soviets underwent a major doctrinal change in their use of armour during the course of '41.

Rather than having endless attached Brigades for the later Armies the armour is incorporated into the Divisional structures.

Overall there are very few attached Brigades or Regiments and those that are there are restricted to the German side. It's a compromise but a necessary one.

10.1.5. HISTORY

Before we leave the overview and dive into the details it's worth touching on research. For a major military conflict that happened only seventy five years ago, the multiple sources of information on the various OOB's display a remarkable lack of agreement.

Admittedly it was wartime. Chaos abounded. Records were lost. But still... It's not the Roman invasion of Gaul we are recreating here. It didn't happen several thousand years ago. There are people still alive who were involved. You'd expect more of a consensus on detail than what is apparent.

Reference books and the web serves up so many conflicting versions that you feel like a detective trying to recreate a crime scene that had twenty eyewitnesses, each of whom has a different version. *He was wearing a red baseball cap, officer. Nope, it was a cowboy hat with a red band. Didn't have a hat at all, no Sir! I swear, Officer, that I saw a red bandanna.*

As the Detective what do you do? Take a mean line and assume he was wearing red on his head in some fashion? Go with the witness that appears to be the most credible? Simplify and state only that there might have been a hat involved?

Research is a frustrating business. Depending on the circumstances and the quality of information on hand I've utilised all three approaches. I've also been ably assisted by people more knowledgeable than myself. You can find their names mentioned in the credits. Any mistakes can be attributed to myself.

10.2. COMMAND STRUCTURES ▶

The game models command in terms of a generic Army HQ → Theatre HQ → High Command structure. Because of the importance of different levels of command and how interwoven into the game mechanics they are it is important to fix on a model and stick with it. The base model is derived from the German command hierarchy that existed on the day. There was, in fact, an additional layer at the top with OKH reporting to High Command in Berlin. OKW has been skipped. Present in effect but not in person.

Most Player's won't know the difference between OKH, OKW and High Command and, from the game play perspective, it's not important. What does matter is that there is a clearly understood hierarchy in place. Divisions are grouped in Armies, or Panzergruppes, and these report to Theatre HQ's which is logical given the theatre separations on the map.

OKH is where the Player resides. The three Theatre HQ's report directly too him. As the Player has superiors there needs to be a higher level. High Command holds down this spot.

It's a straightforward model that aligns with the historical reality. It enables a lot of interesting decisions and mechanics that hinge around the interaction of the various levels of HQ's, the Player's subordinates and superiors.

While it works nicely for the Germans it isn't always a neat fit for the other nationalities involved. An early design question that had to be answered was whether the Command model needed to be changeable to accommodate the different hierarchies on offer or whether those same hierarchies were to be shoehorned into a standard model.

This is an interesting question. The are two main combatants and a number of minor parties. The eccentricities of the minor parties can be safely ignored as they had little impact either way. The Germans are fine as they are already a perfect fit to a model based on them. The Soviets are the wild card.

Lets take a look. At the commencement of Barbarossa they had a convoluted, complicated command structure. There were Armies, Corps, Districts, Regions, Fronts and Stavka (Soviet High

Command). Stavka was officially formed a day after the invasion commenced! Here is a command structure that began morphing into a different shape right from the start. The reality of Stavka and Soviet Supreme Command wasn't quite as clear cut as this but there is no denying the whole edifice was a moving target.

It got worse. A number of minor and major reorganisations followed in rapid succession. Structurally it was all over the place. Like a chameleon unsure of its environment it kept changing. Eventually it settled down and a system of three fronts emerged. Fronts, in fact, that were very similar to the theatre delineations that the Germans utilised.

The decision of what to do about the Soviets wasn't, in the end, very difficult. They were given the same command model as the Germans with the only difference being one of nomenclature - Fronts instead of Theatres. Their initial, complicated, hierarchy at the start of the campaign is shoehorned to fit. As it wasn't a steady state situation in the first place, ramming a square peg down a round hole to cover a situation that appeared to change every time Stalin blinked, is a reasonable compromise.

Yes, there are discrepancies with how the Soviet Command structure is portrayed, especially in the early game. We are willing to live with this. Importantly, the key element of *reorganisation* is picked up and made into an game mechanic for the Soviet Player. While the Soviet Player starts the game with an end state command structure, there is an imperative for him to reorganise and not doing so will create problems later on. While the specific command details have been, to an extent, abstracted the *effect* is retained.

10.3. GERMAN OOB ▶

SS Mot. Div. "LSSAH" (Adolf Hitler) commenced Barbarossa lacking men and equipment. It was more of a Brigade than a Division. By July '41 it had been brought up to full Divisional status and as it was kept in reserve up until when it arrives as a reinforcement in early/mid July rather than commencing the campaign on the map.

The Lehr Brigade (attached to 14th Motorised Div/3rd PG) didn't arrive till the 1st July '41, two week later than depicted in the game.

There was a reasonable amount of Divisional shuffling between theatres. Except for the requirements of the newly formed 2nd Army in Armeegruppe Mitte, this has been ignored. There are also a number of Divisional reinforcements that can arrive, via decisions, earlier than they did historically.

The trend to phase out the 37mm ATG and replace it with the 50mm ATG has been dealt with by the replacement system. Successive waves will have fewer of the smaller guns and more of the larger resulting in a TOE shift over time for the relevant Divisions.

The Germans fielded two types of light tanks, the Panzer II and the Panzer 38(t). While these were different beasts manufactured in different countries they have been combined into a single light tank, the Panzer Mk.II with appropriate tweaks to it's combat stats to reflect a hybrid of the two.

ASK YOUR STAFF

- **Why are there so few tanks in a Panzer Division?** After the invasion of France the Germans wanted to double the number of Panzer Divisions for Barbarossa but were faced with the problem that there weren't anywhere enough tanks to do so. Their simple solution was to thin out the existing Panzer Divisions and basically split one Division into two.

There are a couple of reasons for doing this, the main one being the limit of the number of subformation types that can be displayed for an individual unit. This being eight individual types which you can see in the unit display window, bottom right. The engine can accommodate more but it involves an additional mouse click to access them. Rather than do this I've standardised on the one light tank and made sure that the stats reflect a combination of them both. Having dual light tank types present wouldn't add much other than historical window dressing.

A particular issue with the German OOB was the number of Divisions that were held in reserves. At what point should the Player be able to access these? When they were historically released, from the get go or somewhere in between? In general the Divisions become available around the time that they were released but this is tweaked by a probability factor that can see them turning up earlier or later than they did on the day.

ASK YOUR STAFF

- **Where are the Stugs?**
  The Stugs, in '41, weren't available in large numbers and were organised predominately into infantry support battalions and had no formal role in a Panzer Division. Their use as support battalions is represented by the Command Focus mechanic and they are factored into the Officer cards that represent the secondment of specialist battalions.

10.3.1. SPANISH OOB

The Spanish Blaue Division is shown as a standard German Division. Their signature Blue uniforms were only worn while on leave in Spain. They donned standard Heer issue uniforms in the field and were regarded by the German General Staff (and Hitler) as a bunch of ratbags but excellent defensive fighters who were on par with any equivalent German Division.

10.3.2. FINNISH OOB

Group Oinonen which consisted of a Cavalry Bde., the 1st and 2nd Jager Bde's has been lumped together into a named Division under the command of GenMaj. Oinonen. As you'd expect.

10.3.3. ROMANIAN OOB

There are conflicting opinions as to the strength of particular Romanian formations. Specifically the 1st, 2nd, 3rd & 4th Mountain Divisions which are referred to as Brigade strength (2 regiments strong) in some sources and Divisional in others. My approach is to have them as two third strength Divisions. In a similar vein the 1st and 2nd Fortress Brigades have been combined into a single Fortress Division as each was essentially a reinforced Brigade.

There were quite a few Romanian Cavalry Brigades floating around. These were genuine horse mounted mounted men from another era. Cavalry proved effective in Barbarossa when it was used as a means of mobility rather than one of combat. There were a number of instances of Cavalry charging enemy lines and, in the overwhelming majority of cases, it resulted in only a pointless slaughter of men and horses.

As there were quite a few Cavalry Brigades (5th, 6th, 7th, 8th) at the start of the campaign, (the 1st and 9th turned up later), I've opted to have them as attached units.

The 1st Armoured Division ('Greater Romania') was weaker than a standard Panzer Division and equipped with Romanian R-2 tanks rather than the German Panzer Mk.2's as depicted in the game.

As the 1st Armoured Div actually had a military impact, unlike most of the Romanian Cavalry brigades, I've given it a weakened Divisional status and a place on the map. The game models armour in some detail in terms of mileage, breakdowns and refits. Having a unique type of armour (R-2) adds an additional overhead in terms of programming and processing which isn't warranted when that armour is only used in small quantities by a single unit that played a relatively minor role.

Hence the replacement of the R-2's with Pz. Mk II's. The R-2's were modified versions of the Czechoslavakian Panzerkampfwagen T-35. They were a light tank with any differences (there were a few) being irrelevant from a game perspective. My sincere apologies to the lovers of the venerable R-2.

The Romanian Command structure underwent several changes as the campaign progressed and I've kept it constant as reflecting the changes would add little.

10.3.4. HUNGARIANS

Originally the Hungarians were to be left out. Minor, bit players. Unimportant. They eventually scored a place on the team along with the Spanish. Of all the nationalities involved the Hungarians are the ones who are the most awkward fit. No fault of their own but some major shoehorning has had to be done to accommodate them.

In '41 the Hungarian Mobile Corps arrived at the front with a couple of motorised and cavalry brigades respectively. The motorised Brigades had attached armour, around 10 to 20 Toldi light tanks that were used primarily for reconnaissance purposes. As these had little military impact I've decided to exclude them. Yes, I know that I'll be getting correspondence from the 'I-love-the-Toldi' fan club. My lawyer will have to explain to them that some tough calls have had to be made and that the Toldi, for all it's fine qualities, got left on the reserve bench.

With a total of 4 Brigades I'd be looking to lump them all into a single Hungarian Division but that isn't going to work as half would be motorised and half cavalry. With the inclusion of the support elements there were around 20 to 25 thousand men in total which equates to a couple of standard Divisions, more than you'd expect from 4 Brigades.

Which gives us two full strength Hungarian Divisions with names that are as close as possible to their Brigade notations. Sadly, that's not the end of the Hungarian dilemma. Where do they go? Historically they were assigned to the 17th Army in Armeegruppe South. That's fine but the game mechanics have Armies comprising solely of slow Divisions and there is a fast, motorised, Division that won't fit.

The Hungarians have been assigned to the 1st Panzergruppe instead, the neighbouring formation in AGS, and one that can handle a motorised Division without major alterations being involved. Historically there was a requirement to keep the Hungarian and Romanian forces separate as there was a level of animosity between the two. Or perhaps it was tank envy. Either way the Hungarians are present and accounted for, in their correct theatre and with their Toldi's at a safe distance from the corrupting influence of the R-2 light tank.

10.3.5. ITALIANS

Well behaved. Nothing to report.

10.3.6. SLOVAKIANS

The Slovaks had, apparently, trouble keeping up with the German advance. In August '41 the 1st Slovakian Division was issued with trucks and reorganised into the 1st Slovak Fast Division.

Not in the game. The trucks have been put to use elsewhere. The Slovaks will have to break into a jog although this may not be necessary as they have the same movement ability as a normal German Infantry Division. It would be nice to model these minor bits and pieces but they are well below the radar.

10.4. SOVIET OOB ▶

The Soviets were tricky. They have the largest number of Divisions in the game, over six hundred. Their OOB wasn't a tidy, fixed, exercise. More of a sprawling, rapidly changing and evolving organic process that resulted from having to adapt to fast changing circumstances.

Despite this Soviet forces can be broken down into distinct categories. There were the regular Red Army formations present at the time of the invasion. Badly positioned, poorly lead and undergoing major doctrinal change, but still there, on the map, ready to fight.

Then there were a number of other regular Armies that were elsewhere in Russia. These constituted Stavka's Reserve. Certain of these Armies were already in place but were quickly repositioned by rail to other fronts, eg. Central, to counter developing threats. In all cases these arrive as reinforcements, at the Front that Stavka intended, in the early days.

The mobilisation conscript Armies are a big category that can be broken down into early and late Armies. The distinction is necessary as their

OOB's and TOE's changed as a result of different ways of thinking and the increasing availability of new equipment.

The major differences present are that Conscript Armies are defined by their equipment. Late Armies (October onwards) benefit from having an upgraded ATG (45mm to 76mm), better artillery pieces and T-34's compared to the older, lighter tanks.

T-34's and KV1's are present in the early Armies but in low numbers. There were a lot of teething problems with the early models. Typical Conscript Divisions were formed with lower manpower strengths than the Regular Divisions.

Armour utilisation changed over time. There were only 10 new tank divisions formed before the Soviets switched over to a system of attached Tank Brigades. Rather than being separate these are incorporated into the Divisional TOE's with scope for the massing of Tank Brigades, for offensive purposes, later in the game.

Shock armies have all Divisions with attached Tank brigades.

Finally there were the experienced Divisions shipped over from the Far East, the Siberians.

The tricky bit about all this is the Divisional naming. The Regular Army units that commence the game on the map are all named correctly as information on them is readily obtainable. There is an element of compromise involved in order to fit all the oddities into the games structure but no more than you'd expect.

Reinforcement Armies are another matter entirely. Finding accurate information on these has proved extremely difficult. While there is data available, most of it is conflicting. The Soviet practice of the day with Divisional naming didn't help. If your country is about to be overwhelmed you are probably not going to be fussed about each Division having a unique name which accords to a logical system of nomenclature.

The end result is that any attempt to accurately name the mass of reinforcement Divisions runs headlong into serious conflicts that are difficult to resolve and require an awful lot of fudging.

Rather than do this and end up with a split OOB where some Divisions are named historically correct and others not, because of the contortions involved, I've opted to apply generic Divisional naming to all reinforcement Divisions. This applies to both the Stavka Reserve and Conscript Armies.

The Armies are correct, the Commanders, where possible, are correct, the OOB and TOE's are as correct as the information available allows but the Divisions are named generically.

A final note on replacements. The overall arc of the Soviets in '41 was to create new Armies rather than reinforce existing ones. There are numerous exceptions to this but they were largely focused on reforming mauled, disbanded or destroyed Divisions that were then incorporated in new Armies. In the game the Soviets receive no replacement troops or equipment. All new manpower and materiel is assumed to be consumed by their unprecedented mobilisation drive and arrive as reinforcements, not replacements.

10.4.1. REGULAR RED ARMY

The Northern Front has proven problematic. The 191st Infantry Division has been given to the 7th Army. It may well have been in the Leningrad Military District or held in reserve.

Which is another area of contention. There were many Soviet Divisions, and Armies, in the process of forming up at the time of the invasion. While many OOB's state they were present they fail to indicate when they became active military formations. There is a big difference between Divisions being present on paper to being present on the ground.

The 13th Army in the Central Front is a good example. It apparently was brought to life in the very early days of the campaign. How they managed to do this in any coherent manner when the region in which it formed was being over run by rampaging panzers is a bit of a mystery. I've chosen to have the Divisions involved be part of the existing Western Military District command and forgo the birth pangs of the 13th Army. Probably happened on a Friday.

A number of Airborne Brigades have been combined into named Divisions, for example the 5th

Airborne Group. Technically this was the 5th Airborne Corps comprising of the 9th, 10th and 214th Airborne Brigades but having a Division named as a 'Corps' isn't appropriate so hence the 'Group' tag.

To avoid conflict in other areas of the OOB the 1st Tank Division, Northern Front, appears instead of the 3rd Tank Division. Historically the 1st Tank Division was part of the 14th Army which fought way up north around Murmansk, off the the map.

10.4.2. SIBERIANS

'The Siberians arrived and saved Moscow' is a standard trope of Eastern Front literature and gaming. Whether it actually happened is debatable. There are strongly argued opinions promoting both sides. The recent unlocking of the Soviet Archives tends to favour the 'Siberians had a minimal impact' point of view. They arrived, not as an integral Army but as individual Divisions, spread over time, that were parcelled out willy nilly to help defend both Moscow and Leningrad.

Rather than go with the up-to-date research that contradicts a lot of long held beliefs I've opted for a populist approach. The Siberians will turn up as an integrated Army, in the depths of winter, with the potential to make a difference.

This has been done to align the game with the majority opinion and for reasons of game play. Holding on by your fingernails, waiting for the boost that the arrival of the Siberians will give, is a great mechanic.

An issue with this is which Army should the Siberians arrive under given that it is, most likely, historically inaccurate in the first instance? I've settled on the 58th Army which was sourced from Siberia (not the Far East) and was, in reality, a conscript Army that just happened to be raised in Siberia.

It's a fudge but a good one from a game play point of view.

10.4.3. FORTIFICATIONS AND GARRISONS

At the start of the campaign the Soviets had extensive fortifications throughout Western Russia, especially in the border region. Overlapping this were numerous 'Fortified Areas' that were separate formations tasked with defending a particular area. As the campaign progressed emergency garrisons were formed to defend cities that comprised of a hodge podge of whatever forces where on hand.

This can be dealt with by placing all the required fortifications and defensive formations on the map at game start. Not a good solution. It squeezes the game into an ever tightening historical straight jacket and decreases replayability.

A better approach, one followed in the game, is to give the Soviet Player control over where and when he places his fortifications and forms his garrisons. This becomes a mini-game in itself where he has a limited number of both and has to choose wisely where to use them. It also provides scope for different strategies and enhances the games replayability.

Historically very few fortifications provided much in the way of an obstacle to the Germans. They were, along with their associated 'fortified area' formations, largely ineffective. Later on, with time to prepare, this wasn't the case but in the initial days of the campaign they were minor speed bumps only.

As you'd expect there are a few exceptions that need to be accounted for. The Leningrad region, in the vicinity of the Finnish border, had well prepared fortifications sited in difficult terrain as a consequence of their earlier Winter War with Finland. It's worth prepositioning a handful of these on the map to prevent the Finns from a-historically walking into a lightly defended Leningrad.

It's also worthwhile including some 'fortified areas' but more as representative Divisions than units tied down to a set location. This only really applies to the Baltic Military District and up north around Leningrad. The units are referred to as 'Border Divisions' and are intended to provide a sense of the additional manpower that was positioned in the relevant areas, not as strict historical representations.

10.4.4. SOVIET MARSHALS

Once again another moving target. Lots of senior command changes, at the time, that don't fit easily into the predefined command structure that has been decided upon. Fairly easily resolved as it isn't difficult to discern who mattered and who didn't.

The game allows for the replacement of Marshals. There needs to be a roster of possible replacements. To fill this out I've pulled actual Marshals back through time. Ones that were active later than the time period of the game have been allowed to appear as replacements to those that have been fired or executed.

It's better to provide real life Marshals, even if they need a quick trip in the Tardis, than a collection of mythical, made-up, Marshals as replacements.

Which creates a specific issue with the 19th Army, a Stavka Reserve formation that arrives early on in the piece. It was commanded by one Ivan Konev who served with distinction and went on to become a full Soviet Marshal. He happens to be on the list of replacement Marshals. Having him turn up as a Marshal, for example, in charge of the Central Front, wouldn't be a good look if he was already holding down the job of commanding the 19th Army on the very same Front.

Ivan has been summarily removed from the lesser position and a LtGen. W. Kuznetsov has taken his place instead. Kuzentsov was the actual 19th Army commander who succeeded Ivan when he was promoted so we are still within the realms of the possible here. Ivan will be impatiently awaiting his turn as a full Marshal. You might have to shoot a few existing ones before you get to see him but he is a good man in a pinch and well worth the wait.

11. DESIGNER NOTES – DECISIONS

11.1. DECISION OVERVIEW ▶

Assume that you've been left in charge of a big lump of machinery. There are pipes and valves everywhere, steam vents abound and there a multitude of gauges and controls. It's a complicated mess of equipment and you know that you'll be spending a lot of time twiddling the controls to keep it running. This was me quite a while ago.

I spent most of a four hour watch period trapped inside a never ending feedback loop, chasing my own tail. I'd tweak a control then run around and check gauges. Tweak a few more controls, check again. I never really managed to extract myself out of the loop by achieving an ideal set-up as the dynamics were constantly changing. It turned me off a career as an engineer.

Now consider the same piece of complicated machinery. Instead of having to run around a noisy, hot, dirty engine room there's an air conditioned control room with a window and a coffee maker. All the information you require is right there on a screen. The multitude of controls have been semi-automated. Instead of constant manual intervention, the Engine Control Program (ECP) running the whole show pops up decisions from time to time. It tells you that something is out of whack and asks what you'd like to do about it? Rather than drowning in micromanagement you are making high level decisions and letting the ECP take care of the details.

It would, however, be unwise to be lulled into a false sense of security. The Engine Control Program, left on its own, will, sooner or later, bring everything to a grinding, screeching halt. Typically followed, in quick succession, by a fire. You still need to know what you're doing. You're still in charge, all that's changed is that the system allows you to concentrate on the decisions that matter rather than spamming you with micromanagement irrelevancies.

Which is the aim of the game.

Decisions that matter. Strong feedback. Micro-management not found at this address. Decisions without the fiddly bits.

Take 'Truck Tires' as an example. It's a good one to use as, on a scale of one to ten for potentially interesting game decisions, it would be down there amongst the dead men. If I had to pick the most boring decision in the game, Tires would be it.

Let's see how successful the game is at turning the Tires into something you might want to care about. It's a means of highlighting the individual components of Decisions and to discuss the thinking behind them.

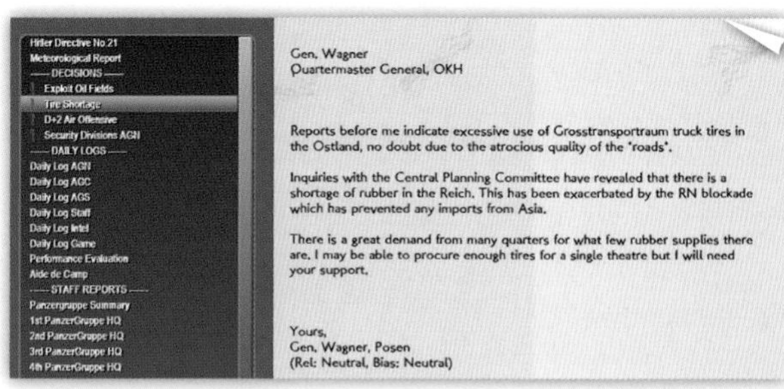

The main decision screen aims to provide all the information you need. There is a primary message indicating the matter at hand, a selection of available options and a list of further, related, reports available on the right. As you're expending a finite currency to exercise decision options, Political Points (PP's), there's also an indication of how many you have available.

How many options should there be? A few, a lot? Research into this consistently states that the ideal number of options that humans prefer, when considering a decision, is around three, four at a stretch. Any more and they tend to feel overwhelmed. Interestingly the research also shows that, when asked, people tend to request more choices than they are capable of processing.

Now this is for the average human. I haven't met that person yet and I bet neither have you. Being average in everything they are probably invisible to those of us who make up the rest of the standard deviation bell curve.

Regardless, three or four choices isn't a bad aiming point. Luckily that's about where the game is. A typical decision involves allocating resources between a theatre. As there are three theatres, that's three options plus a default, do nothing, choice. Mr. Average would be pleased.

Then there are the reports. Each decision has a 'bundle' of reports, explanations and help messages attached to it. Throwing all this at the Player in one go would be too much. It's a lot of reading. It interferes with the natural flow of the game. Which is why there is a single primary report and a means of quickly accessing all the rest at your convenience.

Unlike alternative approaches used by other games, any report is derived from a character. There are no messages from an omni-potent God that tells you of a situation and asks that you respond. Nothing wrong with that approach but as the game already has a cast of characters that you are dealing with, it makes more sense that reports come to you from one of them.

It's also more in line with the Operational Command ethos of the game to have General Wagner, your QuarterMaster Gen., send you a missive when there is a matter that requires your attention rather than have a generic pop-up blandly inform you that you need to do something about Tires.

The downside of this is that there is still, despite my best efforts, a modicum of reading required. The reports are kept short and free of graphical distractions but you still need to read the primary message to understand what is going on. You also need to, at a minimum, glance at the options to determine what choices are available. These have been given a layered approach, with a bold heading that is sufficient on its own and a smaller print line of text directly underneath that gives further information. You can get by without the extras.

Still, there is reading involved. In the early turns of the game, when there is a lot going on, you'll be confronted by a variable number of decisions. Occasionally this will be a sizable number. Each of which requires a minimum amount of reading.

It's a problem that hasn't really been satisfactorily solved. Once it's been decided to provide the Player with a range of decisions, each of which has a meaningful impact on the game, you've moved beyond the simple, generic, decision interface that other designers have made use of. There is also no way of replacing the text with graphics as a certain amount of discussion is required to impart the details of a particular decision.

Some Player just plain don't like reading. They much prefer to shuffle hexes around the map and not be bothered by anything not directly related to the matter at hand. Fair enough. There's a 'No Decision' option available to cater for them and an interim 'Limited Decision' one as well.

For those that are willing to juggle the extra balls that Decisions impart, there is the concept of Delegation that allows you to only deal with the ones that you consider important and to let your Chief of Staff take care of the rest. Feasibly, with a little knowledge of the game, you could scan the list of Decisions and choose which to deal with from the summary notations alone.

A second issue with the Decisions is that not all of them have an immediate impact. There are Decisions that you'll take that won't do anything for a dozen or so turns. Their effect is delayed. These are noted in your Daily Logs but, once again, that requires reading.

The range of Decisions is deliberately broadened beyond the obvious 'direct modifier' effects. As an Operational Commander you're expected to deal with a wide spectrum of decisions. Game wise, they all have an impact on one mechanic or another but that's not always obvious to new Players.

To overcome the, apparent, 'disconnect' between the Decisions and the hex game the pool of Decisions have been buffed up to include more direct effect instances. In the end it probably comes down to personal preferences and the game lets the Player choose their level of involvement in the Decision process.

Still, it'd be a more elegant design if the Decision side of the game could be scaled up or down more easily without the need to tailor it by the use of option settings.

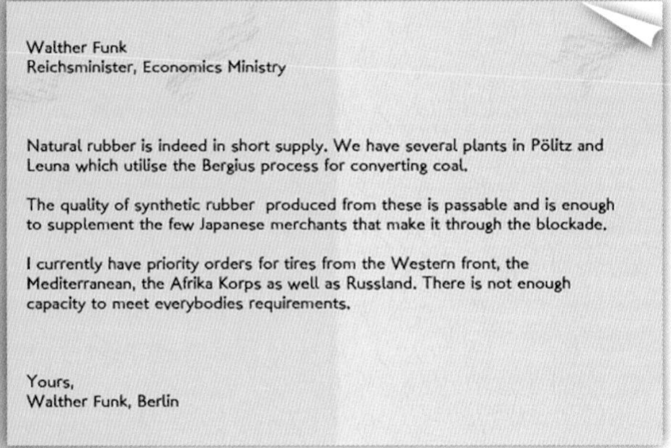

Walther Funk
Reichsminister, Economics Ministry

Natural rubber is indeed in short supply. We have several plants in Pölitz and Leuna which utilise the Bergius process for converting coal.

The quality of synthetic rubber produced from these is passable and is enough to supplement the few Japanese merchants that make it through the blockade.

I currently have priority orders for tires from the Western front, the Mediterranean, the Afrika Korps as well as Russland. There is not enough capacity to meet everybodies requirements.

Yours,
Walther Funk, Berlin

It's a given that each Decision has a minimum of two reports. As Decisions aim to be meaningful, there needs to be a point of conflict. The reports present opposing views. At times there are multiple views on offer.

Any decisions that reach your desk are assumed to be curly ones. If they were straightforward or obvious they would have already been taken care of by your underlings. Hence the conflict. As Operational Commander your role is that of arbitrator. Rather than spell out the conflict in black and white terms the reports provide you with competing perspectives from the characters involved. You deliberately aren't given the full facts. You're provided with sufficient information to make an informed decision, no more, which is in line with everyday reality.

One concession that's been made is to provide a set percentage chance for any option that involves a random roll. Rather than stating that you are unlikely to sway the Führer with a course of action you are instead informed that the chance of a bad outcome is 70%. This is a step back from the situation confronting a real Operational Commander but a necessary one from a game play point of view.

Allocate Tires to AGN This will be at the expense of the other two theatres	2PP
Allocate Tires to AGC This will be at the expense of the other two theatres	6PP
Allocate Tires to AGS This will be at the expense of the other two theatres	5PP
Don't bother me about Tires 75% Chance of a BAD outcome	0PP

The available options for Tires revolve around who will receive them. As previously discussed, this feeds directly into the Theatre system. There is a scarce, needed, resource. Somebody will benefit and others will miss out. It's an archetypal operational decision, one that elevates you above the level of your Theatre Commanders, each of whom feels justified in demanding the Tires.

Their perspective is confined to their individual theatre whereas yours has a broader span that views each of the three theatres as inter meshing parts of the whole. This provides both a sense of command and that of a working hierarchy.

Whatever option you choose for the Tires, some of your Theatre Commanders are going to be pleased

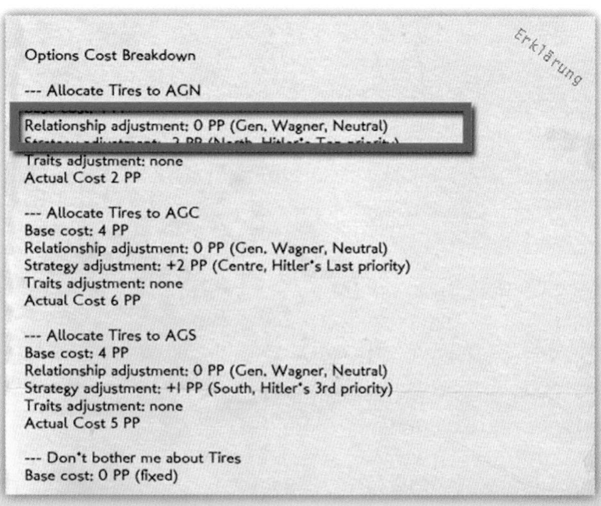

Options Cost Breakdown

--- Allocate Tires to AGN
Relationship adjustment: 0 PP (Gen. Wagner, Neutral)
Traits adjustment: none
Actual Cost 2 PP

--- Allocate Tires to AGC
Base cost: 4 PP
Relationship adjustment: 0 PP (Gen. Wagner, Neutral)
Strategy adjustment: +2 PP (Centre, Hitler's Last priority)
Traits adjustment: none
Actual Cost 6 PP

--- Allocate Tires to AGS
Base cost: 4 PP
Relationship adjustment: 0 PP (Gen. Wagner, Neutral)
Strategy adjustment: +1 PP (South, Hitler's 3rd priority)
Traits adjustment: none
Actual Cost 5 PP

--- Don't bother me about Tires
Base cost: 0 PP (fixed)

Your relationship with General Wagner isn't causing any trouble (0 PP)

and some are going to be unhappy. Having the Decision system mesh directly into the characters reinforces the feeling that you are dealing with people. People who aren't static. They have opinions. They aren't afraid to express them.

Nowhere is this more apparent than in the cost, in PP's, of the individual options. Your relationship with a character directly affects his likelihood of providing willing help or reluctant, begrudging, assistance.

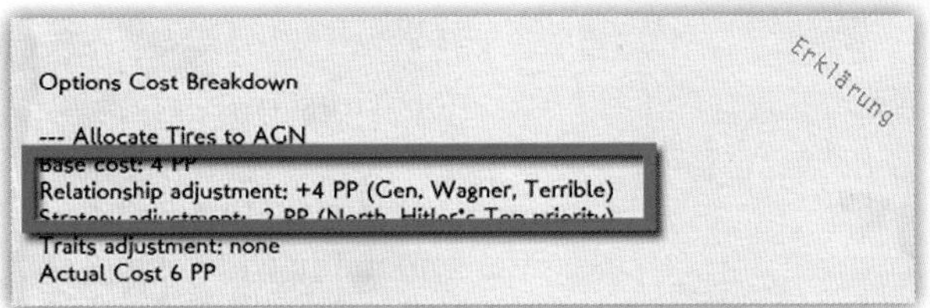

General Wagner is extremely reluctant to assist you given your 'Terrible' relationship

The above image shows the cost of resolving the Tire conundrum at a time when General Wagner is no longer sending you birthday cards. As you can see, Tires, and all other decisions involving General Wagner, have suddenly become a major drama. Because your relationship with him has effectively broken down it will take a greater amount of your time to cajole him into doing something that he'd rather not.

All option costs have increased (+4 PP) due to General Wagner's intransigence

The technical term for this is Command Friction but you can experience it at home. Ask your better half to kindly pass the salt at the dinner table tonight. You'll either get handed the salt shaker with a smile or be rapidly calculating incoming ballistic trajectories depending on your relationship level.

Well if Tires are that important you could resolve to remain in General Wager's good books. Which is achievable but at a cost of other relationships. There is a war on. People are under pressure. They have their own agendas, their own priorities. There were underlying fault lines in the historical command structure of the Wehrmacht that virtually guaranteed that not everybody will get along.

Assume that you've given the Tires to Armeegruppe Mitte. They'll be happy. But the commanders of the other two theatres may not be. Relationships will change. Choose to do nothing and General Wagner, in a fit of frustration, will likely get upset at the lost opportunity.

Then there is the Führer. His strategic vision acts as a changeable background drag, or assist, on most decisions. The game doesn't impose the requirement that the Player conforms to the will of the Führer but it does impart a feeling of consequence when acting in opposition or alignment to his wishes.

Overall the Decision system acts as a central design linchpin that provides a linkage between many other elements. It is a key means of removing micromanagement from a wide range of detailed subjects that would otherwise require them.

Take the Tires. Normally a game of this scale wouldn't be concerned with nuts and bolts down at this level. Which is a valid reason for ignoring it altogether except for the fact that the maintenance of Truck columns was an important aspect of the campaign, one that needs to be modelled.

The game does so in detail, with Tires being one part of it. But at no point is there any micromanagement involved. The game keeps track of a lot of Truck Column statistics. It automatically triggers decisions when required that enable the Player to make a single, hands-off, meaningful choice. The Player is given plenty of feedback and allowed scope to make turn by turn decisions that directly affect the health and efficiency of his Truck Columns (eg. How far does he stretch his Columns? On what terrain does he position his HQ's?).

The alternative approach, maintaining a similar level of fidelity and sans Decisions, would likely involve ticking columns of numbers, truck field maintenance units on the map, truck repair depots and spare parts physically having to be shuffled between this and that. Lots of chrome. Lots of busy work. Meaningless micromanagement.

It's not all roses. Replayability is the lumbering elephant in the room. A big effort has been put into varying the Decisions. They arrive within randomly determined time periods. In a given play through certain Decisions won't appear, others will fail to trigger and a lot of options will only turn up if you have positive relations with the character in question.

Nothing is scripted. The Decisions appear within a set framework but there is a lot of variability in how they do so. But because each Decision is a significant element all on its lonesome, each time it reappears a Player will instantly think, *'yep, been there before'*. Tires, Birthday Present, Werner Molders. *'Yep, already seen 'em'.*

General Jodl
Chief of Staff, OKW

Of course you are aware that it will be F.M von Brauchitsch's birthday next week. I thought it best to remind you in case the demands of the war were preventing you from recalling the smaller details.

While I have no particular interest in the matter I think that you should make a token effort to maintain civil niceties given that F.M von Brauchitsch is your immediate superior. A good working relationship between the two of you is to the advantage of all concerned.

Please remember your position. You are in operational command of the Ostfront and it wouldn't do to spend time away from your duties on frivolities. Give the old man a bottle of confiscated Vodka and be done with it.

Yours,
General Jodl, Zossen
(Rel: Neutral, Bias: Neutral, Traits: Nazi, Toadie)

Show that you care. He's your boss

There are only so many different Decisions. It's not feasible to have a new set for each play through. The system is designed to repeat. After a few playthroughs it's intended you get a feel for what's involved and start thinking about how best to manage them. Which is similar to an Operational Commander.

Imagine yourself, standing to attention, about to invade Russia. There are going to be problems with Trains and Trucks. There are going to be disputes between theatre commanders. The Führer will inevitably poke his oar in. Fuel is going to be an issue. Before the campaign even commences you can confidently predict that all of these will be a given. You don't know when, or in what form, but they are on the radar and won't be leaving.

Yet a lot of Players, conditioned to constantly changing stimulation, will expect that once they have seen a Decision once, it shouldn't reappear. Not in this playthrough, nor the next. The fact that the same Decision appears five turns later in the next playthrough, and that the option costs are markedly different because they have a different set of relations, is drowned out by the act of repetition.

This isn't any fault of the Players. Nor is it necessarily a defect of the design. I'd consider it more a failure of expectations. Perhaps a failure to properly communicate the design intention. It's a nagging question mark that didn't, in the time span available, get satisfactorily resolved.

One reason for this is the nature of a war game portraying a set piece battle. How many times is the average Player going to replay that same battle?

In this instance, because there's a lot of scope for variable outcomes, there are depths to be plumbed and the campaign is both manageable in size and time, the answer is probably more often than most.

Yet not enough to justify spending an inordinate amount of time creating a fully modular, non-repeating, Decision system, assuming such a thing is doable. As it is the system soaked up the most development time of any part of the game.

I'd consider the Decision system to be an evolutionary leap but one that still has some miles to cover. The fun, they say, is in the journey.

11.2. WINTER ▶

11.2.1. WHO FORGOT TO PACK A JUMPER?

Winter Clothing and Equipment

It's historical folk lore that the lack of proper equipment hobbled the Wehrmacht as it endured the harshest Russian winter in over a hundred years.

Which it did. They were horribly unprepared and suffered grievously as a result. With the onset of winter and the failure of Operation Typhoon there was never any hope of winning the war in Russia. They had gambled everything on a fast, decisive, campaign that had them destroying the bulk of the Red Army and crashing through the gates of Moscow *before* the onset of winter.

It didn't happen. Nobody had bothered to consider the possibility of failure. When all you have is Plan A and there is no Plan B or C, that's understandable.

With winter looming, there were no shortage of Field Commanders demanding to know when their winter clothing and equipment was arriving. It wasn't long before Hitler forbade any further mention of winter preparations. The winter of '41 arrived with nothing having been done.

All of which is true. But there is more to the story than this. F.M Von Halder took a preliminary look at the problem as early as the 25th July '41. There were numerous reports and studies thereafter on what a Russian winter would involve and what contingencies would be required to deal with it.

Proper winter clothing, suitable winter quarters, anti-freeze oil, lubricants and how weapon systems could continue to function in ultra low temperatures were all investigated and considered by OKH from early August onward.

Situation, AGN: Enemy before Tikhvin has been reinforced. Very severe cold (38 degrees below freezing), numerous cases of death from cold.

F.M Von Halder's War Diary, 6th December 1941

There is some evidence that winter equipment was available, if required. Whether it was available in sufficient quantities and how accessible it was is debatable but, by all accounts, the cupboard wasn't bare.

Even if Hitler had acknowledged the possibility of an extended campaign and agreed to go ahead with a winter clothing and equipment replenishment there was still the problem of logistics.

At the time of Operation Typhoon the Germans had three separate Panzergruppes in Armeegruppe Mitte, ready for the assault on Moscow. Their network of trains was in crisis. The sudden onset of cold weather had wrecked havoc with the German locomotives. Unlike the Soviet loco's, the water pipes for their boilers were external and they froze and burst in the cold, rendering the locomotives immobile.

Whatever trains they were able to run were fully occupied getting enough fuel and ammunition to the front. There was no spare capacity for the enormous space requirements of bulky winter clothing. The Germans didn't have the logistical capability to resupply, and sustain, their three Panzergruppes, let alone extras.

From a game perspective there are two options. The first would be to go with history and confront the Player with a total absence of winter equipment. That's how it was then, that's how it is in the game.

Not the ideal approach. A better alternative would be to provide a way of gaining winter equipment but doing so in an historical context rather than a straight, 'yes you can have it'.

Situation, AGS: Assault on Sevastopol will start on 10th December. Troop movements from Sixth Army to First Panzer Army are proceeding satisfactorily, but the troops are weakened, and suffer severely from the cold. Ammunition supply to First Panzer Army is disrupted because the railroad must accommodate replacement transports.

F.M Von Halder's War Diary, 6th December 1941

The main factors that can be distilled from the historical record would be Hitler's reluctance, the tightening time frame and the logistical difficulties. While being able to model these is important, above all there should be scope for interesting decisions that present the Player with challenges and opportunities.

The forbidding onset of winter provides a ready made ticking clock. The Player has the foresight of history. He knows what's coming. There's a sense of tension. As the clock ticks down he is becoming increasingly desperate that his forces are adequately prepared. He may have already taken Moscow. But he has to hold it against a Soviet winter counterattack. He needs that winter equipment!

11.2.2. TOUGHEN UP, BUTTERCUP. IT'S ALL IN THE MIND

Gaining Approval

The first big obstacle the Player needs to overcome is that of gaining the Führer's approval. We can take it as a given that Hitler was against the idea. What better way to motivate your forces into an all or nothing final lunge? Warm winter quarters in Moscow beckoned. Failure meant only the prospect of freezing to death in a muddy, frost encrusted, foxhole.

How should the Player be able to change Hitler's mind? On his own, realistically there would be little chance of doing so but if he was able to build a consensus then it might be possible.

It should be more than possible. A Player shouldn't be put in the position of expending a lot of time and effort to get people onside only to have it all fall in a heap when a single random roll determines that the Führer didn't like the idea.

There should be a defined point when the matter is decided, once and for all. Because of the ticking clock it's not a concern that can be deferred indefinitely. The Player can opt to request a meeting with Hitler in early October specifically to discuss winter equipment. This is fixed and known beforehand.

1700 Meeting with Heusinger, Current business: Exchange of views about the future organisation and distribution of forces in Occupied Russia after the Russian Armies have been destroyed. Winter preparations must be initiated now.

F.M Von Halder's War Diary, 9th July 1941

Prior to the meeting the Player is given the opportunity to canvas opinions and garner support from a range of characters.

Before he does this, however, he has the option of ordering a study into the effects of a Russian winter. This happens in July and replicates the actions of F.M Von Halder. It's a gateway decision. It is here that the Player takes a stance on winter. Does he follow an historical trajectory and ignore winter, confident that he can take his objectives and win the game before it becomes an issue?

F.M von Brauchitsch
Commander Armed Forces, OKW

Yes, I have received your request to make a presentation on winter preparations to everybody here at OKW. As winter will shortly be upon us it is a topical issue.

You are aware that the Führer has expressly asked all commanders to NOT raise this issue? Of course you are, as we have discussed winter preparations earlier.

In light of the Führer's position I am reluctant to proceed with your presentation but I will do so if you insist. A suggestion would be to divert the wrath of the Führer by having one of your staff conduct the briefing, rather than yourself.

Yours,
F.M von Brauchitsch, Zossen
(Rel: Neutral, Bias: Neutral, Traits: Anti-Nazi)

Or does he hedge his bets and opt to play it safe? Doing so comes at a cost. He will have to lobby hard and potentially incur the wrath of the Führer who is vehemently opposed. There will be a cost in Political Points (PP's) that could be better spent winning the war.

On the face of it the best strategy would be to ignore winter and go for broke. But this will leave the Player exposed if he manages to capture his objective but is then forced to hold it throughout the worst of the winter. A successful defence here could turn a certain defeat into a tenuous victory.

It's difficult for a Player to accurately judge their prospects of success in July when the Study decision triggers. There is room for the Player to reassess and change direction but, in general, winter isn't something that can be left to the last possible moment.

Having ordered a study the Player will also have the opportunity of presenting it to Higher Command once it is completed. He will also be able to lobby various characters. Each person he manages to sway to his cause will contribute to his chances of success in October, as will the related study decisions.

This is shown as a percentage readout allowing the Player to judge his chances of success. It is designed such that a concerted campaign will result in a greater than 100% chance. This would ensure that Hitler agrees and they can proceed.

F.M Keitel
Military Advisor, OKW

Winter preparations? Nonsense! Are we to win the war or are our men to freeze in their foxholes while the Bolsheviks sit by a warm fire?

The War is almost won. The Soviet Bear has had his back broken and is only waiting for us to put him out of his misery. Stalin is rumoured to have abandoned Moscow.

What could motivate a soldier more than the promise of victory and the warmth of a captured Dacha against the prospect of shivering through a cold winter in his summer uniform?

Yours,
F.M Keitel, Zossen
(Rel: Neutral, Bias: Neutral, Traits: Nazi)

Lobbying F.M Keitel isn't going to be easy

There are wrinkles. Gaining the support of a subordinate (the three theatre Commanders) will have a smaller impact than that of a superior whom is more likely to sway the Führer's opinion.

Conversely it is harder to convince a superior than a subordinate. For superiors the Player has the option of swaying the mind of his immediate boss, F.M Von Brauchitsch. Given they are both professional military officers this isn't onerus. More challenging are F.M Keitel, Hitler's military advisor and Reichminister Goebbels, Minister of Public Enlightenment.

Politics and relations play a part. If your relationship with a particular character is especially bad then the option of lobbying them in the first place won't trigger. If they don't trust you, they won't be willing to countenance your arguments.

If your relationship is good then you are given an additional option, that of asking them for a favour. Doing so will garner their automatic agreement at small cost in your relationship. Favour aren't free.

In summary the Player has the means of mounting a successful campaign which will, by hook or by crook, gain enough support to convince Hitler that winter equipment is a necessity. The Player can also choose to ignore the whole winter question or take a half hearted approach that risks the matter being decided by the whim of the Führer.

11.2.3. WHERE ARE THOSE WARM SOCKS THAT I ORDERED?

Permission Gained

Once the intransigence Hitler has been overcome there is the question of what happens now? Does the Wehrmacht magically sprout winter woollies?

Spell casting wizards sadly aren't a feature of the game (I'd be ordering mine to cast the spell of 'Mud Begone!'). Instead the Player is dropped into the realm of contract negotiations which doesn't sound anywhere near as much fun.

But it's important. Yes Hitler has agreed but it's a reasonable assumption that he would have done so reluctantly. He isn't going to move mountains to assist. More a case of being willing to turn a blind eye.

The Player, as Operational Commander of the Ostfront, wouldn't be expected to have to worry about contract negotiations for the supply of winter equipment. It's a concern well beneath his pay grade. But time is pressing and there is a need for the equipment to arrive sooner rather than later. He could reasonably be expected to be in a position to exert some influence on the process.

A 'Let Contracts' decision triggers the turn immediately after gaining Hitler's agreement. This would be in early October. It may be later as the Player is given the option of deferring his meeting with the Führer by a week or so. Why would would a Player want to do so? Well he might not have enough Political Points (PP's) available when the first opportunity arises so there is a fall back position of deferral to enable him to have a second crack at it.

Gen. Wagner reports to the audience of Gen. Staff Sec. Chiefs on the outcome of his conference with the Supply Chiefs: We are at the end of our resources in both personnel and materiel. We are about to be confronted with the dangers of deep winter. Provision for a sudden break of the weather must be made yet before middle of January. Situation particularly difficult north of Moscow.

F.M Von Halder's War Diary, 27th November 1941

Once the 'Let Contracts' decision fires the Player has the ability to push the process into high gear and get things moving quickly. There are several degrees of 'quick' with commensurate escalating costs.

11.2.4. THE COURIER HAS NO KNOWLEDGE OF MY DELIVERY

Distribution

The Führer has agreed, the contracts have been let and a stockpile of winter equipment has been accumulated. A 'Distribute Stockpile' decision triggers.

There is sufficient stockpile for one theatre only. The Player gets to decide which theatre will receive the initial allocation. This is another typical operational decision where one theatre is prioritised at the expense of the other two. These are excellent decisions as they hammer home the responsibility and difficulties involved in being a true Operational Commander.

Choosing which theatre isn't a challenge. Dealing with the fallout might be. By now it's mid to late November and there is a crying need from all quarters for winter equipment. Everyone has a valid argument as to why they should receive the allocation. You can reassure them all you like that more winter equipment will be forthcoming, enough for everybody. Won't make any difference. They need it NOW, not next summer.

Summoned to the Führer: The Führer is going to take over High Command of the Army himself after departure of F.M Von Brauchistch owing to ill health. I am to carry on my functions, while Keitel will take over the administrative part. New routine: Daily Conference.

Two mistakes have been made 1)... 2)Provisions against extreme cold were inadequate. Army works too mechanically. Air pointed out as the model. Has been educated in entirely different spirit by the ReichMarshal.

F.M Von Halder's War Diary, 19th December 1941

Noses will definitely be out of kilter. Relationships will deteriorate. If you already have a testy relationship with a particular theatre commander can you afford for it to worsen? While this is going to be a secondary consideration to stiffening your military capability in a theatre under pressure, it's certainly a factor to be taken into account.

Is this the end of it? Are those knee length sheepskin sentry coats to be issued automatically?

No. They still have to be transported through your logistical system to the front. There is a decision 'Winter Trains' that asks you to decide what transport priority the shipments of winter equipment are given.

You can choose to put everything else (fuel, ammunition) to one side and concentrate on nothing but. Or you could order that it be sent forward using only spare capacity, when and if it's available. A certain number of trains are required. The engine will keep a tally and provide feed back on your winter equipment transport status.

Depending on the demands placed upon your rail network and your choice of shipment priorities, this could be completed in a single turn or drag on over multiple turns. Once half the required number of train shipments have been made an allocation to all Divisions is conducted automatically to level 1 of winter preparations. When all shipments are completed the remainder is allocated and every Division within the theatre is given another two levels.

The climatic model is very detailed and each level of winter preparations gives protection against a certain amount of cold and frostbite. It applies to both men and machines. As a means of comparison the Wehrmacht starts the campaign with preparations at level 0 throughout. Winter equipment will raise this to level 3. The Red Army, with their greater tolerance for cold, is at level 4 with the Finns and Siberians at level 5 and 6 respectively.

Evening Situation, AGC: Guderian has broken clean through the enemy lines with his central group and has pushed 60km into enemy territory in a sweeping advance. His right wing, still far behind and under enemy attack, is causing concern. All quiet on the rest of the front. The enemy is taking his Divisions out of the line for issue of winter clothing.

F.M Von Halder's War Diary, 1st October 1941

To complete the story the stockpile will continue accumulating, at an accelerated pace due to ramped up manufacturing, and there will be enough equipment to distribute to the remaining two theatres simultaneously. Both theatres still require decisions over shipment priorities and their individual shipments are tracked and reported upon as above.

It's worth noting that I've taken a very benevolent view on the number of trains required. Winter equipment, enough for an entire theatre's worth of men and machines, would overwhelm whatever train capacity was in place. Nor is distribution by Truck Columns considered. It's a game, there needs to be a happy outcome rather than endless frustrations mimicking historical reality.

If we were to go with a high fidelity simulation the decision to supply winter equipment would have needed to be made soon after the campaign began. Shipments would be required to be on hand for progressive transport over an extended period of time and if the process wasn't underway by early October, at the latest, there would be little hope of completing it in time.

Gen. Gercke
Wehrmachttransportchief, OKW

Do you realise how much space Winter clothing consumes? The requirements of a single Line Division bulk load to more than the fuel requirements of an entire Panzer Division.

Yes, we the train service can accommodate the necessities of Winter but it is significant logistical undertaking and we are already over stretched with the need for fuel, supplies and ammunition.

It comes down to priorities. I can gradually train the Winter gear to the front using whatever spare train capacity is on hand or I can push everything else to one side and do it quickly. I will require written confirmation from you either way as I refuse to carry the blame for the ensuring outcry.

Yours,
Gen. Gercke, Zossen
(Rel: Neutral, Bias: Neutral)

But that didn't happen back in 1941. Hitler's intransigence prevented it. The game allows it to happen but it's a prolonged process that requires a solid commitment on the part of the Player. There is a sense of journey here. When your men, frostbitten and shivering in their summer uniforms, manhandling frozen machinery, finally receive their winter clothing you feel that you've achieved something. It's been a long, hard road and despite the difficulties, you've managed to do what others couldn't back in the day.

There is also tension. You may have done everything correctly but the worst of the winter arrives before the clothing and equipment. But this is in the hands of the Player. Various decisions - Contracts, Distribution and Trains allow the process to be prioritised. Whether it is worth doing so at the various inflection points depends on the overall situation and the demands on your stockpile of Political Points.

Tough decisions, trade-offs. That's Operational Command.

11.3. AIR WAR ▶

The Air War over Russia in '41 has been deliberately abstracted. Like artillery there was the imperative to remove all superfluous units off the map, to keep the unit count manageable.

The nature of the Air War lends itself to being abstracted. There is the initial overwhelming destruction of the Soviet Air Force by the Luftwaffe. The textbook acquisition of air superiority. The total absence of strategic bombing and the heavy focus on ground support. The importance of long range reconnaissances. The vital role that aerial resupply played.

Note that none of the above mentions Soviet air activity. Throughout '41 the Soviet Air Force, the VVS, did indeed fight back and cause localised problems. As the year progressed, as the weather worsened, the Soviet edge became greater.

Yet it never really developed beyond nuisance value. From the divisional perspective of the game it had little meaningful impact, apart from in specific areas very late in '41. As 1942 began the air superiority pendulum began edging back towards the VVS (Voyenno-Vozdushnye Sily - 'Military Air Force').

But that is outside the time period of the game. Within it, the Soviet Airforce was, for all intents and purposes, conspicuous by its lack of punch. Certainly it was present but only rarely did the Germans significantly change their plans as a result of activity by the VVS.

The late game, late '41 period where the VVS broke out from being a bit actor, is accommodated by giving the Soviet Player the option of increasing the air defences around a chosen location. This is achieved by an Action Card, not by plonking air units down on the map.

As a drama, the Air War really only had one full time actor, the Luftwaffe. The story arc was all about the slow, gradual, decline of that actor into, relative, senility and feebleness when the war went into its final years of '44 and '45. It's one of introspection and a struggle against the environment, rather than a head to head conflict with an opposing force.

It's also a very typical German pre-invasion planning, head-in-the-sand, ostrich act. There were no shortage of these. The underlying assumption built into all the planning was for a quick, decisive, win. Inconvenient facts that didn't support this were overlooked.

German aviation experts toured Soviet aircraft factories prior to the start of the war and reported back to Reichsminister Göring. Experts from Daimler-Benz Henschel and Mauser informed him that a single aero-engine factory in Moscow had six times the capacity of Germany's largest factories combined. Göring chose to ignore them.

Heinrich Aschenbrenner the German military air attache, toured the Soviet Union's aircraft factories and reported sophisticated and advanced manufacturing facilities with evidence of extensive production already underway. Göring, infuriated, dismissed his report.

It was clear from the start that if German forces weren't going to be wintering in Moscow that the Luftwaffe would eventually be overwhelmed by sheer numbers and superior technology. While this would have been obvious from the reports mentioned above it wasn't as clear cut from the events that transpired in the early part of the campaign.

Stalin's Great Purge had left the officer corps of the VVS in as poor shape as those of the Red Army. Russian aeronautical designers were liable to be shot on charges of sabotage if their prototype crashed. The VVS began Barbarossa with a numerically stronger force but of inferior quality and operated by untrained personnel compared to the Luftwaffe. Reichsminister Göring could well have formed the wrong impression from the Luftwaffe's early stunning victories.

Like the Red Armies motley collection of pre-war armour and poorly prepared crews, it was an illusion. There were vastly superior tanks and planes, along with gradually more experienced crews, waiting just around the corner in '42.

11.3.1. AIRFIELD SYSTEM

The initial design of the Air War component went through a number of iterations. All of them, however, had, at the their core, the removal of specific air units from the map. Right from the start the imperative was to abstract the air war.

The one sided nature of the air war in 1941 was a big help here. If the Luftwaffe had failed to neuter the Soviet VVS in the opening days of the campaign then 'abstraction by design' wouldn't have been viable.

Was there any possibility of the VVS not being chopped to pieces at the start? Should the Players be allowed to have this in their game provided toolbox of possibilities?

No on both accounts. No historical account portrays a 'near miss' or 'unlucky outcome' for the VVS at the start of the Barbarossa. They got what they deserved. Forward deployment. Inexperienced Officer Corps. Planes neatly lined up in rows at airfields. Out of date equipment and the misfortune to be up against an extremely professional, proficient, air force. The outcome was never in doubt. June 22, 1941 was Pearl Harbour done right.

A desire to remove micromanagement and reduce the on-map unit count fed directly into the abstraction decision. Another factor, one not so obvious, was the difficulty involved in balancing the air war once there were actual flight squadrons to shuffle around.

There is a surprising amount of detail that needs to be incorporated into the game to accommodate on-map squadrons. Finding a sweet spot of settings that allow the Players room to move while still adhering to a reasonably realistic outcome is very difficult as a number of other, existing, games covering the same topic have already found.

It's a lot of work and effort involved for the designer and a heck of a lot of busy work on the part of the Players that, even if the balance is ideal, achieves little. The Germans are destined to head shoot the VVS and go on to dominate the ground support war in '41. Much better, in this case, to do away with all the fiddliness and busy work and focus on providing interesting, meaningful decisions.

In keeping with this there are no numbers. Not of planes, anyway. Nowhere in the game can you find an indication of how many He111's there are in Armeegruppe Nörd, for example. Nor can you find a readout of how many Soviet fighters have been shot out of the sky.

This is an, admittedly, heretical approach for a war game design but in a one sided air war where, arguably, the Luftwaffe lost more planes to the environment than it did to enemy action, it's a sensible one.

How many He111's or Bf109E's are available in any theatre are only one part of an effective air power equation where weather, fuel and airfield quality are just as important.

Hence the decision to wrap all of these into a single indicator, 'Net Air Effort'. For each theatre there is a single airfield where it assumed the main Luftflotte resides. It's taken as a given that there will be smaller groups of aircraft scattered around but the main effort derives from a single, designated, theatre airfield.

An airfield has a 'Quality' rating which reflects the standard of runway and infrastructure available. A set number of air worthy aircraft are always going to be more effective operating out of a airfield with a surfaced runway, hangers and adequate repair facilities than one with a dirt strip and a improvised huts and tents.

The longer a particular airfield is utilised the more effective it becomes. Facilities are upgraded, runways are improved, damaged aircraft are repaired. There is a base level for all potential airfields on the map. On the side of the Polish border where they serve hot Bigos (Hunter's stew), airfields are of a high order. Fly east into Mother Russia and there is a marked decline in airfield standards, not helped by retreating VVS forces conspicuously failing to leave an intact and tidy operation for the next occupant.

Moving east also reflects the replacement rate of aircraft. Between June and December of 1941 the new production, in Germany, of bombers, fighters, dive-bombers and close reconnaissance aircraft was below the loss rate (around a 20% shortfall). As an example less than half of the almost 60 close reconnaissance Staffien (squadrons) in place at the start of Barbarossa were still operational by the end of 1941.

Weather has an impact on airfield quality. Provided the sun is shining all's well. Once rasputitsa (mud season) arrives dirt runways become unsafe. Less aircraft fly. There are more accidents. Eventually it snows. Fuel tanks and lines freeze. Engines seize. Lubricating oils coagulate. Metals stress and crack.

Out of one hundred thousand Luftwaffe vehicles (not aircraft) in the east, only fifteen thousand were still operational at the commencement of 1942. That's a mind boggling 85% failure rate.

Fuel acts as an effort limiter. The Luftwaffe normally received priority when it came to limited fuel stocks, especially the high octane, highly refined, petroleum products that it required. But this isn't always the case. The Player has scope to direct some of this precious liquid towards his Panzergruppes. There may not be enough fuel remaining for the Luftwaffe to maintain a full operational tempo.

What's left after airfield quality is marked down for weather and fuel becomes your 'Net Air Effort'. A numerical representation of your ability to project air power within a theatre. How many specific types of planes are available isn't the point. If air power is a spear it's not the composition of the spear, the colour or the length that's important. It's how far and how accurately it can be thrown.

Which is why distance plays an important role. Air power is assigned to an Army, or Panzergruppe. The distance between the theatre airfield and the HQ determines how much of your 'Net Effort' is lost in transit.

Which isn't entirely accurate. Nothing is lost. Planes don't crash into the ground just because they have a longer flight (aircrew are assumed to be professional in their ability to estimate flight time and fuel loads). It's simple maths. If it takes one hour to fly to a location then there is ample time to conduct your business, return to the airfield, refuel and rearm before repeating the process. You can't do that if it's a four hour flight to the objective. The amount of air power you can project is probably halved by virtue of the time required for transits there and back.

Distance matters. Deciding when to relocate your Luftflottes to more forward locations is critical. Automatically rushing them as far forward as you can isn't an obvious answer. You're moving east. The quality of the airfields are declining. You may get overrun. The rail link back to the Main Supply Depot may get cut. Acting precipitously is dangerous. Dithering equally so. Playing safe and keeping your Luftflottes well back in nicely maintained airfields will result in your Panzergruppes outrunning their air support. It's a balancing act.

At least you've got control over it. Unlike the weather. The game takes both the weather at the airfield and at the assigned HQ into account. The best laid plans...

11.3.2. PANZERGRUPPE ASSIGNMENT

Gen Wolfram Von Richthofen, commander of Fliegerkorps VII, noted in his diary that "the Army refused to accept that the Luftwaffe could not be dribbled out to all and sundry. For maximum effectiveness, air power had to be concentrated at major points. Every sortie needed time. Aircraft had to be refuelled, bombs loaded, and then flown to the new objective. Everyone in the Army wanted to take over the Luftwaffe, but the Army was completely unaware of the potentialities of air power" (5th July, 1941).

In accordance with the rest of the design, air power is assigned on an Army, or Panzergruppe, basis. It isn't 'dribbled out'. Who to assign air support is a significant decision as it can be, under the right circumstances, extremely powerful. Typically you'd want to assign it to a Panzergruppe so it can act as a 'mobile artillery' to the spearheads as it did historically. Of course the Player doesn't have to and he can, if he wishes, swing it over to help an Army reduce an encircled pocket or punch through a defensive line.

Anyone can benefit from a Resupply mission and aerial reconnaissance continually updates intel and Soviet on-map force dispositions (the level of knowledge the Germans have on-map is a magnitude higher than that of the Soviets) but air support is dedicated to whoever it is assigned to.

Typically air Power is a fiddly, micromanagement heavy, process in a war game. Lots of counters, lot of low level decisions. Scattered effect. With the games operational perspective the design cuts out all the micromanagement and still has you making decisions but they are few and meaningful.

Who do you assign air support to? Where do you base your Luftflottes? How far are you willing to push your Panzergruppes into, or beyond, the extremities of your air support envelope?

These constitute the key decision parameters that need to be assessed on a theatre by theatre basis. There are a range of secondary decisions that arise but these are of a lesser importance than those stated above.

As Von Richtofen (yes, a direct descendant of the famous, red winged, Baron)pointed out, air power is all about concentration. Having the Player assign each theatre's available air support to an Army, or PG, follows this maxim and provides an interesting decision space.

Like the Garden of Eden, with it's forbidden fruit, there is a terrible temptation to drive your Panzerguppes as far to the east as you can, lunging for your objectives. If you are unable to keep leapfrogging your Luftflotte Air Bases forward at the same pace you can easily find your Panzers way out on a limb without a Stuka or Heinkel in sight.

11.3.3. D+2 AIR OFFENSIVE

The initial Luftwaffe shock and awe air offensive against the unprepared Russian Air force was a resounding success. For the loss of only 78 planes the Luftwaffe knee-capped the VVS with over 2,000 of its aircraft destroyed, many while lined up in neat rows on the ground.

How to model this? Don't even try. Assume that it will happen and move on. There aren't any interesting decisions to be made in slaughtering the opposition. The VVS are going down, regardless of anything the Player does.

What can be done is to give the Player the option to continue the offensive with the consequent disruption to Soviet Command and Control and interdiction to rail and road networks. Do you pursue this policy in the expectation that it will likely hobble the Soviet's ability to react or ignore it and swing all available aircraft into a Tactical Air Support (TAC) role.

Here is a more interesting decision. Disruption and interdiction affects the entire Soviet force while TAC provides the hard hitting punch that the Panzergruppes need for their initial breakthroughs and encirclements.

The German Player, if they choose to interdict, don't get given specific details on the effect of this.

Hermann Göring
Reichsmarschall, Aviation Ministry

Reports are in from all three Luftflotte Kommandants and it appears our initial air offensive has been an outstanding success. In fact, it is hard to believe the extent of our victory but reconnaissance flights have confirmed what the logical mind can't fathom.

Initial estimates are over 2,000 enemy planes destroyed, most on the ground, at the cost of approximately 40 of our own planes. Fragmentation bomblettes used against runways were found to, on occasion, explode prematurely and this accounted for about half of our losses. The few enemy fighters that did manage to get airborne were easily dealt with. A poor level of pilot training was evident.

It is important to not forget that we are fighting a primitive people and we should not expect them to have harnessed the power of flight to achieve military aims. Nor should we be surprised when they manifestly failed to take even basic defensive precautions at their airfields. It will be a short campaign.

Yours,
Hermann Göring, Berlin
(Rel: Good, Bias: Positive, Traits: Nazi)

Nor should they. General, Daily Log, reports give an indication of what's happening. The effect is randomised, within reasonable parameters, and can vary from turn to turn. It is, however, significant and can restrict the Red Armies ability to respond.

11.3.4. WERNER MOLDERS

The Eastern front created many high scoring German fighter aces. Knocking Soviet planes out of the sky wasn't that challenging in circumstances when VVS pilots had strict orders to maintain formation, no matter what.

It made them soft. When the cream of the German aces were transferred to the Reich in order to combat the waves of allied bombers, they didn't last long. They were shot down almost as fast as the regular pilots already on the western frontline. Without a ready pool of trained air crew the Reich's production of new aircraft was pointless.

Werner Molders was a pilot who joined the Condor Legion assisting the Nationalists in the Spanish Civil War. He was an innovative tactical thinker who came up with the renowned 'finger four' formation. He was a resounding success in the Battle of Britain and was an experienced, blooded, fighter pilot before arriving on the Eastern front. Being the first pilot to shoot down over 100 enemy aircraft he was handsomely rewarded, banned from further combat duties, and transferred to the Reich Air Ministry.

Joseph Goebbels
Reichsminister, Ministry of Propaganda

Geschwaderkommodore Mölders has achieved one hundred confirmed kills. He is the first fighter pilot in the world to do so.

This is a major propaganda coup and we must immediately remove Mölders from the front line to avoid the risk of his demise which would be most embarrassing. I consider him to be a national treasure and a most valuable propaganda asset – too valuable to lose.

I will arrange for him to transfer back to the Zone Interior where I envisage he would undergo publicity training prior to an extended tour aimed at demonstrating evidence of our forthcoming victory over the Bolsheviks.

Yours,
Joseph Goebbels, Berlin
(Rel: Good, Bias: Positive, Traits: Nazi)

He died aged 28, not in combat, but when the Heinkel He 111 that he was a passenger on crashed during a thunderstorm while attempting to land. Werner, for all his experience, fatally chose to not wear a seatbelt.

Guderian commented the Soviet bombers made river crossings hazardous for his armour, but he confirmed that the Luftwaffe was always able to secure temporary air superiority where it mattered. "Whenever Mölders showed himself, the air was soon clear."

Werner warrants a decision. He represents an elite officer whose impact extended beyond his own personal efforts. Left in charge of Jagdgeschwader 51 he can reasonably be expected to impart his knowledge and experience onto those he commands. Enough to make a difference.

Yet there is the risk that he may die. He's a hero. It wouldn't sit well with the German people. Morale would suffer. Faced with a similar scenario the Luftwaffe chose to warehouse him back at the Air Ministry. Heroes are a fragile commodity.

The Player can also take a middle course and have him transferred to a Fighter Training School which may result in an immediate drop in air effectiveness in Armeegruppe Mitte but a delayed, overall, increase as the quality of newly trained pilots improve as a result of his imparted wisdom.

There are implications here for all options. Different agendas are in play and there is no obvious answer. It's a fun decision, but an interesting one.

11.3.5. AIR DOCTRINE

The Luftwaffe soon found that their standard operational doctrine parameters were a poor fit for the Ostfront. Poor weather arrived but the requirement to continue flying operations, especially resupply, remained.

Hermann Göring
Reichsmarschall, Aviation Ministry

My Luftflotte Marschalls would like to know what doctrine they are expected to follow on the Ostfront as it is unclear at present and an element of confusion exists.

Standard flight doctrine is for missions to be flown only when the aircraft are operating within their designed environmental parameters. This DOES NOT mean the Luftwaffe only flies when the sun shines and the tulips are in full bloom. We are a professional military organisation and are prepared for a variety of weather.

It would, however, be appropriate for you to issue guidance on what you expect of the Luftwaffe, given Russland's vast geography and range of climatic conditions.

Yours,
Hermann Göring, Berlin
(Rel: Good, Bias: Positive, Traits: Nazi)

Loosening your doctrinal parameters will allow planes to get airborne more often. There will be an immediate boost to the amount of air power you can project. This comes at a long term cost. Operational doctrines are in place for a reason. Bad weather and bad runways make for a higher incidence of accidents. By allowing the Luftwaffe to operate in adverse conditions, those outside of what is normally considered acceptable, you are going to, eventually, lose more aircraft from environmental causes.

Short term gain versus long term pain. The specific outcome has a randomisation factor so the extent of both will vary from game to game. Is the immediate boost to your air power going to help your Panzergruppes punch through the Soviet defences and take a key objective? Perhaps the price paid when the bill is finally presented may be worth paying? If, on the other hand, you're playing the long game then it could be to your advantage to conserve your Luftflottes for when they are most needed.

12. DESIGNER NOTES – INVOLVING THE PLAYER

The games relentless operational focus is expressed in many ways, not the least a plethora of reports that the Player can dig into as they wish. But I think that it's just as important to provide the Player with an immersive experience. If they are going to spend time recreating Barbarossa they should, ideally, have the game reach out and pull them into the experience as much as possible.

This doesn't involve manhandling or virtual robotic arms that extend outwards in an ominous hiss of hydraulic actuators and pnuematics. It's done by providing something you can personally relate to. Movies are the masters of this. Typically a protagonist in a drama, or even a romance, is a larger than life character. But not so large that there aren't a series of clever, subtle hooks that you, the viewer, can latch onto and say, 'hey, that could be me'.

Once you make that leap into projecting yourself into the shoes of the protagonist you are entering the realms of a full on, I'm-having-a-lot-of-fun, immersive experience. You are living out the movie in your mind, thinking 'what would I do in that situation?'. You know that protagonist, or the events, aren't in anyway related to your day to day existence but it doesn't matter. You've made the leap. It's a great movie because you're in it.

Try doing that with a fully digital movie, one without human actors. They are visually excellent. They can tell a story just as well as a movie with warm bodies in it but they aren't the same. It's because there isn't anyone in the digital cast who you can relate to. Nobody to project yourself onto. With their digital disconnect from reality, you are unable to make the leap that allows you to become immersed in the experience.

It's the difference between *watching* a movie and being *inside* one.

Games aren't like movies. Well, that's not actually the case as the lines are definitely blurred. A first person game which places you in the midst of the action can be a tremendously immersive, make your own movie, experience.

War games, hex and turn based war games, are a different beast. You don't receive an adrenalin rush from staring at a map full of counters and deciding to move that unit *two hexes east*. They have nowhere near the level of visceral excitement as popping up, jack-in-a-box like, from behind cover and attempting to hose down the bad guys before they flush you out with perfectly lobbed grenade.

In the immersion stakes they are the gimpy horse at the back of the field that belatedly gallops round the final bend and up to the finish post only after the race has been declared over. No bookmaker will go broke taking bets on Hex the Horse taking out first place in the Inaugural Immersion Stakes.

What can be achieved, however, is to generate the desire to play 'one more turn'. That's a different kind of immersion and one that is just as valid as the pulse pounding kind. But it's a slow burner, cerebral experience. One that requires an investment of time and effort.

It's a lot easier to reach this version of gaming nirvana if the game you are playing is of the 4X genre. One where you start small and gradually build up. There is a threshold that you cross where the time you've spent building up your world matches your desire to hold onto what you have created. Threats that risk destroying an empire that you are personally invested in become more than just a game mechanic aimed at providing a challenge.

It's not just another virtual construction. It's your world. You built it. Nobody is going to take it away from you. You're willing to fight to defend it. What happens next becomes exciting and immersive. You are firmly in the grip of the 'one more turn' addiction.

The further your clunky hexy, turn based, war game deviates from the this 4X sandbox experience the harder it is to pull the Player into the game. A designer can create an excellent simulation of military reality but, if there aren't any people involved, it's going to be a very dry exercise in counter shuffling and number manipulation.

There has to be something to care about. That's people. Tanks, planes and objectives are all tools that are combined to create a military stew according to a recipe. They are ingredients that contribute to the overall taste. But no matter how good the stew is, it's still just a stew. It's the people sitting around the table with you, enjoying the meal, talking and joking, that make the difference.

When you engage in PBEM with another person, you care. Perhaps about beating them or sharing tales of the mutual experience you are enjoying. Put a person in the picture and it elevates the game. Unfortunately most of us, roughly 9 out of 10, will find ourselves sitting at a computer playing the game versus an AI opponent. We are digesting our virtual stew, sitting at the table, all on our lonesome.

We still need to care. There still needs to be people involved. If they aren't at the table with you then they have to be in the game. DC3 has a cast of characters that you interact with. There are portraits of them, they make comments about you and your relationship with them matters.

This is a good starting point for creating immersion. You're dealing with actual people, not numbers. But it can, and should, be taken further.

DC3 uses a number of different ways in order to reach out and grab you. It's a broad palette that befits a broad audience, one that aims to pull you in. As the inherent difficulty of doing so with a fixed campaign recreation is already high, it aims to make the most of any opportunity that arises. It's the sniper on the hill, waiting for you to break cover.

Every time you here the sharp *'Crack!'* of a high velocity bullet zinging past your ears it's probably because of one of the following design mechanics.

- Performance Evaluation
- Loss Assessment
- Halder Extracts
- Leader Quotes
- Battle Reports
- Division Events

12.1. PERFORMANCE EVALUATION ▶

Feedback is important. Nobody likes to be told that they are a dill, nor does the game do this, but all of us like to have the a metric, or two, that allows us to benchmark our progress. Perhaps not against the rest of the world but simply to enable us to strive for a better outcome the second time around.

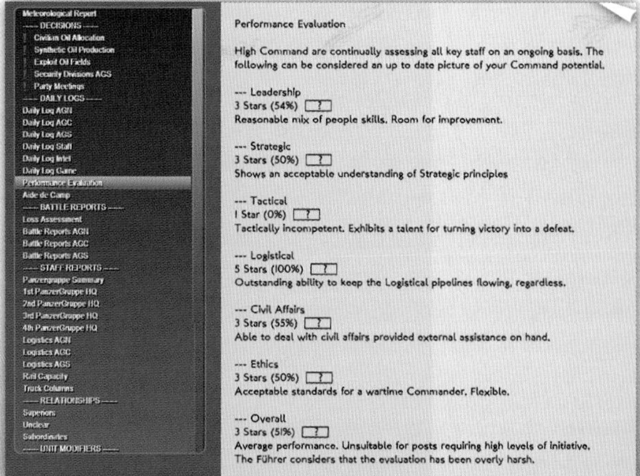

High Command will continually assess the Player's Command Potential. Which, it should be noted, is a different animal to a Player's position on the Win / Loss spectrum. To handle this a more graphical approach is taken which highlights its importance.

High Command's assessment is slanted towards a 'pull no punches' approach with a splash of humour thrown in. Dynamic tool tips let you drill down and see the particular metrics that are being used to judge your performance.

To spice things up the Führer will chime in with an opinion but, as befits the man, this is based more on his intuitive *'feel'* (your current relationship level which is taken as indicative of his opinion) rather than the hard data that High Command uses.

The Player can check this every turn if he wishes. Allowing him insight into how the assessments are calculated is a subtle way of pulling him down the rabbit hole.

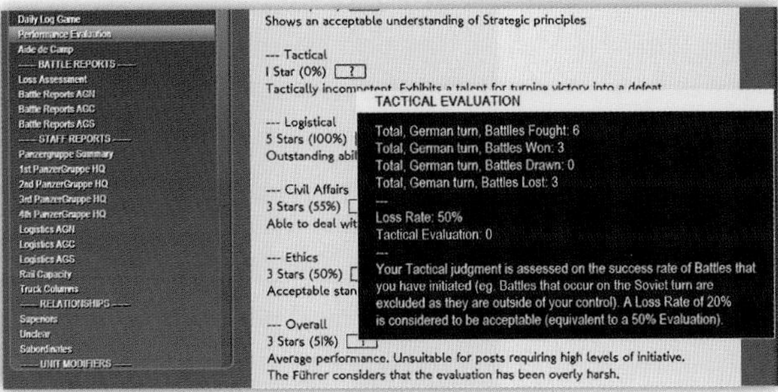

Tucked away in the dark recesses of my resume are six months spent playing professional poker in Las Vegas, which was prior to the boom in online gambling. I'd sit down and play poker for eight hours a day, gradually climbing up the table hierarchy as my 'stake' swelled.

It's not a career that I chose to pursue because I was, it turned out, fatally unsuited for a life of cards. This wasn't initially apparent and it took a substantial amount of time at the tables before I realised that my inclination to seek out the toughest players and try and best them wasn't the way to fame and fortune.

You do the opposite. Find the weak and vulnerable and prey on them like a Great White Shark cruising the beach on a sunny day. Wasn't my thing. However the experience was highly instructive in a number of other ways.

A major insight was that playing cards wasn't hard. There were, like any field of endeavour, a suite of technical skills that you had to master - probabilities, mental tracking, etc. Like driving a car after a certain point they became automatic. There were a similar number of soft skills such as reading and manipulating people, being able to shift gears on a whim, etc. which did, admittedly, require a base level of aptitude. Eventually they became similar background auto-pilot processes just as the hard skills were.

Overall it was a case of aptitude, application and persistence. No different to learning how to become a decent cook or play a musical instrument.

It didn't take long for me to become proficient enough to start making money. I was also sufficiently self aware to be able to recognise the fine line between ability and a good run of luck. *'It all averages out in the end'* is a common misconception about any activity that involves random probabilities, such as poker.

Sure it does. But the 'end' can be a very long, long, way over the horizon. Lady Luck and her husband, Mr Standard Deviation, can really go to town. They hold some wild parties. At times you find yourself standing in the rain, out on the street, peering through a keyhole at all those other people making whoopee inside.

Or you can be having crazy fun with Mrs Luck and the other deluded fools who think they are God's gift to Poker. Parties end. The hangovers can be severe and terminal. You learn to ignore the invitations and become accustomed to wet clothes. You play the long game. Snakes and ladders knowing that there are a lot more ladders out there than snakes. It just takes a while to find them on occasion.

Do all this and you are on track to be successful. You're probably now in the top 5% of all people playing poker, heading for the lucrative top 2%. Until one day you wake up and realise that you aren't playing the other people at the table. Not in the sense of them being a challenge. Because, as a group, they aren't. You'll beat them all. Not today maybe and perhaps not for a couple of months, but sooner or later you'll take their money.

You realise that the toughest opponent you'll ever play isn't any of the faces you see at the tables. It's the one in the mirror. You're a human. You have emotions. Lots of them. You have biases. More than you realise. You have a history. A pattern matching brain that tends to jump to conclusions based on past experiences. Then there is intuition. The urge to do the opposite, just this one time. Why? Because you feel it in your gut.

Being able to manage this riot of internal conflicts and prevent them from interfering with 'optimal play' is hard. So hard that I doubt that anybody manages it. Except those in the top one or two percent of winning players. They still aren't perfect but they have learnt to do it better than anybody else.

Poker is unique. It's not like sport. Or Chess. There is the highly volatile combination of randomised outcomes mixed with the big sums of money at risk that combine to tap straight into the animal part of your brain. If you're not careful it can ram a hot metal poker straight up the rear end of the animal within. Continuous, long term, self control in poker is a Mount Everest sized challenge.

Which is not to say that you should play like a robot, or an algorithm. A perfectly, game theory, optimised computer program would still lose its pants at a table of professionals for the simple reason that there are people involved. People with emotions. Computers are very poor at assessing and manipulating human mental states. But Serious Sid, the emotion free, poker playing software program would probably clean up most non-professionals.

Serious Sid would win a lot of money because it had full control over its emotions. As in he didn't have any. Big advantage right there. The secret to making money at poker, once you've got the skill side down pat, is to play people with less control over their emotions than you have. Which brings us back to the weak and vulnerable. Somebody wound up, or down, by the vicissitudes of the cards, is easily exploited. Like the Great White Shark you can shred them into a bloody pulp. Is that fun or ethical? For me, it wasn't.

But what is fun and a lot more interesting, is playing yourself. The internal game that goes on in your own mind whilst sitting at the table and playing others has a fascination all of its own. Trying to coral your own thoughts and emotions into a semblance of order, being able to dispassionately look down at your own actions, is prime time television at its best. It's infinitely more challenging than the other players. It's the biggest game in town. Right there in your own head.

While I might be an extreme example of the addictive nature of 'trying to beat yourself', there is a part of this in all of us. Which is why the Performance Evaluation report is so immersive. It enables you to play yourself. It doesn't matter if you beat the game, or not, because the most interesting and challenging part of the whole deal is beating yourself. The High Command assessment, while a fairly innocuous looking report, allows you to do this.

At game end there are a whole series of analysis that leverage this even further, but it's the turn by turn Performance Evaluations that will, if you keep playing, grab you by the ankles and not let go.

12.2. LOSS ASSESSMENT ▶

This provides a higher level of detail than the data available in the Statistics tab. It's wrapped up in a more immersive form. Rather than seeing that there are 32,000 infantry casualties, you view it in terms of the number of men killed, wounded and missing. The calculations for these are based on accurate historical data and it serves, in a small way, to bring home the human element of the epic tragedy of Barbarossa.

As Operational Commander you are making decisions that inevitably involve people dying. 32,000 infantry casualties lets you duck the issue as you are dealing with a big bland number that means little. Seeing exactly how many men have died as a result of you pulling the levers of power is another thing altogether.

Yes, it's a game. It's hypothetical. Make believe. But take a look at the number of men currently 'Missing'.

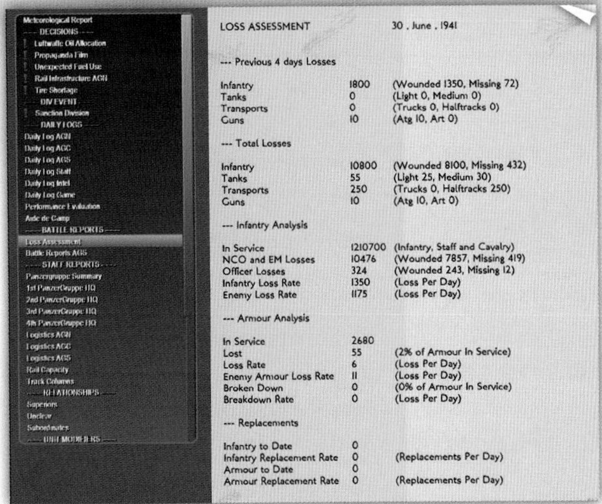

Every one of them would have a family back home praying that they miraculously turned up alive. Waking up every morning hoping for official news.

After a while they would stop caring that it would be good news, only that they were able to gain a sense of closure as it's the not knowing that bites the hardest. Put yourself in their shoes. Think of who you love most. How would you feel if they were 'Missing'?

Watch the number of 'Missing' men climb. Every time you order a division into combat, it'll ratchet higher. Take a moment to multiply whatever number it is by four. That's roughly how many relatives are desperately clutching at whatever slim hope remains or who are resigned to wishing that their loved one died quickly and not in vain. Human misery writ large.

It's an unsettling thought. Not something that you want to be reminded of.

It's Operational Command.

12.3. HALDER EXTRACTS ▶

FeldMarschall Franz Halder graced historians and war gamers with a comprehensive set of war diaries. These are important primary source documents because they were written by a key actor, the person that the German Player is assumed to be. They are an accurate reflection of events as perceived by Halder on the day, not an attempt to reconstruct history with the benefit of hindsight and personal bias as are most books written by other participants, once the war was over.

They are freely available on the web and an excellent read. You can see many of the key campaign themes intertwined through the daily entries. The disconnect between the political leadership and professional military officer corps is clearly evident as is the constant meddling by Hitler.

There are all kinds of interesting tit bits amongst the situation reports and I've included a pool of extracts that serve to ground the game back in 1941. Each entry is applicable for the game date shown and you can visibly track the German trajectory that rapidly arced up into exulted surprise at their unimagined levels of success and then gradually descended through mystification at how the Soviets didn't realise that they were beaten to the sickening realisation that Hitler's great gamble hadn't worked.

26 . June . 1941

Aerial reconnaissance organisations keep closed up to the front. Sporadic attacks on our airfields. Distribution of AA confirms with situation. At Orsha large tank and vehicle parks observed. Photographs show over 2,000 tanks, reconnaissance cars and trucks.

F.M Franz Halder's Diary [?]

30 . June . 1941

In AGS the fight continues successfully despite local crises. The enemy allows himself to be pushed back step by step. No arrivals of new reinforcements from rear areas are reported. Most likely the enemy has already committed the greater part of the forces he was able to muster.

F.M Franz Halder's Diary [?]

12.4. LEADER QUOTES ▶

Every now and then Hitler, or Stalin, will pop up and bestow upon you a quote. These are intended to give you a feel for their personalities. Both of them were dominant characters of their times and both were unsavoury individuals. Not much we can do about that. Sadly nice guys tend to avoid conflict.

While you wouldn't want to invite either of them around for dinner, they are certainly strong characters and would make excellent physiological case studies. Their quotes act as a signpost for the times. There is a wide selection but it's instructive to consider them all in the context of today. Would any of the major world leaders get away with saying similar things? Doubtful.

"It is not truth that matters, but victory."

Adolf Hitler

I've had to be selective in which quotes I used for Hitler. A lot of his are too far out there to be of use as they would upset a large proportion of the players. I've aimed for the less outrageous ones that are more neutral but, even this is tricky given the spaghetti jumble of ugliness that constituted his perceived wisdom.

Still, I think it's worth having him there, along with his less offensive utterances, as he was a key driving force behind Barbarossa. For those that disagree there is the 'Geneva Convention' option which toggles the quotes off and puts the moustachioed one back in his box.

Stalin is allowed to be himself. As an evil, ruthless, dictator he was up there with the all time greats. Whether he was any worse or better, ethically and morally, than Hitler is beyond the scope of the game. He was certainly more entertaining. A superior producer of memorable quotes. I've rounded up as many of these as I can find. If you are able to disassociate yourself from his evil ways, there is some quality historical entertainment to be had here.

"When we hang the capitalists they will sell us the rope we use."

Joseph Stalin

Which is interesting as, once again, nice guys (and girls) come second, both in conflict and famous quotes. They can do memorable, serious and profound but 'entertaining' appears to be the exclusive domain of the genuine bad boys. Maybe it has something to do with the exercise of absolute power. When you aren't answerable to anyone, you don't care what people think. You are unconstrained and free to say what you want.

Or perhaps the serial crazies just had a better sense of humour.

12.5. BATTLE REPORTS ▶

Individual Divisions form the molecular building blocks of DC3. The game tracks dozens of data points for each Division. There is an awful lot of information swirling around under the hood.

Included in the mix are most Divisions having an historical commander. There is a person in charge of each Division. Not quite all as the historical records aren't available but the overwhelming majority do have a commander. A person. Somebody to care about.

Every time a battle occurs the game generates a report. All the information contained within is contextual and relates to a particular aspect of the battle. This is purely chrome and has no effect on the game, with the notable exception mentioned below. It applies only to the German side. With the chaos and communication breakdowns that afflict the Soviet side, reports are an unattainable luxury.

Even as chrome, the battle reports allow you to zoom in and get a feel for the nitty gritty of combat. But it's when an attack fails that the system shines. Higher levels of command aren't fussed about attacks

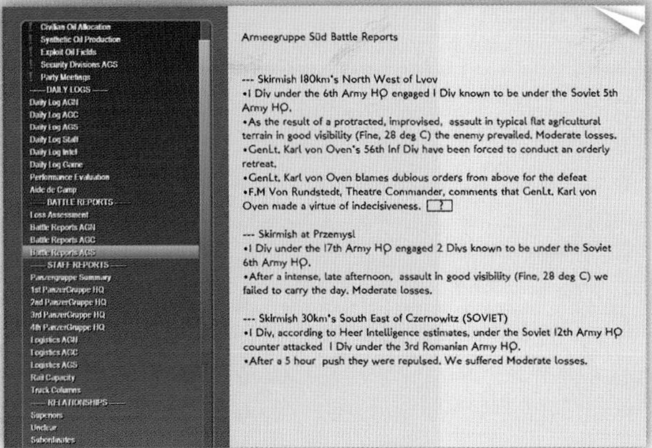

that succeed. Like any organisation, its failure that sparks their interest. They want to know why.

An HQ, if involved, or a Division will be queried. Blame will be apportioned. Fingers pointed. No commander will accept that they were the cause of the failed assault. Perhaps they didn't have air support when it was needed? Or Theatre level artillery wasn't there to prepare the ground.

There is a large pool of possible reasons and a fair bit of underlying logic that is used to determine which one is appropriate. Individual commanders have pet peeves. Others don't hesitate to sheet home the problem to the orders they were given, or other perceived faults of their Theatre HQ based superiors.

Over time you'll find commanders, and their Divisions, begin to tell a story. The battle reports aim to build a bridge between the Player and the counters they are shuffling around on the map.

Take GeneralleutnantKarl Von Oven, commander of the 56th Infantry Division. You've been watching him. He's prickly and pretentious, but he gets the job done. Except for that one time when he was part of the attempt to break the river line north west of Lvov. Fell to pieces. Inexplicably the 56th Infantry failed to carry the day. When asked to explain himself he had the cheek to blame the dubious orders imposed on him by his Theatre Comander!

A lot of the time comments such as those from GenLt. Von Oven, will be accepted as part and parcel of the stress that the burden of command can induce in a man. Von Oven's narky finger pointing will be let through to the keeper and soon forgotten.

But not always. Your theatre commanders have been keeping just as close an eye on events as you have. It's their job to step in when something is awry. Commanders, at times, need to be pulled into line. Or given a timely pat on the back, for example, for deeds well done. You'll see a comment at the bottom of a battle report where your theatre commander has expressed his opinion. These have weight.

12.6. DIVISION EVENTS ▶

Any time a theatre commander feels compelled to comment you know that it isn't the last you've heard of whatever incident has caused him to put pen to paper. The wheels will begin turning and, sooner or later, whatever has been slowly bubbling away, out of sight, will come to a head. A Divisional event will be generated requiring your input.

These are great. GenLt. Von Oven, he of the 56th Infantry Division made some rash comments at the time his Division bolted northwest of Lvov. F.M Von Rundstedt, commander of Armeegruppe Süd took note. GenLt. Von Oven, is, according to Von Rundstedt, not a good example of exemplary, ascendant, Heer leadership but instead a flaky wimp who has just earned himself a provisional Sanction.

You'll be able to note that whenever you ask for a Status Report on the 56th Infantry Division, the Sanction will hang over their, and GenLt. Von Ovens, heads like the Sword of Damocles. Internally the sanction has joined an ever growing list of pending Divisional events.

Usually it's a case of first in, first out as the Heer bureaucracy grinds its way slowly through the accumulated cases but occasionally particular events are fast tracked and it's last in, first out. The Byzantine workings of the bureaucracy are a mystery to all concerned.

Then, BAM! There it is. A decision, demanding your attention. Do you rubber stamp F.M Von Rundstedt's provisional Sanction and make it offical? Doing so will impose permanent combat penalties on the 56th Infantry and jam a skeleton firmly into GenLt. Von Oven's closet.

Why not overrule your Theatre Commander and dismiss the Sanction? You could, but F.M Von Rundstedt isn't likely to be excited at your interference nor do the Political Points you're going to have to expend, to do so, grow on trees. How many PP's is it going to cost you to exercise your veto prerogative? How good is your relationship with F.M Von Rundstedt?

If you weren't paying attention to the story of the 56th Infantry and the wayward Von Oven then you are now. What a mess. All because the 56th Infantry lacked morale fortitude and choked in the grassy steppes north west of Lvov. Who was the dolt who ultimately ordered the attack be made in the first place?

That would be you.

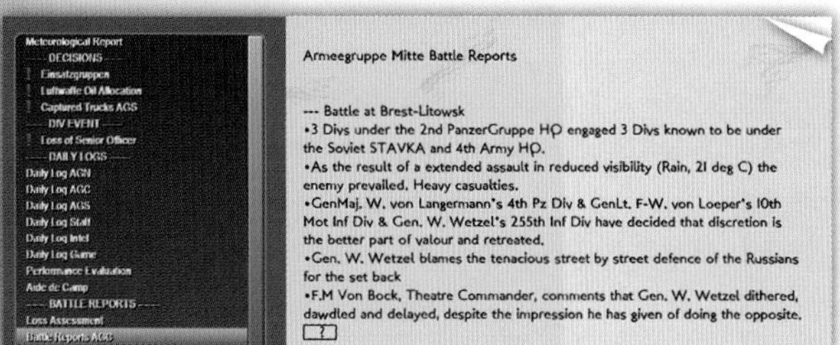

An example of battle report, AGC this time

There are a range of possible Division events that can occur as a result of combat. Various combat parameters can trigger different events. They are all highlighted in the Battle reports and every one of them will eventually generate a Decision that requires your input. They are an even mix of good and bad, but even the beneficial ones still require you to make a, potentially, curly decision.

There is an 'Event Master' that oversees the whole process and attempts to spread the events out evenly so you get a good mix of different types. This isn't always possible given the various triggering criteria required for the events, but it serves to mix it up where ever feasible. The same Event Master keeps a firm hand on the bureaucratic process and ensures that a reasonable mix of events turn up as decisions. Finally it regulates the flow of events so that they only turn up one at a time. It doesn't want to spam you.

Division events leverage the ability of the game to tell a story. They push certain individuals and Divisions to the fore. They provide the means for the Player to develop a personal connection to the units they are shuffling hither and yon.

Importantly they aren't random, drop from the sky, events. They derive directly from Battle reports that, themselves, are a consequence of the actions that the Player has taken. There is a natural flow from the Player's actions to the Battle reports and on to the Division events.

It's an immersive process that pulls Players into the game using a synergy of mechanics derived from their own actions. From a design perspective it's a big win. I'm proud of it.

Printed in China through WorldPrint Ltd.